BY THE SAME AUTHORS

The Academy of St. Martin in the Fields

The War Artists

Opera Today

Sheathing the Sword

Soldiers of the Sun

A Pilgrim Soul: The Life of Elisabeth Lutyens

The
LAST DAYS
of
INNOCENCE

The
LAST DAYS
of
INNOCENCE

America at War
1917-1918

MEIRION AND SUSIE HARRIES

RANDOM HOUSE NEW YORK

Library of Congress Cataloging-in-Publication Data
Harries, Meirion, 1951–
The last days of innocence: America at war, 1917–1918/Meirion and Susie Harries.
p.   cm.
Includes bibliographical references (p.) and index.
ISBN 0-679-41863-6
1. World War, 1914–1918—United States.   I. Harries, Susie.
II. Title.
D570.A46   1997
940.4'0973—dc20   96-21756

Random House website address: http://www.randomhouse.com/

Printed in the United States of America on acid-free paper

24689753

First Edition

Book design by Lilly Langotsky

TO PETER DOWNEY

There lay the best of America,
not dead nor sleeping,
but alive so long as we will them to live.

—HENRY RUSSELL MILLER,
in the aftermath of the
Battle of Soissons, July 1918

Contents

❧✿❧

PROLOGUE   FORGOTTEN SACRIFICE   3

PART 1   FORCED TOWARD ARMAGEDDON   11

1.   The Search for a New America   13
2.   On the Edge of the Vortex   26
3.   "To Hell with Peace Talk": Volunteers on the Western Front   41
4.   "I Didn't Raise My Boy to Be a Soldier":
        The Problem of Preparedness   49
5.   "We Can Do No Other": The Decision for War   61
6.   Launching the War Effort   74

PART 2   BUILDING THE ARMY   87

7.   The Lists of Honor: Conscription   89
8.   "Bring the Liver Out": Officers of a Democratic Army   99
9.   "Are We Still Jim Crow in the Army?"   104
10. "Over There": Pershing and the Plans for an American
        Expeditionary Force   111
11. "I Hope It Is Not Too Late": The First Division in France   118
12. The Military Melting Pot: Into the Camps   127

PART 3   MOBILIZING THE NATION   143

13.   Building the War Machine   145
14.   "Lay Your Double Chin on the Altar of Liberty":
        Food for the Fighters   154
15.   "One White-hot Mass": Mobilizing Minds   164
16.   "I Love My Flag, I Do, I Do": Discouraging Dissent   178

PART 4   THE WINTER CRISIS   191

17.   "The Truth About This War": Mobilization Stalled   193
18.   "The War Is Practically Lost": Crisis on the Western Front   205
19.   American Dreams: Visions of Independence   215

PART 5   INTO BATTLE   225

20.   Ludendorff Attacks: Spring 1918   227
21.   Blood and Propaganda: Setting a Value on the AEF   238
22.   "Know Thine Enemy": The Battle for Belleau Wood, June 1918   246
23.   "Do You Want to Live for Ever?"   260

PART 6   THE END OF INNOCENCE   273

24.   A Time of Reckoning   275
25.   The Will to Fight   282
26.   "The Spirit of Ruthless Brutality"   293
27.   "Nobody Can Say We Aren't Loyal Now"   300

PART 7   THE REALITY OF WAR   309

28.   Attack and Counterattack: July 1918   311
29.   Hope and Glory   322
30.   The Dream Shattered   329

CONTENTS

PART 8   THE DEATH OF INNOCENTS 337

31. The First Battle: Saint-Mihiel 339
32. "The Most Ideal Defensive Terrain": Between the Meuse River
    and the Argonne Forest 349
33. Over the Top: The First Day on the Meuse-Argonne 356
34. "Retrograde Movements": The Second, Third, and Fourth Days .. 362
35. In the Argonne Forest 370
36. "They Are Learning Now": The First Two Weeks of October .. 380
37. Crisis Before Kriemhilde 388
38. "The Big Man": Liggett Pulls the Army into Shape 395

PART 9   LOSING THE PEACE 403

39. Losing to the Allies 405
40. Von Winterfeldt's Tears 415
41. "No Greater Pain" 423

EPILOGUE   THE COST 433

42. Continuing the Search 435
43. The Abiding Enemy 443
44. "When Johnny Comes Marching Home" 451

ACKNOWLEDGMENTS 461
NOTES 463
INDEX 561

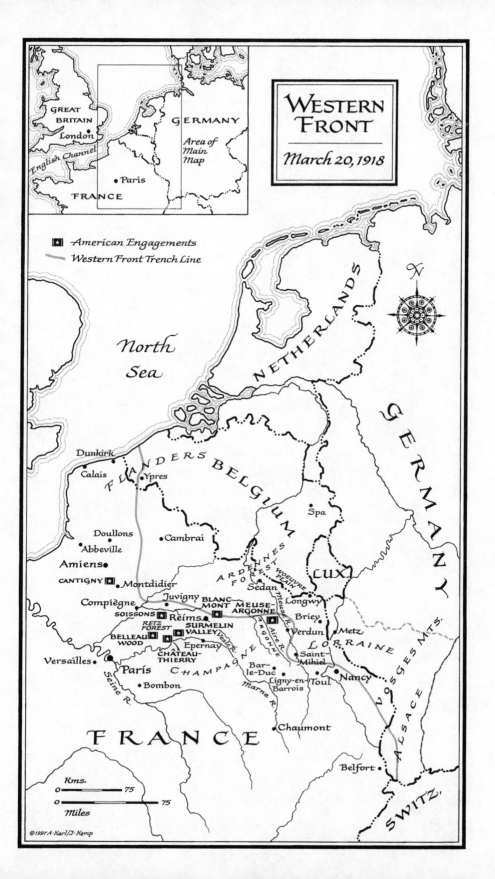

WESTERN FRONT

March 20, 1918

■ *American Engagements*

— *Western Front Trench Line*

GREAT BRITAIN
London
English Channel
GERMANY
Area of Main Map
• Paris
FRANCE

North Sea

NETHERLANDS

GERMANY

N

Dunkirk
Calais
FLANDERS
Ypres
BELGIUM
Spa

Doullons
Abbeville
Cambrai
Amiens•
CANTIGNY ■ •Montdidier
ARDENNES FOREST
WOEUVRE PLAIN
LUX.
Compiègne
Juvigny
BLANC MONT
MEUSE-ARGONNE
Sedan
Longwy
SOISSONS ■ Reims ■
Briey
RETZ FOREST
SURMELIN VALLEY
Verdun
Metz
BELLEAU WOOD ■ ■
Epernay
CHÂTEAU-THIERRY
LORRAINE
Versailles•
Paris
CHAMPAGNE
Saint-Mihiel
VOSGES MTS.
Seine R.
•Bombon
Marne R.
Bar-le-Duc
Ligny-en-Barrois
Toul
Nancy
ALSACE

FRANCE

Chaumont

Belfort

SWITZ.

Kms.
0 ———— 75
0 ———— 75
Miles

©1997 A. Karl/J. Kemp

The
LAST DAYS
of
INNOCENCE

Prologue

Forgotten Sacrifice

In northern France, darkness came early on that bitter, rain-drenched day in the winter of 1917. Seven months had passed since the United States had declared war on Germany, and her first troops had been less than two weeks at the front, picking up experience in a quiet sector to the east of Verdun. The 1st Division's combat units were being methodically rotated into the line, and on November 2 First Lieutenant Willis Comfort led forward the 250 men of Company F, 16th Infantry.

Carrying hundred-pound packs, the men swore softly as they slipped and splashed their muddy way through the darkness over broken duckboards, through shell-shattered trenches, in the wake of their French guides. The relief took several hours to complete. Tired, frightened, exhilarated, startled by the rats scuttling about their legs, they took their positions on the firestep and peered out through the wire at the German lines five hundred yards away in the darkness.

Corporal Tom Carroll and Private Busby were sent out to a listening post in a clump of bushes in no-man's-land. "Dark as pitch, queer shadows and sounds. Have box of grenades. We are both scared." They had foreseen nothing like this when, early that summer, their company had paraded through Paris. On sunlit boulevards, crowds had wept and cheered; young girls had linked arms with them, kissed them, and showered them with roses. Now they looked out onto a landscape of cold and brutal desolation: splintered tree stumps, jagged rusting balls of wire, slimy rat holes, shell craters filled with stinking water, the stench of death and decay. And for three of the company—James "Boo Boo" Gresham, Thomas Enright, and Merle Hay—death was coming closer.

Gresham had charge of a squad of riflemen covering one stretch of the forward trench of the strong point the company was defending, while Privates Hay and Enright were in another squad, under Corporal Frank Coffman, slightly further up the line. Gresham and Enright knew each other well, both being old-timers from the regular army; Hay, a Texan, was a rookie who had only enlisted in May.

"All was quiet," Corporal Coffman recalled, "except for an occasional rat-tat-tat from some nervous machine-gunner further down the line, or an inquisitive Very light from the enemy trenches across the valley." Leaving Hay and Enright on the firestep, he led the remainder of the squad, assigned to day duty, to a dugout in a traverse trench. "Lured on by exhaustion and a sense of safety, we wrapped our blankets around us and prepared for a few hours of restful slumber."

Three hours later, the American position erupted in smoke, din, and debris as ninety-six German guns in rapid fire deluged it with shells. Lieutenant Erickson tried to ignite a flare to call artillery support but burned his hand in the excitement. For forty-five minutes the bombardment continued, collapsing trenches and sending the men scrabbling for the dugouts. Then, ominously, it shifted to the rear, creating a wall of steel around them and shutting off all chance of help or reinforcements.

As the barrage moved back, more than two hundred gray-clad German raiders stormed into the forward trench. These were experienced soldiers of the 7th Bavarian Landwehr Regiment; suspecting that Americans had now moved into the line, they had come to take prisoners for interrogation. This was one of the quickest ways of obtaining intelligence on the Western Front, and for the Germans the operation was little more than routine. But to the men of Company F it was all terrifyingly new. Deafened, stunned, the survivors crawled out of their dugouts and hit back with rifle butts, fists, and bombs, killing two Germans and wounding several more.

"Boo Boo" Gresham had little chance to fight. He was at the entrance to a dugout when a man in an American uniform ran up, shouting "Who are you?" "An American, don't shoot!" exclaimed Gresham. "You are the one I am looking for," said the intruder and shot him in the eye. Private Hay was also taken by surprise—shot dead by "a man in a dark uniform," according to Corporal Coffman, "whom he thought was one of his own comrades."

Almost as soon as they had arrived, the raiders were gone. They took with them their own dead and wounded and every piece of American equipment, and they carried off eleven prisoners. They tried to take Thomas Enright, too, but he fought ferociously for his liberty. Later, in the dawn light, he was found lying half in and half out of the trench he had guarded. The ground around him had been torn up in the struggle to take him prisoner. His body was punctured with bayonet wounds, and his throat was slashed open.

These were the first men of the U.S. Army to die in combat in this most terrible of wars. To the French, their deaths came almost as a relief; at last *les Américains* had spilt blood in the defense of France. With full military honors, the three were buried near where they had fallen. At the graveside, as the ritual gunfire died away, General Paul Bordeaux rejoiced in "the will of the people and army of the United States to fight with us to a finish." On the tombs of the three he promised to inscribe "Here lie the first soldiers of the famous Republic of the United States to fall on the soil of France for justice and liberty. . . . Corporal Gresham, Private Enright, Private Hay, in the name of France, I thank you. God receive your souls. Farewell!"

Eighty years on, Gresham, Hay, and Enright are all but forgotten at home and among the former Allied nations. The other American soldiers, sailors, and airmen—the 50,280 who died in combat, the 205,000 maimed and wounded, the 5 million others who served in uniform—are little commemorated. And America's wider role in the Great War has been largely passed over, seen at best as a bit part, a brief eddy in the gigantic cataclysm that swept Europe between 1914 and 1918.

The British and French attitude is not hard to explain. As the war ended, the Allies were already starting to downplay America's contribution in order to undermine her position at Versailles, where they intended that their peace terms, not those of the idealist Woodrow Wilson, should prevail. And now, at the end of the twentieth century, the French and British remember their lost generations, millions of men killed on the Marne, at Verdun, on the Somme in the years during which America remained neutral and profited hugely from selling supplies to the combatants. The contrast between these losses and those of the Americans in their short war make many Europeans emotionally incapable of accepting the crucial role that the United States actually played in the victory.

In this first modern industrial war, materials, money, and morale played as important a part in total war as the fighting men themselves; and America gave lavishly of all three.

Without the United States, the British could never have become so significant a military power in so short a time. In 1914, the British Army was small and the country had only a limited capacity to manufacture munitions for land warfare. From the earliest weeks of the war America, though technically neutral, acted on a cash-and-carry basis as an auxiliary arsenal for the Allies. The endless stream of ships crossing and recrossing the Atlantic from 1914 onward carried the lifeblood of the Allied war effort: steel, copper, wheat, pork, beef, rifles, howitzers, shells, barbed wire.

The United States spent $50.3 billion fighting this war; a fifth of the total went to the Allies in the form of loans that were never wholly repaid. France, Russia, and Italy had fast run out of foreign exchange and credit to pay for their needs, and from September 1915 their purchases had been underwritten by England. But even the mighty British Empire could not bear the strain of expenditure, which totaled a grotesque $25 billion by mid-1917. At the point when America joined the war, England had exhausted all her foreign exchange, gold, overseas assets, and credit. Outside the Empire, she was effectively bankrupt. She could no longer buy or borrow in America—and she and her dependent allies faced the immediate loss of up to 40 percent of their war supplies. Only continuing loans by the U.S. Treasury Department of billions of dollars kept the Allied war effort alive through 1917 and 1918. As British Foreign Secretary Arthur Balfour told Secretary of the Treasury William Gibbs McAdoo, "Loans stop, war stops."

The French needed more than money to keep going. In April 1917, a cocksure general, Robert Nivelle, launched a huge offensive in the Champagne region—one that he had promised would win the war. When the attack failed, the French Army's spirit buckled. Bitter equally at the butchery and the seeming bad faith of their leaders, the men refused to obey their own officers. Many got drunk and shouted pacifist slogans; by midsummer, half of all of France's divisions had mutinied and Paris lay virtually undefended. Nivelle retired in disgrace, and Henri Pétain—a tough "soldiers' soldier," the hero of Verdun—was appointed to restore morale. Without delay, he visited all his divisions to promise that no more offensives would be launched until *les Américains* had arrived. The hysteria that Company F had experienced on the streets of Paris was gratitude for deliverance; in the eyes of the French, the deaths of Gresham, Hay, and Enright were the down payment on Pétain's promise.

Materials, money, morale—but American manpower played its part too. As the Allies staggered under General Erich Ludendorff's hammer blows in the spring and into the summer of 1918 and German storm troopers advanced on Paris itself, America responded to frantic appeals for help by shipping to France men in their hundreds of thousands—almost 10,000 a day through that critical summer. At Cantigny and Belleau Wood, on the Marne, and across the Soissons plateau to the Vesle river, American divisions helped push the Germans back. Their performance helped brace the Allies; but it was the promise of apparently limitless power to come that buried German hopes. In the fall, two newly minted American armies joined the massive offensive that finally brought Germany to her knees.

So why, given such solid achievement, is America's Great War so little regarded at home? Obviously, this conflict has been overlaid by the wars that followed, the Second World War in particular. But emotion has helped make America's memory selective too—and the strongest emotion in the mix has been shame: the nineteen months of war began in a blaze of patriotic unity, and ended in bitterness, division, and regret.

America went to fight in 1917 with an innocent determination to remake the world; the nation emerged in November 1918 with its sense of purpose shattered, with its certainties shaken, and with a new and unwelcome self-knowledge. Many Americans wanted to turn their backs on the war almost from the moment it ended.

The timing of the war could not have been worse for American society. In 1914, the country was changing more rapidly than at any time in its history. People were trying to come to terms with the massive industrial development that had followed the Civil War—the vast immigration it had sparked, the growth of the cities, the closing of the frontier, the new technologies and their impact on daily life and work. War interrupted all the attempts at social reform and the search for a new, united America, and it aggravated the tensions of a society in flux.

The nature of the war increased the damage. This was total war, the conflict not of army against army but nation against nation, and it required the mobilization of every resource, human, moral, and material; the shock was the greater because few Americans had seriously contemplated the possibility of entering the war and the country had made no preparations to fight a land war in Europe. Unplanned and uncoordinated, the mobilization exploded under a society that prided itself on being quintessentially civilian.

The federal budget grew from $742 million in 1916 to almost $14 billion in 1918, and the balance of political power shifted just as dramatically. Where once power had been widely dispersed and shared, during the war the nation was organized and directed from the center down to the details of its dress, its food, and its conversation. The nation surrendered itself to the draft, to censorship, to repression. Dissent was forbidden, and even honest criticism was outlawed. Worse, ordinary Americans volunteered to police the system, to spy on their neighbors, to condone violence and the abuse of civil rights, to participate in a shameful travesty of their former lives.

By insisting on conformity, the government placed enormous strains on this diverse society. The emotions it whipped up to unite its people against the foreign enemy—hatred, fear, suspicion, intolerance—turned inward and ravaged the people themselves. Blacks, radicals, religious minorities, the foreign-born, all became scapegoats for the country's ills, victims of a nativism that grew more intense as the first shoots of communism appeared on American soil in 1918.

The behavior at home seemed to mock the sacrifices being made on the battlefields of France. Amid the outpouring of public money—some $38 billion by the end of 1919—private greed and self-interest flowered. As American soldiers were fighting and dying on the Western Front, factory workers were drifting from job to job in search of ever-higher wages, while employers tried to use the excuse of national emergency to deny labor the most basic of rights. Though a new class of blue-collar plutocrats arose from the shipyards and munitions factories, the war accelerated the concentration of the nation's wealth into fewer hands than before: in 1900, the nation's wealth stood at $192 billion—50 percent of which was held by 2 percent of the population; in 1929, eleven years after the war's end, the nation's wealth reached $362 billion—and the 2 percent now held 60 percent of the total.

When the peace negotiations at Versailles finally came to an end, America perceived itself as having gained nothing; the prevailing sense was of having participated in a vindictive, dishonorable treaty dictated by the Allies. As far as they were able, Americans turned their backs on Europe and tried to return to normality. But there was no going back for

America, any more than for Britain or Russia. Americans could not re-
capture the innocent optimism and self-confidence of the prewar days.
Wide rents had appeared in the social fabric of America, and the experiment of the melting pot appeared to be over. Rudely, the war had thrust
Americans into the uncertain future of the twentieth century: its consequences are our legacy today.

Part One

FORCED

TOWARD

ARMAGEDDON

1

The Search for a New America

Who were they, these Americans who found themselves caught up in the Great War? And what was their America? Nostalgia for a gas-lit age of livery stables, starched collars, a piano in the parlor, and Teddy Roosevelt at large in the great outdoors conjures up an age of simplicity, security, assurance, and continuity with the old traditions—an age of innocence very different from our own era of turmoil and uncertainty. But nostalgia misleads. The violence of war came upon an America already in transit from that epoch—and the pace of change was accelerating.

Since the Civil War, the country had been transformed by the mightiest industrial expansion the world had ever seen. The United States was already as rich as Great Britain and Germany combined, and three times as rich as France. There were 5 million automobiles and trucks in America in 1914, one fifth of them made by the Ford Motor Company. One hundred and twenty people a year died under their wheels, nearly half as many as were killed by horse-drawn carriages. Production-line models could reach 40 miles per hour, though the newly arrived traffic cops kept the speed limit in New York and other cities to 15 miles per hour. Traveling at top speed, a driver could virtually have covered the length of the nation's paved roads between dawn and midnight. But paved roads were a luxury to those intrepid motorists who drove the "Lincoln Highway" to California; for four weeks, these motorized pioneers plowed through mud, dust, potholes, and swollen rivers, making camp each night as the sun set over the prairie.

Automobiles were America's third largest industry, Detroit the motor city. There, night had been ruthlessly banished by another modern marvel:

electricity. Over several square miles, high towers topped by floodlights bathed the city in garish brilliance. In factories all over America, electric motors were replacing steam engines; in the countryside, gasoline-driven generators brought energy to areas far from power lines. Now farmers could use electric milking machines and light their barns and homes. The internal combustion engine helped to mechanize agriculture and brought the local town within easy reach. It was even suggested that the motorcar, with its potential for long-range spooning, would revitalize the gene pool of rural areas.

The cities were changing at a still more spectacular rate. In 1870, only a quarter of the population had lived in towns; fifty years later, half did so. America had gained a dozen cities with 600,000 inhabitants, including three with more than a million and one, New York, with 5.5 million.

All were testaments to modernity. In this age of steel and elevators, buildings rose to unimagined heights—less for the sake of maximizing land use than for proclaiming the prestige of the owners and those renting space inside. Returning to New York after two decades in Queen Victoria's brick-built London, novelist Henry James was horrified by the skyscrapers of lower Manhattan. The island had become "a pin cushion," the city "a huge, continuous fifty-floored conspiracy." And within these vastnesses businessmen conspired in new ways. Telegraphers were joined by an army of typists, and now came telephones. By 1910, a network of 6 million apparatuses linked home to office and city to city, just as they would soon link a division's artillery to its frontline soldiers.

"America" was a single physical entity now; the frontier was gone, the Redskin was tamed, the land was settled, and exploitation was in full swing. The job of integrating the continent, begun by the railroads, was being completed by trucks, telephones, and the Panama Canal. Control from the center became possible, and the independence of the states was eroded as the federal government asserted its authority over a range of national issues from child labor to the Federal Reserve System.

Modern communications were drawing people closer together, and entertainments designed for instant, easy appeal began to iron out the differences among them. The wind-up phonograph with its steel stylus and brass trumpet spread the treacle of Tin Pan Alley in a thin film over the whole nation. Movies too were big business by 1914. This was the age of D. W. Griffith, Mack Sennett, the velvet luxury of red-and-gilt Roxy theaters showing multireeled melodramas. Ten million people a day went to the movies to sob and sigh over Lillian Gish and Mary Pickford—and, in 1914, to begin laughing at Charlie Chaplin, who within twelve months would be earning the astounding sum of $10,000 a week.

The mass appetite was fed by mass-circulation journals covering all the popular interests: stars, sports, fashion, diets, crime, and high society. They raised the issues of the day and to a certain extent dispensed the new ideas of the age. Atomized, pulped, cannibalized, the novel theories spun through the mass media and contrived to change society: socialism, feminism, cubism, the views of Greenwich Village on Art and Life, Charles Darwin's theories of evolution, Sigmund Freud's psychiatry. (Freud, incidentally, saw his first-ever movie in New York in 1909.)

Not all the new ideas were healthy; this intellectual ferment also produced its share of scum. Worthy academic efforts to explore the characteristics of different ethnic groups were manipulated to give a veneer of respectability to the crudest racism. Blacks were now "proven" to be mentally and morally inferior, lending credence to poisonous tracts such as *The Negro a Beast* (1900) and *The Negro: A Menace to Americanization* (1907).

The findings of "science" accelerated the slide back to servitude for many blacks. Since Emancipation, new chains had been forged in the South. Blacks were disenfranchised, humiliated by "Jim Crow" laws, forced into peonage on the land and virtual slavery as household servants. And where economic and legal bonds could not hold them, there were always the rope and the branding iron.

Black leaders searched desperately for ways to rescue their people. At the turn of the century, Booker T. Washington held center stage. Speaking at the Cotton States Exposition at Atlanta in September 1895, he laid out a manifesto for a black renaissance that, by his own account, brought him out of obscurity and made him a national figure. Washington, the son of a black slave mother and a white father, favored a conservative, pragmatic, ingratiating approach. "Our surest and most potent protection," he believed, lay in "usefulness in the community where we reside," in "friendship and advance" in moral and economic terms, in self-help. Above all, he rejected confrontation. "The wisest among my race," he told the mixed audience at the Exposition, "understand that the agitation of questions of social equality is the extremest folly, and that progress in the enjoyment of all privileges that will come to us must be the result of severe and constant struggle, rather than of artificial forcing."

But as the first decade of the twentieth century drew to its close, many black people began to feel that they could no longer wait. Seventy blacks a year were being lynched or burned at the stake; black women raped by whites could find no legal redress; the Attorney General himself acknowledged that peonage or debt slavery, although illegal, was "extensively carried on." In 1910, southern cities brought in segregationist zoning laws, and black families who bought property in white neighborhoods were likely to have their homes dynamited. Schools were segregated, and allocations for blacks' education declined to the point where black children received, per capita, only half as much as whites. "Jim Crow" still prevailed in streetcars, trains, and government departments. Most labor unions closed the door to blacks and condoned separate washrooms and canteens. Blacks were still denied the vote, a policy the President of the United States himself appeared to endorse: "When a class of persons is so ignorant," declared William H. Taft on a tour of the South, "that they are really political children not having the mental stature of manhood, then their voice in the government serves no benefit to them." Taft made 9,876 appointments, of whom only 30 were African Americans.

Growing numbers of blacks were breaking ranks now, rejecting the policies of "friendship and advance" and urging direct political action instead. In the New York elections of 1910, the United Colored Democracy tried to organize a block vote to achieve its ends. "What Do We Want?" asked the manifesto. "We want Colored Policemen. We want Colored Firemen. We want garbage removed from our streets before noon. We want crooks driven out of the tenements."

W. E. B. Du Bois, a Harvard-educated historian and sociologist, brilliant, emotional, and ferocious, stood at the cutting edge of what was then regarded as black radicalism. In 1910, he was appointed director of publicity and research for the National Association for the Advancement of Colored People (NAACP), a new black activist organization he had helped found in 1905, which was supported by influential whites such as Albert E. Pillsbury, John Dewey, Jane Addams, and Jacob Schiff.

Through his speeches and editorials in the NAACP's journal *The Crisis*, Du Bois urged protest and open agitation: "The function of this Association is to tell this nation the crying evil of race prejudice. It is a hard duty but a necessary one—a divine one. It is Pain; Pain is not good but Pain is necessary. Pain does not aggravate disease—disease causes Pain.

Agitation does not mean Aggravation—Aggravation calls for Agitation in order that Remedy may be found."

Du Bois attacked apartheid in the administration; he led the crusade against lynching; he denounced the toleration of rape of black women by whites—and he took no trouble at all to moderate his language. In *The Crisis* of March 1912, he made an astonishing call for retribution. Three black men had been lynched for killing the whites who had raped their wives; three black victims of rape had been murdered, one of them "a dark and whimpering little girl burned to a quivering crisp." "Everybody knows," wrote Du Bois, "that for three hundred years the most jealously guarded right of white men in this land of ours has been the right to seduce black women without legal, social or moral penalty." But now, he urged, black men should act, they should "kill lecherous white invaders of their homes and then take their lynching gladly like men. It's worth it!"

A less inflammatory part of Du Bois's program for increasing black political power was to get women the vote. This was an issue far higher on the national agenda than the race question. The turn of the century was a time of ferment in women's thinking about themselves and their situation. Suddenly the constrictions of Victorian fashions, the suffocations of the home, the subservience in the workplace, the burden of unwanted pregnancies were obvious as never before. Aroused by activist suffragettes, an army of women marched from New York to the Capitol Building in Washington, D.C., holding the Stars and Stripes high as they crossed the Delaware, to demand justice and an end to discrimination.

Flouting the accepted canons of dress and behaviour, women wore "peekaboo" blouses and tight skirts slashed to the knee, and when young girls went swimming in the heat of the summer of 1913, the delighted press blazoned their outrageous costumes across the front pages. Women in the cities were smoking now, drinking cocktails in public, flocking to the mushrooming nightclubs to dance the tango, the turkey trot, and the bunny hug in "lascivious orgies" of abandon. Alarmed, the Navy Department ordered, "None of the modern dances are to be performed at the Naval Academy under any circumstances." But Secretary of the Treasury McAdoo liked nothing better than to scandalize Washington society with a quick fox-trot.

In small towns and villages, nineteenth-century morals, attitudes, and social hierarchies lingered on. Historian Henry Adams, patrician and pessimist, spoke disdainfully of "the huge polypus waiting to pop over us . . . what we call the Middle West. . . . It has a stomach but no nervous center—no brains." But in its practical details, everyday rural life was often altered out of recognition by the new technologies; and in the cities, the new swept away the old at an increasingly frenetic pace.

Prosperity, however, had a price. Industrialists took no account of the environment. Returning home to Indianapolis in 1914, Booth Tarkington saw from afar his city "nesting dingily in the fog of its own smoke . . . every factory funnel with its vast plume, savage and black, sweeping to the horizon, dripping wealth and dirt and suffocation over league on league already rich and vile with grime." In these decades of unregulated growth, America suffered severe ecological damage: forests were logged to oblivion, rivers and lakes poisoned. Those who tried to defend the country from the ravages of progress, early "green" crusaders, found a staunch ally in Theodore Roosevelt in the movement for national forests and parks.

The Industrial Revolution transformed not only people's daily lives but also the nation's ethnic mix. In an age of mass production, the average worker became a cog in a preset, standardized machine. He needed no skills and little training, and as industry grew, demanding more and more labor, so did the temptation to pull millions of cheap and willing hands in from abroad.

"Of all the mighty nations, From the east unto the west," ran the children's song, "the glorious Yankee nation is the greatest and the best. We have room for all creation and our banner is unfurled, Here's a general invitation to the people of the world: Come along, come along, make no delay, come from every nation, come from every way. . . ." And they came. America's industry was swept to greatness on a flood tide of immigrants—26,377,525 in the half century from 1871, 8,795,386 of whom arrived in the first ten years of this century.

Many of the "strangers in the land" who dropped to their knees in gratitude at the sight of the Statue of Liberty soon found other reasons to stay there, ground down by endless hours of labor in horrific conditions. Too often their homes in the new cities were stinking, crime-ridden tenements, and they sought relief where they could.

Alcohol was the easiest escape. Thomas Edison's son was shocked to see his father's workers, at the end of a twelve-hour shift, heading blindly to the saloons clustered at the factory gates to get drunk on cheap gin. In 1915, each American aged fifteen or over drank an average of 2.4 gallons of pure alcohol a year—roughly fifty bottles of whiskey for every man, woman, and teenager.

Drugs, too, were a release. By the turn of the century, there were 28,000 patent medicines using opium and cocaine to treat colds, flu, and rheumatism. "Gullible Americans will spend this year $75 million in the purchase of patent medicines," reported *Collier's Weekly* in 1905. "In consideration of this sum they will swallow huge quantities of alcohol, an appalling amount of opiates and narcotics, a wide assortment of varied drugs ranging from powerful and dangerous depressants to insidious liver stimulants; and far in excess of other ingredients, undiluted fraud."

As for the substances in their pure form, opium was the narcotic of the Chinese and the bohemian demimonde. Cocaine was the "heaven dust" of blacks, prostitutes, and jazz musicians. Marijuana and peyote were fashionable further up the social scale. Heroin, first made in 1898 and used to wean addicts off morphine, had become the drug of poorer urban whites; one entire area of Boston was known as "Heroin Square." Until 1915, no narcotic was regulated. Drugs were so readily available in New York that around 60 percent of the city's children were estimated to have taken cocaine or opium. Dealers laced sweets with narcotics and passed them around school playgrounds.

Among recent immigrants, poverty was general and extreme. Many turned to crime, prostitution, or the security of the street gang to survive. Thousands of children died of malnutrition and tuberculosis. In defiance of the child labor laws, which by 1912 existed in thirty-eight states, parents took children in their early teens and younger to work in mills and canning factories. Women and girls rarely earned more than $4 a week—at a time when steak cost $1 a pound, eggs 75 cents a dozen, and Ford's Model T automobile around $500.

In the sweatshops of New York, the stockyards of Chicago, and the blast furnaces of United States Steel, Czechs, Poles, Italians, and Greeks faced a new slavery, but not without protest. Demonstrations and strikes for improved conditions were prolonged and bitter. Beatings, riots, and shootings in pitched battles with police or factory guards were not uncommon.

One of the most vicious confrontations took place in April 1914 at the Rockefeller coal mines at Ludlow in the Colorado mountains. Here the men—a mixture of Greeks, Bulgarians, Serbs, Croatians, and other southern and middle European nationalities—earned $1.68 a day, lived in company shacks, and bought from the company store. In the fall of

1913, the United Mine Workers of America had urged them to demand union recognition, a 10 percent pay raise, and the right to trade in any store of their choice. All that winter the miners and their families—twelve hundred men, women, and children—huddled in a tent camp outside the gates of the mine, through months of freezing stalemate.

Then, on April 20, state troopers, who included a significant number of mine guards in uniform, were persuaded by the mine's managers to attack the camp. Moving stealthily into position on surrounding hills, they waited for the signal. As the explosions from three crude, homemade dynamite bombs died away, they began to pour machine-gun and rifle fire down into the tents. The firing continued till nightfall, shredding the tents and killing some thirty men, women, and children. Finally, at 7 P.M., the soldiers charged to burn the camp. During the day, the miners had dug a protective trench into the dirt floor of one of the tents. At 7 P.M., it was crammed with eleven children and two women; all were suffocated as the burning canvas collapsed.

It was here at the bottom of the socioeconomic heap that one labor organization declared war on the capitalist system. The International Workers of the World (IWW, or "Wobblies," a term supposedly coined by a Chinese waiter with an imperfect grasp of the "W") had first come together in Chicago in 1905. They had no intention of working within the existing political or economic structure. Like the French syndicalists, they advocated workers' seizure and control of the means of production and a single, massive union. They believed in direct action, up to and including the general strike. They operated principally among the "lower-level" workers the major unions ignored: the migratory fruit pickers and lumbermen of the West, the miners and unskilled factory workers of the East. They made an active effort to organize Chinese, Japanese, and Mexicans exploited by their employers and denounced the color prejudice that was alive in most other labor organizations.

Threatening though their revolutionary talk was, the Wobblies were feared in their early years less for their real strength or for any action they may actually have taken than for their image, their "fierce and charismatic" leaders, and the lurid language in which they conducted their day-to-day affairs. They were poor and often scruffy, with bad teeth and red faces; they operated in a milieu respectable Americans preferred to ignore. "We are going down in the gutter," boasted one Wobbly, "to get at the mass of the workers and bring them up to a decent plane of living."

William "Big Bill" Haywood, one of the organization's founders, was the quintessential IWW figure: burly, one-eyed, impatient, careless, aggressive, "a son of the Rockies, risen, as he put it himself, 'from the bowels of the earth.' " At nine, he was already working in the mines; later he rose to prominence within the Western Federation of Miners. In 1906, he was indicted for complicity in the murder of a former governor of Idaho; it took the efforts of Clarence Darrow to get him acquitted. In 1914, he was forty-five, a living symbol of insubordination, and his organization was the mouthpiece for the most violent, anarchic expressions of a deep-rooted, widespread, well-founded industrial discontent that was not going to subside.

These social problems—poverty, foul working conditions and swelling labor unrest, ecological damage, corruption in municipal government, alcohol, drugs, vice, discrimination against blacks and women—troubled Americans from all walks of life. In one of the most remarkable books of the time, *The Promise of American Life*, Herbert Croly summed up their conclusions: "The experience of the last generation plainly shows that the American economic and social system cannot be allowed to take care of itself . . . the automatic harmony of the individual and the public interest, which is the essence of the Jeffersonian democratic creed, has proved to be an illusion." Croly's argument—that there must be "interference with the natural course of individual and popular action"—would once have been heresy to a society imbued with the doctrine of laissez faire, but now it found widespread agreement.

As the war in Europe approached, progressives were fighting to control the changes sweeping through the nation and create a cleaner, fairer society. Their prime target was the industrial organization that had generated so many of America's social ills. Woodrow Wilson, who became President in 1912, was one of those who was deeply concerned by a system that seemed to threaten the most basic principles of the Republic. As early as 1889, while still a historian and political scientist teaching at Princeton, he had voiced his anxiety about the modern economic organization that had "so distorted competition as to put it into the power of some to tyrannize over many, as to enable the rich and strong to combine against the poor and weak."

"I like a little competition," mused banker J. Pierpont Morgan, effectively America's financial controller for many years, "but I like combination better." In the last decade of the nineteenth century, Morgan inspired a series of mergers that created giant corporations such as General Electric, AT&T, and the first billion-dollar corporation, U.S. Steel. By the time he had finished resculpting America's economic landscape, just three hundred firms controlled 40 percent of the nation's industrial wealth.

Wilson, who moved from Princeton into elected public office as governor of New Jersey in 1910, had by this time become an outspoken critic of the "money monopoly." He saw his worst fears realized in Morgan's economic megaliths. Campaigning for the presidency in 1912, he warned his countrymen, "If monopoly persists, monopoly will always sit at the helm of government. I do not expect monopoly to restrain itself. If there are men in this country big enough to own the government of the United States, they are going to own it." His answer, in the first two years of his administration, was federal legislation to bring "New Freedoms" to ordinary Americans, including the Federal Reserve System to end the exclusive power of financiers such as Morgan and antitrust laws policed by the Federal Trade Commission.

In battling the monopolies and trusts, Wilson saw himself as a guardian of traditional American democracy. At the same time, he was becoming increasingly sensitive to another threat to "Americanness." Such had been the scale of recent immigration that by 1914 one third of the total population of 100 million Americans was either foreign-born or had one or more foreign-born parent. More than a hundred languages and dialects were spoken across the nation, and there was a flourishing foreign-language press of sixteen hundred newspapers and periodicals.

Earlier immigration had been fairly homogeneous. "Old Americans" of the white rural classes had almost all come from Protestant northern Europe; their image was that of the conservative, restrained, hardworking farmer or small-business man. Now they found their preeminence challenged by an inrush of people whom they saw as fundamentally different from themselves. The new tide of immigrants came largely from Russia, Middle Europe, and the Mediterranean. They were predominantly Catholic or Jewish, many of them Orthodox, and as a body were less easily assimilable than more "Anglo-Saxons" would have been—most obviously because far fewer spoke much English and most clung to languages that few existing Americans could recognize.

A few titles from this era of silent films give some idea of how the newcomers were seen and portrayed. They included *The Wop*, *The Dago*, *The Chink and the Child*, *A Leech of Industry*—the last an epic about Russian settlers in New York. From across the political spectrum came ideas for coping with the foreign influx, for making America a single nation full of "real" Americans.

Simplest and most brutal was the notion of exclusion and racial "purification." New York lawyer Madison Grant wholeheartedly embraced the pernicious theories of racially determined variations in capacity. "Nordics" were larger, cleaner, healthier, and more reliable than other men—and up to now America had been composed primarily of Nordics. In his polemic *The Passing of the Great Race*, Grant warned with venom against the "mongrelization" of America by unrestricted immigration.

Liberals took a more optimistic view. "America is God's Crucible, the Great Melting Pot where all the races of Europe are melting and reforming!", according to the Russian-Jewish hero of Israel Zangwill's 1908 Broadway play *The Melting Pot*. It was a compelling notion and one to which President Wilson himself at least temporarily subscribed, seeing "the great race" as yet to be developed. "There is gathered here in America," he said, "the best of the blood, the industry and genius of the whole world, the elements of a great race and a magnificent society to be welded into a mighty and splendid nation."

But the welding process needed direction; it could not be left to happen naturally. After all, who could say what the end product might be? America's rulers saw it as their right to take charge. Their own Anglo-Saxon ethic, they felt, was as clearly superior as that of the Greeks had been in the ancient world. "These men of many nations," announced Henry Ford, "must be taught American ways, the English language and the right way to live"—and he set up a Sociology Department within his manufacturing empire to mold his employees.

The Ford concept of "Americanization" was dramatically presented in a symbolic pageant at the Model T assembly plant at Highland Park, Michigan. Visiting dignitaries saw workers of every nationality

descend from a boat scene representing the vessel on which they came over [and] into a pot 15 feet in diameter and 7½ feet high, which represents the Ford English School. Six teachers . . . stir the pot with ten foot ladles. . . . Into the pot go 52 nationalities with their foreign clothes and baggage and out of the pot after vigorous stirring by the teachers comes one nationality viz. American.

In schools and factories, churches and nickelodeons, teachers, social workers, employers, and priests peddled the WASP way of life. In 1914, the Department of the Interior, under Secretary Franklin Lane, spearheaded the government Americanization effort. Immigrants were given copies of the Gettysburg Address along with a guide to American money and measures and a list of "American Leaders and Heroes." Their English lessons were cast in sentences that carried supplementary teachings on American etiquette, customs, and morality. "I take off my hat to a lady"; "A white shirt is for Sunday or after work"; "We must wash our hands before eating"; "I can keep my windows open at night all winter if I have warm bedclothes"; "It is not good for us to eat much fried food."

Newly arrived Middle European and Mediterranean housewives received visits from well-meaning American sisters who had been given a brief by the authorities that bristled with racial stereotypes and assumptions of superiority:

> Get the foreign-born woman to show you how to do something which she does well, such as knitting, embroidery, cooking some of the simple but excellent Italian or other dishes. . . . Teach them English. Take any article at hand, dramatize it. Thus, 'I—put—on—my—hat'. Speak slowly and very, very distinctly. . . . While you are teaching the women get some tactful young woman who loves children to amuse the babies; perhaps wash them and turn them back to their mothers clean and happy. . . . Sometimes a bouquet or a little picture will lead the foreign-born mother to tidy up a whole room. . . . As you get to know these people, you will love them for their childlike simplicity, faith and confidence. Everyone does that works with them. . . . Find out about their countries and about their heroes. Most of them fought for democracy centuries ago and prepared the way for America.

This genteel version of cultural imperialism was not to everyone's taste. Trade unions launched their own programs to teach language and civics as well as history and literature—from the perspective of labor. Radical critics such as Randolph Bourne argued fiercely that the distinctive characteristics of each ethnic group should be allowed, even encouraged, to survive in a "federation of cultures" that would allow a kind of intellectual and emotional dual citizenship. The ideal was not a melting

down of the different human elements of the nation but a weaving together of the new ethnic strands.

Immigration, economic change, political division, race, social ferment—it
was a troubled background on which to impose the rising threat of war in
Europe. In 1914, America was neither entirely stable nor united—less so,
perhaps, than several of the nations that were about to plunge into war.
The old certainties were crumbling, and Americans of all kinds were
struggling to find their feet amid the flux of twentieth-century life. The way
ahead was not clear. "Nothing is done in this country as it was done
twenty years ago," Woodrow Wilson observed. "We are facing the necessity of fitting a new social organization . . . to the happiness and prosperity
of the great body of citizens." Considerable progress had been made along
that road; the reformers had not been held back by any fear of the consequences of imposing "social organizations" on a free people. But the quest
for a new America was interrupted, and in some ways halted forever, during that hot summer of 1914.

2

On the Edge of the Vortex

As Europe slid into war in July and August 1914, Americans stood well back. The United States, they felt, bore no responsibility for the outbreak of war in Europe. Nor was America ensnared by the mesh of treaties that had dragged the European powers into the vortex. The immigrant nation had consciously renounced the greed and imperial ambition it saw "over there"; when news of the fighting came over the wires, most people thanked God for the Atlantic Ocean and the wisdom of the Founding Fathers in rejecting entangling alliances. The Chicago *Record-Herald* called on peace-loving citizens to "rise up and tender a hearty vote of thanks to Columbus for having discovered America." As none of the belligerents declared war on America and none of her vital national interests was threatened, the way was clear for the President formally to announce neutrality. And neutral the nation would remain for the next thirty-two months—but not entirely at peace as the backwash of the European war set currents of conflicting interest eddying within her.

President Wilson was personally grateful to push the war to one side. From the end of July into August 1914, he spent much of his time at his wife's bedside, helplessly watching as she died from diseased kidneys. Ellen had been his mainstay, and her death left him bereft, unhinged almost. "Colonel" Edward House, a Texan political operator who had helped secure Wilson's nomination for President and had become his closest adviser, recorded that one night in New York some weeks after her death the President slipped away from his Secret Service agents and walked through the streets, hoping, House believed, that an assassin's bullet or knife would end his agony.

That fall, the horrific casualty toll in Europe—France lost 211,000 men in the first two weeks of fighting alone—put the war news into competition with football and the movies. As neutrals, American reporters could bring their readers stories and pictures from both sides of the front line. Richard Harding Davis, covering the war for the New York *Tribune*, saw the Germans advance into Belgium. "The entrance of the German Army into Brussels has lost the human quality," he wrote.

> It was lost as soon as the three soldiers who led the army bicycled into the Boulevard du Regent. . . . What came after them, and twenty four hours later is still coming, is not men marching, but a force of nature like a tidal wave. . . . At the sight of the first few regiments of the enemy we were thrilled. After, for three hours, they had passed in one unbroken steel gray column, we were bored. But when hour after hour passed and there was no halt, no breathing time, no open spaces in the ranks, the thing became uncanny, unhuman.

To Will Irwin, reporting for *Collier's Weekly*, it seemed as if

> the whole world had turned into a gray machine of death—earth and air and sky. The gray transport wagons rattled past, carrying gray machines of men. The gray motor-cycles and automobiles streaked past, the mufflers cut out, chugging the message of death. Overhead, the gray biplanes buzzed with a kind of supernatural power. . . . And over it all lay a smell which I have never heard mentioned in any book on war—the smell of half a million unbathed men, the stench of a menagerie raised to the nth power. That smell lay for days over every town through which the Germans passed.

These earliest dispatches captured some of the scale of the fighting. On the Western Front, the belligerents faced each other from opposing systems of trenches that stretched in an unbroken line from the English Channel to Switzerland, German mass counterbalanced by French and English mass and no flank to be turned. On the Eastern Front, the Central Powers held off the Russian hordes. The world had seen nothing like it: never before had warring nations been able to bring such immense power to bear—and because it was possible, it was necessary.

All the belligerents needed prodigious quantities of food, munitions, and raw materials to sustain field armies now numbering in the millions and a home population whose labor served the war machine. The resources of the entire globe—nitrates from Chile, wool from Australia, beef from Argentina—were pouring in a steady stream toward Europe, and the demand on the United States was immediate and massive.

In 1913, U.S. exports were worth $691 million. In the twelve months ending June 1916, the figure reached $4,333 million, and in the following twelve months it rose still further, to $6,290 million. In 1916 alone, munition exports were worth $1,290 million; the price of Bethlehem Steel stock rose from 46¼ in January 1915 to 700 in November 1916. Between August 1914 and April 1917, U.S. Steel supplied 6,067,640 tons of steel "for military purposes." In the same period, Du Pont expanded its output of explosives from half a million to 30 million pounds a month.

Trucks, cotton, canvas, rubber, steel rails, submarines, wool, generators, howitzers, Lee Enfield rifles, boots, corned beef, live horses, mules—the Allies bought everything to sustain nations at war. The exports of cartridges rose by 8,490 percent in two years, that of mules by 7,038 percent, and that of barbed wire, an American invention, by 1,710 percent. The house of Morgan placed contracts for the Allies and took a healthy percentage. As the months passed, the Allies built up sophisticated purchasing commissions that ordered, supervised, regulated, transported, and guarded the stream of supplies. Food was a priority. American beef exports to the Allies rose from 180 million pounds in 1914 to 420 million in 1916, and grain sales rose almost two and half times during the same period.

Before the war, America had been a debtor nation, her extraordinary industrial growth having been funded by foreign loans and investment. By 1916, the debt was gone and virtually all foreign-held securities had been returned to American hands. Now America held most of the world's gold, and Secretary of the Treasury McAdoo saw the time approaching when Wall Street would displace the City of London as the leading financial center and the dollar would become the currency of international trade.

The large corporations' vested interests in an Allied victory were colossal. It was a time of riches for individuals too. Brand-new millionaires appeared overnight, but their dollars were worth less. By 1916, prices had risen by 27 percent and inflation was beginning to have an insidious effect on American society. The boom helped only certain sections of the economy, and many of the conservative middle classes, with no involvement in manufacture or commerce, grew relatively poorer as inflation eroded the value of their white-collar salaries, pensions, and savings. These had been the old guardians of culture, and as the redistribution of wealth made itself felt, a new, brasher America began to appear, in a foretaste of the 1920s.

For the workingman, the war brought opportunity. Suddenly, the rate of immigration fell sharply, and, with little dilution of the labor pool, wages rose ever higher for those already in the swim as the economy expanded. Employers, anxious to make the most of the boom, begrudged every working minute lost; an obedient workforce, ready to work long hours, was, more than ever, the key to huge profits. This gave labor leaders a new bargaining power, which they were equally keen to maximize. They pressed hard for all the rights employers had so far been unwilling to grant: the eight-hour day, the closed shop, the universal right to form unions. So intense was the pressure even from the legitimate labor movement, let alone in the ranks of the IWW and other extremist groups, that some employers felt driven to desperate measures.

On July 22, 1916, at the corner of Market and Steuart Streets in San Francisco, a bomb exploded in the thick of a parade. Ten people were killed and forty-four seriously injured, with eardrums shattered, lungs punctured, legs and arms ripped off. Many assumed the atrocity was the work of German saboteurs; the local authorities preferred to believe that it had been committed by socialist critics of the war—who were also, conveniently, troublesome labor activists.

At 2:06 P.M., when the bomb went off, Thomas Mooney and his wife, Rena, had been watching the parade from the roof of the Eilers Building a mile and a half away. Mooney's attorney would produce photographs and witnesses to prove this, and there was no good evidence to suggest that they could have planted the device earlier. But Mooney was a noisy, arrogant, militant labor agitator who had already been charged once with carrying explosives and acquitted only at a third trial after the first two had produced hung juries. If the San Francisco outrage could be attributed to him, the cause of organized labor might well be badly discredited.

The district attorney of San Francisco had been backed in his campaign for office by United Railroads. He was also the protégé of a California Supreme Court justice who was a regular spokesman for the utility companies, and he had many friends in the chamber of commerce. After a trial that bristled with coached witnesses, bogus "identifications," suspect testimony, violations of customary procedure, and systematic vilification of the defendants in the press, Mooney was found guilty and sentenced to death, later commuted to life imprisonment. He served twenty-two years and five months before being given an unconditional pardon in 1939. It was a case that liberals round the world would liken to the Dreyfus Affair, and it provided the American labor movement with one of its most conspicuous martyrs.

Whether or not the "Mooney" explosion was instigated by employers anxious to protect their war profits, a great many Americans had a large financial stake in the Allied cause. But economic forces were not the only dynamics at work during these years. Each of the belligerent nations had children in the New World, and every outburst of passion in Europe was echoed in America. In Chicago, Slavs and Germans battled on city streets. In New York, processions of enthusiastic Germans sang "Deutschland über Alles" while marching up Broadway. German nationals of military age (perhaps as many as 500,000 of them) were summoned back to Europe, and German-American societies feted them on the quays. Irish nationalists wished the Central Powers an early victory over the English oppressors. In Cincinnati, Russian Jews—refugees from the Tsar and his pogroms—tried to raise a volunteer regiment to fight for his enemy the Kaiser. Meanwhile, Italy's entry into the war in 1915 unleashed the emotions of Italian Americans on the other side.

Woodrow Wilson was appalled by the vision of a republic stained with the blood frenzy of European nationalism, and he appealed to his countrymen to be "impartial in thought as well as in action." But partiality was exactly what both the Allies and the Central Powers wanted, and they missed few chances to manipulate the ethnic divides in American society. Subtly—and not so subtly—European propagandists polluted the natural currents of the melting pot with distrust and spite.

The fight was dirty because this was a battle not merely for sympathy but for the keys to victory—the material resources of America. At the start of the war, the Royal Navy had bottled up the Imperial High Seas Fleet in its home ports and swept the ocean clear of German merchant ships. While American materials poured into France and Britain, Germany was slowly being suffocated by the ever-tightening blockade.

It was an imbalance that seemed likely to win the Allies the war. In the murderous, pivotal year of 1916 on the Western Front, when the Germans tried to bleed France white through unceasing attacks at Verdun, they were held and battered by American steel in French hands. And when the

British attacked on the Somme in July, it was Du Pont's powder and Bethlehem Steel's howitzers that helped reduce the German Army to what Ludendorff described as little more than a militia.

The German government did everything in its power to stop the flow of supplies to its enemies. U-boats stole out into the Atlantic to operate a ruthless "sink-on-sight" policy. Within the United States, German interests tried to buy and stockpile essential war supplies to keep them out of British hands. Ingeniously, pro-German companies tendered for munitions contracts important to the Allies—which they then failed to fulfill. Revolution was still spluttering on in Mexico, and the State Department secured evidence "indicating that Germans have aided and encouraged financially and otherwise the activities of one or the other factions in Mexico, the purpose being to keep the United States occupied along its borders and to prevent the exportation of munitions of war to the Allies." German propagandists based in Mexico sent "Mexicans and half-breeds" across the border and into the South to stir up disruptive discontent among blacks by bribing local leaders, spreading rumors of atrocities, and circulating statistics on lynchings and racial injustices.

More directly, the German government paid agents to carry out their own acts of sabotage and terrorism. Production in factories feeding the Allied war effort was mysteriously disrupted. Under the direction of the German naval attaché, Captain Franz von Papen, German employees of the Atlas Steamship Company and the Hamburg-American Line set up a secret laboratory aboard the *Friedrich der Grosse* to manufacture incendiary bombs, which they placed aboard Allied vessels. Papen also paid a man named Werner Horn to blow up the bridge at Vanceboro, Maine, but Horn was intercepted and imprisoned.

By far the most damaging blow was struck on Black Tom Island, the Allies' nerve center for the transfer of munitions from trains into ships. Black Tom was a man-made peninsula jutting into upper New York bay behind the Statue of Liberty. At any one time it was crammed with hundreds of tons of explosives waiting for loading. In the early morning of Sunday, July 30, 1916, two gigantic explosions shook the entire area of greater New York as 2,132,000 pounds of shells, nitrocellulose, high explosives, fuses, and TNT went up.

The Black Tom peninsula disintegrated completely, craters were gouged into the bed of the Hudson River, and a hail of molten metal fell onto Ellis Island and tore holes in the Statue of Liberty. Windows were blown out in

Brooklyn and Jersey City, and in Manhattan as far north as Forty-second Street. People were awakened from their sleep in Maryland and Pennsylvania. Extraordinarily, only seven lives were lost. But the blasts caused $50 million worth of damage and, more significantly, robbed the Allies of crucial arms shipments as the Battle of the Somme was raging.

The German authorities might claim that in all this they were doing no more than trying to enforce genuine neutrality on America. But they also worked to swing American opinion over to their own side by exploiting the conflicting loyalties of the nation's German Americans.

In 1914, 9 million of the nation's population were German speakers, and a further 15 million, almost a quarter of the population, were of Germanic stock. Germans—stable, hardworking, civic-minded—had long been at the heart of American development; the first thirteen families had arrived in the New World on October 6, 1683, on the *Concord*, their own *Mayflower*. Apart from specific religious groups, such as the Amish, German Americans were in the forefront of assimilation—through marriage, acceptance of English as a common language, and involvement in business and community life.

Nevertheless, they did not lose sight of their heritage entirely. "Love of one's mother does not detract from love of one's bride," as the saying goes, and many local German communities had their own societies that kept alive the culture of the old country without denying the new. But an important part of German culture was the beer hall, and the spread of Prohibition in America, spearheaded by the Anti-Saloon League and the Women's Christian Temperance Union, was a direct threat. By 1914, fourteen states had gone dry. "The efforts of the fanatics," commented a prominent German American in Hamilton City, Ohio, "are directed primarily against us Germans. German manners and customs, and the joviality of the German people, are a thorn in the flesh of these gentlemen."

In 1901, to fight the growing menace, local organizations had joined the newly founded National German-American Alliance, which in turn made links with the Ancient Order of Hibernians. By 1914, the Alliance had 2 million members, and within eighteen months it had added a third million. Backed by the brewing interests, the Alliance was well funded, well organized, and closely integrated with the German-language press, and it had sympathizers in Congress. So when the war started, it could offer powerful assistance to Imperial Germany.

The Alliance was never simply the tool of the German government, but it did accept money from the German Embassy and spread its propaganda because the members of the Alliance, who had friends and relatives already fighting and dying in Europe, tended to share the official German perspective on the war. None was more committed than the organization's president. Dr. Charles John Hexamer, a sandy-haired, fleshy Philadelphia engineer, prized his patrimony highly enough to announce at a public meeting that German Americans would *not* assimilate rapidly with the general American population because they would never be prepared "to descend to the level of an inferior culture"—a remarkable statement from a man born and brought up in Pennsylvania, a successful professional product of that "inferior culture."

With a similarly gossamer touch, Hexamer denounced the "lick-spittle policy" of the United States toward Britain. Under his direction, the Alliance promoted a massive publicity campaign to halt the arms trade. Pro-German speakers toured the country, the Alliance's Literary Defense Committee published more than a million leaflets in 1915, and hapless congressmen were swamped with letters and petitions. Resolutions to embargo arms were introduced in the House. Iowa Democrat Henry Vollmer, a German American with close links to the Alliance, accused his country of being "the arch-hypocrite among the nations of the earth, praying for peace . . . and furnishing the instruments of murder to one side only of a contest in which we pretend that all the contestants are our friends." To the Alliance's chagrin, not only did the trade continue but the President proceeded to reverse a ruling that forbade private loans to be made to the belligerents—provoking Hexamer to castigate him as a "dupe of the Wall Street pirates."

The odds had always been against the Alliance. The arms trade was legal—the State Department had said so—and it was extremely profitable. Even more to the point, it had become the only large-scale export trade open to America. Her merchant marine at this point was negligible; in 1914, she had only nine seagoing merchant ships in commission. To trade abroad, she had to use the ships of others, and the bulk of these were controlled by the British, who were now interested only in trade that served the war effort. If America were to drop out of this trade, there was every chance that her expanding economy would be ruined.

But these harsh economic realities did no more than reinforce the natural inclinations of many Americans. True, in these early stages most

people—a poll of newspaper editors suggested two thirds of the nation—
still had no particular feeling about the war either way. Indeed, by early
1915, war news had declined to no more than a few column inches in the
press. But of the third of the population who had formed an opinion, the
majority, for all Hexamer's claims, were more or less warmly pro-Allies.

Perhaps most significantly, the WASP elite, loyal to its much vaunted
roots, was solidly behind England. Individual contacts—professional and
social, administrator to administrator, businessman to businessman—
formed important channels of influence down which prominent Americans
were steered toward the Allied cause. Wilson himself could not claim an
entirely open mind. As a student on vacation in Europe in the 1880s, he
had conscientiously avoided Germany, explaining to a friend, "I have
never liked the way the German mind works nor have I been sympathetic
with the German character." In December 1915, when Brand Whitlock,
ambassador to Belgium, said he was "heart and soul for the Allies," Wilson replied, "So am I. No decent man, knowing the situation and Germany, could be anything else."

Whitlock, of course, had particular reason for his partisanship. Whoever was at fault for starting the war—and in general the American press
laid the blame on the Kaiser—few denied that the brutal German invasion of neutral Belgium was an outrage. Richard Harding Davis gripped
New York *Tribune* readers with his account of but one example of the
widespread German "frightfulness":

> For two hours on Thursday night, I was in what for six hundred years
> had been the city of Louvain. The Germans were burning it, and to
> hide their work kept us [the foreign reporters] locked in railroad car-
> riages. But the story was written against the sky, was told to us by Ger-
> man soldiers incoherent with excesses; and we could read it in the faces
> of women and children being led to concentration camps and of the citi-
> zens on their way to be shot.

Once the butchery was done, the survivors faced famine under German
occupation. The vast majority of Belgian civilians were now living behind
German lines. The invaders not only were reluctant to provide for them
but had seized part of their existing stores. Neighboring Holland was already feeding 700,000 refugees, and in Belgium starvation was imminent.

This was one facet of the European situation of which the American people were intensely aware, largely through the efforts of one man—and their generosity, orchestrated by this man, would keep the Belgian nation fed through the war.

In 1914, Herbert Hoover was forty years old, a tall, dark-haired, smooth-faced man usually dressed in a blue serge suit, to which he paid a minimum of attention, so that the shoulders were scuffed and the back rumpled; his shoelaces were knotted and his shirt studs missing. In private conversation he would stare fixedly at the floor, jingling the coins in his pocket, and he was reputedly the worst public speaker ever to become President of the United States. He was also a congenital pessimist. "If you want to get the gloomiest view of any subject on earth," his wife, Lou, once said, "ask Bert about it." But as a man of action, he had few rivals.

Born on an Iowa farm, Hoover had been orphaned at the age of nine, his father dead of typhoid, his mother of pneumonia. His early education he largely picked up for himself, through the gift of a powerful intellect and prodigiously wide reading. Graduating in engineering from the newly founded Stanford University, he embarked on an extraordinary period of freelance adventuring: hauling trolleys in the mines of Nevada, mining gold in Australia, managing a coal company in China, and acting as a troubleshooter and "engineering doctor" for sick concerns in India, New Zealand, Egypt, and South Africa. By 1914, he was very rich indeed and could have become infinitely richer; he renounced a fortune to head the Commission for Relief in Belgium.

He got the post almost by accident. When war broke out in Europe in the summer of 1914, thousands of Americans had found themselves stranded there. They ranged from wealthy sightseers—"The residents of the Lafayette Square neighborhood seemed to be caught in Europe almost in a body," remarked one critic unkindly—to schoolteachers making a long-planned Grand Tour, porters and clerks employed overseas by American firms, and even a Wild West show working its way through Central Europe. By the time the show was rescued, its food supplies were exhausted and the orangutan had been fed to the lion. (A group of Iroquois, men of the Onondaga Nation, working in another show in Berlin in July 1914, were interned and maltreated by the authorities. On their release, the Onondaga issued a formal declaration of war against Germany.)

Hoover's self-appointed task was, in his own words, "getting the busted Yankee safely home." Preempting a charity that had already been set up, Hoover took charge of a committee of volunteers, all businessmen, and took up residence with it in a suite at the Savoy Hotel. He brought over all the gold and currency he had in his office and used it to lend money to or change money for the castaways who made their way to London. He found them temporary accommodation and, with extraordinary efficiency, arranged their passage home.

He was thus an obvious choice to head the relief operation in Belgium. Once again, Hoover elbowed aside existing organizations. Gathering an army of volunteers and a fleet of thirty-five ships, he launched a massive fund-raising campaign in the American press. The Cardinal Gibbons Fund for Catholic Children, the Belgian Kiddies Fund, the Dollar Christmas Fund, the Flour Fund, and thousands of similar bodies all poured money into the pool; shoes, clothes, and other secondhand goods piled up. "Women all over the world started knitting wool garments for the Belgians," Hoover remembered. "They were mostly sweaters. The Belgian women carefully unraveled them and knitted them over again into shawls—which was their idea of a knitted garment."

Hoover got Thomas Hardy and George Bernard Shaw to write appeals in American newspapers, whose power he understood so well. With money he made from selling rations to those who could afford them, he set up shelters for pregnant women and soup kitchens for children. He extracted subsidies for the commission not only from the U.S. government but also the British, French, and Belgian governments, dealing with their statesmen as an equal. Lord Eustace Percy described his attitude to all governments: "Kindly get out of my way."

America thrilled to his exploits and damned the Kaiser, and the German government, even with the help of the National German-American Alliance, was hard-pressed to explain its behavior over Belgium, not least because the British had cut Germany's cable links with America. British propagandists, with the cooperation of pro-Allied editors, had a free hand to paint an undeniably brutal invasion in the blackest possible colors. The burning of Louvain and other "reprisals" for civilian resistance were simply the beginning of the catalogue of German atrocities. Women raped and mutilated; children bayoneted, their hands cut off; men herded away to slave labor or execution; wanton destruction of libraries, artworks, homes—the bestial Hun was loose.

TOURIST SAW SOLDIER WITH BAGFUL OF EARS proclaimed the New York *Herald* in all seriousness. The claim that Germany had established a factory to melt down soldiers' corpses for soap was accepted unquestioningly. (The photographic "evidence" was later identified as a building where horse carcasses were rendered for their fat.) The propaganda opportunities were too inviting to waste. A British commission formally "investigated" the case against Germany, and Viscount James Bryce, a former ambassador to the United States, lent his illustrious name to the resulting indictment.

The Bryce Report was released on May 12, 1915. Serialized in the American daily press, it achieved all its architects' intentions. The Philadelphia *Public Ledger* declared that Americans would accept the facts as "final"; now, the New York *Evening Post* concluded, Germany stood "branded with the mark of infamy." The timing could not have been better. Only five days before, a young German submarine commander had committed an act of *Schrechlichkeit* ("frightfulness") that made any atrocity story, however exaggerated, wholly believable.

On the afternoon of Friday, May 7, 1915, Toronto newspaperman Ernest Cowper was leaning on the rail of the Cunard steamship *Lusitania*, looking out at the lush hills of County Cork in the southwest of Ireland. "I was chatting with a friend at . . . about two o'clock when suddenly I caught a glimpse of the conning tower of a submarine about a thousand yards distant. . . . Immediately, we saw the track of a torpedo followed almost instantly by an explosion. Portions of splintered hull were sent flying into the air and then another torpedo struck. The ship began to list."

Cowper was wrong about the second torpedo. The explosion he heard was the ship's boilers going up, ripping the life out of a vessel that had been considered unsinkable. The *Lusitania* was one of the world's largest passenger liners, nearly three hundred yards long. Coal-burning, with four stacks, she could maintain an average speed of more than twenty-four knots and had held the Blue Riband for the fastest Atlantic crossing. Launched less than nine years before, she was the last word in luxurious travel: a crew of 700 tended the ship, its 192 furnaces, and the 1,250 passengers. On this trip from New York to Liverpool, she carried, as always, the cream of American and European society, including this time the thirty-eight-year-old Alfred Gwynne Vanderbilt, whose personal fortune exceeded $40 million. And the passengers felt safe: the *Lusitania* could outrun any U-boat, and if by chance she should strike a mine or a torpedo should hit, the 175 watertight divisions in the hull would surely keep her afloat.

But the exploding boilers did to the *Lusitania* what the iceberg (or possibly a coal-gas explosion) had done to the *Titanic*. The damage was so severe that the ship began to list immediately, and within fifteen minutes she had disappeared beneath the waves. As the deck tilted, the port-side lifeboats swung inward and could not be launched. The starboard lifeboats swung out away from the ship and, as the bows began to go down, tipped awkwardly.

Through his periscope, Leutnant-Kapitan Walther Schwieger gazed in horrified fascination from the U-20 that had loosed the fatal torpedo, possibly mistaking the *Lusitania* for her sister ship, the *Mauretania*, known by the Germans to be in use by the British as a troopship. "Many crowded boats come down bow first or stern first in the water," Schwieger observed, "and immediately fill and sink. . . . It appears as if the vessel will be afloat only a short time. I submerge to twenty-four meters and go to sea."

There had been no panic at first. But as the minutes passed and the decks seemed to rear up vertically, hysteria set in. Passengers pushed to the stern, away from the encroaching waters, and then jumped or dived as the ship fell onto her side, smoke and steam hissing from the funnels. One woman, in the water when the ship capsized, was sucked into a funnel and spat out moments later, charred black and scalded—but still alive.

Watching the appalling scenes, Leutnant-Kapitan Schwieger noted, "I could not have fired a second torpedo into this throng of humanity trying to save themselves." There was no need. In the bitter waters, lives were measured in minutes. The *Lusitania*'s radio officer had transmitted a "Mayday" call, but though help was so close, the coast of Ireland no more than ten miles away, 1,198 people died. Vanderbilt's luck, which had previously kept him off the *Titanic*, ran out. He gave his life belt to a terrified woman, and his last reported words were to his valet: "Find all the kiddies you can, boy!"

The tragedy awoke America from the East Coast to the West. "The sinking of the Lusitania was deliberate murder," pronounced the Des Moines *Register and Leader*. In anguish, the German ambassador telegraphed Berlin: "Our propaganda in this country has . . . completely collapsed."

Among the dead were 114 Americans. With their nation still neutral, there could be no excuse for the sinking—and yet, to the disbelief of their fellow citizens, some German Americans set about justifying it. A series of

Alliance resolutions held the British guilty of provocation in using the blockade to drive the Germans to desperate measures. Kansas City's Deutscher Klub sent a public letter to the President: "After due consideration of all the facts of this deplorable incident, we have arrived at the conclusion that England, and England alone, is responsible for the loss of the lives of the Americans." The German government issued claims that the *Lusitania* had been carrying arms, and these were eagerly repeated.

Now the atmosphere turned ugly. Theodore Roosevelt railed at "hyphenated Americans," and at last Wilson himself felt bound to speak. "There are citizens of the United States," he told Congress,

> born under other flags but welcomed under our generous naturalization laws to the full freedom and opportunity of America, who have poured the poison of disloyalty into the very arteries of our national life. . . . [It is] necessary that we should promptly make use of processes of law by which we may be purged of their corrupt distempers. . . . I urge you to enact such laws at the earliest possible moment. . . . Such creatures of passion, disloyalty and anarchy must be crushed out.

It seemed to many that the German-American foundation stone of the Republic had become dislodged and that, with menace swelling rapidly outside the nation, there was also danger from within: faithlessness, ingratitude, even treachery.

War against Germany came close in the summer of 1915, but the President held firm. He desperately wanted America to remain neutral, to save American lives and money, to preserve the reforms of his first term, to avoid conjuring up the specter of militarism. He had, he believed, a large majority of the American people behind him. Nevertheless, he was not prepared for America to abandon her rights just to keep out of trouble. Germany proposed that Congress should forbid Americans to travel on British ships; the idea struck Wilson as interference with American sovereignty: "I cannot consent to any abridgement of the rights of American citizens. . . . To forbid our people to exercise their rights for fear that we might be called upon to vindicate them would be a deep humiliation indeed." Instead, he insisted that the Imperial German government abandon its policy of unrestricted submarine warfare.

Doggedly, for almost twelve months he pressed his case with words alone, while Allied ships went down and more Americans drowned. In

June 1915, twenty-three Americans died on the *Armenian;* in July, two on the *Anglo-Californian* and three on the *Iberian;* in August, three on the *Arabic;* in September, one on the *Hesperian;* in November, seven on the *Ancona;* in December, two on the *Persia;* in March 1916, six on the *Englishman.* On March 23, 1916, a U-boat sank the *Sussex;* four Americans were injured, and eighty Allied nationals died. Then at last the President issued an ultimatum: "Unless the Imperial German government should now immediately declare and effect an abandonment of its present methods of submarine warfare, the government of the United States can have no other choice but to sever diplomatic relations." The threat, wrung from him, was enough; in May 1916, the German government muzzled the U-boats.

3

"To Hell with Peace Talk":
Volunteers on the Western Front

"The man who kept America out of the war"—it was a slogan that would win Wilson a great many votes in the election of 1916. But there were other Americans who were little short of disgusted by their leader and ashamed of their nation's continuing neutrality. "While most of the newspaper despatches from Washington . . . are full of the word 'peace,'" wrote English press magnate Lord Northcliffe, "these husky young American citizens will not hear of it. . . . 'To hell with peace talk,' said a bright-eyed boy from Kansas City, 'while these slant-heads across the line there are enslaving French and Belgian women and children.'"

Some 15,000 "husky young Americans" went to war in defiance of their nation's neutrality, some to fight in the trenches, some to serve in the Allies' medical corps. A mixed and eccentric collection joined the French Foreign Legion—among them Bob Scanlon, a black New York boxer; big-game hunter René Phélizot of Chicago; Algernon Satoris, grandson of General Ulysses S. Grant; retired butcher Eugene Jacobs of Pawtucket; Frederick Capdeville, son of a West Point fencing master; and Alan Seeger, a poet.

Seeger was a Harvard contemporary of John Reed and Walter Lippmann (class of 1910) without having anything in common with either. He was a shy, timid young man who had gone to live in Paris in 1912 to write poetry. Now he was drawn to volunteer by a fervid emotional devotion to his adopted country. He defended the motives of foreign volunteers like himself in an article for *The New Republic*, for which Lippmann was an associate editor. The volunteers, he wrote, "had stood on the Butte [of

Montmartre] in springtime perhaps . . . Paris—mystic, maternal, personified, to whom they owed the happiest moments of their lives—Paris was in peril. Were they not under a moral obligation . . . to put their breasts between her and destruction?"

Seeger was a sentimental poet, no Siegfried Sassoon or Wilfred Owen. Chlorine gas, shell shock, lice, wire, and putrescence have no place in his verse; his images are chargers, cannon, "bright flags," and the legacy of Lafayette:

> I have a rendezvous with Death,
> At some disputed barricade,
> When Spring comes back with rustling shade
> And apple-blossoms fill the air. . . .
>
> God knows 'twere better to be deep
> Pillowed in silk and scented down,
> Where Love throbs out in blissful sleep . . .
> But I've a rendezvous with Death
> At midnight in some flaming town,
> When Spring trips north again this year,
> And I to my pledged word am true;
> I shall not fail that rendezvous.

He was killed, in fact, in summer, on July 23, 1916, at Belloy-en-Santerre during the battle of the Somme.

Other volunteers joined the British forces. Harold and Howard Hudson, fifteen-year-old twins from Bridgeport, Connecticut, were on vacation in October 1914 with an aunt living on the south coast of England. Her house was next door to a military training camp, and they watched the recruits enviously for a few days before giving their ages as nineteen and joining up.

Large numbers of Americans were blatantly enticed by the Allies. The German-language press commented angrily on recruitment drives in the United States by British and Canadian authorities aware that American manpower was "a blank cheque ready to be filled in." The 97th Battalion of the Canadian Expeditionary Force was officially known as the "American Legion"; it was officered largely by West Point graduates, its commander a colonel with twelve years' service in the regular American Army.

Integration was not always smooth. Arthur Guy Empey, an ex–sergeant major in the U.S. Cavalry who served with a British infantry regiment, recalled that when he had been at school in Virginia, he had been "fed on old McGuffey's primary reader, which gave me an opinion of an Englishman about equal to a '76 Minute Man's, backed up by a Sinn Feiner's." But he was quick to adapt, maximizing his social assets. He taught the Tommies to pitch horseshoes and insisted on the superiority of the baseball pitcher to the cricket bowler as a bomb thrower, while the Tommies taught him the vocabulary of the trenches, including the useful tag "R.I.P.—Rest In Pieces."

Agony, courage, and the nature of warfare on the Western Front. . . . "The odor from a dug-up, decomposed human body has an effect which it is hard to describe," wrote Empey. "There is a sharp prickling sensation in the nostrils, which reminds one of breathing coal-gas through a radiator in the floor, and you want to sneeze, but cannot." He found himself haunted by the reflection that "perhaps I, sooner or later, would be in such a state, and be brought to light by the blow of a pick in the hands of some Tommy on a digging party."

George Craik went into the Second Battle of Ypres with a Canadian unit that suffered heavy casualties:

I felt a stabbing pain in my left eye. It was as though I had been bayo-netted in the eyeball. . . . Joe Daugherty, who had been directly in front of me, had disappeared. In the glow of the shells that whistled overhead we made out what was left of him. The Fourth Battalion man's head had been blown off. Corporal Mitchell's right arm was gone. . . . Mitchell was game. All he said was: "If I don't get through this, send my watch to my mother." . . . I started on the journey to the rear, where they took out my eye and fixed up the twelve other wounds I had from the splinters of the same shell. . . . It was here that Lieutenant Campbell of Mount Forest, Ontario, the hick officer of the machine gun section, won his Victoria Cross for letting the gun be fired from his shoulders. The man carrying the tripod had been killed, and it was the only way to stop the tide that was sweeping our men back. Campbell stopped it, but the heated barrel of the little gun that spits 650 shots a minute burned through his uniform, through his underclothes and through the naked flesh. I saw that back when they laid the body of the former lieutenant in the dugout across from me.

Many of the bravest American volunteers were noncombatants. The American Ambulance Field Service included a fair proportion of the four hundred Harvard men who had been in Europe when war broke out in

1914, working in U.S. embassies and legations or simply idling away their time among Europe's ancient fleshpots.

Some were attached as doctors and dentists to the American Ambulance Hospital in Neuilly, outside Paris; in 1915, the Harvard Medical School sent a whole surgical unit. But the majority were used as drivers, operating the corps of motor ambulances provided by the generosity of civilians at home—a fleet that included eighty Fords, eight Sunbeams, and a Pierce-Arrow said to be the finest ambulance on the continent. Harvard supplied 325 ambulance drivers, Yale 187, Princeton 181, Dartmouth 118—and the list went on.

Many of the American hospitals and medical services in France were organized and paid for by the most prominent figures in expatriate society, women such as Mrs. Harry Payne Whitney and Mrs. Robert Woods Bliss. To work at Anne Vanderbilt's American Ambulance Hospital in Neuilly was "a chic way to volunteer." The auxiliary nursing staff included a lavish sprinkling of socialites, actresses, art students disturbed from their studies in Paris, and relatives of the famous (including the daughter of ex-President Grover Cleveland, who taught blinded soldiers to read Braille). These young women are "terribly distracting, I am free to state," wrote one young Harvard doctor.

But despite the picture painted by the most famous of the drivers, Ernest Hemingway, who was serving in Italy, the ambulance services were not playing at war or indulging in heroics. Their task was to evacuate the wounded from the front over ruined roads, from shell holes, through mud and gas clouds, almost always under fire. "They whine, the bastards," wrote Waldo Peirce (Harvard class of 1907) of the German shells in the Vosges Mountains, "and give the flesh a moment to goose itself in, and damned pagans like some of us to find a religion. . . . Mud, manure— down into it, nose first, and make thy world therein, while she whines and whines overhead. . . . Somewhere on the Vosgean steep. . . . there must be a perfect mold—the lifemask of one Peirce, conducteur d'ambulance."

A fellow Harvard graduate, Richard Norton (class of 1902), was a prime mover in the founding of the American Volunteer Motor Ambulance Corps in 1914. Between September 25 and October 6 alone, his drivers carried six thousand cases. "I find a positive added beauty," wrote the novelist Henry James, "in the fact that the unpaid chauffeur, the wise amateur driver and ready lifter, helper, heater and, so far as may be, consoler, is apt to be a University man."

Norton took a more prosaic view. More useful than a degree were the ability to maintain your own vehicle and a grasp of technical terminology in French. "Anyone who thinks he is coming out here to wander over the stricken field doing the Sir Philip Sidney act to friend and foe alike, protected from harm by the mystical light of heroism playing about his hyacynthine locks, had better stay home," he snapped. "What one really does is to look like a tramp who has passed the night in a ditch." Dozens of ambulance drivers and stretcher bearers were killed or severely wounded; others died of the diseases of the Western Front—dysentery, meningitis, pneumonia.

To George Benet, M.D., a member of the Harvard medical unit, the French wounded were "the most amazing patients I have ever seen." He recalled one *poilu* shot during a

very cold night. Raining. Fell in mud and not found until 2 P.M. the next day. No bath for three months. Underwear changed seven weeks ago. . . . When asked what he did until found, the chap said: "Smoked my peep." He had the bone of his thigh sticking out in the mud and he smoked his peep. One chap told a nurse today that he saw his captain killed (by shell) and his head blown off. When he ran to him his "trachea said squeak—squeak." I have no doubt it did; but imagine scenes like that to think about the rest of your life.

The volunteers themselves saw horrors they would never forget. One doctor, William Woolsey, emerging from a spell at a British casualty clearing station, wrote of the "long lines of groaning or morphinised patients awaiting their turn to be put on the table. The task seemed simply hopeless. Seven tables were going night and day. We worked sixteen hours on and eight hours off in rush times. Abdomens followed amputations and as many as twelve shrapnel or shell wounds on the same man would stare you in the face."

Woolsey was a witness of one of war's newest menaces—the air raid:

One night, a week ago, being on night duty, I was plumb in the middle of a radical knee joint operation, the whole patella was laid back over the quadriceps and the tourniquet had just been removed. . . . I had about finished removing a good sized FB [foreign body] from the head of the tibia, when in rapid succession three of the most terrific soul-breaking

explosions occurred. The lights went out . . . groans from the neighboring tents, the rushing of people here and there . . . the realization of catastrophe in the night. I finished the knee joint with the aid of a pocket
electric light.

The explosions were German bombs, and the clearing station had been
devastated. "A few pieces of twisted iron and a big twelve foot hole in the
ground where the cook house used to be. The cook's liver lay up against
my bell tent wall. . . . Brewer's nurse, Miss McDonald, had a small piece
of shrapnel enter her eye and she had to lose it."

Volunteers were watching the air war from above as well as below. By
1914, only a few wealthy and educated Americans had flying experience,
but many of these immediately joined up and were welcomed by the Allies. Their numbers were increased through covert recruiting by the British
carried on from an office on New York's Fifth Avenue. During 1915,
American pilots were scattered through the French and British air services; a few, among them novelist William Faulkner, chose to join the
Canadian Air Force. But in mid-1916, a handful were drawn together
into the "American Escadrille."

The Escadrille was the pet project of Norman Prince, a polo-playing
Harvard Law School graduate from Prides Crossing, Massachusetts,
whose interest in the embryonic science of flying had led him to take
lessons and even to buy an interest in an airplane factory. But his parents,
Boston bankers, also had a hunting estate in Gascony, and by 1914
Prince was a confirmed Francophile. He enlisted in the French Air Service at the outbreak of the war and by 1915 was taking part in aerial reconnaissance during combat. By December 1915, he had won permission
to form a unit of foreigners. The first group gathered at Luxeuil airfield in
May 1916, to take charge of their French Nieuport fighters, on which they
painted the squadron's insignia: the head of an American Indian in full
war regalia.

The volunteer squadron—renamed the Lafayette Escadrille in December 1916 after German complaints at the brash flouting of neutrality—
flew its first mission as protective cover for the bombers of the French 4th
Bombardment Group over Verdun. This was one of the first major struggles for aerial control over the Western Front, signaling the rise to prominence of the fighter, and it provided the Lafayette Escadrille's pilots with
invaluable pursuit experience.

Five days after the first sortie, Kiffin Rockwell gave the squadron its first victory. But the pilots learned, too, the price they would have to pay. Four months later, Rockwell was killed by an explosive bullet in the throat. Norman Prince died in October 1916 after crash-landing on his return from a bombing raid over Germany. His brother Frederick took his place in the squadron.

Great War pilots ran ludicrous, unacceptable risks every time they flew; their planes were primitive and unreliable, safety precautions were minimal, and no one had the depth of experience needed to anticipate disaster. One of the Escadrille's favorite songs was entitled "The Dying Aviator":

> Two valve springs you'll find in my stomach,
> Three spark plugs are safe in my lung,
> The prop is in splinters inside me,
> To my fingers the joy-stick has clung.
> Take the cylinders out of my kidneys,
> The connecting rods out of my brain;
> From the small of my back get the crankshaft,
> And assemble the engine again.

This was only a slight exaggeration. Deaths in the air were appalling in their grotesqueness, variety, and apparent inevitability. Observers, who were not always strapped in, might fall thousands of feet to oblivion as their craft banked steeply. Pilots, who were strapped in, burned in their seats. Not surprisingly, pilots preferred not to speak of dying, using instead the French terms *volatilisé* ("evaporated,") and *refroidi* ("iced").

Death haunted the pilots. Clyde Balsley, operating near Verdun, was hit by an explosive bullet that shattered his thigh. As he lay convalescing, he asked his friend Victor Chapman to get him some oranges. Chapman promptly set off in his plane to search for citrus but came across a dogfight in which some other Lafayette pilots were outnumbered; plunging in, he brought three German machines down before being shot dead in the cockpit. His father wrote, "That our country should have a share in the grief of this war is the only way in which it can partake of the blessings that lie concealed behind the tragedy. It is a kind of world sacrament."

The most brilliant of all the Escadrille's pilots was its most unorthodox. Raoul Lufbery, born of French parents but brought up in the United States from the age of five, was a confirmed adventurer by the age of seventeen. In 1912, after ten years' travel on six continents and a brisk spell as an army marksman in the Philippines, he met French stunt pilot Marc Pourpe. Instantly smitten with a passion for aviation, he toured with Pourpe as mechanic and assistant. In consequence, when Pourpe enlisted as a pilot in 1914, Lufbery followed him to the Western Front. On December 2, 1914, Pourpe was killed, and Lufbery sought permission to become a flier in his own right. On May 24, 1916, he was sent to the Lafayette Escadrille.

By October, he had qualified as an ace, with five kills. He was awarded the Croix de Guerre with ten palms, the Médaille Militaire, and the Légion d'Honneur. (He would later become the first American to receive the British Military Cross.) After one of his extraordinary raids, he returned with a shot in one of his socks, another in his fur-lined flying suit, and three in the engine of the plane.

Lufbery met his end, as he had always expected he would, in the air. On May 19, 1918, by then a major in the United States' own Air Service, he was chasing a German two-seater on a photographic mission when his machine burst into flames. At 200 feet, with no parachute, he jumped to his death. "Americans, rushing to the spot where he lay, found his body already covered with flowers by French peasants who had seen his fall." A villager told them that the flier had crashed through her garden fence. He had gotten up and appeared to bow—but he was already dead. He was buried behind American lines as comrades flew over his grave to drop roses.

4

"I Didn't Raise My Boy to Be a Soldier" : The Problem of Preparedness

American heroism on the Western Front, German barbarities, German spies, Hoover's efforts to feed the Belgians, the fate of the *Lusitania*, German Americans as "the enemy within," the huge profits of war, the mystery of Black Tom, war news, war books, war films, sentimental songs, Allied propaganda in a never-ending stream—the European war permeated American society and brought to the surface a question that had long been debated in informed circles: In this age of total war, how could the United States best ensure its national security? What armed forces, what weapons, what policies should it have?

The Navy was one focus of the debate. How large a navy was needed for a nation bounded by two oceans with interests now spanning the globe? Was Admiral Bradley Fiske correct when he argued that "the importance to a country of her navy varies as the square of the value of her foreign trade"? Should the U.S. Navy aim at parity with the world's great fleets, given the Navy General Board's fear of "a war arising from the present one in which the United States may be confronted by Germany and Japan operating conjointly in the Atlantic and Pacific"?

How could the homeland be best defended—by the Navy or by powerful coastal artillery? And what could the Army do? As things stood, if the enemy broke through the naval shield, he would meet little resistance. On June 30, 1916, the regular army was 107,641 men strong—ranked seventeenth in the world, a pygmy beside the German Army and a generation behind in weapons systems. The National Guard numbered 132,000 men, for the most part poorly trained and equipped, state by state, with feeble coordination at the federal level. The Marine Corps, under Commandant George Barnett, was a highly professional force but small, no more than 15,500 strong, its forces dispersed throughout the Caribbean and elsewhere.

In the unthreatening decades before 1914, when the Army's primary task had been to guard the Mexican border, these limited forces had been adequate. Indeed, an inconspicuous military establishment suited the country's mood: Leo Tolstoy, with his powerful condemnation of war; Alfred Nobel, using the money he had made from the development of dynamite to found an international Peace Prize; Andrew Carnegie and his campaigning for international peace as a facet of national self-improvement—all had helped to raise the prestige of pacifism. By 1914, there were sixty-three separate organizations in the United States that strongly supported measures such as the Hague Conventions and the International Court of Arbitration.

War was distasteful to many of America's elite from the President on down. The son of a Presbyterian minister, Woodrow Wilson was a committed Christian, resolutely opposed to unjustified war. As a historian, he understood and despised the phenomenon of militarism; as a southerner, from Staunton, Virginia, he had actually seen the ravages inflicted on the country by the Civil War. He was the last person to build up armies gratuitously or drag his country into war. Though he had finally threatened to sever diplomatic relations with Germany if unrestricted submarine warfare did not cease, throughout his first term and into his second he deliberately did very little to give America the military strength to back up his threat.

His choice for Secretary of War in 1916 underlined his commitment to peace. Newton D. Baker was once described as a "nice, trim little man of the YMCA type" by English press baron Lord Riddell. Translating the language of British condescension into American terms, Baker was an honest, unassertive Progressive politician with a solid record of liberal reforms carried through in his days as mayor of Cleveland.

He was a convinced pacifist, a spokesman for one of the largest pacifist organizations, the League to Enforce Peace, a man who had declared war to be "an anachronism and professional soldiers left-overs from the barbaric past." He even conformed to the physical stereotype of a pacifist: a very small man, dwarfed by his generals, Baker would sit in his paneled office puffing on his pipe, perched on a cushion with one leg curled under him. "On his desk there was always a fresh pansy," recalled Secretary McAdoo.

With war raging in Europe, Wilson cast the United States, and himself, in the role of peacemaker. He had long believed that America was destined to exercise world leadership in the twentieth century; he saw his own course in foreign affairs as charted "by the hand of God." After the war in Europe was over, he planned to use America's influence to make peace permanent and universal. It could be guaranteed, he believed, not by force of arms but by replacing the present discredited system of a balance of power by a new apparatus of collective security arranged among the nations of the world. The idea was hardly new, having been current well before the war, but it obsessed Wilson—and he believed that as President of the most powerful nation on earth, he had it within his power to bring such a scheme to fruition.

On January 22, 1917, after two and a half years of the worst carnage the world had ever experienced, Wilson appeared before the Senate to call for a "peace without victory" made between equals. And he laid out the principles that should govern this peace: "Every people should be left free to determine its own polity . . . the little along with the great and powerful." "Government by the consent of the governed . . . freedom of the seas . . . moderation of armaments." The list went on, and underpinning the whole was a "peace made secure by the organized major force of mankind," a "league of nations" acting in concert for the benefit of all. These were, he said, "American principles, American policies. We could stand for no others. . . . These are the principles of mankind and must prevail."

It was this kind of resonant idealism, stronger on metaphor and emotion than on technical detail, that maddened British senior statesmen with longer experience of European affairs. There were those even in the Senate who thought the speech might "make Don Quixote wish he hadn't died so soon." But with the youths of Europe lying dead and mutilated in their millions and the terror of starvation, disease, and revolution threatening a whole continent, to many more Wilson's words offered the promise of a new beginning. To one senator it was "the most startling and noblest utterance that has fallen from human lips since the Declaration of Independence." The Pope described it as "the most courageous document which has appeared since the beginning of the war."

. . .

Without doubt, most Americans would have preferred a world peace achieved without arms, specifically without American participation in the European war. But even before 1914 there had been a noisy, active, significant minority—admirals, generals, financiers, doctors, lawyers, veterans of the Civil War, patriots from all levels and brackets of society—who were alarmed by the nation's obvious military weakness in a world that was increasingly menacing. Across the Pacific, Japan was eying the Philippines and gnawing at China's vitals; on the other side of the Atlantic, gigantic, technologically advanced military machines had come into being. Whether America entered this particular war or not, the militant minority declared, she should prepare for a future in which anything might happen.

Among the most aggressive advocates of military preparedness were professional soldiers such as Major General Leonard Wood, a former Chief of Staff. Intelligent, brave, ill tempered and egocentric, a man (wrote Walter Lippmann) with "an apoplectic soul," Wood had begun military life as an Indian fighter, "one of the few white men in the southwest who could ride, run or walk down an Apache": once, while on the trail of Geronimo, he had covered 136 miles of desert on foot and horseback in twenty-four hours.

Wood argued that America must be able to defend her foreign interests: her Philippine empire, the Panama Canal, her investments in China, the Caribbean, and South America. Even on her own shores, she must be on her guard. In 1909, he carried out maneuvers based on the premise that a seaborne enemy was attacking the cities of the eastern seaboard; to his gloomy satisfaction, the "defenders" failed to hold Boston. In 1914, he dismissed the existing army as "just about equal to the police forces of Boston, New York and Philadelphia."

Another leading preparedness campaigner, Yale graduate Cleveland Langston Moffett, took up this theme of invasion in a novel, *The Conquest of America*, that in 1916 seized the public's imagination with a grisly fascination. Manipulating real-life figures as his characters, Moffett had the Germans knocking out the U.S. Navy in a sneak attack and landing on the East Coast. As Hindenburg pushes his men south through New England, Wilson orders Leonard Wood to launch a frontal attack, thus causing the decimation of the U.S. Army. (Moffett was no admirer of the President's skills as a leader.) Wood then tries to hold Brooklyn but is forced to retreat to Manhattan, blowing up the Brooklyn Bridge behind him. As the Germans advance on Washington, D.C., the President cravenly tries to buy peace with a $3 billion indemnity. Hindenburg instead demands the entire East Coast for the Kaiser. In the end, despite the odds, America wins by force of arms. Standard Oil generously supplies enough gasoline to incinerate 113,000 Huns as they lie asleep in their bivouacs, and the enemy retreats, singed tail between its legs.

The scare story was a principal weapon of the preparedness lobby. Moffett belonged to the Vigilantes, a group of prominent writers who agreed to donate a thousand forceful words a month on preparedness issues. Around them, the case was argued loudly by other high-octane organizations, including the National Security League (in the van, a vociferous Theodore Roosevelt), the Navy League, the Army League, and the National Defense League. In 1915, supported by Roosevelt, Wood made effective propaganda out of a series of month-long summer camps at Plattsburg, N.Y., that were attended by professional men—Ivy League lawyers, politicians, and businessmen—who paid to learn how to drill and hold a rifle. The mayor of New York and his police commissioner sweated over kitchen duty. While the flower of British manhood was being machine-gunned on the Somme, Wood and his volunteers sat around campfires, yarning, singing songs, and inhaling the military ethos.

Wilson had turned a deaf ear as long as he could. But slow as the actual progress toward preparedness for war might have been, by mid-1916 the temperature of the debate had begun to rise uncomfortably. On the one side, Wood and Roosevelt blared of Wilson's "criminal inefficiency as regards the United States Navy" and "short-sighted inadequacy as regards the Army." On the other, just as loud and just as angry, stood the Socialist Party of America.

The Socialists had shown themselves to be a significant political force in the presidential election of 1912, when their candidate, Eugene Debs, had polled more than 900,000 votes, 6 percent of the total. With almost a quarter of Roosevelt's own tally and a sixth of Wilson's, they could not simply be dismissed.

War, they declared, was a capitalist tool; wars were contrived by industrialists in search of armament orders and new markets for their goods, and by reactionaries anxious to use military discipline as a means of social repression. War brought "wealth and power to the ruling classes, and suffering, death and demoralization to the workers," and produced a "sinister spirit of passion, unreason, race hatred, and false patriotism." In 1915, the Socialists had taken their stand against preparedness by amending their constitution: "Any member of the Socialist Party, elected to an office, who shall in any way vote to appropriate moneys for military or naval purposes, or war, shall be expelled from the Party."

Women's organizations, too, opposed a military buildup. Not only would it make bloody, murderous involvement in foreign wars more likely, it was a threat to democracy at home: "Military training is bad for the bodies and souls and minds of boys," wrote feminist and socialist Crystal Eastman. "Free minds . . . undrilled to obedience are vital to the life of a democracy." The rights of women became entangled with the right of all mankind to live in peace, and women's leaders such as the great welfare worker Jane Addams added their voices to those of the pacifists and Socialists.

Addams had great faith in what she called "continuous neutral mediation." With other leading peace campaigners, she called in person on the heads of the European governments at war to press peace upon them and gather their reactions as material for the negotiations she hoped would be an ongoing process. Optimistic as the project might have been, it was sincere and apparently constructive, and it fired the imagination of Henry Ford, already overheated with dark suspicions about the origins of the war and the intentions of the United States toward it. The conflict, he proclaimed, had been started by Wall Street parasites: "Take away the capitalists and you will sweep war from the earth." On other occasions he was convinced it had been started by the Jews and fomented by the excessive consumption of alcohol.

Baroque though some of Ford's notions might have been, he was genuinely horrified by the slaughter in Europe and by what he saw as a trend in America toward war-mindedness. "I have prospered much," he declared in something of an understatement, "and I am ready to give much to end this constant, wasteful 'preparation.' " The sum was $10 million, spent on noisy antipreparedness propaganda. But his most dramatic gesture came in the form of his "Peace Ship," a Scandinavian cruise liner, the *Oscar II*, chartered to carry a crew of prominent Americans to Europe to put continuous neutral mediation into practice and, it was boasted, "get the boys out of the trenches by Christmas."

Many were called—the Pope, Helen Keller, Thomas Edison, the head of Sears, Roebuck—but few chose to come. When the Peace Ship finally sailed from Hoboken, New Jersey, at the end of November 1916, amid the competing strains of "Deutschland über Alles," "The Marseillaise," and "I Didn't Raise My Boy to Be a Soldier," it was manned by journalists and an assortment of radical campaigners, several of them internationally renowned cranks. It docked in Norway two weeks later. On Christmas Eve, Ford, suffering from a heavy cold, apparently lost interest in his crusade and had himself whisked home, leaving the boys still in the trenches and the cause of continuous neutral mediation dead in the water.

That an essentially humane, idealistic undertaking should so quickly have degenerated into a ludicrous shambles, material only for cheap jokes in the press, was one symptom of how fast the tide was now running against the opponents of militarism. Throughout 1916, individuals just as prominent as Ford had been throwing their resources behind the preparedness movement. Ralph Pulitzer had put up a prize of $100,000 for an annual transcontinental air race. But he had ulterior motives: "My visit . . . to two of the armies which are fighting on the Western Front," he wrote,

> gave me an exceptionally vivid realization of the vast importance of the air service for national defense. . . . France and Great Britain have over 3,000 aviators each, every one of these being allowed three aeroplanes. We have, I am informed, less than fifty trained military and thirty naval aviators, and of our two hundred civilian licensed pilots only about a dozen have made cross-country flights of one hundred miles.

The National Academy of Sciences established a National Research Council to coordinate "research in time of war." Thomas Edison, one of America's most famous inventors, announced his plan for preparedness: the employment of "only a small number of trained specialists to develop military art through laboratory research." He was immediately invited by Secretary of the Navy Josephus Daniels to found the Naval Consulting Board, with a view to applying such a scheme to the Navy.

Financier Bernard Baruch led the nation's bankers in a parade down Wall Street to raise public consciousness of the need to mobilize economic as well as military strength. (He also privately financed three more Plattsburg-style officer-training camps.) Wealthy engineer Howard Coffin began a scheme to catalogue the entire productive capacity of the nation as the basis of a mobilization plan. "Twentieth-century warfare," he announced, "demands that the blood of the soldier must be mingled with from three to five parts of the sweat of the man in the factories, mills, mines, and fields of the nation in arms."

Others were concerned with how national production should be regulated. In Europe, all economic activity was firmly under centralized control, and by this time a consensus seemed to be emerging among American businessmen as well that the government, with their aid, should create a "Department of Public Defense" to control both the economic and the military aspects of war.

Wilson himself, while still dead set on American neutrality, had gradually allowed himself to be persuaded by the pressure of public opinion that greater defense readiness was necessary. He was now to be found in the front rank of preparedness parades, banner in hand. After years of digging in his heels against a military buildup, the President took a flying leap into the vanguard. As early as July 21, 1915, he wrote formally to his Secretaries of War and the Navy calling on them to "prepare adequate programs for national defense."

But in Wilson's mind, if not Wood's or Roosevelt's, this was preparation for war in the abstract—measures to guarantee the security of America in the years to come, not to engineer her immediate intervention in the current war in Europe. In Hawaii, for example, the National Guard grew from a force of 977 in June 1915 to 5,044 by the summer of 1916 not because of the European war but to ward off an attack by an enemy "who would come from across the Pacific and attack Hawaii as the first blow directed at the United States."

In early 1916, Congress tried to formulate a coherent program for national security. Given the fierceness of the controversy, it was perhaps not surprising that when the legislation was finalized that summer, the result was a compromise; the Army would be enlarged, but not as generously as its champions had hoped, nor was its brief clear cut.

The authorized strength of the regular army was doubled to some 11,450 officers and 223,500 men—infantry, cavalry, field artillery, coastal artillery, engineers, and air squadrons—but the increase was to be spread over five years. The legislators raised the number of General Staff officers from thirty-six to fifty-four—but then provided that only half of them could be in the Capitol at any one time, lest the influence of the military in government rise to unacceptable levels.

Nor was there any question of sending an expeditionary force abroad in the near future. Congress allocated funds for just a single translator for the

Army General Staff and a meager $15,000 to pay for officers to travel to Europe "for the purpose of observing operations of armies of foreign states at war."

To produce the extra officers needed, training corps were set up in colleges and universities, and in the summer of 1916 Congress allocated $2 million to fund Leonard Wood's camps. The National Guard was expanded to a potential 450,000 men—800 men per legislator—and from now on militiamen were to swear a dual oath of allegiance to state and federal government, with the President empowered to call for the mobilization of the entire force, a crucial supplement to the regular army.

The legislation also provided for an Army Reserve to be made up of discharged regulars and militiamen. This was a significant step, but by the spring of 1917 the Reserve totaled precisely eleven men. Passing the legislation had been effort enough; the plans were far from implementation. As 1917 opened, less than half the new authorized strength of the Army had been mustered, and many of these men were abroad, scattered from the Philippines to China, Hawaii, the Panama Canal, Alaska, and Puerto Rico. Of those at home, a large number were needed to man the coastal defenses. The total "mobile" army in the United States was smaller than at any time since the Civil War.

The Navy, too, had been involved in the preparedness battle and the buildup of 1916, and in the spring of 1917 it was slightly further down the road to readiness—though its official spokesman was as unlikely a military leader as Newton Baker. Indeed, Josephus Daniels was perhaps the most controversial Secretary the Navy Department ever had. Brought up by his widowed mother, the postmistress of Wilson, South Carolina, he looked the part of the southern Methodist in broad-brimmed black slouch hat, low collar, and black string tie. A follower of William Jennings Bryan, he was a strict teetotaler and did not like to work on Sundays. His wife, "Miss Addie," called him "Mr. Daniels" in public, "Beautiful" in private.

Daniels had spent more than twenty years as the editor of a North Carolina newspaper, *The Raleigh News and Observer*, nicknamed the "Nuisance and Disturber" on account of its incessant campaigning for good causes. He was a lifelong sympathizer with the poor and underprivileged (provided they were white) and flintily opposed to the power of the great business monopolies, especially those that had made the largest profits from the war—"paytriots," he called them. His affinities, in his early years as Secretary of the Navy, seemed to be less with the Navy League, which was pressing for the expansion of American naval strength, than with the international peace movement.

In the opinion of many serving officers, Daniels seriously hindered the efficient organization of the Navy by sabotaging the development of a Navy General Staff, decrying it as "Prussianism." The Navy under Daniels, wrote one critic, was like "a big, powerful automobile pushing along a crowded street, in the charge of a chauffeur who does not understand his machine, and does not know the Rules of the Road." Others had suspicion and contempt for his amateurism and quoted the "solo from U.S.S. *Pantalette*," an unkind parody of the admiral's song from Gilbert and Sullivan's *H.M.S. Pinafore:*

> When I was a lad a kindly fate
> Preserved my morals in the Old North State.
> I shunned the flagon and the vile cigar
> But I sometimes went a-boating on the raging Tar.
> I went a-boating every now and then
> So now I am Dictator of the U.S.N.

They resented Daniels extending his own "down-home" moral code to the U.S. Navy. "The flagon" was barred from the officers' mess, as he made all ships dry. The issue of contraceptives was banned, and he made a valiant (though unsuccessful) attempt to induce sailors to wear pajamas.

Even more drastic was his campaign against fossilized tradition and reactionary exclusivity. Annapolis was opened to enlisted men, who were no longer segregated from their officers at social functions and who were compelled to attend off-duty schools to improve their educational lot. Hazing at the Naval Academy was abolished, as were admirals' cocked hats; he himself made a point of wearing a naval cap on top of his civilian clothes when visiting naval installations. He admitted women (though not blacks) to the ranks, as "yeomanettes." He abolished the terms "port" and "starboard"; one newspaper suggested unkindly that he would soon have steersmen saying "gee" and "haw." He ordered navy bands, during the period of neutrality, not to strike up "Tipperary." "Why," asked one critic, "should a Navy that has Josephus Daniels for its Secretary wish to sing?"

At the same time, Daniels had ambitions for his department and contrived to engineer a consistent expansion of the Navy through his skill as a negotiator on Capitol Hill, "where the life of a battleship or cruiser is more often in jeopardy than it would be in combat." In 1916, borne up by the wave of public indignation against Germany's brutality at sea after the sinking of the *Lusitania*, the Navy launched itself on a three-year program of expansion on an unprecedented scale, with the biggest appropriation ever devoted to naval expansion by any country. The target was a fleet of sixty capital ships by 1925; the first phase, to be undertaken between 1916 and 1919, would produce ten battleships of the "dreadnought" type, six battle cruisers, ten light cruisers, some fifty destroyers, and about a hundred submarines.

But here again the preparations were not for this war. There was a strong element within the naval leadership that aspired to global naval dominance. Daniels and his Chief of Naval Operations, Admiral William Benson, aimed eventually to build "a great navy second to none," in Woodrow Wilson's phrase, in the world after the war, whoever might win it.

Because the objectives of the program were grand, vague, and remote, in terms of immediate needs its priorities were unhelpful. There were too many large, impressive capital ships, which European navies were busy proving to be irrelevant. There were relatively few submarines, which the Germans had turned into a potentially war-winning weapon. More to the point, by the end of 1916 the program was only just beginning to be implemented. There were simply not enough ships yet—neither enough cruisers to act as the eyes of the fleet nor enough destroyers to combat the submarines. There were hardly any troop transports or auxiliary vessels. Such scouting and screening vessels as did exist were scattered throughout the world. Eight had been sent to Mexico as recently as 1914, with apparent indifference to events in Europe. The only formal naval strategy in existence envisaged a campaign against an enemy fleet in the west Atlantic, with its focus in the Caribbean. There were too few men—at least 35,000 fewer than the official establishment of 87,000—and far too few trained, experienced flag officers. There was no naval reserve.

So as 1917 opened, as her citizens drowned and her President hung on grimly to neutrality, America had stepped up a gear in military power, at least in intent, but it was still very far from parity with the European powers. The buildup of the Army and Navy was still in the idea stage in many respects, and, perhaps more important, the country had not yet come to terms with the essence of modern war. Americans were not yet ready to make the sweeping sacrifices on the home front that total war demanded, nor did the nation have in place the organizations that would be needed to make them.

Three months before the National Defense Act was passed in June 1916, Secretary Baker wrote to Wilson, "Under modern conditions a great war involves . . . such an organization of the industrial, commercial, financial and social resources of the nation as will enable them to be mobilized, both to support the military arm and to continue the life of the nation during the struggle."

The logical instrument for this kind of mobilization was a powerful federal bureaucracy, a "Department of Public Defense" of the type envisaged by American business to control both budget and procurement—but neither Wilson, Baker, nor Daniels could stomach the idea. Such a bureaucracy threatened to bring the nation's industrial leaders into the heart of government. It would give power and influence to precisely the sectors of the economy that the administration and Congress had been fighting since 1912. The "New Freedoms," intended to liberate individual Americans from the thrall of big business, would be impossible in the planned, regulated, controlled economy of a nation at war—and to the President and his supporters, the defeat of monopoly was at least as important as full military preparedness.

Daniels invested heavily in federal plant in Norfolk, Virginia, to insulate the Navy from big business. Baker compromised by recommending the creation of an advisory body, a "council of national strength," to survey the nation's resources and to work for the gradual development of "sympathetic cooperation" with the nation's business interests.

The result was the creation in August 1916 of a Council of National Defense for the "coordination of industries and resources." Set up under Baker himself, the council was little more than a planning body served by a more active Advisory Commission of seven leading business figures—including Bernard Baruch; Julius Rosenwald, vice president of Sears, Roebuck; and labor leader Samuel Gompers. The CND set up a network of 184,000 local defense councils across the nation, and a women's committee nominally directed the energies of some 4 million women. But in practice the council had little real authority, controlled none of the nation's defense budget, and was not truly empowered to direct the nation's economy in time of war.

5

"We Can Do No Other": The Decision for War

The nation's leaders planned a leisurely military buildup with the postwar world in view, not the war currently raging in Europe. But they were wrong to believe that the country could keep clear of that conflict indefinitely and allow them to plan for the future in a comfortable vacuum. With his stern warnings of what might follow if Germany resumed unrestricted submarine warfare, Woodrow Wilson had succeeded once in beating back the flames of Europe's war from America's shores, but it was not a trick he could repeat.

With the balance of power so delicately poised between Germany and her enemies, the mere threat to sever diplomatic relations had been enough to muzzle the U-boats in May 1916. But as the year clawed to its bloody close, the war of attrition was driving the Germans nearer to the brink of desperation, where no outside pressure could restrain them.

By the end of 1916, the year of Verdun and the Somme, Germany had begun the final slide to exhaustion, drained of men, money, and morale. If Germany's plans had been fulfilled, the war would have been over by now. Her military leaders had planned to advance swiftly through Belgium and into France, to encircle and crush the French Army, and then to redirect all of Germany's might against Russia. That strategy had failed. By the end of 1914, the war of swift maneuver in the west had ossified into a static line of opposing field entrenchments stretching from the Swiss border to the English Channel. The German Army could neither outflank its enemies nor break through with a frontal assault, so formidable were the defensive capabilities of artillery and machine guns. With Russia pressing from the east, the country was locked into a war of attrition on two fronts, a battle of men and materials its leaders had not contemplated and for which they had not prepared.

As the British Navy blockaded Germany's ports, food ran short. Supplies earmarked as emergency stores for the Army had to be released to starving civilians to keep public order. "There was no night without the collapse of one or more women at the machines because of exhaustion, hunger, illness," noted a worker at a Berlin armaments factory. "In the canteen, women had almost daily screaming fits, and sometimes fights amongst themselves, because they alleged 'the ladle was not full.' "

The futile slaughter on the Western Front, the growing waves of strikes and protests, rampant inflation, profiteering, and an iniquitous black market were destroying Germans' morale and feeding the fires of revolution. Kaiser Wilhelm II, the icon of German supremacy, was now being blamed personally for the growing crisis, and he was surprisingly vulnerable to the shift in public sentiment.

Technically, Wilhelm was a constitutional monarch who shared power with elected representatives of the people. In practice, however, he was an autocrat who ruled by fiat through a "ruling herd" of courtiers, with some of whom he could covertly express both his homosexuality and his rampant anti-Semitism. ("Jews and mosquitoes are a nuisance that humanity must get rid of in some manner," he once wrote. "I believe the best would be gas.") Wilhelm's obvious passion for power fascinated Sigmund Freud, who interpreted this craving as an attempt to compensate for his mother's rejection of him as a baby because of his withered left arm, whose nerves had been damaged at birth.

Wilhelm's grip on the throne depended in part on placating his subjects. By the summer of 1916, he recognized that for his regime to survive the discontent and revolution brewing in Germany, he would have to provide a victory—and make the resulting peace profitable enough to compensate for the vast sacrifices his people had already made. The people wanted the land their armies now held: Belgium, northern France, some of the eastern territories. Germany's powerful industrialists hungrily eyed the new markets and raw materials that would be the spoils of a decisive victory, not least a large colony in central Africa. And the German people had come to believe that only two men could possibly deliver this kind of victory: Germany's most famous generals, Erich Ludendorff and his nominal superior, Paul von Beneckendorff und von Hindenburg.

They were an unlikely pair. Ludendorff was a boorish, brutal commoner, while Hindenburg was the archetype of the aristocratic Prussian officer, tall and square-shouldered, of massive girth, with close-cropped hair, a walrus mustache, and an air of authority and breeding. But the aristocrat was only an average soldier, while the commoner was recognized as a military genius, an intuitive strategist, and an adept in the technological and managerial skills required by modern warfare.

In the teeth of prejudice, Ludendorff had climbed close to the top of the aristocratic Prussian officer corps. There, however, he stalled. His low caste prevented his appointment to supreme command; for appearance's sake, his nominal superior had to be a noble-born soldier, and Hindenburg, who had been retired from the Army for three years, had been selected for the task. A hero of the Franco-Prussian War, he might have had little aptitude for the complexities of modern soldiering, but he possessed the one trait Ludendorff lacked: the last ounce of nerve for high command.

In August 1916, the Kaiser reluctantly appointed the duo to the Supreme Command. Under their direction, the General Staff quickly conceived a strategy for German survival: the creation of a garrison state that Adolf Hitler, then serving in Ludendorff's army, admired deeply and would come to emulate. Every man, woman, and child in Germany was now to "live only in the service of the Fatherland," and every ounce of the nation's strength, both material and moral, was to be thrown into the war effort. "We can only win," wrote Ludendorff, "if we give our army so much war material that it can face the hostile armies on equal terms. . . . In view of our enemies' greater resources this will only be possible if we lay hands on all the treasures of our country's soil which industry and the plow can make available and then apply them exclusively for the purpose of war."

To enhance Germany's long-term strength, Ludendorff urged the building of a strong resource base through the acquisition of Ukraine and territories in Russia, the formation of a "Middle Europe" under German domination, and, at home, what he called "a strong population program." Given the "excess" of marriageable German women, every healthy man had "a natural duty" to marry and produce children. Blaming the decline in marriage as an institution on "promiscuous sexual intercourse," he proposed the taxation of bachelors and a prohibition on the sale of "articles designed to prevent conception."

To feed the war machine in the short term, he bled the conquered territories, seizing their resources and their able-bodied men as slave labor—workers from Belgium and Poland shipped into Germany at the rate of two thousand a week, many of them to die of tuberculosis and influenza in German camps. "Objections founded on international law must not hold us back," declared Ludendorff. "They must give way before the inexorable necessity of finding the most productive employment in war industries for all labor under German control." When the U.S. State Department protested against this violation of human rights, the German ambassador in Washington explained that, given the current high rate of unemployment in Belgium, the deportations were for the workers' "own moral and physical good."

By turning Germany toward totalitarianism, Ludendorff and Hindenburg hoped for an eventual resurgence of national power. To buy time to reconstruct the state, they decided that 1917 must be largely a year of defense. They planned no major offensives and began to construct modern and massively strengthened positions behind the Army's present lines—a system of fortifications for withdrawal and defense in depth that was known to the Allies as the "Hindenburg Line."

But as Germany retrenched on land, the Imperial Navy advanced its own proposal for winning the victory the Kaiser so desired. The admirals wanted to reopen the campaign of unrestricted submarine warfare that had been halted by America's protests in May 1916. Britain, they argued, was facing a food crisis. The Navy's goal would be to destroy 600,000 tons of British shipping per month and deter a further 250,000 tons of neutral shipping from sailing to English ports. In six months, the U-boats could reduce by 40 percent the vessels available for carrying vital imports to Britain. The ships remaining would not be able to bring in enough grain, and Britain would be forced, by the threat of starvation, to seek peace.

That the theory was full of holes was obvious to many within Germany. The most articulate critic was industrial czar Walther Rathenau. Could the Navy, he asked, really meet its target with only a hundred U-boats on station at any one time? Even if the U-boats sank 600,000 tons per month, would this really be enough to cripple the British merchant fleet before the Allies had a chance to escalate their shipbuilding programs and replace the lost vessels? And even if imports were severely curtailed for six months, would the British really be that desperate for food?

Whether Ludendorff believed the Navy's boasts is not certain, but he did recognize that unrestricted submarine warfare could play a part in his defensive strategy for 1917, maybe a critical part. Submarine raids could impede the menacing Allied buildup, boost the morale of his troops, and buy him time on the Western Front. In addition, unleashing the U-boats would be guaranteed to rally German public opinion—to unite and inspire the people to accept the yoke of total war.

The only potential objection was that the United States would, as its President had threatened, sever diplomatic relations and possibly even declare war. This possibility Ludendorff seems simply to have dismissed. In the words of Admiral Eduard von Capelle, the Minister of Marine, the American menace amounted to "zero, a complete and absolute nothing, a less than nothing." The United States was obviously making no military preparation to join the conflict; one German staff report put the country's fighting value on a level with Romania's—and this assumed its capacity to project force into Europe.

The United States, it seemed, had a President obsessed with peace; her people were riven by ethnic and sectional conflicts; her businessmen were making vast profits from supplying Britain and France that they would be unwilling to abandon. As the American ambassador in Berlin cabled home, the typical German believed Americans to be "a fat, rich race without sense of humor and ready to stand for anything in order to keep out of the war." Ludendorff's gut reaction was to discount Wilson and his threats, and, as was his habit, he acted upon instinct and urged the unleashing of the U-boats.

Supported now by the Supreme Command, the Navy had its way. All that remained was to choose the moment to begin operations. If the submarines were seriously to hamper the Allied buildup, action would have to start early in the year. On January 9, 1917, at his white marble castle at Pless, the Kaiser overruled civilian objections and gave his formal consent to the reopening of the submarine campaign on February 1.

Accordingly, at 4:10 on the afternoon of Wednesday, January 31, 1917, Count Johann von Bernstorff, German ambassador to the United States, arrived at the office of U.S. Secretary of State Robert Lansing to hand over the official Note imparting the news that, as of midnight, America's ships would be sunk on sight.

"He did not smile with his customary assurance," the Secretary recalled later. Nor did Lansing himself as he read the humiliating little document. America would be allowed to sail one vessel per week across the Atlantic, provided it kept to a specified route and was clearly marked with stripes "like a barber's pole, and flying at each masthead a flag resembling a kitchen tablecloth."

Lansing's anger boiled over when he realized that America had been given less than eight hours' notice of the Imperial Navy's intentions. Dismissing Bernstorff, he immediately telephoned the President. Wilson was out of the White House, so Lansing sent the Note over for him to see on his return. There, through "some confusion with other papers," Germany's démarche lay unnoticed until eight that evening—a mere four hours before it would become effective.

The German move was a numbing blow to all Wilson's hopes. Far from being an example to the world, an arbiter of peace, America was in danger of being relegated to the sidelines, dismissed by one brutal nod from a militarist thug.

The President had failed to appreciate the significance of the appointment of Ludendorff and Hindenburg; he had not seen where their policies were leading or identified the strategic alternatives open to them. Yet the warning signs were there. The debate in Germany over renewing the U-boat campaign had been very public and had been well reported in *The New York Times*. Lansing recorded that he had known "that all [Germany's] shipyards had been working to their full capacity in constructing submarines for the past seven months"—ever since Ludendorff had taken power, in fact. But Wilson had taken no action other than to develop his ideas for "peace without victory" and a "League of Nations" to cement that peace.

Perhaps if Wilson had listened to his Secretary of State, he might have been taken less by surprise by Germany's strike. But he disliked Lansing, who, in Josephus Daniels' opinion, was "meticulous, metallic and mousy." Lansing's lifestyle—"out every night attending dinners" and days spent consuming "an infinite number of cigarettes and cups of black coffee"— irritated the puritanical President, as did the company he kept: "Not conducive to a broad outlook, as they are mostly society folk and reactionaries."

Instead, Wilson relied on "Colonel" House, who had become one of his closest friends, not least because House rarely suggested anything he knew to run counter to the President's existing thoughts. Usually a skilled, obsessive observer of foreign affairs, he had been giving Wilson poor advice during these critical weeks, a victim, perhaps, of wishful thinking. "You stand in a position to bring about peace much more quickly than I thought possible," he had told the President on January 15, 1917. On January 20, at least eleven days (and possibly six months) out of date, he reassured his President that "at the moment the liberal element have control of the German government." Reassured, Wilson had continued doggedly in his quest for peace and led America into a dangerous, humiliating crisis.

When they met in Wilson's study on the night of January 31, Lansing, a prominent international lawyer, made himself even less popular with his legalistic appraisal of the situation. In his view there was no alternative to breaking off diplomatic relations, as Wilson had threatened to do back in the spring of 1916. The only question in his mind was whether the President should also expressly warn Germany that any attack on American ships or citizens "would be considered by us to be an act of war."

Still Wilson could not abandon his dreams. While Europe had been tearing itself to pieces, America had become ever stronger and, in Wilson's view, ever more necessary as the life raft of civilization. "White civilization" and its domination in the world rested, he felt, "largely on our ability to keep this country intact."

The next day—"sad and depressed," in House's words—Wilson finally made good his threat and severed diplomatic relations, in the faint hope of "bringing the Germans to their senses." Yet he still insisted that he would not allow the break to lead to war. "I refuse to believe," he argued on February 3, "that it is the intention of the German authorities to do in fact what they have warned us they will feel at liberty to do. . . . Only overt acts on their part can make me believe it even now." His attitude, in the view of British naval intelligence, was "that of a man at poker whose bluff has been called. . . . The Germans have repeated their offenses and the President finds himself obliged to make good his strong words, but having been elected on a peace ticket he prefers to deal by force of typewriters than by force of arms." On February 22, the twenty-two leading peace societies sent Jane Addams and other delegates to Washington to talk to the President. "He still spoke to us," Addams recalled, "as fellow pacifists."

In the days that followed, Wilson was "slower than a glacier," according to Secretary of the Interior Franklin Lane. "His patriotism is covered over with a film of philosophic humanitarianism that certainly doesn't make for punch at a time such as this." The United States, the President ordered, must give Germany no justification for hostilities—which meant that the country could make no military preparations of any consequence.

But passivity was not enough to ease the tension. As the Imperial Navy had hoped, fear of the submarine pinned merchant vessels in their ports. Wilson recognized the unwillingness of shipowners to risk their vessels at sea without insurance or protection; he saw the congestion of commerce that had resulted and feared that this "in itself might accomplish, in effect, what the new German submarine orders were meant to accomplish, so far as we are concerned."

Now, as February drew to its close, he found an avenue for firm action. He asked Congress to permit "an armed neutrality"—the arming of merchant vessels with naval guns and gunners to fight off the U-boats. The House of Representatives passed the bill quickly, but in the Senate there was still a small band of men who, amid the mounting war fever, adamantly opposed any action that might involve America more closely in the European catastrophe. Led by Robert M. La Follette, a progressive Republican senator for Wisconsin and lifelong pacifist, they arranged a filibuster, and the Armed Ships Bill was talked out.

Angry and frustrated, Wilson released the text of a telegram passed secretly to the administration by British intelligence on February 24. The telegram—from the German Foreign Minister, Arthur Zimmermann— had been sent on January 19 to the German minister to Mexico, disclosing a plan for Germany to enter into an alliance with Mexico and possibly Japan, too, if America entered the European war. In the event of successful hostilities, the Mexicans' reward would be the return of their "lost territory" in New Mexico, Texas, and Arizona.

The Zimmermann telegram had little immediate diplomatic or strategic importance (beyond suggesting that Britain had known about the resumption of submarine warfare almost two weeks in advance without sharing the knowledge). But it made explosive anti-German propaganda at home. It had, in fact, a more drastic effect than Wilson had anticipated. He had possibly intended only to secure support for his proposal to arm merchantmen. (He would eventually arm them on his own authority, informed by Lansing that he had the legal right to do so.) But when headlines blazoned the German plot across the country on March 1, public opinion surged ahead to the view that war was now inevitable, even necessary.

Declarations supporting the war poured in from all quarters. "Notwithstanding the difficulties which my race faces in many parts of this country," wrote Robert Russa Moton, principal of the Tuskegee Institute, "I am writing to assure you that you and the Nation can count absolutely on the loyalty of the mass of the negroes."

The American ambassador in London, Walter Hines Page, argued for war on economic grounds. He had been alarmed to discover that the Allies were effectively at the end of their external financial resources and "must have a large enough credit in the United States to prevent the collapse of world trade." Only the government could make loans on the scale needed—but it could not do so while the nation remained neutral. "Perhaps our going to war is the only way in which our present preeminent trade position can be maintained," Page concluded.

In 1936, an investigative commission under Senator Gerald Nye would decide that America's massive arms trade with the Allies had been a positive inducement for the President to declare war. But such a conclusion does not fit with Wilson's character or his mood at the time. Privately, he was in despair at the situation, telling Secretary of the Navy Daniels, "I can't keep the country out of war. . . . They talk of me as though I were God. Any little German lieutenant can put us into the war at any time by some calculated outrage."

As the days went by, the tally of calculated outrages grew. Intelligence reports on German intrigue poured out of Mexico. German merchant seamen tried to block harbors by scuttling their vessels in navigable channels. American citizens in Germany were treated roughly. At the Cabinet meeting of February 25, Lansing confirmed that "the wives of American Consuls on leaving Germany had been stripped naked, given an acid bath to detect writing on their flesh, and subjected to other indignities."

There were rumors that the Allies were facing defeat, that French civilian morale was collapsing, that London was facing food crises. On the Western Front, Ludendorff was systematically laying waste the land he was vacating by pulling his troops back to the Hindenburg Line—burning buildings, poisoning wells, hacking down trees, strewing booby traps, and thus confirming every worst suspicion about German "frightfulness."

During February, twenty-one Americans on various British and French vessels had drowned when German torpedoes struck home. And then on Sunday, March 18, came word of what Wilson had dreaded—the sinking of American merchant ships, three of them, with the reported loss of fifteen lives. Hysteria gripped the country, and the President had to be seen to act.

On March 20, he called his Cabinet together. At half past two in the afternoon they pushed their way through the throng of journalists into the Cabinet room. According to Lansing, "Three minutes later the President came in and passed to his place at the head of the table, shaking hands with each member and smiling genially and composedly as if nothing of importance was to be considered." After making some remarks on a threatened railway strike, he turned to the subject of Germany and invited each member in turn to express his opinion. All ten were in favor of war—even, with misery, the pacifist Secretaries of War and the Navy.

Yet, almost unbelievably, the President was "disinclined to the final break." One more happening of these momentous weeks had still to be assimilated—the revolution in Russia that on March 15 had ousted the Tsar. As this item came up for discussion, Wilson commented, "The glorious act of [the] Russians . . . in a way had changed conditions, but he could not give that as [a] reason for war." To Lansing, on the other hand, the revolution, by dislodging the autocratic Romanov regime from the ranks of the Allied leaders, "had removed the one objection to affirming that the European War was a war between Democracy and Absolutism." Now Lansing was talking Wilson's language; he went on, "To go to war solely because American ships had been sunk and Americans killed would cause debate. . . . The sounder basis was the duty of this and every other democratic government—to suppress an autocratic government like the German."

This meeting seems at last to have turned Woodrow Wilson toward intervention. Lansing's invocation of a war for democracy had opened the way for him to recast the situation in the terms of his long-held policy. America could enter the war not out of self-interest but as a moral crusade.

But the President could not hope to achieve his lofty purpose by joining with France, Britain, and the other Allies in their declared war aims, acquisitive and possibly punitive as they were. The United States would have to remain independent. At the same time, she had to contribute enough to an Allied victory to give her the loudest voice at a peace conference.

To Wilson this meant, among other things, sending a mighty American army into combat. Beyond doubt the Allies, financially drained, urgently needed a transfusion of American treasure, but no one had yet envisaged the outpouring of American blood.

Indeed, in March 1917, the Allies were not desperate for more men and, when Page informally sounded them out, did not call for them. In the United States, there was also strong resistance—even within the Cabinet, from Secretary of the Treasury McAdoo in particular—to the notion of sending American troops into Europe. But in Wilson's view, to have a chance of dominating the discussions afterward, America must be in the fight in Europe physically and not just spiritually or financially. He could no longer realistically propose a *pax Americana* from the sidelines; if he wanted it, his men must fight for it.

Wilson called Congress for April 2. Over the intervening days he put aside his other work and concentrated on his war address, insofar as he could concentrate at all. "Apparently he is not in a working mood these days," an aide confided on March 21. "He spends nearly all his time with Mrs. Wilson, reading, playing pool or visiting."

Forcing himself to focus, Wilson scanned press reports and analyzed the editorial advice of papers such as *The New York Times*, a strong advocate of intervention on an independent footing. He pored over memoranda of German war crimes, took advice from House, and struggled to order his thoughts, "sitting before his own little typewriting machine, and slowly but accurately and neatly typing a message which probably will be his greatest State paper." "If the president is writing as he feels," observed a White House official, "Germany is going to get hell in the address to Congress. I never knew him to be more peevish. He's out of sorts, doesn't feel well, and has a headache."

It was the evening of April 2 before the newly assembled Congress was ready for the President. He drove through a thin drizzle toward the Capitol, whose dome was floodlit from the ground for the first time ever. He was shown into an antechamber and, thinking himself alone, walked to the mirror. Ellery Sedgwick, editor of the *Atlantic Monthly*, who was concealed from Wilson's view, watched closely. "Chin shaking, face flushed, he placed his left elbow on the mantel and gazed steadily at himself until he composed his features." Then he strode out into the corridor and through the swinging doors of the House chamber.

Every seat was taken, and people were standing shoulder to shoulder in the galleries. Supreme Court judges, Cabinet members with their wives, foreign diplomats, and senators wearing or carrying tiny flags were crammed together on the lower floor. The President spoke to the packed joint session for thirty minutes. In a low, dispassionate voice calculated to set off the enormity of his message, he recounted the German outrages, the spying and sabotage, and the barbarities of submarine attacks that now spared neither hospital ships nor ships carrying relief supplies to Belgium. This was "warfare against mankind." The United States could not "choose the path of submission and suffer the most sacred rights of our nation and our people to be ignored or violated. . . . I advise that the Congress declare the recent course of the Imperial German Government to be in fact nothing less than war against the government and people of the United States."

In the remainder of the speech, he sketched the nation's war aims. These, he said, were "exactly the same things" that he had previously described to the Senate on January 22—although then he had hoped to establish peace and justice in the world by keeping clear of war and now he aimed to achieve the same ends by plunging in. Senator John Sharp Williams of Mississippi, who was old and deaf, picked out one ringing phrase—"keeping the world safe for democracy"—and began to clap, leading a roar of approval.

As Wilson's speech drew to its end, his rhetoric assumed its greatest power, in phrases that have carried down the years: "America is privileged to spend her blood and her might for the principles that gave her birth and happiness and the peace which she has treasured. God helping her, she can do no other." The house was on its feet, shouting, clapping, crying. "Think what it was they were applauding," Wilson said to his private secretary, Joseph Tumulty, late that night. "My message today was a message of death for our young men. How strange it seems to applaud that"—and the President wept.

The rhetoric did not silence the opponents of war. "We are going into war upon the command of gold," shouted Republican Senator George Norris of Nebraska as the Senate debated the war resolution on April 4. "I feel that we are committing a sin against humanity and against our countrymen. I would like to say to this war god: You shall not coin into gold the lifeblood of my brethren. . . . I feel that we are about to put the dollar sign upon the American flag."

But that day the Senate endorsed the declaration of war by 82 yeas to 6 nays. On Good Friday, April 5, the House of Representatives followed, with 373 yeas to 50 nays. Among the nays was Jeannette Rankin, Republican Representative from Montana, the first woman ever elected to the House and a suffragette and pacifist. "I want to stand by my country," she said, audibly close to tears, "but I cannot vote for war. I vote No." The male chauvinism of the superpatriots may have spared her most of the indignities heaped on Norris, La Follette, William Stone of Missouri, and others who had voted against war. Leaving the Senate floor on April 4, La Follette was handed a rope, and he would be repeatedly hanged and burned in effigy in the months to come.

On April 6, 1917, the war resolution was taken to the White House. Sitting in a side room off the main lobby, Wilson signed it at 1:18 P.M. A buzzer was sounded in the executive office, and immediately Daniels's personal aide, Lieutenant Byron McCandless, ran out onto the White House lawn and semaphored to an officer waiting at a window in the Navy Department across the street. At once the signal was flashed to every ship and shore installation: "W . . . A . . . R."

6

Launching the War Effort

The atmosphere in Washington was unreal, almost festive, in the days that followed the declaration of war. As men already in office made the necessary mental adjustments, others in their thousands flooded into the capital from all over the country, hoping to serve their country or to profit from the war emergency, often both at once. Temporary offices sprang up along the Mall, and paperwork multiplied at an astonishing rate.

The excitement and the massive burdens thrust on the administrators brought heart attacks and nervous breakdowns and prompted a small circle of senior officials to set up an exercise group for "men in Washington who are necessarily subject to unusual stress and strain." Secretary of the Interior Franklin Lane, Assistant Secretary of the Treasury Oscar T. Crosby, Assistant Secretary of the Navy Franklin D. Roosevelt, and Commissioner of Tariffs William Kent made a pact to do an hour's brisk walking in Potomac Park together four times a week, followed by a healthy breakfast.

Commissioner Kent invited the President to join in the "drills on Tuesday, Wednesday, Thursday and Friday at 7:30 A.M. sharp—sharper than a spankless child." The President passed on the invitation to the Attorney General: "Please do not reply in writing because I know it would involve profanity!"

The banter could not cloak the frightening reality. America was at war with a world power, but she had more or less stumbled in. The grand objective was clear enough: the President had pledged the nation's blood and treasure to the defeat of German militarism. But the militarists were far away across three thousand miles of submarine-patrolled ocean, safe behind a formidable system of field fortifications. How was America to create sufficient power even to trouble their peace of mind? And how could she project that power into Europe?

Though there was a plan of sorts in existence, the joke going around in Washington was that the General Staff knew so little about Germany that they were ransacking the plans drawer marked "J" for a war plan. Joking apart, there was no effective national executive body in place to create a blueprint for mobilizing men, money, and materials. In 1916, resistance to "big government" and the excessive power of big business had left the administration with nothing more than the advisory Council of National Defense. Consequently, every agency from local through state to federal level started the war fending for itself as best it could—without direction and without means of coordination or cooperation.

Hardly surprising, then, if the nearest, softest targets were the first to feel the impact of the American war effort. Ludendorff's men might be safe for some time to come, but German nationals in the United States at once came under fire. All enemy aliens considered "dangerous" were ordered to be interned, with sixty-three suspects rounded up on the first day of the war. Some, it would seem, were a danger largely to themselves: On April 12, reported the U.S. attorney for the District of Connecticut, an alien enemy named Stephen Ruder

> cut the electric wires at Bridge 700 of the New York, New Haven & Hartford Railroad Company, at Fairfield, Connecticut. In performing this act, both of his arms were severely burned, and in falling from the pole, one of his legs was crushed. This leg was amputated. The shock of the burn, the fall and the subsequent amputation have seriously affected the nervous system of Ruder.

Ruder would die in internment of influenza later in the war.

Responsibility for internment lay with the Alien Enemy Bureau within the Department of Justice's War Emergency Division. Although suspects were frequently arrested without a warrant—and none too gently—once they were in custody their cases were carefully investigated and a significant proportion were released on parole. Of the aliens arrested between April and November 1917, only a quarter—1,200—were interned; the rest were paroled, usually at the request of employers desperate for the return of valued workers. Some of their requests went to a young man named

J. Edgar Hoover who was working at a junior level in the parole section. Hoover was not abnormally rigorous in his vetting of applications, though he did recommend internment with no dispensations for a Mr. Otto Mueller, who had called the President "a cock-sucker and a thief."

It was President Wilson's intention that all non-"dangerous" enemy aliens were to be "undisturbed in the peaceful pursuit of their lives and occupations." However, that did not save Carl Muck, conductor of the Boston Symphony Orchestra, who was arrested as he was about to conduct a performance of Bach's *Saint Matthew Passion*. The conductor of the Cincinnati Symphony, Ernst Kunwald, an Austrian, was also arrested on Hoover's recommendation. On the eve of the declaration of war, he had turned his back on the audience and refused to respond to calls for an encore of "The Star-Spangled Banner"; "You all know where my heart and sympathy lie," he said at last, "but I will play your anthem for you." Suspicions aroused, investigators turned up testimony that in 1915 Kunwald had declared, "It would be the greatest pleasure of my life to receive permission from my Kaiser to go to Washington and shoot the President—and I would do it without the slightest hesitation."

As the war began to bite, people began to look for scapegoats. Enemy aliens were turned in to the authorities by women scorned, rivals in love, neighbors bearing a grudge. One German seaman was accused by his estranged Belgian wife of having put dirt into a cargo of ammunition going overseas; he was deported. Underdogs—vagrants and itinerant vendors, cripples and misfits—were also at risk.

But all this was the Department of Justice in action at home, and it could hardly be viewed as a projection of force. Of the armed services, the best prepared in April 1917 were perhaps the Marines. But their determined, efficient commander, Major General George Barnett, had not yet won his fight to permit their deployment on the Western Front. Only the Navy, with its self-propelled weapons systems, could cross the Atlantic and begin immediate action.

In the last days of March, anticipating the actual declaration of war, Secretary Daniels had taken the precaution of sending Admiral William Sowden Sims to London (masquerading as a civilian in obedience to the President's wish to avoid provoking the Germans) to discuss naval cooperation with Sir John Jellicoe, the victor of Jutland and now First Sea Lord.

Sims was a contentious figure. "Preposterously good looking," he was very tall (six feet, three inches) and athletically built, with flaming blue eyes and a trim white spade beard. He was also intelligent, impulsive, and indiscreet, with, in the words of his son-in-law, "a gift for overstatement which at times amounted to real genius." Perhaps unsurprisingly, he was better loved by his subordinates than by his superiors, many of whom considered him to be the military equivalent of a media "muckraker," avid in ferreting out weaknesses in naval preparations and procedures. Daniels acknowledged his quickness of mind and social skills but accused him of being vain, ambitious, disloyal, and prodigal with the truth.

An even greater flaw in Daniels' eyes—and perhaps the heart of the antipathy between the two men—was Sims's love of England and the English. In the last fifteen years, he had spent a good deal of time in Britain studying methods of gunnery, had made close friends of naval officers there, and, in Daniels' view, had imbibed far too many of their ideas. He had even absorbed the British taste for tea and had made it a daily ritual with the officers on his last battleship. "It is the Warrior's beverage," he told the Paymaster General, putting in for a tea service.

In 1910, while commanding a battleship on a goodwill cruise, he had been invited to speak informally at a dinner at the Guildhall in London. His personal goodwill had become too much for him, and he had announced, "If the time ever comes when the British Empire is seriously menaced by an external enemy, it is my opinion that you may count upon every man, every dollar, every drop of blood, of your kindred across the sea." The promise, of course, had not been his to make, and he had been publicly reprimanded by President Taft. But it had not been forgotten by his British hosts, and it stood him in good stead now.

Sims was not indifferent to the Royal Navy's ethos of effortless superiority. "It makes me damn mad," he exploded. "All through their attitude one can see 'He's a damn good fellow and an American into the bargain.'" But he shared their worldview to a great extent, and he was very ready to listen to Jellicoe's analysis of the naval situation.

Without drama, the First Sea Lord handed Sims a record of recent British shipping losses. Since unrestricted submarine warfare had recommenced on February 1, the Germans had sunk more than a million tons and by the end of April seemed likely to have sunk a million more. Britain's supplies were nearly at critical levels; food stocks were estimated at between three and ten weeks, fuel oil was down to six. "I was fairly astounded," Sims recorded, "for I had never imagined anything so terrible. . . . 'Yes,' [Jellicoe] said, as quietly as though he were discussing the weather and not the future of the British Empire. 'It is impossible for us to go on with the war if losses like this continue.' "

The Royal Navy considered the U-boat an "underhand, unfair, and damned un-English" weapon. But its success was remarkable given that in 1917 it was a far from sophisticated instrument. It had to rise frequently to recharge its batteries and immediately became vulnerable, as the Royal Navy had command of the surface. When submerged, the boat had no communications at all; on the surface, it had to rig up an aerial between two masts to transmit a long-wave signal with very limited range, which the crew used with a chattiness that was the delight of British intelligence.

Nor was the rest of the vessel's technology of a very high order. Leading Seaman Stolz described the procedure by which a crew would level a U-boat after firing a torpedo. " 'Five men ready to dress the boat!' . . . The Chief Engineer cannot get his pumps to work as quickly as these smart fellows can dash from the control station into the bows and thus compensate for the lost weight of the fired torpedo. Otherwise the bow would tip out of the water at a most inopportune moment." There was one lavatory and no bath, and no one changed his clothes during voyages lasting weeks. Underwater, it was dark and cold, the walls running with condensation, the vessel always shuddering, often pitching and rolling nauseatingly. "We were," admitted one *Korvettenkapitan*, "the captives of our own smells."

When unrestricted submarine warfare resumed, the Germans had 111 U-boats in operation, divided between the North Sea (the larger, longer-range vessels) and the Flanders flotilla (smaller boats for operating in the English Channel and the narrows off Ostend and Zeebrugge). There was also a group of minelaying submarines. With this modest force, the Imperial Navy in these opening weeks was meeting the target it had so rashly set itself.

Before the war, neither the American nor the British navy had given much attention to submarine warfare, and attempts to deal with the new threat were tentative. Early antisubmarine officers were ordered to hit the periscope of an attacking submarine with a mallet. The Royal Navy toyed with the idea of a barrage of casks of Epsom fruit salts, primed to be detonated from the shore in the hope of frothing passing U-boats to the surface. Gulls were trained to perch on periscopes and sea lions to follow craft underwater; unfortunately, they had trouble distinguishing the German propeller, and obligingly followed anything that moved.

More sensible procedures were equally ineffective. Mines around the British Isles were an inadequate defense, partly because the British had not yet invented a reliable type, partly because the weather and water conditions were too rough. There were too few airplanes available, and they had too short a range, to provide proper cover against U-boats. The Royal Navy had to put its trust primarily in the armed surface patrol.

Destroyers were the best equipped of all fighting ships to deal with the submarine—fast, mobile, and hard to hit, and flexibly armed, but with a draft shallow enough to pass over the path of an average torpedo. The first contingent of U.S. destroyers, a single division of six under Commander Joseph K. Taussig, arrived in Britain on May 4, 1917—the first American forces dispatched to Europe.

Their destination was Queenstown, Ireland, the port commanding the sector where the *Lusitania* had been sunk—the south and southeast coast of Ireland and the outer approaches for North American ships sailing into Liverpool. On the night of May 3, the port's peace had been disturbed by a series of explosions as minesweepers blew up a string of mines laid by U-boats to catch the Americans when they arrived. Now Taussig's contingent was met and welcomed by Commander Edward Ratcliffe Garth Russell Evans, who had been second in command to Captain Robert Scott on his doomed expedition to the South Pole. Asked when the Americans would be ready to go to sea on duty, Taussig, who had just completed a long, anxious, exhausting Atlantic crossing, replied, "We are ready now, sir, when we have fueled."

At Queenstown, Sims and Sir Lewis Bayly, the British Admiral in command, developed a model working partnership, free from the British condescension and American suspicion that plagued the two countries' relations elsewhere. Emotional and affectionate toward close friends, his spaniel, Patrick, and the Australian niece who kept house for him, Bayly was almost pathologically shy with strangers and cloaked his uncertainties in a ferocious public manner. At his first meeting with Sims, he was "as rude to me as one man can be to another."

He was known to the U.S. Navy in Queenstown as "Old Frozen Face," but they also called him, more affectionately, "Luigi" and "Uncle Lewis." Later, Hollywood directors would have had no hesitation in casting Spencer Tracy as Bayly. Admiralty House was thrown open to the American officers. He turned his billiard room into a plotting room, where they could use the green baize for chart tables, and invited them to games of French cricket on the lawn. Unlike the Admiralty, the Americans were able to see behind the bitter, cantankerous exterior. Sims watched him personally greeting the survivors of torpedoed vessels as they came ashore. "I shall . . . keep a vivid recollection of this kindly gentleman, Admiral Sir Lewis Bayly, KCB, KCMG, CVO, RN, serving coffee to wretched British, American, French, Italian, Japanese or negro sailors, with a cheering word for each, and afterward, with sleeves tucked up, calmly washing dishes in a big pan of hot water."

The friendship even survived the issuance of an order banning American troops from the town of Cork to avoid friction with the inhabitants. This was partly political; Sinn Feiners were getting hold of American and especially Irish-American sailors, "trying to persuade them that they are pulling chestnuts out of the fire for England while the English destroyers are doing nothing in English harbors." But almost more inflammatory, the Americans had four times more pay than the British sailor's 28 cents a day and were making considerable headway with the girls of Cork. Fights were frequent; the ban was issued when it was discovered that knuckle-dusters were being manufactured aboard the American ship *Melville*, but not before one Irishman had been killed in a brawl.

The incoming American destroyers were used singly in submarine-hunting patrols, alongside the British. The waters of the Western Approaches were full of drama: loose mines, the derelict hulks of torpedoed vessels, lifeboats crammed with survivors, rafts full of corpses. Press coverage during the years of neutrality about the submarine campaign and German "frightfulness" had left its mark, and the newcomers were quick on the trigger. Sims reported a good many attacks on floating spars that looked like periscopes, and much alarm was caused by "torpedo wake" that turned out to be phosphorescence; at least one whale was depth-charged.

Supplementing the destroyers at Queenstown and elsewhere was the American subchaser force. The chasers, 110-foot wooden vessels with projectors to fire depth charges, were the pet project of Assistant Secretary of the Navy Franklin Roosevelt, but they had severe limitations: they were not strong enough for the wild waters of the Atlantic or North Sea; in the worst weather, ice a foot thick formed on the decks; and those on kitchen duty braved the dangers of cooking on oil stoves in a thirty-degree roll. "This subchasing business is much like the proverbial skinning of a skunk," wrote one officer, "useful, but not especially pleasant or glorious."

Fortunately, the crews were well endowed with the spirit of adventure. "A saucy, high-spirited, devil-may-care lot they were," remembered

Daniels, "and they came capering into the zone of danger and death with laughter and song." Even allowing for Daniels' saccharine literary style, subchaser crews were an intriguing mixture of amateur yachtsmen, newly trained ensigns, college boys eager to get into the war, and an assortment of rootless wanderers; on one vessel a graduate with an M.A. in Arabic worked shoulder to shoulder with a Greek cook who had newly come from operating the lemonade franchise in a circus. They used their own code: three boats constituted a hunting unit, and each unit was named by a phrase or jingle—"High-low-jack" was one, "Corn-meal mush" another—and "Operate at once!" translated as "Quack, Quack, Quack."

Later in the war, when the chasers were used actively to seek and destroy, they were fitted with hydrophones, a crude precursor of sonar. The chaser carried two receivers set slightly apart, designed to pick up the noise of an underwater engine; the operator, sitting between the receivers, turned them until the sound coming into each ear was equal. This would give him the direction, though not the distance, of the submarine; three ships working together could then plot the submarine's position by triangulation. Hydrophones were an advance on any other method of tracking U-boats, but rough seas or other vessels in the area would confuse or obliterate the signals, and their results were disappointing.

Q-ships, or "mystery ships," also had less success than the courage of their crews deserved. The Q-ship was a small merchantman designed to tempt the U-boat. Torpedoes were extremely expensive, and U-boat captains were encouraged to attack their victims with machine guns when it was safe to do so. The crews of Q-ships were trained to act as merchant seamen—groomed, in Sims's phrase, in "slouchy behavior," hanging over the rails, displaying no naval flannel on their washing lines. It was only when a submarine drew near enough to this "soft target" to open fire that bulkheads collapsed and "lifeboats" lifted to reveal naval guns that did their best to blow the attacker out of the water. The British, who had invented Q-ships, sank thirteen submarines with them (German sources say eleven), and the leading Q-ship commander won a Victoria Cross; but twenty-seven ships and many of their crews were lost. The lone American Q-ship, the *Santee*, was torpedoed and wrecked on its first voyage without having claimed a "kill."

Sims reacted to the submarine menace with his usual energy. In April 1917, the U.S. Navy had sixty-six destroyers. Sims sent off urgent requests for them at once and kept up constant pressure on the Navy Department in the weeks to come; between May and July, he sent thirty-two requests. The Navy Department's response was measured: six destroyers were sent on May 4, twelve more by the end of May; ten in June; nine in July.

Daniels was extremely reluctant to strip the Navy of its destroyer screen, especially to protect British trade. The Navy Department was preoccupied with the defense of America's own coast. It had been known since 1914 that submarines could cross the Atlantic, when submarines discreetly bought by the Admiralty from Bethlehem Steel and quietly assembled in Canada had crossed to England under their own power. In 1916, the German submarine cruiser *Deutschland* had visited Newport, Rhode Island, partly to raise the German profile, partly to ship back supplies. That autumn, too, *U-53*, on its way back from Newport, torpedoed British merchantmen off Nantucket Island, Massachusetts.

Daniels was constrained by the real fear that existed on the East Coast and was not confined to the man in the street. "I meant to tell you," wrote Roosevelt to his wife, Eleanor, "that if by any perfectly wild chance a German submarine should come into the bay and start to shell Eastport [Maine] or the Pool, I want you to grab the children and beat it into the woods." It was useless for Sims to point out that even if the U-boats came (and it would in fact be a year before they did so), they could not operate for long so far from their bases and the damage they could do would be negligible compared with the havoc being wrought in European waters. "There are at least 17 more destroyers," he complained bitterly on June 26 to Walter Page, the American ambassador in London, "employed on our coast *where there is no war.*"

But even as Sims fired off his requests, it was obvious that, however many destroyers were sent, patrols were not going to be enough to contain the threat of submarines in the shipping lanes. A single vessel roaming around nine hundred square miles of ocean was at a lethal disadvantage against an invisible enemy. One obvious alternative was the convoy. By drawing together the ships that were the U-boats' targets and escorting them in groups, the Navy would be concentrating instead of dispersing its strength and luring the enemy to declare himself.

The system was already in use for troopships, as well as for the ships of the French coal trade, where it had reduced losses considerably. But the Admiralty, as well as naval officers reluctant to abandon the thrill of the chase for the dubious delights of escort duty, had produced a rich variety of arguments against applying it to the whole merchant trade: The targets would be too large and inviting, and the convoy would be constrained to move at the speed of the slowest vessel. Merchant captains, who traditionally were loners, would not be able to conform to the strict discipline of sailing in convoy: keeping a regular distance, zigzagging, sailing without lights at night. Ports would be clogged with ships all arriving and unloading at once. And anyway, there were not enough escort ships available, given the number of vessels to be accompanied and the Admiralty's conviction that the escort should be twice as big as the convoy.

The U.S. Navy too had its opponents of convoying. "Daniels said we must not convoy—that would be dangerous," exploded Franklin Lane. "Think of a Secretary of the Navy talking of danger!" Daniels clung to his faith in the armed merchantmen in whose cause Wilson had released the Zimmermann telegram. In this as in much else, he was staunchly supported by Admiral Benson. Benson liked to describe himself as "a plain sailor"; he was correct, conscientious, patriotic, and devout but not reckoned to be one of the Navy's "bright men." "Not very quick at grasping any ideas other than his own," declared Walter Long, First Lord of the Admiralty.

"The real truth," wrote John Jellicoe early in July 1917, "is that Admiral Benson has an idea in his head that the gun and a sharp pair of eyes are the answer to a submerged submarine. One would hardly believe that such ideas could be held by any naval officer—but there it is." Sims was mortified; he pointed out to Washington that in the last six weeks thirty armed ships had been sunk by submarines they had never seen, and he complained to Page of "the embarrassment and delay which is caused by the insistence of our people on the other side trying to advise these people over here in the *direct lines in which they have had the most experience.*"

When Sims arrived in London, the officer in charge of the successful French coal convoy had recently demonstrated that the Admiralty had inflated the current number of sailings from British ports to make the number of sinkings look proportionately less alarming; there were in fact fewer ships to be escorted than originally suggested, and these did not need to be outnumbered by their escort. Other strands of opinion were now coming together in favor of the convoy system, including those of Admiral Sir David Beatty and Prime Minister David Lloyd George. Sims at once added his voice, but it took a direct request from British Foreign Secretary Arthur Balfour to President Wilson, jointly engineered by Page and Sims, to obtain American support for the policy of convoy, almost three months later than the British had approved it, in early July 1917.

The convoy system would in time prove remarkably successful. Shipping losses would drop steadily, and the U-boats would be forced closer inshore, where they were more vulnerable to mines and subchasers. Even in midocean, convoys would bring about more actions and sink more U-boats than either hunting groups or patrols would. And in this war, the German Navy would find no viable tactics for attacking convoys; the "wolf pack" would not begin to run effectively until the next war.

As for aggressive tactics against the submarine, mines would eventually account for more submarines than any other weapon. They were deployed most dramatically in the Northern Barrage, a pet project of Franklin Roosevelt—a barrage stretched all the way across the North Sea between Norway and the Orkney islands off the Scottish coast to pen the U-boats into their bases.

The idea of a barrage had occurred to the British Admiralty, and it had been applied in the Straits of Dover. But bad weather disabled mines, which were anyway so unreliable that some German vessels carried them on deck as souvenirs, confident of their harmlessness. It was the invention of a greatly superior American mine, with longer antennae that were better adapted to the greater depth and breadth of the northern passage, that persuaded the Admiralty to cooperate with the scheme. In the end the United States would be responsible for 56,000 of the 75,000 mines laid in the Northern Barrage.

Mines might have been the most effective weapon against the submarine, but the barrage was not necessarily the most effective way of utilizing mines. After the war a German U-boat captain concluded, "The closure of such great depths as in the Northern Barrage is irrational as well as completely impracticable"—a reference to the fact that inevitably U-boats were always slipping through or under the barrier. Beatty agreed: "All we have done is to waste valuable vessels, time and material, in planting the North Sea with stuff which debars us from using it and can do no harm to the enemy."

From the British perspective, the U.S. Navy's contribution to containing surface raiders also seemed slightly pointless. U.S. capital ships and submarines joined the Allied fleets in Northern European and Mediterranean waters, but to little effect.

Although the United States could claim the credit for evolving the first working submarine in 1900, underwater technology had not received much attention since then. Of the "K-boats," the first batch of submarines sent to Europe, only half survived the Atlantic crossing, and these got only as far as the Azores. The strain of the journey was appalling; the second officer of *K-1* was sent home on sick leave, "a mere shadow of the former 200-pound Captain of a navy crew and a football end"; he died soon after his return.

The major preoccupation of later American submarine commanders was getting off recognition signals to trigger-happy American destroyers. *L-10* was depth-charged by the destroyer *Sterett;* the two commanders had been roommates at the Naval Academy, and when *L-10* surfaced, conversation was brisk and to the point. As a parting shot, the *Sterett*'s commander warned *L-10* to beware the *Trippe*, which was on the way. Sure enough, although *L-10* was now on the surface and waving the American flag, the *Trippe* fired six shots. Wearily, *L-10*'s commander radioed, "Three over, three short. Deflection fine."

As for capital ships, despite the prevailing wisdom against dividing the fleet, the Navy came to see that there would be practical advantages in joining the British Grand Fleet at Scapa Flow. Their battleships had had no recent war experience; participation now would be good training and possibly even a source of useful technical information. Morale aboard the capital ships would be damaged if theirs were the only crews to be left out of the war; worse, Congress might shrink from subventing capital ships if there appeared to be no part for them to play in modern conflict. Above all, in Benson's words, "It is of the first importance to our present and future prestige that the Navy of the United States shall act in a principal role in every prominent event."

Admiral Beatty, commanding the Grand Fleet, would have agreed that the importance of the American presence was largely political. The American ships were enviably well equipped with labor-saving devices such as laundries, motor-driven potato peelers and dough mixers, and luxurious levels of heating. "British ships are notoriously too cold for the comfort of men brought up in American homes." The American commander with the squadron, Admiral Hugh Rodman, was a genial, popular man who referred to the Prince of Wales as "a peach" and the Kaiser as "Bill H. [Hohenzollern]." But the American ships lacked experience, their gunnery was poor, and in Beatty's view they were more of an "'incubus" than an asset. "I am sending old Rodman out on an operation of his own," he wrote patronizingly to his wife, "which pleases him and gives them an idea that they are really taking part in the war. I trust they will come to no harm."

Part Two

BUILDING
the
ARMY

7

The Lists of Honor:
Conscription

Admiral Beatty might condescend to American sailors, but at least they were there in Europe, while the Army was at home, confronting an impossible task. Shackled by its political masters until the race was almost run, it found itself on the starting line in April 1917 ranged against a military machine that had virtually exhausted the Russian, French, and British Empires—free to fight but with few of the tools to do so.

No greater task ever faced a soldier than that now confronting the Chief of Staff, Major General Hugh L. Scott. Little in his experience had fitted him for the task ahead. Scott had joined the 7th Cavalry Regiment as a replacement for a lieutenant killed with George Armstrong Custer at Little Big Horn. He had become expert in Plains Indian languages, both spoken and signed, and Indian chieftains visiting his office in Washington discussed their concerns with him in their native tongues. He was a fine soldier, but he belonged in spirit and experience to the frontier army of the nineteenth century, and indeed he was due to retire that fall.

Scott was eons removed from the professional staff officers who were running the war in Europe; had he been typical of the bulk of the officer corps, the United States would have been hard-pressed to make a significant contribution to the Allied war effort. Armies as large and complex as the British and German forces required an infrastructure of skilled managers simply to feed, supply, clothe, transport, and arm them, before even considering doctrine, training, strategy, or tactics.

Fortunately, the foresight of General William T. Sherman after the Civil War and the reforming zeal of Secretary of War Elihu Root at the beginning of the century had created an army school system in America that had made the generation of officers under Scott at least as well qualified for command and staff work as the officers of the British Army had been in 1914. And Root, by introducing the General Staff system, had established a blueprint for the development of effective military management.

To these new professionals fell the task of raising, training, equipping, and transporting to Europe an army that could wage modern war and win. It was a staggering burden, placed on them by a President who had not seen fit to consult them before deciding to commit men to combat.

The most fundamental problem confronting the planners was how to provide a continuing supply of men in the quantity required by and consumed on the modern battlefield. Most staff officers argued that war on the European scale would be impossible without resorting to the draft. Leonard Wood, himself a former Chief of Staff, had seen the military developments in Europe. "The war resources of a nation can only be employed to the greatest advantage," he wrote, "when used as a national force under national control and direction. . . . Voluntary enlistments based on patriotism and the bounty cannot be relied upon to supply men for the army during a prolonged war."

The war boom in industry had given men every reason to stay at home, and drastic measures might be needed to prise them out. Walter Lippmann told Wilson that it was impossible "to raise such an army by voluntary enlistment . . . in view of the present condition of the labor market, except by a newspaper campaign of manufactured hatred that would disturb and distract the morale of the nation." But while conscription was being debated, the Army was dependent on volunteers—and almost at once the "manufactured hate" that Lippmann feared began to appear on walls and billboards and in newspapers. THEY CRUCIFY, proclaimed one recruitment poster showing a husband and baby murdered by marauding Germans and a stripped and bleeding woman with her arms pulled up over her head and her hands nailed to the wall. THEY MUTILATE—a Belgian child in clogs standing on a pedestal inscribed KULTUR, holding out arms amputated at the elbows—FOR HUMANITY'S SAKE ENLIST.

Conscription, its advocates argued, was a fairer way of spreading the burden of service; it could be operated more efficiently and with a higher degree of order and predictability than the volunteer system and with less emotional turbulence. It was a means of ensuring that all ethnic groups played their part and possibly a means of bringing those groups closer together in national harmony. Indiscriminate volunteering, on the other hand, as England's example proved, could have disastrous effects on industry and agriculture.

Before the present crisis, these arguments of military necessity and social desirability had always foundered on the rock of Wilson's hostility. The President had seen himself as the bringer of new freedoms, the defender of the individual against the growing might of the collective; to him and his supporters, conscription had seemed the antithesis of the American way. "Why introduce Prussianism to fight Prussianism?" asked Daniels.

But Wilson had changed his views. Having decided on war to achieve his war aims, he could cast conscription as a tool with which to advance the cause of liberty. Even before the decision for war was finally taken, he had called for draft legislation. His war address spoke of augmenting the armed forces by "at least 500,000 men, who should, in my opinion, be chosen upon the principle of universal liability to service"; and a conscription bill was presented to Congress immediately following the declaration of war.

Not all Democrats were as quick as Wilson to ditch their principles and the American tradition of volunteering. Daniels refused to take conscripts for the Navy, as did Barnett for the Marines. There was also fierce resistance in Congress: "Oh, you call us pacifists, we who fear this great shadow of militarism that overhangs the land." "I protest with all my heart and mind and soul," burst out Champ Clark, Democratic Speaker of the House, "against having the slur of being a conscript placed upon the men of Missouri; in the estimation of Missourians there is precious little difference between a conscript and a convict." The Democratic chairman of the House Military Affairs Committee refused to introduce the bill, and the task fell to a Republican who had been born in Bavaria. "What do you know about that?" commented Scott.

The emotion generated in Congress by the draft bill was, as the General Staff well knew, merely a shadow of the nationwide resentment of the notion of coercion by the federal government. When Senator James Reed of Missouri told Newton Baker, "You will have the streets of our American cities running red with blood," he spoke with the force of historical precedent. In the second year of the Civil War, conscription had caused widespread protests and rioting on the streets of New York. Even the Judge Advocate General, Enoch Crowder, protested, "A military draft is not in harmony with the spirit of our people. All of our previous experience has been that it causes trouble and that our people prefer the volunteering method." A group of protesters spanning the entire political spectrum took the fight to the Supreme Court to challenge—unsuccessfully—the constitutionality of the draft law.

The debate dragged on, and now it was clouded by Theodore Roosevelt, who wanted to lead a division of volunteers on to the Western Front. Busily he drew up lists of the officers he wanted to take with him, and he received applications to be included from friends and the sons of friends. Before long he was requesting permission for four divisions, and valuable time was lost while Congress debated the issue of whether he was to have his way, before Wilson finally poured the coldest of water on his pretensions. "It would be very agreeable to me," he enunciated,

to pay Mr. Roosevelt this compliment and the Allies the compliment of sending to their aid one of our most distinguished public men. . . . But this is not the time or the occasion for compliment or for any action not calculated to contribute to the immediate success of the war. The business now in hand is undramatic, practical, and of scientific definiteness and precision.

"This is the twenty-fourth day of the war, and nobody knows how to raise a force," Scott noted anxiously. He continued:

I think the best efforts of every patriot should now be concentrated on Congress to cause them to pass the [conscription] bill. . . . If Russia should weaken and make peace, forty-one divisions of the German army will be freed from that front and cast at once on the English and allied lines, in which case we would have to conscript million after million of men. It requires not a few volunteers, but a nation in arms.

The Selective Service Act became law on May 13, 1917. It did not forbid volunteering. Only the ranks of the new "National Army" were to be filled exclusively by the draft; the regular army and National Guard were both to be brought up to war strength and kept there by volunteers "until, in the judgment of the President, a resort to selective draft is desirable." But the old American way, the way of the gallant amateur, was now subordinated to modern realities.

Getting the legislation passed was only half the battle. The administration was well aware that it did not have the resources to enforce the draft if there was widespread resistance. Apart from objections to the principle of conscription, Wilson and Baker knew there were still pockets and pools of opposition to the war itself from socialists and German Americans. As the initial euphoria of the declaration faded away, the old attitudes of apathy and straightforward antagonism could be expected to reappear. The draft would succeed only if the War Department could persuade a highly individualistic, disparate, geographically scattered cross section of the population—10 million men between the ages of twenty-one and thirty—to surrender themselves willingly to the federal government. Some form of draft machinery had to be found to which the average patriotic citizen could not object.

Ironically, responsibility for this conjuring trick fell to Enoch Crowder, who had been one of the first to speak out against the draft. It would be hard to imagine a less likely candidate for what was essentially an exercise in public relations. Crowder was a bony, vile-tempered bachelor whose hobby was work and whose creed was efficiency. Aware of his reputation as one of the best brains in professional administration, visitors to his office were startled by the absence of filing cabinets, accumulated memoranda, or any of the other impedimenta of the bureaucrat. His secret, as he explained, lay in a generous supply of tags marked EXPEDITE; dust never settled on his desk.

But however grim his exterior, it was Crowder who found a way of appealing to American loyalties. He proposed to keep the Army out of sight as far as possible. The operation would be planned by the War Department but put into effect by specially created boards of unpaid civilian volunteers. On a certain day to be specified, every eligible male in the country would be required to go to his local polling station and register his name at a table manned by his "friends and neighbors." Then, from among the registrants in their area, boards of local people would make the selection of those to be inducted into the Army. The method relieved the War Department of the impossible task of building a vast bureaucratic machine overnight, and it preserved some flavor of voluntarism. Men were not taken from their homes by the Army; they were delivered to the Army by their neighbors.

The people, Wilson artfully maintained, had "volunteered in mass." Ignoring the fact that should a man fail to "volunteer" he would be subject to a year in jail, the authorities pursued this theme relentlessly in propaganda both during the passage of the Selective Service Act and immediately thereafter.

To cut down on the time between legislation and implementation and thus prevent resistance from flowering, Baker and Crowder had millions of registration forms printed covertly (and wholly illegally) and distributed them around the country while the bill was still before Congress, swearing printers and distributors to secrecy. So that there could be no possible mis-understanding, the documents were translated into all the languages in use in this most polyglot of countries. In Hawaii alone, they were printed in Japanese, Chinese, Korean, Portugese, Spanish, Hawaiian, and three Fil-ipino dialects.

With the machinery set up, Wilson was able, the moment he had signed the Selective Service Act, to issue his "call to arms." On June 5, between the hours of 7 A.M. and 7 P.M., all men between the ages of twenty-one and thirty were to present themselves for their names to be inscribed on "the lists of honor." In rhetorical cadences, committed to paper partly in imposing Gothic script, Wilson did his best to confer nobility on the pro-ceedings. Let men approach the day, he intoned, "in thoughtful apprehen-sion of its significance and . . . accord to it the honor and meaning that it deserves."

Baker had taken state governors, city mayors, and the chairmen of local chambers of commerce into his confidence and given them advance notice; they responded by turning Registration Day into a carnival. All across the country, from Hawaii to Brooklyn, America's young men streamed toward their appointed polling centers:

> Ore-passers in Ashtabula, lumbermen in Bangor, cow-punchers in Cheyenne, cotton-farmers in Dallas, miners in Leadville, shoe-workers in Lynn, sophomores in New Haven, grocery-clerks in Syracuse, apple-growers in Walla-Walla, city boys from Third Avenue, country boys from Main Street and Bear Notch, youths white, black, and of alien birth, every type and condition of man between twenty-one and thirty to be found in the country.

Boy Scouts marshaled them into lines as bands played, and matrons pinned small flags to their chests. They were the heroes of the moment, ad-mired by their elders, eulogized by the local dignitaries, hung upon by young girls. The fever of the day gripped the nation, and its sons dutifully turned out to give their names. The speed of Crowder's hand had deceived the eye.

On top of the regular army, the National Guard, and those who had already volunteered, a further 687,000 men were to be conscripted. To spread the burden fairly, Baker fixed quotas for each state and territory according to population, reduced pro rata if men from the state or territory had volunteered. Thus New York had to provide 122,424 men; Pennsylvania, 98,227; Texas, 48,116; Tennessee, 22,158; Puerto Rico, 13,480; Alaska, 710.

Each of the 4,500 registration boards had numbered its registrants serially beginning with 1; the shortest list numbered less than 100, the longest 10,500. In Washington, D.C., the numbers 1 through 10,500 were written on slips of paper and inserted into black capsules; the capsules were placed in a large glass bowl and stirred with a long wooden spoon swathed in red, white, and blue bunting. Then Baker pulled the first capsule: number 258. Across the nation, the men holding that number would be the first to be called up. There was no broadcast radio, so the word was passed by telephone and telegraph—and it spread quickly. "Thanks for drawing 258," wired a Mississippi man. "That's me!" In New York, number 258 was a peanut vendor. For seventeen hours, relays of blindfolded dignitaries pulled the capsules from the bowl until all 10,500 were drawn. Anxious wives and mothers waited to learn how high up the list their men were, how close they were to the fighting. Suddenly, the war had become very real.

In the order determined by the draw, the registrants were called before draft boards to be examined and declared eligible or exempt. The law specified a narrow band of categories for exemption: state and government officials, employees of armories, those with provable dependents, and the medically unfit.

"Unfitness" covered a multitude of physical shortcomings. "Thousands of doctors tapped chests, scratched abdomens with a wooden stick, commanded 'Say "ah,"' and culled out the myopia, dipsomania, barbers' itch, flat feet, and such other marks of the less-than-perfect man as the Surgeon General directed." John Barrymore was rejected for varicose veins. Some 30 percent eventually fell by the wayside. James Thurber, then a student at Ohio University, was blind in one eye and shortsighted in the other but found it hard to convince the examiners of this drawback:

I was called almost every week, even though I had been exempted from service the first time I went before the medical examiners. . . . There was usually a letter for me on Monday ordering me to report for examination on the second floor of Memorial Hall the following Wednesday at 9 P.M. The second time I went up, I tried to explain to one of the doctors. . . . "You're just a blur to me," I said, taking off my glasses. "You're absolutely nothing to me," he snapped, sharply. I had to take off my clothes each time and jog around the hall with a lot of porters and bank presidents' sons and clerks and poets. Our hearts and lungs would be examined, and then our feet; and finally our eyes. That always came last. When the eye-specialist got around to me, he would always say, "Why, you couldn't get into the service with sight like that!" "I know," I would say.

Those who passed the medical were given seven days to claim exemption on other grounds. Only American nationals could be drafted, which meant passing over almost 4 million nonenemy aliens who were resident but had not begun the process of obtaining citizenship. With exemption for citizens hard to obtain, there was intense resentment of this group of seeming parasites, especially in the northern industrial areas, where they were concentrated in the greatest numbers. (Draft boards gave very short shrift indeed to naturalized aliens who expressed a wish to return to their former, exempt nationalities.)

There was no exemption for men opposed to war on humanitarian or political grounds—"enemies of the Republic, fakers and active agents of the enemy," in Leonard Wood's view. They were either inducted to fight or, like Roger Baldwin, director of the National Civil Liberties Bureau, tried and imprisoned.

Partial exemption was granted by law to bona fide members of religious sects whose creeds forbade their members to participate in war. They were excused from service in combat units, but they were obliged to serve in the armed forces "in any capacity that the President shall declare non-combatant." Almost 21,000 accepted these terms, were granted the partial exemption, and were sent to work on relief and reconstruction in Europe, in the medical services, or, a lucky minority, on the land. Others considered these activities to be as much a part of the war effort as carrying a weapon and refused so-called noncombatant service. They were promptly inducted, along with many other religious objectors whose spiritual credentials were not acknowledged by draft boards.

Large numbers of pacifists from small, unrecognized sects ("nut societies," in the phrase of one examiner) had their claims for exemption rejected—among them Alvin C. York, an elder of the fundamentalist Church of Christ in Christian Union, from the mountains of Tennessee. Men who had converted to a religion since the beginning of the war had difficulty convincing the draft boards of their sincerity. Some invariably failed, such as the members of the International Bible Students' Association (later the Jehovah's Witnesses), whose founder, Charles Taze Russell, was in jail for selling "miracle wheat" with magic powers. All were sent to the camps to face an uncertain future.

Throughout that summer of 1917, the draft boards worked hard to meet their quotas. The system was widely regarded as a success, and Crowder basked in praise from all sides. Little of the expected resistance materialized. A few individuals, between fifteen and twenty of them, were killed resisting the draft, but there was virtually no collective action. On Registration Day in Butte, Montana, some six hundred Irish Americans protested, and military intelligence reported suspiciously that "300 Indians bought ammunition lately and 100 tried to buy guns."

But the positive effectiveness of the system was harder to gauge. There was no method of measuring the number of eligible men who did not register. Crowder himself estimated that during the war as many as 3.6 million never entered the system at all. Then, of those who registered and were passed as fit to be inducted, some 12 percent, or 2.8 million, dodged the draft.

Some simply ran away. Others employed an astonishing variety of evasive maneuvers. A very few succeeded in bribing draft board officials. Far more discovered a pressing need to marry, in order to take advantage of the exemption for those with dependents. New York's municipal marriage chapel saw 164 marriages in one day, as compared with the usual 15, and U.S. marshals were dispatched to forbid the banns to men with registration cards. The deputy clerk was disappointed; he had gotten the marriage ceremony down to sixty seconds.

Many took more drastic action. A Kentucky man poured carbolic acid over his face to escape service. A chemist in New York successfully marketed a drug "that will make men unable to pass physical examination." In San Francisco, another entrepreneur was sentenced to ten years for "the fitting of eyeglasses to make the vision temporarily defective." Virgil S. Phipps, who had already been rejected as unfit by a Los Angeles draft board, was given eighteen months' imprisonment for standing in at the medical for his inconveniently healthy friend George S. Baldwin. On occasion, unwary foreign-born Americans wishing to evade the draft wrote to relatives abroad, declaring their intentions. Draft authorities, primed by the censors, were doubtless intrigued to read careful directions from one father to his naturalized son on how to feign malaria during the medical examination.

More serious than the evasion rate was the system's initial failure to fulfill the prime purpose of a manpower policy—that of protecting the supply of essential labor while siphoning off the nonessential into the Army. Crowder had omitted to build into the original machinery any criteria for assessing a man's dispensability as a worker, and it took an outcry from organized labor, agriculture, industry, and the railroads to prevent the draft authorities from solemnly repeating England's mistakes. Organized labor was given fuller representation on draft boards, and a more detailed procedure for grading registrants was introduced.

Other inherent injustices were harder to remedy. Draft boards were appointed by the President, but he relied heavily on the advice of state governors, and he was well aware that the composition of some of the boards was determined as much by political inclination as by patriotism. Too often, it seemed, Republicans were granted deferments at the expense of Democratic youths. Baker was resigned: "In dealing with so political a people as ours, I fear that it is impossible to prevent at all times the manifestation of partisanship."

For all its blemishes, the system began to provide the men almost immediately. At least one of the 258 group was in uniform by the end of July. By the end of August, the draft boards had met their quotas and call-up papers were being issued. The problem now was how to train this mass of civilians in the ways of war.

8

"Bring the Liver Out":
Officers of a Democratic Army

America might have entered a state of war with the basic planning left un-done; but at least the War Department could avoid the British mistakes of 1914. As Hugh Scott's deputy, Major General Tasker Bliss, observed, the British had rushed all available men to France to help stop the Ger-man drive and as a result had "sacrificed their regular army—their only means of training raw levies. . . . You can imagine what a helpless mob a body of a million or more men is when it has not an ample leaven of trained officers and veteran troops to organise and train it."

But not even the regular army was sufficient to train the mass of Amer-ican conscripts. Though experienced soldiers could leaven the ranks and provide noncommissioned officers, most of the regular officers would be needed to provide the command and administration expertise for the million-man army. The actual day-to-day training had to be done by new men: 26,000 new company-grade officers, lieutenants and captains, were needed overnight.

All through that spring of 1917, the War Department groped for a method of training the trainers. In May 1917, it set up a series of officers' training camps across the country, on the model of Wood's Plattsburg ini-tiative. Speed was of the essence if officers were to be available to train the conscripts before winter set in. The General Staff was realistic about what could be achieved—"Manifestly a fully-trained officer cannot be produced in any three months' course"—and they set clear priorities. From the start, the camps concentrated on a single aspect of an officer's duties: "The primary object . . . is to produce instructors—men capable of intelligently and successfully training others."

It became clear almost at once that the success of the scheme would depend on the initial quality of the candidates for commission. Reserve officers, who already had some training, met part of the need. In addition, some of the necessary specialists—engineers, communications experts, doctors, veterinary surgeons—could be recruited directly from civilian life. Of the officers employed by the Army during the war, a third simply transferred their civilian skills to the military, while one in six came from the reserve. For the rest, the War Department turned to a sector of society not usually attracted to service in the Army. Hugh Scott proclaimed the need for the "educated, athletic, bold"—and he looked to the Ivy League colleges.

At first, to the General Staff's chagrin, the educated, athletic, and bold went after shellproof commissions in ordnance and quartermaster departments. But when the draft law became a reality, Ivy League men, professionals, and businesspeople applied for officer training in droves; 40,000 were selected and admitted into the first camps. "The officer corps is drawn almost entirely from the rich, cultured bourgeoisie," remarked French military observer Inspector-Auxiliare Mignot in amusement.

This middle-class influx did nothing to bring together an already divided officer corps. Regular officers educated since the Spanish War at the Leavenworth Schools and the Army War College were professionally distanced from the older, more antiquated breed of officer, and all regulars habitually disparaged the National Guardsmen. Now a third ingredient was added to the mixture—a seasoning of gilded youth and highly educated professional men in their late twenties and early thirties. In an officer corps drawn mainly from the earthier elements of American society, the result was a kind of inverted class warfare. Experience, professionalism, and authority rested with the humbly born, while their social superiors filled the lower orders.

To civilian outsiders, unaware of these distinctions and conscious only of the relationship between the new officers and the conscripts at their beck and call, the accession of the "cultured bourgeoisie" to military power was the fulfillment of every darkest fear. An officer caste, it seemed, was emerging in America, an instrument of Prussianism in which military and civilian elites would interlink and reinforce one another. Labor representatives protested at commissions going only to the "privileged class," and in the months to come, there would be widespread antiofficer feeling, with military intelligence agents reporting uneasily on hostility to officers in uniform when they walked city streets. The Washington *Times*, the agents complained, was pursuing a "vicious policy of ridicule" against members of "the so-called 'officer class' " because they undemocratically insisted on being saluted with due deference.

In the early summer of 1917, however, the War Department's sole concern was to push the scions of the moneyed classes through the necessary training courses as quickly and effectively as possible. On May 15, the camps opened their gates and the candidates for commission faced the bewildering process of induction: issuing of uniforms and equipment, allocation to barracks, a sequence of medical examinations and vaccinations, the first encounter with the drill instructor. "Discipline, precise and exacting, must be the keynote," ran one training directive. "The salute, bearing, demeanor and address of instructors and candidates must be required to meet the highest standard of correctness at all times."

While the candidates—some of them quite senior executives and managers in civilian life—reeled at their first brush with army discipline, the physical conditioning schedules took more account of their frailties. "Many of the candidates have been accustomed to indoor work and cannot, at the time of reporting, undergo great physical exertion without danger of injury to health." In the first week, the candidates had only one march of one hour's duration with a light pack—though all too soon these would become route marches with a full pack.

For a minimum of ten hours a day, they drilled and studied, preparing to participate in a war that for three years had been no more than a series of exciting newspaper reports. They learned about the Army and its regulations; about musketry; about signals and codes; about the seven seconds that was all they would have in which to raise their respirator during a gas attack "from the slung position to complete protection."

The first courses were based on the British and Canadian officer-training courses and were largely dedicated to the art of trench warfare. The cadets spent five days and nights in continuous occupation of a "typical network of trenches," facing an imaginary enemy. They grew familiar with entanglements, dugouts, strong points, listening posts, machine-gun emplacements, observation posts, points of command. They learned the principles of scouting in no-man's-land and some of the habits of German snipers. They were taught the tricks of successful trench raids: the disciplined advance behind a rolling barrage, the "mopping up" of captured trenches. They became adept in the use of rifles and hand grenades, the method of relieving other units, the procedures of supply, sanitation, liaison. In microcosm, they were introduced to the new and horrific world that awaited them "over there."

As company-grade officers, they were taught that their relationship with their men was paramount. Several hours a week were allotted to training in giving commands: "Never hesitate" and "Never argue with an enlisted man." They were urged to cultivate the men's loyalty and trust: "Treat men with respect," "Be impartial," "Look to their food," "Take care in the selection of non-coms," "Be a daddy as well as a commander."

With varying degrees of shock, they learned the importance of "the spirit of the bayonet" in instilling fighting quality, honing aggression, and building élan in the attack. "Bring the liver out on the bayonet—bring his kidneys out—bring his breakfast out," yelled the instructors. "Never pass a wounded enemy without running him thru. . . . When bayoneting, always listen for the cough—if he doesn't, stick him again." And the Ivy Leaguers learned to grunt loudly as they thrust the bayonet in, "for the purpose of drowning the squeal that comes from a man who knows death has come"; to butt the enemy with their helmets; to "gouge eyes out"; to "use a slug of shrapnel as brass knuckles"; and to free a deeply embedded bayonet by firing a round into the victim.

As the weeks passed, the actuality of war began to sink in. "I shall never forget one night in the barracks just before taps," recalled one candidate who had already experienced the Western Front as a war correspondent.

In our company was a group of college boys, always singing, quite often rough-housing, brimming with young animal spirits. I wondered if they had comprehended the seriousness of it all. . . . I began to tell them of the front, of the No-Man's Land I had seen between the trenches; the fragments of things that used to be men dangling from barbed wires, tossed there by the bursts of shells. . . . The college boys became serious. Then one of them gave a quick nervous laugh and exclaimed, "You know what they say: see Paris and die!" The others joined in the laugh. Then someone cried: "On to Paris! On to Berlin!" . . . Yes, they were the stuff.

They would need all their resilience. In France, Britain, and Germany their counterparts were already well on their way to mythological status as the "lost generation," tragic icons of the Western Front. The stereotype of courage was the junior officer, whistle in mouth, leading his men up the ladder, out of the trench, and into the inferno of flame, gas, machine guns, and shrapnel. Twenty-one days was the life expectancy of British subalterns, and the War Department estimated that there would be a "wastage" of two thousand officers a month when combat began in earnest. Much depended on the luck of the draw; only 4 percent of those young American officers destined for the newly forming 38th Infantry Regiment would survive the war.

The candidates of the summer course of 1917 struggled to meet the pace set by the War Department. Of the 40,000 who started the course, only 27,341 were commissioned three months later, in August 1917; the remainder were unequal to the physical strain, the rigid discipline, or the psychological pressure. Some attempted suicide. Those who failed to graduate returned, humiliated, to civilian life. Some of those who passed would instruct the next batch of candidates in the same camps; the rest were to become junior officers in the National Army as soon as it was constituted, under senior officers from the regular army.

The graduates impressed Inspector Mignot. "Some of the officers are really good. . . . One encounters again the real qualities of the race: intelligence, judgement, level-headedness, energy, tenacity. . . . [Their] intention is certainly to go to the limit, whatever the sacrifices might be. . . . On the whole, the spirit of the American officer corps would appear to be remarkable and entirely worthy of our confidence."

Motivation was a subtle blend of ideals and pragmatism. According to Inspector Mignot, many echoed the theme of Moffett's *Conquest of America*, believing that "if the Allies were beaten, the Boches would be able in several years' time to attack America." But they were convinced too that America was fighting a moral crusade. "Almost to a man, they share the theories of President Wilson. . . . [They fight] to uphold the principles of humanity and liberty . . . to punish the many crimes committed by the Boches . . . to come to the aid of France and repay her for the assistance which she rendered the U.S. during the War of Independence."

Secretary Baker wanted this spirit to infuse every act of his army. "I want you all to remember," he told one newly commissioned group in August 1917, "that you are officers of a democratic army. . . . We are in the business of making, in the words of the President, 'the world safe for democracy' but we are also in the business of showing to the world what we for a long time have known—that democracy is safe for the world." Whether or not democracy could be stretched, however, to include the notion of equality for black Americans remained to be seen.

9

"Are We Still Jim Crow in the Army?"

From the beginning, Secretary Baker wanted the American Army to be "homogeneous." "We do not want any German, Slav, Italian or Irish regiments," he told Hugh Scott; nor, to Scott's intense disappointment, was his suggestion of an Indian regiment considered. The policy pleased those who were doubtful of America's ability to absorb the seemingly unending influx of immigrants. They saw the new conscript army as a nation-building tool—a compulsory melting pot, a centrally controlled mechanism for "Americanizing" the strangers in the land. "The Selective Service Act," remarked *The New York Times* bluntly, "gives a long and sorely needed means of disciplining a certain insolent foreign element in this nation."

But Baker's plan for an unsegregated army did not include black Americans. "There is no intention in the War Department," Baker stated firmly, "to undertake at this time to settle the so-called race question." In any event, the scale of the problem was far beyond his powers. By 1917, the downward spiral of prejudice and discrimination, violence and abuse that had provoked Du Bois and other black radicals to break with the passive policies of Booker T. Washington had spun virtually out of control.

In the years since 1914, while the war industries had been booming, immigration from Europe had virtually ceased. Manufacturers had to compete for labor to meet the huge Allied orders for matériel—and they drew on the previously untapped labor of the cotton fields. More than half a million whites had moved into the cities, and now the factories needed blacks too. Southern newspapers carried advertisements exhorting black workers to leave the fields and serve the war industries, and agents employed by munitions companies trawled the southern states, netting men with the bait of high wages: 50,000 blacks went from Georgia, 90,000 from Alabama, 100,000 from Mississippi.

The pull of these appeals was reinforced by the push of serious flooding and a boll weevil plague in the cotton fields. Together with a general shift in agricultural practices that was taking place in the South, they precipitated a migration of blacks that by 1920 would total 500,000—a watershed in black history to rival that of Emancipation.

A large proportion of the new arrivals were virtually destitute—hungry, dirty, and dazed. To many white middle-class northerners, they seemed to be a ready-made underclass, badly educated, immoral, unmannerly, menacing. Blue-collar workers simply saw cheap-labor rivals for their own jobs. Very rapidly, tensions in the cities reached alarming proportions.

Violence was often the result, and none worse than that in East Saint Louis, the chief railway and manufacturing center of Illinois. In 1917 alone, twelve thousand blacks arrived there—and it took them very little time to realize that they had been duped. True, they did find work, often ahead of the whites who clustered around the factory gates each morning; more than ten thousand whites reckoned they had lost their jobs to the black "scabs." But the blacks were paid worse than whites and were forced to live a hand-to-mouth existence, huddled in slums or sleeping rough in boxcars or on the streets.

The city administration, leprous with corruption, provided no relief; on the contrary, it joined with the swarming pimps, gamblers, and saloon keepers in preying on the new arrivals. For some, stealing was the only way to survive, drink the only way to forget. Now whites began to fear not only for their jobs but also for their homes and families.

On the night of July 1, an automobile drove through a black district, its occupants firing indiscriminately into people's homes. The black community gathered itself and retaliated. A white policeman was killed, and the city exploded in a frenzy of race hatred. The news reached the War Department in a telegram: EAST LOUIS IN HANDS OF MOB ENTIRELY BEYOND CONTROL. For a day and a night, "scenes of horror that would have shocked a savage were viewed with placid unconcern by hundreds whose hearts knew no pity, and who seemed to revel in the feast of blood and cruelty." At the very least (the exact figures were never known), thirty-nine blacks and nine whites—men, women, and four (black) children—

were clubbed down, shot, stabbed, scalped, hanged, and dragged through the streets. The chant went up: "Get a nigger! Get a nigger! Get another!"

Among the black victims was Edward Cook, on his way home to Saint Louis with his wife and teenage son after a morning's fishing in nearby Alton. The streetcar on which the family was traveling was stalled when thirty whites pulled its trolley arm off the overhead wire at an intersection. Cook was pulled to the rear platform and shot; his son was clubbed over the head with a revolver. The crowd dragged Mrs. Cook out of the streetcar, ripped her dress, and tore her hair out; she was saved from being kicked to death only by the intervention of a tall white man who shielded her body with his and screamed, "In the name of the Lord, don't kill the woman!" "And then some way or other," she testified later, "they got me into the ambulance. I . . . wiped the blood out of my eyes and when I looked down I saw my husband lying there and my boy right under me. They had their eyes open and they were dead."

The venal, murderous city of East Saint Louis may have represented the far end of the spectrum of racial hatred, but in a lesser degree tension was universal, and it was not a problem that Baker could put to one side. In a situation of total war, with manpower equally at a premium in field, factory, and armed forces, the black tenth of the population could not be ignored. As a General Staff memorandum pointed out, "In the old regular army, the handling of colored troops was of comparative simplicity. Such negroes as were in the army were there because they wanted to be. . . . Now, however, the government is asking the entire colored population to take a full share in the war. Their men, their money, and their devotion are needed to the greatest possible extent." The war could not be fought, let alone won, without their willing participation.

The situation presented black leaders with a dramatically improved bargaining position from which to advance the cause of civil rights. "Prominent negroes," the memorandum continued, "have raised, even more than in civil life, the question of the 'equality' of the negro, and agitators have made what capital they could of the situation. 'Why should we fight for America?' they ask. 'What has she done for us?' 'Are we still Jim Crow in the army?' "

Black leaders viewed military service from the perspective of the good it could do the black community at home. Specifically, they wanted black combat units. Historically, service in the Army had provided one of the few opportunities for the black underclass to make a mark; their triumphs had provided valuable ammunition for promoters of black rights.

Many white Americans, however, were equally adamant that black combat troops could be a menace at home. "In talking with southern members of Congress," remarked Tasker Bliss, "I find . . . it is not that they disbelieve in more or less universal training on principle. But they do not like the idea of looking forward five or six years by which time their entire male negro population will have been trained to arms."

SOUTH ALARMED BY THREAT OF NEGRO UPRISING screamed the New York *Tribune* in the feverish summer of 1917. "US acts to prevent revolt. Insolence of blacks increases. . . . German plan to stir plantation hands." Women rushed to buy firearms, and their target practice became a daily spectacle.

Race relations deteriorated on the administration's doorstep. Military intelligence cited several instances of black males in Washington, D.C., inviting white women to go out with them; when they were turned down, "practically the same answer was made in each case, that the white women were high and mighty now, but they would not be so superior in a short time." The War Department took the threat seriously enough to pull the District of Columbia National Guard's "First Separate Battalion (Colored)" off duty at the White House and replace it with a battalion of white regulars.

Disastrously for the black cause, the danger supposedly presented by black soldiers materialized in Houston in the summer of 1917. On the evening of August 23, white law officer Lee Sparks beat up two black soldiers—one a private who had protested at Sparks's brutal treatment of a black woman, the other a provost guard in uniform investigating the first assault. The relationship between the black troops and the local people had been sour from the start. The troopers were almost all northern blacks, and they jibbed at the city's Jim Crow laws. Because many of the regiment's officers were newly assigned, they did not realize quite how high emotions were running. That night, about a hundred of the men armed themselves and set off into town through the darkness and drizzle to find and kill Lee Sparks. As they marched, they fired indiscriminately at any whites they saw, killing sixteen and wounding eleven more before the night ended.

In the midst of this desperate deterioration in race relations, Baker met with black leaders in a high-profile public relations exercise to discuss their grievances. Robert Russa Moton, principal of the Tuskegee Institute, objected to any scheme that would deny blacks a combat role. Baker had already decided to commission significant numbers of African Americans into company grades; in June a special black officer-training camp opened at Des Moines. Now he agreed to create black combat units: one from drafted troops, another to be based round National Guard units. And as a token of blacks' involvement in high-level policy making, he appointed Emmett Scott, a former aide of Booker T. Washington, as "Special Assistant for Negro Affairs."

This was enough to satisfy black Americans temporarily. Apparently, the two combat units counterbalanced the creation of infinitely more numerous labor battalions, which is where Baker intended the vast majority of black troops to serve—performing a menial though vital role at ports of embarkation and along the lines of communication without being trained to arms. Black leaders rewarded Baker with their support.

But Baker could not fulfill his side of the bargain alone. In practical terms, the fate of black troops in the Army lay with the senior regular officers, and they were far from proof against the prejudices prevailing in civilian America.

From the early 1890s, as the Army had become more professional and placed a far heavier emphasis on technical education, the War Department had been recruiting an ever-smaller proportion of blacks. Increasingly, senior officers had come to accept the widely held stereotype of the African mind as unable to cope with scientific matters.

Prejudice appeared to claim an important victim almost at the outset of the war. Lieutenant Colonel Charles Young, the most senior black officer in the U.S. Army, was a man of dignity and humor and a distinguished soldier. He was also one of only three black officer candidates to have survived the loneliness and hostility of West Point in the 1870s and '80s. "He had no comrades at the Academy," a classmate recalled. "I remember him conversing in German with some foreign-born shoe black." As a major in the 10th Cavalry, Young had gone with Pershing into Mexico, where he had led a force to relieve a besieged squadron of the 13th Cavalry. "By God, Young," exclaimed Major Frank Tompkins, grateful to be saved, "I could kiss every black face out there!" "If you want to," Young replied, "you may start with me."

Other white soldiers were not as enamored of Young. White officers, mostly southerners, wrote to the President, Secretary Baker, and various southern senators declaring that it was "not only distasteful but practically impossible to serve under a colored commander." Young was fully equipped to move up to general grade; it would have been a huge step for black America, and it would have applied pressure for equality that the Army would have been unlikely to withstand. But the threat to white supremacy never materialized. Young was declared medically unfit for active command and sidelined. In fact, he did have serious kidney damage, and he was to die of nephritis in 1922. But the decision looked dubious—the more so when Young, in despair at his rejection, rode on horseback from his home in Ohio to the door of the War Department to demonstrate his fitness.

There were other, more certain victims of racial prejudice, most conspicuously the 1,200 candidates at the black officer-training camp at Des Moines, Iowa. Prejudice was underwritten by the fact that the vast majority of blacks in America had low educational attainments. In 1910, only 45 percent of blacks five to twenty years of age were attending school, and a high proportion of those were in first grade, with attendance tailing off rapidly to fifth grade. Consequently, many of the candidates, not least the 250 noncommissioned officers drawn from regular and National Guard units, were not equipped to cope with the academic demands of the course. Some of the candidates had been to college, but according to the testimony of two men who attended Des Moines, "very few had even a fair education."

In addition to academic pressures, the men suffered from discrimination in the drugstores, theaters, and movie houses of Des Moines, and tensions mounted, occasionally erupting into violence. In the wake of the Houston massacre and the hanging of thirteen of the ringleaders, the commandant at Des Moines, Charles Ballou, called the candidates together and lectured them:

> You who form 10% of the population of the United States can't force social equality down the throats of the white 90% of our population. What you get you must win . . . by your modesty, your ability and your character. . . . And I say to you now that these down-town broils . . . are going to stop and stop now. . . . I simply will not tolerate having the success of this camp, and all that the success means to your race, ruined by the acts of a selfish and conceited handful of men.

Ballou seems to have been well meaning, but the attitude of his staff was not conducive to creating officers capable of initiative and command.

The white instructors, from regular army units, treated the candidates like the lowliest of enlisted men in the regular army. And it was claimed that they awarded commissions—seven hundred passed—to "those who were more likely to fail than succeed. [One man] won a commission by singing plantation songs."

10

"Over There": Pershing and the Plans for an American Expeditionary Force

In May 1917, with the draft law secure and officers' training in hand, Chief of Staff Hugh Scott left America with Elihu Root on a mission to Russia to see what aid the new revolutionary regime would need to keep on fighting the Germans. Now the burdens of war fell on the broad shoulders of Scott's deputy, Tasker Bliss. In his early sixties, also approaching retirement, Bliss was a bulky man with a luxuriant mustache, a figure exuding maturity and reassurance. But for all his avuncular solidity, he had an agile mind and an extraordinary breadth of learning. The son of a professor, he read Latin and Greek in the original (though he wrapped his classical texts in plain brown paper in order not to seem unduly highbrow).

Like Scott, Bliss was an officer of the old army, no war manager on the Ludendorff model, and his appointment did not seem to add much to the General Staff's potential for organizing a modern mobilization. Nevertheless, Bliss had important contributions to make. Wilson and Baker admired and liked him, and his ability to cross into their civilized civilian ambience was important for serving officers. Until then, they had not had a voice in the highest circles; indeed, the decision to wage war against Germany had been made without the advice of the military professionals being sought.

Bliss had clear and convincing views on grand strategy. His President wanted the Army to fight at the heart of the war so that the United States could be at the center of the peacemaking. But in 1917, even the Allies were undecided where the war should or could be won. After two and a half years of stalemate on the Western Front, some highly placed Europeans—including the British Prime Minister—were arguing that it was time to shift the fighting to other theaters.

David Lloyd George favored a more oblique approach partly to protect the far-flung British Empire and partly because, in his view, the Western Front was an unproductive charnel house and his generals well-bred butchers and blunderers who were throwing precious lives into the maw of German machine guns and artillery. "The policy we have pursued hitherto," he wrote urgently to Wilson, "has been to concentrate all our attacks on Germany, on the ground that Germany is the mainspring of the hostile alliance." Believing that the battering frontal attacks were failing to break down German resistance, he asked Wilson "to consider very carefully whether we cannot achieve decisive results by concentrating first against Germany's weaker allies"—to knock away "the props on which the German military power is now increasingly dependent."

Wilson was much struck by Lloyd George's denunciation of the "wastage" of the Western Front. "Something different should be done in the conduct of the war," he wrote to House. It was a critical moment. The United States was being offered an opportunity to redirect grand strategy, but should the gamble misfire, the cost would be enormous. Bliss stood firm. He had the General Staff's War College Division draw up a memorandum for the President, discussing and unequivocally dismissing the notion that America should apply her military power anywhere but in France.

The reasoned arguments ranged over logistical problems, the effect on French morale of the diversion of American troops, tactical and political problems in countries other than France, and the fact that the interior lines of communication of the Central Powers made nonsense of the idea of an outflanking thrust. More than this, Bliss asserted that American participation would end the stalemate in France. "While matters are at a deadlock on the Western Front," he argued, "a preponderance of two or three million men which we hope to place there on the side of the allies in the near future promises a possibility of success."

In France, the U.S. Army might win the war; but even though it had fewer problems than other battlefronts, it was by no means an easy theater for operations. The Atlantic was a three-thousand-mile barrier not only to the transportation of men and matériel but even to communications. There was no telephone link; all messages had to be sent either by ship, in which case any exchange of letters took weeks, or by telegraph, with all the problems of coding, garbling, and incomprehension.

The commanding officer of the American Expeditionary Force in France would be isolated and out of touch with Washington, surrounded by Allied generals and politicians, trying to dodge their obvious self-interest while protecting America's position. The War Department needed to find the right man, and soon. Groups of officers were being sent to Europe at intervals to assess conditions and gauge the needs of a future American Expeditionary Force, but a permanent commander was urgently required over there to provide focus and take responsibility.

Given the modest size of the officer corps, Secretary Baker had very little room for maneuver in his choice. To everyone outside the administration, the obvious candidate was Leonard Wood. He had filled key administrative posts in the army hierarchy, including Chief of Staff; he had also studied in Europe, and, through his close association with Theodore Roosevelt, who had served under him in the Rough Riders, he had strong contacts with Europe's political elite.

But Wood, once the equal of an Apache brave, was now in uncertain health. Sometime previously, he had crushed part of his skull by jumping up hastily from his desk and hitting a heavy chandelier immediately above; despite two operations to relieve the pressure on his brain, the impacted fracture had left him dragging one leg. More damning still, his loyalty was highly suspect in the eyes of Wilson and Baker. He had ignored orders to stop calling for preparedness, and he was a devout Roosevelt man; when Roosevelt had tried to force his volunteers on Wilson, Wood had been his staunchest ally, even supplying him with the names of the best officers for his purpose. In Wilson's eyes, he was "an agitator."

Age and inability ruled out all other serving major generals except John Joseph Pershing, the most junior of them all. Born in Laclede, Missouri, into a poor family, Pershing taught school before taking several years off his age to get himself into West Point in 1882, at the age of twenty-two. He passed out in 1886 and served on the frontier with the 6th Cavalry, after which he was assigned to the university at Lincoln, Nebraska, as an instructor in military science. There, in his spare time, he took a law degree, even considering leaving the Army to practice. Then came the Spanish-American War, in which his courage under fire was conspicuous. He served three tours in the Philippines and went to Japan as military attaché in the aftermath of Japan's successful war against Russia. Exposure to the battle-fields of Manchuria brought him face to face with twentieth-century warfare.

Now his star began to rise rapidly. A Republican, in 1905 he had married the daughter of a Republican senator, a fact that, when added to the approval of all but one of the serving generals, may have encouraged Theodore Roosevelt to raise him to brigadier general over the heads of 862 other officers. At this rank, Pershing took posts beyond the reach of his contemporaries, including the governorship of Moro Province in the Philippines. Then, in 1915, he was selected for the politically sensitive task of bringing Pancho Villa to heel. His handling of the Mexican adventure, in particular his strict obedience to orders, impressed both Baker and Wilson and it gave him valuable experience in running an expeditionary force with long supply lines.

This tough, middle-aged cavalryman did not quite have the intellect of Wood or Bliss, nor was he a student of war to the depth attained by a man like Douglas MacArthur, then a major, but he more than compensated with other qualities, not least an iron will. He was highly charismatic, powerfully affecting both men and women, and he was a born leader; at West Point, he had been first captain of cadets and president of his class. Although Pershing was only five feet, nine inches tall, his combination of robust health, square jaw, and dynamism consistently made people see him as well over six feet tall.

His restless energy sometimes made him an uncomfortable companion. "He was never still," one junior officer remembered. "Always he was adjusting his clothes, fingering his gloves, looking away in impatience, striking a pose, making those about him ill at ease." But he had, when he needed it, an extraordinary capacity for listening to advice and for recognising and using the good qualities of others. One young captain, George C. Marshall, had personal experience of his tolerance. During an inspection, Marshall had been incensed by Pershing's misplaced criticism of the commanding officer. As Pershing had turned his back to leave the room, Marshall had lost his temper. Stepping forward, he had grabbed Pershing, spun him round and angrily set the record straight. Rather than having Marshall put into custody, Pershing had heard him out, and on later visits to the unit he had taken him aside to ask his opinion.

If Pershing had a weakness, a chink in the psychological armor required by commanders on the Western Front, it was of recent origin. He had been devoted to his wife, Frankie, and their three daughters and one son. Normally they had traveled with him on assignment, but in 1915, when trouble was brewing on the border, Pershing and his brigade had been sent to El Paso, Texas, and the family had remained at home in San Francisco. On a hot August night, the family house had burned down, and only his son had been saved. At the peak of his profession, this fifty-five-year-old soldier, who had become a father late in life, had lost almost everything dear to him. His duties on the border and preparations for the expedition against Villa had helped him sublimate his grief, but he would face the trials of the Western Front with a misery that was always close to the surface.

Pershing was appointed to "command of all the land forces of the United States operating in continental Europe and in the United Kingdom of Great Britain and Ireland, including any part of the Marine Corps which may be detached for service there with the army." He was ordered to establish "all necessary bases, lines of communication, depots etc and make all the incidental arrangements essential to active participation at the front," and he was invested with all the authority available under existing legislation to "carry on the war vigorously in harmony with the spirit of these instructions and towards a victorious conclusion."

The scope of the command, necessary given the primitive state of communications with Europe, was fantastic. To a major extent, the War Department had passed the responsibility for shaping America's war effort to Pershing. Unlike the German Supreme Command, which kept power at the center because it needed to balance the demands of east and west, the War Department, having decided to fight only on the Western Front, existed, in effect, to do as Pershing asked. Tasker Bliss, now Chief of Staff in Washington, even went so far as to say that he regarded himself simply as an assistant to Pershing's own Chief of Staff in France.

The news of Pershing's appointment raced through the regular army, and Pershing was inundated with pleas to be taken "over there." "I write now to request that my two sons, Theodore Roosevelt Jr., aged 27, and Archibald B. Roosevelt, aged 23, both of Harvard, be allowed to enlist as privates under you," wrote one ex–commander in chief.

For his Chief of Staff in France, Pershing chose a man he described as "the ablest officer I know." James G. Harbord, born in Bloomfield, Illinois, was the son of a Union cavalry officer. Brought up on a farm in Kansas, he had attended the State Agricultural College. After failing to get into West Point, he had taught school for two years before enlisting as a private. In 1891, he had been commissioned a second lieutenant of cavalry, and he had served in Cuba and the Philippines. In 1917, he was fifty-one years old, a major, and a student at the Army War College in Washington, D.C. One passage in his efficiency report could stand as a symbol of the whole regular army's unpreparedness for combat against Germany in France. One of the principal assets of the officer who was to be Pershing's right hand in France was his ability "to speak Spanish with fair fluency," with the main highlight of his active experience being "over ten years . . . in the Philippine Constabulary."

Baker had intended Pershing to take no more than a few carefully chosen officers to France on his personal staff, but, sensibly, Harbord recommended taking a full complement of specialists to study every feature of the Allied armies. The initial party comprised 131 clerks, translators, and orderlies and 58 officers, 2 of them marines. Among the officers were some of the most brilliant men in the Army, including Fox Conner, Hugh Drum, and, on Pershing's personal staff, the Army's richest soldier, George Patton.

Pershing had found something of a refuge in the Patton family in the months after Frankie's death, to the point where the press had spread rumors (firmly denied by Pershing to Frankie's father) of an engagement to Patton's sister Nita. Patton was no administrator and appears to have been selected for Pershing's staff as a social asset. Certainly, Haig was very taken with him on their first meeting and placed him at his left at dinner. On such occasions, Patton refrained from the "earthily profane" vocabulary that Omar Bradley believed he used in order to compensate for a voice that was "almost comically squeaky and high-pitched, altogether lacking in command authority."

Pershing and Harbord worked quickly, and on a gray, drizzling day at the end of May 1917, the commander's party assembled on Governors Island in New York Harbor. They were met by George Marshall, then a thirty-seven-year-old captain, who was in "a most depressed frame of mind" at being left behind. From the island they boarded a tugboat to take them out to the liner *Baltic*, already en route to the open sea. Pershing was anxious not to alert German submarines, hence the decision to board covertly in midchannel. He need not have bothered. For two days, supplies labeled FOR GENERAL PERSHING'S HEADQUARTERS, PARIS, FRANCE had lain around in open view on the pier. And, in case the German spies were not paying proper attention, the battery on Governors Island fired a salute as the *Baltic* sailed. It was with some trepidation that the party entered the U-boats' killing grounds in the seas off Ireland, and they were relieved and grateful to slide within the protective circle of Admiral Sims's four-stackers.

The contingent landed first at Liverpool, England, which Pershing had visited with his wife in the autumn of 1908. Now he had the use of the King's private railway carriage in which to travel to London. If Pershing had any illusions about the difficulties of his appointment, his reception quickly destroyed them. After lunching with the King at Buckingham Palace (the usual royal fare was one egg, some bread, and lemonade), he met Prime Minister Lloyd George and took tea with the Chief of the Imperial General Staff, Sir William "Wully" Robertson—a cumbersome, whiskey-drinking, flat-footed individual known to his juniors as the "ambulating refrigerator."

Though he had risen from the ranks through sheer intellectual ability, Wully remained a blunt man. The British knew that the United States intended to form its own army, and they had resisted the idea from the start. By 1917, they had a training, procurement, and logistical infrastructure that could equip men as replacements for existing units in nine weeks. The British wanted America to supply raw levies to feed into this tried and proven system and believed that it was a waste of effort and, more important, time—an estimated eighteen months—for the United States to construct a separate army.

However, Pershing's orders, approved personally by the President, made the position quite clear. He was directed "to co-operate with the forces of the other countries employed against the enemy," but—and it was an all-important "but"—"the underlying idea must be kept in view that the forces of the United States are a separate and distinct component of the combined forces, the identity of which must be preserved." For Wilson to have influence at the peace negotiations, an American army must have triumphed on the battlefield. Merely supplying levies would leave all the laurels in the hands of the Allies—a point not overlooked by the Allied leaders.

As Wully sipped his tea, Pershing patiently explained the Americans' plan for the organization of their independent forces. But it was obvious that the British were not going to give up easily. Pershing had to acknowledge that the War Department's plans depended on British shipping to get his men across the Atlantic to France—and this gave Robertson the opportunity to play the British ace. It was, he said, "entirely out of the question" for the British to provide America with any shipping, since they were already struggling to find vessels for their own national necessities. No levies, no ships. The battle lines between Britain and America had been clearly drawn.

11

"I Hope It Is Not Too Late": The First Division in France

On June 13, Pershing left London for Paris to meet a reception very different from the cautious machinations of the British. Massive crowds lined the route to his hotel, cheering, screaming, and weeping. The Americans were taken aback by the force and openness of the feeling. During the brief cavalcade, the misery of three years' excruciating war poured out. "Though I live a thousand years," wrote James Harbord, "I shall never forget that crowded hour. One may easily believe that not quite the same emotions have swayed a Paris throng since the first years of the nineteenth century."

The French were exhausted to the edge of defeat and badly afraid. That summer, their army was reeling from the aftereffects of Nivelle's abortive offensive in Champagne. The bitter, widespread mutinies had not yet been resolved, and Paris lay virtually undefended. Many Parisians had already experienced the humiliation of defeat at the hands of the Prussians in the war of 1870–1871, when their city had been occupied and the palace at Versailles used for the Kaiser's coronation. Indeed, Hindenburg, then a young officer, had represented his regiment at the ceremony. Now, the Parisians feared, it was about to happen again—but here was Pershing, the forerunner of an American army that would surely save them.

As Pershing arrived, the new French commander in chief, Henri Pétain, was desperately trying to quell the mutinies with a "pacification" program founded on the promise that the French Army would launch no more offensives until the Americans arrived. But though Pétain inspired his troops, he had no real faith that American blood and treasure could rescue the situation. The hero of Verdun, the stoic who had redeemed his immortal pledge, "*On ne passe pas,*" whispered to Pershing when they met, "I hope it is not too late."

"It was most touching and in a sense most pathetic," Pershing wrote of the flow of emotions in Paris that summer. "It brought home to us as nothing else could have done a full appreciation of the war-weary state of the nation and stirred within us a deep sense of the responsibility resting upon America." In the short term, it was vital that America send troops as a visible commitment to the defense of France—but this could at best amount to no more than a token division.

In April, in Washington, Marshal Joseph Joffre had begged for men to be sent over. The War Department, not realizing the importance of such a gesture, had been reluctant to cooperate at first. While perfectly willing to send specialist noncombatants such as railway engineers, Bliss had intended to keep every available soldier at home to train the National Army. But the decline in French morale was so serious that Wilson had intervened and personally approved Joffre's plea.

The Army did not then possess a tactical unit it could call a "division" in the Western Front sense, long though the General Staff had mulled over tables of organization. One would somehow have to be manufactured from elements of the regular army, supplemented by volunteers in the ratio of one regular to four volunteers. Hastily, the necessary troops were scrambled together, and this "1st Division" left New York for France only two weeks after Pershing—with Captain George Marshall, after some deft string pulling, as its assistant chief of staff.

It was a miserable voyage, cramped and suffocating belowdecks. Tom Carroll, who had enlisted at Cincinnati at the end of April, noted in his diary, "Food is very bad. Yellow corn meal and stew mostly. . . . Am put on puke detail." Few had any conception of what they might expect at the end of the voyage. (One of the officers in charge of marshaling troops at the Hoboken port of embarkation as they came off the ferry noted that many, after a matter of minutes at sea, believed they had already arrived in France.) Smoking was forbidden on deck once dusk began to fall—a lighted match, it was said, could be seen two miles away—and likewise the wearing of white caps. Spotting "raiders" was the principal pastime during the day; at night, when most of the U-boats operated, there was nothing to do but huddle together in darkness, fully dressed including life belts, and hope.

Once on board, Marshall began to realize precisely how unprepared the American forces were; many of the officers were meeting for the first time aboard the boat, and together they spent the voyage trying to digest the mass of papers that had been turned over to the War College by the Allies. The division's senior officers were regulars, but the company grades were filled with men culled from the new officer-training camps. "I have never seen more splendid looking men," Marshall noted; in the years after the war he could not recall a single one of them surviving.

He was not as impressed with the men in the ranks. "Many of the men were undersized and a number spoke English with difficulty." The need for experienced troops at home meant that the division had been allowed to contain only about 20 percent experienced men. The rest were regulars in name only, recent recruits hurriedly thrown together—"perhaps the most motley array of 'regulars' that ever left our shores," in the view of the commander of the 7th Field Artillery—"undisciplined, untrained, untried, but full of life and spirit." Sailing with the Army was the 5th Marine Regiment, which held a high proportion of veterans and had benefited from a superior marine training program.

Marshall was the second man ashore at Saint-Nazaire, a little port at the mouth of the Loire River. In an imposing automobile, probably the Cadillac brought over by the Marines, he set off to inspect the camp being prepared for the division. "Riding with a French officer," he recalled, "I decided to initiate a policy of . . . speaking French on every suitable occasion. Intending to comment on the wonderful morning, I remarked *Je suis très beau aujourd'hui.*' He gave me an odd look and I mentally translated my remark ['I am very beautiful today']. I never spoke French again except when forced to."

The men made their own contact with the locals. "Camp surrounded with barbed wire fence," wrote one, "but guys were sneaking thru and getting loaded. Company commander catches Sergeant Hooker coming back with two bottles wrapped in newspaper; gives him hell and puts guard along the fence." One unfortunate, led on by a village girl, amorously pushed her to the ground; though matters went no further, the division commander made an example of him: court-martial and a thirty-year sentence. They were certainly a tough bunch; their surviving diaries and letters document brawling, gambling, and drinking on a major scale. "These first troops," wrote one French soldier to his parents, "professional mercenaries, aren't the cream; the civilian troops coming later will give us more reason to hope, I think. There is a large proportion of brutes in these contingents, of all origins—English, Spanish, Italian, German."

But however variable their quality, the Americans in France were already serving their immediate purpose. Although aware that military observers could not fail to note the troops' rawness, Pershing ordered elements of the division to appear in Paris on the Fourth of July. At the Invalides, with full ceremony, in the presence of the President of France and Marshal Joffre with his staff, Pershing was presented with flags by the descendants of the Frenchmen who had fought for America against the British in the War of Independence and by the people of Puy, Lafayette's hometown. In return, the flag of the American volunteers who had been fighting with the French was handed to veterans of the Franco-Prussian War. "This signified," wrote William "Billy" Mitchell, later one of Pershing's most prominent officers, "that the work of the American volunteers was ended and that the regular troops of the Government had taken over their part."

For their part, the men of the 1st Division looked around, somewhat awestruck by their surroundings, waiting for the order to form up. When the moment came, these Americans, many of them untrained civilians in uniform, clutched their rifles, pulled down their peaked campaign hats, and stepped out with unbridled enthusiasm—but little symmetry. "They looked," Mitchell conceded, "totally unprepared for war." German cartoonists ridiculed these first American combat troops, depicting them as "tin soldiers, an incompetent regiment of billionaires and cowboys." But the tin soldiers hit the mark with the Parisians, who showered flowers over them as they paraded from the Invalides until the procession looked like a moving rose garden.

Since Pershing's arrival, the French had taken him to their hearts. Only weeks before, he had been largely unknown to them—most Frenchmen had been expecting and hoping to see Roosevelt or Leonard Wood lead the American contingent. But, wrote one observer, "the French are intensely personal in everything they do. They ascribe much more to personalities than to systems or organizations. . . . [They] are now saying that we shall have two 'pères' [fathers] running the war: 'Père Joffre' and 'Père Shing.' "

As for Pershing, he had already succumbed to French allure. On the day of his arrival in Paris, he had met a twenty-three-year-old artist, Micheline Resco. She was regularly commissioned by the French government to paint

official portraits; images of bravery and determination made valuable propaganda among the middle classes. Admiral Sims had already sat for her,
and, not surprisingly, the French authorities wanted to add Pershing to the
gallery. They got the portrait, and Pershing acquired a mistress.

Pershing's women were a subject widely discussed in the Army.
Leonard Wood, in a moment of particular bitterness at having been passed
over, once repeated to President Wilson the story that Pershing had fa-
thered several illegitimate children during his bachelor days in the Philippines; Wood had himself, he said, been involved in the cover-up. But
"Michette" was no passing fancy. The relationship endured for the rest of
Pershing's life.

Whenever he could, Pershing would slip away from his staff late at
night and drive through the dark cobbled streets to her apartment. There
he found peace and comfort; they never talked about the war or the job he
had been sent to do. He needed all the strength he could muster, whatever
the source, because the burdens on him were bearing down with ever more
crushing force.

Pershing knew only too well that if the American land forces were to
have any practical value beyond the reassurance they brought the French,
he and his staff must quickly draw up a blueprint for their active participation in the conflict. Packed into a tiny house in the rue de Constantine on
the left bank of the Seine, close to Napoleon's tomb, he and his staff
sweated through the hot summer in a welter of anxious study and planning.

One of the earliest questions had been where precisely to deploy the U.S.
forces. Pershing wanted a zone with strategic possibilities, but his choice
was restricted by logistical considerations. The massive nature of combat on
the Western Front meant that major offensives required months of preparation. To achieve the necessary buildup of men and matériel, Pershing
needed a part of the front that had easy links to large-volume port and rail
facilities. But in 1917, his options were limited. Douglas Haig's British
Army was operating through the Channel ports and (with the Belgians)
held the line covering those ports. The British offered to share their communications routes with America, putting the AEF into the line between
the British and French, but Pershing felt this was not consistent with an independent army. (The French, too, objected, according to Billy Mitchell,
on the grounds that they frequently had to go to the assistance of the British
and it would be a mistake to interpose a mass of raw troops between them.)

Of the remaining sections of the line, the French would not give up the defense of Paris, which pushed the Americans to the east and south.

Here in Lorraine, birthplace of Joan of Arc, Pershing could establish satisfactory and, above all, independent lines of communication using the Atlantic coast ports, with rail lines looping east and north, supplemented by the Mediterranean port of Marseilles, with its direct line north. There was also a tempting target. At the town of Saint-Mihiel, the German line bulged, enclosing a triangular tongue of land twenty miles across at its base and ten miles deep. If the AEF could take this salient, they would open the door to the iron- and steel-producing areas of Longwy and the Briey Basin, as well as to the enemy's main rail line serving a major portion of the Western Front.

This was the hinge of the German line, and much depended on the German Army's standing firm. Consequently, the salient had been heavily fortified, making it, in Billy Mitchell's words, "a nasty part of the front . . . where the French have been able to make practically no headway." But the AEF, Pershing felt, could do better in Lorraine, not least because the defensive system was by this time outmoded. In places it lacked the full depth of the new Hindenburg Line, which had been designed to absorb the crushing weight of steel that Allied artillery could now throw. The Saint-Mihiel operation was at the forefront of Pershing's plans from the start.

With this in mind, Pershing's staff concluded that they needed an army of one million men—"the smallest unit which in modern war will be a complete, well balanced and independent fighting organization." Pershing emphasized that a million men was only the start: "the force which may be expected to reach France in time for an offensive in 1918, and as a unit and basis of organization." "Plans for the future," he continued, "should be based, especially in reference to the manufacture etc. of artillery, aviation and other material, on three times this force. . . . Such a program of construction should be completed within two years."

While men and company-grade officers could be drafted and trained from scratch in sufficient numbers for an army this size, command and senior staff appointments could be filled only by experienced professionals. Some of the National Guard officers had the requisite ability, but the burden fell most heavily on regular army officers, of whom there were desperately few. Consequently, Pershing confirmed a decision that had been made provisionally before he left Washington: There must be the lowest

ratio possible of senior officers to the rest of the command—in other
words, the services of each senior officer must be spread thin. The corol-
lary was that the United States would fight the war with divisions 28,000
strong—999 officers and 27,173 men, roughly twice the size of any Allied or German division.

To Harbord, a large division had the major advantage of sustainability:

> With the deep and very powerful defense developed in the world war,
> no decisive stroke could be secured in battle without a penetration ne-
> cessitating several days of steady fighting. . . . The infantry of the divi-
> sion must be of such strength as to permit it to continue in combat for
> such a number of days that the continuity of battle would not be inter-
> rupted before decision was reached.

For the time being, however, Pershing had only the 1st Division and the
5th Marine Regiment. He set the marines to work as stevedores and as
military police, while he sent the soldiers to Gondrecourt, a tiny town in
Lorraine not far from the Saint-Mihiel salient. As if claiming the sector for
the AEF, he moved GHQ from Paris to Chaumont, in the rolling countryside of the upper Marne.

In the rural backwater of Gondrecourt, some twenty miles behind the
front line but within the sound of the guns, the Americans saw at first hand
the ravages endured by the French. At dawn each day a pathetic file of the
old and the very young trudged to the fields in a struggle to save the harvest. The soldiers came to know these peasants intimately. With no camps
yet built or barracks available, the 1st Division had to be billeted with families across a zone twenty-five miles long. Sleeping in damp, draughty
barns amid cows and chickens, the men endured the stench of manure that
had been piled in the village streets, as was the French custom. The vil-
lagers for their part stood around in awe as the troopers produced tooth-
brushes and performed unheard-of maneuvers in dental hygiene.

The first careless rapture of the relationship took some time to wear
off. "The Americans are the most lovable people in creation," enthused
one village representative. Another was fascinated by the ethnic diversity
of the units:

> You can't imagine a more extraordinary mixture than this American
> army; there's everything—Greeks, Italians, Turks, Chinese, Indians,

Spaniards, even lots of Germans—to tell the truth about half the officers are of German origin. It doesn't seem to bother them. . . . As for the men, it's often even more obvious. Did I tell you the story of the man . . . who was disembarking in France and saw his brother working in the port as a German prisoner-of-war?

Money eventually ruined the romance. For the first two months, the troops received no pay. Then, in an outbreak of bureaucratic idiocy, bags full of francs were solemnly distributed to men who had spent a good part of the journey to France gambling. Whooping, they threw the flimsy war currency into the air and watched it blow through the village streets—and into the teeth of French village women whose husbands and sons in the French Army earned a quarter of a franc per day.

The Americans' generosity, extravagance, and occasional ostentation generated an uncomfortable blend of greed and resentment in the locals. Food prices skyrocketed to 50 francs for a goose, a franc for one egg—far beyond the reach of the average family. The awesome American concern for personal hygiene created a booming laundry industry, but this too was tainted. "Business is too good," a customer complained, after being turned away from the door of one washerwoman despite having offered twice the usual allowance of soap, "the scarcest article in France. . . . They use little of the soap we furnish, and then sell the remainder."

Even the troops' attempts at kindness often rebounded on them. "The Americans are doing all sorts of peculiar things at Besançon," reported a French liaison officer. "They scoop up children on the streets and take them off to dinner." Most seriously, the Americans' success with the local girls undermined morale among Frenchmen at the front and morality within strict Catholic communities at home. It did not help that a few soldiers found it funny to teach the girls outrageously obscene American expressions on the pretext that they meant "How do you do?"

As more and more Americans arrived, the problems would multiply. At Valdahon, where the 1st Division's artillery trained, prostitutes and pimps congregated to the point where "honest country women" dared not go out. Wherever Americans gathered, alcohol was freely available, in joyous contrast to their hometowns, over which the clouds of Prohibition had gathered. In later months, it was quite common to see soldiers tipsy, even dead drunk, in daytime. Soldiers went on long debauches. "Some stayed eight days in Ligny-en-Barrois without going back to camp. They went on a binge with the women and were drunk all day," reported one scandalized French observer. And drink bred crime: the rape of an eight-year-old girl at Ligny by a drunken soldier terrorized the inhabitants.

On the heels of the 1st Division, specialist troops requested by the Allies poured into France. Their vessels were unloaded by the marines and by hastily trained black labor troops. By the end of August, nine regiments of railway engineers had been sent to France and temporarily assigned to the Allies. These soldiers suffered what were probably the first American casualties: Sergeant Matthew Calderwood and Private William Branigan, 11th Engineers, were wounded by German artillery fire on September 5, 1917, while serving with the British Third Army near the village of Gouzeaucourt.

The troops were also joined by the medical units that had originally come to France as volunteers to serve with the Allies and were now told that they should transfer to the AEF or go home. "I was in a dilemma," wrote one young medical orderly to his parents. "Was I to come home now and be thought a coward by future generations? I thought of Grandpa who enlisted as a private in the Civil War. Did anyone force him to join up? And he wasn't an American citizen! No, but he had America in his heart. I signed up."

12

The Military Melting Pot:
Into the Camps

Back home, there were thousands of others with America in their hearts, both conscripts and volunteers. Across the country, bands played, mothers wept, and men cheered as the young men made their final parade through their hometowns to the railroad station. William P. Hawley, assistant manager of the Woolworth's store in North Adams, Massachusetts, was so overcome by emotion after watching the local National Guard contingent leave town that he rushed down to the recruiting office to enlist. His reward for this flush of patriotism was assignment to the 3rd Division, promotion to first sergeant, and eventually a place in a trench on the banks of the Marne River at midnight with Prussian Guards advancing at him behind a hail of gas and high explosives.

In the early fall of 1917, watchers by the rail tracks would have seen a remarkable display of young Americans riding to their appointed camps and cantonments, an unrehearsed pageant of America's ethnic diversity: Chocktaws and Cochin Chinese, "Hebrews" (the Army's classification) from everywhere in the Diaspora, Greeks, Italians, English, Irish, Scots, Slavs, Swedes, Germans, Austrians, Albanians, Poles, Armenians, Syrians, Finns, Hispanics, and Japanese. (In Hawaii, the National Guard gained its first Japanese company.) Blacks went on separate trains.

To this army of Babel came men of all shapes and sizes: lanky recruits of Scots blood from the mountains of North Carolina, short and stocky Mediterraneans from the Northeast, where recent immigration had been heaviest. The minimum size was five feet, one inch and 128 pounds; any smaller, and the man would have been unable to carry the regulation army pack (though occasionally lighter men were accepted if they had special skills). The maximum was six feet, six inches; any taller, and the man was likely to have poor circulation. The weight limits were 190 pounds for infantry, engineers, and artillery and 165 pounds for the cavalry.

The average recruit measured five feet, seven and a half inches and weighed 141½ pounds, a meaningless statistic in this miscellany of manhood—except at the unit level, where the average was crucial in determining the sizes of uniforms to be supplied and quantity of rations allocated. Divisions with a high proportion of immigrants from eastern Europe received a smaller average ration and smaller uniforms than midwestern divisions formed of strapping Scandinavians and Germans. Few were racially as mixed as New York's 77th Division, whose theme song ran: "The Jews and the Wops,/ The Dutch and the Irish cops,/ They're all in the Army now" and which boasted forty-two different languages or dialects spoken in its ranks.

During the war, some 400,000 first-generation immigrants were drafted, including some who were alien enemies and ineligible. This influx was too much for Major General George Bell of the 33rd Division, whose contingent of around 15,000 National Guard volunteers had been fleshed out with conscripts. He complained to the Adjutant General that "the local boards in Illinois had very evidently spared men of the draft age of American birth or stock at the expense of those of foreign birth or patronage."

Many who had known only the ghettos of the East Coast cities could not speak English or understand commands. Bombarded with unintelligible instructions and forced to eat such unfamiliar substances as boiled potatoes and stewed apricots, they created serious morale problems in their units. Recent German or Austrian immigrants had the additional anxiety, so military intelligence reported, of having been warned that "if it were known in their home countries that they were in the American army, their families would be hunted out and killed." This rumor was recognized as one of many deliberate propaganda attempts to disrupt recruitment and ruin morale in the camps. Army authorities believed the Lutheran Church Board to be one of Germany's instruments, noting "its efforts to place its pastors in as many camps, forts and other military establishments as possible."

The plight of these first-generation immigrants was compounded by prejudice. Anti-Semitism inevitably surfaced. One night, six weeks after his induction from the Bronx, Private Otto Gottschalk found himself dragged from his tent, stripped, and thrown into a ditch of black muck. He was forced to drink the filthy water and was then badly beaten.

In the early days of the draft, a high proportion of "unsuitable" immigrants appears to have been sent straight back to the ghetto. Later, attempts were made to fit them for service. Where there were enough of them, immigrants were banded together into "development battalions" under officers of their own. At one point, Camp Gordon, in Georgia, had two Slav companies and two Italian and one Russian-Jewish battalion. They quickly became well disciplined and proficient in drill, and when asked how many of them were ready and willing to go abroad immediately, 92 percent stepped forward.

This jumble of colors, cultures, and languages, European, Asian, and Latin, mercilessly underlined the isolation of the black Americans who formed a large section of the intake—larger, perhaps, than was just. No blacks were appointed to the draft boards, and local boards often used their powers to conscript a far higher proportion of blacks than whites relative to population. In part, this was to compensate for the higher number of whites enlisting voluntarily. (Blacks, after all, had very few units to volunteer for.) But draft boards also had a tendency to use selective service as a means of "cleaning up" the neighborhood. A General Staff report noted, "The physical condition of a large part of the colored draft is very poor. Many must be entirely eliminated and a large proportion of those left are not fit for combat duty. The Surgeon General reports that 50% are infected with venereal disease." There was no organized conspiracy to fill the Army with the poorest and "least socially desirable" blacks, but, judging from the results, that is often what happened.

Whatever damage the draft boards had inflicted by their "selection" techniques the Army compounded by its treatment of its black draftees. Few received more than six weeks' training, and their living conditions were often appalling. In October 1917, black stevedore and labor battalions were formed at Camp Hill, Virginia. Six thousand men arrived at the camp to find "no barracks, no mess halls, no clothing, no sanitary arrangements of any kind." In the coldest winter in Virginia for twenty-five years, those who could find room packed themselves into small, dirty tents pitched on the bare earth, while the less fortunate were obliged to stand in front of fires all night. Those who inevitably fell sick were taken to the crowded large tent that served as a hospital, where they lay on the frozen ground with neither cots nor thick blankets.

Camp Hill was an extreme case, but a War Department inspector criticized the white officers of all these black noncombatant units for their indifference to their men. The NCOs, he continued, had often been promoted to their positions "because of previous knowledge of negroes, usually gotten on plantations, public works, turpentine farms and the like." At Camp Hill, an NCO was often selected from the ranks "because he is a 'husky' and will beat and abuse the men. Two such sergeants are in the guard house now for killing other soldiers under their command." The seeds of hatred, inefficiency, and even mutiny were being sown.

The inevitable consequence was low morale and indifference among black labor units when they got to Europe. "We have experienced considerable difficulty in getting the proper amount of work out of the negro stevedores at the various ports," W. W. Atterbury, Pershing's Director General of Transportation, was later to complain. "Fining them and putting them in the guard-house is very little punishment for them and to be dishonorably discharged and sent home is just what they desire." From Liverpool, one of England's major ports, the commanding officer of a detachment of stevedores reported that police and local citizens had begged for them to be withdrawn. "They are without exception the most worthless aggregation of humanity that was ever collected in one unit."

As for the black combat troops, who had originally been intended to share facilities with white troops, they were eventually consigned to segregated units; worse, they were at no point allowed to assemble and train as complete divisions in the United States. While white divisions could seek to develop esprit and identity from the beginning of their training, the fragmented black divisions barely knew what their senior officers looked like, so infrequently could these officers visit the various units scattered among the cantonments in which the National Army was training.

Arriving at the railheads, the new recruits were marshaled into columns by newly commissioned lieutenants trying to summon up the principles of command. The officers at least had the advantage of being in uniform; the recruits were still in civilian clothes, many wearing their best suits as if they were going to a wedding and clutching a few belongings or the remains of the food they had been given for the journey by the send-off committees in their hometowns.

After a brisk march, they got their first sight of the camp or cantonment that was to be home for months to come: "a far-spreading city of wooden buildings," one remembered, "whose flat roofs extended one after another in exact order like the biscuits in a baker's pan." (He was describing one of the sixteen hutted cantonments built for the National Army; members of the National Guard, who were used to living in tents, were housed in sixteen canvas cities farther south.)

If the recruits still cherished any spark of chivalry or romance about their induction, the medical orderlies waiting inside the gates soon introduced a note of gritty realism. Inspections for vermin and venereal disease and a vicious schedule of inoculations against smallpox, typhoid, and other contagious diseases left the new arrivals with barely the strength to crawl to their barracks.

And what they found there was rarely inspiriting. The basic design of the company barracks was sound. Each was to be a two-storied wooden building, the second floor a vast dormitory lined with iron cots, the first floor equipped with kitchen, storerooms, mess hall, and captain's office. Unfortunately, few of the buildings were ready. The delay in deciding on the precise size and structure of the infantry division had entailed constant alterations to the cantonment blueprint. Infirmary buildings, for example, were planned at a time when the Table of Organization prescribed thirty-three men for the medical detachment of an infantry regiment. This number was increased to forty-eight, and the building was too small before it was ever used.

The quality of the work that had been done left much to be desired. Far to the south, near a Houston still in shock after the summer massacre, the officers and men of the Illinois National Guard—now designated the 33rd Division—found Camp Logan "in a decidedly unfinished state." The hospital had been built without heating or running water—the construction quartermaster had put in two faucets on his own initiative—and the engineers pronounced the storehouses to be so faulty that it was only a matter of time before they collapsed. At Camp MacArthur, Texas, the builders laid water mains made of wood that had been lying around for months, and when the water was turned on, typhoid ran through the camp.

All these camps were huge, and the numbers rose as the war progressed. Camp Dix, near Trenton, New Jersey, was built for 38,000 men but at one point housed 54,500. The sanitation demands of such concentrations of human life were immense, yet little thought had been given to them. Camp Sherman, Ohio, produced without effort 982,500 pounds of garbage a month and its horses 120 tons of manure a day. The men of Camp Custer, Michigan, filled 1,200 garbage cans a day. None of the camps had waterproof surfaces where the trash cans could be kept, so the earth around the cans became a morass of mashed and rotting waste, magnificent breeding grounds for flies—but nothing compared to the lakes of sewage that loitered in the vicinity of most camps.

At Camp Lee, Virginia, home to the 80th Division, a single creek carried the daily consignment of effluent into a marsh nearby, where it settled. The division's engineers decided to clear the marsh by dredging a channel, but in damming the creek to permit dredging to begin, they created, in the words of a visiting entomologist, a "semi-solid mass of sewage 600 feet long and alive with fly larvae." The comfort levels of latrines matched their sanitary standards; the seats in most had a square hole—an easier shape to cut than an oval.

Among the new arrivals at the camps and cantonments were the conscientious objectors. The Selective Service Act had forced the draft boards to induct them for combatant or noncombatant duty, depending on the nature of their objection, but several months passed before the War Department laid down a policy as to their treatment.

Newton Baker's intention was that the government's attitude to those who had "personal scruples" about the war should be reasonably liberal, especially in the case of those whose objections were religious: Mennonites (who had come from Russia specifically to avoid war), Quakers, Dukhobors, Seventh-Day Adventists, Plymouth Brethren, Christadelphians, and so on. He specifically ordered that Mennonites and the members of certain other sects should not be compelled to wear uniforms, as their raiment was a tenet of their faith. It was his express wish that conscientious objectors should be segregated from serving soldiers, given noncombatant duty if they had been deemed eligible for it, and treated with "tact and consideration."

The military authorities had far less sympathy. Going "soft on slackers," they felt, was unfair to ordinary conscripts. Many objectors, now that they had been inducted, flatly refused to perform even noncombatant duties, since these still served the purpose of the war, and declined to obey army discipline, wear uniforms, march, drill, or even, in extreme cases, keep clean. Most of the division commanders, like Leonard Wood at Camp Funston, Kansas, felt it their duty to convert them to the ways of war. The pressure they applied took various forms—verbal abuse, humiliation, courts-martial and exaggerated legal penalties, beating, and, in extreme cases, what amounted to torture.

Hutterites, whose faith forbade them to cut their hair, had their beards shaved off by force. Dukhobors were forced into military dress or tormented if they refused. One who was ducked under a faucet on a freezing day subsequently died of pneumonia; his widow, upon receiving his body for burial, was appalled to find it in full uniform, a desecration of his faith.

The most brutal treatment was generally reserved for those whose scruples were ideological rather than religious—and this included not only socialists and others with political objections to the war but those whose objections were made in the name of humanity rather than that of any recognized creed. A great many were eventually "persuaded" to accept military discipline or noncombatant duties, but almost four thousand held out.

Sheldon W. Smith refused to sign the Army's clothing slip. "They put a pen in my hand and held it there to make a mark. . . . Next I was stripped in a violent manner and taken inside and dressed [in uniform] amidst arm twisting, thumping etc." Then he was taken to the bathhouse, where he was stripped again, held under the shower, and scrubbed with a broom. His captors whipped him with their belts, put a rope around his neck, and lashed it to a pipe, hauling on it until he could not breathe and all the while shouting at him to give in. "The bathing was continued until I was chilled and shook all over; part of the time they had me on my back with face under a faucet and held my mouth open. They got a little flag ordering me to kiss it and kneel down to it."

When the severity of the treatment being handed out in some camps was brought to Baker's attention at the end of 1917, he was horrified and ordered that, from the start of 1918, all "personal scruples," including nonreligious ones, should be classed as objections of conscience and his previous strictures observed. Baker would ultimately review all court-martial sentences, disapproving a tenth of them altogether and mitigating a further 185 out of a total of 540. None of the seventeen death sentences was carried out.

But in the interim neither he nor the President would intervene any more closely to protect individual rights. The force of public opinion—from the press, the parents of serving soldiers, even the clergy—was against the objectors, and it was a factor neither Wilson nor Baker was prepared to ignore.

Far more worrisome to the Army than either immigrants or conscientious objectors were the draft boards' peculiar ideas as to what constituted physical suitability for service on the Western Front. Of the conscripts inducted during the war, an estimated 196,000 had venereal disease on arrival at camp. Of the 22,000 men examined at Camp Lewis, Washington, 5,000 had thyroid enlargement. Orthopedic problems, particularly foot defects, were commonplace; in one camp, 18 percent of the men had foot trouble, which drill soon revealed. The dentists at Camp Lee examined 38,963 draftees and found 10,596 suffering from infected root canals.

Problems varied with the conscripts' ethnic stock. According to Army Medical Department statistics, French Canadians had the poorest overall health in general: a high incidence of stunted growth, tuberculosis, and nervous and mental defects. Germans and Austrians were prone to alcoholism, varicose veins, and flat feet. "Sections of the black belt of the South," medical officers reported, showed higher-than-average arthritis, manic-depressive psychoses, and heart valve disease, lower-than-average obesity.

From an intake of 6,600 at one camp—and these were men who had passed through the mill of the draft boards—1,600 were immediately discharged as unfit and/or "unsuited, worthless, non-English-speaking, illiterate and venereally diseased." Where there was some hope of remedying the defects, the men were assigned to holding units. Camp Devens, Massachusetts, for example, had a battalion including 134 venereal, 151 neuropsychiatric, 368 cardiovascular, and 1,271 orthopedic cases.

Whatever their vital statistics or their moral standards, the raw levies all had one thing in common; they were in the camps and cantonments to be trained individually in the skills of the soldier and collectively, with their officers, molded into efficient units ready for war. The War Department's strategy had no frills. Besides instructors sent over from Europe by the English and French, they produced company-grade officers—captains and lieutenants—to train the men and then depended on the regular army (and, to a lesser extent, National Guard) officers—majors, colonels, and above—to weld the companies into battalions, regiments, and brigades. The objective was a division that was militarily efficient, a responsive organism of great power.

Many of the professional officers had theoretical knowledge of how to handle large units, but none had any practical experience of anything resembling a 28,000-man division; nevertheless, they rose to their task. The newly commissioned company-grade officers, in the Army for less than

half a year, were even further at sea, each finding himself suddenly responsible for the welfare, discipline, and instruction of 250 men, with no protective shield of seasoned drill sergeants to cow the insubordinate.

Black company-grade officers of the 92nd Division struggled to create
cohesion and maintain morale. Not only was the division never assembled
in one place, but hanging over it was General Ballou's warning that
"white men made the Division, and they can break it just as easily if it be-
comes a trouble-maker." The officers hardly advanced their own cause.
"The vast majority of colored officers," remembered the regimental surgeon of the 349th Field Artillery, "held themselves distinctly aloof from
the colored enlisted men . . . [who] used to nickname their colored officers
'Monkey Chasers.' "

At first, not surprisingly, the key figures in the National Army cantonments were the eight hundred or so British and French instructors. They
were all veterans, often with wound stripes on their sleeves, and they
brought the callousness of the front with them. "We made an attack one
day," one told his pupils.

As our first wave carried the enemy trench, they heard shouts from a
dugout: "Kamerad!" The Germans surrendered. The first wave rushed
on, leaving it to the second wave to take the prisoners. As soon as the first
wave had passed, the Germans emerged from their dugout with a hidden
machine gun and broke it out on the backs of the men who had been white
enough not to give them the cold steel. So now, men, when we hear
"Kamerad" coming from the depths of a dugout in a captured trench we
call down: "How many?" If the answer comes back "Six," we decide that
one hand grenade ought to be enough to take care of six and toss it in.

It was impossible in these home camps for either men or units to be made
fully ready for combat. Communications being what they were, the knowledge and experience accumulating daily in France was simply not crossing
the Atlantic. After six months of war, the General Staff in Washington
recognized that it was receiving information that was at best three weeks
old. In France, Pershing created an elaborate system of schools to provide
instruction for every branch and level of the service: staff officers, unit
commanders, candidates for commissions, specialists from every staff and
supply department, artillerymen, intelligence officers, pilots. Ideally, all
the incomers should have achieved a basic level of competence before

crossing to France, but the AEF schools were equipped to improve on the training of any unit in any branch, with the benefit of having more immediate knowledge of field conditions.

At Langres, forty miles south of Chaumont, Pershing established the critically important Staff College, which, in a frenetic three-month course, attempted to turn out war managers. In addition, his Training Branch developed a three-month training cycle for divisions in France, covering small-unit training, staff work, and combined arms practice and ending with a period in the trenches brigaded with Allied units.

Infantry training was only one of the specializations that together created the complex mechanism of a division. A man's occupation in civilian life would often dictate his role in the Army: typists were assigned to headquarters staff, garment workers to the quartermaster, construction workers to engineer battalions, pharmacists to medical units, cooks to the kitchens, backwoodsmen to sniper units. In theory, motorized transportation units should have been especially hard to staff. There were usually men who knew how to handle horses, but in 1917 truck and tractor drivers were few and far between. Nevertheless, the appeal of driving was irresistible and men often lied about their experience with motor vehicles in order to get behind the wheel.

Native Americans made some of the U.S. Army's most awe-inspiring soldiers. Though Americanization was accelerating, and as many Indians were lawyers, doctors, and engineers by 1914 as were employed in hunting, trapping, or guiding, many still brought skills that adapted remarkably well to conditions on the Western Front. Possibly because of Chief of Staff Hugh Scott's deep interest in their culture, they were not discriminated against, provided there was "no colored admixture." In all, 6,509 were inducted and the same number volunteered, a total of almost 30 percent of all adult Indian males. The percentages varied from tribe to tribe: roughly 40 percent of the Oklahoma Osage and Quapaw served, while less than 1 percent of the Navajo did so. In the federal Indian schools where Americanization had free rein, almost 100 percent of males enlisted, many lying about their age. "I felt no American could or should be better than the first American," explained one Siletz volunteer.

In 1917–1918, young Indian males were still in touch with traditional hunting and fighting skills. In the cantonments, they provided an object lesson to the urban conscripts in techniques of concealment and stealth by slipping across "no-man's-land" to snatch a "German" from the trenches opposite. Their languages were regarded as excellent substitutes for code, though a new vocabulary had to be evolved to deal with the terminology of modern war: machine guns became "little guns shoot fast" and battalions were indicated by "one, two and three grains of corn."

Zane Grey, touring Wild West shows, and other more authentic by-products of a culture so recently vibrant had all imprinted the Germans with stereotypical images of "Red Indians." They were terrified of the specter of the "red man" and drafted extra snipers into sectors where Indians were spotted, "specially to pick off these dangerous men." Recognizing an opportunity for psychological warfare, the War Department gave serious thought to "attempting a limited number of night raids with men camouflaged as Indians in full regalia."

In the early days of sorting and allocating men, the Army relied a good deal on personal impressions and the direct question "What can you do?" But this was the second decade of the twentieth century, when the psychologist had begun to make an impression, and when Pershing complained that "too many mental incompetents were being shipped abroad," it seemed time to try newer methods. Psychologist Robert M. Yerkes was able to persuade the War Department "to adopt a scientific basis for assessing the quality of the new recruits."

During the war, 3 million soldiers were given intelligence tests—one test for the literate, another for those considered illiterate. (The literacy test itself provided perhaps the biggest shock: throughout the Army, 24.9 percent of men could neither read the paper nor write a letter home—in English, at least—and this was the criterion employed.) Men who were rated "feebleminded" because they scored so low on the intelligence test were immediately discharged from the Army without review by a disability board—until the authorities realized that many college graduates were using this as an ingenious escape route from the Army.

By today's standards, the tests were obviously flawed, geared remorselessly to the middle-class native English speaker with questions on literature, tennis, and the like. Even so, a grading of "A" to "E" offered a simple, convenient reference tool to personnel officers struggling to allocate thousands of new recruits in a hurry. Once the men with relevant experience had been assigned, each company would receive a mixture of grades. Men who had scored lower than "C" would not be permitted to apply for commissions.

Life in the Army offered the clearest demonstration that the grip of the federal government was closing ever more tightly around the individual. It was a protective as well as coercive clasp. In the late 1890s, William Gibbs McAdoo (then a dealer in railway bonds) had helped the "penniless and starving" wives and families of servicemen in the Spanish-American War. Now, as Secretary of the Treasury, he urged that "the basis of the family's support . . . should be an allotment of a fixed proportion of the soldier's pay." Enlisted married men were obliged to make over half their $33 monthly pay to their families, which the government then supplemented.

The allotment could not fully compensate for the induction of a husband or son. Draft boards seem to have applied the "genuine dependency" exemption very narrowly, and across the country division headquarters were inundated with applications for the release of enlisted men or for more money in lieu. Desperate letters told of starving children, sick and bedridden relatives. In their bemused incoherence and their combination of greed and optimism with genuine hardship, these were a constant source of amusement to headquarters staff, who circulated a list of the choicest pleas. "My boy has been put in charge of a spittoon. Will I get more money now?" "I didn't know my husband had a middle name, and if he did, I do not think it was 'None.' " "You ask for my allotment number: I have four boys and two girls." "I am writing to ask you why I have not received my elopement." "I have not received my husband's pay and will be forced to lead an immortal life." "Please return my marriage certificate. Baby has not eaten in three days."

Material support was only one aspect of the government's paternalism. McAdoo and Cabinet colleagues such as Daniels, Baker, and Wilson made the soldier's moral welfare in camp their concern as well. Baker, a reformer by inclination, remembered the public outrage in 1916 at the plague of brothels spreading along the Mexican border with the soldiers. He knew people were afraid of the effects of these huge new concentrations of troops, and he threw his weight behind a morality campaign; by the end of 1917, some 110 red-light districts near camps had been closed. At the level of private enterprise, the concerned citizens of the National Allied Relief Committee raised funds to bus vulnerable American servicemen through "the London danger zone" and save them "from the distressing and terrible dangers of the streets."

For help in finding something to take the place of the customary army pleasures, Baker turned to a friend, Raymond Fosdick, a thirty-three-year-old moralist and social reformer and the brother of the well-known clergyman Harry Emerson Fosdick. Baker asked him to provide the men with "wholesome recreation and enjoyment." This he was to achieve by coordinating the various voluntary organizations operating in the camps—bodies such as the YMCA, the Jewish Welfare Board, and the Knights of Columbus, up to thirty-six of them in some camps. Under Fosdick's Committee on Training Camp Activities, the men came to enjoy community songs, Liberty Theaters (occasionally graced by the singing of the President's daughter Margaret), YMCA huts (blacks usually excluded) where they could read magazines and write letters, Hostess Houses (separately provided for blacks) where they could meet female visitors in civilized surroundings, athletics, football and baseball, and educational programs aimed particularly at illiterates and the foreign-born. A small pamphlet published by the YMCA in 1917 offered the man about to go overseas a remarkable selection of handy French expressions: "I should like very much to see the periscope of a submarine"; "I have pawned my watch"; "A piece of shell hit me in the arm"; "Do not stick your head above the trench"; "Here I am, here I stay."

The young American male in those days was deemed by the War Department to be remarkably ignorant about sex; Fosdick's committee set out to put him straight. He was taught the facts of life and the risks of low life. "A German bullet is cleaner than a whore," announced one poster, showing a surprising lack of tact. "You wouldn't use another man's toothbrush. Why use his whore?" The potentially horrific results of normal intercourse seem so to have traumatized the youths of America that some of the young men moved swiftly from a state of ignorance to a widespread preference for alternatives, or so the Paris prostitutes claimed.

The motive of the military authorities for combating vice was military efficiency, not spiritual improvement. Where Fosdick's civilians concentrated on deterrence and moral suasion, the Army blandly provided prophylaxis at any hour of the day and night, somewhat undermining the credibility of the righteous. Contracting a venereal disease was a punishable offense, but this was because it was careless and unnecessary and detracted from the soldier's usefulness, not because it was wicked.

Neither military personnel nor civilians were entirely successful in combating venereal disease. At some camps the scale of the problem verged on the unmanageable. So many conscripts on leave from the camps in Kansas and Missouri headed for the prostitutes on Kansas City's Twelfth Avenue that it had been nicknamed "Woodrow Wilson Avenue—a piece at any price." Local authorities often refused to cooperate in the campaign against the local red-light district, which might be a useful factor of a community's economy. Seattle had to be declared off limits, New Orleans failed to see the point of the campaign, and Galveston, Texas, remained an open city. Where prostitutes were pushed out, they often took up residence in the black districts of town, beyond the reach of the authorities' interest, and into the vacuum stepped the amateurs, hero-worshiping girls, some as young as twelve, who were determined to give themselves to the uniform.

In France, Pershing was very much more draconian, certainly more so than the natives. The French provided licensed brothels for their troops, and in 1918 Premier Georges Clemenceau offered similar services to the AEF. When Baker saw the letter, he exclaimed to Fosdick, "For God's sake, Raymond, don't show this to the President or he'll stop the war." Pershing personally inspected the VD returns every day. He declared red-light districts off limits and had them patrolled; MPs were then found to have the highest incidence of VD in the AEF. Men returning to camp drunk were automatically assumed to be infected and were treated, by force if necessary.

The Army also fought a constant, if losing, battle at home against the temptations of alcohol. In the "dry" states, soldiers helped bootleggers make a killing; in "wet" ones, the authorities created "dry" zones around the camps, but the regulations proved nearly impossible to enforce. Men found lemon or ginger "extracts" with a 9 percent alcohol content perfectly satisfactory. The punishment for selling liquor to men in uniform was a year's imprisonment, so the soldiers took off their tunics or paid the proprietor in advance, whereupon the barman "treated" them to drinks.

In Pershing's domain, beyond the reach of the moral crusaders, military efficiency was again the only criterion. Spirits were forbidden, but the men were allowed to buy beer and wine, and "Major Van Rooge" and "Captain Van Blank" became constant companions. Pershing did curb the intake by supporting the move to retain half the pay even of men without dependants. The soldiers' spending power worried him because of the impact it was having on the morale of French and British soldiers, who were paid far less. "$10 a month," he remarked, "is more spending money than a man in the trenches ought to have."

Drugs, which were widely used in society, duly made their appearance in the Army. Military intelligence gave warning of the sale to troops in southern cantonments of "the Chihuahua or Marihuana weed. This is a plant smoked by Mexicans of the lower classes; its use produces insanity and homicidal mania." The death-dealing weed proved popular, and by the summer of 1918 it had spread as far as Seattle. At Camp Devens, Special Agent Kelleher surprised a narcotics dealer in barracks at six one evening "with a complete outfit of hypodermic syringes, a spoon for heating the concoction, and quite a lot of morphine." Waiting in line were three conscripts with their sleeves rolled up.

Part Three

MOBILIZING
the
NATION

13

Building the War Machine

With a division in France, a million soldiers flooding into training camps at home, and Pershing urging the General Staff to think ahead in terms of an army of 3 million, the burden on America, coming on top of the continuing Allied demands for money and materials, was sudden and immense.

As other combatants had found in this new age of total war, to achieve victory a nation must be mobilized behind its fighting men. The American people would have to be willing to struggle, pay, and produce on a gargantuan scale; their leaders would have to find ways of channeling and coordinating these efforts—and they would have to do it fast or pay a heavy price for the fact that America had entered this war unprepared.

To train and equip such vast numbers of men required day-to-day materials in quantities that defied the imagination. The sixteen hutted cantonments alone, cities of 40,000 inhabitants built in just two months, had used enough wood to have made a boardwalk eighteen inches wide and an inch thick stretching to the moon—plus piping for drinking water and sanitation, lighting, heating, and miles of roads to connect the hundreds of barracks, kitchens, laundries, hospitals, stores, latrines, stables, and other buildings. The tented camps for the National Guard divisions economized on wood, but the infrastructure still had to be built. And this was by no means the end of the construction program: for the duration of the war, 200,000 men were kept continuously employed building for the Army.

And then there were the uniforms, equipment, and weapons: By November 1917, the Quartermaster General's department had placed orders for 17 million blankets, 33 million yards of flannel shirting, 125 million yards of canvas for tents. By the end of the following year, the armed forces would have ordered 29 million pairs of shoes, 82,500 trucks, 16,000 automobiles, and 27,000 motorcycles—and mechanized vehicles could meet only part of their transportation needs. They also required one horse or mule per five to seven men, and this in turn meant millions of tons of forage, a veterinary service, and hundreds of miles of leather harness.

By the fall of 1917, the Ordnance Department had ordered "for delivery in France" 2,137,025 rifles; 57,000 light Browning automatic rifles; 102,450 heavy machine guns; 5,490 75mm field guns with 2,850,000 high-explosive and 2,750 shrapnel shells; 700 75mm antiaircraft guns; and 3,315 155mm howitzers with 950,000 high-explosive and 50,000 shrapnel shells.

The AEF had also to be prepared to cope with German shells. A vast complex of hospitals, dressing stations, hospital trains, and ambulances was required for France. But, as Surgeon General William C. Gorgas pointed out succinctly, shell wounds tended to be "large and mutilating," and he expected that for every million men in the field, 100,000 would be returned from France to the United States for long-term hospital care. He anticipated the need for specialist hospitals at home: for "oral surgery . . . where a man has had the whole lower jaw taken off"; for shell shock—"we will have special hospitals for the insane, which is a fair share of the disabled"; for the blind, for those who contracted tuberculosis in the trenches, for amputees. "One hundred thousand beds for reconstruction in the United States is not going to be near enough."

The new technologies also made their demands, both for offensive and defensive purposes. The Navy subcontracted the manufacture of the antenna mines needed for the Northern Barrage to the automobile industry, which eventually produced more than fifty thousand mines, each carrying three hundred pounds of TNT. On land, tanks, gas, and flame had become integral parts of modern warfare.

On July 19, 1917, Pershing set into motion a study of tanks. "I think it advisable not to publish any orders on the subject," he wrote, "but to give oral and very confidential orders." Tanks were not in themselves warwinning weapons—they moved at scarcely more than walking pace, were hard on the men operating them, and were limited in range. But they were more than adequate for infantry support, particularly against machine-gun nests, and as the heavier tanks could flatten barbed wire, they made it possible to dispense with the bulk of the initial artillery barrage, thus economizing on shells and permitting surprise attacks. They acted as a force multiplier: the British estimated that one division plus seventy-two tanks was the equivalent of three without. They also crushed enemy morale as comprehensively as they did the wretched foot soldier in their path.

On September 14, Pershing cabled the War Department for 1,800 tanks. Six hundred were to be the heavy British Mark VI model—350 for fighting, 20 for signals, 40 for carrying gasoline and oil, 140 for carrying twenty-five soldiers each, 50 "with upper platform for field gun"; 1,200 were to be the light Renault model—1,030 for fighting, 130 for supply, 40 for signals. It was anticipated that 15 percent of these machines would need replacing each month, and to service the force the War Department was asked to supply 300 six-ton trucks, 90 three-ton trucks, 270 one-ton trucks with trailers, 93 one-ton trucks with kitchen trailers, 90 Ford automobiles, and 180 motorcycles. On top of all this, Pershing mentioned that the French "desire about 2,000 Renault tanks from United States."

As for chemical warfare, since the Germans' first use of chlorine in the Second Battle of Ypres in April 1915, poison gas had become an integral part of any assault—to kill or cripple men and horses, to neutralize artillery, to mask forces' advance, and to create chaos along supply routes and in rear areas. Despite reservations among some generals on humanitarian grounds—Pershing himself was resigned rather than eager—the American chemical warfare program grew rapidly to the point where, had the war gone on longer, it would have swamped those of the Allies.

Pershing set up laboratories and a research station in France, and at home 1,500 highly qualified scientists congregated in what was then the largest research organization ever assembled for one specific purpose. The arsenal at Edgewood, Maryland, near Baltimore, comprised a variety of chemical plants, including the largest chlorine plant in the world and a filling plant with a daily capacity of 200,000 shells. Scientists also developed a number of gases more deadly than any of those currently in use, including one that "rendered soil barren for seven years; a few drops of it on a tree-trunk would cause the tree to wither in an hour." The British reported that a large number of dogs had been collected on which each scientific breakthrough would be tested.

Ironically, America owed much of this success to Germany. Before the war, the domestic chemical industry had been insignificant, crushed by the might of the German conglomerates, which had grown rich in America—

and which now found their patents confiscated and shared among American manufacturers by the recently appointed Alien Property Custodian.

The search for new military technology was continuous. Among other research, American manufacturers experimented with various types of armament for tanks. At a meeting of the Inter-Allied Tank Committee the following summer, the American representative would speak proudly of American tanks "fitted with steam and heat projectors," prototype flamethrower tanks: "At a distance of 30 meters from the machine, glass and metals were melted."

The Science and Research Division of the Army's Signal Corps worked at full stretch. The hunt was on, for example, for a wireless method of communication that would be effective on the battlefield. The Signal Corps came up with "voice command equipment," a radio telephone apparatus for air-to-air, ground-to-air, and air-to-ground communication. It was a considerable achievement but not yet combat ready, as it required an antenna made of flexible copper wire several hundred feet long, unreeled by the aviator to trail behind his craft.

Thomas Edison's Naval Consulting Board of inventors was hard at work to find ways of winning the war at sea. "Mr. Edison came in," recorded Josephus Daniels in the fall of 1917, "and said he now felt quite sure he could put an end to Fritz and end sub menace. . . . I gave him Dewey's room and told him he could have anything except my job—and he could have that if he made the discovery." The board focused primarily on underwater listening devices, an area in which American technology had taken a clear lead.

Lesser brains, too, were invited to contribute. Both the War and the Navy Departments had "Inventions Sections" to consider ideas submitted by the general public for the nation's defense. "I have invented a medicine what will stop the Germans," wrote one correspondent. "Mind is evidently unbalanced," noted the receiving officer wearily. "Labors under the impression that Germans in this country are trying to poison him." One correspondent who had invented an aerosol system to spread droplets of water onto fruit trees suggested adapting it for gasoline—spreading vapor across the battlefield and then igniting it over the advancing German infantry. Blueprints for electrified bayonets, chlorine-gas revolvers, tunneling machines, and processes for rendering ships invisible poured in. Some inventors accompanied their designs with working models, to the alarm of the mail-room staff.

A few inventions—such as color filters for field glasses—were invaluable. The vast majority amounted to little more than elaborate expressions of fear, frustration, and hatred. "The cause of this invention was prompted by the frightfulness of German gas cruelty," wrote one inventor about his wrist-mounted "Liberty Lance," eight feet long with twisted, vicious serrations. "The deepest cut with the largest claw of this Lance will express my kindest resentment for the enemy. So let the boys have a weapon ever at hand to dominate the devil's own hell."

One recent invention had brought warfare, as far as Europe was concerned, into the third dimension. On both sides of no-man's-land aircraft were playing an important part in the battle, observing, photographing, directing artillery, strafing ground troops, bombing rear areas, bombing civilian targets (London was bombed by airplanes—the giant Gothas—for the first time on the day Pershing left for Paris), dropping propaganda leaflets, and fighting to deny the same opportunities to the enemy.

There were men in America who had been arguing the case for military aviation for years. In March 1917, the Council of National Defense called for an air armada of five thousand aircraft; Congress was unmoved. But then, in May 1917, in a direct and remarkable appeal, the then Premier of France, Alexandre Ribot, begged the United States to come to the Allies' aid in the air and repeated the call for "a flying corps of 4,500 airplanes" for the campaign of 1918. His telegram arrived just as Congress was coming to terms with conscription and the prospect of high casualties on a land battlefield of terror and squalor. If they did as Ribot asked, could they not save American lives by putting a clean, rapid end to the war—and do it cheaply?

Aviation's champions evoked images of "winged cavalry sweeping across the German lines and smothering their trenches with a storm of lead, which would put the 'Yankee Punch' into the war." This could be America's kind of combat, the argument ran, with dogfights between aces offering far more scope for rugged individualism than the dirty, bloody, depersonalized struggle on the ground. Carried along by a gust of popular enthusiasm, Congress appropriated $640 million for this new miracle weapon, a sum equal to the federal government's entire annual prewar budget.

The detailed plan based on Ribot's request and provided for in this budget required an air force considerably larger than that currently possessed by the French themselves, totaling "22,625 aeroplanes plus 80%

spares and 45,250 engines," according to the Aviation Section of the Signal Corps. This represented enormous quantities of spruce, Douglas fir, cedar, mahogany, walnut, and cherry wood; linen, cotton, and balloon fabric; and castor-seed lubricating oil and dope for the fuselages alone, not to mention thousands of air-pressure gauges, altimeters, fire extinguishers, safety belts, rotating map cases, oxygen masks, radiator thermometers, and other precision instruments, basic equipment for the machines before they were even armed or powered.

But none of these machines and equipment and none of the men now training in the cantonments would be of any use unless they could be transported to Europe. The most pressing need was ships, and ships were in desperately short supply. The U-boats were sinking them at an average rate of 600,000 tons per month, and with only 20 million tons of shipping on the Atlantic routes where the submarines were most active, the outlook was bleak. Urgent demands for new merchant vessels to supply the AEF compounded the difficulties of an administration already struggling to arrange the building of the destroyers demanded by Admiral Sims and the Royal Navy.

In April 1917, the United States was as short of merchant vessels and transports as it was of submarines and destroyers. As a first step, the government commandeered eighty-seven enemy vessels, including passenger liners, that had been in American ports when war was declared. The British were also persuaded to relinquish their claims to the merchant ships being built for them in American yards. Yet more tonnage was obtained by pressuring neutrals into putting their vessels on charter to American interests. But ultimate salvation lay in building new ships.

To take hold of the merchant shipbuilding program, Wilson called on one of the great administrators of the day, George Washington Goethals, a military man who had orchestrated the most remarkable engineering feat of the last fifty years, the construction of the Panama Canal. Goethals—voted "seventh most useful American" in a 1913 magazine poll—was a bull-necked, no-nonsense dynamo, and he made his presence felt at once. The Shipping Act of 1916 gave him the legal framework for his task, but when he met the men with whom he was notionally to work, he was less than impressed. "The US Shipping Board has some excellent hot air artists," he told his son. "When I got to Washington I found the air still hot but I increased the temperature by giving them my opinion of them, from which they gathered that I couldn't serve under them or with them. . . . The result was that a separate corporation was formed and I am it."

As head of the Emergency Fleet Corporation, semi-independent of the "hot air artists," Goethals got to work. He swiftly drew up plans, specifications, and bills of materials and by early June 1917 reported to the President that he hoped to be able to build "3,000,000 tons in eighteen months" by applying the techniques of American mass production to shipbuilding. In the past, ships had been built on site, each component being shaped in the yard before being riveted into place. Now Goethals arranged for steel producers to supply standardized parts for simple assembly at the shipyards. (Seamen were similarly procured en masse when the president of the United Drug Company put his nationwide chain of 6,854 drugstores at the disposal of the Shipping Board to act as recruiting agencies.)

The scheme had huge potential, but the burden on the nation was proportionately heavy. Facilities did not exist to lay down keels in these quantities, so the administration embarked on an expensive bout of infrastructure construction that gave the United States double the rest of the world's shipbuilding capacity in the process. At Hog Island, on the Delaware River near Philadelphia, the biggest yard in the world was created on 846 acres of desolate marsh. Hog Island had 246 buildings, eighty miles of railroad track, a hospital, a hotel, a school, a labor force of 34,000, and the capacity to build fifty ships at a time while another twenty-eight were being fitted out at the piers. It received three hundred carloads of materials a day; the rivets were delivered in trainloads.

All this cost money on an unimagined scale. The cost of shipbuilding alone was $2,645,451,000. At the center of the maelstrom, in the hushed paneled office of the Secretary of the Treasury, sat the man who liked to shock Washington with his fondness for dancing: William Gibbs McAdoo. In this time of crisis, America needed men capable of expanding their horizons, and none was more flexible than McAdoo. He was a lawyer; he had gone bankrupt trying to build an electric streetcar system for Knoxville, Tennessee; he had sold railway bonds on Wall Street; he had succeeded, where many had failed, in driving tunnels under the Hudson River, connecting Manhattan with a new station built in the fields just outside Newark—the Manhattan Transfer; he had also married the President's daughter Eleanor and was regarded by many as the heir apparent. He took the onset of war in his stride.

McAdoo's first guess at the cost of the war effort was $3.5 billion, a figure that would balloon to $13.771 billion by May 1918, with a $24 billion estimate for the next twelve months. And he had more to worry about than just the cost of America's own mobilization.

Since 1914, the country's economy had effectively been colonized by the Allies, who had stretched it to its limits. In the thirty-two months of war before America's entry, the economy had grown by 60 percent. The rail transportation system, for example, was so hard-pressed that in April 1917 it needed a further 145,000 freight cars just to meet current demand.

Procurement in America had kept the Allies in the war, but it had left even the mighty British Empire—which since 1915 had been funding all the Allied purchases abroad—with almost no exportable wealth. Even the stockholdings and other assets of its citizens in America had been requisitioned to pay for munitions. In the spring of 1917, McAdoo was faced with the incredible truth that within weeks the Allies would no longer be able to pay for the materials they so desperately needed from America.

This spelled catastrophe both for America's economy and for Allied military power. Not only would the flow of supplies from America dry up, but sterling would crash in the international markets and the British would be unable to buy from any other supplier. She would be left with only the resources of her far-flung, overstretched empire with which to sustain herself and her allies.

Ambassador Page cabled frantically from London, "France and England must have a large enough credit in the United States to prevent the collapse of world trade and of the whole of European finance." Lord Northcliffe saw the President in June and insisted that Britain "must have $200 million regularly each month," a figure that represented approximately 40 percent of all British war expenditure.

It was a time of immense strain for the Allies. McAdoo recalled the members of the foreign missions being "war weary, jangled, nervous . . . on the edge of hysteria." One Englishman, Sir Richard Crawford, was completely worn down by the crisis. "Often when he came into my office to discuss the war and the needs of his country . . . his emotions got the better of him and tears streamed down his face. . . . 'You must forgive me—overstrain,' he used to say with a smile when I noticed his emotional state."

On July 1, 1917, the Allies finally reached the brink, and the British Foreign Office passed on the grave news that "the ability of His Majesty's

Government to effect payments in America from today onwards will be in jeopardy." McAdoo spelled out the consequences to the Senate Ways and Means Committee: the United States must lend the Allies the money they needed to continue buying supplies in American markets. The Senate should think of it as a means of saving America's young men by keeping the Allied war effort alive. And from the summer of 1917 onward, America shouldered the financial commitments of the Allies in her own markets—another $9.5 billion to be added to the bill.

14

"Lay Your Double Chin on the Altar of Liberty": Food for the Fighters

Apart from money, the most basic material required for waging total war was food. Long before April 1917, it had become clear that without food from America, the Allied armies and civilian populations would starve. The war had seriously damaged the Allies' usual sources of supply. The prewar trade routes had been disrupted; wheat could no longer come to western Europe from Australia or Romania, nor beef from Argentina, and the closure of the Baltic and Dardanelles had cut off all supplies from Russia. A large proportion of Europe's sugar had been coming from the beet fields of Germany, Belgium, and France, now either closed to the Allies or devastated by the fighting. As men were called up in ever-growing numbers, labor shortages crippled the Allies' own production of staples, and they turned to America to supply them.

During the neutrality period, American farmers had enjoyed boom conditions, with the result that, by the start of 1917, food prices in the United States were high. In February 1917, Jewish housewives in New York orchestrated a boycott of perishable foods: chicken, fish, and vegetables:

Whenever a woman, basket or bag on arm, approached a poultry market there were dozens to tell her that she must not buy fowl of any kind. If she ignored the warning and emerged with a chicken she was seized, as was the chicken, which was torn limb from limb. . . . Several hundred women in the chicken market at Stanton Street and the East River became frenzied by the sight of a crate of chickens, and set upon it. The crate was destroyed, the chickens were seized and dismembered, and the crowd poured through the street, waving the heads and wings and mutilated bodies of chickens.

With a little encouragement from the Socialist Party, another street protest against the cost of living turned into a demonstration in Madison Square by more than five thousand women—and an attack on the Waldorf-Astoria.

Real shortages, however, were not considered a possibility until America entered the war and the balance of her own demand and supply was disturbed. The War Department required copious quantities of food; the man taken from an office desk to the parade ground eats almost twice as much as before, and most American soldiers put on weight during the war. The increased demand, compounded by expectations of a poor wheat harvest, meant that Allied purchasers and the American armed services would now be bidding against each other.

Unpalatable as it might be, some kind of food regulation was going to be necessary, and with some prompting Wilson proposed that Congress establish a Food Administration to regulate the supply and consumption of American foodstuffs and guarantee supplies to both the AEF and the Allies. The man he nominated to head it was Herbert Hoover.

Hoover was an extremely complex man. His memoirs are wise, funny, erudite, perceptive, unreliable, and self-serving. There can be no question of his sincerity, idealism, and desire to serve suffering humanity. Equally, there is no doubt of his ambition—not for present fame, which he disliked, but for power and a place in posterity. He wanted to be a player in the "big game" of public life, and Woodrow Wilson's invitation to him to become America's Food Administrator brought him into the front row.

He possessed a genius for problem solving and crisis management and was perfectly suited to America's ad hoc war effort. His ideal was the professional man. He preferred westerners, especially Californians, to easterners, especially New Yorkers, and self-made to inherited wealth; his *bêtes noires* were Phi Beta Kappa and the Royal Navy. In the eyes of the American public, he became one of the few unchallenged American heroes of the war—square-jawed, with a rags-to-riches background, a love of action, a contempt for tradition and rank, and a generous spirit.

His work with the Commission for Relief in Belgium had given him the chance to observe at close quarters the British government's attempts to control food supplies. "Let the nation as a whole place its comforts, luxuries, indulgences and elegancies on the country's altar," David Lloyd

George had demanded in his first speech as Prime Minister. Among the first "indulgences" to go was the British Sunday roast beef; to produce a "Motto for Meatless Days," the satirical magazine *Punch* rifled the pages of *Hamlet* and came up with "The time is out of joint."

By February 1917, even the institutions at the heart of the British establishment had come under attack. Luncheon in gentlemen's clubs was restricted to two courses; there were to be no sugar bowls on the tables of the Lyons' Corner Houses; Masters of Foxhounds were shooting foxes to forestall the destruction of vital crops by the hunt. By April 1917, the King and Queen themselves had adopted the voluntary Scale of National Rations, a move that upset the American ambassador, who had formerly been an enthusiastic lunch guest at Buckingham Palace.

These were useful precedents. Brushing aside criticism of his powers as "food dictator"—"a King, a Potentate, a Caesar, a Kaiser"—Hoover began to implement his plans. "My notion of organization," he declared, "is to size up the problem, send for the best man or woman in the country who has the 'know how,' give him a room, table, chair, pencil, paper and wastepaper basket—and the injunction to get other people to help and then solve it." At the upper levels of the Food Administration he did just that, gathering from a wide variety of businesses and professions a body of skilled, versatile, dedicated volunteers. Since he was receiving no salary himself, he had no scruple in press-ganging them with the force of his personality. Like Wilson, he took pride in the concept of an American war effort rooted in free will, the antithesis of Prussian militarism; unlike Wilson, he managed on the whole to preserve the notion in practice.

While the Department of Agriculture was to stimulate production, the Food Administration's primary task was to control the supply, distribution, and movement of the food produced. The Food Administrator was heavily dependent on the transport system for success. Any breakdown could result in local gluts and dangerous fluctuations in prices. The Food Administration had also to ensure the conservation of scarce goods; control food exports; prevent dealing in food futures and all forms of hoarding, wasting, or profiteering; and stabilize prices.

Price-fixing, in Hoover's view, was preferable to requisition and rationing, which smacked of coercion. "I was well aware that every farmer in the world believed it was his family's divine right to consume any of the food he produced. . . . General requisition not only was the antithesis of American character but in a country as large as ours was a practical impossibility without [a] hundred thousand bureaucratic snoopers." Better to encourage the farmer to produce than forbid him to consume.

To stabilize the price of wheat, a national Grain Corporation was set up with a capital stock of $50 million, from which the corporation undertook to purchase the entire wheat crop of the country at $2.20 per bushel, a price determined on August 10, 1917. It would then resell to home or foreign buyers more or less at cost. If private growers could get more than $2.20, they were free to do so; but purchasers were not allowed to buy for less. A Sugar Equalization Board attempted to regulate the price and allocate the supply of sugar fairly in a nation that spent as much on candy in six months as would feed Belgium for a year. The greatest effort went into manipulating the price of hogs in relation to the price of corn, to guarantee pork production; should the price of corn rise proportionately too high, the farmer would see no sense in feeding it to hogs.

Not all the controls were imposed on the producer. Hoover, who came from farming stock, had no particular love for middlemen. He was trying to keep prices up for the producer and down for the consumer, and as often as not he did it at the expense of the men in between. Excess profit, Hoover proclaimed, was "money abstracted from the blood and sacrifice of the American people." Manufacturers and wholesalers were allocated fixed profit margins, which were not to exceed their normal prewar profits. Particular attention was paid to the hugely powerful meatpackers, whose cooperation was essential to the war effort but whose past record of profiteering had been black.

These regulations were enforced partly by the persuasive force of the government's purchasing power; no major manufacturer or wholesaler cared to offend the largest client of all. But to keep smaller businesses in line, all manufacturers and wholesalers of commodities listed as important to the war effort, as well as all retailers whose gross sales exceeded $100,000 per annum, were required to have a license to trade, which could be revoked for any infringement.

For the conservation of vital foods, those most needed by soldiers and by civilians threatened with starvation in Europe, Hoover and the Food Administration depended heavily on the goodwill of the public. But they did not wait for it to arise spontaneously. Hoover was perfectly aware of the power of public relations. He had friends in the press and in advertising, and with their help he launched the jingle, the poster, and the slogan at the heads and hearts of the American public.

Wheat, meat, and sugar were the staples most easily transported to the front line. Hoover had to persuade the American people to alter their diet and consume less of these foods, and he was aware that this might be considered an attack on the American way of life. "It isn't 'in' any other country to fight a war the way the Germans are doing it," wrote one American observer in Berlin. "Imagine people in New York paying any attention if they were ordered not to serve milk before 11 o'clock on three days in the week, or if they were told not to cook with fat . . . on two days in the week! They would get up particularly early in order to be able to do both."

This was the attitude that Hoover had to change. He did it by appealing to different aspects of the all-American character. Generosity was to the fore—charity toward Allies who, in Christian conscience, could not be left to starve. But pragmatism was there too. Without food the Allies must fall; America could share or "wait in plenty and face a conquering enemy alone." Soon, doughboy, Tommy, and *poilu* would be fighting shoulder to shoulder, and all would have to be fed. "Perhaps it will not be long before we will read each day long lists of American boys killed or wounded in the trenches of France. There will be boys in those lists that you know, boys that I know. And as our eyes film over with tears it will be at least some comfort to us to be able to say, 'I am helping too. I am saving food for the boys who are fighting.' "

There was, too, a puritanical streak in the national character, a legacy of the first settlers; Hoover felt it strongly in himself. "Go back to simple food, simple clothes, simple pleasures," he urged. "Pray hard, work hard, sleep hard and play hard. Now is the time to lay your double chin on the altar of liberty. . . . If we are selfish or even careless, we are disloyal, we are the enemy at home. . . . We need but get back once more to the old fashioned home, the kind of home in which many of us older folks were raised, where . . . the waste of foods, as we were taught by our mothers, was *sin*. . . . Can we not all of us . . . help spread that sense of sin?"

At the heart of his program were the wheatless and meatless days—wheatless Mondays and Wednesdays, with one wheatless meal every day for the rest of the week; meatless Tuesdays, with one meatless meal every other day. (This did not include poultry or game, and servicemen and war workers were exempt.) The American was resourceful; let him find substitutes for his wheat bread, his beefsteak, and the syrup on his pancakes. Let him eat the perishable foods that could not go overseas: fish, fruit, vegetables, eggs, and cheese. Let him not hoard. Let him not waste.

"The world lives by phrases," cried Hoover, and a flood of phrases and snappy sentences poured from the Food Administration. "Don't let your horse be more patriotic than you are—eat a dish of oatmeal"; "If U fast U beat U boats—if U feast U boats beat U." Chicle put slogans onto its gum wrappers, Sears, Roebuck on the envelopes containing its catalogues, theaters on their drop curtains, Child's Restaurants on their menus, the Chicago Telephone Company on its bills.

Pastors appealed to their flocks to fill in weekly reports on what had been accomplished in each household by way of wheatless meals and dishes made from leftovers. The Food Administration then planned to announce the results weekly, by denomination. "This will produce a splendid emulation in patriotic service between the various denominations," concluded the idea's originator happily. The Loyal Order of Moose, the Modern Woodmen of America, the Mystic Order of Veiled Prophets of the Enchanted Realm, and the Improved Order of Red Men were among the fraternal organizations that pledged themselves to urge restraint among their members.

Douglas Fairbanks suggested tacking a short scene onto each of his films in which he would deliver a food message; Mary Pickford and Billie Burke appeared in "picturettes" with such titles as "Raise a Pig in the Right Way" and "The Food Stuffer." The Marx Brothers kept chickens and planted Victory Gardens, with great verve but little output. Movie producer Thomas Ince called for the elimination of all cinematic banquet scenes using real food. "Americans were called upon to forsake the drama of the custard pie."

"The House of Every Hoarder Is Haunted by the Specters of Those His Greed Has Slain" warned the caption of a picture in an exhibition touring state and county fairs. No one could possibly ignore the message. Hoover targeted every sector of the community. Food messages went out in German, French, Spanish, Italian, Swedish, and Yiddish (though a member of the administration noted sadly that "notices requesting readers of the foreign language press to eat less meat were withdrawn since it appeared that most of them could not afford to eat meat much anyway"). Jewish rabbis were persuaded to circulate a letter pointing out the advantages of vegetable oils over animal fats from the point of view of keeping kosher. Less successful was the Food Administration circular that instructed Jews to eat shellfish, in violation of dietary law, and used the words "synagogue" and "pork" in unacceptable proximity.

Black women were informed that they had a double opportunity to further the food program—in their own kitchens and in the white kitchens where so many of them worked as cooks. The traditional practice of "pan toting" was now deplored; black servants had been allowed to take home leftovers from their employers' kitchens and thus had been encouraged to make too much food.

Children, too, were targeted twice—directly, at school and in the public libraries, and through their parents. During the New York State campaign to encourage potato eating, children were compelled to write potato essays, while at the library they found potato posters and storytellers relating potato tales with titles such as "The Crowning of the Little Brown Prince." At home, Hoover acknowledged, "saving food became a sort of game. Parents took advantage of it to impose upon their children the disciplines which had been the griefs of their own youth—and blamed it on me." "Do not permit your child to take a bite or two from an apple and throw the rest away," *Life* magazine instructed parents. "Nowadays even children must be taught to be patriotic to the core."

Hoteliers, restaurateurs, and their staffs were in the front line of the food battle. Hoover issued a steady stream of orders and exhortations, conscious that on a single meatless Tuesday one New York hotel had saved two thousand pounds of meat. Tin could be saved for munitions, hoteliers were told, if they would make their cuspidors and champagne coolers from wood pulp. The ammonia used in the making of ice could be better employed in the manufacture of ammunition; and the White Sulphur Springs Hotel in West Virginia was commended for cutting three hundred tons of ice from the lake on its golf links to put into its Scotch on the rocks. Waiters were urged to return all meat fat to the steward for soap.

Barbers in Texas abandoned egg shampoo, and glass manufacturers restricted their use of arsenic to guarantee supplies to the chemical warfare authorities. But the pivot of the program was the American housewife, the principal instrument the food pledge. Every woman in the country was invited to sign a card pledging herself "to carry out the directions and advice of the Food Administrator in the conduct of my household, in so far as my circumstances admit." Some women's circumstances admitted more than others. Eleanor Roosevelt embarrassed herself by describing to a delighted *New York Times* reporter the economies she had been able to make in the Roosevelt household. "Making the ten servants help me do my saving has not only been possible but highly profitable," she was reported as saying.

Franklin Roosevelt wrote, "I am proud to be the husband of the Originator, Discoverer and Inventor of the New Household Economy for Millionaires! Please have a photo taken showing the family, the ten cooperating servants, the scraps saved from the table, and the hand book." Mrs. Woodrow Wilson put her pledge sticker into the White House window and planted a war garden, while her husband kept a flock of Shropshire Downs sheep on the lawn. He held the yarn from his sheep while his womenfolk rolled it—which would have been a slightly ludicrous scenario had the wool not raised $100,000 when the Red Cross auctioned it.

It was the housewife who bore the brunt of recipes for delicacies such as cottonseed sausage—three parts meat to one part cottonseed—or a table syrup made of mesquite beans. She was urged to can and dry: Mrs. Robert Lansing, wife of the Secretary of State, gave a lunch consisting entirely of dried foods. Reduce waste, the Food Administration urged, by keeping fewer pets and refraining from giving too much protein to old and sedentary people. The household garbage was solicited for salvage: fatty acids for soap, glycerine for explosives, fruit pits and nut shells for the carbon that went into gas masks, the rest for pig food and fertilizer. In one month, ran a proud statistic, enough grease had been recovered from the garbage of eleven cities to produce explosives for half a million 75mm shells.

By European standards, America was not a fish-eating nation, but the housewife was told how to win her husband over. "De wise ol' owl . . . he say, sezee," wheedled one of Hoover's staff in the guise of Uncle Remus, " 'I gwine ter sprize you all wid a mess er fishes 'cause you all mus' save de meat.' . . . Den he kotch a big fish and say, sezee, ''t-hoot, 't-hoot, 't-substi-toot,' sezee." "Catch the carp; buy the carp. Cook the carp properly and eat it. Eat the roe; can the roe. Make carp jelly," barked the Food Administration. There was, women were told, as much leather on a shark as on a steer.

From these economies and increased production, America shipped overseas to the Allies and the AEF nearly 10 billion pounds of meat, fats, dairy products, and vegetable oils, as well as one and a quarter billion bushels of cereals and cereal products. From the political point of view, food, and the capacity to withhold it, would be a useful lever in the postwar negotiations. From the military point of view, Hoover's contribution to the fighting power of the AEF and the Allied armies was immeasurable. From the humanitarian point of view, he was averting a great deal of suffering.

Hoover was aware, nevertheless, that the system of voluntary cooperation was not a foolproof method of achieving his ends. The Food Administration knew, too, that its regulations were often violated. The most
common offenses were hoarding—salt, sugar, flour, matches, laundry
blueing—and failing to use substitutes for wheat. Hoover's men used the
Treasury's Secret Service Division to trace the sources of damaging food
scares, to expose hoarders, and to detect excessive retail prices. A retailer
could be punished by revoking his license, but the only sanction against an
offending consumer was an appeal to conscience and a sense of shame—
and often these were not enough.

A report entitled "Where the Food Campaign Fails to Get Across"
published the results of a survey of one thousand people who had refused
to sign the food pledge, analyzing the reasons they had given. Discounting
the people who claimed to be pro-German (147 of them), the most frequent complaint was that while the citizen was asked to make do with
adulterated bread, the brewers were allowed to use wheat for beer.

Hoover did reduce the permitted alcohol level of beer and limited the
amount of grain used in it by 30 percent, but he stopped short of halting
beer supplies altogether, fearing that if beer supplies were cut off completely, drinkers would turn to whiskey. (Distilling had been halted, but
two years' supply remained in bond.) Many protested bitterly at the double standard. "*I do not like corn meal. I do not like rye bread. I do like meat
and I am not wasteful. Why should I be asked to go without food that I do
like and eat food that I do not like and save wheat to be made into liquor
that destroys men's souls?*" Even worse, grain was going overseas for
British beer; barley was being shipped to Britain marked "for munitions
purposes." To this the Food Administration's answer was that it did not
feel it right to pass judgment on the social habits of other countries. "How
do you suppose the people of this country would take it if the British government were to ask why we don't stop lynching?"

Farmers were another discontented lobby, exasperated at seeing the law
of supply and demand set aside just when they stood to profit by it. Dairy
farmers envied wheat farmers for the security of having a stable price for
their goods. Grain farmers resented the pegging of the price of wheat while
the cost of farm machinery was escalating. Beef producers felt they had
profited far less than the packers, whom they suspected of having undue
influence with the government.

There were women who resented being the focus of the campaign and perpetually scolded by the government. "As a being with no political rights in Massachusetts," snapped one, "I fail to see why my signature on one of your cards would have the slightest weight."

Some complained, not without justification, that it was pointless saving food for soldiers who then would waste it; the authorities at Camp Oglethorpe made it a misdemeanor to throw away more than six ounces of food per person per day. Some feared that the pledge campaign was a covert census and that the government would raid their houses looking for hoarded goods. Others balked for reasons the researchers could hardly bring themselves to write down; they refused to sign "unless their wishes were carried out in some matter entirely irrelevant to Food Administration work, as, for example, the closing of motion picture theatres"; because they were on a diet; because the window card was unattractive; because the cook would object. Many were impeded by a vague feeling that the whole enterprise was un-American.

15

"One White-hot Mass": Mobilizing Minds

Men for the Army, food in vast quantities, huge demands for steel for shells and rifles, wood for aircraft and cantonments, frightening estimates for money to pay for it all—the burden of the war was squarely on the shoulders of the American people, and they had to carry the burden willingly and with full commitment. Victory would bear a high price tag, and the unknowing, innocent patriotism that had swept the nation into the war in April had somehow to be maintained if the nation was to continue to make the sacrifices necessary in the months and years to come. As Hoover came to realize, however, support for the war was far from universal and far from automatic.

In a country of 3 million square miles, regional differences did matter. Embracing a vast diversity of religious and ethnic groups, including a mass of unassimilated black Americans and a class hierarchy no less powerful for being unacknowledged, the United States had no universally recognized political center and a strong resistance to the idea of a powerful federal government.

Unfortunately for the administration, Americans lacked the prime motivation mobilizing the peoples of Europe. There was no immediate or obvious threat to American towns or villages, wives and children, farms or businesses, nor were there daily lists of casualties to prick the national conscience and feed the desire for revenge. With the war still so remote, the authorities had to create their own sense of urgency, they had to fuse the American people into "one white-hot mass" ablaze with "fraternity, devotion, courage and deathless determination," ready to enlist, to give money, to make any sacrifice that was required of them.

These were the words of George Creel, the tousled, exuberant Irishman to whom, at Josephus Daniels' suggestion, Wilson entrusted responsibility for "war publicity." The son of a Confederate officer from Independence, Missouri, Creel had had for the last twenty years a vigorous career as a "muckraker," a liberal (some said socialist) crusading journalist with a wickedly sharp pen and an impressive list of conservative enemies. He had fought hard for female suffrage and for legislation against the use of child labor and had put in a term on the police board in Denver as part of his battle for social reform. By 1912, he had been a vocal Wilsonian Democrat, and as part of the presidential campaign of 1916 he had written the inspiring *Wilson and the Issues*—which also spoke warmly of Josephus Daniels.

Wilson was greatly attracted by Creel's blend of idealism and outrageousness. They shared the same likes and dislikes—Creel maintained he could get to see the President anytime simply by entering the White House and loudly cursing Henry Cabot Lodge. Creel too was a fiery orator and never hesitated to offend if he felt it was in a good cause. Mobile-featured, with curly dark hair and burning eyes, he was a vivid talker and excellent mimic, and Wilson relaxed in his company.

Creel set out his program for selling the war in a long memorandum forwarded to Wilson by Daniels on April 11. "Administration activities must be dramatized and staged," he wrote, "and every energy exerted to arouse ardor and enthusiasm. . . . In the rush of generous feeling much that is evil and nagging will disappear."

To a greater or lesser extent, all the war agencies—War, Navy, Food, and Fuel, as well as the Shipping Board—carried out their own propaganda, but Creel held center stage, supporting the agencies and blending their separate messages into a single propaganda voice addressing the nation as a whole. His Committee for Public Information (CPI) took over the offices, staff, and facilities of the Carnegie Endowment and began work immediately.

Creel was an innovator. His work and the organization of his department were demand-led—if there was a need for propaganda in a specific area, he would see that it was satisfied. "The world's greatest adventure in advertising," he called the career of the CPI, with the war as the product to be merchandised. Creel's men gathered material from government departments and shaped it into what were early prototypes of the PR handout, which they gave to the press. Publication was not compulsory, but there were no alternative sources of news.

The remoteness of the war gave Creel the huge advantage of being able to control virtually all the information that came into the country from the battle front. At that time America could still be cut off quite effectively from Europe, so that all news of the war would have to pass through official channels. Private citizens did not possess radio receivers for trans-Atlantic messages, and there was no broadcast radio at home. Since no American troops were in action in the early months of the war, none would be coming back wounded to describe the rigors of life on the Western Front; and because of the shortage of shipping, none would be coming home on leave. Soldiers' mail and press dispatches from Europe were subject to AEF censorship, and the trans-Atlantic cable was controlled by the Navy.

Then, in October, the government's power to control incoming information was completed when Congress passed the Trading with the Enemy Act, which permitted censorship of civilian communications with foreign countries by mail, cable, radio, or any other means. Under the act, a Board of Censors was established, with George Creel as chairman. A full-blown postal censorship organization soon followed, with its main office in New York and censorship stations spread all over the country, especially densely along the coasts and the sensitive border with Mexico.

In each station, staff pored over thousands of letters. Their brief was wide. Domestic mail was at first exempt (though later the censors would be given power to open the letters of individuals suspected of disloyalty). But in letters going to or coming from abroad, they must be alert not only for details of military operations and casualties but for hints of sabotage, labor disturbances, pacifist activity or incitement to revolution (most particularly in Latin America), plans to evade the draft or desert, industrial secrets, and applications for patents on mines or submarines; they must also watch for "all letters referring to chess problems or chess magazines," all letters to Spain for people with non-Spanish names, all letters in code or with "peculiar markings," all picture postcards of public property, and all criticisms of the censorship.

The mechanism for controlling information was easy enough to establish; however, the issues the government had raised by introducing censorship were very sensitive. Freedom of the press, for one, was a keystone of American democracy, protected by the First Amendment, and no one wanted to be the first to tamper with it. At first, the administration hoped that common sense would be curb enough, and newspapers were merely given "guidelines" to assist their self-censorship: Editors should refrain

from mentioning the movements of ships or troops, the names of line officers, the existence or location of minefields and coastal defenses, serious
differences of opinion among the Allies, threats against the life of the President. They should check before repeating disquieting rumors or giving the
names of military units and the details of technical inventions. Otherwise
they might use their own discretion. Though there were occasional crass
lapses, such as the article in William Randolph Hearst's *San Francisco
Examiner* entitled "Why the U-boats Can't Get Our Troopships," for the
most part the press complied fairly graciously.

But though Creel could control the information available to the newspapers, he also needed to put reins on their ability to analyze and draw
conclusions that might be detrimental to public morale. Editors could see
the point of discretion where factual information was concerned, but ideas
and opinions were a different matter. It was their right, they insisted, to express their views on America's war aims or criticize the conduct of the war
effort. The government was equally adamant that they should not undermine confidence in the nation's cause and erode the people's will to win.

Before the war, the government had had no power to interfere with free
speech. During the neutrality years and on into the first months of war,
pessimistic rumors, criticism of America's military preparations, and
overtly pro-German propaganda had all gone unchecked. Democrats'
moves to introduce press censorship as part of wider antiespionage legislation had been blocked by Republicans claiming that censorship could be
used by the President to screen himself from criticism.

But with war fever mounting all the time, a modified Espionage Act
(subsequently to be supplemented with the even more stringent Sedition
Act) became law in June 1917. Suddenly, any statement that might interfere with the success of the armed forces, incite disloyalty, or obstruct recruiting to the Army became a punishable offense. A crucial weapon had
been added to the government's armory. It now had the legal power to
control what its citizens said in public. And rather than simply trusting
newspaper editors to be discreet, it had the power to suppress their publications if they spoke out too roughly. In some cases, suppression was temporary; for others, it was permanent. Postmaster General Albert Burleson
was given the power to ban offensive material from circulating through the
mail. Under postal regulations, if a journal missed one issue, for whatever
reason, it automatically lost its second-class mailing privilege—and for a
great many publications, this spelled financial death.

Burleson was able in this way to counter German propaganda infiltrating from Mexico, India, and elsewhere; he also found other targets nearer home. The black press—some two hundred weekly papers and a half-dozen monthly magazines ranging from half-apologetic moderation to hardening radicalism—came in for particularly close scrutiny. These publications could not be allowed to stir up unrest by claiming that America was unfit to lead an international crusade for democracy, having failed to honor the rights of black people at home. Make the world safe for democracy? "We would rather make Georgia safe for the Negro," wrote the *Messenger*. Black editors were flattered, cultivated, and encouraged to formulate long-range programs and bills of rights. But in the end it was the threats of closure and prosecution under the Espionage Act that persuaded them to subordinate their political objectives to the war effort. "*The Crisis* says: First your country, then your Rights!"—strange words, coming from the pen of W. E. B. Du Bois.

Controlling information was not a purely negative business; George Creel was also anxious to inject positive thoughts into the nation's psyche. In its regular news bulletins, the CPI aimed at a colorless, objective style for good and indifferent tidings alike. In its special publications, it trod a finer line between reportage and rhetoric. A slim volume entitled *The Battle Line of Democracy: Prose and Poetry of the World War* marshaled Henry Wadsworth Longfellow and Rudyard Kipling; Maurice Maeterlinck and Robert Burns; Ralph Waldo Emerson and Alfred, Lord Tennyson; Walt Whitman ("O Captain, My Captain!") and W. E. Henley ("England, My England!") in small doses to rouse the children of America.

Once roused, the children were invited to channel their energies into a hundred different schemes. "Victory Boys" pledged $10 a head toward the war effort and to earn it busied themselves "raising guinea pigs . . . painting barns . . . sifting ashes . . . making stocking stretchers for ladies who were knitting for soldiers . . . making needed household articles such as andirons, umbrella racks etc. . . . tutoring backward students . . . waiting on table as 'extras' in boarding houses." Less venturesomely, "Victory Girls" were invited to mind children, gather nuts, black shoes, clean silver, and put money into a "self-denial fund from allowances."

The Loyalty Leaflet "Friendly Words to the Foreign Born" was aimed at the workingman, with simple vocabulary and syntax. The "To Make the World Free" leaflet went to black communities. "Negroes were held in slavery until Abraham Lincoln set them free," the leaflet reminded its readers. "Since then there has been no slavery in America and there never will be—unless Germany wins this war. . . . This war will be won for freedom by the soldiers in the trenches—and Negroes are among them doing their brave part; by the sailors at sea—and the Negroes are among them as courageous as any" (albeit confined to the lower decks as mess boys and stokers).

The pocket-sized pamphlet "The Kaiserite in America" went to commercial travelers, whom Creel cast as a flying squad against the spreading of idle rumors. It listed and poured scorn on "One Hundred and One German Lies" reputed to be circulating among the credulous—among them the notions that half the funds given to the Red Cross would be handed to the Catholics; that German spies at the Government Printing Office were injecting government bonds with bacteria so that they would crumble to dust in a few months; that Joseph Tumulty, the President's secretary, (a Catholic) had been shot for treason; that the bodies of two soldiers sent back from Europe for burial had been found to have bullet holes in the backs of their heads. Other lies received their share of scorn:

Lie No. 60 . . . That men at Camp Funston are so poorly cared for and are so despondent because of their unwillingness to serve in the army that they end their lives by throwing themselves under trains. (*This is so plainly a lie that denial is not necessary. . . . Newspaper correspondents at the camps do not report any such loss of life.*) Lie No. 18 . . . Schools in towns at or near training camps are to be closed because girls are about to become mothers. (*Investigators declare this is utterly without foundation. . . . The morale of men at the training camps cannot be better.*) Lie No. 84 [an obvious legacy of the Zimmermann telegram] . . . Some 150,000 Japanese and 50,000 Germans are massed in Mexico, waiting the word to swing an attack upon the United States. (*There are a great many Japanese and a great many Germans in Mexico. There is nothing at this time to make Washington believe the Japanese are allied with the Germans in Mexico, or that the Japs plan an attack upon America.*) Lie No. 93 . . . Fifteen to eighteen aviators are killed daily at Scott Field. (*The War Department is giving to the public information of every death that occurs anywhere in the army without regard to whether death results from natural or accidental causes.*) Lie No. 16 . . . That sweaters knit by St. Louis women for soldiers in the trenches wear out in less than two weeks because of the inferior workmanship in the garment. Many women have quit their knitting because of this lie. *(Members of the Red Cross Society here say this is the most outrageous lie they have heard.)*

Truths about the Germans were circulated in the form of postcard-sized reproductions of German proclamations issued to civilians in the occupied territories. One announced the death sentence passed on British nurse Edith Cavell for alleged treason. Another confined inhabitants to their houses except for errands to procure food. "Potatoes can be dug only with the commandant's consent and under military supervision." A third ordered the adult population of Lille to prepare themselves for transportation in an hour and a half's time:

> An officer will definitely decide which persons will be taken to the concentration camps. For this purpose all the inhabitants of the house must assemble in front of it. . . . All appeals will be useless. . . . It is absolutely necessary that people should provide themselves in their own interest with eating and drinking utensils, as well as with a woollen blanket, strong shoes and linen. . . . Anyone attempting to evade transportation will be punished without mercy.

The CPI Division of Advertising's literary style was just as pungent. Patriotic messages were framed in a brisk paragraph of copy. "He will come back a better man!" American mothers were assured.

> A broad-shouldered, deep-chested, square-jawed YOUNG MAN . . . that's who will throw himself into your arms when "Johnny Comes Marching Home Again." . . . Help him, keep him happy NOW—by cheerful, newsy letters—for your sake—and for Uncle Sam.

> In gas warfare there are two classes—the quick and the dead. . . . The folks at home should not fail to urge their boys to "Go strong on the gas drill."

> Poison gas, the flame thrower, the tear bomb, the saw-tooth bayonet— these are the contributions of Germany's scientists to modern warfare. But that peculiar combination of high spirits and vigor called "pep" is a distinctive American invention. . . . "Pep" will win the war. Let's cultivate it!

Then the Division of Advertising's staff prepared suitable illustrations and approached magazines and newspapers with the plates. The papers were not asked directly to donate space, but the CPI did not pay for it; public-spirited advertisers bought the space and gave it to the government. Others were persuaded to carry CPI messages on their billboards, on displays in their shop windows, on placards inside their trolleys and cable cars.

Creel had also to reach those who could not read. The CPI's Speaking Division rapidly enlisted the nation's most effective professional speakers and sent them around the country in the service of the various war agencies. Veteran women's rights campaigner Jane Addams and Secretary of the Interior Franklin Lane were among the most persuasive; Wesley Frost, the former American consul at Queenstown, Ireland, tirelessly reprised his dramatic narrative of the sinking of the *Lusitania*. "It was quite black out there on the Atlantic," Frost would declaim, with as much conviction as if he had been there,

> and in the blackness the life-boats alternately rose on the crests of the waves and sank into the black valley between. The boats carried women and children whose hair hung in icicles over their shoulders. . . . Now and then a half-dead passenger uttered a shriek of pain or of anguish as she realized that a friend or relative had died in her arms. . . . Meanwhile, in the dark hull of the German submarine, the captain watching through the periscope finally turned his head away. Even this man, agent of Prussian cruelty, had witnessed a scene upon which he did not care to gaze.

"A thousand Denverites," wrote the *Rocky Mountain News*, "sat in the Auditorium last night and alternately sobbed and cheered."

War veterans, especially disabled European heroes, had a tremendous impact—men such as Arthur Guy Empey, of "Over the Top" fame, and Lieutenant Paul Périgord, the French "warrior priest," a Catholic father with a degree from the University of Chicago and a record of great gallantry at Verdun. Sergeant Empey's fees were a little steep, but Périgord, with a face that reminded Creel of Saint Francis of Assisi and a voice like an organ, was considered one of the government's most effective mouthpieces.

With speeches lasting anything from thirty minutes to two hours, these were the CPI's heavy artillery. The infantry of the propaganda battle were the Four-Minute Men, who delivered a rapid fire of pithy phrases and elevated sentiments in the four minutes it took to change the reels of film at a movie show.

"It became difficult for half a dozen persons to come together without having a Four-Minute Man descend upon them," wrote chronicler Mark Sullivan after the war. In movie houses, public parks, lumber camps, charity balls, factories, ferries, and streetcars, the volunteer orators delivered their texts, orchestrated by the CPI to bolster each successive drive for men, money, or increased output. The organization had started life as a handful of Chicago businessmen impatient with the administration's timid progress toward war and eager to galvanize public opinion with their own more positive views. But Creel recognized the idea's potential at once, and in June 1917 the Four-Minute Men came under the CPI umbrella.

Most of the speakers were professional men used to having to make their case in public—lawyers, business executives, schoolteachers. But in Georgia a barber, a paperhanger, a ship's carpenter, a shoemaker, and three preachers were among the first black Four-Minute Men to tackle issues of special interest to blacks. Mexican speakers operated along the southern border and Indian agents in the reservations; there was a separate Jewish section and, in New York, an Italian section as well. Four-minute singing found particular success in the South; tenor Vincent Kelley was engaged to sing "We'll Lick the Kaiser If It Takes Us Twenty Years" from the roof of the Woolworth Building in Birmingham, Alabama. In the intervals of band concerts, before the Army-Navy football game, at games during the World Series, Four-Minute Men would rise to their feet. In eighteen months, 75,000 of them delivered 7,555,190 speeches to 314,454,514 people.

The Germans, determined to downplay the impact of America's entry into the war, doubted whether the Four-Minute Men would have much to talk about. "The time of the speeches will be limited to four minutes," sneered the *Frankfurter Zeitung* in November 1917, "because America has done so little up to the present." But the CPI found plentiful grist for its mill. Regular bulletins from headquarters provided speakers with themes, useful phrases, even whole specimen talks. "You will want 'Somebody's Boy' to have an anaesthetic when they take out the bullet," suggested one briefing to speakers appealing for funds for the Red Cross. Alternatively, "My rule for a man's finding out just how much he should subscribe to the Red Cross is this: In the evening when the house is quiet put down your name and the best figure you dare on the white paper. Then go upstairs a minute and look in the crib. Then look at your blank when you come down once more."

Much advice was offered on technique, invoking the examples of Jesus Christ, "the Master Four-Minute Man," and the Gettysburg Address as the greatest four-minute speech of all time. The speaker should consider the race or former nationality of his audience as well as their politics, likely educational standard, industrial conditions, religion, sex, and age, and he should select the "impelling motives" most likely to move them, be they duty, pride, shame, or greed. He should refrain from criticism of the government's past neutrality and avoid irritating the Allies by boasting that America would win the war. He should present an imposing appearance. "Most speakers wear their trousers too long. A man appearing on a stage should hitch his trousers up higher than ordinary." He should be dignified without being dull, waste no words, and above all observe his time limit. "Finish strong and sharp. . . . You recall the hornet because he ends with a point."

There were those who deviated from the ideal. Violence was used against at least one Four-Minute Man who persevered for twenty minutes. "Cut out the bunk on the Red Cross and get on with the show," an incensed moviegoer shouted at one Four-Minute Man in full flight. Unwisely, the speaker had allowed himself to be introduced between reels. "I had butted into the middle of a love-story. The girl was pining, the villain was . . . seemingly triumphant just at the moment I stepped on the stage."

Charles Dana Gibson, America's best-known illustrator, headed the Division of Pictorial Publicity. He was the creator of the "Gibson Girls," and their buxom, wholesome images stared out of some of the division's most successful posters. Gibson worked to inject imagination and emotion into such mundane themes as the need to economize on coal and the importance of killing rats to preserve grain stores. His artists took liberties with the facts—the German soldier was regularly portrayed in the menacing spiked helmet that had actually been discarded by the lower ranks years before—and occasionally they overstepped even the bounds of wartime taste, depicting bayoneting and rape with too much relish. But their posters prompted a fervent response to appeals such as the one for the French Workingman's Fund: "French comrade, your children shall be as our children!" ran the slogan over a picture of an American soldier kneeling at a poilu's grave beside the weeping orphans.

Cartoons struck a lighter note but still a carefully orchestrated one. Every week the division sent out a collection of topics to prick cartoonists' imaginations. "The Red Cross versus the Iron Cross" ran one proposed caption during a major Red Cross recruiting drive, or, alternatively, "Useless Christmas Present versus Red Cross Memberships." The Internal Revenue Bureau managed a nice turn of phrase in exhorting the public to pay their taxes—"If you pay now, the Kaiser can't prey later"—though they set the illustrator a difficult task with slogans such as "Our boys are shelling the Huns. It's up to us to shell out the hun-dreds."

Movies probably gave the CPI its widest audience. The Film Division succeeded in recruiting the best part of the burgeoning American film industry, taking advice from, among others, D. W. Griffith, a devout believer in the power of the movies to mold public morals. The division worked with all the rising companies—Pathé, Universal, Paramount, and others—supplying them with suitably uplifting scenarios and supervising production. Patriotic producers made the pictures at their own expense and distributed them in the normal way, partly disguising the scent of propaganda that would otherwise have hung about movies such as *Keep 'Em Singing and Nothing Can Lick 'Em, There Shall Be No Cripples*, and *Reclaiming the Soldiers' Duds*, a deathless work on delousing units on the Western Front. *The American Indian Gets into the War Game* was launched under Universal's aegis. "By showing the heroic part the Indian men are playing in voluntary enlistment and the part the Indian women are playing in Red Cross work . . . the white man is shamed into a higher patriotism," claimed the CPI handout.

Creel saw every American as a potential audience and broadcast the message of every government department in the attempt to sell the war. But always he had three basic preoccupations: men, money, and industrial morale.

Once the draft law had been passed, the CPI's objective was to help induce men to register for conscription without using sanctions. Getting their families to apply the pressure could be very effective. "I'd rather you had died at birth," ran one widely circulated ditty, "or not been born at all / Than know that I had raised a son who cannot hear the call. / To save the world from sin, my son, God gave his only son. / He's asking for MY boy, today, and may His will be done."

Creel's men were just as uninhibited in their calls for money. From the start, businesses had strongly resisted the notion of paying for the war even partly through taxation, and McAdoo had resolved to raise the phenomenal sums needed through "loans" from the people of America by selling them something called "Liberty Bonds."

McAdoo wanted Liberty Bonds to appeal to the masses rather than to the big financial institutions; he wanted their purchase to be "the expression of a fundamental patriotism." So, for the first Liberty Loan, he went for a dangerously large issue, $200 million worth—dangerous because he also wanted to keep the rate of payable interest low in order to hold down the cost of the war, and this made them less attractive. Should the bonds not be taken up, it would mean the collapse of government finances—and possibly the loss of the war. McAdoo looked gray and drawn on his tours of the country to promote the bonds, and he pulled no punches in his rhetoric: "I have three sons myself who are in the Navy of the United States. I expect nothing more of them and nothing less of them than what every gallant boy intends to do in this conflict—die, if need be, that liberty may be safe. . . . The least you can do for them is to give them the means of defending themselves."

The CPI was no less passionate in its "multi-media convulsions" in support of the Liberty Loan campaigns. War-loan posters easily outnumbered any other category and produced some of the most lurid images of the war, repulsive more often than not for their brutality and sentimentality alike. The approach was rarely subtle, and some played queasily on a mixture of guilt and fear in the noncombatant observer, laced with sexual innuendo.

The Boy Scout kneeling at the feet of the figure of Columbia, clasping a sword emblazoned with the motto "Be Prepared," was straightforward enough, and the Scouts would sell more than $350 million worth of bonds to sympathizers. Artist Ellsworth Young's "Remember Belgium" aimed lower, with its gross silhouette of a corpulent, walrus-mustached, middle-aged Hun dragging a nightgowned child of no more than twelve or thirteen into the darkness against a backdrop of flame and devastation. Other war-bond posters stripped their female victims to the waist and stained their clothes with blood. Joseph Pennell employed the same vocabulary of atrocity propaganda more obliquely in his hugely popular "That Liberty Shall Not Perish from the Earth." In it, German bombers head away from a bloodred Manhattan wreathed in smoke and pass over a headless Statue of Liberty, its uplifted arm a shattered stump—mutilated just as it was claimed the women and children of Belgium were being mutilated.

Four-Minute Men bombarded their audiences with catchphrases: "Bonds or bondage"; "You can't keep your money and your self-respect"; "If you don't come across, the Kaiser will." In New Jersey one Friday night, a "shock battalion" of Four-Minute Men swung into action; at 6 P.M., 467 of them began to speak from booths spread along the streets of Jersey City. Each delivered ten addresses, in two bursts of twenty minutes each; speaking for an aggregate of 18,600 minutes, they sold $373,600 worth of bonds.

In movie houses, audiences were encouraged to squirm in their upholstered seats with a mixture of vicarious excitement and guilt:

> It will soon be 10 o'clock here—3 A.M. in France. . . . The usual hour, so I'm told, that the Germans start their artillery fire. So while we are sitting here, all comfortable, well-fed, secure, our boys are standing in the trenches down in the mud. Shells are bursting over their heads— right now—there's a fire in one place—roaring cannon—poisonous gases creeping through the trenches. Perhaps a moment ago while I was talking a giant German bomb struck a squad of our men—some are dead, others dying, mangled bodies are being taken away in stretchers. Yes, that's what is happening perhaps right now.

Reproaches were aimed straight between the eyes of the stonyhearted and closefisted:

> In later years, when you try to sleep, other eyes will haunt you, eyes of soldiers dead will look upon you. [*Spoken in a low voice:*] Perhaps your son, a nephew, some of your friends' sons will be among them. And the white lips will murmur: "But for you, you slacker, and such as you, we might be home with you."

Clergymen delivered Liberty Loan sermons:

> If the Christ who was merciful to the harlot is conscious of the outraged womanhood and motherhood of France, with what utter scorn and contempt must he look upon that American citizen calling himself a follower of the lowly Nazarene who, having the means, still refuses to buy these bonds. . . . As you value your Christianity, buy these bonds.

Sousa dutifully produced a "Liberty Bond March," and the famous used their charisma as a marketing tool. Douglas Fairbanks, Mary Pickford, and Theda Bara raised thousands, even hundreds of thousands, of dollars with their tireless professional charm. Enrico Caruso, Amelita Galli-Curci, and John McCormack raised $4,800,000 from a single audience at Carnegie Hall.

But though money changed hands, the Liberty Bonds did not reach the mass market of McAdoo's designs. The first issue was taken up less by the man in the street, who needed to look for a higher return than 3.5 percent, than by the rich, who were attracted by the bonds' generous tax exemptions. Inadvertently, the first loan had created a class of rich nontaxpayers, and from then on Liberty Loans were aimed more obviously at the better off or at financial institutions.

The money of the masses was tapped by different means, through the more modest War Savings Certificates and War Savings Stamps, sold over the counter in post offices and banks, table to table in restaurants and cafés. To receive a War Savings Certificate, the purchaser filled a pocket folder with twenty stamps, each with a face value of $5. Thrift Stamps were cheaper still—25 cents apiece, sixteen to a card, which could then be exchanged, plus the balance of the cash, for a War Savings Stamp. Thrift Stamps were even within the reach of the patriotic child. In Kona, Hawaii, the *Honolulu Advertiser* reported, "Japanese children are working by lantern light in the coffee groves gathering the berries in order to make extra money with which to purchase Thrift Stamps." The purchase of a Thrift Stamp in Kona entitled the buyer to drive a nail into a wooden effigy of the Kaiser; a War Savings Stamp bought the right to clip his mustache. Then the effigy would be dragged through the streets and burned.

Finally, and perhaps most important of all, the CPI had to keep Americans working—in the factories, the shipyards, the mines, the forests, and the fields. Materials would win this war, and nothing could be allowed to interfere with their flow to Europe. But in the quest to maximize production, the old traditions of tolerance and individual freedom were meeting their sternest test—and in the white heat of mobilization, American democracy was showing signs of melting away.

16

"I Love My Flag, I Do, I Do":
Discouraging Dissent

In this age of total war, the industrial landscape of America became as much of a battleground in its way as the trenches of France. "The industrial forces of the country," declaimed Woodrow Wilson, "men and women alike, will be a great national, a great international service army." But American labor had none of the unity, conformity, or discipline that the term "army" implied. The ranks of labor were distorted by sectional, political, occupational, and ethnic differences, all of which had been heightened in the turbulent prewar years. The CPI had to make sure that these separate interests were reconciled and subordinated to the nation's need. The motivation and loyalty of the workingman had become as critical to the war effort as the courage and obedience of the soldier.

The foreign-born worker was an obvious target, on the assumption that his loyalty to his homeland might complicate his attitude to the war. Creel created a new CPI division for work with the foreign-born. It was split into twenty-nine subsections, each pouring out propaganda in a different language, adjusted subtly to appeal to its particular audience.

These efforts were reinforced by Secretary of the Interior Franklin Lane, who called prominent businessmen and state governors to a conference in Washington and urged them to throw themselves more enthusiastically into the Americanization of immigrants, along the lines of the prewar program. "The real melting pot for the adult foreign-born is the industrial plants of America," he declared, attacking the collected captains of industry for "the indifference that has been shown by this nation in the education and enlightenment of those whom [you] have invited to these shores."

Lane had a full-time staff of thirty-six working on the developing Americanization program, guided by "over 100 men in racial conference groups so as to understand their needs, help work out a sound policy and program of racial relations and carry the message to their own people." The objective was simple: to "create in the immigrant a better understanding of America and his duty to America."

Eight hundred industrial plants established "Americanization Committees" all over the country. Men's pay packets were stuffed with loyalty leaflets printed by the American Chamber of Commerce, which also distributed a fortnightly national bulletin "telling what the industries are doing for Americanization." The Missouri Council of Defense declared itself ready to "thoroughly Americanize all groups of Missourians, without regard to their racial origin." In Indianapolis, foreign-born citizens participating in the "Americanization Day" parade of July 4, 1918, were astonished to be offered an official apology for having been treated "as a mere economic unit, to be used, worn out and cast aside."

The native-born worker too had to be bound into the war effort. But controlling labor was no longer something that could be taken for granted. With immigration at a standstill and the draft in full swing, the labor pool had shrunk even as demand was escalating. Labor leaders now had a degree of leverage that they had never before enjoyed; the war had provided a unique opportunity for them to press for better pay and conditions, perhaps even for recognition of the universal right to form unions.

The administration was faced with a dilemma. The activities of the labor movement must not be allowed to jeopardize the war effort. Was the government to side with employers to crush the demands of labor for the duration or to conciliate labor as far as it could in order to guarantee war output? For a number of reasons, the President and his administration preferred conciliation. Since 1912, Wilson had dedicated a significant part of his energies to restricting the influence of big business, and he had achieved genuine reforms in labor law; reinforcing the power of the employers was not part of his plan. In any event, given the limited ability of the federal government in 1917 to impose its will physically on the people—even the draft had to be "voluntary"—coercion on a large scale was not a genuine alternative.

Fortunately for Wilson, the principal figure in labor circles also saw cooperation as the way forward. Samuel Gompers, president of the American Federation of Labor (AFL), the country's largest organization of trade unions, supported the United States' entry into the war for patriotic reasons—but also as a means of advancing the cause of labor.

In 1917, Gompers was in his sixties, a stocky, grizzled man, born in England of Dutch-Jewish origins, who had risen to power in labor circles through the Cigar-Makers' Union. (In his old age he remained addicted to nicotine; he smoked forty cigars a day, though his doctor tried to restrict him to twenty "for his health's sake.") He was in many ways a natural ally for the government. He was no wild-eyed ideologue; he had no interest in abstract theories of social and political change, no feeling of solidarity with a world proletariat, only a passionate, stubborn devotion to improving the material conditions of the American workingman, inch by inch. His enemies were unjust employers and those more extreme activists who challenged his control of the labor movement.

In late 1916, before war with Germany had even looked likely, he had accepted an invitation from Wilson to join the Advisory Commission to the Council of National Defense. Now he saw a chance to recruit the power of the state against employers. His price for cooperation was high: guaranteed wages on government contracts, equal pay for women, and an eight-hour maximum workday. All these the government imposed on employers for him. In the government sector, the right to collective bargaining was recognized more widely than ever before. Experiments were made in workers' housing that were not to be bettered for decades. Gompers also had unions represented directly on the committees that decided who should receive government contracts, in order to prevent their being allocated to nonunionized companies.

In return, to maintain industrial peace, he held back from insisting on major principles—either on unionism as an absolute right or the closed shop. He undermined more radical unionists, on his own account and to the benefit of the government. An official intelligence report on the activities of the troublesome president of the Laundry Workers' Union included the observation that a "discreet word" to the AFL might help to get him out. Again, the AFL letterbook for 1917 reveals Gompers' collusion, or at least acquiescence, in a plan to discredit a socialist labor organization on New York's Lower East Side by publishing claims that it had tried to influence Jewish socialists in Germany's favor.

Gompers had enormous influence in persuading the workingman that this was a "people's war" that must not be undermined by strikes. "We understand now," he declared, addressing a rally in Saint Paul, Minnesota, "that we are engaged in one common cause—the defense of justice, the defense of the ideal of the common brotherhood of the people of the United States. If we fail, the Lights of Freedom go out over the whole world. We cannot fail! We must not fail!"

His willingness to work with Wilson's war managers and, on occasion, take cigars from the captains of industry made him a controversial figure, despised by the left wing as a lackey of the ruling class. Even moderate members of the labor movement questioned where his loyalties lay. The president of the Pennsylvania Federation of Labor wrote to him in October 1917 to ask whether certain of his activities had been "financed wholly or in part by the widely recognized enemies of labor with whom you have lately been appearing. . . . Who paid the expenses of the special train from New York to Minneapolis? . . . Who pays the rent for the halls you have been using? . . . Who paid the tremendous expense of the Minneapolis Convention?"

The answer to several of these questions would undoubtedly have been the American Alliance for Labor and Democracy (AALD), formed under Gompers' presidency in 1917. Designed to "stimulate labor morale," the AALD poured out a flood of leaflets and articles explaining the worker's role in the war and aiming to defuse potential conflict between workers and management. Patriotic posters, printed by the government, were put up in factories by employers and miniature pamphlets were inserted into paycheck envelopes. Lapel buttons were circulated with service flags for workers to put in their windows; mass meetings, pep talks on a gigantic scale, became regular events. Gompers and the AALD were given thousands of columns of publicity in the press—and here skeptics were right to query Gompers' independence. For however carefully the work of the AALD was camouflaged to look like "the spontaneous action of labor itself," the organization was effectively run by the CPI.

A wide variety of inducements, both moral and material, were being used to keep the American Federation of Labor working, with Gompers as the middleman. But there were other workingmen beyond Gompers' control, and it would take more forceful action to suppress their hostility to the employers—or even to the war effort itself.

To the majority of America's socialists, this was no "people's war" for justice and democracy but a "capitalist venture," a profitable enterprise run on the blood of the people. They made their opposition known, and it was a challenge the authorities did not feel able to ignore.

During the immediate prewar period, socialism had been a growing force. In 1912, Eugene Debs had run for the presidency and had polled almost a million votes (while Theodore Roosevelt had received 4 million, Woodrow Wilson 6 million). In mid-1917, the American Socialist Party (ASP) continued to attract electoral support; Morris Hillquit became mayor of New York with five times the usual vote. An eloquent minority of socialists—men such as Upton Sinclair, John Spargo, and Charles Edward Russell—did accept the picture of the war as a fight for international democracy. But most continued to project it as a battle between different groups of capitalists for ill-gotten gains. The administration dared not let them work on the feelings of the workingman and -woman in this way. It was now that the Espionage Act proved its usefulness.

Leading socialists such as Debs and Rose Pastor Stokes went to jail— Stokes for denying that every citizen should support the war and claiming that the government was "for the profiteers"—and most of the party leaders were eventually indicted. Further down, in the lower federal courts, sentences were handed out lavishly. One socialist got twenty-one months in jail for maintaining that Germany's actions in Belgium were no worse than America's in the Philippines.

More damagingly, as far as the spread of socialist ideas was concerned, their publications were banned from the mails under the authority conferred by the Espionage Act on Postmaster General Burleson. "Newspapers cannot say that this Government is the tool of Wall Street or of munition makers," declared Burleson. "There can be . . . nothing that will interfere with enlistments . . . or the sale of authorized bonds or the collection of authorized revenue." On this basis he suppressed issues of the *Masses*, the *Internationalist Socialist Review*, the *Milwaukee Leader*, and dozens of other publications.

Burleson was "a Southerner of the old type," a Texan introduced to his job on the recommendation of Colonel House and a close personal friend of the President. In the opinion of McAdoo, who had mixed feelings about him, Burleson "acted the part of a homely, uncouth politician, which he was not. In reality he was a gentleman of education and ability," though his black coat was often rumpled and rusty. "I think he intended to create the effect that he was no better than the humblest citizen of the republic. The effort was successful."

Burleson was a curious mixture of pomposity and eccentricity, but he was not insensitive to the moral and intellectual ambiguities of his job. "To those who have the will to launch assaults against public officials who are discharging their duty," he wrote, "I commend a careful reading of the eighth stanza in Tennyson's 'The Grandmother.' " ["A lie which is all a lie may be met and fought with outright / But a lie which is part a truth is a harder matter to fight."]

Wilson often sought Burleson's advice, and he relied on him to a surprising degree. "You know," he wrote in September 1917, "that I am willing to trust your judgment after I have once called your attention to a suggestion." But in his zeal to protect both the fighting men and the administration from destructive rumor or criticism, Burleson went well beyond the President's intentions on censorship, toward the infringing of civil liberties.

Wilson may have had qualms about crushing the dissent of what had been very recently a legitimate and important part of the political scene. But he had no such reservations when dealing with the most radical of the labor organizations, the International Workers of the World, (IWW, or "Wobblies"). The Wobblies had been grit in the economic machinery since their inception in 1905; with the onset of war, influential voices were heard calling for these "troublemakers" to be crushed.

The authorities had to move with care. Originally, the Wobblies had vigorously opposed America's entry into the war. They endorsed all the economic antiwar arguments: "General Sherman said: 'War is Hell!' Don't go to Hell in order to give the capitalists a bigger slice of heaven!" They also deflated the noble imagery of war:

> I love my flag, I do, I do,
> Which floats upon the breeze,
> I also love my arms and legs,
> And neck, and nose and knees.
> One little shell might spoil them all
> Or give them such a twist
> They would be of no use to me;
> I guess I won't enlist.

Nevertheless, since the declaration of war they had been more discreet than the socialists, which made them harder targets for legal repression. The most extreme activists may have preached resistance to conscription, for example, but most branches left the issue to individual members, and in some areas as many as 95 percent of IWW members registered for the draft. They realized that imprisonment would remove them from the labor scene at a crucial time—and besides, there were other blows they could strike against the war.

For years the IWW had been advocating sabotage as a tool in the class struggle; in the context of war, this could be a deadly weapon. What the organization's theorists had in mind was less the destruction of property than the withdrawal of efficiency. "Of course you will be honest with the boss," argued J. T. "Red" Doran, speaking to an audience of lumbermen in Washington State in September 1917. "You give him in return for whatever he gives you. That's honest, isn't it? He gives you rotten hours and rotten pay—and you give him rotten work. . . . We do not advocate violence or destruction of property. We are dead against such a thing." But, he continued, " 'Accidents' of course cannot be guarded against entirely. If tools are mislaid, if the belting should be worn away so that it snaps, if a wrench or a large bolt should get in the machinery . . . that is an accident."

Some Wobblies took such homilies to heart. Spikes were driven into lengths of timber to break planing machines and band saws as logs passed through the mills; when the spikes went under the band saw, one intelligence agent reported, "the saw teeth flew about like bullets." Blacklegs found cow itch in their bedding, stumping powder rubbed into their hat bands.

The Wobblies were never as dangerous as they made themselves sound. They threatened vastly more sabotage than they actually carried out, and they tried to keep their strikes peaceful and within the law. But they could not escape the threatening image that had been firmly in place before 1917—an image reinforced by their wartime speeches and songs. "Big Bill" Haywood's language remained exaggerated and incendiary, the language enshrined in the *Little Red Songbook* of the legendary martyr Joe Hill. Subtitled "To Fan the Flames of Discontent," the little red book contained "Songs of the Miseries That Are. Songs of the Happiness to Be. Songs That Strip Capitalism Bare." In it, IWW messages were carried to a huge audience on the backs of the tunes of popular hits or familiar gospel or revival hymns.

Church and flag were rejected as tools of the exploiter to the tune of one of the best loved of all marching hymns:

Onward, Christian soldiers, rip and tear and smite!
Let the gentle Jesus bless your dynamite,
Splinter skulls with shrapnel, fertilize the sod!
Folks who do not speak your tongue deserve the curse of God.

And Wobbly leader Ralph Chaplin commandeered one of the nation's most sacred anthems, "Glory Hallelujah," for his "Solidarity Forever":

It is we who plowed the prairies, built the cities where they stand;
Dug the mines and built the workshops, endless miles of railroad laid;
Now we stand outcast and starving, mid the wonders we have made;
But the union makes us strong.

In the early years, the Wobblies had been distrusted as enemies of the social order, opponents of the American way. During the years of neutrality, their menace became more sharply defined. In threatening to slow down or even halt production in coal mines and steel factories, the Wobblies were curtailing the industrialists' opportunities to profit from the Allies' demands. Now, with America in the war, they became a threat to the nation's security and its chances of victory in battle. With their influence over the copper miners, the lumbermen, and unskilled migratory field hands in the West, the Wobblies were in a position to check the flow of crucial materials and manufactures to the front—and they showed no reluctance to do so.

In 1917, lumber became one of the most important of all war materials—spruce for aircraft manufacture, Douglas fir for the building of army cantonments. At the same time, lumberjacks endured some of the worst working conditions in the country. Seasonal and migratory workers, they were wide open to exploitation by the mill owners and lived on lamentable pay, packed into repulsively filthy camps, in an atmosphere of hatred and lawlessness. A campaign for better pay and an eight-hour day was already under way when the IWW decided to take a hand. In June 1917, strikes began to disrupt timber production seriously.

At the same time, the Wobblies were waging guerrilla warfare among the fruit pickers of Washington and California, riding freight cars all over the two states and bringing impetus and direction to an already existing upsurge of rebellion. By July, with the fruit and grain harvests approaching, the Washington Council of State Defense was beginning to panic. The IWW organization, it reported, recognized "no flag except its own flag of freedom that is the quote red quote flag."

On Haywood's own home ground of the mines, the IWW faced the most hard-nosed opposition. The major companies producing copper, for instance, had flatly refused to arbitrate grievances. Butte, Montana, was one of the principal hotbeds of unrest. Here the employers, led by the Anaconda Copper Company, had decided to drive out radical labor and were operating a primitive blacklist against union men. After a disaster at the Speculator Mine, where 164 miners were suffocated or burned to death, strikes began to erupt, and the IWW set up a headquarters in Butte.

As the strikes spread in the summer of 1917, employers, local businessmen, and patriotic citizens alike depicted IWW activities as a treasonable conspiracy and called for federal aid. Many looked first toward the Department of Labor, in whose hands lay the power to deport undesirable aliens, a weapon of which much was hoped, on the basis that the majority of labor agitators were not native-born Americans. As an administrative rather than a judicial procedure, deportation had the great advantage of bypassing the need for criminal prosecution with all the constitutional safeguards a trial entailed, such as rules of evidence and the right to counsel. The main problem in labor disturbances was establishing individual guilt, but the immigration laws seemed to offer scope for acting on guilt by association—in which case mere membership in the IWW, an organization that apparently advocated destruction of property, could have been a basis for deportation.

But Secretary of Labor William B. Wilson—the first man to hold that office—had been a union man himself, a member of the United Mine Workers, and the principle of guilt by association offended him. He insisted that if immigration officials wished to move against the IWW, they must establish individual guilt, and the organization's enemies had to look elsewhere for a quick solution.

The military seemed the obvious ally, and it was certainly willing. "It is not a labor organization, in the ordinary acceptance of the term," reads one analysis of the IWW. "It is a glorified hoboism. . . . It is anti-order. It is anti-restraint, social or economic. It is anti-Christ. It is immoral—or unmoral—and wholly irresponsible. . . . It typifies, under thin disguise, the incarnation of anarchy." The case against the IWW was blackened by rumors that it was financed by Germany: "Imperial Wilhelm's Warriors."

Federal troops were used to break strikes, raid IWW premises, close down meetings, arrest and interrogate labor organizers. They were violating the law and the Fourth Amendment, but they gave near-hysterical citizens the reassurance they craved that "something was being done" about radicalism.

Rarely did the situation justify the use of the Army; law officers were often induced to call for help by public frenzy deliberately whipped up by mine and mill owners, who saw a chance to turn the power of the state against unruly workers. In these circumstances, the Army did not always move swiftly enough to satisfy local "patriots."

At Bisbee, Arizona, unionists were pressing for strike action by workers in mines that accounted for 28 percent of the national output of copper. IWW strike organizers were also operating in the town. "No violence nor disorder," reported a War Department official from Bisbee. "Two largest companies only are operating with 40 to 50% force. . . . Troops would expedite production but cannot be justified on ground of disorder." Sheriff Harry Wheeler, an ex–Rough Rider, disagreed. Ignoring the broad base of discontent in the mines, he declared, "The IWW *strike* here is most serious. . . . Majority strikers seem foreign, the whole thing appears pro-German and anti-American"—and on June 28 he called for federal help, an appeal vigorously backed by the mine owners.

When intervention was slow in coming, "volunteer organizations" took direct action. Local businessmen under the leadership of the Phelps-Dodge Copper Corporation conspired to remove all labor agitators from their town. On July 12, two thousand citizens of Bisbee formed a mob that was headed by Sheriff Wheeler but armed and paid by Phelps-Dodge, and marched on the strikers. They rounded up some 1,200 men, a mixture of IWW members, suspected IWW members, and local sympathizers, and led them to a baseball park converted into a temporary concentration camp. There the strikers—a motley crowd of shopkeepers, lawyers, and clerks, besides the miners—were given the choice of returning to work, going to jail, or being deported from the state. Furious at the violation of their civil liberties, they refused to call off the strike. So the vigilantes herded them into twenty-seven cattle cars and sent them across the border into New Mexico. When the first town they reached refused to accept them, the train plowed on into the desert until it reached the village of Hermanas, and there the deportees were left, with little food, water, or cover from the blazing sun.

Now the Army did take them in charge, on the instructions of Newton Baker. "Secretary of War desires proper provision made for protection of people referred to until some means are devised for getting rid of them." They were held in a camp at Columbus, New Mexico, where a census was held on August 6. Of 1,008 present on that date, 804 were indeed foreign-born, and 530 of these had not been naturalized. But of the foreign-born, only twenty were Germans and only five Austro-Hungarians. The loyalty of 179 Austro-Hungarian Slavs and fifteen Swedes might have been questioned, but they were outnumbered by the 268 Mexicans, 141 Britons, and 93 Russians and Finns. How many of them actually belonged to the IWW was not established.

The Bisbee deportation, in the view of Felix Frankfurter, then secretary to the President's Mediation Commission, was "wholly without authority in law, either state or federal." But Attorney General Thomas Gregory saw no grounds for a federal case against Sheriff Wheeler and took no conclusive action against the vigilantes. Nor was there any outcry in support of the IWW from the rest of the labor movement. Gompers could not curb the IWW's activities, and, as John Reed angrily pointed out, he had no intention of allowing the AFL to be contaminated by association: "Samuel Gompers protested to the German trades unions against the deportation of Belgian workingmen. But even the Germans didn't deport Belgians into the middle of a desert, without food or water, as Bisbee did—and yet Gompers hasn't uttered a single peep about Bisbee." Some of the deportees were still under military guard at the end of September.

In Butte, an orderly strike was aggravated by the brutal murder of one of the IWW's leading activists. Frank Little looked the stereotype of a hobo agitator—part Indian, tall, spare, one-eyed, and beat-up. After twenty-five years on the road following the action, he was crippled by rheumatism and in July 1917 had a broken leg in a plaster cast. He had recently made a speech encouraging the strikers to stay out, larding it with antiwar remarks. On the night of July 31, he was pulled out of his cheap hotel room in his underclothes and dragged through Butte behind an automobile, scraping his kneecaps off. Then, some miles outside town, he was lynched, with a piece of paper pinned to his undervest bearing the old vigilante sign "3—7—77," the dimensions of a grave: three feet wide by seven feet long and seventy-seven inches deep.

To deal with the aftermath and break the strike, troops were called into the copper mining camps. With the cooperation of the Anaconda Copper

Company, they carried out searches and seizures and broke up public meetings. Military intelligence planted agents in the IWW ranks, watched their mail, and monitored their movements.

By now Baker was having serious misgivings about this use, or abuse, of troops, who were anyway needed overseas. "Great care should be exercised," he directed, "that no basis exists for the charge that the military is partial to either side of any existing labor difficulty. . . . The anxiety of the Department that the civil rights of strikers be respected should be tactfully conveyed to the civil authorities with whom every discreet cooperation for the maintenance of peaceful conditions should be made."

In the end, it was the Department of Justice, guardian of the Espionage Act, that moved most effectively against the IWW, with raids on IWW offices throughout the country on September 5, 1917. These were ordered not by the Attorney General himself but by Hinton Clabaugh, the superintendent of the department's Chicago branch.

The raiders seized paper clips, rubber bands, and Ralph Chaplin's love letters as well as a mass of the organization's official correspondence. But they seem to have known, amid the detritus, what they were looking for. "Copies of letters, telegrams, circulars, etc. showing the connection of each possible defendant with the illegal activities of the IWW organization," according to an intelligence report, "were assorted, assembled, and sent to the Chicago office as promptly as possible soon after the receipt of the telegram from Division Superintendent Clabaugh." One hundred sixty-six of the men named in advance as "possible defendants" were later indicted under the Espionage Act. One hundred thirteen, including Haywood and Chaplin, would be tried in Chicago in April to May 1918, each charged with more than a hundred crimes, all to be found guilty on all counts and sent to prison: Haywood, Chaplin, and thirteen others for twenty years each.

As 1917 drew to its close, Wilson's administration had done its best to discourage dissent in the newspapers and among the workforce, and it had worked hard to project optimism and confidence. But there was still criticism the President could not silence and some truths he could not hide. As the winter snow began to fall, some of the most senior and eminent figures in the country began making their own protests over issues that were plain to all. Despite what the propaganda said, the Republic's glorious charge to victory was not going according to plan.

Part Four

The

WINTER

CRISIS

17

"The Truth About This War": Mobilization Stalled

To the cynical outside observer, it sometimes seemed as if George Creel was doing his job too well. "It will never do to let the people at home find out the truth about this war," one American in France wrote bitterly, hardened by two years' experience as a volunteer on the Western Front. "They've been fed on bunk until they'd never believe anything that didn't sound like a monk's story of the Crusades. Every time I get a paper from home, I either break into a loud laugh or get mad."

In fact, the people at home had not altogether lost their collective critical faculty. After nine months of mobilization of men, materials, and minds, many were still opposed to the war on principle; even more disapproved of the way in which it was being run. In the New York *Tribune* Heywood Broun kept up a constant sniper fire at the inefficiency of the administration. The Army in France, he sneered, had less than a day's reserve of fodder for its horses and mules but 180 days' supply of coffee beans. Broun's barbs were sharp, but he did not need much skill to hit a large, soft target. By the end of 1917, whatever the CPI might say and however determined the attempts to suppress socialist and IWW dissent, there were few Americans who did not realize that there was much that was seriously wrong with the American war effort.

Wilson was trying to organize it without a strong central bureaucracy, relying on newly formed agencies such as the Food Administration and the CPI, on the American tradition of voluntarism, and on the procurement systems already existing within the armed forces. To coordinate these operations and somehow harness the nation's economic strength in support

of them, there was only his office and the underpowered Council of
National Defense. The administration needed luck as well as determination to mobilize the nation effectively—and at the end of 1917 luck was
against it.

That winter was the worst in living memory; people walked over the
thick ice from the Jersey shore to Staten Island. As the chill took hold, fuel
supplies ran out. People froze to death; pneumonia reached epidemic proportions, with 263 people dying in one week in New York alone. Across
the Northeast, gangs of normally respectable husbands and fathers broke
into coal yards and rail depots to steal coal. In Ohio, citizens tore up railroad tracks to prevent the movement of coal to other areas.

In the Army's camps, with their close concentrations of men, diseases
spread with horrifying speed. Camp Funston reported 922 cases of influenza in November and 2,480 four months later; there were also 3,384
cases of mumps. At Camp Beauregard, Louisiana, dozens of cases of
measles were followed by influenza turning into bronchopneumonia;
seventy-one died of cerebrospinal meningitis, which was killing an average
of three men a day at Camp Funston. At Camp Greene, North Carolina,
the men lived in crowded barracks with poor mess halls, filthy kitchens,
and noisome latrines; they contracted gangrenous dermatitis to go with the
routine outbreaks of measles, mumps, TB, and influenza. There, even
horses and mules died of the flu—almost a thousand of them.

The winter crisis and the sufferings of these civilian soldiers provoked
public outrage, which was eagerly fanned by the administration's critics.
"Never in the history of any country has there been more incompetence
than in our preparation for this war," stormed Leonard Wood—and he
demanded a full exposé. "It is pitiless publicity we want," he wrote.
"This Democracy will have no chance to win the war if the truth is concealed and the facts are hidden from the people." On December 12, Democrat Senator George Chamberlain, chairman of the Senate Military
Affairs Committee, instigated an inquiry into the War Department's conduct of the war.

After three weeks of listening to a catalogue of failures and a list of un-
convincing excuses, Chamberlain could contain his rage no longer. Regardless of party loyalty and of the comfort he would surely give the enemy,
he took the platform at a meeting of the National Security League, a Republican bastion, and before an audience that included Leonard Wood,
Henry Cabot Lodge, and a cheering, whooping Theodore Roosevelt, he

denounced the administration. "We are still unprepared, without a definite war program and still without trained men," he thundered. "The military establishment of the United States has broken down. It has almost stopped functioning."

His claim was largely true. "Nine months after we entered the war, and three months after our men were gathered at cantonments," declared one of the senators involved in the investigation, "we found, in the dead of winter, tens of thousands of men without overcoats, tens of thousands lacking woolen breeches, tens of thousands without woolen blouses." Eighty percent of the soldiers had been given shoes too small for their feet, made of the wrong kind of leather, which let the water in.

The pneumonia epidemic, the Surgeon General maintained scientifically, had little to do with these shortages: "Control of the germ was the principal point to be considered." The Chamberlain committee would have been more impressed had there been any evidence of a successful attempt to control infection. But hospital buildings had been last on the construction schedule, and many were still incomplete when pneumonia first broke out. The existing wards were dangerously congested, and the overflow found themselves in half-finished shacks with neither heating nor sewage facilities.

The Ordnance Department too came under fire when investigators found "hundreds of thousands of men training with wooden sticks for weeks and months because of mistakes and delays in ordering rifles last spring." At that point, America had possessed the best rifle so far developed in any military service. The Springfield was a weapon so accurate that it would still be in use as a sniper weapon some four decades later in Korea. But the War Department was creating a mass army, and for technical reasons, the Springfield could not be easily mass-produced. Hastily, Baker decided to adopt the British Lee Enfield rifle but decided to rechamber it for the slightly different Springfield-sized ammunition, of which there was a substantial supply. The rechambering process involved the redesigning of fifty parts, interrupting the mass production that had been the Lee Enfield's main advantage in the first place. Worse, the AEF was now tied to production facilities in America; in an emergency, it could not procure any rifle ammunition in Europe. A "hideous travesty on standardization," Leonard Wood called it, castigating the authorities for sending over "any old calibers which happened to be the fad of an obsolescent Ordnance Department."

For its artillery, the War Department had decided to adopt French models and French ammunition, to be produced by American manufacturers. Production, inevitably slow because of the long lead time required to construct the large machine tools and construction facilities, was further delayed as the manufacturers waited for the drawings to arrive from France—and when they came, the drawings of the shells were so poor and inaccurate that they were reckoned to be "the ones the French had intended the German Government to obtain through secret sources." This did not stop members of the French Purchasing Commission in America from criticizing the finished products from every possible perspective. The steel specifications, design, method of manufacture, and tests, they claimed, were all inadequate, and they declared themselves "fearful that a large number of prematures would occur when our shells were put into use."

Even this was less serious a failure, in Senator Lodge's eyes, than the machine-gun fiasco. Writing to Theodore Roosevelt to praise him for speaking "the burning truth about our amblings to disaster," he described how the Ordnance Department had stopped making the Lewis gun:

> They took months to consider a new gun, and then that expert ordnance officer, the Secretary of War, decided on the Browning gun, which never had a field test and of which there is only one in existence—the model. . . . After deciding on their gun, they have made none. [Senator] Wadsworth says they will not have any before April [1918]. We have no machine guns and no prospect of any.

Here, in the field of weapons procurement, where a long lead time was needed, the lack of preparedness was most keenly felt. The economy was already at full stretch when the war began, trying to meet the Allies' needs as they ground painfully toward crisis after crisis. There was no slack—and the few facilities that were not under contract to the Allies were made over to the Navy, which enjoyed priority for demands that could be met within the first twelve months.

But even if the infrastructure had been ready to cope with demand, the Army's own procurement systems would have created problems. In peacetime, each of the Army's supply bureaus—Ordnance, Quartermaster, Medical, Signal Corps, Engineers—had bought its own supplies on the open market (other than munitions manufactured in government arsenals), out of its own separate budget allocated by Congress. The bureaus were independent equally of one another and the General Staff, and there was no mechanism for coordinating their purchases. Often they found themselves buying the same articles, everyday items such as rope, motorcycles, linseed oil, machine tools, linen, leather, paint, stationery. When the Army had been 125,000 men strong, the system had worked; the economy had been big enough to absorb the Army's demands without dislocation or shortages. But now, suddenly, the handful of officers running the bureaus were issuing uncoordinated procurement orders amounting to billions of dollars that badly distorted the already overstretched economy.

Efficiency was threatened still further by the fact that the bureau chiefs had little idea of the precise size of the army they were notionally providing for, nor were they working toward any specific deadline. They had no idea what allowances they should make for reserves, wastage, or consumption. The General Staff, from whom the information should have come, had no central plan for reference; desperately understaffed, they were themselves waiting for guidelines from Congress, from various investigative missions that had been sent to Europe, and from Pershing. So the Gun and Carriage Division made its initial orders on the basis of 1 million men, while the Small Arms Division based its estimates on an army of 2.3 million.

In the crisis, each bureau chief did his duty as he saw it. The commandant of the Rock Island Arsenal admitted that when the war began he had gone out and bought up "practically all the equipment leather in the country. . . . I had it all. Well, that was wrong, you know, but . . . it was up to me to look after my particular job." Even the Adjutant General got into the act. One morning Baker arrived at the War Department to find typewriters piled up by the thousand. "I have them all. I have every free typewriter in the United States. I will not be caught short in typewriters." Defending their separate corners, the bureaus and the different war agencies used public money to outbid one another for scarce commodities.

The men on whom these enormous responsibilities devolved were far too few in number, and they were woefully inexperienced in business matters. In April 1917, the Ordnance Department had only ninety-seven officers; to supply an army on the scale envisaged by Pershing, it would need a hundred times that many—and new officers took two years to train. The Quartermaster's Groceries Section had only one officer, one inspector of produce, and five clerks when the war began.

These meager forces confronted a daunting range of tasks. The Quartermaster General's department as a whole was responsible for procuring

1,500 separate commodities from lawn sprinklers to beef (corned, roast, salt, and sliced canned), from shovels and puttees to fish (dried cod, canned salmon, and pickled mackerel). Men broke under the load, and the suicide rate in Washington rose to demoralizing heights in 1917.

Overloaded military bureaucrats with no commercial experience had to take on trust their contractors' ability to deliver; they could not supervise production nor even, in some cases, verify credentials. One construction company was awarded a contract on the basis of its estimate of $600,000. When the actual cost reached $15 million, the Quartermaster General's department discovered that the company had had no previous experience whatsoever but had been formed simply to tender for the job. Other companies took contracts they knew they could not fulfill.

The problems of mobilization were not confined to the War Department. The ship construction program had also gone disastrously off the rails. As manager of the Emergency Fleet Corporation, George Goethals had achieved a miracle of organization by May, when he put his construction plan to the President. But there it had languished. "The president continues his waiting policy," Goethals wrote to his son. "He's a peculiar type and runs everything." As time passed, the bullnecked shipping supremo inevitably fell out with the "hot air artists" on the Shipping Board and in particular with its head, William Denman. Goethals wanted the kind of independence and degree of control that Hoover possessed at the Food Administration and told his son that if he could not have it, he would "just throw up the whole thing."

In the end the matter was taken out of his hands. His fracas with the Shipping Board became public, to Wilson's embarrassment and anger, and both Goethals and Denman were replaced. In the ensuing chaos, the shipbuilding program, with its multiplicity of plans for steel, wooden, and even concrete ships, foundered. In August, Goethals visited his successor, Admiral Washington L. Capps, and found his desk "filled up with paper and telegrams which he lets lie around untended. . . . The contract division is all out of joint and growling, the legal division is broken up, the labor division is talking of disbanding, the naval architect is going back to New York. . . . The whole situation is sickening."

Aircraft procurement, too, was in crisis by year's end. The $640 million program launched with such fanfare had failed to put a single "winged crusader" into the air over the front. This was more of a disappointment than a surprise. In 1917, the country did not have an aeronautics industry worth the name. There were only twelve factories manufacturing airplanes, and the industry as a whole had barely the capacity to produce a thousand machines a year. Suddenly, it found itself being asked to make two thousand aircraft a month—and its failure was total.

The decision-making framework was partly to blame. There was no separate department for the air force and no unified policy on aerial warfare. Once the $640 million appropriation had been granted, civilians had to be recruited to direct the expansion program. The Council of National Defense formed a subsidiary body, the Aircraft Production Board, to supervise the purchase of materials and production of planes. It contained representatives of both the Army and Navy, but at its head was a civilian: Howard Coffin, president of the Hudson Motor Car Company. His background would have a crucial influence on the direction the American air program took.

As with guns, so with airplanes—America had to decide whether to design and produce her own models, to produce European models in her own factories, or to buy direct from the Allies. The Allies themselves reduced the appeal of one alternative: airplane designs were both militarily and commercially very valuable, and the French in particular were unwilling simply to send them over to America for copying. In several cases they wanted royalties before they would send their patents—a demand resisted by those who did not see why Americans should pay a license fee for the privilege of defending France.

So: to invent, or to buy? National pride or quick results? An investigative mission sent over to Europe in the summer of 1917 recognized that America was too far out of touch with the air war, too ill informed and geographically remote to keep up with the constant innovations in aircraft technology. Fighters in particular were at the cutting edge of technological development, evolving all the time. Here the Americans would have to order the latest models from the French, merely supplying the necessary raw materials.

The aircraft American factories could most realistically hope to produce were long-range bombers, trainers, and observation craft, whose designs remained comparatively constant. In the event, they chose to concentrate their efforts on one aircraft: the British de Havilland DH-4 reconnaissance bomber.

These aircraft were, however, to be powered by American engines. The "Liberty Engine" was designed in just four days in a hotel room in Washington, D.C., by J. G. Vincent of Packard Motors and E. J. Hall of the Hall-Scott Motor Company. The aim was simplicity and speed of production; the engine was an ingenious compound of already proven components and principles with no untried elements, and it lent itself well to mass-production methods.

This, at base, is why both the Liberty engine and the DH-4 were chosen—not because they were the best possible machines but because they seemed suited to each other and to the capabilities of the manufacturers who were so intimately involved in determining policy: automobile manufacturers, mostly, who were geared to standardization and mass production.

But disastrously, the techniques evolved for automobile production proved to be unsuited to the manufacture of aircraft. "An airplane engine is not simply a refined truck engine," one commentator pointed out. "Elements enter into flying two to ten thousand pounds of balanced, inert material that will not be bulled into space by simply machine force." Aircraft production, he felt, should be in the hands of a specialist designer and engineer. "He should also be a man who knows propellers. This latter item has almost been forgotten and today no reliable propeller exists that can safely be standardized for even one machine!"

American aircraft production was in the hands of unskilled laborers operating machinery according to the accepted methods of mass production; the Aircraft Production Board was expecting these men to carry out designs that had been prepared in Europe for execution by craftsmen working on a single machine at a time, drawing heavily on acquired skills and experience.

Both airframes and engines were slow in coming; the confident predictions of 22,000 planes a year began to seem ridiculous almost at once. (This would be the one area in which Creel was caught purveying undeniably false information, when the CPI declared that thousands of planes were on their way to the front and illustrated its generous claim with misleading photographs.)

When the machines did arrive, they proved to be a very mixed blessing. The quality of materials supplied and the standard of workmanship were often dangerously low. "In the first type of De Havillands manufactured in this country," Billy Mitchell later reflected, "many lives were uselessly lost due to lack of skill in workmanship and in the imperfections of the design of the plane and to the early unreliability of the Liberty motor. Flyers at the front were generally afraid of this plane." The Inspector-General's department recorded the comments of a pilot who had just had his fourth engine installed: "I don't mind getting killed if necessary, but we're just as apt to meet an unnecessary death as a necessary one, and it gets on our nerves to think about it every day."

Loose bearings, leaking radiators, rotten fabric, warped wings, short control wires, faulty magnetos, and engines assembled incorrectly made it hard for American pilots to acquire flying experience safely. In combat, the DH-4 proved murderous: it had unprotected gas tanks and a pressure-feed gas system—a lethal combination. French gas tanks were coated with asbestos-rubber that automatically sealed holes. If a bullet pierced the DH-4 tank, the pressure system forced gas through the hole and over the fuselage, where a single spark or tracer bullet would guarantee a horrible, fiery death for the crew and earned the plane its nickname: the "Flaming Coffin." Leading ace Eddie Rickenbacker flew missions to protect these craft with their "criminally constructed fuel tanks." During just one brief fight, he saw three go down in flames, an American pilot and gunner in each "coffin" "dying this frightful and needless death."

The Liberty engine, strong and reliable if it was properly assembled, was also crude and heavy, capable of racking a lighter plane to pieces. As a power plant, however, it was used successfully for trucks and tanks, and the Allies requested as many as Detroit could produce. Even this project became badly mired down; the engines were slow in arriving, which in turn badly delayed the output of Allied tanks.

Senator Chamberlain criticized individuals for inefficiency and failure, and both the Chief of Ordnance and the Quartermaster General were "promoted" to a supervisory board within the War Department. But the investigating committee recognized that the real problem lay at the foundations of the mobilization—in the White House and with the President. The nation's leaders had no way of bringing focus and efficiency to the war effort. If America were to have any impact at all on the war, the nation would have to be able to analyze its needs, fix its priorities, allocate the work and the relevant materials, regulate prices, draw up schedules and manufacture goods according to them, and transport and distribute the end products—all in the shortest possible time.

The Chamberlain committee and every one of Wilson's critics demanded once again a powerful centralized bureaucracy to take hold of every aspect of the mobilization. The president of the American Chamber of Commerce warned that "if further time is lost in planning to centralize control of the industrial energy and the material resources of the country, serious disaster is inevitable." Even the "seven wise men," the Advisory Commission appointed by Wilson to advise the Council of National Defense, had urged him in March 1917 to create a body "analogous to the Ministry of Munitions in England [to] take charge in a general way of all purchases for all departments of the Government."

But Wilson was still dead against this kind of superbureaucracy. Such an organization would most naturally be constituted from the leaders of American big business, and he refused to give them the opportunity to increase their influence over the economy. Already, 1917 had seen more corporate amalgamations than any year since 1902. To tolerate the emergence of a powerful "economic general staff" would be to give big business carte blanche to fix prices, to rationalize industries and control markets, to sculpt the economic landscape of America irreversibly.

War seemed to some to have made such abstract political ideals a luxury. But Wilson continued to work actively against centralization and coordination by maintaining the antitrust laws once mobilization was under way. The effects were often disastrous. Attorney General Gregory prosecuted coal mine operators in West Virginia for allegedly operating a cartel to keep prices high. With the case in the pipeline, businessmen all over the country delayed ordering coal in the belief that the price would fall. As demand slumped, so did production.

Wilson had acknowledged the importance of fuel to the mobilization by creating a Fuel Administration alongside the Food Administration. On August 23, he appointed Harry Garfield, a former colleague from Princeton, to be Fuel Administrator, responsible for maintaining supplies of coal and oil. Garfield, son of former President James Garfield, was an optimistic soul. In October, he wrote to his wife, Belle, "The world is still full of kindly, wholesome and amusing things—in spite of pain and suffering and war." But more than optimism was needed to solve the present crisis.

As soon as the Attorney General had lost his case in West Virginia (the judge blaming inflation, not conspiracy, for the price hike), Garfield raised prices to encourage mine operators to produce more coal. Then, with the help of the CPI, he began a campaign urging the public to use less: "COAL—the coal you are going without is forging the key to—

VICTORY." He preached the virtue of the "cool house," introduced "heatless days" and "lightless nights," appealed to people east of the Mississippi to observe "gasless Sundays." Non-war-related industries, from brick manufacturers to florists, were required to reduce fuel consumption by set percentages. And he tried a little moral blackmail on the miners, informing them that their failure to increase production would be reflected in the casualty lists. But it was too late. The lost production could not be regained. By November, the country was facing a 50-million-ton shortage for the following twelve months.

Wilson's stubbornness had an equally damaging effect on the transport system. The country's 397,014 miles of rail track were owned by a hodge-podge of 2,905 companies operating an inefficient net of competing lines. When the war began, these companies formed a coordinating committee but held back from rationalizing their operations to any meaningful extent for fear that they too might be accused of monopolistic practices. So there was no effective regulatory body to contain the crisis when it came.

The draft, the demand for railmen for France, and the pull of high wages in the munitions industry severely depleted the railways' labor force in 1917. As for rolling stock, the country had been 145,000 cars short even before the mobilization had gotten going, and poor planning had worsened the situation. Throughout the fall and into the winter, the War Department and other agencies blithely dispatched goods without any assurance that the cars could be unloaded into ships or warehouses at the other end. As the shipping shortage worsened and all available storage facilities filled up, cars began to tail back miles up the line from the ports. With the tracks congested, coal could not get through, ships could not be bunkered and leave, and the ports themselves clogged up.

By mid-January 1918, as winds blowing 50 miles per hour brought savage blizzards to the Northeast, the nation's transportation system was locked solid. On January 17, Garfield gave an order that the New York *World* considered "worthy of a Bolshevik government": he instructed all the factories in the Northeast to shut down for five consecutive days and on each Monday thereafter until further notice. All Senator Chamberlain's fears were realized. The war effort had indeed stalled. Even the loyal Colonel House was shaken:

> There is nothing that the Administration has done that I regret so much. . . . I look to see an instant demand that some change be made in

the organisation responsible for the conduct of the war. . . . Men of every shade of political opinion condemn the organisation as it now exists. The President and Secretary Baker seem to be the only ones that think the organisation is as it should be. . . . I do not think that [the President] has an effective war organisation.

18

"The War Is Practically Lost": Crisis on the Western Front

The mobilization crisis at home could not have come at a worse time. The world war was entering its most critical stage, and American arms were desperately needed in the line. The campaign of 1917 had drained the Allies' strength. In April, General Robert Nivelle had launched the disastrous attack on the Chemin des Dames ridge in Champagne that had broken the spirit of the French Army. There had been small successes at Vimy Ridge in April, in Messines in June, and in the Russian advance in the east launched in July; the Italians were also pushing hard against Austria through the summer. But then had come the catastrophic month of November, which opened with the shattering defeat of the Italians at Caporetto. Ludendorff had sent four divisions there just to "keep Austria on her legs"—but when his divisions spearheaded an attack, they broke through at once and pushed fifty miles through northern Italy to the Piave, capturing 300,000 prisoners and a third of the Italian Army's supplies and wiping out all the Italian gains of the war.

During those same weeks, the British were forced to call off their great offensive in Flanders, which they had hoped would win the war. Instead, the fighting around Passchendaele, the culmination of the third Ypres offensive, became a synonym for military ineptitude and pointless slaughter in the Flanders mud. Then, on November 20, hope flamed again as 381 British tanks burst through the Hindenburg Line before Cambrai—only to be doused by German counterattacks, which by the end of the month had almost entirely reversed the territorial gains and had obliterated the fleeting psychological advantage.

Worst of all, by the end of the year Russia had gone out of the war, free-ing Germany of the nightmare of war on two fronts. After the abdication of the Tsar in March 1917, a provisional government under Aleksandr Kerensky had taken power in Russia and fought on against Germany, warmly encouraged by America and the Allies. On July 4 in Petrograd, for example, John F. Stevens, heading the U.S. Railways Advisory Com-mission, issued a "Message to the People of Russia." To "cheer the nation and convince it that the United States stands shoulder to shoulder with its great ally," Stevens promised to ship over on credit 2,500 locomotives and 40,000 freight cars. But the help did not arrive in time, and by fighting on under Kerensky, Russia only propelled herself deeper and faster into the abyss of revolution.

With Ludendorff's active support, the Bolsheviks returned to Russia to subvert Kerensky's government by propagating an irresistible gospel: the triple promise of peace, food for the urban masses, and land for the peas-ants. During this critical period, the powerhouse in the Bolshevik move-ment was not Vladimir Lenin, who was absent for much of the summer of 1917 in Helsinki, but Leon Trotsky, who had come to Russia in March from the Bronx, where he had been a leading figure in socialist and anar-chist circles (besides studying the American economy closely in the New York Public Library). "Judging from what I see here," wrote an American observer in Petrograd, "I am convinced that the anarchist movement in the United States must be dead, they've all come over here. And they've been busy hating America at the top of their voices ever since."

Realizing that the Bolsheviks, if they came to power, would take Rus-sia out of the war, America and the Allies tried to fend them off by every possible means. The Root mission, to which John Stevens was attached, promised more material aid to the Kerensky government, while the CPI's Foreign Section began a campaign to raise Russia's morale and stiffen her backbone for the fight against Germany. Then, as the Bolsheviks' power grew, a committee was formed specifically to counter their propa-ganda and keep Kerensky in place. To Creel's puzzlement, the American ambassador was excluded from this committee. There had been a leak of information at the embassy, an informant explained, and suspicion rested on a woman named Matilda de Cramm. "I was surprised and disgusted," Creel recalled, "to find that the woman in question was supposed to be the Ambassador's mistress. . . . She helps the old man put his dispatches into code!"

In his place, Colonel William B. Thompson, though technically head of the (nonpartisan) American Red Cross in Petrograd, represented the War Department on the committee (besides giving a million dollars to the fighting fund). General W. V. Judson, head of the American Military Mission at Petrograd, estimated that this committee's efforts did indeed set back the Bolshevik coup and the withdrawal of Russia from the war for a crucial six weeks. Not until December 15, 1917, did Russia agree to an armistice with Germany.

With the guns now silent on the Eastern Front, America struggled to minimize the damage. The State Department gave General Judson a million dollars "for the purpose of purchasing supplies to prevent them falling into the hands of the enemy," and Colonel Thompson tried to postpone a formal peace between Germany and Russia, which would release yet more German troops for the Western Front. The Germans' greed helped Thompson in his mission. The Germans demanded vast territorial and economic concessions from the Russians, including control over Poland, Ukraine, and the Baltic provinces. Ludendorff then intended to exploit the food and raw materials of these regions to fuel the German war machine. The Allies feared he would also conscript the peasants: "The Germans are frankly pagan and opportunistic and will not hesitate to employ any methods that may be necessary. . . . Starvation and flogging, backed by machine-guns, soon produce the required effect in a community of illiterates with centuries of serfdom behind them."

Colonel Thompson saw Lenin and Trotsky daily and persuaded them that the Germans were asking too much and that the Russians could get better terms the longer they waited. He told them that "the United States would probably assist the Bolsheviks if they came to a final falling out with the Germans." Whether or not credit is due to Thompson, Lenin and Trotsky did delay—until Ludendorff forced them to sign the peace treaty by ordering fifty-two divisions to march on Petrograd.

But Germany's military survival in the west and triumph in the east had not been achieved without immense sacrifice—a net annual loss of 1,150,000 men, according to War Department estimates. This was a war of attrition, and the drain on German blood and treasure during 1917 had been enormous. These losses were more significant than ever before now that America was helping to cut off Germany's supply routes. Economic warfare had been an important element of the Allies' strategy since 1914, but their blockade had always resembled a leaking sieve, with goods from

America and other nonbelligerents filtering into Germany through neutral countries. From April 1917, the blockade became absolute as neutral countries were subjected to economic discipline.

The instrument of America's economic warfare was the War Trade Board (WTB), headed by the chairman of the Democratic Party, Vance McCormick, a shrewd operator and close friend of the President. The WTB had the power to control America's foreign trade, and its intelligence agents collaborated with their Allied counterparts in worldwide surveillance of trade and traders to keep vital supplies out of German hands. In league with the Alien Property Custodian, who was empowered to seize all American businesses owned by Germans or their sympathizers, McCormick was able to stop at the source the export of contraband either direct to Germany or indirectly via neutral countries. Such was the WTB's power and its knowledge of world trade that it was able not only to starve Germany but also to ration her neighbors, allowing them just enough food and basic supplies for their own populations and leaving none to travel discreetly over the borders.

"There is a considerable shortage at the moment of the most important war material of all kinds," Hindenburg noted bleakly. The U.S. War Department reported that the official ration for German civilians was "about one half of the normal requirement of a person engaged in a moderate amount of activity." People could survive only through the black market, and that created greed, corruption, and crime on a scale massive enough to tear German society apart. Starvation fed revolution, and in the winter of 1917 Germans listened avidly to the Bolshevik message, convincing Lenin that Germany would be an easier target for revolution than Russia.

Germany's rulers, both military and civilian, recognized that time was running out. Germany was sinking, while the Allies, sooner or later, would be buoyed up by American reinforcements. Ludendorff was forced to act: he would have to return to the offensive in 1918 and risk all by a series of heavy blows on the Western Front. Allied and American intelligence quickly picked up the new mood. On December 15, the General Staff warned of extensive German preparations for a large-scale onslaught along the Western Front in the spring. And the critical importance of the coming offensive was well understood: "The German internal situation is more critical than generally realized abroad and unless this offensive is successful, Germany will be compelled to seek the most favorable peace terms possible."

Ludendorff was gambling, but with Russia out of the war, the balance of power had tipped in his favor. In November, Germany had had 150 divisions on the Western Front; three months later, there were more than 190. Where in March 1917 there had been three Allied soldiers to every two Germans in France and Belgium, now there were four Germans to every three Allies. Douglas Haig noted that "all British Divisions were very weak and tired," with few drafts to bring them up to strength again. Nor was the French Army fully recovered from the mutinies following the Nivelle débâcle. Though in December the French assured Haig that their forces were back in harness, the truth was that France was nearly finished. Pétain confided to Bliss that the war had cost his country 2.6 million men killed, permanently disabled, or captured. At the end of November 1917, the total French combat strength on the Western Front stood at 1.1 million men divided into 100 divisions, with a further 8 divisions in Italy. Each division was 4,000 men short—"and they have no more," Bliss reported, "that they can or are willing to call out."

Italy too was virtually exhausted. After Caporetto, "Wully" Robertson told Bliss he doubted whether Italy could be held in the war during the coming winter. "Should she remain in, it would require the presence of considerable numbers of troops from the English and French forces on the Western Front to be maintained in Italy for the remainder of the war."

In Bliss's view, the crisis now facing the Allies could be blamed only in part on events in Russia and Italy. "It is also largely due to lack of military coordination, lack of military control on the part of the allied forces in the field." Remarkably, after three years of war, the Western Front had remained a patchwork of separate commands. There was no supreme authority to coordinate Allied forces, reserves, or supplies, nor to direct strategy. If the Allies continued to ignore the axiom of single command on the battlefield, then, Bliss warned somberly, "our dead and theirs may have died in vain."

After Caporetto, David Lloyd George had engineered a Supreme War Council, made up of Allied political leaders advised by chosen military experts. Wilson appointed Bliss as military representative but did not appoint a political representative because he was not prepared to relinquish his personal control over the political aspects of the war. Whatever the diplomatic repercussions of his gesture, the effect on the Allied war-fighting capability was minimal, for the Supreme War Council, despite its name, was at best a policy and planning body, not an organization for command and control in battle.

Weakened, divided, and facing a determined and numerically superior enemy, the Allies began to ask one pressing question: Where are the Americans? "We expected to see two million cowboys throw themselves upon the Boches," complained the French, "and we see only a few thousand workers building warehouses."

The American sacrifice had so far been minimal. Ten months into the war, 136 Americans had been killed in action. Another 134 had perished by accident, and five times that number had died of disease. As for the casualties they were inflicting in the heat of battle, when an American on leave in Paris ran over and killed a local, observers remarked sourly that the AEF seemed to be more ready to exterminate French than Germans.

At the turn of the year, the AEF numbered 9,804 officers and 165,080 men. Pershing had only four full divisions at his disposal so far—all regular army or National Guard. No soldiers would come from the new National Army being assembled in the training camps until the following April, a year after the declaration of war. The 41st Division (National Guard), elements of which arrived in France in December, was designated a replacement division. The four full divisions—the 1st and 2nd (regular), 26th and 42nd (National Guard)—were "combat" divisions, but in name only. None except the 1st could possibly be sent to the front line yet for any purpose except training.

The 26th Division, under its controversial commander, Major General Clarence "Daddy" Edwards, had arrived in September. Edwards was far more popular with his men than with his superiors; volatile, argumentative, intractable, he trod a fine line between independent initiative and outright insubordination. His men spent most of their first four months in France manning the lines of communication.

The 42nd Division had initially been designed as a propaganda showpiece. Secretary Baker, anxious that every state in the nation should identify equally with the war effort, wanted each to feel that its boys had been among the first to land "over there." Douglas MacArthur pointed out to him that most National Guard divisions had spare units that could be banded together in a composite formation that would be seen to "stretch over the whole country like a rainbow." The first elements of the "Rainbow Division," with MacArthur now its Chief of Staff, landed at the end of October. Almost at once it faced threats—but not from the enemy. Its commanders had to fight hard to prevent its being broken up to supply replacements for other units, thus instantly wiping out all its propaganda value. After initial training, units from the "Rainbow Division" entered the line in the care of the French 7th Army Corps in the Baccarat sector, near Luneville in the Vosges mountains, a very beautiful spot—and very quiet.

The 2nd Division, organized from regulars and marines during the last quarter of 1917, was initially under the command of Brigadier General Charles A. Doyen of the Marines and then under Major General Omar Bundy, not a man whom Pershing would respect for long. The infantry regiments spent their first weeks working on the lines of communication, and they were the last to enter the line for training—though their sector was a more active zone on the western side of the Saint-Mihiel salient. Here the division faced troops the French called the "Verdun Boche"— enemies who "seemed to inherit the aggressive spirit of the locality"—and they would suffer a continual toll from shelling, sniping, and raids.

As 1917 ended, only the 1st Division (regulars) had actually approached the realities of life on the Western Front, taking their first trophies, their first prisoners, their first casualties. In a large complex of training trenches they dug near Gondrecourt and called "Washington Center," they had struggled in the late summer and fall to learn the elements of trench warfare from the French Chasseurs Alpins. The "Blue Devils" taught them the use of the Chauchat automatic rifle, the Hodgkiss machine gun, and the grenade, and set them tactical problems.

Conditions could hardly have been more different from the desert heat and open, uninhabited terrain of the Mexican border, which had been the last posting for many of the 1st Division's regulars. A new approach was called for—and some found it hard to make the change. The French instructors admired their pupils' fighting spirit but had no faith in their efficiency. They paid too little attention to supply and liaison. They called for impossible artillery barrages. They failed to position their machine guns properly or space their waves of attack sensibly.

Perhaps with these reservations in mind, the French selected a very quiet sector near Sommerville for the 1st Division to receive its frontline training. Its infantry battalions were rotated up to the trenches in turn as parts of the French 18th Division, and the first battalions were in position in the line at dawn on October 21. The 1st Division's artillery brigade trained near the Swiss border, and on October 23, Battery C of the 6th Field Artillery fired America's first hostile artillery shot of the war. Where it landed is not recorded; but the gun was later sent to West Point and the shell case was presented ceremoniously to President Wilson. The Germans also marked the Americans' entry into the war. Here, on November 3, their raiders, anxious for information on the new enemy, made Gresham, Hay, and Enright the first American dead. Three weeks later, the 1st Division's infantry went back to Gondrecourt to train with its artillery and aviation as a combat division. The battalions had lost forty-three wounded and ten captured. They had inflicted unknown casualties and taken one prisoner.

Not until January 1918 was the 1st Division given a divisional sector—on the south side of the Saint-Mihiel salient. The zone was considered to be safe from a general attack, but it offered the 1st Division trench warfare at its worst. The front line lay along the bottom of a low valley, in a sea of mud. The main line of resistance, some two thousand yards back, lay on a ridge along which ran a busy road, neatly marked on the skyline by a double row of trees, that joined the various regimental headquarters and provided limited shelter for the divisional artillery drawn up along the ridge. German shells aimed at these pleasantly varied targets whistled over the heads of the frontline troops day and night, while the troops came under more direct fire from the enemy's position on Mont Sec, a conical hill rising high above the valley bottom and overlooking the entire sector, heavily fortified with tunnels, concrete dugouts, and observation posts.

Throughout these first months, Pershing and his staff at Chaumont were more preoccupied with problems of transport and supply than with getting their untrained troops into combat. They had to prepare for a vast army—though estimates showed that the projected 1 million men would be in France by the end of July 1918 only if the oceangoing tonnage available for military purposes was increased from its present 4.4 million tons to 7.7 million tons. And if America herself had to supply all this shipping, it would mean, according to Bliss, "a curtailment of our import trade to an amount of approximately fifty per cent."

Progress in France was slow, impeded by the growing chaos at home. Pershing, calling urgently for ammunition, pile drivers, truck engines, mule harnesses, boots, and winter clothing, was infuriated to find valuable shipping space wasted. "Recommend no further shipments be made of following articles," he cabled tersely. "Bath bricks, book cases, bath tubs . . . cuspidors, office desks, floor wax . . . step ladders, lawn mowers . . . settees, sickles, stools, window shades."

As for the articles Pershing did desperately need, to some extent he was able to procure them locally through his own agencies, which were coordinated by his close friend Charles Dawes (later Vice President and architect of the Dawes Plan). In Europe the AEF bought munitions, steel helmets, mules, horses, leather, and cork for insulating refrigeration plants. American Army engineers went into the French forests to cut the wood the AEF needed: 200 million board feet of timber, 4 million railroad ties, and thousands of timber pilings. The experts of the War Trade Board in Europe helped locate new sources of supply and used lucrative AEF contracts as a tool for economic and political warfare, to maintain stability and stimulate pro-Allied sentiment in neutral countries.

Even where suitable supplies were available, the AEF's logistical system in France was desperately weak. Before he could handle an army on the huge scale proposed, Pershing had to complete a number of massive construction projects: a new ten-berth port at Bassens, a sixteen-berth port at Montoir, and a rail bridge 2,190 feet long across the Loire. Then he needed to rebuild large tracts of the decrepit French rail network and equip it with 1,183 locomotives and 21,900 freight cars. And to supply his men on the battlefield, he needed miles of light-gauge railway, thousands of trucks, and 200,000 horses and mules. As matters stood early in 1918, even if he had had the fighting men he wanted, he would have been unable to amass and move forward the supplies they needed to sustain combat. The men-supplies-transport equation was one he would never completely solve.

To make matters worse, that winter in France, as at home, was one of the coldest in living memory. American soldiers faced subzero temperatures without adequate supplies of blankets, gloves, or overcoats. Some of the doughboys had no shoes that would fit and were marching through the snow and ice with rags wrapped round their feet. The 42nd Division was forced to make an epic forty-seven-mile march through a blizzard on Christmas Day 1917, and "many a foot left its red trail of blood in the snow." To Pershing's anger, allotments of winter clothing and blankets had been reduced because they were needed at home. "Weather conditions in France are far more severe than in southern part of United States," he telegraphed acidly. Rations were short, and as the reserves of forage petered out, the AEF's horses, still the locomotive power of the artillery and supply trains, began to die of starvation.

Depression hung over the divisions like a cloud. On December 13, Pershing wrote grimly to each of his division commanders, "Americans recently visiting our training areas and coming in contact with officers in high command have received a note of deep pessimism, including apprehension of . . . the great numbers of our enemy, and a belief in the impregnability of his lines . . . and generally have come away with an impression that the war is already well along toward defeat for our arms." The fault, he felt, lay mainly with his generals, and he warned them that anyone deficient in "the lofty attitude which should characterize the General that expects to succeed" should yield his position to another "with more of our national courage."

This letter was copied to Major General William Sibert, whom Pershing had relieved from the command of the 1st Division the previous day. Sibert was an engineer, reticent and undemonstrative, not at all the warrior type Pershing favored. Pershing undoubtedly considered his approach to be too negative, though when Sibert asked for a court of inquiry, Pershing claimed his relief had "no connection" with the warning about pessimism, which would be repeated to his successor. The real reason for his dismissal was more likely the slow progress of the 1st Division to combat readiness, underwritten by the list of defects in Sibert's leadership style that Pershing had been gradually compiling since July. "Slow of speech and of thought," he noted. "Slovenly in his dress. . . . Has an eye to his personal interests. . . . Utterly hopeless as an instructor or as a tactician. . . . Loyal as far as it suits his purpose. . . . Opinionated withal and difficult to teach."

Whatever his other advantages, the new commander was no more optimistic than Sibert. Robert Bullard was a tough, sinewy Alabaman who thought Pershing "soft"—but he too was soon confiding to his diary, "The war is practically lost. . . . Alas, I think we came too late."

19

American Dreams: Visions of Independence

With America's mobilization in disarray, the burden on the Allies' shoulders was heavy. "We shall be hard pressed to hold our own and keep Italy standing during 1918," David Lloyd George confided in a note to Lord Reading, now British ambassador in Washington. "Our manpower is pretty well exhausted. We can only call up men of 45–50, and boys of 17. France is done. The American soldiers will not be ready to fight as an army until late in 1918. Our experience proves that meanwhile we must keep the fight going."

And to keep it going, the Prime Minister naturally had a plan: American soldiers must be brought directly into the ranks of the Allied armies. England and France had the infrastructure to train and equip more men than they could conscript in their own countries, and once again they pressed both the administration in Washington and Pershing in France to permit American troops to be combined with their own at the small-unit level.

The orders given Pershing in May 1917 had insisted that the identity of American forces should be preserved. In the face of Allied pressure, however, Newton Baker modified his instructions, cabling Pershing that the desire to maintain an independent identity was "secondary to the meeting of any critical situation." Now, amid the deepening gloom on the Western Front, the onus was on Pershing to make perhaps the most critical decision of the American war effort to date.

On January 2, 1918, he replied to Baker, "Do not think emergency now exists that would warrant our putting companies or battalions into

British or French divisions." It was a bold decision; Pershing was with-
holding the only immediate help that America could give. But his assessment of the situation was not perhaps as foolhardy as his critics suggested.
Marshal Joffre himself assured Pershing, a fellow Freemason, that as the
Germans had not been able to break through in 1914 when they had
greatly superior forces, they were unlikely to do so now. And for all their
public protestations, in private neither Haig nor the British War Cabinet
was convinced that Ludendorff would succeed in 1918.

During the winter months, the Allied leaders seem to have been trying
to use the impending threat of a German offensive as a lever to divert
America from her central purpose of forming an independent army. In
calling so loudly for American drafts, Lloyd George may also have had an
ulterior motive: to release British troops from the Western Front so they
could defend Britain's possessions in the Middle East. But whatever the
reasons, the pressure for amalgamation failed: Pershing never for a moment lost sight of the objective of an American army fighting its own campaign under its own flag.

Nor in the Navy, despite Sims, was there a general readiness to abandon America's independence. "My first thought in the beginning, during,
and always," wrote Admiral William Benson after the war, "was to see
first that our coasts and our own vessels and our own interests were safe-
guarded. Then . . . to give everything we had . . . for the common cause."
On this basis, he argued fiercely that the Navy must give a higher priority
to transporting American troops than to convoying food supplies to
Britain.

In Benson's view of grand strategy, the powerful American navy to be
built under the 1916 legislation was a weapon less for immediate action
than for long-term diplomacy and defense against future conflicts. He
wanted the Navy to be second to none after this war—whoever won. Germany might be the present enemy, but Britain was equally likely to be the
major rival for naval domination after the war, and America feared Japan
as well. Officially, Japan was allied to England, but she had joined the war
in order to capture German possessions in Asia and to tighten her already
cruel grip on China, which was in chaos after the collapse of the Manchu
Dynasty. In the Navy Department the prospects of war with Japan were
openly discussed; from Benson's perspective, whatever the Navy did now
must be done with a view to preserving its own independent strength for
afterward.

Sims, on the contrary, saw the Navy as a weapon to be used to the full in the present war. He was swayed by his instincts as an officer actually in the field, bound by military imperatives, and by his loyalty to other field officers. But those officers were in the Royal Navy, and his superiors were quick to accuse him of kowtowing to British imperialist interests. "Don't let the British pull the wool over your eyes," warned Benson. "It is none of your business pulling their chestnuts out of the fire. We would as soon fight the British as the Germans."

America's assertive independence in military and naval affairs reflected real differences that had existed between the New World and the Old in the neutrality period and even before 1914. America had increasingly been engaging in economic competition with the Allies all over the globe, and in some areas the war had barely interrupted the trend. By early 1917, *The New York Times* was warning, "Growth of Britain's trade with South America in cotton goods and other manufactured products even in wartime points to the competition that must be faced after the declaration of peace." William McAdoo, perpetually alive to the competition underlying America's relations with the Allies, forbade the Allies to spend federal money anywhere except in the United States, in order to boost the domestic production capacity.

Elsewhere the pressure of war forced some community of interest. By the turn of the year, the United States had joined a multiplicity of Allied boards and committees dedicated to the international control of war resources: munitions, wheat, rubber, wool, shipping. These were valuable instruments in the economic battle being waged against Germany and could be used to discipline neutral nations that tried to exploit war conditions. Chile, for example, was virtually the sole source of essential nitrates for the Allies and America. Speculators there tried to drive up the price but were stopped dead by a cartel organized through the international Nitrates Executive.

But regardless of the efforts at economic cooperation, there remained an unbridgeable gulf between the fundamental war aims of the Allies and those of the United States. At the outset President Wilson had deliberately steered clear of formal alliance with Britain and France in order to pursue his independent aims, closing his eyes to the objectives he knew them to have agreed on already. In April, just after America had joined the war, British Foreign Secretary Arthur Balfour had mentioned that the Allies had already reached certain agreements and understandings for the eventual disposal of their enemies' possessions—but Wilson had silenced him and forbidden House and McAdoo to listen to and relay the details of these agreements. Ignorance was some defense, albeit an unworthy one.

Unfortunately, fate would not allow Wilson to continue to avert his face this way. On November 8, 1917, Vladimir Ilich Lenin, a short, stocky figure "with a big head set down on his shoulders, bald and bulging," appeared before an excited, roaring crowd in Petrograd. As John Reed recalled:

> His great mouth, seeming to smile, opened wide as he spoke. . . . "We shall now proceed to construct the Socialist order! . . . The first thing is the adoption of practical measures to realize peace. . . . We shall offer peace to the peoples of all the belligerent countries upon the basis of the Soviet terms—no annexations, no indemnities, and the right of self-determination of peoples. At the same time, according to our promise, we shall publish and repudiate the secret treaties."

These "secret treaties" were the very agreements and understandings that Wilson was trying to ignore. They made unsavory reading. England and France greedily apportioned the Ottoman Empire and Germany's colonies in Africa, while Italy's price for joining the war in 1915 on the side of the Allies was revealed as including the Trentino, the southern Tyrol, Trieste, and various holdings around the Adriatic, plus a share of German Africa.

As for the German homeland itself, Russia (then still ruled by the Tsar) had promised to "accord entire freedom to France and Great Britain as regards the fixing of the western frontiers of Germany, counting that those allies will accord Russia equal liberty in the establishment of her boundary with Germany and Austria." France wanted more specific assurances than this, so Russia had obligingly agreed that the left bank of the Rhine should be separated from Germany and made into an autonomous, neutral state, to be occupied by France until Germany had completely satisfied the terms of the peace treaty that would end the war.

Until Lenin's démarche, Wilson's strategy for ensuring that his world vision would prevail had been to wait until Germany was defeated. By then, he hoped, America would be in a position of such economic and military strength that he would be able to bend the Allies to his will whatever their previous arrangements, which need not be acknowledged. But now the Bolsheviks had forced his hand by dragging the Allies' war aims before him, offering their own alternative of unilateral peace, and making it necessary for him to state his own position.

Wilson and House agreed it had become imperative "to return some sort of reply to [the Bolsheviks'] demand for a logical statement of why the war should continue." Wilson must repudiate the secret treaties and put something worthier in their place, pledging the Allied governments, if he could, to "the principles of a settlement which would justify the sacrifices of the war and maintain the enthusiasm of the liberal and labor circles in Britain and France"—circles he would have seen as his natural constituency.

Certainly, a broad spectrum of public opinion in the Allied countries had been swayed by Lenin's appeal for peace, seeing little justification for sacrificing blood and treasure to achieve the sleazy objectives of the secret treaties. "Reports of increasing unrest in Great Britain are reaching us," military intelligence noted; "50,000 aeroplane and munitions workers in England have been on strike since November 26. There is no sign of settlement as yet. . . . Mr. Hudson, the former labor member of the Cabinet, is traveling through England advocating peace."

The pressure forced Lloyd George to readjust Britain's public war aims. On January 5, 1918, he delivered to the Trades Union Congress a speech based, as Balfour explained to Wilson, on "declarations hitherto made by the President on this subject." Indeed, when the text arrived in Washington that afternoon, phrase after phrase evoked Wilson's past pronouncements: "the sanctity of treaties," "territorial settlement based on the right of self determination or the consent of the governed," and an "international organization to limit the burden of armaments and diminish the probability of war."

The gap between the British and American objectives seemed to be closing. But even as he justified the war on one set of grounds, Lloyd George was exploring the possibility of making peace on another. Privately, even Haig was reasoning that there was little to be gained and a great deal to be lost by continuing the war. At the end of another twelve months' fighting, Haig felt, "we would be much more exhausted and our industrial and financial recovery would be more difficult, and America would get a great pull over us."

Lloyd George agreed, and in the Russian situation he saw a means both of silencing Lenin and of ending the war. It had occurred to him, pragmatist that he was, that Germany might accept a peace by which she surrendered her conquests in the west and made other concessions in exchange for a free hand in Russia. After all, he reasoned, "the Russians had acted badly and must take the consequences."

But Wilson was not interested in a compromise peace, certainly not one bought at such a ruthless price. To him there was "a voice calling for . . . definitions of principle . . . thrilling and more compelling than any of the many moving voices with which the troubled air of the world is filled. It is the voice of the Russian people. They are prostrate and all but helpless . . . before the grim power of Germany." Wilson seems at this point to have regarded Bolshevism as less of a threat than Prussian militarism to the development of democracy in Russia. Indeed, he intended to use American power to release the Bolsheviks from German exploitation. In a real sense, his defense of Russia—Bolsheviks and all—at this critical point made him the godfather of what was to become the Soviet Union.

It was not enough for Wilson simply to distinguish his position from that of Lloyd George. America must deliver an answer to Lenin; the continuation of the war must be justified on American grounds. Since September 1917, a War Data Investigation Bureau (known as the "Inquiry"), staffed by Walter Lippmann and other loyal Wilsonians, had been gathering material for the President's use when the precise terms of peace would be debated. Called in now to advise, the Inquiry recommended that the President launch a "powerful liberal offensive," setting out the terms upon which America would accept peace. This would win him the leadership of liberal opinion in Britain and France, important support to have at the war's end. It would also, the Inquiry hoped, "assure the Administration the support of the great mass of the American people who desire an idealistic solution."

On the afternoon of Friday, January 4, 1918, Colonel House traveled to Washington from New York to discuss the proposals drafted by the Inquiry. "I did not reach the White House until nine o'clock. They had saved dinner for me, but I touched it lightly and went into immediate conference with the President." By 12:30 P.M. the next day, they had finished "remaking the map of the world."

On January 8, Wilson presented Congress with a program of fourteen points. "God only needed ten," remarked Premier Clemenceau, sourly. But to the peoples of a world dissolving in blood, the program had an aura of grandeur and held the promise of a deliverance they had begun to think was impossible. With the help of Creel's mechanisms for projecting the voice of America abroad, Woodrow Wilson became the most famous man on the planet, his picture pinned up at family shrines all over the globe.

"We demand," he said, "that the world be made fit and safe to live in," and he set out "the only possible program." First, and most pointed, there should be "no private international understandings of any kind." (Specifically, he called for the evacuation of all Russian territory and "an unhampered and unembarrassed opportunity for the independent determination of her own political development"—a fairly unequivocal snub to Lloyd George.) Second—another shaft aimed at Britain—there should be "absolute freedom of navigation upon the seas . . . alike in peace and in war." He went on to call for the removal of all economic barriers and the establishment of "an equality of trade conditions among all the nations." And he insisted upon the reduction of national armaments "to the lowest point consistent with domestic safety."

Several articles dealt with the details of postwar territorial adjustments. All colonial claims must be decided impartially. Belgium and northern France, including Alsace-Lorraine, must be restored. Italy's frontiers should be readjusted. The peoples of Austria-Hungary and the Ottoman Empire should be given the opportunity of entirely autonomous development, the Turks should be guaranteed secure sovereignty, and all the nations should give guarantees of the political and economic independence of the Balkan states. An independent Polish state should be created, with free access to the sea.

Last, the President identified the means through which all the other points might be secured. The old system of power balances must be replaced by a new system of community of interests: "A general association of nations must be formed under specific covenants for the purpose of affording mutual guarantees of political independence and territorial integrity to great and small states alike."

These were not simply America's war aims. In Wilson's eyes, there ran through his Fourteen Points a universal "principle of justice." All peoples, he insisted, had the right to live on equal terms of liberty and safety with one another, whether they were strong or weak. And he reaffirmed the pledge he had made to the world in his war address: "The people of the United States could act upon no other principle; and to the vindication of

this principle they are ready to devote their lives, their honor, and everything they possess. The moral climax of this the culminating and final war
for human liberty has come."

It seems likely that on the day he delivered this address, Wilson felt his
life had found its ultimate purpose. He believed, as he had written in
1908, that the United States was destined to assume the leadership of the
world—that the President himself was "one of the greatest powers of the
world," holding the initiative in foreign affairs in a country that had now
risen to the first rank in power and resources. At this "midday hour of the
world's life," it was ordained that he, Woodrow Wilson, should exercise
this astonishing power on behalf of "the common people of the world" who
recognized that the old armed diplomacy was bankrupt. And to carry out
this mission, he was empowered to sacrifice the lives and wealth of his
countrymen.

With the mobilization grinding to a halt around him and his soldiers
fearing the worst in France, Wilson's pronouncements during early January were remarkable—"one of the great documents in American history,"
the New York *Tribune* called one utterance, "and one of the permanent
contributions of America to world history." To others, however, his remarks seemed in the circumstances to be positively mystical. Psychoanalysts and physicians have repeatedly tried to explain his behavior. Sigmund
Freud regarded him as "psychotic." More recently, Edwin Weinstein has
suggested that he was suffering from progressive arteriosclerosis accompanied by a series of strokes of increasing severity but that he responded to
his illness by burying it under a manic determination to reach his goals.

Leaving aside all consideration of the moral and practical validity of the
Fourteen Points, Wilson's personal behavior in delivering them was odd
and extreme. He did not consult his Cabinet over the Fourteen Points
speech—"the limit of humiliation," in Secretary Lane's view, "as far as
the Cabinet was concerned." He did not even tell Congress he was going
to speak until the last moment. Colonel House appears to have been
alarmed by the extremism of some of the remarks he was making privately
at this time. "The President has started so actively on the liberal road that
I find myself, instead of leading as I always did at first, rather in the rear
and holding him back." Most disconcertingly, Wilson told House that he
"did not believe the Democratic Party could be used as an instrument to
go as far as it would be needful to go." What was needed, he suggested,
was a new political party to achieve his objectives.

. . .

Wilson, Pershing, Benson—all cherished dreams of America standing apart and triumphing entirely through her own efforts on the world stage. These dreams grew out of a particular vision of America's character, standing, and capabilities—a vision of the future that would be unable to withstand the grim pressure of the present. But as Wilson conjured up the images of a new political force in America, a new international role for her President, and a new world order, events on the Western Front were rushing away from him.

Part Five

INTO BATTLE

20

Ludendorff Attacks:
Spring 1918

At 4:40 A.M. on Thursday, March 21, a "crushing, smashing power" woke General Sir Hubert Gough, commanding the British 5th Army on the Somme, with brutal suddenness. A forty-three-mile stretch of the British line had come under the heaviest bombardment of the war, a devastating barrage launched by 6,473 German guns and 3,532 trench mortars. The hail of death fell for four and a half hours with appalling accuracy. Frontline trenches and their occupants simply evaporated; in the rear areas, the headquarters, artillery positions, strong points, lines of communication, and munitions dumps were wrecked by high explosives and saturated with gas. By 9:30 A.M., the British line was a smoking ruin, its defenders dead, maimed, or stunned. And then Ludendorff unleashed his storm troopers.

If the power and precision of the artillery barrage had come as a surprise, so did the tactics employed by these shock troops. During the winter, Ludendorff had effectively reconfigured his army. The best of his men he had put into "assault divisions," consigning the rest—a motley crew of the underaged, the middle-aged, and the semi-invalid—to "trench divisions." He had then taken the assault divisions and armed and trained them to exploit the opportunities that would be created by the devastating artillery barrage. Lavishly supplied with automatic weapons and flamethrowers, the storm troops were ordered to infiltrate the enemy lines. Each unit was to push on independently, utilizing the terrain and bypassing strong points. Behind them would come heavy machine guns and field artillery to support the advance, then more heavily equipped units to mop up the strong points.

Most startling of all after the years of attrition, Ludendorff had again inspired his army with a belief in itself. "The whole thing can only be compared with the gigantic general mobilisation of 1914," exulted artillery-man Herbert Sulzbach. "After years of defence on the Western Front, Germany is moving to the attack; the hour eagerly awaited by every soldier is approaching." On that March morning, the Germans were ready to meet Ludendorff's call for aggression, initiative, speed, and self-sacrifice.

Wreathed in gas, smoke, and a heavy mist, his specially trained divisions launched a human blitzkrieg. The tactics worked to perfection, and they stabbed through the enemy line like the fingers of a steel-clad hand. The British, by now unused to fighting anywhere except from their trenches, were routed. Desperately, their officers tried to shore up the defenses. At a rail depot, in the path of the storm troopers' advance, was a three-hundred-strong detachment from an American railroad regiment. They were soldiers in name only—civilian railroad engineers who had come to France to help restore the decrepit French rail system, not to train for combat. Nevertheless, when the British called for help, the Americans found some abandoned machine guns—a weapon none had ever fired before—and fought back.

Ludendorff's divisions had broken through at the point in the line where the British and French fronts joined. Now the Allies would pay the price for having no supreme commander—for having failed even to agree to form an Allied reserve. Haig appealed to the French commander in chief, Henri Pétain. They met on the night of March 24, but Pétain, whose armies were not even under attack, looked like a defeated man. He told Haig he intended to wheel his line back to cover Paris.

"Do you mean to abandon my right flank?" Haig asked disbelievingly. Pétain nodded. "It is the only thing possible." The man who had whispered, as the first Americans arrived, "I hope it is not too late," was on the verge of turning his own gloomy forebodings into fact by parting the wall of flesh and iron shielding France and allowing Ludendorff to strike where he wished.

Haig now realized that he could no longer rely on his previous loose arrangement with Pétain for "mutual support," and he did what Bliss and Pershing had been pushing the Allies to do since November: he urged the appointment of a supreme commander on the Western Front to consolidate authority, resources, and strategy. On March 26 at Doullens, a small town on the Somme in the path of the German advance, the British and French signed an agreement appointing Ferdinand Foch to "coordinate the action of all the allied armies on the western front." And the Allies indicated their disregard for Pershing by not even informing him that this meeting was taking place.

"Un bon cadeau!" said Foch in response to his appointment. "You give me a lost battle and tell me to win it." But few generals were better equipped to take charge in such a crisis. A tiny, ebullient, energetic man, Foch was the ultimate optimist, an intelligent soldier and sound strategist. Haig admired him deeply as "a man of great courage and decision" who had proved his mettle in 1914, during the very first German offensive. He was a soldier's soldier, but he was also politically astute. His elevation to supreme command brought into the arena a man who could be as devious as the politicians when it suited him and who could use military strategy for political ends. In the complex, volatile alliance now existing on the Western Front, Foch was a useful tool for Premier Georges Clemenceau, and a new foil for Pershing.

After hearing of Foch's elevation on March 26, Pershing motored over to Clermont-sur-Oise to repeat the offer he had made to Pétain the day before—to put his handful of divisions at the disposal of the French command. The military benefit was small, but the gesture was the basis of a propaganda *coup de théâtre*. Soon all France read of "Pershing's pledge": "Infantry, artillery, aviation, all that we have are yours; use them as you wish. More will come in numbers equal to requirements. . . . The American people will be proud to take part in the greatest battle of history."

A flourish such as this could and did stiffen the French backbone, but it could not affect the progress of the battle. By March 28, the marauding storm troopers had captured 1,100 guns, taken 70,000 prisoners, and inflicted 185,000 casualties on the British and French. On the southern flank of the attack, the Germans swept clean through the line and were denied a major strategic victory only by the French reserves sent in by Foch and the resilience of the British, defending their stronghold of Arras to the north against the German battering.

The situation remained critical. On April 3, a second conference was held to discuss extending Foch's authority. This time Pershing was invited, and he urged the Allies to cooperate. "The principle of unity of command is undoubtedly the correct one for the Allies to follow. . . . I am in favor of a supreme commander and believe that the success of the Allied cause depends on it." It is possible that the Allied representatives did not care for his lofty tone. To Pershing's anger, they promptly drafted a resolution giving Foch "the strategic direction of military operations" and omitting to mention the AEF.

"I think this resolution should include the American Army," protested Pershing, to which Pétain retorted baldly, "There is no American Army as such." "There may not be an American army in force functioning now," Pershing replied grimly, "but there soon will be." He had his way, and the agreement was amended accordingly.

In the field, the Germans pushed on, but their momentum was perceptibly decreasing. Here at the southern end of their front, though the Allied troops were spread thin and vulnerable to blitzkrieg, there was nothing of strategic importance behind the lines until Amiens, a vital rail and communications center fifty miles away. Haig had room to allow his men to retreat—and Ludendorff lacked the means to catch them.

Once his storm troopers were through the enemy lines, there was little technology, apart from aircraft, to support their advance. The Army had few trucks, so the soldiers had to carry their own supplies on their backs; the surviving horses and mules were so debilitated that they had difficulty pulling the guns forward. Most tragic of all from the German perspective was the lack of any capability for rapid pursuit. There were no light tanks. The Army did have cavalry, and the retreating British infantry anxiously scanned the horizon for the glint of drawn sabers; but Ludendorff's mounted divisions were all in Russia, unavailable at a moment when their shock effect could have shattered Haig's command.

As the days and nights passed, the German lead troops became exhausted. They had outpaced their supporting arms, and their supplies were running low. Morale began to crumble, and troops who had fought with extraordinary skill and courage began to give in to the temptation to loot and malinger. They were struck dumb by the riches they discovered in the supply dumps and towns they captured—not simply food, forage, weapons, and clothes but medical supplies of almost unimaginable superiority. In the German Army, crepe paper had long replaced linen bandages. "Instead of cotton wool," one medical orderly remembered, "we used a kind of cellulose paper which in no time got soaked in blood and pus and just dissolved into a wet, stinking mess." Hungry after days in combat, the storm troopers fell like wolves on the food and drink and rapidly passed beyond the control of their officers. Tipsy, their weapons discarded so they could carry off more booty, they lost interest in the fight.

On April 5, Ludendorff abandoned the offensive and, as he had always planned, switched his attention north to Flanders and the Channel ports. The magnificent lateral communications behind the German line enabled him to concentrate men and matériel rapidly and with great flexibility at chosen points for attack or defense, and to bring up reserves to exploit success. On April 9 he launched his second assault, this time against the British First and Second Armies on a narrow front between Armentières and Béthune, east of the Lys River. Again he had chosen his point of attack brilliantly. The weak Portuguese division in his path was brushed aside, and the vital ports supplying the entire British Army were threatened as the storm troopers poured forward.

Haig saw this attack on the Lys as the greatest crisis so far. On April 11, he issued an exhortation to his men: "Every position must be held to the last man: there must be no retirement. With our backs to the wall, and believing in the justice of our cause, each one of us must fight on to the end." He meant this literally: he was not going to evacuate his armies from France. He knew this was part of Ludendorff's final offensive, and he meant to meet the challenge. His men would hold, or they would die where they stood.

And the British line held. Worn by the overextended offensive on the Somme, the German machine lacked some of the penetrative power it had possessed only weeks before. For their part, the British were fighting more stubbornly now. Close to the coast—a mere twenty-five miles or so from Dunkirk—there was no longer room for a tactical retreat, and they gave ground only when absolutely compelled to do so. By April 29, Ludendorff's second great offensive had come to a halt.

But the Allies were not yet safe. Ludendorff still had men and resources, and he held the initiative. Now he ordered a third attack, a strictly limited push across the Aisne toward Paris to draw in the Allied reserves. This feint was to be followed by what was intended to be a final blow in Flanders to drive the British into the sea and end the war. But this time the pieces of the jigsaw failed to fall into place, and in the gap between Ludendorff's plans and the reality, Pershing and his soldiers would find their foothold in the war.

In those crisis days, the Allies saw salvation in American manpower. Ludendorff had inflicted 350,000 casualties on the British and French in his first two assaults, and there would clearly be many more when he attacked again. The Allies were not broken, but they faced an acute manpower shortage. Frantically, Lloyd George cabled President Wilson: THE DEFICIENCY MUST BE MADE GOOD BY AMERICAN TROOPS IF WE ARE TO MAKE CERTAIN OF HOLDING THE ENEMY. Britain could raise 400,000 to 500,000 men, he said, "by taking boys of eighteen, by raising the military age to fifty," but this would take time, and Haig would be dangerously short of men during the summer months.

But even at this moment of crisis, Lloyd George had lost none of his cunning. He still had no wish to receive integral divisions from the Americans; he wanted only infantry and machine-gun troops that Haig could amalgamate with British units. In this way alone, he insisted, could the hundreds of thousands of trained or partially trained men now in the United States be "made available."

Once again the full weight of the Allied High Command, bent on amalgamation, bore down on Pershing's shoulders. Even Tasker Bliss, believing the situation to be desperate, had joined the other military representatives on the Supreme War Council in urging this policy of feeding troops into the Allies' armies. Now he went further and individually endorsed Lloyd George's message: "I have carefully considered the Prime Minister's despatch and I fully concur in the action recommended by him."

Pershing, however, held firm. "A better procedure," he countered, "would be for the Allies to amalgamate their weakened divisions into a lesser number and let the American divisions take their proper places in the line." He added trenchantly, "I am prepared to put the American divisions in the line as fast as they arrive."

The Allies' fury beat down on Pershing. "You are willing to risk our being driven back to the Loire?" inquired Foch in outrage. "Yes, I am willing to take the risk," replied Pershing. "The time may come when the American Army will have to stand the brunt of this war, and it is not wise to fritter away our resources in this manner."

"America declared war independently of the Allies and she must face it as soon as possible with a powerful army," he insisted—and despite the Allies' scheming and Bliss's apparent disagreement, neither the President nor Secretary Baker was about to overrule Pershing. In the aftermath of the winter chaos, Wilson was already under quite enough pressure at home without it being suggested that the AEF was incapable of contributing independently to the defense of the Western Front.

Nevertheless, Pershing was shrewd as well as stubborn, and he realized that he could gain by unbending a little. American ships could carry no more than 52,000 men a month across the Atlantic; if he were ever to realize his ambition of an independent American Army in France, he would need access to British transports and merchant vessels. He therefore agreed that from the available divisions in the United States, the British could ship 120,000 infantry and machine gunners over per month—without artillery or supply trains. These incoming troops would stay, as Haig wanted, on the British section of the front for "training and service" though still be available to Pershing on demand.

The British seem to have hoped that this arrangement would compel amalgamation, because the American combat troops would have to form part of British organizations if they were to be supplied and used in battle. But Pershing, who was perfectly alert to the danger, extracted three crucial concessions. First, he guaranteed the units' American divisional identity by insisting that their signals, engineer, and headquarters staff accompany them. Though few in number, the staff officers in particular gave each division coherence—and if Pershing had identifiable divisions, he could at a suitable moment recall them from service with the British and assemble them in corps and armies under the Stars and Stripes.

Then he demanded that if any troops were to come over in excess of the agreed number, they must be of the types designated by him: artillery and supporting units or specialist troops for his lines of communication. Finally, Pershing compelled the Allied leaders formally to acknowledge that "in order to carry the war to a successful conclusion, an American Army should be formed as early as possible under its own commander under its own flag."

Inevitably, a deal like this, made in haste under the threat of Ludendorff's continuing assaults, was a compromise. Neither party had gotten precisely what it wanted. Pershing was prevented from building up his logistical infrastructure to keep pace with the growth of his army. He knew that at all times during the coming summer and fall he would be dependent on the Allies for transportation and artillery. By the spring of 1919, a balanced force, a genuinely independent American Army, might exist, but not until then.

The Allies, for their part, had permanently forgone the chance of acquiring American troops to flesh out their horrifyingly depleted divisions. But at least American combat troops were coming—the proof was everywhere to be seen. At the end of March 1918, the AEF numbered 318,000 men; at the end of April, 430,000; and at the end of May, 650,000.

Given the chaos into which the country and the War Department in particular had been plunged at the turn of the year, it was remarkable that the United States was able to ship this number of men. The credit was due to one of the forgotten heroes of this war, the Chief of Staff appointed to pull the war effort into shape: Peyton March.

A towering, austere man with a steel-trap mind, March was one of the leading voices among the new modern, professional breed of officers. The problems facing the new chief after a year of mismanagement would have daunted lesser men. March, a wiry, ruthless administrator, imposed his authority at once, eliminating from his new organization anyone who fell short in the slightest degree. He spoke his mind coldly and ignored criticism: "One is proud to be hated, if it is a consequence of doing one's work well."

His vision of modern professionalism was one he had acquired outside the United States. In 1904, he had been the American observer attached to the Japanese Army as it defeated the Russians in a campaign east of Lake Baikal. The Russo-Japanese War had brought March face to face with twentieth-century warfare, in particular the crucial need for centralized direction of all aspects of an army through an efficient and dominant General Staff.

When he arrived at the War Department in February 1918, he had absolutely clear ideas as to what was required. "The conception of a true General Staff which I had acquired in my observation of [the Japanese] General Staff in operation in the field in Manchuria formed the basis of the orders which I issued in the reorganisation of our own General Staff." He was not blind to the irony of the situation: the Japanese version was "in its essence, a complete copy of the German General Staff Corps"—the modern Japanese Army having been built with the help of a Prussian officer, Jacob Meckel.

The American Army needed modern, albeit Prussian, methods if it were to defeat Prussianism. A mass army could not operate through a labyrinth of checks and balances and divided authority, however democratically inspired. For March, the only organization for the Army was a strict hierarchy with authority flowing from the top—and this also applied to the supply bureaus, whose independence had almost succeeded in crippling the war effort. But though March provided the vision, in his first months in the job he was fully occupied with the urgent problems of building the Army and getting men to France. Thus the huge task of rationalizing procurement fell primarily to George Goethals, who had returned to the General Staff after the débâcle at the Emergency Fleet Corporation.

Empowered by legislation to "coordinate and consolidate executive agencies," Goethals applied copybook management-consulting reforms. Consolidating purchases; standardizing army matériel, contracts, and requisitioning and commandeering procedures; introducing statistical analysis and modern accounting methods; creating an internal "Committee on Priorities" to resolve conflicts among the various supply bureaus—his innovations took many forms, and all headed toward the eventual abolition of the bureau system.

It was, however, not plain sailing: "The Bureau chiefs are agin it," Goethals confided to his son. March helped by replacing some of the old bureau heads with younger men, and they were prepared to cooperate with Goethals and with one another—up to a point. Where specialist equipment was concerned, none would trust anyone else. The Surgeon General objected bitterly to any department but his own buying X-ray machines, while the Chief of Engineers wanted to restrict the purchase of items such as timber piling for piers to his experts. But Goethals was adamant. By July 19, there had been fifty meetings to rationalize procurement, and by August 6 there remained "only five more consolidations to be effected." By the end of the year, the bureaus themselves would have been merged and the whole task of supply centralized.

March's insistence on a logical hierarchy inevitably brought him into conflict with Pershing. "My sole desire," Pershing had told him on May 5, "is to establish the fullest cooperation between you and me. You can count on me to do my best to play the game." But March, it seemed, was playing by different rules; the foundation stone of military efficiency was authority, not cooperation.

Tasker Bliss, during his tenure as Chief of Staff, had been happy to coast along as "assistant to Pershing's chief of staff," implicitly conceding priority to the man in the field. March, on the contrary, now saw the AEF as an integral part of a larger whole, all under the control of the General Staff in Washington. His refusal to rubber-stamp Pershing's recommendations for promotion was a symptom of his attitude. "With reference to promotions," snapped Pershing, "I think we have not entirely understood each other's view point."

March's prime objective was efficiency through centralization and logically this meant limiting the scope of Pershing's authority in France. He phrased it in terms of concern for Pershing's ability to carry the heavy, complex, and rapidly increasing burden of command alone. Government activities, he argued, fell into three distinct groups: "1st, the Army proper—the fighting command; 2nd, the general divisions of finance and supply; and 3rd, the governmental and intergovernmental questions." Any one of these "would require an unusual man to make the conduct of its affairs a success."

No one could be expected to handle all three any longer, and to Pershing's intense irritation, March therefore suggested appointing George Goethals to take charge of the supply side in France, restricting Pershing to operational command as "our fighting soldier."

Purchasing in France appeared to need the same kind of rationalization as it was receiving at home. "The various Services of the AEF have independent appropriations and . . . independent Purchasing Bureaus," explained George McFadden, the War Trade Board's representative in Paris, "[and] it is very difficult to obtain a Consolidated Program of Purchases . . . covering all Services of the AEF." Goethals, still radiating energy, was patently the man to extend the War Department's grip on logistics through to the combat zone. But the proposal threatened Pershing's absolute rule in France, and it was firmly rejected: "There can be no dual control. All matters pertaining to the use of American forces and their relation to the allies must remain in my hands."

March's scheme was strictly in line with his overall theory of an efficient General Staff system, and as a plan for the future no one could fault it; but the immediate practical reality favored Pershing. In a wider war, with American forces operating in strength in a number of theaters, central control based in Washington would be vital. But America's grand strategy in this war was to concentrate solely on the Western Front. Here the situation was shifting rapidly and dangerously all the time, and it was crucial for the AEF to react quickly. So the ultimate authority for the war effort must logically be located in France, as information and instructions could not travel quickly or reliably enough across the Atlantic. The reasoning that had shaped the terms of Pershing's original appointment still held, and he was probably right to resist the Chief of Staff's initiative.

Nevertheless, March was reluctant to back down, and Pershing wrote directly to Baker, clearly registering dissatisfaction with the General Staff:

"There is an impression here that our cablegrams are not being carefully studied and thoroughly co-ordinated. There seems to be energy enough behind things, but perhaps it is not as well directed by the Staff as it might be. . . . There may be some of the personnel that is not entirely satisfactory." In case Baker was not concentrating, he added, "I have at times doubted whether you will get [the system] going smoothly without taking someone who has actually gone through this organisation here from beginning to end." And just in case Baker had still not taken the hint, Pershing concluded, "All this comes to my mind following the idea of an occasional change, of which you spoke when here as being your intention."

Baker recognized more clearly than most how much March was contributing to the war effort in rationalizing the War Department, and he was reluctant to replace him at this crucial stage in the war. Nor did he want to offend Pershing by insisting that Goethals should go to France to take charge of supply. For the moment, he left March and Pershing in charge in their respective domains, but he threw his support behind March in his long-term plans. With Baker's approval, March promulgated General Order 80, which redefined the structure of the General Staff along modern lines—and began by reasserting that "the Chief of Staff by law takes rank and precedence over all officers of the Army . . . [and] is the immediate adviser of the Secretary of War." The order would have important repercussions for the future. But in April 1918, Pershing remained in place, his power in France undiminished and his eyes still firmly fixed on the ultimate triumph of the American Expeditionary Force.

21

Blood and Propaganda:
Setting a Value on the AEF

March's organizational talent put 332,000 more men onto the Western Front in just two months. At such a desperate moment, this incoming tide of fresh vigor had a remarkable effect on morale on both sides. Whether or not the Americans were actually in combat, their physical presence in France seemed to spell the ultimate defeat of the Central Powers. Allied propagandists nagged at the German psyche with constant updates on the hordes of fresh, enthusiastic, Class 1 American soldiers pouring through the ports of England and France on their way to kill Germans, emphasizing that the U-boats were failing to sink a single troop-carrying ship.

The German leadership had somehow to minimize this threat to the nation's morale. They had available a massive propaganda machine that used all the media, all the men of influence from priests to professors, cartoonists to photographers. This they now turned against the Americans, picturing them as degenerates and wastrels, ridiculous millionaire cowboys, reluctant conscripts weeping as they were herded on board the transports. "Our soldiers despise them and do not consider them worthy enemies," German newspapers reassured their readers.

But the propagandists also needed hard evidence of American worthlessness in the face of German arms. In the spring and early summer of 1918, desperate battles were fought, within the wider war, to establish the true worth of the AEF. German soldiers had to inflict an early humiliation on an American unit—ideally, to capture a newsworthy landmark defended by Americans. The sector held in the spring of 1918 by the 1st Division, on the south side of the Saint-Mihiel salient, contained just such a spot—the village of Seicheprey. Ludendorff planned to use the 259th Infantry, reinforced by a special raiding force known as "Hindenburg's Traveling Circus," to break through the 1st Division's lines in a swift and brutal operation.

The 1st Division was now the AEF's elite unit. Its aggressive commander, Robert Bullard, had turned what had been a quiet sector into a frenetic combat zone. His artillery fired an average of four thousand shells a day and the Germans responded in kind, mixing high explosive and shrapnel with phosgene in the first significant gas barrage to be directed against American troops, taking eight lives.

Bullard's troops had seen a good deal of fighting, much of which they had brought on themselves. But just as the "Traveling Circus" was preparing to wreak mayhem, the 1st Division was being reassigned. On April 4, its place had been taken by a far less experienced contingent: the New England National Guard, the 26th "Yankee" Division, under Major General Clarence R. "Daddy" Edwards.

Pershing was not an admirer of Edwards. The only National Guard general to command a division on the Western Front, he owed his position, Pershing suspected, less to talent than to powerful patrons in Congress. Constantly on trial in Pershing's eyes, Edwards was about to face his sternest test. Not only had the 26th taken over the 1st Division's sector, it was also given the stretch of line previously held by a French division to its right—nine more miles of muddy trenches dug through marshes, the entire defensive system overlooked by the four-hundred-foot vantage point of Mont Sec, which was firmly in German hands.

Twice the Germans raided Edwards' lines. During the second raid, the Guardsmen captured forty of the raiders—but then came the stage-managed humiliation. In the early morning of April 20, while it was still dark, German guns opened up with a heavy barrage on a two-mile front to the far right of the sector. The troops in the American forward line were killed almost immediately—very possibly because when the barrage opened they had left the cold, foul-smelling, muddy safety of the trenches for the hazardous comforts of open ground; certainly the dead lay in neat rows in front of the trenches.

At 5 A.M., 1,200 German troops led by the "Traveling Circus" burst through the shattered front line. Within an hour, they had penetrated nearly a mile into the American sector and were in Seicheprey itself. The village was well defended and the raiders were repulsed, but they retreated only a little way to the north of the town, where they dug in. The "Yankees" were under the tactical command of the French, and that afternoon Clarence Edwards was given orders to counterattack the following dawn. By 4 A.M. on April 21, two of the companies assigned to the assault were still not in position, and the officer immediately responsible for directing the counterattack called off the operation on his own initiative. He would later be court-martialed.

The German raiders, however, had never intended to stay. By 5 A.M. they had retreated to their own lines, leaving the Yankees to count the cost of Seicheprey: 669 casualties, 81 of them dead, 187 captured or missing. The German propaganda mill had been fed with the blood-soaked grist it needed. Details were broadcast all over the world from the radio station in Berlin, and German airplanes dropped photographs of the raid in neutral countries. The débâcle made Pershing's life no easier, as it allowed the Allies to be openly skeptical about the fighting efficiency of American troops under American leadership. Somehow he had to prove them wrong.

When the raid on Seicheprey took place, Bullard and the 1st Division were 140 miles to the northwest in the rolling chalklands of Picardy, holding almost three miles of the line near the apex of Ludendorff's first advance. Each day the Germans shelled them, and there was little protection as the sector was, in the words of one survivor, "wholly disorganized . . . no dug outs and no communication trenches." Even light artillery could collapse the trenches, burying men alive, and the heavy guns wrought havoc. The strain began to tell. One morning, the witness remembered, as the bombardment started for the day, a soldier named Jackson "commenced to shake badly and he showed his terror in his face. . . . He lay flat on his stomach in the mud and water on the bottom of the trench and wept and wept."

The 1st Division had been sent there to join a counteroffensive against what Allied intelligence had initially believed would be the flank of Ludendorff's third thrust. When it became clear that the next German blow would instead fall further south, on the French on the Aisne, the operation was canceled—but Pershing nevertheless decided that the time had come for the AEF to make its mark. The 1st Division was to wipe out the stain of Seicheprey with a localized demonstration of American military prowess.

At first sight, the plan mirrored the Germans' attack on Seicheprey. The target was the ruined village of Cantigny, a strong point in the local

German defense system. But Cantigny was not simply to be raided. Pershing intended to advance the Allied lines permanently and ordered that Cantigny was to be held after capture.

Though it would take place in the French sector, this was an American operation, and the French divisions on either side of the 1st would not be directly involved. Bullard would have to protect his flanks and reorganize the new front line out of his own resources. Consequently, he was obliged to limit the operation essentially to a single regiment. He selected the 28th Infantry, not least for its commander, Colonel Hansen E. Ely, one of the toughest officers in the regular army. A West Point football player, "six-feet-two with 220 pounds of bone and gristle," Ely epitomized the hard, aggressive, uncompromising type of officer Pershing wanted to have leading his combat troops.

This operation must not fail, and to make quite sure that it did not, Ely would have under his command, besides his own 28th Infantry, elements of the 16th and 18th Regiments, one machine-gun company per battalion, the Stokes mortars and 37mm guns from other regiments, a company of engineers, a detachment of French flamethrower troops, and a squadron of twelve French tanks; flying overhead would be observation aircraft supplied by the French.

The key to success, however, was artillery. "Artillery conquers, infantry occupies" ran the conventional wisdom on the Western Front, and the provision of artillery for the operation was substantial—a total of 250 guns, American and French, up to the huge caliber of 280mm. For several days before the attack, the German defenses in and around Cantigny were subjected to intermittent destructive fire. Bullard planned a one-hour concentrated barrage of extreme violence followed by five minutes of smoke and gas shells just before the advance began.

Nothing was left to chance. Ely's force spent two days rehearsing the operation over similar terrain in the rear. The flamethrower troops and infantry assigned to flush out the cellars and caves studied maps and models of the village. Even the routes to the jumping-off points were carefully reconnoitered and marked so there would be no confusion in the darkness as the troops moved up.

Then, barely seventy-two hours before the assault, this smooth progress was disrupted. A young lieutenant detailed to place entrenching equipment in the jump-off trenches set off in the dark with his squad, got lost, and landed up in the German trenches. He was carrying a map with details of the various dumps being made for the assault. No one knew precisely what German intelligence had made of this windfall, but with twenty-four hours to go, the Germans drenched the area with 15,000 gas shells and sent over a small raiding party that managed to capture another man—another possible source of information.

Ely must have known he might now be walking into a trap, but Bullard was insisting on pressing ahead when there arrived even more dramatic news: at dawn, fifty miles to the east, on a front running from Soissons to Reims, Ludendorff had launched his third offensive across the Aisne toward Paris. Still the American operation was not canceled or even postponed. At 5:45 A.M. on May 28, right on schedule, the massed guns turned Cantigny into "an active volcano," in George C. Marshall's words, "with great clouds of smoke and dust and flying dirt and debris which was blasted high into the air."

At 6:45 A.M., Ely's men moved out in perfect alignment in three lines, the center preceded by tanks. As rehearsed, the first line stayed within fifty yards of its own rolling barrage while concerted fire from sixty-four heavy machine guns tore apart likely counterattack positions in the surrounding woods. Meeting almost no resistance, they swept up the steep ridge to Cantigny and on through the village, leaving the flamethrowers to clear out the cellars. Revolted, one lieutenant saw a panic-stricken German scramble out "just as I had seen rabbits in Kansas come out of burning strawstacks. . . . [He] ran ten to fifteen yards then fell over singed to death."

Now the fighting turned vicious. "An enemy officer with about forty men indicated his willingness to surrender," reported Lieutenant Colonel J. M. Cullison, commanding the 3rd Battalion,

> but when approached by an American Lieutenant, he fired on the latter who had lowered his weapon. A German sergeant major held up his hands until a sergeant approached within a few feet, when he threw a bomb at the latter. A machine gun crew kept firing while half of the crew tried to surrender. . . . Owing to these incidents the men were rather bitter. . . . The bayonet was used freely and with effect.

On schedule, at 7:20 A.M., Ely reached the crest of the ridge, just beyond the village, where he intended to hold. His men worked desperately to fortify the line. Its keystones were three strong points—one just to the east of the Château de Cantigny, one in the cemetery north of the village, the third controlling the northeast sector. Each was in the shape of a cross, so that the defenders could fire in any direction, and was manned by a platoon of infantry with two automatic rifles and five machine guns. Elsewhere in the front line, the men adapted shell holes for cover, while behind them engineers dug a continuous trench, three feet deep and shielded by barbed wire.

For four and a half hours the 28th Infantry consolidated the position without interference. By noon, however, the Germans had brought up heavy machine guns and alerted the artillery, forcing the Americans into their hastily dug gun pits while the earth around them shook with the detonations of shells. Ely realized at once that this fire included heavy guns—and the danger of his predicament began to dawn on him.

The maximum depth of the advance on Cantigny had been set at 1,600 yards, through the infantry trenches but well short of the German gun line. Ely had been relying heavily on big guns supplied by the French to suppress the German artillery, but, panicked by Ludendorff's new offensive on the Aisne, the French had largely abandoned the Americans to their fate. "Orders for the withdrawal of more French artillery arrived before the advance had been completed," Marshall recalled bitterly, "and we discovered that at least one French regiment had started its withdrawal without having fired a shot."

Ely's troops were now cannon fodder, and the German guns, directed by aircraft flying over the position, fired accurately and relentlessly. "A 3-inch shell will temporarily scare or deter a man," Marshall noted, "a 6-inch shell will shock him; but an 8-inch shell, such as these 210mm ones, rips up the nervous system of everyone within a hundred yards of the explosion."

Throughout the late afternoon of May 28, the Germans probed the American lines, and the rain of 150mm and 210mm shells peaked in intensity. At 6:45 P.M., waves of Germans in field gray advanced from the woods toward the center of Ely's lines. Fortunately, the German division that had been holding Cantigny, the 82nd Reserve, was a third-class unit. Watching them advance, Ely had the impression that "the troops had been forced to make the counterattacks against their desire." Certainly, the coordination with their artillery was poor. They stayed 200 yards behind their rolling barrage, giving Ely's men time to emerge from cover and cut them down.

Though the French had withdrawn their heavy guns, Ely still had at his disposal the divisional artillery under Charles Summerall, the AEF's best gunner. Signals troops succeeded in maintaining a telephone link between Ely and Summerall, and, as the German counterattacks took shape, Ely could have Summerall break them up with shrapnel and high explosives. The first wave of Germans had gotten through before Summerall could respond and had to be taken out by rifle and bayonet; but succeeding waves were simply scythed by shrapnel.

Just after dawn the next day, the Germans made two more small counterattacks. Slightly before six that evening, they launched a far more ferocious assault but were again beaten back. At first light on May 30, they attacked once again—and once again the Americans held. It was virtually the end of the struggle. The Germans had lost 800 dead, 500 wounded, and 255 captured. The German fire slackened, and Cantigny passed into American hands. As night fell on May 30, the survivors of Ely's command were relieved and went back down the hill.

Ely's men showed their greatest heroism in their resistance to the deadly barrage that fell on them as they defended what they had taken. For three days and two nights, the big guns had pounded them. Eighty men had been casualties in the advance on Cantigny, but holding it had cost 13 officers and 186 men dead, 31 officers and 636 men wounded or missing.

In his report, made only hours after his return, Hansen Ely verged on the insubordinate:

> The great strain on men holding a front line trench or being practically without sleep for three or four days and nights seriously weakens them; and when there is added to this casualties amounting in some Companies as high as 40%, with casualties among Company officers of Infantry Companies of from 33% to 100%, it is believed that as soon as a force has gained and fairly consolidated its objective, having suffered any such losses . . . it should be relieved by fresh troops.

Few would have argued with Ely's conclusions, but once again he had been dogged by bad luck. Bullard had felt not unwilling but unable to relieve him; anticipating a more general German attack after Ludendorff's third offensive, he wanted to keep his remaining units fresh.

With great courage and even greater cost, the 1st Division had taken the heights of Cantigny. But what had they gained? George Marshall has testified that the objective was "of no strategic importance and of small tactical value." Given that any propaganda value in the demonstration had been submerged under the tide of Germans advancing on Paris, should the division have attacked at all? Or, if the attack was still valid, should there have been an immediate withdrawal once the village had been captured?

The reason for the 28th Regiment's sacrifice seems to have lain in Pershing's fanatical determination to reply to the Seicheprey débâcle—to restore American pride and defend against the continuing Allied pressure for amalgamation. He could argue his case effectively only if his units were seen to perform to the highest standards in battle. There was no way the inexperienced AEF could avoid suffering in comparison with the well-tried Allied war machines—but Pershing would not relax his demands. By replacing Sibert with Bullard, he had shown he would ruin any officer who did not deliver on time. Toughness was necessary if the AEF was to achieve combat readiness quickly, but it made Pershing inflexible. Once news of Ludendorff's third attack had come through, the Cantigny operation should have been postponed at the very least; this was not the time to waste lives. And when the French withdrew artillery cover, Ely should have been pulled back. Instead, Pershing ordered Bullard to hold, and the 28th furnished German gunners with three days of target practice.

No one was better acquainted with Pershing's uncompromising nature than James Harbord, who had sailed with him on the *Baltic* nine months before. No longer Chief of Staff, Harbord now commanded the 4th (Marine) Brigade of the 2nd Division. Word of Ely's exploits had already reached the marines as they marched toward a small hunting preserve that stood in the path of Ludendorff's drive for Paris. Its name was Belleau Wood; it would be their own private Armageddon.

22

"Know Thine Enemy": The Battle for Belleau Wood, June 1918

Ludendorff's third offensive, the attack on the Reims-Soissons front, was essentially a feint. He still believed that the way to win the war was to launch a final thrust at the British Army in Flanders; with American troops pouring into France and time running out, he would have to do it soon. But for the assault on the British to have the best chance of success, he must prevent the French from sending reinforcements. By menacing Paris, he hoped to frighten them into keeping their reserve divisions on that front, far from Flanders. If the behavior of the French gunners in abandoning Ely and his men to their fate was typical, Ludendorff's strategy was working perfectly.

Ludendorff had instructed his storm troopers to drive south over the Aisne River toward the Marne valley and then stop. A penetration of about twelve miles, he had calculated, would be enough to pin the French to the defense of Paris. When his troops reached this "terror line," he had intended to make the "real" attack—to unleash his forces in Flanders and push Haig and the British Expeditionary Force into the sea.

He had dressed his feint, however, in all the trappings of a genuine offensive: meticulous planning, intense secrecy, formidable artillery support, heavy allocations of assault divisions. Ironically, the attack succeeded even better than the preceding two; in the center, General von Conta's troops reached the "terror line" on the evening of the first day, May 27.

At this point, Ludendorff should have turned and attacked the vulnerable British, but his troops' fantastic achievement had loosened his grip on grand strategy. He now chose to reinforce their success, to transform the feint into a real offensive, arguing that he might at least capture the Marne valley and open a road to Paris.

Onward rolled the German war machine toward the Marne. The government prepared to abandon Paris, and Pétain appealed to Foch and Pershing for help. Foch, who was more conscious of Ludendorff's gifts as a strategist, continued to believe that this was only a feint and refused to part with precious reserves, holding them ready for the "real" attack. Pershing sent to the Marne the only divisions he had available: the regulars of the 3rd Division and the regulars and marines of the 2nd Division.

The 3rd Division's motorized machine-gun battalion raced through the pathetic files of French refugees to meet the German advance as it bore down on Château-Thierry, a town on the Marne some fifty miles east of Paris. While the bulk of the unit dug in below the road and rail bridges on the south side of the river, Lieutenant Bissell led fifteen men with two machine guns across to fight in the desperate, futile defense of the northern suburbs of Château-Thierry. Late that evening, the French blew the road bridge—fortunately leaving the rail bridge, over which Bissell was able to sneak his weary command two days later. By this time, the rest of the division was strung out to the east for ten miles, holding the south bank of the Marne; at the Jaulgonne bend, it lent its weight to a French attack forcing back German advance guards who were trying to establish a bridgehead.

The 2nd Division also moved up on May 31. In any circumstances, to be called so urgently to the front would have been a trial for a commander and his staff. In this case the division had not completed its training as a unit and its senior officers had no experience of warfare on this scale. The commanding officer, Major General Omar Bundy, a short, dapper, punctilious disciplinarian, was considered at General Headquarters to be better behind a desk or on the training square than in the field. "He is attentive to duty and appears to be trying to learn his duties as a division commander," reads a confidential assessment sent to Pershing during the latter stages of the division's training, "but gives no evidence of unusual ability for this position." His Chief of Staff, Colonel Preston Brown, was a sharp-tongued, razor-witted veteran who had once been accused of illegally executing insurgents during his service in the Philippines. Neither seems to have possessed the qualities that inspire personal loyalty and build a division that functions as a responsive, organic entity. The brigade and regimental commanders were considered to be better material, though they inevitably lacked experience with large units. Harbord, leading the Marine Brigade (5th and 6th Marine Regiments), acknowledged that he "had never commanded more than a squadron of cavalry."

The Marine Brigade was a unique formation in the AEF, and its presence on the Western Front was a tribute to the determination of the Marine Corps' commander, Major General George Barnett. Though there were plans afoot for amphibious landings in the Adriatic, the reality was that, with the German fleet bottled up, there was little scope for marines to fulfill their traditional mission. The British Royal Marines, with much the same problem, had formed a Naval Division to fight as infantry on the Western Front, and George Barnett decided that his command should fulfill a similar role. During the neutrality period, he made sure marine officers saw the conditions on the Western Front.

Barnett kept the Corps' entrance requirements at a high level. "Lads" had to be able to read, write, and understand English; be at least 64 inches tall and weigh 124 pounds, be sound of limb with good eyesight and hearing, and have "at least twenty teeth." The marines, all of whom were volunteers, were well aware of having a special aura of rakish glamour—"I am a two-fisted fighting rover," declared a recruiting pamphlet— but it clothed a solid substructure of the most rigorous training.

When war broke out, Barnett had quickly acquired and developed sites at Quantico, Virginia, and San Diego for large-scale expansion of the Corps. By the summer of 1917, Quantico had become one of the most up-to-date training camps in America, offering "a post-graduate course in the actual work of war." While the old-timers of the 5th Marine Regiment had gone to France with the 1st Division in June 1917, the rapidly assembled 6th Marine Regiment (of which 60 percent were college men) had drilled and hiked, strung wire, sent wigwag messages with flags from hillside to hillside, fought "duels" with rubber bayonets, practiced grenade throwing between movable wooden "trenches," and above all learned high levels of marksmanship. With 60 shots, a man had to score 202 out of a possible 300 (the bull's-eye counted as 5, the next ring 4, and so on), or he would not be admitted to the Corps.

In France on the last day of May, these elite soldiers moved southeast toward the front in convoys of trucks driven, in Harbord's phrase, "by little, yellow, dumb-looking Annamites," conscripts from a French colony in Asia. For twenty-four hours, longer for some of the units, they bumped and slewed their way through the rolling Marne countryside—broad-leaved woods and wheatfields speckled with bloodred poppies—toward the sound of the guns.

The marines too met the chaos of refugees pushed south and westward by the German assault, but turned their backs on drunken, looting, fleeing French soldiers, who shouted, *"La guerre est finie."* In fact, it was the German advance that was almost over.

The success of Ludendorff's third thrust had been miraculous in all but one vital respect: to support such a deep drive, he required excellent communications. For this purpose he had targeted the important rail centers of Soissons and Reims. Soissons had fallen, but Reims, the capital city of the Champagne region, had not. Despite repeated German assaults, the city and the high ground to the south remained French—a solid shoulder constricting the left of the German advance.

Without Reims, the Germans had only one inadequate railroad through which to supplement their dwindling stock of trucks and horses. The forward troops were poorly supplied, some of them desperately hungry. Abandoning the attempt to take Reims, Ludendorff urgently ordered a new offensive that would widen the Marne salient to the west, toward Montdidier, near the 1st Division's sector. In the interim, however, he would have to halt his present attack, except where it would assist the new operation in the west.

The obvious place for the Germans to stop east of Château-Thierry was the Marne; the 3rd Division was putting up spirited resistance along this line. But west of Château-Thierry, the advance could profitably push on along the Paris road. On the day the marines arrived at the front, Conta ordered the advance to continue in the west; his left flank was to pivot on Château-Thierry until it rested on a line running west to Gandelu, the sector to which the 2nd Division was headed. Early on June 1, as Conta continued to push the French back, General Jean Degoutte, commander of the French XXI Corps, to which the 2nd Division was attached, warned Bundy that his travel-weary troops must be ready to go into action by eleven that morning.

The French had aimed to plug the rapidly expanding gaps in their own line with the Americans as they arrived, but 2nd Division Chief of Staff Preston Brown was equally determined that his troops should not lose their identity. He argued fiercely that tired, scattered, and unprepared as they were, the Americans should form a support line behind the French. Hastily, a line was agreed on. West of the Paris road, it stretched from the village of Le Thiolet, around the north of Belleau Wood, and along the crest immediately overhanging the villages of Belleau and Torcy to Hill 142. These were precisely the strong defensive positions Conta wanted for his own troops.

Unknown to the Americans, there was a race in progress and the German advance was still accelerating. "It is absolutely imperative that one of your regiments should occupy the line we agreed this morning," Degoutte urged Bundy at 1:10 P.M. on June 1. "As a matter of extreme urgency . . . I ask that you send the first available regiment to hold that line." But, he conceded, "it is possible that enemy progress might prevent your regiment from arriving in time." He suggested, just in case, a line further back, running from Le Thiolet south of Belleau Wood to Hill 142. This far more modest objective, which left the Germans with Belleau Wood, the village of Bouresches east of the wood, and much of the high ground, was indeed the line Bundy sent the Marine Brigade to hold.

At 5:05 P.M., Harbord reported the Marine Brigade to be in position, confirming among other details that they were "going into line from Lucy [Lucy-le-Bocage, a village just south of Belleau Wood] through Hill 142." Locally, Hill 142 was the dominant ground—not a single hill as such, more a long crest running north to south. But despite Degoutte's orders and Harbord's confirmation, the marines actually took up position to the south of Hill 142, leaving the high ground to be occupied by the Germans. It was to prove a costly mistake in the days to come.

With the French fighting in front of them, the men of the 2nd Division tried desperately to pull themselves into shape for combat. The chaos of the deployment, combined with serious delays in assembling all the units, greatly complicated the task of organizing and consolidating the line. Then more gaps opened in the French line, which forced the Americans to spread wider until at one point they were holding nine miles of the front. Their orders were to "maintain at all costs the line of support they occupy," and from June 2 onward the enemy tested their resolve. "The Germans have been repulsed today along our entire division front," Harbord proudly reported to Bundy at 6:25 P.M. on that first day of fighting.

In repelling these German thrusts, the marines showed both their determination and their marksmanship. While their artillery shredded the advancing waves of troops with shrapnel, their machine guns and rifles devastated the survivors. "Three times they tried to break through," remembered Private Gulberg later, "but our fire was too accurate and too heavy for them. It was terrible in its effectiveness. They fell by the scores, there among the poppies and the wheat. Then they broke and ran for cover." Here the marines learned at first hand the effectiveness of machine guns in the defensive. "Oh, it was too easy; just like a bunch of cattle coming to slaughter," wrote one machine gunner later. "I always thought it was a fearful thing to take a human life, but I felt a savage thrill of joy and I could hardly wait for the Germans to get close enough."

At the same time, the marines were perpetually under enemy observation and had to take punishment. "The hum of German airplanes is almost constant over our front lines," Harbord complained, asking that "the French authorities be called upon to show some of that superiority in the air which is referred to in almost every French and British paper recently." He walked the front from Lucy to the Paris road and found not one section from which a German balloon was not plainly visible. "Any activity or appearance of people along that line in sight of these balloons," he noted grimly, "is followed within a very few minutes by shell fire."

Major Berton Sibley's 3rd Battalion, 6th Marines was caught by a barrage as it moved into position and four men died. The division's gunners also suffered from counterbattery fire: "Corporal Kirkpatrick was all but killed," reported a fellow officer. "An H E . . . blew off both arms. In addition he had 30 odd other wounds. He did not even lose consciousness. . . . When I went on at 4 am, I found Kirkpatrick's thumb." One unit was caught by German shrapnel: "Fragments glittered in the air like a shoal of small silver fish. The blow was quick, sudden, destructive, and eleven of our men went down. One or two cried out in surprised pain, but four lay inert and silent. Faces turned white and the company showed a tendency to huddle and mill about. 'Get going! . . . What do you think this is, a kid's game? Move out!' "

But while the 2nd Division had contact, the French were taking the real force of this last German push. Their resistance bought time for Bundy to bring up supplies. On the evening of June 3, the French, finally exhausted, began passing through the American lines. As they fell back, a major suggested to Captain Lloyd Williams that the marines might be wise to withdraw as well. "Retreat?" said Williams. "Hell, we just got here."

Shortly after daybreak on June 4, the French formally handed over responsibility for the sector to the 2nd Division, and that afternoon Pershing

motored over to stiffen the resolve of his officers and men. At this crisis of
the war, Americans stood alone on the front line—and they were proud to
do it. "I thought trench warfare was bad," wrote twenty-two-year-old
Lambert Wood to his mother,

> but this open warfare is plain hell. Plastered by high explosives in the
> open is no joke. We have had extremely heavy fighting, but the Boche
> are stopped on their way to Paris. . . . We piled them up by hun-
> dreds. . . . Five letters from you today from the beach. How I would like
> to be with you. . . . My best sergeant was killed yesterday, 15 feet from
> me. A true and fine soldier. I wish every German in the world were
> dead. . . . Don't worry. I am alright and it is worth while; no matter
> what the hardship or who must die. We are blocking the road to Paris.
> So we don't die in vain.

But with Paris and the main line of lateral communications with Verdun
still under threat, the Americans were required to do more than defend.
On June 5, Degoutte ordered them to push the Germans back. The
French 167th Division moved up on Bundy's left, allowing him to shorten
his lines and concentrate his troops. The plan of attack, quickly formulated had three objectives: to take the dominant Hill 142; to push through
Belleau Wood from the west and south; and then to emerge from Belleau
Wood and, with support on the flanks, take both Bouresches and the high
ground to the north and west.

Degoutte's impulse to attack was understandable, but the timing was
dangerous, for the 2nd Division was not yet fully prepared. On the night
of June 5–6, the men were still securing supplies and establishing lines of
communication, and the relief of the western units by the French 167th
Division was in progress. It is perhaps a symptom of disorganization that
Harbord did not issue his written orders for the attack until 10:25 P.M.
Major Julius Turrill of the 1st Battalion, 5th Marines, only got his orders
at 1 A.M., less than three hours before he was due to launch the first phase
of the operation, the attack on Hill 142.

Even more dangerous was the almost complete lack of operational intelligence. The maps of the area with which the French supplied Harbord—
drawn in 1832 and revised in 1912—were less than informative. Nor, as
Harbord had complained, were the French able to provide much aerial reconnaissance. The marines had little detailed knowledge of the terrain and,

worse, no precise idea of the strength of the enemy, let alone its exact position—but they do not seem to have done much reconnaissance of their own.

The fluid nature of the front since June 1, the lengthening and shortening of the division's line, the piecemeal arrival of the various units, the daily attacks and shelling, had all contributed to the lack of reconnaissance. Harbord later attributed it to "inexperience," an opinion supported by the division's Assistant Chief of Staff, G-2 (Intelligence), Colonel Arthur Conger: "The division was confronted with a situation in open warfare which had not been anticipated in the training of intelligence personnel," geared as it was to the demands of trench warfare.

However, on the afternoon of June 4, according to the brigade diary, Harbord had instructed the regimental commanders "to have small patrols pushed out to the front tonight in an endeavor to locate the enemy." That night, the 6th Marines' intelligence officer, Second Lieutenant William Eddy, led a three-man patrol north from Lucy-le-Bocage along the road to Torcy. Away to his left was Hill 142, the first objective of the attack, and on his right the dark mass of Belleau Wood.

The intelligence Eddy gathered about enemy activities to the left, in the direction of Hill 142, was meager: "Coughing distinctly heard . . . repeated four or five times. . . . Between 12 and 1 am three carts passed rapidly, two from east going west . . . one cart going in the opposite direction."

Intelligence about the second objective, Belleau Wood, was a little more substantial. Eddy saw a searchlight and heard a man's voice in the wheatfield on the western edge of the wood; he reported "considerable activity" in the wood itself and heard "distinct sound of heavy wagon apparently moving south through the northern half." A French pilot had already reported being shot at on June 3 by a machine gun located in Belleau Wood. Harbord later claimed, however, that "the French had informed us that Belleau Wood was not occupied except by a very short line across the northeast corner which was entrenched," information current no later than June 4, as the French retired through the American lines.

Thus as Harbord considered his plans on the eve of the June 6 operation, he did so in ignorance of the numbers and disposition of the enemy. It was then too late for reconnaissance, and neither Bundy nor Harbord considered delaying the operation by twenty-four hours. The only concessions made to the possibility that the advance on Hill 142 might be contested were the instruction given to the marines to proceed by "infiltration" and the attempt to retain a degree of surprise by ordering the artillery to make no preparation "properly speaking," the idea being "not to attract the attention of the enemy." Instead, the divisional artillery brigade, supported by two French *groupements* of 75s and 155s, was to execute "raking fire" on the objective and "interdiction fire" on the surrounding roads and ravines. Then, just before the marine advance, "violent annihilation fire" was to be placed on the objective, and during the operation "a boxing fire enclosing the whole area of attack."

Turrill, who was in charge of the attack on Hill 142, was a tough, stocky regular. His command was meant to be augmented by two machine-gun companies and a company of engineers. To their right, the 3rd Battalion, 5th Marines, under Major Benjamin Berry, another regular, tall and thin, would advance "to conform to the progress made by the 1st Battalion in its attack."

But Turrill was not ready. When he launched his attack at 3:45 on the morning of June 6, he had only two companies of marines and "half a machine-gun company"; the other two companies and the engineers were waiting for a French relief that was six hours late. Nor had his men been issued with hand grenades or Stokes mortars. He attacked regardless. At 3:45 A.M., in the first light of dawn, the marines came out of woodland cover and advanced, wading through mist, across a wheatfield toward Hill 142.

The injunction to proceed by infiltration had not sunk in. Instead, the men advanced in neatly dressed waves, a formation that Bundy, three weeks earlier, had informed his commanders would "insure the highest degree of control by subordinate commanders." The fifty-eight-man platoons were certainly under control, but they presented an open target to the enemy. And unknown to Turrill, waiting in the woods opposite were skillfully positioned Maxim guns with a firing rate of one thousand bullets a minute.

For fifty yards the marines advanced unmolested. Then a storm of machine-gun fire scythed through the wheat, killing and wounding. Now it was they who went like cattle to the slaughter and took the kind of punishment they had been handing out to German attackers. But rather than sensibly withdrawing, as the Germans had done, Turrill's men became the first to demonstrate the chilling marine theory that the only sure way to overcome machine-gun positions of this kind was to rush them.

Inspired by the extraordinary leadership of Captain George Hamilton, the marines surged over the German gunners, pushing through the wheatfields and woods of that long ridge time and time again. Behind them they left a trail of dead and dying Americans and Germans. Hamilton lost all his junior officers, but the survivors' aggression carried them to their objective, the far end of the crest running from Hill 142—and, for two brave marines, beyond it into the village of Torcy, which they attacked by themselves.

Such was the speed, the ferocity of Turrill's battalion's assault that neither the French on its left nor Berry's battalion on its right could keep up. Now Turrill's men were on their own, their flanks exposed, and the Germans counterattacked. Using infiltration tactics, one squad got within twenty feet of the Americans before being noticed. It was too close for safety. With hideous yells the marines charged with fixed bayonets and killed or captured them.

The fight would actually rage on through the day—Turrill would lose 9 officers and 325 men—but the reports passing up to Brigade HQ led Harbord to believe that the action had been completed successfully within three hours, a conclusion encouraged by triumphant descriptions of the taking of prisoners. At 5:50 A.M., Colonel Wendell Neville, Turrill's commanding officer, declared, "About 15 prisoners and one officer captured by his men are coming to the rear. All are young, ragged and looked badly fed. 3 deserters from the Boche surrendered. The prisoners have no morale."

At 7:30 A.M., Colonel Manus McCloskey issued orders to the divisional artillery confirming that "the enemy has been driven back." Consequently, the 155mm guns were to abandon their protective screen, turning instead to shell the towns behind the German lines, while for the 75mm guns firing would "be lessened gradually and then cease."

While Turrill fought on, his superiors turned east to center Belleau Wood and Bouresches in their sights. At 2:05 that afternoon, Harbord issued orders to the Marine Brigade (including the beleaguered Turrill) to attack "in two phases": to take Belleau Wood, then Bouresches village, its railroad station, and the high ground to the north and west of the wood. At the same time, the division's infantry regiment, the 23rd, which was linked with the marines in the east, decided to advance its lines to maintain a defensible liaison.

Belleau Wood, the first objective, was no more than a thousand yards at its widest, in the north, and about three thousand yards long from north to south. On all sides farmland stretched away from it, pasture and wheatfields dotted with poppies, a beautiful sight in the June sunshine.

Harbord's plan was to have Berry's battalion, which had attacked with Turrill that morning, move into the west side of the wood, turn north, and emerge to take Hill 133 and the high ground. For this latter phase, they would be supported by Turrill's battalion, to be augmented and placed under the command of Lieutenant Colonel Logan Feland.

On Berry's right, Major Berton Sibley's 3rd Battalion, 6th Marines would strike at the southwest corner of the wood. When Sibley had pushed through the wood, his battalion was to take Bouresches and the station. On their right Major Thomas Holcomb's 2nd Battalion, 6th Marines would advance in alignment with Sibley. Holcomb's easternmost company, the pivot of the whole sweeping movement, was to stay put, but the commander of the 23rd Infantry Regiment remained in ignorance of this fact, and his orders to the regiment to advance would cost many lives.

Jump-off was to be at five that afternoon, but once more the marines were hardly prepared. As the orders were being drawn up, Turrill's men were still fighting on Hill 142, Sibley's were a mile away from their intended starting point, and Holcomb's were carrying out reliefs. Berry did not receive precise orders until fifteen minutes before the attack was due to start, though, according to Holcomb, "verbal warning" had been given at noon.

Nor, once again, had the strength and disposition of the enemy been established. There is little doubt that Harbord knew that there were at least some Germans in the wood. Among his papers at the Library of Congress is a copy of Eddy's report with a pencil sketch on the back marking the patrol's findings, which strongly suggests that he had seen and registered them. However, he seems to have based his plans on the French assertion that the main line of resistance was in the northeastern corner alone.

The orders issued to Sibley's battalion, for example, stated, "The enemy holds the general line Bouresches-Torcy-Montecourt"—a line clipping the northeast corner of Belleau Wood. The artillery order for the attack reflected the same belief: "In order to avoid attracting the attention of the enemy, there will not be any artillery preparation other than . . . raking fire on the northern and eastern slopes of the Bois de Belleau," together with interdiction fire to the north and east of the wood. At Hill 142, "violent annihilation fire" was ordered just before the attack, suggesting at least a suspicion that the objective was occupied; here no such barrage was felt to be necessary for the rest of Belleau Wood.

From ignorance would come tragedy. Unknown to the marines, Belleau Wood was already an enemy stronghold. The Germans had entrenched and wired almost the entire western edge of the wood and carried this line east and north to link up with the main defenses just north of Bouresches. Only the southwest corner was relatively empty of troops. Everywhere there were lines of barbed wire, sharpshooter pits, heavy mortars, artillery zeroed in, and, most deadly of all, machine-gun emplacements echeloned to give one another virtually perfect cover.

Colonel Albertus Catlin, commander of the 6th Marines, later claimed that he had reported to brigade headquarters that very morning that "the Germans were organizing in the woods and were consolidating their machine gun positions." This may have been an attempt to justify himself after the event; for Harbord had made him responsible for the attack. The diary for Sibley's battalion contradicts Catlin's claim: "The enemy holds the general line Bouresches-Torcy-Montecourt. . . . There was no other information concerning the enemy or the terrain." With a mixture of resentment and resignation the diary adds, "And as there was no time for scouting, the company commanders were shown the above order, also their objectives on the maps and were conducted to the line from which the Battalion would start the attack."

From their superb vantage points, the Germans appear to have been forewarned of the attack. The marines' orders said nothing about moving up by stealth, and their preparatory movements would have been readily interpreted by an experienced observer. By 5 P.M., as Berry's battalion readied itself to attack, the wheatfield it had to cross was already alive with shrapnel and machine-gun fire. But Berry was under orders, and he obeyed them. With the sun slanting their shadows toward Belleau Wood, the marines rose up and, in waves of four ranks, like any Civil War formation, they advanced. The shrapnel and machine-gun fire slicing across the field brought them down, mangled and bleeding, still in those ranks. "Come on, you sons of bitches," yelled Gunnery Sergeant Dan Daly. "Do you want to live for ever?" And the survivors scrambled to the edge of the wood.

"What is left of battalion is in woods close by," Berry reported at 6:10 P.M. "Do not know whether will be able to stand or not." By 9:50 P.M. he was reported missing—he had received a bullet in the elbow that eventually lodged in his palm—and, despite optimistic reports of German positions "taken," his battalion's attack had failed. All over the field lay the dead and dying. Medics worked heroically to bring in the wounded, but many were recovered too late.

Meanwhile, at the southwest end of the wood, Sibley's battalion had fared better. "Troops started out in beautiful deployment in beautiful line," Major Edward Cole of the 6th Machine-Gun Battalion reported at 5:39. "It was one of the most beautiful sights I have ever seen," Colonel Catlin confirmed. "The battalion pivoted on its right, the left sweeping across the open ground in four waves, as steadily and correctly as though on parade. . . . They walked at the regulation pace, because a man is of little use in a hand-to-hand bayonet struggle after a hundred yards dash."

The two companies on the right, outside the wood, soon ran into the storm that had decimated Berry's command. Pinned down, they stayed put while the two companies on the left entered the southwest corner and started pushing through. Now at last the marines realized what they had to contend with. Even without an occupying enemy, Belleau Wood was an inhospitable jungle of massed trees, heavy tangled undergrowth, huge tumbled boulders, ridges, and sudden small ravines. It was impossible to maintain direction or even to keep in touch with units to the right and left. And it was an ideal place for defense: the brigade diary for the day acknowledges that the nests of machine guns were "so protected in the rocks that [they] could not be gotten out by our men, who were without hand grenades or Stokes mortars."

On the left, Sibley's men ran into machine guns and turned to the north; on the right some managed to push through the wood to a point opposite Bouresches. Their orders were now to take the village—but it had already been captured.

At the last moment, Major Holcomb had been ordered to put one company into the sector south of Bouresches and support Sibley's men as they emerged from the wood to take the village. The 96th Company, under Captain Donald Duncan, moved off; almost at once Duncan fell with a Maxim bullet in the stomach. He was carried to cover in a clump of trees; seconds later an eight-inch shell landed there and killed Duncan and all but one of his rescuers.

Believing Sibley to be ahead, Lieutenant Robertson, who had taken Duncan's place, veered off, taking the remains of the company with him— and so the 96th Company advanced on Bouresches by itself. On the outskirts, Robertson struck off to gather reinforcements; Lieutenant Clifton Cates, with the only two surviving officers and twenty-three men, went in. Some fell to a machine-gun nest, and Cates himself collected a bullet through the rim of his helmet and another in his tunic, but the remnant held Bouresches until darkness allowed the two companies of Sibley's 3rd Battalion, which had been pinned down south of the wood, to move up.

As darkness fell, the southern portion of Belleau Wood was cupped by dead and dying marines. That day the division had lost 1,087 men, 222 of them killed. And that night, as the Germans pounded the men in the wood with high explosives, their commanders tried to come to terms with the catastrophe. "The Brigade can hold its present position," Harbord told Bundy, "but is not able to advance at present. Figures on which to base call for replacements will be submitted as soon as possible." While they waited for the dawn, the marines held fast in almost total ignorance of what the new day would bring.

23

"Do You Want to Live for Ever?"

Harbord and his marines had no real choice but to go on. During those early June days, all France knew that Ludendorff had broken through and was on the road to Paris. The pitiful files of refugees mingled with the ragged, exhausted soldiers fleeing the German storm troopers and did dreadful damage to French morale. And to coincide with his military onslaughts, Ludendorff had launched a propaganda offensive aimed at "sowing dissension and creating distrust in the minds of the French people." In Paris he turned the mood of defeat and depression into near panic with bombing raids and his new terror weapon: long-range guns that could shell the city from seventy-five miles away. The government readied itself to flee, but whether France would fight on no one knew. Analysts in Washington were pessimistic: "Competent observers believe Paris is the backbone of French resistance and should the city fall, France would accept peace on reasonable terms."

The U.S. reinforcement, France's only hope amid the gloom, continued to be singled out for special treatment by Ludendorff's psychological warfare specialists. Where are these vaunted saviors, the whispers asked—and what are America's motives? Woodrow Wilson was denounced as "a tool of American financiers" who had "pushed America into the war." The "real aim" of American policy was no less than "the Americanization of Europe. . . . This is already being accomplished in France where the Americans have usurped in a most shameless way French industry and administration. French workmen are sent to the Front and replaced by Americans. These are the methods adopted by the country of trusts and dollars in order to make war pay." Innuendoes of this kind reinforced the French socialists' own defeatist propaganda, and morale threatened to plunge even lower than in the desperate days following Nivelle's bungled offensive a year before.

After the Nivelle fiasco, it had been the Americans who had restored French nerve; at the beginning of June 1918, they were just beginning to do so again. "We cannot afford to allow their morale to become too low, as there is a danger of their breaking at the wrong time," Pershing warned March, confiding in him his idea for "strengthening some of their divisions by placing some of our best regiments in them temporarily." The presence and courage of the 3rd Division at Château-Thierry and along the Marne, and the 2nd Division's Marines before Belleau Wood, were an answer to the German suggestion that America had no real will to help France. "The morale, not only of the French Army but of the entire nation, has greatly improved as a result of the show made by our men," military intelligence reported proudly. The Americans could not now be seen to fail—whatever the cost.

Victory was also crucial to morale at home, as well as to Woodrow Wilson's personal standing. *The New York Times* heaped praise on "Our Gallant Marines. . . . I never saw such wonderful spirit. Not one of our fellows hesitated in the face of the rain of machine gun fire. . . . The German dead are piled up three deep in places." For Pershing too, the fighting was important. This kind of élan in attack seemed to substantiate his claim that America was ready for its own army fighting under its own flag. Harbord, closer than most to the commander in chief, wanted very much to give him a victory to brandish alongside Cantigny. He was also anxious on his own account to acquit himself well in his new role as field commander, having already been moved once from a senior position as the AEF's Chief of Staff.

But the Germans were just as highly motivated. Ludendorff was well aware of the undercurrents on the other side, and on June 8 he ordered that United States troops should be "hit particularly hard in order to render difficult the formation of an American Army." Belleau Wood itself was taking on an exaggerated significance in Germany and among the troops in the field in terms of its propaganda value. General Böhm, commanding one of the divisions opposing the marines, regarded the battle as crucial in evaluating "the Anglo-American claim that the American Army is equal or even superior to the German Army."

Almost at once, Belleau Wood had become a battle of more psycholog-ical than strategic importance. Caught in a web of national fears, vanities, and ambitions at a critical stage of the war, Harbord had only one possible course; to fight on and win. For the marines in the front line, tragedy was guaranteed. For on the German side too, as a prisoner later revealed, the orders were to hold "at all costs." Despite the parlous supply situation, the German commanders were willing to lavish extraordinary resources of men and matériel on the defense of this wood.

On the morning of June 7, the second day, the village of Bouresches was in American hands. But Berry's attack from the western edge of Belleau Wood had failed; and Sibley's men, starting from the southwest corner, had made some ground across the wood to the east but very little progress upward toward the north. During the day, while the brigade consolidated its lines and braved machine-gun fire and snipers to rescue the wounded lying out in the open, Harbord ordered Sibley to renew the attack up into the wood at dawn. The Germans, however, stole the initiative; that night, pouring shells and heavy machine-gun fire on the entire length of the brigade's line, they attacked in force. But the marine line held, and, as the enemy faltered, Sibley launched his attack.

Tragically, thirty-six hours after the original attack, Harbord still had no idea of the true strength of the German fortifications in Belleau Wood. The previous afternoon, he had ordered German prisoners to be "interro-gated with a view to ascertaining as accurately as possible what is now in the Bois de Belleau." He seems to have gleaned little because he provided Sibley with only "a short bombardment" of Stokes mortars to break down what turned out to be very strong German defenses.

With dense forest and huge boulders sheltering the German machine gunners, the short mortar barrage was useless. The enemy's machine guns were "mowing our men down pretty fast," according to one report at 5:45 A.M. Then, as the remaining marines worked their way closer to the rocks, the Germans started hurling hand grenades. Still the marines pushed on. "We were able to capture four machine guns and to kill many of the enemy. . . . Much execution was done by automatic rifles. Bombs [hand grenades] were scarce. The rifles played the most important part and many enemy were killed by the bayonet."

Just after 6 A.M., Lieutenant Colonel Harry Lee, Catlin's second in command, was telling Harbord that there were "many more machine guns than expected." Still taking heavy casualties, the marines fought on until 8:30 A.M., when Sibley "became convinced that he could not carry these forts without artillery preparations even by expending all his forces." Already he had lost 42 percent of his officers and 40 percent of his men. Deciding to hold at least some of the ground gained, he pulled back the survivors sufficiently to gain cover and dig in.

Now, at last, Harbord began to suspect the strength of the opposition in the wood. "Let your men rest," he told Sibley. "I will have artillery play on the wood." His plan was to begin a barrage at dawn on June 9, "which by the late afternoon is expected to obliterate any enemy organizations in that wood."

The barrage continued throughout June 9, and Harbord ordered a third attack for dawn the next day. This time he limited his immediate objective more realistically to the southern portion of the wood. Belleau Wood fell neatly into two halves, with a thin neck joining them in the middle. So far the marines, for all their struggles, had gained no more than a thin fringe of ground along the southern edge. Now the 1st Battalion, 6th Marines, commanded by Major John Hughes, was ordered to push up through the southern half to the top end of the neck and establish a liaison with Bouresches to Hughes' right and units linking across to Hill 142 on his left.

The artillery barrage continued unabated until Hughes attacked at dawn on June 10—and then the messages flowing back to brigade headquarters justified the expenditure of shells. At 4:51 A.M., Hughes reported, "Artillery barrage working beautifully," and later, "Artillery has blown the Bois de Belleau to mince meat." Hughes lost no men crossing into the wood and found little resistance once inside. By 5:40 A.M., the 6th Regiment's intelligence officer was reporting to Brigade: "Action in woods deemed finished." There were reports of machine-gun fire and some casualties, but as far as Harbord, and indeed Hughes, were concerned, the southern operation had been a success.

By now the troops were near collapse. Water was short, and most were living on "monkey meat"—greasy, stringy Madagascar corned beef—or raw bacon and hardtack. Diarrhea and fever were common and debilitating, lice universal. "Men fall asleep under bombardment," reported Harbord, and he planned for their relief. Nevertheless, he intended that the marines should finish the job. Late that afternoon, he ordered Major Frederic Wise to take his unit (2nd Battalion, 5th Marines) and clear the northern end of the wood.

Wise was a hard-boiled, paunchy veteran with service in the tropics, something of a martinet with his men. In thick cover like that of Belleau Wood he favored shooting from the hip. Among his other tips to his troops was the observation that a prisoner made an excellent shield against enemy machine-gun fire. "It is a safe method," he added, "to bayonet all men on the ground, as some are not wounded." ("Safe" only in the short term, as Harbord pointed out: "The enemy have been told that Americans do not take prisoners, which makes their men fight to the death. . . . This idea . . . undoubtedly costs us many lives.")

Even Wise might have been daunted by the order for a fresh advance. Tired and understrength as they were, two of his companies, side by side, were to hit the northern half of the wood at dawn on June 11. Attacking on a southwest-to-northwest axis, Wise would virtually be repeating the disastrous attack made by Major Berry on the first day. But this time, Harbord assured him, there would be support from Hughes in position in the neck of the woods, as well as a heavy artillery barrage.

Unknown to Harbord or Wise, however, the confident messages of the previous morning had been hopelessly misleading and Hughes had failed in his operation. He had not in fact established a line across the neck of the woods. As Wise struck across from the west, Hughes was still struggling against the lines of machine guns in the southern half, almost half a mile south of where Harbord supposed him to be, and he was not in place to cover Wise's right flank. The German hold on Belleau Wood was virtually undisturbed; in a tragic rerun of Berry's attack, Wise's men were being sent through the wheat against the waiting German gunners.

At 4:30 A.M., the nightmare repeated itself. The men emerged in regular waves, and machine guns and shells engulfed their lines. One marine later remembered a high-explosive shell dropping and a squad of automatic riflemen "which was there a moment ago disappeared, while men on the right and left were armless, legless, or tearing at their faces."

By the time the survivors reached cover, Wise was losing control as support troops ran into the back of those leading the assault. With great bravery but little discipline, his battalion clawed its way through the wood—but in the wrong direction. Gravitating, according to Wise, to where the enemy fire was heaviest, the attack turned off the northwest axis and cut due east across the narrow waist of the wood. This exposed the left flank, and the Germans filtered in and attacked.

Now it was kill or be killed; tactics were an irrelevance. One survivor recalled how in those deep woods

the Germans fought their machine-guns with desperation and courage and mostly died at their guns. They did not hesitate to close with the bayonet and both sides threw grenades that killed both enemy and friend. There were absolutely no prisoners taken during the heat of the attack and anything on the ground received a bayonet thrust to make sure of death. When the 55th and 43rd companies pushed the enemy's third line down into a ravine and were fighting hand to hand, two German machine guns on the far slope opened up on the line, killing as many Germans as Marines, if not more.

Wise no longer had any idea of the true situation and now he began sending back misleading reports. In ignorance, Harbord told Bundy that "the north half of the wood was taken and the line established on the north-east side" and that "two companies of engineers . . . are employed on the east and north edge . . . in consolidating positions." The marines had taken three hundred enemy captives: "the biggest thing in prisoners the AEF has yet achieved." Effusive congratulations poured in, and Bundy telegraphed Pershing with the good news; it would feature the next day in *The New York Times*. All was complacency. "German officer complained that they had been up against Canadians and British," reported one staff officer, "but that they had found us a bit worse."

Back in the wood, the truth was dawning on Wise. More than half his battalion were dead or wounded, and the remainder were strung out along a thin line of foxholes. The enemy was very close, at some points no more than fifty feet away, and a counterattack could be expected at any time. Harbord began to realize that Wise had taken heavy casualties and that the enemy were still in the wood in some numbers. But Wise was unable—or unwilling—to say exactly how far back the battalion's line was, how far short of its objective. Instead, he told Harbord what the commander wanted to hear: that "with a certain amount of artillery preparation he could capture the remainder of the Bois de Belleau." Accordingly, Harbord arranged a preparatory barrage on the northwestern section of the wood "until 5 pm when an attack is to be made."

With his original force in ruins, the weight of Wise's attack would have to come from two companies of engineers and 150 replacement troops, some of them only two months in uniform, who had been marched up from the rear and thrown into the battle. This motley group waited anxiously for the barrage that was to clear their way. But when it came, it missed the German defenses completely; because Wise either did not know or would not say how far to the south his lines really were, the barrage dropped too far north to trouble the enemy.

Nevertheless, the marines advanced. Now their preparation at Quantico served them well. The replacements and engineers attacked with fury, and some did reach the northern edge of the trees. Briefly, the best part of the wood was at last in American hands, but the grip was too precarious to be maintained. At 11:07 on the night of June 12, Wise calculated his strength: "Have now 350 old men left and 7 officers."

That night, June 12–13, the marines were subjected to the most devastating shelling they had endured so far. Wise was attacked, but his lines held. A heavy assault also crashed into Bouresches. A young replacement officer, overwhelmed by the force of the attack, reported the village lost, and the American field artillery was asked to prepare a counterbarrage. The order was revoked in some haste when it was discovered that the despair was premature and Bouresches was still in marine hands.

Now Major Holcomb was ordered to relieve Wise on the night of June 13–14; but just before his battalion was due to move off, the enemy sent over a mixed barrage of mustard gas and high explosive that disabled two of the four companies. Many took their masks off before it was safe to do so, with agonizing results. "Probably more or less gassed through removing their respirators to attend their wounds," reported a medical officer of the 160 gas casualties in Holcomb's companies.

Wise, expecting 800 men to relieve him, was presented with no more than 325 effectives when Holcomb's battalion eventually arrived early on the morning of June 14. "My men physically unable to make another attack," Wise reported at 6:05 A.M., and now a note of panic was beginning to creep in. Fortunately, at this moment, Harbord assigned local command to Lieutenant Colonel Logan Feland. He agreed to launch another attack from the west to clear Wise's left flank and, by 8 A.M. on June 15, this latest push had succeeded in completing the marines' lines right across the northern part of the wood.

Unfortunately, Feland himself became confused about the precise line held. He reported to Harbord that the Germans had been pushed back into a V-shaped stronghold in the northwest corner with the open end fac-

ing the German lines. "He [Feland] could force this position in a few minutes," Harbord was told, "yet he realized that it would mean a considerable loss of life and felt certain that with a little more time these men could
be taken or driven out without much loss of life." Harbord agreed to the
delay, perhaps feeling that the job was as good as complete already.

At this point, in mid-June, the marines had fought themselves virtually
to a standstill. To a man, they were exhausted, dirty, sick, hungry, and
stunned by incessant noise and squalor. They had suffered, and seen others suffer, hideous injuries. "The character of the wounds encountered
here fall chiefly into the tearing, lacerating, crushing and amputating
types, accompanied by all degrees of fractures, haemorrhage, and destruction of soft tissue," a battalion surgeon noted concisely.

The wood was filling with refuse, excrement, and, increasingly, putrefy-
ing corpses, the ground was alive with decay, and infection killed many before they could receive medical treatment. No American hospital service
had yet been organized behind their lines, and the French could barely
cope with their own wounded. Before the fighting had started, the American evacuation hospital at Juilly had had 250 beds, two surgeons, and
twenty nurses; between June 4 and 8 alone, they handled more than two
thousand cases.

After two weeks' fighting, the brigade as a whole had taken almost 50
percent casualties. Some units had been entirely wiped out. Sibley had lost
14 officers and 400 men, Turrill 16 officers and 544 men, Wise 19 officers and 615 men, Holcomb 21 officers and 836 men. The French 167th
Division on the left had saved the marines' manpower by extending its line
to hold the crest running from Hill 142, while on the right the infantry
brigade had taken over the defense of Bouresches. This had allowed the
marines to shorten their lines, but they desperately needed relief. Fortunately, the 3rd Division's 7th Infantry Regiment was available; beginning
on the night of June 15–16, soldiers began moving into the wood to release the embattled marines. The relief was intended to be only temporary,
and Harbord retained control of the sector.

He still seems to have believed that the Germans held only the small
V-shaped bastion that Feland had described. Consequently, on June 18,
when Lieutenant Colonel Adams, commanding officer of the 1st Battalion, 7th Infantry, attempted to strengthen the defenses in the wood, he received a withering rebuke from Harbord: "It is understood that you are
wiring an east and west line through the woods between you and the party

of Germans on whom you are supposed to exert pressure. It is not believed that you have anything to fear from any aggression on the part of these people"—an extraordinary, revealing remark in the circumstances—"and it is not desired that you wire yourself in to prevent the pressure which it is desired you exert steadily until those people are killed or driven out."

The 7th was relatively poorly trained and lacked frontline experience, and on June 20 the edge of Harbord's contempt was even sharper. "Attack ordered on machine gun nest on northwestern edge of Bois de Belleau failed because companies of 7th Infantry [the 1st Battalion again] fell back when a few casualties [63] occurred." Patently, Harbord felt he had diagnosed serious weaknesses in some elements of the 7th. His remedy was kill or cure. "Your battalion will be relieved tomorrow night," he told Adams. "Tomorrow morning is its only chance to redeem the failure made this morning. If you clear the northern half of the Bois de Belleau the credit will belong to the 1st Battalion, 7th Infantry and will be freely given. The Battalion cannot afford to fail again."

Unhappily, it did, as Adams forecast it would. "I can assure you," he told Harbord, "that the orders to attack will stand as given but it cannot succeed. . . . The woods is almost a thicket and the throwing of troops into the woods is filtering away men with nothing gained." Adamant, Harbord directed the attack to go ahead at 3:15 A.M. on June 21. By 7 A.M., Adams was reporting, "Everything is not going well." By 8:20 the battalion's A Company was "all shot to pieces" and the attack was effectively over.

Company A's commanding officer would later give his version of what had happened. The company, he said, had reached the top of a knoll to confront massed machine guns, with no sign of Company B, which was supposed to be advancing on the left. At this point, he had been stunned by a grenade. The report continued, "That when he recovered consciousness he saw sixteen or seventeen men of his company running back toward their former position. That he tried to rally them but could not. That he stopped to attend to a wounded man and then got lost and reported at the PC of the 3rd Battalion."

"This officer," Harbord observed grimly,

has no marks of any kind on himself or his clothing. The PC at which he reported is a full kilometer west of where he claims to have been stunned, and in the opposite direction from his company. Company B, which was to have attacked on the left of Company A, turned up without reported casualties . . . entirely outside the Bois de Belleau. . . . This whole situation arises in my opinion from the inefficiency of officers of the 7th Infantry and the lack of instruction of the men. The 1st Battalion is untrustworthy for first line work at this time.

"Imagine the poor Army boys that have not been under fire before," Lieutenant Cates had written when the 7th Infantry had first come into the line. "It's a tough spot to put them in for their first baptism of fire." On June 21, the conditions were no better, and Adams' attack was complicated by surprise enemy tactics. The Germans seen by his men

were in groups of 6 to 10 to 12, manipulating machine guns and rifles, and were dressed in American uniforms. . . . Certain of them mixed with our troops and attempted to interfere with the plan of attack saying that the line should not advance as our own people were up there and we should not kill our own people. At one point in the attack a German in American uniform approached Lieutenant Paysley of Company A saying to him: "My God you are not going to fire on your own men out there in front of you, are you, you are not going to kill your own men." It being so apparent to Lieutenant Paysley that this officer was an enemy in our own uniform that he immediately shot and killed him.

That night the 7th Infantry was withdrawn, and the marines went back into the wood to occupy more or less exactly the line they had left a week earlier. Harbord had chosen to blame the failure of June 21 on the weaknesses of the 7th Infantry, but he did finally have a realistic understanding of the strength of the Germans.

He reported the truth to Bundy on June 22 with cold anger: "The statement made by a German deserter last night that the German line ran through the north end of the Bois de Belleau proves to be practically true. . . . The undersigned has been misled as to affairs in that end of the woods, either consciously or unconsciously, ever since its first occupation by the battalion under command of Lieutenant-Colonel Wise and later by the battalion of the 7th Infantry." (The brigade diary for June 24 records that Wise departed that day "for School." It is possible that he was suffering from a temporary nervous breakdown. "I personally can say," he wrote later, "that towards the end of our stay in the sector from excessive work that I was not at my best in giving clear reports.")

The marines would pay the penalty for Harbord's anger: "The commanding officer 3rd Battalion 5th Marines [Major Maurice Shearer, who had relieved the wounded Berry], now in there, has been told that this is intolerable and that he will clear the woods by ten o'clock tomorrow night; further that the space does not permit the use of more troops than he now has and that it is not practicable to make artillery preparation by withdrawing his troops."

Shearer's attack went in at 7 P.M. on June 23. Harbord's 10 P.M. deadline turned out to be fantasy; by one the next morning, one of Shearer's companies had been virtually obliterated and another had made only twenty yards, which it was unable to hold. The lines were so close by then that conversation had to be held in whispers. "The Boches on one or two occasions, when they had heard talking, had pitched hand grenades into our lines," Shearer reported.

Despite his original impatient hard line, Harbord now pulled the battalion back to make way for a maximum intensity artillery barrage starting in the early morning of June 25. "Every gun that could shoot was turned on the place," recalled one artillery captain. "By dark it was practically kindling." Then, at 5 P.M., Shearer's men attacked again. An hour and a half later, they were being shelled by their own artillery firing short.

"General Harbord had promised us that if we cleared the woods he would relieve the battalion on the following night," Shearer remembered. "The 47th Company, with this in mind, did most of their work with the bayonet and grenade." Terrorized, perhaps, by this ferocity, the Germans began surrendering dozens at a time—only to find their own machine guns turned on them as they tried to come over.

To the end the attackers were uncertain of their success. "*We have taken practically all of woods*," Shearer reported frantically, "*but do need help to clean it up and hold it. Do we get it?*" At 11:20 P.M., Harbord reassured Shearer's regimental commander that there would be no counterattack: "You are in charge of the Bois de Belleau."

He was, at last, right. Worn down like the marines by hunger, thirst, fatigue, tension, and the added scourge of influenza, with their deadly machine-gun nests finally knocked out of alignment, the Germans were abandoning the bloody, grinding struggle. Just before ten the next morning, June 26, Shearer reported "Woods now U.S. Marine Corps entirely."

Statistics conflict, but at a conservative reckoning the Marines had lost more than 100 officers and 5,500 men killed, wounded, or missing. Harbord's estimate was 670 dead, 3,721 wounded. No survivor would ever forget the astonishing and horrifying sights of June 1918 in Belleau Wood; bodies decapitated, torsos eviscerated, joints shattered, eyes put out, jaws shot away, hands, feet, arms, legs blown off and scattered on the ground, men blistered and blinded by gas, sweating and gibbering with shell shock.

Nor would they forget the extraordinary courage of those who fought. Harbord saw the interior of the wood for the first time on June 29. "No-one who has not visited that wood can comprehend the heroism of the troops which finally cleared it of Germans," he wrote. A machine-gun officer in the division's infantry brigade gave perhaps the highest accolade when he wrote home on July 1, "I have seen Chicago papers of June 6, 7, 8 and 9 and they might give one a vague indefinite idea of what the Marines did during the whole month of June. . . . If I could transfer my commission from the army to the Marine Corps, I would do so. It is an honor to serve with them."

However, the infantry brigade did not emerge from the encounter without credit. There was to be one final flourish in the area—to give the 3rd Brigade a chance, cynics suggested, to rival the Marines. Further over to the right, toward Château-Thierry, the 9th and 23rd Infantry had all this time been holding their own sectors of the front, taking more than three thousand casualties in the process. On July 1, they launched a brisk, carefully orchestrated attack on Vaux, the village opposite the crucial Hill 204 overlooking Château-Thierry, to secure the end of the Americans' defensive line.

In stark contrast to the situation at Belleau Wood, the intelligence work before Vaux, under Colonel Conger's direction, had been immaculate. By the time the 3rd Brigade attacked, its commanders were familiar with every corner of the village. Aerial photographs had revealed the layout of the streets; patrols had spotted wire entanglements, machine-gun posts, and other strong points; prisoners and captured documents had given away the whereabouts of enemy units. Refugees from the village had been happy to talk; one old stonemason who had lived in Vaux and had been building and repairing its houses for fifty years had been able to describe virtually every interior in the village, locate the windows from which sniper fire might come, and identify the houses that had cellars and other potential shelters. The artillery knew where to aim, the infantry knew where to storm, and every escape route was blocked to survivors. The attack was technically perfect. Now the French and American defensive line ran, as they had planned that it should, along the dominant ground from Château-Thierry through Vaux, Bouresches, and Belleau Wood to Hill 142, standing indeed between the Germans and Paris.

The 2nd Division had won the battle, both physical and psychological. German intelligence reports acknowledged it to be "a very good division, perhaps even assault troops. In Belleau Wood, the various attacks were carried out with dash and recklessness." More important, the victory restored French morale and confidence in the Americans. Military intelligence reported French comments with pride: "They are in the fight in full force. How admirably they are fighting for the love of France, as well as for the honor of everything human and divine. Let us bear in mind the immense importance of their material and moral contribution." The wood from then on would officially be known as the "Bois de la Brigade de Marine."

It was an important first major display. Serious questions would be asked about the performance of the division's staff, many of whom were undertrained, and of Bundy in particular, but there was less doubt now about the crucial role of America in the war. Public opinion throughout France, reported military intelligence, was "unanimous in believing that when *our* armies are large enough, the war will be brought to a victorious conclusion." Belleau Wood had altered everyone's view of America's capacity—and they adjusted their demands accordingly.

During 1915 and 1916, summer camps were organized to train volunteers: this kind of Civil War massed charge would have provided fodder for German artillery and machine guns.

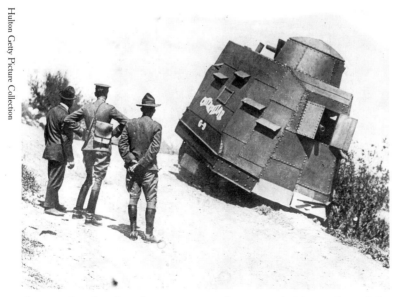

A metaphor for American unpreparedness: a primitive tank stuck in a ditch three days before America declared war on Germany.

ENTER THE DOLLAR

Possibly the most important moment of the war: Secretary of the Treasury William Gibbs McAdoo signs the first of America's loans to the bankrupt Allies.

The supply of men was as critical as the supply of money: the Marines borrowed Barnum & Bailey's elephants to pull volunteers into the Corps.

Liberty Loans from the American people were the principal source of war finance. Here a rather more sophisticated tank roars past Manhattan's Flatiron Building during a Liberty Loan parade.

In the fall of 1917 a million young Americans (labeled) filed into hastily constructed training camps across America. Many wore their best suits to enter the service of Uncle Sam.

A shortage of experienced officers meant that the troops had to be herded into vast, 28,000-man units. This rare photograph of an entire division shows the Big Red One spread across the landscape like a whole medieval army.

As the young men left for war, young girls like this Vassar alumna took over their jobs.

In this new world of industrialized warfare, victory depended as much on labor as on the soldier in the front line. Samuel Gompers, great labor leader, compromised some of his principles in the patriotic quest to motivate his fellow workers.

Even the huge sums of money poured into the American economy could not boost output overnight. It took almost twelve months to build the infrastructure for shipping construction, with a capacity twice that of the rest of the world; and though prefabricated ships could quickly be riveted together, only a handful were finished before the war was ended.

Imperial War Museum

British Field Marshal Douglas Haig walks with Pershing (left) at an English tea party. Haig's daughter follows.

The enemy (left to right): Hindenburg, Kaiser Wilhelm II, and Ludendorff plan strategy.

For ordinary soldiers, life was full of new encounters—meeting the French peasants with whom they were billeted and, for many, making their first acquaintance with modern dentistry.

A WHITE MAN'S WAR

Imperial War Museum

Blacks were used for labor at the front and in rear areas but excluded from the combat that they had hoped would bring them equality at home. No black troops advanced on the St. Mihiel Salient, and no black gunners gave support to this first American Army attack.

Imperial War Museum

Conditions for fighting in the Argonne were close to impossible—thick brush, dense growths of trees, soldiers feeling their way forward into well-emplaced German machine guns.

Hoover Institution

Rain ruined any hope of sustaining the army's advance. Here German prisoners of war are used to push a laden Packard truck back onto the muddy track.

Death at long range: shattered bodies and guns were all too common a sight behind the AEF's lines.

The loneliness of combat: men of the First Division pushing through the Exermont ravine in the teeth of machine-gun fire and shrapnel. Their isolation contrasts with the almost festive comradeship of the massed charges of early training.

There were one hundred thousand "stragglers" on the Meuse-Argonne battlefield. Stigmatized rather than shot, they were herded forward again.

Individuals and groups of Germans surrendered, but the Imperial German Army as a whole remained undefeated and marched home, ragged but still armed.

SHAPING THE PEACE

The prime ministers (left to right) of Italy (Vittorio Orlando), France (Georges Clemenceau), and England (David Lloyd George) joined with U. S. President Woodrow Wilson to shape a vindictive peace, the price Wilson was prepared to pay for a League of Nations.

Occupying Germany: the peace found America with a foothold in Europe from which she would find it hard to draw back in the years to come.

Part Six

The
END
of
INNOCENCE

24

A Time of Reckoning

The events of the last four months had brought the Allies within sight of the end of their resistance. Four times Ludendorff had assaulted the Allied line: his first great offensive on the Somme; the second against the British on the Lys River; the third, coming to rest at Belleau Wood and the Marne; and a fourth, further northwest, between Noyon and Montdidier, during June. Each time the Germans had been repulsed—but the cost in blood and treasure had been enormous on both sides.

The Allied losses were such that, had they stood alone, victory, or at least a compromise peace, might yet have been within Germany's reach. The British, French, and Italian prime ministers had warned President Wilson at the beginning of June, "There is a great danger of the war being lost unless the numerical superiority of the Allies can be remedied as rapidly as possible by the advent of American troops." And Pershing had echoed the call. On June 4, he cabled Secretary Baker: "It should be fully realized at home that the time has come for us to take up the brunt of the war." General Foch was prepared to be more specific; what he wanted from America, he had already made plain, was one hundred 28,000-man combat divisions.

The AEF staff discussed this proposal in detail with Foch's staff, and on June 25 Pershing gave his official endorsement: "We have reached the inevitable conclusion that, in order to beat the Germans next year, the Americans must have . . . 80 divisions here by spring and, if possible, 100 by the end of June [1919]."

This was a colossal figure and in some ways a puzzling one. Though Ludendorff's offensives had cost the Allies dear, the Germans themselves were locked in a downward spiral of material and manpower shortages; they had used up their best troops with their human blitzkrieg tactics and were now being forced to pull 200,000 boys from the graduating class of 1920 into training camps to ready them for the front by September 1918. Analysts in Washington were estimating that the Germans' material resources could last no longer than November 11. Where "the Huns" were getting the men and munitions from, noted George Goethals in his diary, "continues to be a mystery."

Against this declining, even puny force, Foch and Pershing were claiming they needed to open the 1919 campaign with the equivalent of more than 350 European-sized divisions (French, British, and American), massively augmented by artillery, tanks, and aircraft. No good military rationale seems to have been offered for this, and Pershing may well have become embroiled in the Allies' machinations. The British were still anxious to reduce their presence on the Western Front in order to counter the German and Turkish threats to the imperial possessions in the east, while the French, themselves almost at their limit, were anxious to insure against a defection of this kind. In 1919, if the British did go, only the Americans would have strength left for the fight.

Neither the figures nor the reasoning seems to have been questioned at home. The Chief of Staff, Peyton March, backed Pershing in principle: "I am thoroughly convinced of the absolute necessity of a very large American force, in fact a force to the limit of our powers." But could the nation actually create an army 100 combat divisions strong, equip all those millions of men, ship them, and supply them over three thousand miles of ocean and the overstretched French rail network? The time of reckoning was upon the United States: Foch's demand was at the same time the ultimate test of national capability and an opportunity for the nation to assume leadership on the world stage.

Fourteen months earlier, when Wilson had declared war on Germany, a burden like this might have been shouldered virtually without question, and the opportunity to lead would have been eagerly welcomed. The confidence with which Americans viewed themselves, their abilities, and their destiny had never been higher than in the heady days of spring 1917. But America had been mauled in different ways by twelve months of war. Collectively, Americans had failed to harness the immense strength of the country; during the winter, production had all but stopped. Their simple trust in overwhelming material strength had been shattered. So too had their self-image. By the summer of 1918, in the eyes of many liberals America was no longer a place of tolerance, openness, and democracy; it was divided, intolerant, vindictive, and submissive to the demands of a central authority that attempted to control people's lives down to the details of the food they ate, the newspapers they read, and the conversations they were permitted to hold in public. In the crucible of total war, the nation had lost its innocence; few could now claim with absolute conviction the moral superiority over the corrupt nations of the Old World that it had once possessed.

As to material strength, Peyton March saw clearly that the burden of 100 divisions was beyond America at present. The immensity of the demands defied the imagination. The 2 million pairs of shoes that had been on order in November 1917 had mushroomed to 29 million pairs. For the next winter, which was not that far off, the Army would need 16 million wool coats, 22 million pairs of woolen gloves, and 40 million sets of underwear. An army this size needed 15,400 guns of all types, consuming an estimated 691,000 tons of projectile steel and 97 million pounds of smokeless powder every month. And all this was on top of supplying the Allies' own vast procurement programs in America and meeting the needs and demands of the home population.

March must have despaired at the opportunities that had been wasted in the months before he had taken up his position. No one could say he had not done his best since then. He had prussianized the Army, established a responsive hierarchy, and ensured that army supply officers, rather than simply looking out for their own bureaus, provided commodities for the Army as a whole. "The reorganization of the War Department is about reaching a point where the machine is completely in hand," March informed Tasker Bliss in July.

Goethals, too, was waging war on waste in the Army. Sixty percent of supplies to France were needed simply to fill the pipeline in accordance with the official policy on reserve stocks. Now Goethals suggested reducing the reserves at ports of embarkation from two months' supply to one and cutting the allowance made for losses to submarines from 10 percent to 5 percent. Taking the bull by the horns, he directly challenged the AEF's estimates of its needs: "Smokeless powder estimated for AEF is practically double that of Britain and France for equivalent combat groups," he cabled Pershing. "Total requirements calculated on basis of this expenditure are considered excessive."

In the civilian sphere, however, there was no equivalent economic general staff. President Wilson's guiding ethic as a war leader had been not efficiency but a determination to maintain continuity with peacetime methods. Like many of his fellow Americans, Wilson preferred a "democratic" approach to war management, one faithful to the country's voluntarist traditions. His strategy was based on targeting particular aspects of the mobilization and entrusting them to temporary, unconnected organizations that would automatically disappear when the war ended. To ensure that their corporate attitude was correct, he put gifted (and trustworthy) amateurs in charge: Herbert Hoover in charge of food, Harry Garfield of fuel, Edward Hurley of shipping—men who shared his philosophy. He allowed his son-in-law William McAdoo to take command of the railroad system and rationalize it, blasting competition away and creating links between the multitude of different companies.

But as Senator George Chamberlain had pointed out, in the economic sphere there was no system to enable these individual agencies to cooperate efficiently either with one another or with industry, other than through a feeble offshoot of the Council of National Defense known as the "War Industries Board" (WIB).

The War Industries Board had initially been set up to oversee the placing of government contracts in war-related industries, thus avoiding the need for the various war agencies to deal directly with business (an obvious opportunity for corruption) and, in theory, providing expert advice on where the best and safest deal was to be obtained. Clearly, business leaders could make an invaluable contribution here; the problem in the President's mind was how to draw on their knowledge without giving them access to the levers of power.

In the spring of 1918, Wilson's preferred method was to make the WIB's chairman his personal envoy to industry. Once again he was pinning his hopes on the gifted individual, and the choice of chairman was critical. Here McAdoo lobbied hard—for a friend who was quietly supporting his own plans to run for the presidency in 1920. Bernard Mannes Baruch was a loyal Wilson supporter who had contributed lavishly to the President's reelection fund in 1916 and even had plans to buy a New York newspaper as "a major vehicle for Wilsonian liberalism." (Wilson was delighted: "Your newspaper plans . . . They are bully!")

Baruch—who always believed he could have been president himself "if I had not been a Jew"—was a formidable operator. Forty-eight years old, he was a multimillionaire who enjoyed a life of private railroad cars and estates in South Carolina and Scotland. He was a dazzling figure, six feet, four inches tall with a physique kept in shape by boxing and weight training. Women found his combination of blue eyes and an Iberian profile (inherited from his Portuguese Jewish mother) irresistible, and, married though he was, he cut a wide swathe through society; only Eleanor Roosevelt seemed openly to dislike him. Wilson enjoyed his style and wit and always sat him on his right at the weekly meetings of the informal "War Cabinet" that the President had instituted at the end of March.

Baruch worked hard at his celebrity, shamelessly manipulating his own image in the national press. But he did know a great deal about raw materials—he had, in fact, made his money speculating in metals and railroad stocks—and he also had well-informed views on industrial mobilization. Wilson wanted him, as chairman of the WIB, to act as a catalyst for voluntarism—to rally America's industrial forces not through any formal authority but through the power of his personality and the skillful use of his high-level contacts.

With Baruch at its head alternately bullying and wheedling, inspiring and menacing, the WIB was able to achieve some rationalizations. Though Goethals (now director of the Purchase, Storage and Transportation Division of the Army's General Staff) personally disliked Baruch and never went to WIB meetings, the Board nevertheless served as a "universal joint" between the Army and other war agencies and the nation's resources.

The WIB did more to militarize the nation's economy than the pure pull of government dollars ever could have done. Military needs were given strict priority over civilian ones in the allocation of capital and materials. Non-war-related production would decrease during the war: $24.3 billion worth of war materials were produced, of which only $1.9 billion came from increased output while $22.4 billion came from diverting civilian production to war needs. If they could, manufacturers turned to war production. Detroit switched almost entirely to producing tanks and aircraft engines, while companies such as the Akron Tire Company turned to producing army cots; the Black and Decker Company used its machinists' skills to manufacture gun sights; the Evinrude Motor Company of Milwaukee suspended its manufacture of outboard motors to make grenades and trench pumps. The war even threw a lifeline to the whiskey makers cramped by Prohibition as they turned their stills to the manufacture of ethyl alcohol for explosives.

Companies that tried to struggle on making civilian goods were required to conserve and use materials not needed for the war effort. They took the tin out of children's toys, and there were no more brass, bronze, or copper coffins to be had. To save wool, men's coats and jackets were shorn of their wide lapels and pocket flaps; Parisian couturiers were persuaded to promote pencil-slim silhouettes in skirts, reducing the consumption of dress material by 25 percent but posing problems for the portly, as at the same time Baruch was denying corset manufacturers the steel for stays. The leather in women's high boots went to make horses' harnesses and Sam Browne belts for officers; rubber boots and tires lost their shine, saving 30,800 gallons of varnish. The authorities harnessed "wasted labor"—the 493,000 inmates of America's prisons—to reclaim the $5 billion worth of garbage that Americans discarded annually.

The American consumer had enjoyed and demanded variety—but with the WIB surveying whole industries through the prism of business efficiency, standardization became the watchword. By reducing their lines to a mere handful, manufacturers released labor and avoided the need to stockpile a wide range of materials. The types of plows available to the farmer were reduced from 326 to 76, washing machines for his wife from 446 to 18; little boys now had a mere 100 types of pocket knife to choose from, instead of the 6,000 or so that had been available before the war. The 155 shades of typewriter ribbon were slashed to 4; shoes too came in only 4 colors now.

These economies may have generated a satisfying aura of earnestness and self-sacrifice, but the activities of the WIB came nowhere near solving the major practical problems dogging the mobilization of American industry. By the summer of 1918, the condition of the industrial heartland of the Northeast, America's powerhouse, was deeply worrying. Harry Garfield predicted that it would soon be impossible to meet both domestic and industrial fuel requirements in the area if the demand grew much heavier. And even if the production figures from the mines and factories could somehow be miraculously improved, the transportation system could not carry the load. In 1916, the railroads had carried 2,256 million tons of goods; in 1918, this figure rose only to 2,306 million tons.

Wilson and Baker had accepted these inefficiencies for the sake of preserving the New Freedoms, but after the war it would emerge that their efforts to curb conglomerates and protect small operators had been largely futile. In the drive to maximize production, mergers became as commonplace as in the bad old J. P. Morgan days: a congressional committee, reporting in 1921, commented that "trusts and combinations sprang up like weeds, until . . . there was hardly an industry or business interest that was not thoroughly and completely organized; competition was at an end." It was the final irony: in refusing to create an economic general staff with real power, Wilson had forced American industries to form their own internal systems of cooperation and control—far more damaging to the New Freedoms and more permanent than an economic general staff would ever have been.

Nor was this new network entirely successful in meeting the extraordinary demands pouring in from the AEF. By the summer of 1918, several vital commodities—wool, cotton, steel, and coal—were running short, and the situation could only worsen as the Army ballooned. Even more serious, there were signs that America simply could not provide the manpower that was needed to staff an army of more than 5 million men and keep the wheels of industry turning as well. "The limiting factor controlling production of war materials is going to be labor rather than transportation," concluded the WIB.

Peyton March acknowledged the inevitable. As he explained to Bliss, far from fielding 100 divisions in France by the summer of 1919, at best America could support a program of

> 80 divisions of all kinds, with the necessary proportionate amount of corps and army troops in France by June 30 1919, together with 18 divisions in the United States. . . . Pershing's cablegrams have been based upon something we do not understand here, and I am advising him that the 80 divisions does not mean 80 combat divisions, but 80 divisions including combat and base divisions.

Though this would give Pershing only 67 combat divisions, it would mean an American army, including the divisions in training at home, of 4.8 million men by June 30, 1919. It was still a colossal program. Whether the nation had the material resources or organizational ability to meet it was one question; whether it had the will to do so was another.

25

The Will to Fight

Cotton and steel were not the only commodities running short by the summer of 1918; there were also worrying signs that support for the war was ebbing away. Even George Creel, the ebullient architect of the whole edifice of public morale, seems to have had his doubts about the people's commitment. In June, as the marines were battling in Belleau Wood, the CPI issued a leaflet recounting a conversation among soldiers behind the lines on the Western Front:

> They were not laughing or joking as is often the case with soldiers who have just been given a few days' relief from the horrors of the front lines. These men were talking seriously, for it was a critical time in the affairs of the Allies. Finally one of the men said: "I wonder if they'll hold?" Another soldier who had just joined the group asked: "You wonder if who will hold?" "Why, the folks at home," was the reply.

The heartland of support for the war, the industrial Northeast, remained enthusiastic. The war meant prosperity for many northern factory workers—as well as for Wall Street; the economy was now too closely tied to an Allied victory to permit any option other than seeing the war through to a triumphant end. The administration too could take comfort from the queues outside Marine recruiting stations. Creel's sanitized presentation of the savagery in Belleau Wood inspired some young men for whom the war still seemed an adventure.

Across the nation, many Americans worked and fought for the vision of the world that their President described, for specific reasons such as the blatant infringement of American rights at sea, or because they believed Creel's warnings that German expansionism might even stretch as far as the American continent itself. Others served not out of hope or anger or fear but from a simple conception of their patriotic duty.

The worry for Wilson's war managers was that, as 1918 wore on, these increasingly seemed to be small islands of support in a wider sea of apathy mixed with eddies of opposition. In some parts of the country, the President's war aims had made no impression at all: "Comprehension of object of the war by farmers unsatisfactory," reported the intelligence officer for Fargo, North Dakota. Elsewhere, the first glow of enthusiasm for his vision of the future had died down. In the midterm elections, after Wilson had personally appealed for a vote of confidence, the electorate returned both houses to Republican control.

This result would have pleased the radical critic Randolph Bourne as a blow struck against the East Coast WASP elite whom Wilson seemed to represent. Old-stock Americans, Bourne had argued in 1916, could not afford to ignore the "strong and virile insistence that America shall be what the immigrant will have a hand in making it, and not what a ruling class, descendant of those British stocks which were the first permanent immigrants, decide that America shall be made."

Certainly, the ethnic diversity of America made itself felt in differing attitudes toward the war. Many Irish Americans, German Americans, Scandinavian Americans, and others had objected to their country joining the Allies and in 1918 continued to harbor resentment. (Russian-Jewish Americans, on the other hand, who had refused in 1917 to fight for a cause espoused by the Tsar, reversed their stance in 1918, after the Bolshevik Revolution.)

Blacks' support, freely offered by some leaders and hard-won from others, was beginning to fall away now, as African Americans realized that their sacrifices would not after all automatically win them equality. William M. Kelley, a black resident of Quincy Street, Brooklyn, who was drafted in the summer of 1918, sent his protest to Secretary Baker: "I go forth to battle, not as a patriotic soldier eager to defend a flag that defends me and mine, but as a prisoner of war, shackled to a gun that shall spit fire in the defense of a humanity which does not include me." The treatment of the all-black 92nd Division, the apparent unwillingness to develop an efficient black officer corps, the consigning of the majority of black units to stevedore and laboring jobs, the executions of the Houston rioters—all gave the lie to hopes of advancement.

"Unrest among the colored people of the United States is greater at the present moment than it has been for many years," noted military intelligence agents anxiously at the end of June 1918. "We find today among the better educated negroes a decided increase in the desire for radical agitation, with the view of achieving real as well as theoretical civil and political equality. At no time have the colored people resented the discrimination as keenly as at present."

Even where no issues of color, race, or principle were involved, a great many people were becoming weary and disenchanted, ground down by the day-to-day realities of wartime life. No one was immune from suffering. Theodore Roosevelt wrote:

> Archie is badly crippled; whether permanently or not it is not yet possible to say. . . . Ted was seriously wounded. . . . He will be back at the Front in a few weeks. If the war lasts long enough he will either be killed or crippled. In his battalion, all his four captains and two thirds of his lieutenants have been killed or wounded. . . . Kermit is trying to get with the machine guns in the infantry; if he succeeds he will do admirably, but will at no very distant time share the fate of his brothers.

And Roosevelt's beloved youngest son, Quentin, a pilot, was already dead, shot down over the Western Front. So too was Peyton March's son, also in training to be a pilot, killed before ever reaching France.

Even for families that had not been touched by death, the economic and social effects of the mobilization were inescapable. Many goods were scarce, some were completely unavailable, and prices across the board were rising almost out of control.

Wilson doggedly rejected all calls for a nationwide price control system. In part this was simple pragmatism: the WIB believed it "wise to fix prices only in those cases where there is some means, direct or indirect, of compelling obedience. . . . It is obviously impossible for the government to seize and manage lumber mills, forests, etc."

Temperamentally, too, the President preferred a piecemeal approach. He chose to rely on patriotic restraint, reinforced by the operations of the

Food and Fuel Administrations, the influence of the WIB—and the Price Fixing Committee, another ad hoc creation whose chairman, the patrician Robert Brookings, also reported directly to him.

Brookings' job was to negotiate prices for raw materials, the roots of the mobilization tree, at levels that the government could afford but that would still stimulate production. His committee had not, however, been created to stem the tide of rising prices that threatened to engulf ordinary Americans, and if Wilson had hoped that reduced costs for the manufacturers would be passed on to the consumer, he was to be badly disappointed.

The cost of living increased by 20 percent between 1914 and 1916 and by 73.8 percent over the next four years. By 1918, food prices were up by 63 percent, fuel and light by 45 percent, and clothing by 77 percent over their 1914 levels. Secretary of Commerce William Redfield told the President that before the war, "Mrs Redfield paid 12 cents a pound for beans and perhaps 20 cents a pound for pork to cook with them. Now she is asked 40 cents a pound for beans and 60 cents a pound for pork. This may not trouble her seriously, but it is ruinous to a man on a daily wage."

The administration itself was to blame for much of the inflation. In 1916, federal expenditure had stood at $742 million. The war had increased this annual budget by 2,454 percent—excluding loans to the Allies. As only 23.3 percent of this amount came from taxes, the rest had ultimately to come from Liberty Loans. At the beginning of the war, faced with the urgent need for Liberty Loans to succeed, Secretary McAdoo had tampered with the strict controls regarding credit in the United States: he had allowed Liberty Bonds to be used as collateral for bank loans. Since the banks, under the Federal Reserve System, then used these bonds as collateral for their own borrowing from Federal Reserve banks, the government was in essence printing money to lend to itself. Though the disruptions caused by mobilization caused the economy to shrink by $1.8 billion (about 4 percent of the 1917 total), the volume of money flowing through the system bulged from $376 million to $2,685 million.

Inflation slowed during 1918, but the damage was done. Watching people sell their bonds below face value, the Treasury Department acknowledged that there was real hardship. This was made the more painful by the obvious signs of immense prosperity that war had brought to the few. While the administration called for patriotic sacrifice, many of those in a position to profit from the war were exploiting every opportunity.

Even well-known companies took advantage of the situation. The Anaconda Copper interests offered to spend $1.5 million on developing manganese resources, crucial to the manufacture of steel, provided that "they would receive a guarantee that the government would not regulate the price." Similarly, Pierre Du Pont offered to build a new company plant to produce desperately needed smokeless powder—on a commission basis. "On the basis of a ninety million dollar investment," Secretary Baker stormed, "this would have yielded them gross profits of from twenty to forty million dollars." His counterproposal, however, was completely inadequate in Du Pont's eyes, as it promised only "a small profit unless we attain complete success. . . . We cannot assent to allowing our patriotism to interfere with our duties as trustees."

Companies fell over themselves to secure government contracts, regardless of whether they could realistically hope to fulfill their obligations. (Even a well-known company like Bethlehem Steel proved incapable of meeting the orders it accepted; the General Staff accused it of having "overcontracted its facilities.") The incentive was terms that were potentially very lucrative indeed. The demand for materials was immediate, and saving money was not a priority for the war agencies. The type of contract—cost plus a guaranteed profit—offered endless opportunities for spurious management or rental charges and other types of creative accounting.

Colonel W. A. Starrett reviewed some of the contracts for the Army's construction program and found that they had given a construction company

> carte blanche as to what constituted cost, exacting no particular accountability and setting no limit on the amount of profit that might be made by reason of increased cost of the work. . . . Projects that were estimated to cost two or three million dollars would be discovered to have run up to eight or ten million dollars before they were fairly started, and bad as it was to allow contractors 10% on so vast a sum as the original estimate, no limitation of fee had been named in case of an overrun of the cost of the work.

Wilson told Congress that the existence of profiteering was "indisputable," citing the findings of the Federal Trade Commission, which had uncovered "inordinate greed and barefaced fraud." Secretary of the Treasury McAdoo recalled looking through the 1917 income tax returns for coal-mining companies and finding "as fine a specimen of war profiteering as I have ever seen." He took a random sample of twenty-four returns: "Two had profits of more than a thousand per cent in one year. . . . Ten earned between one hundred and six hundred per cent, four between fifty and one hundred, and only eight made profits of less than fifty per cent."

The profit margins for munitions producers were staggering. Bethlehem Steel's profits were 800 percent higher during the war years; the value of Du Pont's stock rose by almost 600 percent; and senior executives were not averse to awarding themselves large bonuses. One executive of the American Metal Company received a $350,000 bonus in 1917; had he been conscripted, he would have earned $35 a month.

Profiteering on this scale jeopardized the nation's ability to pay for the war: shipowners, charged an incensed President Wilson at one point, were "doing everything that high freight charges can do to make the war a failure." Worse, it was a permanent threat to social and industrial harmony.

"The law of supply and demand has been replaced by the law of selfishness," protested Herbert Hoover, and he went on to warn the President of a storm brewing. The workingman was confronted with the spectacle of naked greed among the upper echelons of business and industry, while he himself struggled to keep up with the spiraling cost of living. Families were coming under great strain, a situation reflected in the statistics for juvenile crime—up 16 to 30 percent across the country. "Parents are having a hard struggle to maintain their livelihood," explained Saint Louis's Chief Probation Officer, "and consequently are not able to give the proper care and attention to the children in the home."

In this situation, why should a worker set aside his own aspirations for better wages and conditions simply because there was a war on? "The fact that there are so many employers who put greed before patriotism," wrote George Creel, drafting propaganda directed at labor, "makes it very difficult to level any blanket attack against workers who are likewise guilty of thinking of themselves before their country."

"We cannot hope to restrain the constant demands of labor," warned Hoover, "with its reactions on national efficiency, unless we bring the advances in prices to a stop." Secretary Redfield echoed his conclusions: "Just as we can hardly preach religion to a starving man, so patriotism is a cold thing when the breakfast is scant and a strike seems the only way to make it sufficient."

Despite all the efforts of Samuel Gompers and the propaganda of the CPI, during 1918 strikes flared all over the country. Many were settled but others dragged on, and some grew violent. The governor of Georgia turned in panic to the Army to restore order in Columbus, where there were riots. "Some men had been killed," he explained, "and conditions were beyond the control of the home guards." At Bethlehem Steel, the workers went on strike because the eight-hour day in force for War Department contracts was not considered to apply to Allied contracts, on which the men were required to work a ten-hour day without overtime. The objection was perfectly well founded, but the three-month delay in the delivery schedule caused by the strike meant that no American-made guns would be delivered to the AEF during 1918.

Even where men were not striking, they were showing an alarming tendency to move from job to job in search of better wages. Bethlehem Steel's executives defended their delay in fulfilling contracts by blaming other manufacturers, who had lured away "fifty per cent of their trained men." Creel appealed for unselfish concentration on the job in hand. "Why does drifting from job to job give comfort to the Kaiser?" inquired a CPI poster. "Because idle machines reduce production and weaken our Army. . . . A chain is only as strong as its weakest link. You are a link in the chain of production. . . . STICK TO YOUR JOB."

While Samuel Gompers used all his influence to persuade union men to put the nation's interests first, there were other voices encouraging the workingman to stand up for labor's rights, whatever the cost to the country. Even after the government swoops of 1917, the IWW continued to be a catalyst for disruption. Though its leaders were mostly in jail, the organization showed remarkable resilience. At the end of January, Omar Bradley had taken his company of infantry to Butte, "the principal hotbed of unrest in Montana." His wife was heavily pregnant, and her health worsened in the bitter cold, which touched 40 degrees below zero. She lost the baby, but Bradley had to remain in Butte. On Saint Patrick's Day, the IWW "attempted to stage an all-out strike to shut down the Anaconda mines. . . . Main Street was soon teeming with literally thousands of agitators, many armed with brass knuckles and knives. Forewarned, I deployed the entire company [five officers and eighty-six men] with loaded rifles and bayonets fixed. . . . This show of force had a decisive effect."

But that was by no means the end of the IWW challenge. That summer, an order "written on tissue paper and rolled up until it was not much larger than a pin" was sent from Chicago, where "Big Bill" Haywood and other IWW leaders were on trial, to Butte, Seattle, Spokane, Los Angeles, and Arizona. The IWW intended to stage a series of strikes in the copper mines, shipyards, and lumber camps; thousands of leaflets were printed, and IWW organizers held torchlight meetings to rouse workers to action.

The situation in the shipyards of Seattle was regarded by the authorities as "particularly menacing." But then military intelligence agents in the city had a stroke of luck:

At 4 o'clock this morning, the police of this city received a telephone call from a person unidentified stating that a man had taken poison in a certain room of a local hotel. The police were asked to come at once with an ambulance. The police went to the hotel but the clerk knew nothing of the report. The police then went to the room mentioned. The door was locked and all was quiet within. The police unlocked the door and went in. Mrs Collier . . . wife of C E Collier, leading IWW attorney in this district . . . was in bed, nude, with a man other than her husband. . . . Mrs Collier said that if her reputation would be protected, she would . . . give the intelligence officer complete details of her husband's IWW activities and turn over all the documents and data she could obtain. . . . It is probable she will prove a source of information for some time to come.

The Wobblies were still regarded with loathing as radical agitators by employers and military authorities alike. But that summer a new threat to law and order (and the pursuit of profit) was emerging beside which the Wobbly menace would pale into insignificance. Bolshevism was making its appearance in America.

In February, Bolsheviks had already been spotted in the Bronx, "where Trotzky lived," and on the shores of Puget Sound; in April, "Bolos" bobbed up in Buffalo, and in Passaic, New Jersey, and Los Angeles the following month. America's first encounters with the new ideology had not been antagonistic, rather the reverse. In January 1918, two months after Lenin came to power, Woodrow Wilson had been insisting that America would be "privileged to assist the people of Russia to attain their utmost hope of liberty and ordered peace." But then, with the signing of the Treaty of Brest-Litovsk, the new regime took Russia out of the war; suspicions gathered, and attitudes began to harden. Now, in the public mind, their associations were no longer with aspirations toward "liberty and ordered peace" but with pacifism, disruption—and the IWW, which was sometimes labeled "Lenin's advance guard."

The tentacles of Bolshevism seemed to many God-fearing citizens to be creeping ever nearer the throat of America herself. From the Marxist perspective, the country had a promising gulf between rich and poor, between the WASP plutocracy and the seething proletariat of new immigrants, downtrodden and caged in their urban slums. Lenin had written directly to these people, the "American Workers," reinterpreting American history in terms of the Marxist dialectic and "pointing out," as military intelligence analysts explained it, "what a wonderful illustration of proletariat power our Revolution against the Bourgeois English populace was, and that the Civil War was a similar rising against the Bourgeois South for the sake of the proletariat slave." The first anniversary of the Bolshevik revolution was a gala event. In Chicago, several thousand people turned up to hear the keynote speaker express his heartfelt desire: "Let us hope that in the near future we shall see the Soviet Republic of the United States."

In fact, the authorities were worried less by the remote threat of revolution than by the spirit of selfish noncooperation with which radicals, whether Wobblies or Bolsheviks, seemed to infect the entire workforce. "There is . . . a very large percentage of wage workers," reported military intelligence,

> who, while disavowing any sympathy with the IWW or with doctrines akin to their propaganda, have, nevertheless, a feeling of toleration for the IWW, or any other radical organization, who by their efforts create a condition out of which they may secure some advantage for themselves. While they do not indulge in sabotage, disloyal utterances or diminish the returns they make for their wage, they are, nevertheless, just as ready, just as willing, and just as sure to take their "Pound of Flesh", from employer or nation when the conditions permit the opportunity. While not positively disloyal, they are more than unpatriotic [and] not the least percentage of this element may be found in trade unions affiliated with the American Federation of Labor.

.   .   .

To keep labor in line behind the war effort, the authorities toyed with the notion of using the draft as a tool—an idea that would have been unthinkable and un-American even twelve months before. Captain Neal Johnson, leading the Army unit sent to suppress the Bethlehem Shipbuilding strike in Alameda, California, took pains to emphasize in his report that some of these men were of draft age and should have their exemptions withdrawn. He made his point crudely, but the sentiment was echoed in more sophisticated form by no less a person than Secretary of War Newton Baker in his suggestion that the Provost General should squeeze the nation's manpower more efficiently with an order to "Work or Fight." All men with deferred classifications who were not currently working or whose jobs contributed little to the war effort automatically passed into the highest class of eligibility for the draft.

This "Work or Fight" order of May 1918 was highly contentious. To labor, it appeared to be a device to penalize strikers—and there was some truth in the suggestion. Woodrow Wilson himself openly threatened striking machinists at Bridgeport, Connecticut, with being banned from war-related industry for a year—which would instantly render them liable for the draft.

Now it was not only the well-paid factory or shipyard worker who looked with disfavor on the draft. The huge surge in the demand for troops for the Western Front put the nation's enthusiasm for the war to the test— and the results, as an indicator of whether or not an eighty-division army was feasible, worried the War Department.

The original screening for the draft had made only one broad distinction: between the eligible and the exempt. By December 1917, Enoch Crowder had begun to categorize the eligible more precisely into five classes of descending suitability for service. By the summer of 1918, Class 1 was on the verge of being exhausted, and to maintain the quality of the intake, the age limits of the draft had to be extended—down to eighteen and up to forty-five, making an additional 13 million men eligible.

These millions were subjected to even more ardent and inspiring efforts at persuasion than the first registrants. But the men did not come forward with the same enthusiasm. There was no sense of a crusade, only the cold realization of imminent transportation to a shooting war. Military intelligence sources reported that the draft was seen now as "an unpleasant necessity rather than as an opportunity to serve," adding, "The extension of the age limit for the draft is believed by the average man to have been forced with a view to controlling the labor situation."

The rot had set in even among the gilded youths; a General Staff memorandum of August 1918 noted a "perceptible slackening" of morale among the cadets at Princeton's School of Military Aeronautics, the former epicenter of volunteerism. And according to Attorney General Thomas Gregory, draft evasion was now a serious national problem: "There are many deserters and slackers at large in this country."

The Department of Justice had already, in Pittsburgh that spring, launched the first of a series of "slacker raids" aimed at catching the estimated 350,000 men who had not registered at all ("slackers"), had registered but failed to report for the medical examination ("delinquents"), or had been inducted but deserted. Now, with practice, the raids became more sweeping, reaching a peak in New York and New Jersey at the beginning of September.

In hotels, cafés, saloons, dance halls, poolrooms, the show ground of the Ringling Bros. Circus, every man who appeared to be of draft age was rounded up and asked for his registration or classification card. If he was not carrying it, as required by law, he was detained. In Chicago the municipal pier was turned into an internment camp, while elsewhere city armories were used; public buildings were crammed with men taken off the streets, in many cases by soldiers, sailors, and volunteer vigilantes. In New York, early risers found all the subway exits blocked at 6:30 A.M.; thousands of men were taken, sometimes forcibly, to detention centers, where they waited all day and into the night to be interrogated. The protests reached Congress, but the raids netted Crowder the vital extra thousands of men. In New Jersey alone, 28,875 men were detained, of whom 789 were inducted at once and a further 12,515 had their classification amended.

Conscripts reluctant to go to war; blacks unwilling to put national unity ahead of their own battle for equality; labor set on pursuing better pay and conditions whatever the risk to the war effort—in many ways, the country that faced the challenge to raise 100 divisions was not the one that had rallied to the President's inspiring war message little more than a year before.

26

"The Spirit of Ruthless Brutality"

The failure of Woodrow Wilson and his war managers to unite the country behind the war did not mean that the CPI's gigantic effort had been without effect. What the propaganda had done was intensify many of the pressures that had been building up within American society before the war, to the point where an explosion was inevitable. The war effort, as much as the fighting itself, was inflicting damage on the American psyche that in some ways was irreversible. This became most obvious in the summer and fall of 1918, a period of mass paranoia to rival the later McCarthy era, when hatred, mistrust, and hysteria would grip the nation.

With the prime motivations of any war—the threat of invasion and the fight for survival—missing from the American matrix, Wilson's propagandists had concentrated on two main themes: hatred for the enemy and loyalty to the flag. The one was far easier to inspire than the other, as Wilson himself had predicted before the fighting had even begun. "Once lead this people into war," he had told newspaper editor Frank Cobb in March 1917, "and they'll forget there ever was such a thing as tolerance. To fight you must be brutal and ruthless, and the spirit of ruthless brutality will enter into the very fiber of our national life, infecting Congress, the courts, the policeman on the beat, the man in the street."

It was not hard to generate hate for the Hun, particularly after American soldiers began to be killed. But Germans were not just an external enemy, they were woven into the fabric of the Republic itself; for decades they had been a solid, successful, integral component of communities across the nation. Then the machinations of Dr. Hexamer and the National German-American Alliance in the neutrality years had helped place a question mark over their loyalty—and now, everywhere, the hate Creel stirred spilled over them.

At the outset, the CPI insisted on a degree of calm and atrocity stories were outlawed. But as the temperature of the war effort rose, cool reason dissolved. "It is difficult to unite a people by talking only on the highest ethical plane. To fight for an ideal, perhaps, must be coupled with thoughts of self-preservation."

In April 1918, the CPI began screenings of its most famous hate movie, the film "that blocked Broadway": *The Kaiser, the Beast of Berlin.* This epic portrayed the burning of Louvain and the agony of the *Lusitania,* and depicted the Kaiser telling the American ambassador that he would "stand no nonsense from America after the war." In Omaha, Nebraska, 14,000 people saw the film—"the largest number that ever saw a motion picture in Omaha in one week."

In print, one of the CPI's most popular publications, *Why America Fights Germany,* picked up the theme of invasion so skillfully exploited by prewar preparedness campaigners. Having made a successful landing on American soil, the Hun advances until he reaches Lakewood, New Jersey. There the apostles of *Kultur* demand wine, beer, and money. "One feeble old woman tries to conceal $20 which she had been hoarding in her desk drawer; she is taken out and hanged. . . . Some of the teachers in the two district schools meet a fate which makes them envy her. The Catholic priest and Methodist minister are thrown into a pig-sty while the German soldiers look on and laugh." Then, inevitably, the invaders get drunk and "robbery, murder and outrage run riot. Fifty leading citizens are lined up against the First National Bank and shot. Most of the town and the beautiful pinewoods are burned, and then the troops move on to treat New Brunswick in the same way."

The British had used atrocity stories shamelessly to aid their propaganda, most notably in the Bryce Report on German atrocities published at the time of the sinking of the *Lusitania.* In November 1917, Creel's committee issued its own report, *German War Practices,* and urged the Four-Minute Men to arouse their audiences with choice examples of *Schrecklichkeit* ("frightfulness"). Some duly responded with calls to string up "Withered Willie" from the tallest tower in the Wilhelmstrasse and to keep "those goose-stepping, baby-killing gorillas" away from U.S. shores.

Rumor was an effective catalyst of hatred. Germans, it was whispered, were putting ground glass into food, poison on Red Cross bandages; there was sympathy for the Hun in high places (Attorney General Gregory had to defend his wife's German antecedents). Spy fever reached epidemic proportions: the flashes of light refracted from the stained-glass windows of William Randolph Hearst's apartment on Riverside Drive were read as being signals to German submarines skulking in the Hudson River below.

Across the country, all things German came under attack. Beethoven's music was banned in Pittsburgh. King George III was lambasted anew in American history lessons, but now for his German origins. German Americans anglicized their names (as had the current King of England). Frankfurters were euphemized into "Liberty sausages," dachshunds became "Liberty dogs," sauerkraut (where it continued to be served) was "Liberty cabbage," hamburgers were "Salisbury steak."

The New York Times put German publications into intellectual quarantine: "Any book whatever that comes to us from a German printing press is open to suspicion. The German microbe is hiding somewhere between its covers." The eminent publisher Irving Putnam signed a pledge, declaring, "I am opposed to opening the markets of America to the products of Germany for the next 25 years, and I will knowingly buy and use no German-made goods during the said period of time."

The Kaiser's conspiracies were laid bare:

We all know this, that though disguised in a hundred ways, sly, stealthy, ruthless, the German propagandists are still at work in every city of our land, striving by every means to make America accept the supremacy of Kultur. . . . The surest way to defeat Kultur's ambition is to destroy its grip on the schools. . . . Fort Wayne, Indiana spent last year $14,672 for teaching German to immigrants, and $108 for teaching English; Columbus, Ohio, spent nothing for teaching English and $16,000 for teaching German; Philadelphia spent $11,000 for English instruction and $70,000 for German.

German-language teaching was banned in many schools and the books burnt, in fear of the insidious threat of cultural slavery. "Behind the chair of innumerable teachers we have seen the shadow of the spiked helmet," raved one speaker at a conference of the League to Enforce Peace.

Festering through 1917, paranoia deepened after Ludendorff's 1918 offensives and now more often erupted into violence. Gangs of vigilantes ransacked German Americans' homes and daubed yellow paint onto the walls; they tarred and feathered the men and made them crawl down the main streets of cities. The Cleveland *Plain Dealer* reported that in Willard, Ohio, on March 28, a Mr. and Mrs. Zuelch "were taken by a crowd of men to the city hall and there before a crowd of 200 persons compelled to salute the American flag and then kiss it. A flag was given to Zuelch and he was commanded to display it in front of his cigar store. It was waving there tonight."

Other mobs were not so restrained. Early in April, a young man named Robert Prager, a drifter with an argumentative manner and vaguely socialist views, fell foul of a group of miners in Maryville, Kentucky. Prager was German by birth, but as soon as America had entered the war he had taken out his first papers applying for citizenship and tried to enlist in the U.S. Army; being blind in one eye, he had been rejected.

The miners now jeered and hustled him and paraded him through town as an enemy spy. The next day, Prager posted a characteristically disputatious document demanding his rights. That night a mob of about seventy-five men left the saloon and made its way to his house. They pulled off his shoes, shirt, and trousers, draped him roughly in a flag, and made him march through the streets singing a patriotic song. Police officers extricated him and escorted him to the police station, but the mob forced its way in. They took him to the outskirts of town, where they put a tow rope around his neck. Prager asked to write a letter to his parents in Dresden, telling them he was about to die. Then he said, "All right, boys, go ahead and kill me, but wrap me in the flag when you bury me." Half an hour after midnight, they lynched him. The ringleaders of the mob who hanged Prager were themselves put on trial. At their trial, the mob leaders wore red, white, and blue ribbons in their buttonholes. As the jury acquitted them, one of the jurors cried, "Well, I guess nobody can say we aren't loyal now."

African Americans, too, were smeared with the taint of disloyalty. The authorities, unable to ignore black radicalism any longer but still unwilling to credit its seriousness, concluded that German agents must have been at work. German agents, it was rumored, were approaching blacks in the South, "taking peculiar advantage of their illiteracy and consequent credulity" and telling them "that if they do not oppose the German Government or help our Government, they will be rewarded with Ford automobiles when Germany is in control here." Blacks were no longer just getting uppity, it seemed, they were subversive as well. A fresh brand was added to the fire.

Thirty-eight blacks had been lynched in 1917, in addition to those killed in the riots in East Saint Louis and elsewhere, and in 1918 the number was heading toward the eventual tally of sixty-four. In some areas there was evidence that the Ku Klux Klan was taking advantage of the new atmosphere of hatred to resurface. "Night riding and negro baiting around Athens, Georgia, without hindrance from local authorities," reported one intelligence source in July. "Local policemen and Internal Revenue officer reported to be members of the Klan."

In much the same way, the government used hatred of the Hun to repel the advance of the Bolshevik. Not only had blacks been bought by the Germans, it was insinuated, Bolsheviks too were little more than German puppets.

The arguments were superficially convincing. Certainly in Russia that summer Lenin and Trotsky, though technically neutral, were moving from opposition to the German invader toward a policy of military and economic cooperation. But the U.S. government's motives for discrediting Bolshevism were complex. At home, the Bolshevik was one among a number of enemies of law and order, making speeches, denouncing the war, encouraging strikes. Abroad, however, thanks to the administration's confused, inept policy toward Russia, he was killing American soldiers. The government had to portray the Bolshevik as an enemy worth fighting in order to justify a particularly ill-advised intervention on Russian soil.

In pulling Russia out of the war, the Bolsheviks had enormously relieved the pressure on Germany. The German leaders were now free not only to mass troops on the Western Front but also to look around for the resources they so desperately needed—not only in Russia itself but also in the Middle East and possibly even India. To defend their interests in Russia—and in Japan's case to extend them by grabbing the riches of Siberia and the Maritime Provinces—the Allies landed troops on Russian soil and demanded that America do the same.

Wilson was dubious. Neither he nor Peyton March could see any military value in such a venture, nor any point in diverting precious resources away from the AEF. On June 24, March restated the policy laid down by Tasker Bliss the previous fall: "All responsible military opinion believes that the war will be won or lost on the Western Front, including Italy, and that any substantial diversion of troops from that one object is a serious military mistake."

But the need to remain on good terms with the Allies was pressing and Wilson eventually agreed to the demand for intervention. The reason he gave the American people was that he wished to rescue a large body of Czech troops who were battling along the Trans-Siberian Railway in order to make their way to Europe and fight the Germans there. In fact, the President was far more concerned by Japan's obvious expansionist ambitions.

He did not, however, ignore March's warning against sending "substantial" forces. He sent a small force to Vladivostok to watch the Japanese, and to show solidarity with the British and French, he dispatched a single regiment to the Murman coast, just east of Finland, to help secure Archangel and Murmansk, to prevent their being used as U-boat bases and potentially to use them as a base for Allied military operations against Germany in 1919.

In Vladivostok, as the various expeditionary forces eyed one another suspiciously and jockeyed for advantage, the American troops simply studied Japanese imperialism in action. They were not involved in combat with the Bolsheviks and would finally be withdrawn, leaving Manchuria and Siberia east of Lake Baikal in Japanese hands.

In North Russia, however, American forces would see action of a kind, remaining long after the war was over, attempting to push south under British command to the Trans-Siberian Railway, and scattering Bolshevik resistance to cement Allied control of the railroad.

The North Russian campaign, launched in the fall of 1918, was distinguished not by its results, which were negligible, but by its squalor. From the start, the American troops were hardly cut out to be a first-class attacking force. Peyton March had grudgingly selected the 339th Infantry Regiment, supported by other troops from the 85th Division. The large majority of the men were from Michigan; a significant number were Russian speakers, which made them a curious choice. They had been drafted only in June, had trained for a month, during which time they had fired only twenty-five rounds each on the rifle range, and since then had been in transit. Almost all of them had been under the impression they were going to France, and few had any idea what they were supposed to be doing in Russia.

Many were ill when they arrived from influenza they had caught on the transports. Others sickened and died as they traveled south, packed into wet, stinking coal barges. "Blood from underneath coffin trickles across floor of barge while we eat our hard tack and black tea. . . . Our faces and uniforms are black with moist coal dust." Living conditions in their camps and outposts were filthy enough to make the manure heaps of France appealing:

> It's the land of the cootie and bed bug,
> The herring and mud-colored crow
> My strongest impression of Russia
> Gets into my head through my nose
> It's the land of the infernal odor
> The land of the national smell
> The average American soldier
> Would rather be quartered in hell.

Food was British issue: bully beef, dried vegetables, rock-hard biscuit, rhubarb and ginger jam, tea and no coffee. Worst of all was the climate, which ranged from the muggy heat of the swamp in September to the appalling cold of a Russian winter, down to 55 degrees below zero, that stuck hands to weapons and destroyed toes with frostbite. Misery bred brutality on both sides, and American officers' reports routinely spoke of prisoners being shot.

But messy and ineffectual though the fighting was under these conditions, from the beginning it cost American lives. The Bolsheviks had all the tactical advantages; they were fighting what was essentially a guerrilla campaign, and the Americans would eventually suffer 472 casualties. Back home these casualties had to be justified; in the fall of 1918 they were presented as necessary losses in the fight against a Soviet-German conspiracy.

The evidence for this conspiracy was contained in a remarkable collection of sixty-eight documents brought back from Petrograd by Edgar Sisson, once editor of Hearst's *Cosmopolitan* magazine and now associate chairman of the CPI. On September 15, they were released to the press: DOCUMENTS PROVE LENINE AND TROTZKY HIRED BY GERMANS screamed a *New York Times* headline. The documents purported to show, in George Creel's words, "that the Bolshevik revolution was arranged for by the German Great General Staff, and financed by the German Imperial Bank and other German financial institutions." Their authenticity (disputed both then and since) was guaranteed by the National Board for Historical Service and accepted by Wilson himself. Genuine or not, they were used to magnificent effect—and the virus of hatred and suspicion spread.

27

"Nobody Can Say We Aren't Loyal Now"

Though hatred of the enemy proved a powerful emotion in wartime America, even more powerful was the demand that every citizen show himself entirely loyal to the flag—100 percent American. But the quest for total loyalty was another phenomenon whose roots were deep in the prewar years, which made its influence the stronger, and its by-products the more malign.

At the end of the first decade of this century, many native-born Americans had come to believe that the nation was losing its identity. There were now huge communities of the foreign-born, immigrants of a different kind from the northern European pioneers, settlers whose "America" meant not rugged independence, man pitted against the wilderness, but the struggle for a living wage in mills and factories. Unlike their predecessors, they were not being absorbed across the broad spectrum of American life; rather, they formed a solid industrial proletariat that seemed impervious to the heat of the melting pot.

"We are trying a great experiment in the United States," Franklin Lane claimed. "Can we gather together people of different races, creeds, conditions and aspirations who can be merged into one? . . . If we do this, we will produce the greatest of all nations, a new race that will long hold a compelling place in the world." Many had begun to fear that the great experiment was failing, that America was being submerged under an alien tide and, far from carving out a new place in the world, would lose even the one it already had.

When war came, these fears were magnified out of all proportion. The industrial proletariat moved to center stage as the power driving the machinery of total war, and its wholehearted commitment and conformity to the nation's stated objectives became crucial as never before. Yet workers made trouble, went on strike for better wages, and swelled the ranks of seditious organizations such as the IWW. It seemed to be significant now that so many of them were foreign-born—in the steel works, the copper mines, the shipyards, and all the other key war industries. Then, in 1918, the doubters' worst fears were realized with the infiltration into America of Bolshevism, a patently alien creed that struck at the very roots of the Republic.

"We deem it necessary to abolish the present social order based on private ownership of land and the means of production . . . and replace it by a socialistic order," proclaimed the constitution of the new Soviet Republic. No notion could have run more contrary to the American way, and it is hard to overstate the shock effect that communist ideas had in America even before the Bolsheviks were securely established as Russia's rulers. In 1918, American Communists were probably to be counted in the hundreds rather than the thousands, but undeniably the great majority were foreign-born. For the first time since the founding of the Republic, ordinary Americans felt threatened; the Atlantic was no insulation against the revolution that was threatening most of Europe, even Ludendorff's Germany. It was time for defenses to be put in place.

Linking Bolshevism with Germany by means of the Sisson papers was one form of defense; another was to bring all Americans to a full awareness of their own national identity. This had been the thrust of the Americanization program before the war; Bolshevism simply made the need more urgent, as Franklin Lane made clear in a speech to employers in April 1918. Immigrant workers, he warned, could not be exploited indefinitely; employers should show them the benefits of the American way or run the risk of repeating the events of November 1917 in Russia, where, he considered, "they had no sense of nationality."

For those without the patience to wait for the Americanization program to mature, the war appeared to have provided much quicker methods of gauging and enforcing Americanness. The government's demands for people to buy bonds, register for the draft, and conserve food and fuel were innocuous enough in themselves—until they were applied by some people as a measure of the loyalty of others.

Had you registered for conscription? Had you bought bonds? How many? Were you hoarding coal? Had you eaten beef on a meatless day? If the answers to such questions were wrong, the questioners began to take it on themselves to enforce conformity to the nation's wishes. The Banque de France's representative in New York admired the finesse used in selling Liberty Bonds. The philosophy behind the third loan campaign in May 1918 was "to *compel* as many people as possible to subscribe as much as they could afford; at the same time to wage an enthusiastic propaganda campaign to persuade them that they were subscribing voluntarily." Elsewhere there was no such comforting fiction, and "persuasion" took the form of violence. In a few short months, the old traditions of openness, trust, tolerance, and welcome—already under threat before the war began—disappeared completely.

For all his misgivings before the war, Wilson, in calling for unity, obedience, and unquestioning loyalty, had helped to generate the new spirit of the age. To some extent, he had then institutionalized it by seeking the legislative power to enable him to curb dissent. Worse, by allowing his agents to involve patriotic amateurs in policing the law, he had put the levers of oppression into the hands of men whose actions could neither be monitored nor called to account. The jurors who saw the lynching of Robert Prager as a demonstration of loyalty to the nation were very far from alone.

By the summer of 1918, the instruments for repression were almost perfect. On May 16, 1918, the President signed the Sedition Act, which reinforced and extended the Espionage Act. Disloyalty was now a crime, and the penalty was a $10,000 fine or twenty years in prison. It was now an offense to obstruct the draft, to oppose the Liberty Loan scheme, or to call for revolution along Soviet lines. As the courts interpreted the act, it was an offense to call the Secretary of the Navy a fool or to spread depressing rumors about the war—to whisper, for instance, that privates in the AEF were being issued a quart of wine and rum a day; that blacks in the AEF would never get home except in the form of soap; that two hundred beds in a New York maternity ward were reserved for Red Cross nurses returning from the AEF. Abuse hurled in the heat of the moment could, if it had the faintest political tinge, be incriminating. As one senior law officer observed, the Sedition Act "gave the dignity of treason to what were often neighborhood quarrels or bar-room brawls."

To implement the espionage legislation, the existing law enforcement agencies—the Treasury's Secret Service Division and the Justice Department's Bureau of Investigation (BOI)—expanded their operations, and now they were joined by a rapidly multiplying military intelligence establishment, the Military Intelligence Department, later Division (MID), which operated within the United States. These official agencies could be held accountable if not always controlled, but when they actively recruited volunteers to assist them, they sanctioned ordinary Americans to take the law into their own hands.

The self-styled "American Protective League" (APL) was the largest of the volunteer agencies. It had begun its insidious rise even before war had officially been declared. In the weeks immediately after the resumption of unrestricted submarine warfare in February 1917, spy hysteria had mounted, and the different intelligence agencies had jockeyed for the lead in antiespionage activity. Frustrated by Congress's failure to increase the Bureau of Investigation's financing and anxious not to be superseded by McAdoo's Treasury agents (at that point more assertive than the youthful military intelligence organization), the BOI's zealous head, Bruce A. Bielaski, accepted an offer of volunteer help.

The offer came from Albert Briggs, the president of a Chicago company selling billboard advertising, who had assembled a group of patriotic citizens anxious to stem the tide of subversion. Under the title of the American Protective League, the group took up headquarters in the People's Gas Company, Chicago, under Briggs and his second in command, Thomas B. Crockett, a descendant of the legendary Davy. The majority of the early members were too old to be drafted but longed to serve; many had been involved in the campaign for greater military preparedness. To a large extent, they came from the wealthier and more influential levels of society: bankers, hotel managers, retired police chiefs, insurance executives, railroad presidents, company directors.

These were the chiefs; under them was a quasi-military hierarchy of captains, lieutenants, and operatives who were spread through communities across the nation. The size and aggressiveness of the organization made many in government uneasy, including Wilson, who was sensitive to the atmosphere of xenophobia and intolerance that had generated the APL. When it was pointed out to him with a nudge that the White House had a German-born cellarman, he retorted, "I'd rather the blamed place should be blown up than persecute innocent people." Not long after the APL had been given official authorization by the Department of Justice, he was already asking Attorney General Gregory, "I wonder if there is any

way in which we could stop it?" The Justice Department, however, preferred the informal, civilian APL to the threat of extended military surveillance, and the volunteer vigilantes survived.

At no cost to the government (agents had to have an assured income
and cover their own expenses), the APL went around ferreting out disloyalty wherever it existed—and in thousands of cases where it did not—operating in the miasma of hearsay, gossip, and slander that enveloped
America in 1918. APL headquarters provided its agents with the broadest of guidelines. They must seek out all "organizations . . . or individuals
influenced, exploited or used as cover by the enemy in furtherance of his
activity. Example: Labor unions, the International Workers of the World,
the Sinn Fein, religious organizations, pacifists, educational institutions,
educators, racial groups, cults, fads, the demi-monde, vice etc"—in other
words, "persons of character or mentality in keeping with activities of sabotage or crime."

"I am not shure of how much athority I have," wrote one Los Angeles
member. "Do I have power to arest also cary a weappon?" From the beginning, the APL's operations were riddled with abuses of power. In hard-
line Minnesota, the police did deputize the APL, giving them the power
of arrest. Elsewhere, members simply went their own way, breaking and
entering, tapping phones, bugging offices, impersonating gas repairmen
and plumbers to gain entry to homes, interrogating ministers about members of their congregations and schoolteachers about their pupils' parents,
and peering into bank accounts, medical records, real estate transactions,
legal files, private investigators' dossiers, and even the mails. "Let us call
the APL sometimes clairvoyant as to letters done by suspects," remarked
one insider with satisfaction.

They took a vigorous part in rounding up aliens for internment and
identifying alien property for sequestration. They threw themselves into
slacker raids, pointing the finger at suspects and even making (wholly illegal) arrests with a crude enthusiasm that threatened to become a serious
embarrassment to the administration. "Contrary to my express instructions," admitted Attorney General Gregory, ". . . and contrary to law,
certain members of the investigating force of this Department . . . used soldiers and sailors and certain members of the American Protective League,
I am satisfied, in making arrests. I am convinced by the inquiries which I
have made that they were led into this breach of authority by excess of zeal
for the public good."

Many prominent APL members were simply gratifying the urge to play detective and bolstering their own sense of self-importance—lurking on street corners, whispering in hotel lobbies, flashing their badges. There were more than 100,000 of them actively investigating and perhaps another 100,000 passing on information.

Their greatest coup was to put behind bars the man Lenin had described as "The beloved leader of the American workers": Eugene Debs, the Socialist who had polled almost a million votes in the 1912 presidential election. TEN YEARS IN PRISON FOR EUGENE V DEBS, crowed *The Spy Glass*, the APL journal.

> The speedy outcome of the trial which occupied less than five days was a striking testimony to the careful way in which the evidence against Debs had been prepared. Knowing that Debs was scheduled to speak at the socialist convention at Canton on June 16, [1918], Chief Arch C Klumph, of the Cleveland Division, sent operatives and stenographers to cover the meeting and take down the Debs address verbatim. . . . [This] transcript of the speech was the principal evidence introduced. It showed that Debs had ridiculed the army and navy, had criticized the conduct of the war, had questioned the ideals for which the flag stands and had made further remarks calculated to encourage disloyalty and obstruct the draft.

The APL also served the War Department. In reporting on morale and potential opposition to the war effort, local intelligence officers relied heavily on APL sources. APL operatives reveled in enforcing the regulations for the control of vice and liquor around military camps. In some areas they dressed up (entirely illegally) in military uniforms and boarded trains with departing draftees in the hope of detecting drinking. They carried out character investigations on applicants for commissions in the Army and jobs in the civil service, interviewing their friends and acquaintances as well as their referees, and checked the credentials of potential jurors.

Beside the APL, the MID had other keen amateurs working for it at county, state, and federal levels. Each trained agent had a force of volunteers reporting to him who were looking out for loose talk, sabotage, suspicious delays in the production of war supplies. All over the country, railroad employees, private investigators, traveling salesmen, and post office clerks were on the alert for treachery. These volunteers were given a small, highly confidential reference collection of "suspect cards" with the photographs and details of targets on them. There was a proposal that the cards should also be given to bellboys and house detectives in hotels, but this was swiftly rejected on the grounds that bellboys were "not a trustworthy class, and might turn their information into purposes of blackmail." The MID was equally unreceptive to the notion that a bevy of society ladies, reporting to a "matron of undoubted loyalty," might patrol cocktail parties and buffet luncheons. To detect signs of pro-German wavering among blacks, MID recruited other blacks—among them, improbably enough, W.E.B. Du Bois, who then spent the rest of his life on its list of targets.

Volunteers were used to ensure security in factories producing war materials. An agent from the MID's Plant Protection Section (PPS) would visit a plant or factory to carry out a fire or safety inspection. In the process, he would get the name of a plant official who might be recruited as the head of an "Interior Secret Service Organization." This official supplied a list of trusted employees to serve as captains, the captains named their lieutenants, and the lieutenants drew up lists of privates. Then all the volunteers reported back up the line on the loyalty and efficiency of their fellow workers, current plans for strikes, and rumors of sabotage or go-slows, until the information reached the agent at the top. Arguably, this system was even more valuable as a means of keeping troublesome labor activists under surveillance than it was as a means of catching spies.

At the state level, legislators gave their councils of defense extraordinary powers to punish disloyalty. In New Mexico, the council printed standard letters to be handed to people who had made remarks unbecoming to persons "enjoying the liberty and protection of the United States." The Nebraska council formed its own secret service; those it arrested had no right to representation, nor were they told the names of their accusers. South Dakota advised councils at the county level to subpoena slackers and interrogate them about their finances, to find out why they were not subscribing adequately to Liberty Loans. Each Federal Reserve District had a network of "Economic Vigilance Committees" dedicated to ensuring that no capital investment was being wasted on non-war-related projects such as new buildings or road improvements.

Below these official surveillance bodies and feeding dangerously on their activities were literally thousands of half-formed, ad hoc groups that could barely be dignified with the title "organization," all dedicated to ferreting out disloyalty. By the beginning of August, there would be enough to alarm the MID seriously. "In New York City alone, during the past month, over fourteen thousand such organizations were active. It will be seen that drastic steps should be taken with a view to securing Government supervision over their activities."

But the genie was out of the bottle. In Washington State, the Minute Men, a volunteer security force, planted agents in school German classes to detect subversive grammar or disaffected literary criticism. Elsewhere there flourished the Boy Spies of America, the Terrible Threateners, the Knights of Liberty, the Sedition Slammers, and the Anti–Yellow Dog League, a group of children organized to listen for antiwar talk among their families and acquaintances.

Floating free were countless individuals who saw in the emergency conditions of wartime an opportunity to work out personal paranoias or settle private scores. As the months passed, the CPI urged citizens not simply to be loyal but to inform the authorities of any disloyalty in others. This was an invitation to trouble; through accusations of un-American behavior, people could persuade the authorities to move against business competitors, political rivals, annoying neighbors, social upstarts, heterodox ministers, and "advanced" schoolteachers whose "offense" against their country had frequently been no more than an unguarded remark.

In the summer of 1918, Attorney General Gregory was receiving fifteen hundred letters a day, each pointing a finger at someone. Cases brought under the Espionage or Sedition Acts poured through the courts, and local law officers were swamped with information and demands for action. In Eureka, California, a man was sentenced to five years' hard labor for criticizing the President, on the testimony of his own daughter. The young playwright Eugene O'Neill, on vacation in Massachusetts, took his typewriter to the beach to work; the sun glinting off the machine was spotted by a man who leaped to the conclusion that this was a signal to enemy ships offshore. O'Neill was arrested at gunpoint and spent several hours held incommunicado in the basement of the town hall.

Unpleasant though they were, such activities were within the confines of the law. But all too often people's desire to enforce loyalty, like their hatred of the enemy, carried them beyond the boundaries of what was lawful into beatings, ritual humiliations such as forcing people to kiss the flag, tarring and feathering, and worse. Without meaning to, by working on the fears and prejudices already latent in society, Wilson and Creel had helped to shape a divided, fearful, intolerant nation.

Satirist H. L. Mencken, himself of German extraction and a savage critic of "nativism," drew up a list of "patriots" in line for imaginary decorations for "varying services to democracy":

> The university president who . . . heaved the works of Goethe out of the university library [and] cashiered every professor unwilling to support Woodrow for the first vacancy in the Trinity. . . . The authors of the Sisson documents. . . . Every patriot who bored a hole through the floor of his flat to get evidence against his neighbors the Krausmeyers. . . . The patriotic chemists who discovered arsenic in dill pickles . . . bichloride tablets in Bismarck herring. . . . The Methodist pulpit pornographers who switched so facilely from vice crusading to German atrocities. . . . Judges whose sentences of conscientious objectors mounted to more than 50,000 years.

In his Flag Day address of June 1917, Wilson had declared, "Woe be to the man or group of men that seeks to stand in our way!" It was now obvious that this had been more than a rhetorical flourish. In the twelve months since then, America had passed from a free, tolerant civilian democracy with the emphasis on government at the local and state levels to a country dominated from the center. By the summer of 1918, coercion had replaced voluntarism as the mainspring of the war effort at home.

Only in France, where the enemy's menace was real and his cruelty obvious, did the spirit of willing sacrifice remain unmuddied by self-interest or cynicism. And it was soon to be needed; for on July 15, Ludendorff swung yet another hammer blow at the Allied lines.

Part Seven

The
REALITY
of
WAR

28

Attack and Counterattack: July 1918

Ludendorff's new attack had two objectives. First, it continued his grand strategy of drawing in Allied reserves so that his powerful forces in Flanders could push the unsupported British into the sea and win the war. His second aim was purely practical: to enlarge the salient his May attack had created. Curbed by the huge Retz Forest on the west, Belleau Wood to the south, and Reims to the east, this "Marne pocket" was so deep and narrow and so lacking in road and rail capacity that he would not be able to sustain it if the Allies counterattacked.

In early June, Ludendorff had tried—and failed—to outflank the Retz Forest in the west; now, in mid-July, he pinned his hopes on expansion to the east in a pincer attack to the left and right of Reims. But he had no new tactics or weaponry to bring to this, his fifth assault in as many months, other than a handful of tanks hot from the factory. He was if anything less well equipped than before, because he was consistently forfeiting the weapon most crucial to his blitzkrieg tactics: the element of surprise. With the decline in his army's efficiency, preparations were becoming sloppy; once again the Allies knew precisely where and when Ludendorff would strike, and they made their preparations.

The right pincer of the German attack was formed by the Seventh Army under General von Boehn. Tasked to cross the Marne west of Épernay and break out of the pocket to the south and east, von Boehn faced only a polyglot French Fifth Army that included two Italian divisions, elements of the newly arrived American 28th Division, and, at the westernmost edge of his thrust, the 3rd Division under General Joseph Dickman.

Von Boehn launched his troops across the Marne in the early hours of July 15. Artillery and heavy machine-gun fire carved a route through the French lines in all sectors except on the western flank, the Surmelin valley, which was guarded by the 3rd Division's 30th and 38th Regiments.

The 38th Regiment was commanded by Colonel Ulysses Grant McAlexander, a soldier in the Hansen Ely mold and equally as determined. For weeks the 3rd Division had been standing guard against a German crossing of the Marne, and McAlexander had taken every opportunity presented by the terrain to cover the river, the opposite bank, and likely enemy assembly zones with machine-gun and artillery fire. When the crossing finally began, the Germans were badly mauled—and on the other side they faced a careful disposition of forces.

Well aware of the penetration that German blitzkrieg tactics could achieve, McAlexander put three of his companies in the forward zone to hold the riverbank while the rest were disposed to the rear of his position in three further lines, the last one continuous to prevent infiltration. He anticipated that the French division to his right would employ a "yielding," or "elastic," defense, giving ground in the face of pressure, so he had three more of his companies dig in facing the French sector to cover his flank as the French dropped back. Dickman, one of the best of the American generals, had ordered him to hold the line, and he intended to do just that.

In the forward zone, Company G—251 men under Captain Jesse W. Wooldridge—held 600 yards of riverbank on the left of the 38th's sector. Knowing that the Germans could get a bridge across the 80 yards of river "in exactly 120 seconds by the watch," Wooldridge put one platoon into slit trenches dug into the riverbank itself. Five hundred yards back, across a wheatfield that gave a clear zone of fire, he placed a second platoon in front of a railway embankment. The third he put behind the embankment, the fourth on the spur line behind that.

At 3:30 A.M. on July 15, as Wooldridge explained in a letter home, the enemy's creeping barrage started, "behind which at forty yards only, mind you, they came two regiments strong—with more machine guns than I thought the German army owned." Company G had lost no men from the artillery barrage, and at first the platoon on the riverbank stood its ground; with rifles, automatic weapon fire, and grenades, supported by the division's artillery, the men smashed many of the enemy boats and rafts, and gradually the water filled with wreckage and corpses. But through it all, the German attackers poured across the river in large numbers. One German regiment veered off westward into the zone of the 30th Regiment, while the other attacked Wooldridge's position head-on.

"The regiment which came over at my center," reported Wooldridge,

> fought thru my first platoon on the river bank, exterminating same except for three wounded men, one of whom was later killed by our own shell fire on the railway bank. They gradually eliminated my second platoon on forward edge of railway bank, their place being taken in desperate hand-to-hand fighting by my third platoon, the fourth platoon being simultaneously deployed in place of the third.

"Any of the enemy," he concluded laconically, "who battled their way through the three platoons were easy prey for the fourth and there was absolutely no infiltration on my sector."

Wooldridge's situation was complicated by the withdrawal of the battered 30th Regiment on his left to the first support line. General Dickman was on the verge of ordering an immediate counterattack to push the invaders back to the river, when the French corps commander instructed him to wait. "We regret," Dickman replied with dignity if not candor,

> being unable on this occasion to follow the counsel of our masters, the French; but the American flag has been forced to retire. This is unendurable, and none of our soldiers would understand their not being asked to do whatever is necessary to remedy a situation which is humiliating to us and unacceptable to our country's honor. We are going to counterattack.

He issued orders accordingly; but the counterattack was not made. Instead, at 10:30 A.M., seven hours into the battle, some of the Germans who had veered off westward into the 30th's zone now launched an attack from that direction. Wooldridge, his riflemen decimated, thereupon gathered up "kitchen personnel, company clerks, two runners and three buzzer operators" and repelled an attacking force 250 strong.

During the battle for the Surmelin valley, which lasted well into July 16, the French on McAlexander's right did fall back, as he had expected. The defensive precautions he had taken now paid dividends; all his companies performed well, and the 38th held firm. But it paid heavily. Overall, it lost 19.8 percent of its strength; Wooldridge's Company G lost 3 lieutenants and 147 men, and Wooldridge himself found fourteen bullet holes in his clothing. Tragically, some of the losses were caused by the division's own artillery, which, in Wooldridge's opinion, "seemed to think the whole line had withdrawn because the French did."

The 38th Regiment had fought solidly for two days, beset on all sides, firing in three directions, giving ground only as each position became untenable; they took prisoners from six different enemy regiments. Under constant shell fire, and bombing and strafing by a dominant German air force, they held the line on the Marne in a display of resilience that, as Pershing wrote, was "one of the most brilliant pages in our military annals." The grateful French put the Croix de Guerre onto the regimental colors.

One German officer confided his impressions of the 38th Regiment to his diary: "The Americans kill everything. That was the exclamation of terror that lay in the bones of our men. . . . We left on the field, dead and wounded, more than 60% of the troops brought into the conflict on July 15." The 38th had indeed succeeded in standing off two German divisions and effectively destroying two Guards regiments, denying von Boehn the Surmelin valley and compressing his right wing by about three miles.

But further upstream to the east of the 3rd Division, where the French and Italians were struggling, the German general was prevailing in the planned wide sweep around the west side of Reims. It was perhaps the most dangerous moment in four years of fighting. "If Reims falls, we have lost the war," exclaimed Foch without exaggeration, and he embarked on a bold gamble. While General Henri Gouraud and the French Fourth Army, assisted by the American 42nd Division, used the famous elastic defense to absorb the shock of the other German pincer striking to the east of Reims, Foch launched a violent attack on the flank and rear of von Boehn's advancing army.

He had been planning this offensive-defensive strategy for almost a month, intending to pinch out the Marne pocket and remove the threat to Paris. Now he stood the chance of cutting off and destroying von Boehn's army as well. Supported by nearly 1,200 guns, 500 tanks, and 1,100 aircraft, the French Tenth Army (sixteen divisions under General Charles Mangin) and the Sixth Army (eight divisions under General Degoutte) were to attack on a line looping northwest from Château-Thierry to Belleau Wood and along the edge of the Retz Forest back up to the Aisne. Degoutte's divisions in the southern sector were to press forward only slightly; it was Mangin who was to make the main thrust, in the northern sector.

Mangin's objective was to cut the road and rail links leading into the pocket and, in particular, the road from Soissons to Château-Thierry. The task of capturing it was entrusted to the strongest assault divisions at Mangin's disposal: the crack Moroccan Division (which included the French Foreign Legion), flanked on either side by the best of the American divisions, the 1st and the 2nd. Haig had doubted whether the French Army "would have any offensive spirit left without American support"; Mangin's choice seemed to confirm his suspicions.

Though Foch had been considering the Soissons counterattack for some time, the American divisional commanders were not informed of their key role until just before the assault—and both commanders were new in their posts. Charles "Go Through" Summerall had replaced Bullard in command of the 1st, while James Harbord had replaced Omar Bundy at the head of the 2nd. (Bullard and Bundy had both been promoted to corps command.)

The lack of advance warning was not inefficiency on the part of the French but the result of a ruthless policy decision. Foch's strategy depended on taking the Germans utterly by surprise. He intended to bring up his divisions only the night before the attack, so that German intelligence could not forewarn the defenders in the pocket, and he decided not to risk any American breaches of security, regardless of the suffering to which he might be exposing the American troops by denying them time in which to prepare for a major assault. (The divisional surgeons, for instance, did not know the real purpose of the impending troop movements, and some units would enter combat "without litters and with only the dressings contained in the field belts.")

The insistence on surprise was a strategy essentially made in Detroit, rooted in Foch's awareness of the material strength of the Allies with America behind them. Sufficient trucks and locomotive power were available to the French to carry all the attacking divisions in one movement to concealed sites within marching distance of the line on the night before the attack, as well as to position artillery hub to hub along the line with stockpiles of ammunition. Had Ludendorff possessed this level of logistic capacity with which to support his storm troopers in the spring and early summer, the war might already have been over.

To complete the surprise, Mangin planned to dispense with even a preparatory artillery barrage. The French colonials and the Americans would be given their objectives and would advance toward them behind a rolling barrage. The Germans had no entrenched positions and no wire, and Mangin hoped to reach his objectives before they could bring up reserves.

The night before the attack, thick cloud and heavy rain helped to blind German aircraft and balloon observers; but it made the concentration of troops on the ground a nightmare. The Retz Forest was a vast, ancient broadleaf wood pierced by a network of dirt tracks, with here and there a modest paved road. In the last hours before the assault, it was thronged with artillery, ammunition trains, tanks, trucks, staff cars, cavalry, ambulances, Signal Corps cable-laying carts, and tens of thousands of men, all jostling for position and fighting their way toward the jump-off line.

"Weary drivers were constantly falling asleep," recalled Harbord, "halting the teams, and causing the most heartbreaking delays for a man who was in a hurry." Whole companies, even battalions, lost their way and groped through the gloom by compass, each man holding on to the pack of the man in front, until frantic staff officers found them and directed them toward the front. Slogging through the mud for hours in "Plutonian darkness" merely to reach the start, the men were already exhausted; soon the entire attack was in jeopardy. So tight was the schedule that at 4 A.M. on July 18, with the jump-off set for 4:35, the 2nd Division's lead battalions had not arrived in the line. It was too late now to halt the attack; years later, a participant remembered the leading battalions literally running into battle, "covering the last few hundred yards in double time, [reaching] their positions just as the first streaks of dawn strike the eastern fringes of the forest behind them and as the artillery barrage comes down with a crash upon the enemy's lines in front of them."

The dawn was clear and beautiful as Harbord's 2nd Division advanced behind the rolling barrage and twenty-eight tanks. Three regiments—the 9th and 28th Infantry and the 5th Marines, with the 6th Marines in reserve—marched abreast. It was the first large-scale offensive in which the division had taken part and the first for Harbord; the Allied generals to the right and left of him were sufficiently afraid of disaster to offer to write his divisional orders for him. (He declined with dignity: "To draw Battle Orders requires not only professional knowledge and tactical judgment. . . . It also involved in this case a knowledge of the American temperament and character.")

The division was to advance three miles due east across the plateau to the village of Vauxcastille and then swing through a twenty-degree turn to the southeast, cross the Vierzy ravine, occupy the village of Vierzy itself, and press on to Hartennes and the road to Soissons.

The task would have been daunting even for an established division with a seasoned commander and experienced officers and NCOs. But the 2nd Division's training had been truncated because of the spring emergency, and the ranks were full of replacements for the casualties of Belleau Wood. The men had been in transit not only for the night preceding the attack but also the night before that. Their last hot meal had been at lunchtime two days earlier, and on the day of the attack they had only a single canteen of water each plus what remained of their emergency rations. Worse in its way was the complete lack of information available to Harbord, his staff, and the officers in the line. There had been no opportunity for reconnaissance or study of the ground to be covered, and the plateau had few features to make orientation easier.

But the element of surprise had its initial effect, and after three hours the division was two and a half miles into enemy lines. Then came the right wheel—and the organization disintegrated. The 5th Marines slewed over into the Moroccans' zone, losing their machine-gun support in the process; the Moroccans complicated matters by straying into the 2nd Division's zone. All the units became hopelessly intermingled, and the support troops now caught up with them, adding to the confusion. By midday, there was chaos on the 2nd Division's front. There were no telephone links to the rear, and headquarters had little idea of the situation in the front line. Lieutenant Robert Winthrop Kean went back to report his unit's position. He was taken into a deep dugout, where he found Harbord. Spinning around, the anxious commander asked, "Lieutenant, where are the infantry?" "It was the first 1/20,000 map of the sector I had seen," Kean remembered, "but I showed him best I could where I thought the infantry were. 'I did not think that they had gone so far,' said the general."

As the day wore on, German machine guns and artillery became increasingly effective; the wheat was waist high, the ground was dotted with woodland and heavy brush, and it was difficult to locate the guns, let alone silence them. As Kean had crossed the battlefield, all around him had been American, French, and German wounded, crying out for help or water or babbling incoherently in the blazing heat of the day. This now was the price of French secretiveness; unprepared, the medical services could evacuate only a few of the wounded. Many got dressings for their wounds only if they could be taken from the German dead. But Kean saw one sight that touched him—an old French soldier who had dressed himself in the tattered blue uniform of an earlier war, "walking slowly down the road carrying on his back, toward the dressing station, a wounded American doughboy."

The general confusion blunted the attack. Vauxcastille held out until about 6 P.M., and the village of Vierzy, taken once, was snatched back by the Germans and had painfully to be retaken even later that evening. As Harbord surveyed the situation just before midnight, he was forced to admit, reluctantly, "It is not practicable for me to state my intentions for the morning." At an estimated cost of 1,500 casualties, the division had succeeded in advancing further than the Moroccans to the north, and its left flank was exposed. The French division to the right had veered off sharply to the south, leaving that flank also "somewhat up in the air."

These tactical hazards were magnified by the poor physical state of the troops. By the end of the day, straggling was adding to the disorder. "The large number of recruits and the exhausted condition of the men," concluded Major Keyser, commanding the 2nd Battalion, 5th Marines, "accounted for the large number of stragglers that in previous activities have been conspicuous by their absence."

Harbord knew better than anyone that Pershing would not accept failure, and one can imagine his state of mind as he made his report to his corps commander. Citing in his troops' defense the sequence of sleepless nights, the forced march, the shortages of food and water, and the fact that the division had been fighting "practically continuously . . . since the 1st of June," he concluded stiffly, "It is regretted that [the 2nd Division] is not believed to be equal to further offensive tomorrow."

The 1st Division, under Charles Summerall, had also suffered severely that first day. The men had gone forward behind forty-eight tanks with all four regiments in line, battalions deployed in depth. Advancing on a front of 2,900 yards, they had an average of 4.65 rifles per yard. On the right of the divisional sector, this weight of numbers was enough to bull through the German line. On the left, however, the steep, rocky ravines slicing through the plateau before Soissons provided good defensive terrain and the Germans had placed their machine guns to maximum effect.

During the night, the Germans rushed artillery and reinforcements into the beleaguered salient. They also threw "Baron von Richthofen's Flying

Circus"—now commanded by Hermann Göring—into the fight. The red-nosed airplanes drove the Allies from the sky, permitting wholesale strafing and bombing of infantry and rear areas.

With von Boehn pulling back across the Marne, German resistance on the ground, too, was stiffening. Mangin needed the worn 2nd Division to fight on—so Harbord kept his mauled frontline units in place while Lieutenant Colonel Harry Lee brought the 6th Marines and the 6th Machine-Gun Battalion out of reserve and into the attack. But with the element of surprise gone, Lee's advance on the morning of the second day turned into an appalling ordeal reminiscent of the initial assault on Belleau Wood. The marines were supported by tanks, but this was a mixed blessing. The slow-moving tanks made easy targets for the enemy's artillery on such open ground, and Lee's men behind them took many casualties before even crossing the starting line.

As they moved forward under the crippling barrage, the marines found themselves flanked by machine guns. The wheat was high enough to make the going nightmarishly slow, too low to offer any cover. On the right, the 1st Battalion advanced toward Tigny, and at 9:50 A.M. Lieutenant Colonel Lee sent a cheery message: "We are advancing nicely, think Tigny ours. Tanks are doing fine work. The enemy are retiring. Things going well. Casualties normal."

But Tigny had not been taken and was being defended fiercely; the commander of the 74th Company reported machine-gun fire from windows and doors. Then the tanks failed, and the men were pinned down, unable to advance. On the left, the story was the same; when relieved at midnight on the second day, the 2nd Battalion had taken 70 percent losses and was down to fewer than two hundred effectives.

Enemy prisoners blamed the Americans' own tactics for the high casualty rate. One German officer, with a mixture of awe and disapproval, called Americans "inhuman" in their disregard for hostile fire. (He echoed, unknowingly, the Australian comment, made that month, that the Americans were "good in battle, but terribly rough"—a compliment indeed, coming from the notoriously pugnacious Australians.) But aggressiveness had its price. "The Americans sacrifice their troops needlessly by close formation, by needless headlong rushes at machine-gun nests, and by insufficient attention of soldiers to their shelter from German fire. . . . One prisoner declared, 'I am sure that my company without casualties on one occasion mowed down three American companies.' " Harbord estimated the 2nd Division's losses at 5,000; they had struggled on to within half a mile of the objective before being relieved.

For the 1st Division there was no relief yet. Summerall had kept control of his command during the first day and was able to attack as ordered on July 19. Resistance in his sector was now intense, particularly on the left, as the Germans protected Soissons. But Summerall was perhaps the most remorselessly determined of all Pershing's generals. On the eve of battle, he had told his officers, "Let no man feel that he is tired so long as he can put one foot in front of another, demand the impossible in order that the possible may be accomplished." Mangin ordered him to take the high ground directly overlooking Soissons, and Summerall was perfectly prepared for his division to die in the attempt.

On the second day, the casualties were heavy. On the third, July 20, as the Germans battled increasingly desperately to keep the pocket open long enough to extricate men and precious materials, the losses were even worse. "Machine-gunners of the Prussian Guards," recalled one survivor, "lay in the small clearings they had made in the wheat, and as the waves of attacking troops approached they loosed off belt after belt of ammunition, firing at top speed, regardless of the certain death that would come to them when the Americans came through that galling fire. There were no prisoners taken in this fierce assault."

Summerall's division reached its objective, but the French failed to take theirs: the village of Berzy-le-Sec, sited on a commanding knoll. So on the third night, Summerall gathered together all the remaining men of the 2nd Brigade—"cooks, kitchen police, orderlies, clerks from regimental headquarters, military police, engineers"—and with the battered remains of each of the infantry regiments launched a dawn assault on Berzy. The brigade commander, Beaumont Buck, who was doubtless more in awe of Summerall than of the Germans, took personal command. "When most of the officers of his Brigade had fallen . . . [Buck] led the first wave of the culminating attack which stormed and captured the town." On Buck's right, the 1st Brigade crossed the road to Château-Thierry, and the mission was accomplished.

In four days on the Soissons plateau, the 1st Division lost 8,365 men, 1,252 of them killed. The infantry lost 50 percent of its enlisted men and 60 percent of its officers, 75 percent of those above the rank of captain and all its battalion commanders. "Everywhere I looked," wrote newspaper correspondent Henry Russell Miller,

the trampled wheat was dotted by recumbent figures. There was one field, two or three acres, on which it seemed you could not have stood ten feet from some one of those figures. They might have been wearied troops that had thrown themselves down to sleep. They slept indeed, the sleep no earthly reveille could disturb. I wish you could have seen that silent company under the summer twilight. It was not gruesome then, and it was not all tragedy. There lay the best of America, not dead nor sleeping, but alive so long as we will them to live.

29

Hope and Glory

The success of the Soissons counterstroke and the pursuit that followed forced Ludendorff to cancel his planned offensive in Flanders and go onto the defensive. For the first time in 1918, the Allies had the initiative—and the Supreme Commander, the ebullient Ferdinand Foch, was not one to waste such an opportunity. On July 24, he called Pershing, Haig, and Pétain to his headquarters at Bombon and urged that they "abandon the defensive attitude that had been so long imposed upon them and continue the offensive without cessation." He proposed a swift series of operations to take place consecutively at selected points along the front. These limited attacks were designed to improve the Allied position by freeing railroads and resources as well as to continue Foch's fundamental strategy for victory through attrition.

As part of this strategy, Pershing was to create an army—he issued formal orders calling the American First Army into being on August 10—to pinch out the triangular salient that still jutted into the Allied lines around the town of Saint-Mihiel. This had always been Pershing's intended first target. The AEF had focused its communications and its logistical infrastructure on this section; many of the divisions had trained here, and American blood had been spilled in its defense—most notably at Seicheprey.

In his preliminary study dated August 6, George Marshall (now with the operations staff at General Headquarters) identified three objectives for the Saint-Mihiel operation: "To free the main line of the Paris-Nancy railroad. . . . To carry out a purely American major offensive operation before the start of the rainy season in 1918. . . . To prepare the way for the 1919 offensive."

The phrase "the 1919 offensive" had an almost talismanic quality. All of America's work, in France and at home, had been predicated on joining the war then, in earnest, on the scale of the Allied fighting since 1914— when the eighty-division program had been completed. If America picked up the gauntlet as Britain and France inevitably faded, Woodrow Wilson would have the authority he required to dictate the terms of peace to the Allies.

It was with such visions of grandeur that Pershing confided to Peyton March on July 27:

> I have had under consideration for some time the question of limiting the grade of lieutenant-general to commanders of armies and groups of armies, leaving the corps in command of major-generals. . . . Counting eighty divisions, we would have by spring [1919] something like ten or twelve such armies, and these will have to be arranged in groups of two or three armies in each group, which would give us fifteen or more lieutenant-generals in command of troops.

Dreams of a future peopled with American lieutenant generals and groups of armies were pleasant, but for the harsh present, Pershing had quickly to patch together a "First Army" from what he had available— and his resources were limited by the compromise deal that had been forced on him by the British and French during the panic of Ludendorff's spring attacks. In shipping over a great majority of infantry and machine gunners at the Allies' insistence, Pershing had left the AEF's auxiliary arms and support systems seriously undermanned. In return for replacement raw materials from the United States, the French and British willingly supplied artillery, shells, and aircraft, but neither could meet the wider demands of the support services.

According to Johnson Hagood, Chief of Staff of the Supply Services, in August, when the First Army was formed:

> We did not have the engineers, pioneers and labor troops to build the roads, the medical troops to attend the sick and wounded, the ordnance troops to handle the ammunition, the signals troops to establish tele-

graph and telephone lines. We were short of chauffeurs and auto-
mechanics. We did not have the supply trains nor the military police to
regulate traffic. . . . In transportation we were short of wagons, horses,
ambulances, trucks, locomotives, and railroad cars. We were lacking in
replacements of all kinds, both of personnel and matériel.

These were deficiencies for which the AEF would pay a very high price in
the weeks to come.

Pershing also had serious worries about the combat readiness of his infantry divisions. He could rely on the units that had been in France the
longest; some of them—the 1st, 2nd, 3rd, and 42nd Divisions—were as
impressive as any troops on the Western Front. But the bulk of his men
were in divisions that were barely coherent units, formed of inexperienced
officers and poorly trained men.

He had already confided his fears about the quality of his officers to Peyton March: "We cannot hold our standards so high as formerly because we
simply have not the qualified officers to fill the places. We are now in very
straitened circumstances as to the staffs for the various corps and field
armies, and I feel anxious about the question. It is certainly one of the weak
links in our chain, another being division and brigade commanders." Indeed, in early August, the AEF possessed only two operational corps.

Pershing had tried to remedy the deficiency by establishing an AEF
staff college at Langres, but, as he admitted to March, "Officers cannot
learn the art of war in three months. They can get some considerable smat-
tering of staff duty, but they must have experience before we can have
much confidence in them. . . . I cannot tell you how hard put we are for
staff officers, and I need not tell you how important it is."

Like the officers, the bulk of the men were new to France and without
battle experience of any kind. Peyton March's driving force and organizational genius had pushed troops over to France—the AEF numbered
61,061 officers and 1,354,067 enlisted men by the end of August—but
not even March had been able to cancel out the consequences of twelve
months of chaos at home.

Recalling his training at Camp Sherman, Ohio, Private William J.
Schierholt described using "broomsticks for make-believe guns and rocks
for grenades. We had lots of squad drills and when we were not drilling,
we would be trading clothes to get a better fit. After the fall [of 1917] was
over, winter set in and it sure got cold and lots of snow so that put a stop to

our drilling and training." Military efficiency was further undermined by Baker's reluctance to set up training centers for replacement troops. Divisions going abroad were topped up either with raw recruits or with men from other divisions, which then received raw troops. Both methods were damaging. The 79th Division, for instance, had suffered so many calls on its manpower for other units that it ultimately trained 80,000 men. Many of the hastily assigned troops had not yet fired their rifles, and French veterans along the route to the front were said to be earning healthy sums teaching them how to load and aim.

The AEF had devised a three-month program of instruction for divisions when they reached France, including frontline experience with Allied units to come to grips with combat on the Western Front. But in the desperate circumstances of that summer, there had been no time for familiarization under controlled conditions. Most of the little experience the incoming divisions possessed had been acquired through becoming occasionally embroiled in fighting, more or less haphazardly.

There were also serious inconsistencies in fundamental doctrine, as there had been from the start of the war. The General Staff in Washington had long been at odds with Pershing and the AEF staff in France over the kind of war they were training the men to fight. Under the influence of Allied training missions, the troops in the cantonments at home had been taught trench warfare. Pershing, however, believed that the war must be won "by driving the enemy out into the open and engaging him in a war of movement" and had consistently urged the War Department to train the army "mainly for open warfare, with the object from the start of vigorously forcing the offensive."

In France, Pershing had built the AEF's training program around open warfare; and when, at the end of 1917, the generals responsible for training the new divisions had visited the front on a tour of inspection, he had urged on them the need to give it priority. On returning home, the generals had obeyed with enthusiasm—to the horror of the French military mission: "It seems to have been misunderstood that there was no more need for trench warfare training and it has been replaced by open warfare training. . . . The teaching of trench warfare as well as the use of specialities has suddenly ceased." The French response was simply to subvert Pershing's instructions, and confusion reigned until the summer of 1918, when the training course for officers at home was modified once and for all to meet Pershing's requirements.

The choice of infantry weapons was equally controversial. Luden-dorff's storm troopers, rushing headlong through the Allied defenses, seemed to prove Pershing right in insisting that his men free themselves of the trench warfare mentality. At the same time, their success suggested that he was wrong in relying on the rifle and bayonet as the principal infantry weapons. "The company of infantry has become, so to speak, a company of light machine guns," Ludendorff had declared. "Its main fire strength, in the attack as well as in the defense, rests in the light machine gun, which corresponds to the power of 30 rifles or even more." Machine guns, grenades, Stokes mortars, and one-pounders were now the standby of the average Allied soldier as well. But to Pershing, while they were all valuable weapons for specific purposes, "they could not replace the combination of an efficient soldier and his rifle."

After Soissons, however, the upper echelons of the AEF could hardly ignore the losses American riflemen were sustaining every time they faced machine guns. A staff paper prepared by Hugh Drum and circulated to regimental commanders in the first week of August suggested adopting different tactics and shifting the emphasis away from the rifle. Commanders were urged to make use of natural cover, to attack in greater depth, and to precede the first advance with groups of automatic rifles and machine guns widely spaced, working forward to positions under cover where they could neutralize hostile machine guns. On August 29, Drum issued a more detailed eight-page memorandum on "combat instructions" that George Marshall had prepared, drawing heavily on Ludendorff's instructions to his storm troopers.

It is not clear that Pershing himself ever abandoned his belief in the supremacy of the rifleman, but certainly, after fourteen months in France, his senior staff officers had begun to recognize the value of automatic weapons. Among Harbord's papers, there is a document dated July 5 suggesting that high-ranking officers, including Pershing, had even then been discussing the possibility of replacing the rifle with "a semi-automatic rifle that can fire 100 shots per minute effective up to 400 yards" and reviewing the changes in organization and tactics that this would imply.

Pershing needed time and resources to produce well-officered, tactically modern units. There were at least six, and possibly nine, months before the 1919 campaigns would open, so he could hope that things would have fallen into shape by then. In the meantime, with Allied assistance, he could create around the kernel of his elite divisions an army sufficiently powerful to undertake the Saint-Mihiel operation—and have it supported by an American-led air armada under extraordinary and charismatic leadership.

Lieutenant Colonel William Mitchell was the great American prophet of airpower. Born in 1879, the son of a former senator, he had left school to enlist in the Spanish-American War and spent almost twenty years in the Signal Corps. By 1916, he had been bitten by the aviation bug and on weekends took himself off to learn to fly. In April 1917, as his country declared war, he went to France as a military observer. Taking on himself the task of discovering the nature of modern air warfare, he made flights as often as possible with French pilots over the battle lines of northern France. He first accosted Pershing at a Paris railway station as the general arrived in France for the first time on June 13, 1917, and had soon been appointed chief aviation officer on Pershing's staff.

Bursting with energy, confidence, and initiative, Mitchell was not a modest man, and he would make some powerful enemies among those whose abilities he openly despised. But he was right in supposing that he was among the very few Americans to understand the strategic potential of airpower. Much of his insight stemmed from a visit he had made in May 1917 to Major General Hugh Trenchard, commander of Britain's Royal Flying Corps, during which he had become totally convinced by Trenchard's view of the airplane as an offensive rather than strictly defensive weapon.

Mitchell accepted that the air force must be the eyes of the army—feeding the infantry with information and providing fire adjustment for the artillery—and it must also provide a defensive shield preventing enemy air forces from interfering with ground operations. This was Pershing's view. But airpower could also, Mitchell argued, be a strong right arm, reaching out to strike behind enemy lines, bombing rear areas, destroying roads and railways, and laying enemy forces open to attack on the ground.

Mitchell believed that the Saint-Mihiel pocket offered particular scope for a triumphant display of airpower of this sort because of the critical role aircraft could play in destroying the vital German communications so near the battle zone. "If we create a strong enough aviation, it has a good chance of being the decisive element in this area."

The AEF could now draw on a pool of seasoned American pilots who had flown during neutrality with the British and French air forces. That spring, when the AEF Air Service was formed, 93 fliers from the Lafayette

Escadrille had transferred to it, supplying many of the unit commanders. Mitchell gathered his aircraft for the Saint-Mihiel operation: some 1,500 planes, of which 600 would be flown by Americans, the rest by British, French, Italian, and Portuguese pilots.

His strategy was adapted to the triangular shape of the salient. As he pointed out, along most of the Western Front the line was

> more or less straight, and the Air Service acts out from it more or less homogeneously all along the front. Now, we are attacking a salient so I intend to change the ordinary procedure and employ massed air attacks against the vital points in the enemy's rear. In this case we can hit from first one side of the salient and then from the other, just as a boxer may try a right hook and then a left hook successively against his opponent.

With overwhelming air strength and elite American divisions supplemented by a number of French units, including tanks and artillery, Pershing could feel confident he had the resources to tackle Saint-Mihiel. The United States, he predicted, would be guaranteed an independent triumph with which to end the 1918 campaign and set the scene for the anticipated glories of 1919. It was an innocent dream—and all too soon the realities of the Western Front in 1918 would intrude.

30

The Dream Shattered

Pershing's vision of glory would be shattered, ironically, not by the Germans but by the Allies—by a rush to victory that left no room for America's more leisurely triumphs.

On July 15, as he attacked to the east and west of Reims, Ludendorff had scented success. But his armies had been held, the enemy's counterthrust had cleared the Marne pocket, and more than a quarter of a million American soldiers had made their presence strongly felt as the Germans retreated. With America's weight at last in the scales, the balance of power on the battlefield tipped irrevocably against Germany. Then, on August 8, began the slide to oblivion. In a rapid, limited jab at the German line, the Canadians and Australians, supported by British tanks, inflicted a stunning defeat at Amiens—"the black day of the German Army in the history of the war," in Ludendorff's words.

Two days later, American military analysts concluded that "in view of the rapid development of American strength and the increasing shortages in manpower which the enemy is beginning to feel, the enemy will not dare to undertake further offensive operations at the present time." Foch was inclined to agree, and he issued an exhortation to his forces: "Yesterday I said to you: Obstinacy, Patience, your American comrades are coming. Today I say to you: Tenacity, Boldness, and Victory will be yours!"

Ludendorff, too, was being forced to accept that Germany could no longer win. His losses since the spring had been crippling, his formidable assault divisions shattered. On August 13, he made a momentous announcement to the German Chancellor. The Army, he said, was no longer able to "force the enemy to sue for peace." And as "defense alone could hardly achieve this objective," he continued, "the termination of the war would have to be brought about by diplomacy."

But though he now recognized he could not force a victory on the battlefield, he was far from recommending abject capitulation. Germany could not win, but she need not lose. Ludendorff believed that his army was still powerful; it had proven itself in defense throughout 1917 and still held the awesome fortifications of the Hindenburg Line. He wanted an early end to the war, but he intended peace overtures to commence only after he had inflicted a bloody repulse on the Allies. Then, undefeated, Germany could still negotiate a favorable peace—even if the terms fell short of those that would have been imposed on the enemy had she won.

His faith in his army, however, was misplaced; indeed, his grip on reality had begun to slip under the intense pressure, and he would be relieved of command before the end of August. The speed with which Germany was disintegrating was all too obvious on the battlefield. Divisions were being disbanded and the numbers of effectives in the remaining units reduced. Each Allied attack pulled in an ever-larger haul of prisoners with tales of deprivation and influenza, of Bolshevik soviets being formed in some regiments where the men now refused to obey the commands of their superior officers, and of pilfering from depots reaching such proportions as to "imperil the supply of the army." In the spring, Ludendorff had performed a miracle to inspire his men with belief in victory. Now, after the sacrifice of a million of their comrades in just five months, morale had plummeted and with it discipline and unit coherence.

The home front was also in terminal decline. After four years of war, Germany had little left with which to stave off ruination. The MID estimated that "70% of the male population of 18 to 50 have been called to the colors since the beginning of the war. . . . The number in hospitals at present is 500,000, while the grand total of German casualties killed, badly wounded and mutilated . . . is 4,760,000." Starvation beckoned for soldier and civilian alike. The MID reported that the authorities had released reserves of food "in the expectation of their prompt replenishment from the Ukraine." But nothing was coming from Ukraine, and by August meat was often unavailable for weeks on end, the bread ration was lower than at any time since the beginning of the war, and the potato ration had been cut drastically.

In the fourth week of August, further Allied attacks all along the line met ever-decreasing German resistance. By August 26, no fewer than six Allied armies were pushing the Germans back toward the Hindenburg Line. As he watched the German resistance crumble, Pershing proposed revising the Saint-Mihiel operation. On August 16, he issued preliminary instructions for plans to be made for the First Army to punch through the pocket and out into the Woeuvre Plain beyond, to bring the American line to within five miles of Metz. Here the AEF would be poised for a war-winning thrust in 1919.

But he was not the only one with expanding horizons; Foch and Haig saw an even greater opportunity. They began to believe that the German Army was so weakened and demoralized that it could actually be defeated in 1918. Haig was the first to smell blood. "We ought to hit the Boche now as hard as we [can], then try to get peace this autumn," he was recorded as saying at dinner on August 11. Ten days later, he told Winston Churchill, then British Minister of Munitions, that the Allies should do their utmost "to get a decision this autumn. We are engaged in a 'wearing out battle' and are outlasting and beating the enemy." Distrusted by Lloyd George, Haig received no more than lukewarm support from the civilian authorities. He was permitted to continue, he confided bitterly to his diary, "if I think it right to do so. . . . What a wretched lot of weaklings we have in high places at the present time!" He knew he could expect few replacements for his army, but he backed his instinct: through August (during which he lost 100,000 men) and beyond, he expended his troops in a final gamble to end the war.

As the Allied successes continued, Pershing too became convinced that the end was near, and on August 29 he cabled the President that the war could be won in 1918. Clearly there needed to be a high-level discussion of strategy—but, unknown to Pershing, this had already taken place. The very next day, on the evening of August 30, the tiny Supreme Commander descended from his automobile at Pershing's residence to communicate the decisions made.

Foch's message was simple: he wanted the Americans to throw their weight behind the strategy proposed by Field Marshal Haig—which was that the Allies attack the Germans along the whole length of the Western Front from Verdun to the sea in a convergent, mutually supportive operation. It would be the biggest battle in all history—deliberately so in order to swamp the German defenses and prevent Ludendorff from using his magnificent lateral communications to deploy his reserves.

The conception was superb, but the part reserved for the First Army was no more than a supporting role. Foch wanted Pershing simply to collapse the Saint-Mihiel salient, abandoning his thrust into the Woeuvre Plain. Then he wanted the American First Army broken up—some divisions allocated to the French Second Army in Champagne, some placed around the Saint-Mihiel salient, the rest as an "American Army" (but temporarily under French command) operating between two French armies to attack toward Sedan.

Pershing was furious. "Each time we are on the point of accomplishing this organization," he raged, "some proposition is presented to break it up." Foch, intoxicated with Haig's scheme, asked acidly, "Do you wish to take part in the battle?" "Most assuredly," Pershing stormed, "but as an American army."

The next three days saw a frenetic round of negotiations as each side jostled for advantage. Pershing was adamant that his army should not be broken up, but he had to offer to fight with it on any front that Foch chose. He kept his army—but the price was grotesque. Under the new plan, the American First Army would undertake two major operations within the space of roughly three weeks: the first, to pinch out the Saint-Mihiel pocket; the second, to shift forces rapidly north and west and break through the Hindenburg Line between the Argonne Forest and the Meuse River.

At this point, it would have been prudent, despite the months of preparation, to cancel the Saint-Mihiel operation completely. But Pershing refused to relinquish his long-cherished scheme, arguing stubbornly that the Germans could launch attacks from the pocket against the rear of his army while it was fighting on the Meuse-Argonne front. Foch did not agree that the Saint-Mihiel salient was a threat to the First Army's rear, but he was still willing to see a limited interim attack there, as a means of maintaining pressure on the Germans.

On September 2, Pershing committed the First Army to the two-battle operation. To preserve the integrity of his army, he had placed the most horrifying burden on it. Why Foch had allowed him to do so is not quite clear. It was almost as though Foch, as a Frenchman rather than Supreme Commander, a politician as well as a soldier, was reluctant for the Americans to distinguish themselves, content to see them bite off more than they could comfortably chew.

The Saint-Mihiel operation, at least, was well in hand. Pershing had already stockpiled ammunition, engineers' equipment, and the components for light railways; he had built railheads, made his medical arrangements, and concentrated his aircraft, tanks, artillery, and men. But the Meuse-Argonne was a different proposition. It was entirely out of the American zone and had never been considered by the First Army planners. All they knew of it was its reputation as one of the most formidable killing grounds on the Western Front. Could the AEF concentrate the materials, the munitions, and the men to fight there and win—and all within three weeks, when even an experienced staff would really have required three months?

George Marshall realized at once that in order to assemble the necessary resources for the Meuse-Argonne operation, they would have to start pulling some units away from Saint-Mihiel on the evening of the first day's fighting there:

> I could not recall an incident in history where the fighting of one battle had been preceded by the plans for a later battle to be fought by the same army on a different front, and involving the issuing of orders for the movement of troops already destined to participate in the first battle, directing their transfer to the new field of action. . . . This appalling proposition rather disturbed my equilibrium and I went out on the canal to have a walk."

As far as President Wilson was concerned, it made no difference whether or not the AEF could pull off the double attack successfully. By its very nature, the new strategy had demolished his hopes for an overwhelming American victory. Between the evening of August 30, when Foch had arrived at Pershing's residence, and September 2, when the plan was agreed upon, the nature of America's military contribution to the war had changed fundamentally. In those three days, Pershing abandoned his carefully worked out buildup to the 1919 campaign and an American-led triumph and agreed instead to throw an unready army at the Germans. He risked the total collapse of his command in order to support a strategy devised by the Allies that, if it succeeded, would quite possibly give them and not him the lion's share of the credit. And this in its turn would make it harder for his President to exert anything but a modest influence at the peace conference.

Pershing made this crucial decision to seek victory in 1918, a decision as much political as military, on his own, without seeking guidance from

Washington. In retrospect, he might seem to have betrayed his President's trust. Wilson had entered into no formal alliance with France and Britain; he had his own war aims set on a moral plane high above those of the Allies; he had refused close military collaboration in the form of amalgamation; and he had appointed no political representative to the Supreme War Council to coordinate policy. Yet here was his military captain assuming the role of a minor cog in the Allied war machine in a gamble to finish the war quickly.

But Wilson and Baker had delegated military questions to Pershing, and this was fundamentally a matter for military judgment. Pershing seems to have accepted that Germany would be beaten in 1918, with or without his help, and that by 1919 there might be no war for America to win. In breaking the news of the dual battle to Johnson Hagood, the man responsible for supplying the armies and sustaining the men in combat, Pershing's staff told him, "It was now or never. . . . The time had now come when America was to show its teeth and . . . the great drive must go through."

In fact, though Pershing had accepted a subsidiary role, he could still see a glimmer of hope—a means of snatching an impressive, even decisive victory from the jaws of Allied triumph. The final objective of the Meuse-Argonne offensive was the Sedan-Mézières stretch of the four-track lateral railroad that linked Ludendorff's armies with Germany. This railroad, carrying a huge volume of Germany's men and munitions, was vital to the entire German defensive system on the Western Front. If the First Army could advance swiftly and cut this railway, Ludendorff would be compelled to make an immediate withdrawal from France.

This stunning prize was only twenty-two miles from the jump-off line— but to get there the First Army would have to push through some of the strongest defenses on the Western Front. Pétain said they would be lucky to get as far as the hill at Montfaucon—not quite four miles into the combat zone—by Christmas. But Pershing lacked neither the will nor the confidence. "No Allied troops had the morale or aggressive spirit to overcome the difficulties to be met in that sector," he conceded; but his were the men to do it. His army could take the Meuse-Argonne sector, even though his best divisions would already be locked into the Saint-Mihiel offensive and in the Meuse-Argonne he would have only a residue of largely inexperienced and undertrained units. At this moment of crisis, his staff set out to perform miracles—to shape the soft clay of a novice citizen army into an effective fighting tool within a time scale that verged on the ludicrous.

Pershing's decision to accept the dual challenge of Saint-Mihiel and the Meuse-Argonne was the more extraordinary for having been made only days after the British had delivered a body blow to his army's potential strength. Throughout August, according to Brigadier General Samuel Rockenbach, chief of the tank corps, "the whole plan of attack" for the Saint-Mihiel operation "was based on having heavy tanks, able to cross the trenches and make a path for the light tanks and infantry, get at and crush the wire." Only the British had heavy tanks, and Pershing was expecting 150 of them to be made available. Then came catastrophe. On August 22, Haig, deeply embroiled in following up the Amiens offensive and building on Germany's "black day," informed Pershing that he could not "for the moment furnish any tanks, all . . . available tanks being employed in the battle which is now going on." There would be no heavy tanks for Saint-Mihiel and none for the even stronger defenses of the Meuse-Argonne.

Without tanks and with serious doubts about the quality of many of his divisions, Pershing nevertheless committed himself. The success or failure of America's wider policy lay firmly in the hands of her soldiers. While desperate staff officers plunged into the maelstrom of preparations for the Meuse-Argonne offensive, the minutes ticked away to the assault on the Saint-Mihiel pocket.

Part Eight

The
DEATH
of
INNOCENTS

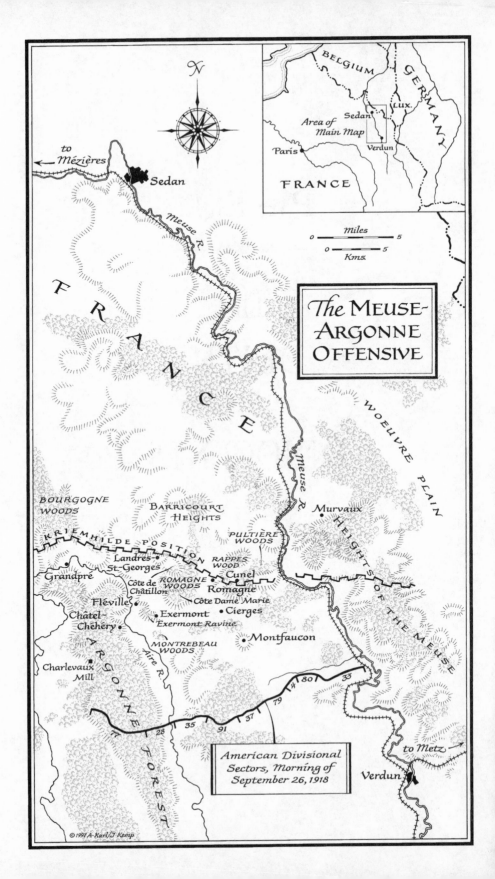

The MEUSE-
ARGONNE
OFFENSIVE

American Divisional
Sectors, Morning of
September 26, 1918

©1991 A·Karl/J·Kemp

31

The First Battle: Saint-Mihiel

"L'Hernie"—"the Hernia"—the French called it, this triangular bulge into Allied lines about twenty miles southeast of Verdun. Its western face was formed by the heights of the Meuse River; the town of Saint-Mihiel stood at the apex of the triangle; and the southern face ran across flat, swampy ground, skirting the ill-omened village of Seicheprey and running on toward the Moselle, where the terrain became hilly and wooded. Across the base of the salient, the Germans had built the Michel Position, twenty miles of modern defensive emplacements.

The Germans had held the pocket since 1914, and since Verdun both sides had regarded it as a quiet stretch of the front. A great many American soldiers had spent their first months in France here, in the old Toul sector below Mont Sec, cursing the rain of northern France and wallowing in the sticky mud.

In early September, the Germans were manning the fifty-two-mile perimeter of the salient very thinly; two divisions had been taken out for the spring offensive and not replaced, and the remainder each held an average of seven and a half miles of front. Among these units, besides some indifferent Austro-Hungarian troops, were the 192nd Division ("completely used up," on the German Army's own assessment), and the 10th Division, which had suffered heavy losses at the hands of McAlexander and the 38th Regiment on the Marne in July. The 77th Reserve Division caused the German commanders the most concern: It contained "a large number" of Alsace-Lorrainers—men who believed themselves to be French but had found themselves sent to a town in Lorraine to guard it for the Germans.

Against these weak forces Pershing now planned to send a total of eighteen divisions—twelve in the line, six in corps and army reserves, a total of almost half a million men—to attack no more than 23,000 German troops. The concentration of American troops was extraordinary. With an infantry rifle strength of 13,000 per division, the 2nd, 5th, and 42nd Divisions each had approximately five riflemen for every yard of their divisional fronts.

Pershing's problem was to create this concentration without alerting the Germans to his every move. Pétain suggested an intricate deception, a ruse to convince the Germans that the real Allied attack would occur somewhere else—far to the southeast, at Belfort on the Moselle River. Intrigued, Pershing adopted the subterfuge, taking it to such lengths that in sending Omar Bundy, former commander of the 2nd Division, to the southeast with his skeletal VI Corps, he concealed from him that his mission was merely a ploy. Happily ignorant of the ludicrous figure he cut before the handful of officers who were in the know about the Belfort ruse, Bundy departed to "prepare detailed plans for an attack" and "definitely select the bridgeheads on the Rhine." With him, in equal ignorance, went staff officers from six divisions (beside the 29th Division, already at Belfort), their transfer designed to signal to any curious German agents a significant concentration of force in the southeast.

Bundy played his part loyally—though he must soon have guessed his true role as he observed light tanks maneuvering with bizarre ostentation in the vicinity and signals units manufacturing a heavy radio traffic in gibberish, while his only liaison with headquarters was through intelligence chief Arthur Conger, his former intelligence officer in the 2nd Division. Conger added a cloak-and-dagger flourish to the charade. In his hotel room in Belfort, he typed out details of the proposed Allied "attack," negligently discarded the carbon, and went out for a walk; when he returned, the carbon was gone.

The Belfort ruse provoked some reaction—three German divisions were sent south to cover the possibility of an Allied assault—but the deception failed in its principal objective of persuading the enemy that there would be no attack at Saint-Mihiel. Lax security was partly to blame. "Both the French and the Americans have talked," Pershing reported despairingly, "and it now seems certain that the enemy is aware of the approaching attack." But the best security in the world could not have concealed the prodigious quantities of men and materials being marshaled behind the perimeter of the salient—columns of infantry footslogging through the September rain, horses, trucks, and guns struggling in the mud. According to Eddie Rickenbacker, "Every taxi driver or waiter in Paris could have told one just where the Americans were concentrating. . . . The number of guns, the number of troops and just where they were located, how many aeroplanes we had . . . were discussed by every man on the streets."

German intelligence had indeed reported "indications of an impending hostile offensive," and Lieutenant General Fuchs, commanding the bulk of the enemy troops in the salient, was becoming decidedly uneasy. When intelligence officers began to predict a simultaneous attack on both sides of the salient, he pressed the panic button. On September 10, two days before Pershing's planned D-Day, without waiting for superior orders, Fuchs instructed his officers to remove materials from the Saint-Mihiel area and to destroy buildings, bridges, roads, and water supplies preparatory to abandoning the salient altogether and pulling back to the Michel Position.

Aerial reconnaissance and the plumes of black smoke rising behind enemy lines confirmed that the Germans were getting ready to leave. The Americans were less than astonished; according to Fox Conner, "documents captured in June 1918 had shown that the enemy had a plan for evacuating the salient in case this became necessary." Indeed, only days before, Foch had given it as his opinion that the Germans "would fall back from Saint-Mihiel at the first sign" of pressure.

Now Fuchs's hasty preparations suggested that the Americans might catch the Germans at a disadvantage, between standing and retreating, provided they acted quickly enough. Billy Mitchell later recalled that on the evening of September 11 Pershing had gathered his staff to consult them on whether the attack should proceed the following day:

> Our Chief Engineer recommended that we delay the attack because there had been considerable rain. This, he said, had held up our light railways used for getting up artillery ammunition. The question of adequate water for some of the troops would be difficult and a thousand and one things which could not be done were mentioned. I was surprised to see that several of the old fossils there had agreed with this foolish view of the situation.

By his own account, Mitchell then pleaded for the assault to go ahead. He had flown over the lines himself and seen the enemy preparing to withdraw; all the First Army had to do, he said, was "to jump on the Germans, and the quicker we did it the better." In his view, the problem of artillery supply was irrelevant: "Our troops might be better off without artillery as they would probably shoot a good many of our own men anyway." Pershing, he recalled, smiled and ordered the attack.

The first and heavier of the two assaults on the salient was to hit the south face at dawn the next day, September 12. Hunter Liggett's I Corps (the 82nd, 90th, 5th, and 2nd Divisions) and Joseph Dickman's IV Corps (the 89th, 42nd, and 1st Divisions) were to move up at 5 A.M. from the old Toul sector, supported by the entire light-tank force led by Lieutenant Colonel George Patton. They were to drive north toward Vigneulles, a village roughly in the center of the salient, on the road leading east from Saint-Mihiel toward Metz. Three hours later, General George Cameron's V Corps (the 26th, French 15th Colonial and 4th Divisions) were to launch themselves against the western face of the salient and drive south and east to link up with Liggett and Dickman at Vigneulles, cut the road, and trap the German troops. French divisions under Pershing's command would surround the nose of the salient and apply enough pressure to keep the defenders in.

Much of the salient's perimeter, the south face in particular, was protected by dense entanglements of wire. Until the British bombshell of August 28, the planners had assumed that this would be crushed by the heavy tanks. Accordingly, Pershing's staff had accumulated artillery and ammunition on the basis that they would not need to cut the wire—and they now faced a serious problem. The troops attacking from the south, on a seven-mile front, needed fifty-five breaches to be made in the wire—eight gaps per mile. To make a breach twenty-seven yards wide in wire sixty-six yards deep would normally require 1,600 rounds. With the resources available, it would have taken the First Army's gunners eighteen hours, totally eliminating any element of surprise, giving the Germans more than enough time to man their defenses, and turning Pershing's rapid thrust into a battle of attrition.

Knowing that the wire was poorly maintained—"posts rotted and wire rusted"—Pershing and some of his staff now resolved to send the troops over without either heavy tanks or preliminary bombardment. They would be led by pioneers and engineers carrying wire cutters and Bangalore torpedoes. And where the wire could not be cut, the men would have to go over or under it. Aghast, Marshall argued strongly that some barrage must be put down—on rear areas, on communications and command posts, on the frontline trenches, and as much as possible on the wire. After agonized debate, Pershing decided that there should be four hours' bombardment before the attack on the southern face of the salient (seven hours on the western side)—the maximum that was possible without forfeiting the advantage of surprise completely.

At 1 A.M. on September 12, the 2,971 guns of the American First Army opened up in unison with a barrage that split the night sky. "The enemy's attack struck . . . by surprise," the official German report would concede later. Their intelligence had predicted a September 15 offensive; the American attack found the German divisions with their heavy artillery in transit and some companies away from the front laboring on the defenses of the Michel Position.

But though caught out, the Germans did not immediately abandon the salient. The American barrage seems not to have troubled the defenders as much as it should have done. At 4:20 A.M., Fuchs informed higher authority that "the evacuation would not be begun as there were no compelling reasons for such action at that time."

At 5 A.M., behind a rolling barrage, the U.S. divisions on the south face moved out. "Caked with the slimy yellow clay they looked like nothing human as they plodded on." Agonizingly slowly, they moved forward into the wire. Some gaps had been cut, Fox Conner maintained, by artillery fire; others had been made by light tanks, according to Patton. But in the main, the men appear to have coped for themselves with their wire cutters and Bangalore torpedoes, as Pershing had thought they would. Where there were no gaps, the troops—blessed, as the French put it, with big American feet—often simply walked over the sagging entanglements. The trick had been to carry forward rolls of chicken wire as a carpet to lay over the rusting coils.

As the I and IV Corps poured across, the southern face of the salient crumbled as the Germans fled. From the skies overhead, Rickenbacker looked down on the fight:

Closely pressing came our eager doughboys fighting along like Indians. They scurried from cover to cover, always crouching low as they ran. Throwing themselves flat onto the ground, they would get their rifles into action and spray the Boches with more bullets until they withdrew from sight. Then another running advance and another furious pumping of lead from the Yanks. . . . I flew above this scene for many miles watching the most spectacular free show that ever men gazed upon.

The troops entered villages whose French occupants had been prisoners for four years. "They laughed and wept and kissed everybody in sight." Some of the Germans, too, were glad to be out of the war. In one dugout, troops of the 42nd Division found an officer sitting at a table with a bottle of schnapps, waiting to welcome his captors. One of the Austrians taken prisoner was a reservist who had lived in the United States in 1914. "Can I go back now to Sharon, Pennsylvania?" he asked.

Sergeant Harry J. Adams saw an enemy soldier run into a large dugout. Pelting after him, he fired his two remaining rounds through the door, yelling to the fugitive to surrender. Solemnly, more than three hundred Germans filed out of the dugout; swallowing hard, Adams brandished his now empty pistol and marched them back to his startled platoon.

By 11:50 that first morning, the German losses from one cause or another were very high. Staff officers were afraid that their 77th Reserve Division might have been "annihilated." Many had indeed died in the barrage—but most had simply thrown down their arms and surrendered. Knowing that his troops were needed to man the Michel Position and assuming that the American objective was to press forward against this line as soon as possible, Fuchs threw his two reserve divisions into a counterattack against Liggett's I Corps, which was moving inexorably north toward the meeting point with Cameron. The reserves gained no ground, but when the Americans did not advance to the Michel Position, Fuchs congratulated himself and continued to pull his troops back. The carefully planned withdrawal was becoming an undignified scramble.

The retreat from the nose of the salient lay along the road from Saint-Mihiel through Vigneulles. Rickenbacker saw the Germans fleeing along the road and swooped down to attack. "Dipping down at the head of the column, I sprinkled a few bullets over the leading teams. Horses fell right and left. One driver lept from his seat and started running for the ditch. Half way across the road he threw up his arms and rolled over upon his face. He had stepped full in front of my stream of machine-gun bullets."

American artillery now began shelling the road, and Rickenbacker watched the enemy abandon "huge quantities of guns, wagons and supplies" and take to the woods to cover their flight north and east. Their fate now lay in the hands of Cameron and V Corps. To trap them as planned, his nearest division (the 26th) had to advance eight miles. But his attack, starting three hours later than the main assault and unsupported by tanks, was moving more slowly. Nevertheless, by 1 P.M., he had pushed the Germans off the plateau of the Meuse Heights. Fuchs now ordered the units facing Cameron to hold him off "at all costs"; on their determination depended the safety of all the troops remaining in the pocket and, it seemed, the fate of the Michel Position itself.

As darkness fell on that first day, the Germans were retreating from the salient as quickly as they could, in a race, as they thought, for the Michel Position. Pershing was indeed racing, but his battle was with the clock as the Meuse-Argonne offensive grew ever nearer. Seeing enemies escaping to fight again, he personally telephoned orders for the advance to continue through the night. The gap was closing all the time.

By morning, units of Dickman's 1st Division and Cameron's 26th, muddy, exhausted, and hungry, had joined up at Vigneulles and cut the road from Saint-Mihiel. The salient was sealed off—but too late to achieve the original objective fully. Fighting a heavy rearguard action, by far the largest part of the German "Mihiel Group" had covered nineteen miles with the loss of "only 1,100 men and three guns," according to their own figures, to reach the Michel Position early on September 13. In the process, they had been able to destroy water supplies, set fire to "the majority of the villages and camps," blow up some important road crossings, and take with them many civilian prisoners.

After four years, "the Hernia" had been repaired. The American First Army had captured 13,251 prisoners with 466 guns. By French calculations, the Allied losses had been light for an assault on fixed defenses such as these; Fox Conner gave the total as 11,000. Most importantly, the operation had taken no longer than had been allocated to it, and the Meuse-Argonne offensive was still on schedule.

For public morale purposes, the French press was ecstatic in its praise of the First Army; but Pershing received little credit from Allied soldiers. French staff officers acknowledged "the superb state of morale amongst the American troops" but attributed their success to "favorable conditions . . . a debilitated enemy, a withdrawal in progress, the larger part of the artillery already withdrawn." The Americans, they said, had merely "relieved the Germans."

Fuchs, overwhelmingly relieved at not having to explain to his superiors that he had lost the Michel Position, considered that the Americans had failed to press their advantage. He had, after all, succeeded in withdrawing four fifths of his troops and holding on to a viable line of defense. There were many within the First Army itself who agreed that an opportunity had been missed. For several hours, they argued, a key stretch of the Hindenburg Line had lain largely undefended; had the First Army been intent on pushing through, it could have done so with impunity. Proving the point, Douglas MacArthur sneaked through the Michel Position and into the German rear areas. He scanned Metz through his binoculars, saw few defenders, and forever after would believe that the First Army should have pushed on, as Pershing had originally wanted. MacArthur's corps commander, Dickman, thought the same. Even Marshall considered that if the operation had not been deliberately limited from the outset, there was "no doubt" that the First Army could have captured Metz on September 14.

Pershing, who had been the one to accept the limits placed on the operation and had made only a vague reservation of the right to exploit success, was forced to agree with Marshall, but both knew that it was too late to act now. On the night of September 13, with the salient sealed, Pershing had asked Marshall whether the advance should continue. Marshall had replied in the negative. The attack had been planned as a limited operation and had now been halted; the momentum had been lost, and it would take time to initiate a new advance, time the First Army did not have. Liggett, too, was opposed to going on; it would have been practicable, he thought, only if the First Army were "a well-oiled, fully-coordinated machine, which it was not, as yet."

Liggett's remark highlights the real significance of the Saint-Mihiel operation. The territorial gain was not, in the end, particularly important, as it was not to be followed up. But this was the First Army's baptism as a complex organization, an event that was expected to have momentous consequences for the future. Staff officers appraised their army's performance with interest and honesty, finding much both to praise and to blame.

Despite heavy rain and wind, the air operation had been largely a success. Command of the air had been ensured by "perhaps the most important air concentration the western front ever saw," in Fox Conner's opinion. Billy Mitchell himself had played a typically energetic part in the action. With physical courage not called for by his rank, he went up to direct ground troops in their attack, for which he later received the Distinguished Service Cross. On the ground, he showed great skill in marshaling and controlling his mixed forces and succeeded in throwing the German air forces onto the defensive, keeping a large number of their planes away from the fighting at the front by making them guard installations in the rear. The strategic value of large offensive air formations working in front of the troops on the ground had been convincingly displayed.

In general, too, the light tanks manned by the Americans had proven effective. Fox Conner noted, "In spite of heavy rains which had made the ground soggy and difficult, many of the tanks accompanied the infantry through the trench systems and did valuable work in wiping out machine gun nests that constituted the main reliance of the German in his effort to cover his withdrawal." Patton reported proudly that eight of his light tanks had advanced without infantry support and driven the Germans back to Jonville, on the Michel Position itself. "From a point of view of training," commented Rockenbach, commander of the tank corps, "this maneuver was worth months to the little force of American tanks." He had unbounded pride in his embryonic force: "It met its first call with all the vim, dash and courage of its splendid young manhood. It could not be held back and . . . led wherever it operated." Even more fortunate, with the Meuse-Argonne operation coming up, only 4 of the 144 tanks now in American hands were out of commission.

In Fox Conner's eyes, "The greatest result of the operation was the development of the First Army as an effective offensive weapon for more vital fighting." But many faults had first to be corrected, and French observers were only too ready to list them:

Command, Staff—Lacking in foresight and decision. The 82nd Division eluded its commander during the morning of the 12th.

Troops—Not up to scratch. The officers were sometimes deficient in the basic skills (map-reading, for example).

Artillery—Supplies far from secure, traffic badly regulated. Too many guns brought forward and not enough ammunition.

Liaison—Mediocre. Some units had never exercised together. The infantry responded poorly to the air services.

Traffic—Gave rise to serious criticism. Problems were increased by the presence of French units.

Food supplies—Remains a weak point, especially where front line units
are concerned.

Road discipline had indeed been appalling; the supply trains showed a
total disregard for standing orders, and the military police lacked any experience in an operation on this scale. Patton reported that three trucks
loaded with gas for a detachment of his tanks were stopped dead by the
military police at Flièrey. "This fact materially hampered the operations of
the tanks on the morning of the 13th." IV Corps's Chief of Artillery,
Major General W. Lassiter, was equally concerned at the breakdown in
the supply of ammunition: "The machinery for this purpose was almost
non-existent."

There was little time to solve these problems. Units were already being
withdrawn from the salient and dispatched toward the Meuse-Argonne
front. In just twelve days, the First Army would again have to engage the
enemy—but this time they knew there was no prospect of the Germans retreating.

32

"The Most Ideal Defensive Terrain": Between the Meuse River and the Argonne Forest

With good reason, Hugh Drum, the First Army's Chief of Staff, regarded the front between the Argonne Forest on the left and the Meuse River on the right as "the most ideal defensive terrain." At first sight, from the center of the American line, there are no startling features to warrant this claim. The map shows Montfaucon, the hill standing in the center of the battlefield, to be 1,250 feet high—but as the whole area is about 1,000 feet above sea level, the net effect is modest. In the fall, the most significant characteristic of the region is the weather: *"Pas de neige, toujours la pluie, pluie, pluie"* ("No snow, always rain, rain, rain"), as the locals will tell you, raising their eyes to the heavens.

Looking north from the center of Pershing's line, woods and farmland gently rise over a progression of east-west ridges to the Barricourt Heights, some twelve miles away. On the left, running all the way to these heights, is the fordable Aire River and beyond it the Argonne Forest—an ancient broadleaf forest growing on ridges that rise 300 feet or so above the surrounding land. On the right of the sector is the Meuse River. Beyond the river, running parallel to the Argonne, are the Meuse Heights, a range of hills rising on occasion to 600 feet above the battlefield.

The effect of the high ground to left and right is to turn the sector into a long, shallow channel. This configuration, with the ridges running across the sector and Montfaucon in the center, gave the Germans good observation over perhaps 80 percent of the battlefield, with the remainder visible from balloon or aircraft. Small though Montfaucon is, it had twenty-three artillery observation posts on it because the lie of the land gave it panoramic views as far south as Verdun. In 1918, with artillery at a peak of accuracy, the sector was effectively a shooting gallery, with the attacking troops and rear areas exposed to shell fire at all times.

The Germans had held the sector since 1914, and they had made magnificent use of the advantages nature offered. To advance only as far as they could see, about four miles to Montfaucon, the Americans would have to force their way through a tightly woven tracery of defensive lines.

The first line of defense would once have been sufficient by itself to keep them out; in 1916, the wire entanglements and trench systems just the other side of no-man's-land had been a virtually impenetrable barrier of concrete, stone, and steel. But by the late summer of 1918, the methods of defense on the Western Front had changed considerably. Tanks and artillery could now blast a path through fixed defenses, and the Germans had changed tack: "We must, above all things, consider," a senior officer was reported as saying, "how we may prepare for resistance according to the basic principles of echelonment in depth."

Fortunately for the German planners, an extensive infrastructure for in-depth defense already existed, a legacy of the years of bloody fighting in the area. There were six hundred artillery emplacements west of the Meuse to add to the five hundred on the heights. Patchworks of barbed-wire entanglements had been cunningly distributed to funnel attackers into lethal fire zones covered by artillery and machine guns. More recently, the Germans had added minefields and tank traps and established a strong air force to target enemy infantry.

So once the Americans crossed the front line of defense, now only lightly held, their problems would really begin. Immediately they would find themselves in an "outpost zone" of strong points and machine-gun nests leading to a line of resistance running across the heavily wooded sector below Montfaucon. If they penetrated this line and pressed on through the fire raining down on them from front and sides, they would face a second line of resistance: the Etzel Position, anchored on Montfaucon itself. This was the point that, in Pétain's view, they would be lucky to reach by Christmas.

And this was only the preliminary hurdle. Once through Montfaucon, Pershing's men would find themselves in yet another outpost zone, the Giselher Position. This series of carefully sited machine-gun and mortar emplacements used the succession of woods and ridges that ran for five more miles covering the Germans' principal defensive line: the Kriemhilde Position.

Begun in October 1917, the Kriemhilde Position took full advantage of the Côte de Châtillon, the Côte de Romagne, and the other significant ridges that lay across the battlefield here like a shield. Kriemhilde also had the considerable advantage of being beyond the range of all but the heaviest artillery. And beyond the Kriemhilde Position, if there were any attackers left, the Germans had emplaced yet more machine guns as a buffer zone before their final fallback position on the commanding Barricourt Heights.

Not surprisingly, the Germans regarded the sector as impenetrable— but there were chinks in the armor. The Etzel Line, running through Montfaucon, had never been completed. Throughout its length the trenches, though they were well sited and the wire in front of them was in place, were only one spadeful deep. The Kriemhilde Position, too, was incomplete in stretches. The fearsome wire was set out and ready, but the trenches remained shallow and there were few dugouts to protect the infantry from shell fire.

The greatest weakness, however, was the shortage of troops; the Germans had only five divisions actually manning these splendid defenses, and many of the gun emplacements were empty. If Pershing could keep his attack a surprise, he might hope with a numerical superiority of eight to one to burst through even the Kriemhilde Position before the Germans could rush reinforcements in. Pershing's staff calculated that four German divisions could be brought up within twenty-four hours, two more in forty-eight, and a further nine in seventy-two hours, at which point the sector would become impassable. Success depended on the Germans' having no warning of the strike; and, once launched, it must be extraordinarily rapid.

"Absolute secrecy," ordered Pétain, "must be maintained until the last moment." In response, though it added to the complications facing the staff, the First Army changed its code from the one used at Saint-Mihiel only days before. The AEF used a series known as "River Codes": "Potomac," "Wabash" (used at Saint-Mihiel), and "Colorado." Each had the same carefully chosen code groups, but in preparing each book, the connection between each code group and its plain-text equivalent had been established by chance drawing "as in a lottery, so that there was no rule or law about it." Later it was claimed that at Saint-Mihiel the Germans had broken the code "within a few hours." At the time there was no suspicion of this (and indeed, it is unlikely to have been true, given the complexity of the River Codes). In any event, Pershing was taking no chances.

But simply ensuring the security of the code could not conceal the increased volume of communications nor do anything to disguise the physical presence of 600,000 American troops, 3,980 artillery pieces, and 90,000 horses moving over the three roads leading to the front—as well as the outflow of 200,000 *poilus*. The only hope of obscuring so vast a movement was to execute it by night. By day, men and beasts with materials huddled under cover in the woods or under camouflage netting while intelligence staff tried hard to distract the Germans' attention from the area.

Pétain's headquarters spread the notion of an American attack in the east and the First Army staff tried to arrange a ruse to support this disinformation. On September 18, the Signal Corps' Radio Detachment was requested to have

> some camouflage radio stations installed between the Moselle and Luneville to operate for the next two or three days. . . . These stations should be located on the ground so as to give the impression of a Corps or possibly a larger force concentrating in that vicinity. Say five or six stations operating. . . . The messages should be comparatively few and in an entirely meaningless code . . . and occasional apparently indiscreet service messages in clear should indicate that the stations are American.

At a distance, some of the enemy commanders were unsettled. On September 21, General Max von Gallwitz was positive that Pershing would ultimately attack to the east of the Meuse, probably toward Metz, given that the AEF's experienced divisions were in the Saint-Mihiel area. The civilians in Metz were evacuated, and as late as September 25 the German artillery around the town was still regrouping. Most significantly, though the number of German reserves in the Meuse-Argonne area had remained stable, those further east, from the Woeuvre Plain to Switzerland, had increased.

But locally the German forces were keenly aware of the real threat. However carefully the Allies were hiding by day, their feverish nocturnal maneuvers could hardly go unnoticed. "The circulation in hitherto quiet sectors," observed a German intelligence summary on September 24, "points to the possibility of an attack along the whole front from Reims to

Verdun. . . . At night great activity reigned along our front. The noise of narrow-gauge railways, the unloading of heavy material, loud cries, sirens and klaxons could be heard throughout the whole night."

French units continued to hold the forward trenches, screening the American buildup—but with less than complete success. "Brown uniforms having been observed along our front on September 23," commented German intelligence, "it would appear, although not definitely, that the presence of American troops must be taken into consideration. . . . On the left of the neighbouring groups, in sectors previously held by the French, the presence of the 79th and 80th American Infantry Divisions has been confirmed." That presence was established beyond doubt when the Germans succeeded in capturing a private from the 79th Division.

Divisional staff officers in the area may even have predicted the exact date of the offensive; prisoners from the German 5th Guard Division told intelligence officers from I Corps that an Allied attack was expected on September 26. American intelligence noted that the enemy "appears to be extending his policy of echeloning in greater depth." But the evidence was not weighty enough, it seemed, to persuade Gallwitz to reinforce the Meuse-Argonne sector specifically.

Against the scarce defenders, Pershing intended to throw nine divisions: one in the Argonne Forest, eight from the eastern edge of the forest across the eighteen-odd miles to the Meuse River. On the left, Pershing placed the three divisions of Hunter Liggett's I Corps: the 77th, 28th, and 35th. The 77th would advance through the Argonne Forest, while the 28th and 35th would drive north along the Aire valley. George Cameron's V Corps (the 91st, 37th, and 79th Divisions) had the unenviable task of advancing in the center through Montfaucon. And on the right, Robert Bullard's III Corps (the 4th, 80th, and 33rd Divisions) would advance along the Meuse, peeling back to secure the flank.

Pershing intended that his army should reach the approaches to the Kriemhilde Position by the end of the first day and go through on the second. He was giving the First Army less than two days to advance over heavily fortified and difficult terrain for a distance of ten miles—which would mean advancing at twice the speed achieved at Saint-Mihiel, where the Germans had been in full retreat.

On the face of it, it was a foolhardy gamble, but Pershing had little choice. His army was brand-new and unblooded. None of the best divisions was available; four of the divisions chosen for the attack in the Meuse-Argonne had no experience of the front even in quiet sectors, and for many of the men, as Private Vernon Nicholls recalled with grim humor, "going over the top" was "still but a figure of speech." They had neither the training nor the discipline for complex maneuvering or to "bite and hold" their way north. Nor did the Army—or the AEF as a whole—have the logistical capacity to support such a strategy: to equip the First Army, Pershing had been obliged to strip the Supply Services, leaving "only 25% of the personnel necessary to do our work."

Pershing had to finish the battle as soon as possible, and he put his faith in the one great asset his green troops possessed: élan. Either they would go through quickly, or the Germans would arrive in force and slam the gate shut. "The attack must be pushed with the greatest vigor. . . . Division commanders will deploy their infantry in sufficient depth to give fresh impulses to the attack when necessary." The orders passed down to the infantry sketched a blueprint for rapid penetration. The rate of attack, which was tied to the speed of the rolling barrage, would be well over 100 yards every four minutes—an extraordinary pace to set given the abundance of wire and obstacles and the absence of heavy tanks. The infantry would maintain this rate by "utilizing lanes of least resistance, outflanking"— shades of Ludendorff's storm troopers!

As forward elements pushed on, special teams would deal with the enemy strong points that had been outflanked. Private Nicholls remembered the "moppers up" in the 91st Division: "They had some strange-looking camouflage on their helmets and were armed with trench knives, hand grenades and several of them carried the new US riot gun, a 12-gauge pup-gun shooting a heavy charge of buckshot. These guns were designed for close quarters."

Like Ludendorff's storm troopers, the infantry needed firepower to blast through the defenses for them. The First Army had a huge number of guns allocated to the attack: 3,980 of various types and calibers, 70 percent of them placed west of the Meuse. Had they been evenly distributed, there would have been one gun for every thirty-three feet of front. Unfortunately, the Navy's fifteen-inch guns, mounted on specially constructed trains and firing 1,400-pound shells more than twenty-five miles with almost pinpoint accuracy, were not available for the opening barrage, though five would eventually join the operation.

Patton's light tanks and Billy Mitchell's squadrons were tasked to support the advance; the infantry would carry with them Stokes mortars, two-man-operated 35mm guns, and rifle grenades, and each battalion was supposed to be accompanied by two 75mm guns. Nevertheless, it was crucial, given the depth of the German defenses, that as much artillery as possible should move up in support, and division commanders were ordered (in typed capital letters) to "GIVE THEIR ESPECIAL ATTENTION TO THE PROMPT CONSTRUCTION OF EFFICIENT ROAD COMMUNICATION ACROSS NO MANS LAND."

The planners could do no more. By the evening of September 25, the First Army staff had in any case achieved little short of a miracle. They had assembled a platform of guns, tanks, aircraft, matériel, and men from which to launch the greatest offensive in the history of the United States. What they could not know was whether the parts would combine with a destructive power sufficient to rip through some of the most powerful defenses ever devised.

33

❧❦❧

Over the Top:
The First Day on the Meuse-Argonne

The massed guns began a harassing bombardment at 11 P.M. on September 25. Three hours later, every battery let loose, filling the sky with a blinding, deafening sheet of flame. Nothing their instructors had told them in camp, no newspaper reports or veterans' memoirs, nothing they had heard in France had prepared the green troops for this mind-numbing noise and terror. Their nerves were already raw. "The troops were tired when they went into the fight," George Marshall reported later. "They had been held in the woods in wet clothes and wet feet for a week or more, made a long march the night before going in, without any sleep." Now they cowered, awed, in the mire of the forward trenches as the ground shook beneath them.

"Fix bayonets!" The order passed along the line from man to man. Then, at 5:30 A.M., the whistles blew, and young officers led their men up the ladders and over the top. For fifteen miles, from the Argonne to the Meuse, Americans were advancing virtually shoulder to shoulder. Fog laced with acrid powder fumes stung their eyes and burned their throats as they roared and cheered. Private Milton Sweningsen had been drafted from his home in Fargo, North Dakota, only on March 28. He had never stepped onto a firing range, let alone benefited from any training; battlefield tactics were a closed book to him. "Now here I was, at the bottom of a hill, in a pit of fog, and on the attack." His division, the 35th under Major General Peter Traub, advanced along the east bank of the Aire River in wonderful order. There were only a few telltale traces of their unfamiliarity with the Western Front—the men, for example, whom Sergeant William Triplett saw proudly carrying a flag.

For the moment, the whole line was shrouded in thick fog and untroubled by the Germans. With visibility down to barely forty feet, the men stuck close to their platoon commanders, each of whom had a luminous compass and orders "to follow the azimuth 330 degrees to the corps objective regardless of obstacles, machine gun nests etc." No one had realized that the weight of steel embedded in this old Verdun battlefield had its own magnetic polarity that distorted compass bearings.

In the center of the line, facing Montfaucon, the 79th Division advanced like the rest. Their good order lasted only as far as their own wire, which they had been given twenty-five minutes to hack through while shell fire cut the German wire ahead. It was not long enough, and when the rolling barrage started, the men of the 79th were marooned.

Then as gaps in the wire began to appear, they bunched up, waiting impatiently to go through. Units broke up, and as they pushed on the fog, old wire, shell craters, and winding trenches quickly turned the careful formations into a rabble. Supporting battalions that had set out a thousand yards behind the front line now caught up and added to the jumble. At 8:55 A.M., Brigadier General F. S. Foltz sent back an agonized message to his divisional commander: "Fields are covered with barbed wire and 'cheveaux de frise'. Men cannot get through. The men are disorganized and are under heavy shrapnel fire. As soon as sun raises fog, men will be cut to pieces by machine-gun fire."

Confused, deafened by the noise, and blinded by the fog, the men formed their own ad hoc units and pushed on across the German front line into the first outpost zone. Shell fire had plowed up the earth all around them. "Debris of every kind strews the ground," reported twenty-two-year-old Leroy Y. Haile. "Many dead are lying around and many who have been buried are tossed out of their graves. The stench is terrible."

American shells had caught the Germans in the front line. These were the first victims of war many of the doughboys had ever seen. "Some of them were terribly wounded," one private remembered. "A slight feeling of sickness came over me as I looked at them, but I fought it off. I must get used to this." On they went, the dense fog and smoke keeping their own casualties light. PFC Casper Swartz, Company C, 314th Regiment, was faced with another astonishing sight: "We came across two men and a boy about 14 or 15 years old chained to a heavy machine gun. . . . They were left there to hold the American troops back and kill all they could."

Colonel Howland, commanding the 138th Regiment, 35th Division, navigated through the fog by compass, completely ignorant of the progress of his regiment. With him stumbled a little group of staff officers, runners, and regimental bandsmen, their numbers augmented at one point by men of the 91st Division, who were totally lost. They were well up on their objective by midmorning, when the fog lifted—and then at once they found themselves under fire from the crests of the Argonne to their left and Montfaucon to their front and right. "The shelling was so heavy," Howland remembered, "that more than a score of [my men] were instantly killed, several blown into shapeless masses of blood, flesh and clothes. Simultaneously, enemy machine guns opened a terrific fire from both flanks and front." The survivors took cover in a ditch while a French officer, with great bravery, went to call some nearby tanks to the rescue.

Howland decided that when the tanks returned, he would charge the machine guns with every man at his disposal. "Deciding to bring into the ditch such men as might still be alive . . . I crawled . . . into the road behind, and over the shelled area, but found none but dead." For three hours Howland and his men lay under intense shelling and machine-gun fire. Then, when the tanks arrived, his little band—raw recruits who had been in combat for less than six hours—formed up and launched their charge. "All unwounded men went forward with dash. . . . In a few moments all of the enemy machine guns on the flank were wiped out, the crews killed or captured." Howland himself was wounded, and three days later he cabled Traub from the hospital: "My left hand shattered, but hope to be patched up and back for duty soon. Would break my heart to lose regiment."

This kind of piecemeal engagement was repeated up and down the front as the fog lifted and the German gunners gained sight of their enemy. But though the rolling barrage had progressed too far ahead of the advancing Americans to be of any immediate use to them, and though they had lost a fair degree of unit coherence, they had gained the surprise they so desperately needed. The Germans showed little fight and mounted no counterattacks; traversing the first outpost zone, the First Army crossed the first real line of resistance without difficulty.

By 11 A.M., the 28th and 35th Divisions on the far left, astride the Aire River, had reached the objective set for Liggett's I Corps. Now, as ordered, they halted, waiting for Cameron's V Corps to come up in the center.

Liggett had tried to persuade Pershing to abandon the scheme of corps objectives and obey Foch's call for unrelenting advance, but the First Army
staff feared that individual divisions would drive too far ahead and be outflanked. It was a bad mistake; the battlefield was so chaotic that six hours
passed before orders could be given and I Corps's attack relaunched.

On the right of the attack, on the Meuse side, the three divisions of
Bullard's III Corps also advanced steadily. "No substantial resistance to
our advance," Bullard reported at noon. Pershing, waiting anxiously at
headquarters, was not prepared to hear anything else. His entire plan was
based on an unopposed progress. The two outer corps were to advance,
guard their respective flanks, suppress fire from the heights of the Argonne
and the Meuse, and assist V Corps as it swept up over Montfaucon and
fought on toward the Kriemhilde Position itself.

While Liggett and Bullard drove forward to their flanking positions, in
the very center of the attack Major General Joseph E. Kuhn's 79th Division approached Montfaucon. These men from Pennsylvania, Maryland,
and the District of Columbia were almost the newest to combat of any in
the First Army, and their training had been among the worst. More than
half the division's personnel had been assigned to it since May 1918, from
camps all over the United States. A War Department inspector looking
over the division that summer at Camp Meade, Maryland, had recommended that it be kept there for further training, but before his report could
be published, the 79th had begun the journey overseas. The last units had
reached France only on August 3. Then, just after the division had begun
training in France, its senior officers had been transferred and replacements
appointed. The division was in no sense an organic entity; its artillery
brigade had remained behind in training and new gunners were assigned,
arriving just as the infantry took up position in the front line.

Now, as soon as the 79th was put to the test, its attack formation was
ruined by the fog and the wire. The 314th Regiment lost entire sections
and gained two companies of the 315th, supposed to be in support. When
the fog lifted, the lead units found that they had stumbled into a thicket of
German machine-gun nests: bullets streamed at them from all points of the
compass.

That afternoon stretched the division to the limit. The 4th Division to
the right had omitted to mop up the extreme edge of its sector, leaving a
line of enemy machine guns entrenched on a ridge on Kuhn's flank. Kuhn
had no means of communicating with his artillery to have them take out

these guns, and morale dipped. "Toward 4 o'clock," recalled Colonel
Oury, commanding the 314th Regiment, "there was a little evidence of
panic. A number of retrograde movements were started."

As darkness fell, Colonel Claude Sweezey's 313th Regiment to the left
of Oury's men was also short of Montfaucon. Sweezey reported that the
313th owed their advance thus far entirely to their riflemen, who had taken
on machine-gun nests with nothing more than rifle grenades. The regiment
was not equipped with Stokes mortars, and the machine guns and 37mm
guns had been unable to keep up with the advance. "The tanks I had expected much from," Sweezey remarked, "due to the extensive laudation of
them which I had seen in the daily press." But, he concluded, "the tanks
with this regiment were of little use."

After fourteen hours of combat, the men were badly in need of food and
rest, but there could be no respite. The 79th Division, spearhead of the
First Army's attack, was already lagging badly; the divisions to the right
and left had all pushed well past Montfaucon, and Kuhn ordered
Sweezey to take the stronghold that night.

V Corps artillery pounded the hill, and two tanks arrived to help the infantry cross the open ground into the lashing machine guns. The tanks
"went forward about 200 yards," noted Sweezey with scorn, "stopped,
turned around, withdrew and left the field of action." Nevertheless, he ordered his men to advance through the twilight. The hill commanded clear
fire lines; out in the open, the attackers were cut down mercilessly and
forced to retreat.

Kuhn had wanted Oury's 314th Regiment to attack at the same time,
but they were temporarily out of contact, so Sweezey and the 313th were
advancing unsupported. When their attack failed, Kuhn summoned
Brigadier General Robert Noble, who was commanding the support
brigade, and ordered him to take Oury's regiment and, with the 315th
Regiment from his own brigade, to attack "at once." It was an appalling
order to be given. The division had been in combat for nearly twenty hours
by now, with heavy casualties, and was disorganized; its telephone communications were out, it was pitch dark, and now it was raining.

At 2:15 A.M., Noble tried to establish contact with his regimental commanders. He managed to get a message to Colonel Knowles, commander
of the 315th Regiment, and ordered him to assemble his battalion commanders for a conference. Noble went forward to meet them but the road
was so congested with traffic that he had to walk, and did not reach the

rendezvous until after 5 A.M. As far as he knew, Oury and his regiment had simply disappeared, and neither artillery nor tank commanders would act without knowing their whereabouts.

Here in the dawn of September 27 a major crisis was building. Pershing's strategy of rapid penetration before the Germans could reinforce was being prejudiced by the failure of the 79th Division to take Montfaucon. The division should by now have been some six miles forward, confronting the Kriemhilde Position. At 6:30 A.M., Kuhn, grimly determined to drive his men on, went forward personally to Noble's command post. Finding him still there, with no attack in progress, Kuhn relieved him of command.

Unknown to Noble, and too late to save his commission, one of his aides had succeeded in locating Oury several hours before. He had passed on the message that "the attack had not been aggressive enough and that it must be pushed on." But Oury, possibly because he had been informed that the 4th Division to the right was on the point of making an attack in support, had decided that his men "should have a little rest and attack again at 4 o'clock" that morning. (The 4th Division's attack never materialized.)

Oury was promoted to command Noble's brigade, and he assessed the situation. Sweezey had attacked and been repulsed; his old regiment had now finished its little rest; the two regiments in his brigade were waiting to move. Oury was now able to establish liaison with the artillery, and at last the 37mm guns arrived. The 79th was ready to try again.

With Pershing frantic to get the advance moving, every available gun fired at Montfaucon, deluging the little hill with gas and high explosive, while all four regiments tried to envelop the defenders in a coordinated attack. Everywhere the fighting was savage. By 7:30 A.M., the Germans had beaten the Americans back, and frantic demands came for more artillery support. With the aid of a barrage that turned the hill into "one great belching spout of dirt and dust," Sweezey pressed home his attack. Finally the message came back: "Montfaucon captured 11 H 45."

For all the pounding the citadel had endured, the men of the 313th found the German barracks still standing. Inside were thirty wounded Germans "with two wounded Americans whom they were caring for." But outside brutality reigned. Sergeant Davies wrote in his diary, "The 313th dead and wounded all around us. One boy with a terrible hole in his chest was lying in a shell hole about ten yards from me and kept calling for help." A sniper was waiting for any one who tried to reach him; the boy's cries were quieted only by his death later that afternoon.

34

"Retrograde Movements": The Second, Third, and Fourth Days

With Montfaucon taken, the First Army entered the combat zone covering the approaches to the Kriemhilde Position. Now, on the second day of the attack, the element of surprise had gone. The Germans were fully alert, their guns more numerous and effective, and reserves were desperately rushing to shore up the defenses. Three new German divisions appeared on Liggett's I Corps front alone. With resistance stiffening, the First Army needed to maintain all its destructive power and momentum if the strategy of rapid penetration were to succeed. But at this crucial time, the attack faltered.

After twenty-four hours of combat, many of the divisions were disorganized and disoriented. The men were tired after a night spent in cold, muddy holes under the noise and sudden glare of star shells, artillery bursts, and machine-gun bullets. Vernon Nicholls, with the 91st Division, woke up on the second morning in the drizzle, stiff, cold, and thirsty. He drank from a nearby stream and then sat watching "infantry and artillery, tanks and supply wagons moving around in the mud and rain, most of them trying to locate their respective outfits. . . . The carcasses of four horses were lying a few yards away and not far from where we sat were four Yanks, killed by one shell as they slept together in a shell hole." Eventually he and his buddies were gathered up by an officer they had never seen before, who tried to push them on.

The disorganization in the front line, however, was a pale reflection of the situation in the rear. Since midmorning the previous day, guns, artillery trains, food and water supplies, ammunition trucks, and divisional staff had all been trying to move forward. None of the units had sufficient trucks or animals to carry forward all it wished; Liggett reported his corps as 7,000 mules and horses short, and the First Army as a whole was an estimated 50,000 horses short of requirements. But what they did have was more than enough to jam the tracks leading to the front. As they tried to cross no-man's-land, trucks and horses alike slipped and sank and bogged down in shell holes, wire, and collapsed trenches. Eddie Rickenbacker observed, "As far as the eye could reach, the shell holes covered the landscape. . . . The soil was familiar yellow clay. Since the rainfall, the country . . . resembled a desolate fever-stricken swamp. Trees were sheared of their branches and even the trunks of large trees themselves were cut jaggedly in two by the enemy's shells."

This three-mile band of murderous man-made swamp running across the entire front proved virtually impassable. The orders to divisions to construct roadways, emphatic though they might have been in their capital letters, were almost impossible to fulfill. As fast as roadbeds were laid down, the press of traffic caused them to collapse. Nothing could get forward, not even the guns—and this spelled disaster for the infantry, which was even then passing beyond the efficient range of its field artillery. Desperately, gun teams wheeled off the road, set up in the mud, and began firing indiscriminately just to give the men ahead some sort of support. Some infantry units could not even locate their artillery, and effective coordination between the two broke down.

The burden of the advance now rested squarely on the shoulders of the infantry, and the going was tough right across the front. Throughout this second day and the next, Traub's division, the 35th, labored painfully up the valley of the Aire, harassed by enemy planes above, machine guns and artillery below. Ammunition was short and medical attention scanty; many of the growing toll of casualties lay where they fell, crying out for help that would never come.

The forward elements of the 35th Division spent the third night of the attack concealed in the distant fringes of Montrebeau Wood, a patch of woodland little more than six miles north of the jump-off line, in the shadow of the Argonne Heights. In the early dawn of September 29, the 137th Infantry Regiment prepared to attack Exermont, a strongly held village lying just ahead in a ravine 50 feet deep and 300 yards wide running east to west. Jump-off was set for 5:30 A.M., and the men were promised a squadron from the 2nd Cavalry to reconnoiter the flanks, with a rolling barrage and tanks to lead their advance.

Major Kalloch, detailed to lead the assault, sent word to the regiment's company commanders to get their units to the north edge of the wood, above the Exermont ravine. Few arrived. "Picking up all the men that could be found," Kalloch recalled bitterly, "I had a force of approximately 125 riflemen and two Chauchat rifles, having three or four clips of ammunition apiece."

After three days of attrition, the vaunted "staying power" of the double-sized American division was nowhere to be seen. These men had been in bivouacs before the attack, had lain the night of September 25–26 in the mud of the front line, and had now spent three more days and nights in the open, tormented by incessant machine-gun fire, high explosives, shrapnel, and gas, and strafed and bombed by enemy aircraft. Influenza was spreading rapidly, and while the food supply was adequate, the men had been driven to drink water from shell holes and were now ravaged by dysentery. Kalloch himself was a replacement officer sent forward during the battle. He now discovered, aghast, just how many of the other officers and NCOs were already dead or wounded. As a functioning organism, the 35th Division was all but extinct; only the extraordinary willingness of the raw, battered troops permitted Kalloch even to think of obeying the instruction to move forward.

Anxiously, the 137th Regiment waited for the cavalry, the rolling barrage, and the tanks. None materialized. At 5:34 A.M., Kalloch led his men out without protection. In the dim light, they got to within a hundred yards of the line of German machine guns on the near edge of the ravine before they came under fire. Charging the guns with a courage born of having little left to lose, Kalloch's men plunged down into the ravine. Now they were encircled by a murderous fire from flanking machine guns and artillery firing from the Argonne and Exermont the length of the ravine. They had been caught in a carefully prepared death trap.

Kalloch sent back word that he could not advance further without help. At 6:15 A.M., he watched as a line of one hundred Americans advanced out of the tree line. "I saw this support coming up over a hill north of the wood, but upon looking again several minutes later, they were nowhere to be seen."

These new troops were under the command of Major John O'Connor. "It was now broad daylight," O'Connor later reported, "and lively machine gun fire was coming from bushes on front and flanks. Very heavy artillery fire with flat trajectory was coming from left flank and in front. The men, very much willing, were very much disorganized and officers were unable to maneuver them." Then this pathetic remnant of the 137th Infantry broke altogether. "I do not know how it started but without command and apparently without panic, most of the men got up and retired to the wood."

Without support, Kalloch could not stay down in the ravine, and at 8 A.M. he ordered the survivors of his group to withdraw. "Every effort was made to bring in all wounded but owing to the intense fire and the German advance around the wood shortly after our retirement, there were several wounded who could not be brought in."

The 35th Division's other regiments suffered equally. The machine-gun company of Howland's 138th found itself between two German batteries firing point-blank. "We executed 'by the right flank,' " Sergeant Leavitt remembered, "and found ourselves . . . in a mined field which was full of trip wires that exploded the mines. We retired . . . under heavy gas shelling." Howland's 2nd Battalion, however, succeeded in driving the enemy through Exermont and made a stand on a ridge just above and to the west of the town. The 1st Battalion of the 140th had also broken through, and together these units tried to hold. They lasted three hours; then, swamped by advancing Germans, they too were ordered to withdraw.

By late morning on Sunday, September 29, the 35th Division was in serious trouble. It was deep within the German killing grounds, without an effective organization to repel a determined counterattack. Sergeant Triplett's outfit "looked terrible . . . exhausted, sleepy, hungry, worn down and sick. Worse—they didn't feel lucky any more. They'd lost the soldier's bullet-proof ego, that feeling of 'others might get hit but never I.' . . . Not even the clowns were wise-cracking any more." With casualties totaling around seven thousand, Traub had no option but to withdraw his shattered columns to a entrenched position on a ridge behind Montrebeau Wood, well short of the line they had reached on the second day.

Traub's division was not the only one to have been broken by the fourth day. That Sunday, Major General C. S. Farnsworth, commander of the 37th, watched his men attack Cierges-sous-Montfaucon, to the east of Exermont, then falter and stall under intense shelling. Their failure exposed the right flank of the 91st Division, but Farnsworth could not move his left flank up because "the physical condition of his men on account of exposure and fatigue was such that it would be impracticable to advance."

On Farnsworth's right, Kuhn's 79th, having taken Montfaucon at immense cost, had found themselves virtually cut off by the stream of shells pouring onto them from the reinforced German defenses. They could not push on, nor could they bring up supplies or even set up dressing stations that were at all safe. The troops were practically without food for three days, and their only water was scooped, foul and lethal, from shell holes. By Sunday morning, demoralization was starting to show. After an attack on a strongly fortified farmstead, the Ferme de la Madeleine, was driven back, the 315th Infantry "drifted to the rear." Staff officers stopped what was politely termed "the retrograde movement" and tried to relaunch the attack. But at 5 P.M., the 315th "again drifted to the rear without orders and this time was permitted to remain." A report on the 79th Division's performance would conclude that German artillery fire had "come nearer than anything else to destroying the morale of the units. Troops with three months service will stand the ordeal but a short time, as was proved, as there were many retrograde movements."

The First Army's difficulties were caused not by lack of will or courage but by the failure of its staff to overcome the fearsome logistical problems of this stretch of the Western Front. "Once the attack commenced," the French staff officers attached to the First Army concluded, "this army behaved as if it had been struck by paralysis. . . . It was just one more demonstration of the old truth that an army cannot improvise."

From the second day on, the worsening chaos in the rear not only denied units the support they needed in order to push forward, it also began to function actively as a brake on their progress. Even after four days of struggle, none of the hideous problems of crossing no-man's-land had been resolved. "The congestion on all highways furnished a horrifying spectacle," French observers reported, "unimaginable." In places, vehicles stood stationary for anything between sixteen and thirty hours; elsewhere the average speed was just over one mile per hour.

So desperate were the men becoming for food that the divisional rolling kitchens and food trucks, stalled in the traffic snarl, were being looted by men of other divisions. Hunger forced men to drop back; military police often found men from the front line heading back toward YMCA stalls in search of cigarettes and a mug of coffee. While some of the lighter guns were getting forward, the heavy army artillery was immobilized for seven days; the nine-foot-wide tracks of the 155mm GPF guns blocked the roads unaided. Even command decisions could not get through. On September 27, Pershing had sent orders at 11:30 P.M. for V Corps to attack at seven the next morning; the orders did not arrive until four hours after the appointed jump-off time.

This monstrous traffic snarl, which was an anxiety and a frustration for the commanders, spelled torture for the sick and wounded. Essentially, the First Army's medics were equipped to cope with static trench warfare; the forward movement of the troops grossly overstrained the system, especially the hopelessly inadequate arrangements for transport of the wounded.

The Table of Organization for Cameron's V Corps provided for a sanitary train with 4 ambulance companies, 4 field hospitals, 44 cargo trucks, 8 motor cars, 20 motorcycles, and a staff of 50 officers and 800 men. On September 26, however, there was no such admirable institution in existence. Frantic, the medical officers borrowed anything the Allies could offer: automobiles, trucks, buses. If a wounded man were lucky, he would be collected by a stretcher party and carried to the first-aid station. From there he would be taken through the traffic jams into the back areas, a journey that could take twenty-four hours, with a further forty-eight hours in transit back to the nearest field hospital if major surgery were called for. If he were unlucky, he would lie on the battlefield for days. V Corps, now to the north of Montfaucon, had no roads due south, and all its wounded had first to be carried across to the I or III Corps's areas to join the throng of maimed and suffering there.

The First Army had taken 45,000 casualties in four days, and its attack had at best slowed, at worst stalled. Frontline troops were in retreat in places, and several of the divisions were incapable of even defending the line against German counterattack. The rear areas were gripped by chaos. The difficult terrain and foul weather, the haste with which the offensive had been thrown together, the inexperience of so many of the divisions involved, all had played a part in the breakdown. But no rationalizations, no excuses could soften the fact that there had been no breakthrough. On the evening of September 29, Pershing accepted the inevitable and suspended the offensive. He had lost his gamble, and his men had paid the price.

At headquarters, the First Army staff analyzed the débâcle. Poor tactics, an enemy who had resisted far more fiercely than expected, transport problems beyond anyone's worst nightmares—all were acknowledged to have played their part. But as he jotted down his thoughts on the evening of September 29, Colonel Willey Howell, Assistant Chief of Staff, G-2, was brutally frank about the principal reason for the failure: "I believe that the Germans were overwhelmed by our original advance, but that the advance has been so mismanaged and has been so dilatory as to enable them to recover from their first surprise, to readjust and establish themselves."

He was not alone in blaming the First Army for its own misfortunes. Within hours, the Inspector General had compiled a terrifying list of defects within the organization:

> Failure of artillery to support infantry advances. . . . Lack of definite information by artillery commanders as to location of infantry lines. . . . Artillery not pushing far enough forward, resulting in shells falling on or behind our own advancing lines. . . . Brigade PCs not connected by telephone lines to division PCs. . . . Division PCs not informed as to location of Brigade PCs. . . . Failure to mop up machine gun nests immediately after advancing of infantry lines. . . . Trucks going to front only partially loaded. . . . Carrier pigeons not made full use of by battalion commanders. . . . Liaison not maintained laterally between battalions. . . . Enlisted men . . . without gas masks. . . . Enlisted personnel having only summer under-clothing and no overcoats. . . . Shortage of animals and those on hand in poor condition. . . . Shortage of divisional supply of rifles, helmets, gas masks, and gun oil. . . . No panels for front line signaling. . . . Reserves being ordered into line without knowledge of the division commander or his chief of staff. . . . No radio messages because signal officer did not know the Corps code call. . . . Radio messages sent in the clear. . . . Officers not with their organizations in the front lines. . . . Organizations becoming mixed and company leadership bad. . . . Men in the front line being stampeded because officers were not there with them, because organizations were mixed, and because of pessimistic talk among officers and men about their severe losses. . . . Many stragglers from front line

and so on, in a catalogue of inefficiency that drew a stark profile of a raw, vulnerable army.

Stragglers apart, the Inspector General had no complaints about the courage of the men. From end to end of the line their bravery had been remarkable—and one of the most conspicuous displays took place the very day the attack was suspended.

The key to the dominance of the German artillery in recent days had been its unimpeded observation of the battlefield from high ground and from balloons. American and French batteries had been tasked to neutralize observation posts on the ground, while one of Billy Mitchell's principal concerns was to eliminate aerial observation from the equation. His best pilot was Frank Luke, the "Arizona balloon buster" of the 27th Squadron.

Luke was a notorious wild man, arrogant, boastful, and insubordinate; his first victory had been officially queried because he had not sought permission to set off on the hunt by himself. But he possessed to an almost unique degree the ideal combination of nerve, marksmanship, flying ability, and the will to win. He was also a survivor who five times returned to base in planes so riddled with bullet holes as to be write-offs.

Luke had only one close friend. Lieutenant Joseph Fritz Wehner was another loner, but not by choice; during training he had been under almost constant surveillance as the son of a Boston cobbler of German descent. A brilliant flier and gunner, he protected Luke's tail while Luke homed in on the target. In one period of seventeen days, they shot down eighteen German craft, mostly balloons. At Saint-Mihiel, they destroyed nine in two days. It was an intense, complex, emotional relationship. Then, on September 16, the pair engaged two more German balloons. Preoccupied with the kill, Luke failed to notice the arrival of six Fokkers and Wehner had to face them alone. To give Luke time to escape, he flew straight at them—"a deliberate sacrifice of himself for his friend," according to Eddie Rickenbacker—and was shot down.

A week later, Luke went up with another pilot and witnessed his death. At this point Luke, distracted with misery at the loss of Wehner, seems to have lost his mental balance altogether. This may explain why, on the second day of the Meuse-Argonne offensive, he went absent without leave. The following day, he made another unauthorized flight (accounting for one more balloon) and went AWOL once more. Then, on September 29, he was informed that he was being grounded. His immediate response was to take off for enemy lines in his Spad. An order went out for him to be arrested as soon as he landed, but it proved to be superfluous.

As the sun was setting over the chaos below, Luke dropped a note to his squadron commander, alerting him: "Watch three Hun balloons on the Meuse, Luke." Turning, he flew back down the river. He shot down the first balloon with ease but was badly wounded eliminating the second. This did not stop him from destroying the third and strafing German troops in the streets of the village of Murvaux. Then at last he was forced to land. Surrounded by a horde of enemy soldiers, he refused to surrender and continued to fire at them with his pistol until they shot him to death.

35

❦

In the Argonne Forest

Pershing's decision to suspend operations went unheeded in the depths of the Argonne Forest. There, New York's so-called "ghetto" troops, the 77th "Liberty" Division, were fighting their own private war. This bloody, brutal test of endurance was almost totally unexpected. In Pershing's original scenario, the 77th would merely have rolled the Germans back up through the forest as the French in the west and the Americans in the east outflanked their defenses. But when the First Army stalled, the 77th's commander, General Robert Alexander, had to set his division the task of pushing the Germans out by force. The Argonne, its heights bristling with artillery and heavy machine guns, so threatened Pershing's left flank that it could not be permitted to remain in German hands. If it did so, Pershing's staff warned grimly the very day he suspended operations, "it may be found necessary to draw back the line of resistance south of Montfaucon and eventually to our old positions."

How was the forest to be cleared? This was no compact hunting preserve; it was the size of Manhattan, and the 77th was jumping off from about Fourteenth Street. Its support weapons—artillery, mortars, 35mm guns, even grenades—could make little impression on this terrain. "Huge trees," recalled Lieutenant Arthur McKeogh, "tower protectingly above their brood of close-grown saplings, branches interlacing branches overlaid until no patch of sky is visible and the light is the sickly half-light of early dawn. The ground hides under a maze of trailing vines, prickly bushes, rheumatic tree branches, embedded in soggy leaves and rank fern." It was a deeply alien environment for urban conscripts.

The New Yorkers quickly learned that the "streets," the network of trails through the forest, were dangerous killing grounds covered by emplaced machine guns. They had to learn woodlore: how to advance through the undergrowth in single file, stealthily following officers who were themselves navigating by compass. Time and again they would be caught by hidden snipers or machine guns buried in the undergrowth, muzzle flashes invisible behind their screens—emplaced not in ones or twos but every fifteen yards along one overgrown ridge.

The fighting was at close quarters and savage. Company K of the 306th Regiment came across a group of Germans "who held up their hands and said 'Kamerad.' . . . The Americans thought they had surrendered, whereupon they started forward and the Boche produced hand grenades and caused a considerable amount of loss." As at Belleau Wood, only the highest level of commitment could weather such brutality. On the face of it, a polyglot division of foreign-born Poles, Jews, Italians, Greeks, Irish, Armenians, and the rest might not have been expected to cohere. But the heat of battle warmed the melting pot, and men who could communicate only in broken English phrases risked their lives for one another.

With the division thinly spread across the forest among the trees and crags, split up by gullies and ravines, there was no weight to its advance, no chance of punching through the enemy lines. In the tangled undergrowth it was difficult to maintain contact at all, and the fighting evolved into a recurring pattern of small units pushing forward stealthily, with the Germans, equally furtive, infiltrating behind to cut them off. Units trapped like this were under orders not to surrender; they were the forward base on which the advance could build. "Any ground gained must be held," Brigadier General Evan Johnson told his officers. "The troops holding it must be supported. . . . If I find anybody ordering a withdrawal from ground once held, I will see that he leaves the Service."

On September 28, the third day of the advance, the 308th Regiment's 1st Battalion under Major Charles W. Whittlesey was cut off and was not rescued for seventy-two hours. During this time, there was no panic. The battalion carried a supply of pigeons for sending out messages. "We can of course clean up this country to the rear by working our companies over the ground," Whittlesey signaled on September 29, when he realized his predicament, "but we understand our mission is to advance and maintain our strength here." He requested rations and ammunition, which were brought up by a relief party led by Lieutenant Colonel Fred E. Smith.

When the colonel found his way barred by a machine gun, he attacked it single-handed. "Badly wounded in his side," the official report records, "the fearless Colonel continued to advance alone upon the enemy, pouring fire from his automatic until he was hit again and fell dead." He was awarded a posthumous Medal of Honor. When other units finally came abreast of Whittlesey, he was not relieved, merely resupplied and ordered to push on into the forest.

Centering on small-unit operations, the fighting in the Argonne might have seemed to present an ideal opportunity for the 92nd "Buffalo" Division's company captains and lieutenants to demonstrate the "equality of the negro in battle," the black soldier's frequent rallying cry. They were given their chance when their 368th Regiment was taken from I Corps reserve and assigned to the left flank of the 77th, under the control of the French XXXVIII Corps, to link the two armies.

These were hardly the easiest circumstances in which to prove themselves, and the 92nd's black officers failed even before they had begun. Liaison was quickly lost, exposing the left flank of the First Army and forcing the 77th Division to extend its lines west to connect with the French.

The division's white officers had no sympathy with their black colleagues. Major J. N. Merrill, commanding one of the battalions that had failed, complained bitterly:

> Every time the many halts under none too severe fire were made, I personally and often at the point of the pistol literally drove forward the battalion. Without my presence or that of any other white officer right on the firing line, I am absolutely positive that not a single colored officer would have advanced with his men. The cowardice shown by the men was abject. . . . Under the slightest fire the men either diverged into the forest and laid down, or laid down where they were in the majority of cases without any officers near—who were conspicuous by their absence, the men firing in all directions and even into the trees.

The French had the 93rd Division's four black regiments in their own army, where they had done well, and they looked hard at the poor performance of the 92nd. They found the commanding officer, General Charles Ballou, "a cold, authoritarian man" with "only very superficial ideas about the actual conditions of this war." They observed that some 20 percent of the men were raw recruits who had been assigned to the division immediately before embarkation. And they strongly criticized the training methods. "The relatively restricted area of terrain available for exercises, the lack of ranges (because of the lack of material), the habits of the officers, especially the black ones, have all meant that at the moment there is far too much emphasis on drill and on exercises in rigid massed formations." In consequence, the 92nd Division might be considered "still to be ignorant of the current use of arms and equipment other than the rifle, the practice of open, linked formations and the uses of liaison."

But the real problem, as the French saw it, was that the black officers, most of them career NCOs, were "very mediocre" company commanders. They were to blame for the indifferent training of the men and for leaving their battalion commanders, such as Major Merrill, with "crushing responsibility," exercising the command of their units "down to the smallest details." Lacking courage and competence, the French concluded, the black officers could hardly expect to command confidence or respect. One private was reported as having said to his captain, "You are of the same black meat that I am."

To militant and even moderate black Americans, the miserable performance of these troops was the consequence of a deliberate and cynical exercise in destructive manipulation. Candidates at the black officers' school in Des Moines, Iowa, had claimed at the time that officers were being assigned without regard to experience or expertise. Infantry officers were sent to artillery and machine-gun units for which they had no special training. A graduate of Sheffield Scientific School was sent to the infantry, while a senator's butler, "commissioned by graft," went to the heavy artillery.

While the 92nd Division was forming, observers had accused the authorities of assigning the best black officers to noncombatant units, while the worst went to the fighting regiments. *The Crisis*, which had once been supportive of War Department policy, protested, "Unless this decision is reversed, the 92nd Division is bound to be a failure as a unit organization. Is it possible that persons in the War Department wish the Division to be a failure?"

Other examples of flagrant discrimination suggest that *The Crisis*'s suspicions were not paranoiac. General Ballou was not sent to France for a tour of inspection like other divisional commanders. The 92nd was always poorly equipped. In France, its senior officers were constantly being reassigned. Though it was a combat division in corps reserve, its riflemen were assigned to the corps engineers for labor duty. A report to the Director of Military Intelligence, responding to various accusations in *The Crisis*, would eventually agree that the 92nd's Chief of Staff, Colonel Allen Greer, "actually did more to destroy its effectiveness than to promote its morale. . . . If the Division was not a success the fault rests with the division commander and his field and staff officers and not with the men. . . . Colonel Greer should be ordered before a general court martial for trial, thus placing the blame where it justly belongs."

It is not clear exactly what Greer did or said, but without doubt the officers of the 368th Regiment went into battle with low morale. General Ballou had already threatened fifty of them with demotion, and there was a widespread belief that they had been "put into the hardest fighting to kill them." More objectively, the French pointed out that the 368th was "the least well-trained [regiment] of the division," and that there had been "a lack of direction given by the 184th Brigade [which] resulted in hiatuses in supply."

Whether, as seems likely, white officers did set out to destroy the 92nd's reputation by pointing to the 368th Regiment's débâcle, the slur was bitterly resented by the rest of the division. French liaison officer Captain Metz Noblat reported:

> Aware that their future destiny depended a good deal on their present conduct, the black officers and men believed that they would be adjudged incapable of doing well. There were two demonstrations of this: General Ballou, visiting the 368th regiment, found himself surrounded on getting out of his car by enlisted men asking him not to judge them on what had happened, telling him that they didn't want to discuss their differences with him, that they wanted to be given another chance to show that they knew how to behave and, if not advance, at least to hold their ground. Then came Colonel Moss, commander of the 367th regiment, bringing a petition from the officers and NCOs of his regiment, asking not to be judged on what their neighbours had done, but to have their own chance.

Meanwhile, the New Yorkers continued to struggle. On October 2, their painful advance stalled in front of a strongly wired and entrenched position deep in the forest. Goading them on, General Alexander, a tough professional who had worked his way up from the ranks to command the division, telephoned the command post of the 154th Brigade with a message for his brigadier general: "You tell General Johnson that the 154th Brigade is holding back the French on the left and is holding back everything on the right." He added caustically, "You report heavy machine gun fire, but the casualty lists do not substantiate this. Remember that when you are making these reports."

Alexander's rebuke was unfair. Neither the French on the left nor the 153rd Brigade on the right had come up, but Johnson reacted smartly and pushed on his brigade's attack. The immediate objective for the left flank of the 154th was the old mill at Charlevaux, a mile ahead. The orders, as usual, were for each unit to advance independently, regardless of exposed flanks, and on reaching the objective to dig in and hold until the rest of the division came up.

Major Whittlesey, having only twenty-four hours earlier been rescued after three days in an advance pocket, was on the far left of the brigade. At 12:30 P.M., he pushed forward and found that the Germans had left unwired a ravine that conveniently ran due north. He fought his way up the ravine for a thousand yards, until it opened into another ravine running west. This he followed virtually all the way to Charlevaux Mill, taking about ninety casualties in the process. It was still daylight as he approached the mill. Choosing a position on a suitable reverse slope, his rear protected by the ravine, he dug in and sent a message back indicating his precise position.

That night, the Germans filtered in behind him, closed the gap down the ravine, and sealed his unit off. Whittlesey, a neat, bespectacled, slightly built graduate of Williams College in Williamstown, Massachusetts, could hear German shouts around him, but he realized he was in a pocket only the next morning, October 3, when the patrols he sent out returned decimated. Again there was no panic. The sounds of American guns could be heard in the distance, and clearly his comrades were trying to break through to him.

There were about seven hundred men under Whittlesey's command. It was a motley force, with elements from the 306th and 307th Regiments as well as his own 308th. The men carried only one day's rations and had no water, but they did have a plentiful supply of ammunition for the machine guns, Chauchat automatic rifles, and Lee Enfields. To make sure the various company and detachment commanders realized what was expected, Whittlesey circulated a message: "Our mission is to hold this position at all costs. Have this understood by every man in the command."

At about 8:30 A.M., German artillery opened fire, but Whittlesey's men were shielded by the reverse slope and the shells passed overhead. Other than rifle and machine-gun fire, the only weapon the Germans could bring to bear that day was a trench mortar. This fired intermittently, and during the day the Germans also tried two attacks, which the men fought off. By evening, the command was tired, hungry, and depleted by fifty-six more casualties, but morale was high; the wounded men earned admiration and gratitude by stoically suffering in silence while the German wounded cried out all around them.

After a cold, sleepless night, the men faced the dawn of October 4 still optimistic and looking forward to relief. In their improvised foxholes, they were safe from machine-gun and rifle fire, but the high-trajectory mortar shells took their toll, and only the fact that many were duds stopped the dwindling command from being wiped out. At 10:35 A.M., with only 520 effectives left, Whittlesey sent back another, more explicit message, by carrier pigeon: "Germans are still around us in small numbers. We have been heavily shelled by mortars this morning. . . . Situation is cutting into our strength rapidly. Men are suffering from hunger and exposure. Cannot support be sent at once?"

Brigadier General Johnson ordered Colonel Cromwell Stacey to make two attacks that day, but both failed to penetrate the German defenses. Instead, Alexander ordered artillery fire to shield Whittlesey. The barrage was a disaster. Although Whittlesey had provided his exact coordinates, the division's guns zeroed in on his command. The wounded were buried by the shell bursts, and if any man tried to shift his position, the German machine gunners and snipers were waiting. The misery was ended only when Whittlesey sent out the last pigeon: "Our own artillery is dropping a barrage directly upon us. For Heaven's sake stop it."

As night fell on the second day, some of his men crept down to the muddy stream in the ravine to fill canteens for the wounded, who were now suffering terribly. At 8 P.M., they heard the sound of American small arms in the distance and their hopes revived even as they settled into their foxholes for another damp and chilling night. Suddenly, they were lit up with flares as the Germans attacked, throwing grenades into the position. The attack was repulsed; the casualties mounted.

That night, Johnson ordered Colonel Stacey to make another attack the following morning, but Stacey "protested against the use of his men, saying that they were worn out and could not do this work, asking to be relieved of his command and sent to the rear." Stacey's nervous collapse put Johnson into an impossible position; he refused to relieve Stacey or his men and told the colonel that "it was necessary to relieve the situation at the front and that we had no other troops at our disposal but those on the line." Alexander took a different view: he pulled Stacey out and ordered Johnson to reach Whittlesey some other way.

Johnson's problems were multiplying. He had an acute manpower crisis. Apart from the 700 men Whittlesey had with him, the brigade had taken about 1,600 casualties since September 26. The survivors were suffering the effects of ten days' continuous fighting in awkward terrain with serious supply problems; food was hard to work through the forest to the troops, and they had gone into action without blankets, overcoats, or shelter halves.

Of the men Johnson did have available, almost a quarter were virtually useless. To fill the gaps left in the ranks of his brigade by the 77th's fighting on the Vesle in the summer, he had been sent about 2,100 raw recruits, who arrived just before the jump-off in the Argonne. One battalion commander testified that

> many of them ... had never fired a rifle. Some had only fired 15 rounds, and some had fired 30 rounds. They ... seemed to be absolutely ignorant of the bayonet and its use. ... Not one of them had seen a hand grenade. ... Under fire each man had to be told by an officer or non-commissioned officer where, how and when to shoot. ... They were excellent material individually, but they lacked the training and discipline, which made the majority of them uncontrollable in battle. ... Their faculties seemed to be dulled or paralyzed when under severe shelling or machine gun fire.

On the morning of October 5, the Germans around Whittlesey stayed quiet as French and American aircraft circled overhead. Then, in the midafternoon, shells began shrieking into his position from the southwest—from French guns, presumably armed with the same faulty coordinates. For an hour and twenty-five minutes the nightmare barrage continued. And when it finally lifted, Germans came pouring up the slope. Leaping to the firing line, the Americans beat them back once again. But now they were down to 375 men.

The noise of this encounter was heard by the rest of the division, and a short time later American planes flew over to drop supplies of food and ammunition and orders to retreat. Not one parcel landed on target, and soon German voices were heard gloating over the unexpected bonus.

Now Alexander ordered Johnson personally to force a passage. Johnson gathered up such men as he could find and made frantic but futile attempts to break through. Ironically, the reasons for his failure were precisely those that Stacey had given him for refusing to attack: "All the time I was within 75 to 300 yards of the actual firing line . . . so when I say that these men are not fit to be sent against the enemy, I speak not at any distance. . . . They went without complaint and willingly, but their physical condition was such that it precluded the possibility of success."

That night, Whittlesey's men took the dressings off the dead to put onto the newly wounded; they took off their puttees and used them as bandages for shattered limbs.

By the next day, October 6, they were near the end: starving, thirsty, exhausted, their nerves tortured by the cries of their own comrades; gangrene had set in, and the wounded were delirious with pain. Of those who could still walk, "many requested permission to attempt individually to work their way back through the lines at night. Permission was refused." Whittlesey had gone too far to surrender now. In the middle of the morning, another American aircraft flew over, and shortly afterward a terrific barrage opened up—only this time it landed on the German positions, and it caught the enemy forming up to attack.

That afternoon, the Germans tried another grenade attack. Beaten back, in a frenzy of frustration they turned every machine gun they had on Whittlesey's men. The first bursts caught some out of their foxholes, and the rows of wounded lengthened; now there were fewer than three hundred still able to rise to their feet, though many of the wounded still worked their guns.

On the night of October 6, the men left their foxholes to strip the German dead of their rifles and ammunition. With these weapons they repulsed one more attack at noon the next day, the fifth day of fighting. Then, at 4 P.M., Private Lowell R. Hollingshead, who had been taken prisoner earlier that day, was seen coming slowly up the slope under a white flag. Blindfolded, he was carrying a personal message for Whittlesey from the German commander, Leutnant Heinrich Prinz, who before the war had spent six years as a businessman in Seattle. "The suffering of your wounded men," he wrote, "can be heard over here in the German lines, and we are appealing to your humane sentiments to stop. A white flag shown by one of your men will tell us that you agree."

Whittlesey said nothing, except to order that the white panels his men used for aircraft signaling should be rolled up and carefully concealed. The men hurled abuse and defiance at the Germans. Everyone knew that another attack would not be long in coming. This time when it came, it was led by flamethrowers.

36

"They Are Learning Now":
The First Two Weeks of October

The agony of Whittlesey's ordeal simply added to Pershing's humiliation. Along 250 miles of the Western Front, British, French, and Belgian armies were fighting the greatest battle in the history of mankind while the Stars and Stripes lay mired. Pershing's hopes of piercing the Kriemhilde Position in two days seemed almost laughable now. The American forward thrust was trapped under the German guns emplaced in the Argonne, on the heights of the Meuse, and on most of the high ground in between. Whole divisions were literally bogged down in the rear amid a chaos of torn roads, jammed vehicles, dying horses, hysterical transport officers, and the groans and cries of the wounded. It seemed all too likely that the First Army would have to retreat—pull back, as its staff had warned on September 29, "south of Montfaucon and eventually to our old positions." And where could Pershing go from there?

The French High Command was merciless. Pétain blamed the First Army's failure not on the ferocity of the enemy's resistance, but on "the problems which the American general staff had experienced in transporting and supplying their troops." He suggested that French staff officers should now manage the American divisions—an insulting idea, which Foch translated into a firm proposal for the French Second Army to take over Liggett's I Corps and operate both west and east of the Argonne, leaving Pershing to command on the Meuse alone.

This was a less extreme solution than the one proposed to Foch by French Premier Clemenceau. After becoming hopelessly snarled in traffic during an ill-advised sightseeing trip to Montfaucon, Clemenceau had declared that the AEF was in "complete chaos" and Pershing should be relieved of his command. "The Americans have got to learn some time," replied Foch. "They are learning now, rapidly." Ignorant of this exchange, Pershing was outraged by the proposal that he should relinquish any of his divisions to the French. Considering Foch to be exceeding his authority by trying to dictate tactical dispositions, he absolutely refused to divide the command of the American troops. Foch, having made his point, agreed to leave the First Army alone—provided, as he told Pershing, that "your attacks start without delay and that, once begun, they are continued without any interruptions such as those which have just arisen."

Pershing was goaded into action. With most of the problems that had bedeviled his first attack still unsolved, he now ordered another. This time the First Army had apparently even less chance of breaking through. They had lost both their advantages—surprise and overwhelmingly superior numbers—and faced the daunting prospect of advancing through the Giselher Position. This five-mile-deep outpost zone was on hilly, wooded ground cut by ravines, terrain even more favorable to the defenders—and all this before they reached the Kriemhilde Position itself.

The Germans too had nowhere to go: "There is no question of voluntary withdrawal," declared Gallwitz. Urging on his troops, General Georg von der Marwitz issued orders reminiscent of Haig's "backs to the wall" order. "It is on the unconquerable resistance of the Verdun Front that the fate of a great part of the Western Front, perhaps even of our nation, depends. The Fatherland must rest assured that every commander and every man fully realises the greatness of his mission and that he will do his duty to the very end." Once again the scene was set for tragedy.

Pershing's guiding strategy remained virtually unchanged. The objective was still to penetrate the Kriemhilde Position, and the method was still frontal attacks. Liggett's I Corps, on the left, was to take the Argonne bluffs and the heights northeast and north of Exermont, the southern switch line of the Kriemhilde Position; Cameron's V Corps, in the center, was to capture the heights northwest and west of Romagne; and Bullard's III Corps on the right was to hold the line of the Meuse and capture the heights northeast of Cunel.

The new attack was ordered for the entire army for October 4. Fresh divisions were in place, some of them veterans, including the 3rd, the "Marne" Division. But at this pivotal moment, perhaps inevitably, Pershing pinned his hopes on the division whose shoulder patches bore the

"Big Red One." Under the command of the brutally determined, self-opinionated but outstandingly capable Charles Summerall, Pershing could see no limit to what could be expected of the 1st Division.

The 1st had replaced the 35th after the massacre at Exermont. Simply to take back what the 35th had given up, the division would have to advance through Montrebeau Woods, across the open killing grounds beyond, and into Exermont ravine. It would then be confronted with a barrier of hills and ravines three miles deep and three miles wide, infested with machine guns and artillery and flanked by the Argonne with its well-sited artillery and heavy machine guns. These had destroyed the 35th and were already causing five hundred casualties a day while the troops waited for the attack to begin.

Despite suffering 10,000 casualties at Cantigny and Soissons, the 1st remained an excellent fighting machine. The staffs and support units were experienced, and, unlike some of the newer divisions, it had a full complement of equipment, including Stokes mortars, 37mm guns, and rifle grenades. Perhaps most important of all, the signals sections could maintain communications on the battlefield; for virtually the whole of the coming advance, except under the very heaviest of fire, the frontline units would be in telephone contact with their command posts. In a war in which voice control had almost disappeared, Summerall could direct the movements of even his furthest frontline units and, crucially, provide them on request with accurate artillery fire from the rear to supplement the single 75mm guns that accompanied the frontline battalions.

The 1st Division, as part of Liggett's I Corps, formed up along a two-and-a-half-mile front with its left resting on the Aire River. All four regiments were in line, battalions echeloned in depth, with the 1st Brigade (the 16th and 18th Infantry Regiments) on the left and the 2nd Brigade (the 26th and 28th Infantry) on the right.

The division jumped off at 5:25 A.M. in darkness and fog, as did all the other divisions across the front. Following the same compass bearing of 335 degrees north, they advanced behind a rolling barrage for just over a mile. Underfoot, as they pushed through the 35th Division's old killing field, they saw the pitiful sight of hundreds of the wounded of that battle, who had patched themselves up with their field dressings and died waiting for help to come.

For the 2nd Brigade the attack proceeded slowly. "Casualties were heavy," one survivor recalled. "Few prisoners were taken, the enemy showing the general disposition to fight to the death." But the brigade reached Exermont ravine by dusk and dug in, preparing to spend a miserable night sheltering from shells and aircraft bombs. On the left, under the guns of the Argonne, the 1st Brigade made better progress, advancing partly through the open terrain of the Aire valley. By the evening they were just south of the village of Fléville on the river, bending their line back to link up with the 2nd Brigade south of Exermont.

Donald Kyler, who had enlisted in April 1917 at the age of 16, was a company runner with the 16th Infantry advancing on the far left of the 1st Brigade's sector. He would never forget that first day on the attack. So close were the German guns that their shells were traveling on a flat trajectory that gave no warning, only a final terrifying shrieking sound just before they hit. "One of the shells hit almost on a man nearby. When it exploded I felt a sharp blow on my cheek. At first I thought I was wounded by a shell fragment, but it was a finger blown from his hand."

Slaughter by a remote enemy was a far cry from the glories of combat promised by the recruiting sergeant, the CPI, and the regiment's morale officer. But this kind of horror barely touched the young Kyler:

I had seen mercy killings, both of our hopelessly wounded and those of the enemy. I had seen the murder of prisoners of war, singly and as many as several at one time. I had seen men rob the dead of money and valuables, and had seen men cut off the fingers of corpses to get rings. Those things I had seen, but they did not affect me much. I was too numb. To me corpses were nothing but carrion. I had the determination to go on performing as I had been trained to do—to be a good soldier.

On the second day, October 5, the fighting was vicious in the extreme as the men of the 1st Division edged forward past Exermont. Four German divisions opposed their advance across the ravine with artillery and machine guns. "The 2nd Battalion of the 26th Infantry, 30 officers and 1,000 men, went over the crest," remembered Captain Shipley Thomas of that regiment, "down into the ravine, and up the steep banks on the far side and established the line on the other side in a little clump of woods. When the count was made, there were left of this battalion but 6 officers and 285 men." By the end of the second day, it was obvious that the 1st would suffer the same fate as the hapless 35th if the guns of the Argonne were not silenced.

On October 6, there were three American divisions in the area: the 77th, which was actually in the forest; the 28th, which was advancing between the Argonne cliffs and the Aire River; and the 1st itself, to the right of the Aire. The 28th had not succeeded in moving up between forest and river as far as planned. Nor had the 77th made any progress through the Argonne thickets, despite having the burning incentive of rescuing Whittlesey and his "Lost Battalion," which, despite all the odds, was still hanging on grimly in the depths of the forest.

The 1st Division, however, had advanced and created a wedge in the German line jutting a mile and a half ahead of the 28th, which was coming up on the left. This gave Liggett the chance to try a daring strike across the Aire. He proposed to Pershing that a strong unit be sent up behind the 1st Division's line, to pivot left, cross the Aire in front of the 28th, and assault the artillery-infested heights of the Argonne to seize the targets he had been given: Hills 180, 223, and 244.

The raid on October 7 was actually carried out by a brigade of the 82nd Division, brought up into the 1st's sector the previous night. It would have been hard to regard the assignment as a privilege. These troops—who were relatively inexperienced and wholly new to the area—were being required to turn their own flank invitingly to the enemy forces north of them while trying to storm heavily defended crests up to 800 feet high.

Against the odds, the attack went well at first. Hill 180 was the first to fall. Then attention switched to Châtel-Chéhéry, a tiny town of a single street clinging to the slope of the Argonne plateau, flanked to the north by Hill 223 and to the south by Hill 244. By 7 A.M., Châtel-Chéhéry was taken; by noon, the men of the 82nd had advanced partway up the slopes of Hill 223 and were entrenched along the ridge of Hill 244.

The troops partway up Hill 223 included the 2nd Battalion, 328th Infantry, who had been tasked to capture the light railroad a mile into the forest that supplied the German troops to the south. As they advanced over the slopes toward their target, they were caught in enfilade fire from a hill on the extreme left. Sergeant Harry Parsons (who had been an actor before being drafted) ordered Acting Sergeant Early to take two squads and put those machine guns out of action.

Early's men circled around the hill and climbed steadily. For the first time in days the sun came out, and they surprised a party of Germans sunning themselves by a stream. Gathering up the sleepy, startled prisoners, they were about to continue when, on the steep slope less than thirty yards in front, a clutch of machine guns opened fire. Six of Early's men were killed immediately, several others wounded. All the Germans dropped to allow their comrades free fire, and the survivors of Early's patrol threw themselves flat—all except one.

Squatting down on his haunches, Private Alvin C. York, a backwoodsman from Tennessee, started firing back. It did not occur to him to surrender. Equally, as an elder of the Church of Christ and Christian Union, inclined to pacifism, he had no wish to kill more than he had to. "His problem," Early remembered,

> was to make the enemy give up as quickly as possible, and he kept yelling to them "Come down!" Bang! Bang! "Come down!" York would shout, precisely as though the surrender of a battalion to an individual soldier was the usual thing. . . . And with every shot he brought down an enemy. No, I am wrong. He showed me a crease on a bole of a tree later and confessed his belief that he had missed one.

"If I'd moved, I'd have been killed in a second," York explained later.

> "The German [prisoners] were what saved me. I kept up close to them, and so the fellers on the hill had to fire a little high for fear of hitting their own men. The bullets were cracking over my head and a lot of twigs fell down. . . . I don't know how many I did shoot. . . . All the Boches who were hit squealed like pigs." "You killed the whole bunch?" someone asked him. "Yes, sir. At that distance I couldn't miss."

The final tally was twenty-eight dead.

The attack of the 82nd brought home to the German forces in the forest precisely how precarious their situation had become. They began to withdraw, and the ghetto troops of the 77th Division could at last press forward. No one can have been more profoundly relieved than Major Whittlesey. At 7 P.M. on October 7, he recalled, "the 307th Infantry [77th Division] was reported coming up through the woods on our right. The relief felt by our men is indescribable. The 307th generously gave up all the reserve rations which their men were carrying and nearly everyone had food before going to sleep." Only 231 of the original 700 walked out the next day.

On October 9, the 82nd at last completed the silencing of the guns on the heights of the Argonne. Further west, thanks to the heroic efforts of the

2nd Division in penetrating the German defenses at Blanc Mont ridge, the French Fourth Army had been able to push well up. Outflanked on both sides of the forest, the Germans were forced to evacuate it.

Now Pershing could concentrate on the original objective of breaking the Kriemhilde Position. Once again he was looking to the 1st Division, which he had transferred to the center of the offensive, under the control of Cameron's V Corps, with orders to push forward.

At daybreak on October 9, in a thick fog, the 1st began once again to battle northward. Summerall, an artillery expert, had divided his force into three separate groups to attack consecutively, each in turn supported by the entire weight of the division's artillery. For what he hoped would be a last push, he brought up all his reserves, as he had done at Soissons, including the divisional engineers; but they were reinforcing a spent front line.

In six days, the 1st Division had advanced a miraculous four and a half miles through the most difficult terrain, through filthy weather and appalling conditions, and had faced eight separate enemy divisions. They had made possible the capture of the Argonne Forest and made it unnecessary for the First Army to pull back behind Montfaucon. Now, with casualties of 177 officers and 8,370 men—the heaviest suffered by any division in the Meuse-Argonne offensive—the 1st was beginning to show the first signs of disintegration. There was a note of panic in Lieutenant J. N. Canby's report: "I can only find 70 men—I have no officers." At 2:50 P.M., Captain R. M. Youell, commanding the 2nd Battalion, 26th Infantry, signaled: "Lt Hyde reports Boche coming in on his left. He seems very *much excited*. On account of this several of our men have straggled to the rear. Not enough of officers and NCOs to watch them."

Forward elements continued to advance and could still rely on artillery support, but there were ever-fewer men left. On the morning of October 10, Major Legge totaled up the manpower of a battalion (1/26) that had once numbered 1,000 men: "A Co—61; B Co—38; C Co—37; D Co—56; M[achine]G[un] Co—23." On the morning of October 11, Major L. S. Frazier (3/26) made his report: "My phone will not work. Have no more wire. . . . Most of the men have had nothing to eat in 48 hours and no water. . . . Some of my officers and many of my men are sick and cannot go much further. I do not want to complain but I would like the CO to know the situation we are in."

Fortunately, there was now less fighting for them to do: "No sound of small arms ahead. . . . Everything seems to be going nicely." On October

11, they reached the dense wire fronting the main line of the Kriemhilde Position—and there they stopped. "Division commander directs," ran the order, "that as resistance has been met on Côte de Châtillon you will withdraw your patrols and consolidate along the Bois de Romagne."

On the night of October 11–12, what remained of the 1st Division, minus its artillery, was relieved by the 42nd "Rainbow" Division under Major General Charles T. Menoher, with Douglas MacArthur now commanding the 84th Brigade. The men of the 42nd knew something of what faced them. All the way up to the front, across Exermont ravine and beyond, they had seen the rough graves and unburied remains of the 35th and the 1st Divisions. Now in front of them, within striking distance at last, lay the main line of the Kriemhilde Position.

37

❧❧❧

Crisis Before Kriemhilde

The horrors confronting the 42nd Division, the graves, the chaos, all were ultimately Pershing's responsibility, and he felt it acutely. He had gambled on untried and largely untrained divisions to advance rapidly through difficult terrain against well-organized if lightly manned defenses—and he had lost. He had been justified in his faith in the bravery of the American soldier, but bravery was enough in itself only when the fighting man was face to face with another fighting man. Artillery, aircraft, minefields, mortars, gas, machine guns firing from long range or concealment kept the German soldier remote from the American rifleman. "Enemy line held by MGs and artillery—apparently no infantry," wrote a bewildered intelligence officer on September 28. Charging in groups, head-on and upright, into the path of automatic weapons, the AEF's foot soldiers were buying their experience of modern warfare at a very high price.

General Jean-Henri Mordacq claimed he could read clearly in Pershing's eyes that "he realized his mistake. His soldiers were dying bravely, but they were not advancing." Their suffering almost broke Pershing's spirit. These first weeks of October "involved the heaviest strain on the army and me," he later admitted. "The strain was too great," wrote one of his officers, "this last battle overloaded him." Another was with Pershing in his staff car when the general suddenly buried his head in his hands and cried out his dead wife's name: "Frankie . . . Frankie . . . My God, sometimes I don't know how I can go on."

He was in a better position than any of his staff to appreciate that the Americans had stalled at a most critical moment in the war. Foch and

Haig's grand strategy of coordinated attack along the entire front from the Meuse to the English Channel had proved triumphant. Under the weight of the remorseless pressure applied day after day, relaxing at one point only to be reinforced with double vigor at another, the Imperial German Army had come to accept the inevitability of defeat.

The day after Montfaucon fell to the 79th Division's Marylanders and Pennsylvanians, before the Germans had grasped the full extent of the chaos behind the American lines, Ludendorff's nerve had finally failed him. Since Soissons, his mental equilibrium had been as savagely battered as his armies. Prey to uncontrollable rages, vindictive to his staff, blindly obstinate in his refusal to withdraw from impossible positions, he had lost the confidence of his senior officers. In a moment of panic that he lived to regret, he went to Hindenburg and, with tears in his eyes, confessed that Germany must seek an immediate armistice.

The decision had patently been precipitated by the military crisis, but neither Supreme Commander intended the Army to take the initiative in ending the war. The civilian government must be seen to bear the blame: the Imperial Chancellor must ask for peace. But from whom? Not from the Allies, who were hell bent on revenge—and compensation. Since Lenin's publication of the secret treaties, the entire German nation had known of the unbridled lusts of France and England for German territories as well as German blood. So now Ludendorff played his last strategic card: Germany would ask Woodrow Wilson to arrange the "peace without victory," the "soft peace" that his Fourteen Points promised.

Fully aware that the President despised Germany's military masters, Ludendorff recommended that Prince Max von Baden, a recognized parliamentarian, be made Chancellor, heading a newly created "democratic" government to be formed immediately from the leading parties in the Reichstag. With the purest and most transparent hypocrisy, Ludendorff engineered a "revolution from above" designed to appeal to the man who wanted to make the world safe for democracy.

The German initiative, received in Washington on October 6, created an embarrassing gulf between the United States' diplomatic and military profiles. While the President bestrode world affairs, his captain crouched, seemingly nearly paralyzed, in the narrow confines of the Meuse-Argonne. Had the 1st Division failed to make progress and the Argonne Forest remained in German hands, Pershing's humiliation would have been complete. But the 1st Division had advanced, in the process saving

Pershing's career and enabling the First Army to secure its lines before the final heights of the Kriemhilde Position. By October 9, the situation had become sufficiently stable for a review of strategy, which produced three crucial and positive changes.

First, Pershing resolved to create a Second Army under the tough Alabaman Robert Bullard to conduct operations to the east of the Meuse Heights. By dividing the American front this way, he was giving himself more room to maneuver as well as wider strategic options.

His second decision grew out of the first: two armies must have an army group commander. He thus took steps to promote himself out of the front line. This left the command of the First Army vacant, and on October 10 he informed Hunter Liggett of his elevation to the post. It was another demonstration of Pershing's extraordinary capacity for putting talent above all else.

Liggett was "a big man" in every sense—"one of the ablest, broadest and wisest military men I have ever talked to," remarked that quintessential civilian, Josephus Daniels. He had gained Pershing's respect through sheer ability. Liggett, a direct and modest man, was temperamentally incapable of intriguing or scheming for self-advancement; a letter he wrote after the war to his Chief of Staff, Malin Craig, suggests that he had felt something of an outsider, remote from Pershing's "Chaumont crowd." Certainly, he shared some of the disadvantages that had kept other able generals at home; at sixty-one he was technically too old for active command, and he was authentically fat. But he was an experienced commander who had worked his way up in the field and a profound student of the art of war with a mature and capable military brain; the fat, as he put it, stopped at the neck. A fighting general, Liggett had the resilience, patience, and strategic sense that make for greatness.

He demonstrated this instinct for strategy at once by refusing to assume command of the First Army until Pershing had seen his third decision through himself. The Commander in Chief had resolved that within days there was to be yet another frontal attack on the German line. As Liggett waited in the wings, doubting the wisdom of the move, Pershing ordered his corps commanders (including Summerall, who had replaced Cameron in the command of V Corps, and Joseph Dickman, who had replaced Liggett in I Corps) to build on the 1st Division's drive and occupy key strong points in the Kriemhilde Position itself.

The scenario for the attack was familiar: the enemy solidly entrenched on the high ground ahead, the treacherous terrain underfoot, the wire, the machine-gun nests, the artillery on the flank as well as to the fore—though now the firing was only from the Meuse Heights, not from the Argonne. Pershing had brought fresh, experienced divisions into the line, but the rest of his force was in such bad shape that the newcomers would have to attack the bastions of the Kriemhilde Position with only limited support.

The First Army had taken 100,000 casualties in two weeks, and thousands more men were ill. Desperate for water in the front line, many had filled their canteens from streams and shell holes in ground littered with the corpses of men and horses. Food too was becoming hazardous. Doctors blamed some of the dysentery on the bread supplied to the troops—soggy in the middle, its crust covered in mold. One officer saw a railcar of loaves arrive at a divisional salvage and forage dump and get shoveled out onto the dirt, to be left there overnight under a filthy tarpaulin. Next day, they were hurled into the back of a truck parked some twenty feet away; those that fell into the mud were promptly tossed back onto the pile.

Still in their summer clothing, without blankets or overcoats, and worn down by constant exposure to shelling and gas attacks, the men were easy prey for the new killer loose on the battlefield: an influenza virus of the most virulent kind. That fall, the entire world was in the grip of an epidemic that would kill 21 million people before its course was run. At home, March told Pershing, "the overwhelming epidemic of influenza has cut down the production of the plants to one third"; there were 286 cases on the War Industries Board alone. In the AEF, there were 11,910 cases in September and 37,904 new cases in October.

Even more costly was a new plague that Liggett diagnosed in the First Army: of the 100,000 "stragglers" who had fallen behind their frontline units, some had deliberately absconded, though the exact proportion was not clear. (In the whole of the army, only 4,316 men were ever court-martialed for desertion and only 3,362 convicted.) These deserters hid in foxholes, ravines, thick underbrush, abandoned dugouts; one enterprising trio stood guard, turn and turn about, over a pile of salvage they had found in a safe zone. In later investigations, the Inspector General blamed "limited disciplinary training" as the prime reason for dereliction of duty.

Probably the majority of stragglers were simply lost, separated from their units by accident. Many had been detailed to carry the wounded to the rear and had then been unable to find their units again in the 115 square miles of battlefield. One division had only 1,600 men in the front line, but when it was relieved and roll call was taken in the rest area, the infantry regiments alone contained 8,418 men.

Others were sick or shell-shocked, not visibly wounded but completely unable to function. Still more were starving; the YMCA came in for criticism from senior officers for bringing canteens up close to the front, where desperate men would sneak back to them for hot coffee and a sandwich. (They were criticized by the men for different reasons; Rickenbacker was shocked to find a YMCA canteen in Montfaucon *selling* cigarettes and coffee to the men of the 79th Division while all around their dead comrades lay unburied.)

When the dead, the wounded, the sick, and the stragglers were counted, it was clear that a manpower crisis was looming at the heart of the apparently limitless American Army. Pershing had to reduce his companies from 250 to 175 men each; doctors kept sick men in the line because there were no replacements for them. And now, just when reinforcements were most needed, the flow of troops from home was checked. Omar Bradley recalled arriving at Camp Dodge, Iowa, on September 25: "We immediately went into intensive field training, coached by officers recently returned from combat in France. However, within a week or so, the great and dreadful influenza epidemic of 1918 hit Camp Dodge. Hundreds of men collapsed, many died. Our hospitals were jammed with the sick. The epidemic drastically curtailed our training schedule and decimated our ranks." When men did sail, they often took the disease with them; during one crossing on the *Leviathan,* they were dying at the rate of fifty-five a day.

The Meuse-Argonne offensive, which had been designed as a swift strike, had turned into a battle of attrition, for which the AEF had never been prepared either mentally or practically. Short of men, short of horses, short of trucks, the supply system was near collapse, and maintenance of equipment was little more than a fond dream. The lack of spare parts alone threatened to immobilize the First Army. The transport system was equally skeletal; with infantrymen and machine gunners having effectively been monopolizing shipping space since the spring, the motor transport section was receiving only 19 percent of the equipment it had ordered, and Pershing had 50,000 fewer horses and mules than he needed. By September, more than one division was literally unable to move. Nor was there ever enough ammunition to permit maximum artillery fire; at this crucial moment, some divisions were ordered to economize with their ammunition.

Cold, unkempt, depressed, ill fed, in a landscape of wreckage and filth, the attack divisions moved into the line, numbed by the never-ending sweep of shrapnel, gas, and high explosives sent over by the waiting enemy. On his way to the front, Father Duffy, chaplain to the 42nd Division, saw five German prisoners and their four American escorts scattered in the mud by a shell that exploded in their midst.

> We ran up and I found one of ours with both legs blown completely off trying to pull himself up with the aid of a packing case. In spite of his wounds, he gave not the slightest evidence of mental shock. . . . He told me his name was Conover, and that he was a Catholic, and said the prayers while I gave him absolution. He had no idea his legs were gone until a soldier lifted him on a stretcher, when I could see in his eyes that he was aware that his body was lifting light. He started to look down, but I placed my hand on his chest and kept him from seeing.

The First Army desperately needed to suspend major operations; Liggett intended to take a ten- or twelve-day pause when he took charge. But the French were putting Pershing under severe pressure. On the western flank of the Argonne, the French Fourth Army (profiting from the capture of Blanc Mont) moved forward some seven and a half miles between October 11 and 12. Confronting Pershing in his headquarters on October 13, Foch pointed out that once again the Americans were not keeping up. Pershing began to blame the terrain, but Foch was not interested. "Results," he said, "are the only thing to judge by." His whole strategy from the start had been based on unrelenting attack: the enemy must not be given time to reorganize on any part of the front. However badly disrupted it was, he needed the First Army to keep attacking; whatever the cost, he required Pershing's divisions to be thrown against the wire and guns of the Kriemhilde Position.

Foch's refusal to let Pershing off the hook was all part of his determination to impose a hard peace on Germany. The American President might want a "soft peace" as a prelude to creating a new world order in the future, but the French were interested in the immediate practicalities. Foch and Clemenceau wanted to make quite sure that their country would never again be menaced by German military power. To Frenchmen of their age, the humiliations of the Franco-Prussian War—the crushing defeat at Sedan, the occupation of Paris, the theft of Alsace-Lorraine—were living memories. The Germans had to be battered into giving the French what they wanted—above all, the right to occupy the Rhineland.

But as October wore on, it seemed increasingly unlikely that the weary French and British could achieve a victory that would be crushing enough. Besides, the British had no wish to occupy Germany and were prepared to settle on more lenient terms. Only America still had the reserves and the potential vigor to achieve the French objectives—but America too, according to her President, wished to stop well short of inflicting such a humiliating defeat.

Fortunately for Foch, Pershing did not agree with his President. Whether he was influenced by his mistress, Michette, or his fellow Freemason "Père" Joffre; whether he was driven by ambition for his American armies ultimately to make their mark; or whether he was really moved, as he later explained, by his personal reading of history, he decided once again not to serve his President's interests. The Atlantic Ocean, it seemed, was an effective barrier to the coordination of diplomatic and military policies. On October 29, Pershing would make it known to the Supreme War Council in Versailles that he favored demanding unconditional surrender from the Germans—not, after all, surrender on the basis of the Fourteen Points.

In the meantime, his actions spoke louder than words. Germany must be beaten as quickly as possible, before his President could negotiate the kind of peace he wanted. To that end, it seemed Pershing would do precisely what Foch asked. He would attack the wire and fortifications of the Kriemhilde Position without sufficient artillery, without preparation, without mercy on his own men.

38

"The Big Man":
Liggett Pulls the Army into Shape

One division that was due some mercy was Alexander's 77th. For nineteen days, the "ghetto" troops had suffered in the Argonne Forest. Now Pershing asked them to attack the Argonne's northern extension, the Bourgogne Woods, which flanked the Kriemhilde Position on the left. But just to reach these woods the 77th had to attack across the valley formed by the Aire River as it curved westward, totally exposed to German fire. Then they had to take the fortified town of Grandpré, sited on a bluff above the river, before pushing up onto the plateau of the Bourgogne and into the woods.

This was an important element in Pershing's plan. But the primary objective, in the center of the First Army sector, was the keystone of the Kriemhilde Position: the Côte Dame-Marie. Recognizing that this crescent-shaped ridge and the huge Romagne Woods in which it stood were the strongest parts of the German line, Pershing commanded two divisions, the 5th and 42nd, to drive east and west of the Côte Dame-Marie and take the ridge in flank and rear. Meanwhile, a third division, the 32nd, was to occupy the defenders by making a frontal attack.

Both sides recognized the crucial importance of the coming battle. The Kriemhilde Position was the last major defensive system in this sector. Once through, the Americans had only to storm the lesser redoubts of the Barricourt Heights, and then the way would lie open to the Sedan-Mézières railway, the jugular vein of the Western Front. If they could cut it, the Germans' hold on France would be broken. "There is no question of voluntary withdrawal," General von Gallwitz told his troops on October 13.

The next day, October 14, the First Army attacked into a storm of steel. On the far left, the 77th advanced hardly at all that day, but on October 15, propelled by the sheer willpower of General Alexander, they battled across the Aire and up the slope to the outlying houses of Grandpré. Now, after twenty days in continuous combat, the decimated New York division was relieved by men from New Jersey, James McRae's 78th Division.

The three divisions facing the Côte Dame-Marie had an equally bloody and unsuccessful first day, during which the American line barely advanced. By the second day, however, John McMahon's 5th Division, coming up on the east of Côte Dame-Marie, had pushed through the dense Pultière Woods, and some units had even reached the far edge of Rappes Woods, the divisional objective.

This success, however, owed little to the skills of the divisional commander. McMahon should perhaps not have been commanding a division at this point, given his exhausted mental state. At Saint-Mihiel he had fallen asleep at his post, and he had generally become so sluggish that he was taking forty-five seconds just to sign his name. In this attack, he had overloaded his front line and kept back too few reserves. Now, receiving reports of heavy casualties, he panicked and, not realizing that success was in his grasp, ordered a withdrawal from Rappes Woods. This was a mortal blow to the strategy of envelopment, and when Pershing, with the new III Corps commander, John L. Hines, visited McMahon's headquarters, he immediately relieved him, placing Hanson Ely, who had led the assault on Cantigny, in charge of the 5th.

Disaster on the right was compounded by murder on the left, where Menoher's 42nd "Rainbow" Division was under orders to take the twin villages of Landres-et-Saint-Georges and the Côte de Châtillon, a steep hill occupying a commanding position at the western edge of the Romagne Woods.

General Menoher attacked with his brigades, the 83rd and 84th, side by side. The 83rd, on the left, had men from Ohio (the 164th Infantry) and the "Fighting Irish" (the 165th Infantry) under William "Wild Bill" Donovan, the most decorated officer in the 42nd Division. Spurred on by Donovan, who was notoriously immune to fear, they scrambled the two miles from their start line to the wire of the Kriemhilde Position, under devastating fire all the way, only to face a near-impossible task. In unbroken ribbons ran three lines of trenches fronted by barbed wire chest high and twenty feet wide.

"Groups of our lads dashed up to the wire only to be shot down to the last man," remembered Father Duffy. He continued:

Soldiers of ours and of the Engineers with wire-cutting tools lay on their faces working madly to cut through the strands, while riflemen and grenadiers alongside of them tried to beat down the resistance. But they were in a perfect hail of bullets from front and flank, and every last man was killed or wounded. Further back was a concentration of artillery fire, of bursting shells and groans and death that made the advance of the support platoons a veritable hell.

Donovan was wounded in the leg; he refused to be evacuated and spent the night sheltering in a hole waiting for the promised tanks to arrive. The next morning, without tanks and apparently with very little artillery support, the 83rd attacked the wire again and once more were hurled back. Unsupported infantry advancing against wire, machine guns, and artillery was a sight no longer seen elsewhere on the Western Front; the Americans were learning the grim lessons already paid for in blood by the French and British.

That evening, General Summerall, the 42nd's corps commander, visited the 83rd Brigade and demanded "results, no matter how many men were killed." For good measure, he relieved the brigade commander, the commander of the Ohio National Guard—and a captain and lieutenant who had the temerity to ask him where the tanks and artillery had been.

Summerall was no softer with Douglas MacArthur and his 84th Brigade. On the evening before the attack he had demanded, "Give me Châtillon or a list of 5,000 casualties!" To which MacArthur had replied, "If this brigade does not capture Châtillon, you can publish a casualty list of the entire brigade, with the brigade commander's name at the top." "Tears sprang into General Summerall's eyes," MacArthur recalled. "He was evidently so moved that he could say nothing. He looked at me for a few seconds and then left without a word." It was a condition to which MacArthur frequently reduced people; but posturing aside, Summerall was deadly serious in his desire to take the Côte de Châtillon, and MacArthur knew it.

Châtillon was not the fearsome Côte Dame-Marie, but it was steep, wooded, and tricky, thick with wire and machine guns. On the first day, the brigade could only inch forward, though MacArthur left his command

post to lead the attack in person. The second day was just as bloody and
no more productive. That evening, Summerall pushed MacArthur hard
for results; MacArthur's reaction, in his own version of the story, was to
take a patrol out along the German wire to probe for weak points. Suddenly, the patrol was enveloped by shell fire and all except MacArthur
were killed. "God led me by the hand, the way he led Joshua," reflected
MacArthur, never one to underrate his own significance.

The next day, while MacArthur led a diversionary attack to the front of
the hill, Major Lloyd Ross's battalion worked its way around to the weak
section the ill-fated patrol had located, cut the wire, and burst through.
Châtillon was taken and held. Whether or not the story of the patrol was
true, MacArthur had personally contributed a great deal to the success;
the citation accompanying his second Distinguished Service Cross (with
Oak Leaf Cluster) noted, "On a field where courage was the rule, his
courage was the dominant factor." His battalions, however, had suffered
80 percent casualties.

Châtillon was an important thread in the MacArthurian tapestry, but it
was only one step toward the ultimate objective. For all the 42nd Division's
efforts between October 14 and 16, which had cost them 2,895 killed and
wounded, the 83rd Brigade had failed to advance on Landres-et-Saint-
Georges and the 84th had suffered devastating losses in securing only a
partial success. Combined with McMahon's error of judgment on the right,
the offensive would have been counted a misfire had it not been for the Wisconsin and Michigan National Guard, the 32nd Division under Major
General William G. Haan.

When the offensive kicked off, the 32nd Division was barely operational. It had helped push the Germans out of the Marne pocket and had
captured the town of Juvigny in late August. By the beginning of September, its casualty roll stood at almost 7,000. To fill the ranks, Haan had
been given 5,000 raw recruits, to many of whom, according to one company commander, "a gun was about as much use as a broom." Then
Haan's division had joined the October 4 offensive on the right of the 1st
Division and was now sorely depleted and ready for replacement. For all
these reasons, Pershing had intended it simply to pin the Germans into
place on Côte Dame-Marie while the 5th and 42nd made their deep
flanking drives.

But no one appears to have convinced Haan of this, nor was he swayed
by his division's weaknesses. The men of Wisconsin and Michigan at-

tacked the ridge for real, to be cut down in their hundreds by the massed machine guns and preregistered artillery—but not before a battalion of the 126th Infantry had found a gap in the blanket of wire. Time and time again they hurled themselves at the gap in massed attacks, but the Germans had machine guns trained on it and the casualties were horrifying. In desperation, the battalion commander sent forward a party of eight men with instructions to silence the guns. Under a hail of fire they crawled up the slope to within rifle-grenade range, fired their missiles, and seized the terrified survivors as prisoners. The 32nd had its route to the top of the Côte Dame-Marie; within hours the keystone of the Kriemhilde Position was in their hands.

Though bought at appalling cost in an operation that arguably should not have been mounted at that point, the successes at Châtillon and Côte Dame-Marie were invaluable to Liggett, taking command of the First Army on October 16. Exploiting Pershing's success in a series of piecemeal operations, he dismantled much of what remained of the Kriemhilde Position, putting himself in "a very advantageous position for a general attack." This, for all Pershing's pushing, he intended to make only on October 28, in conjunction with the French Fourth Army to his left. In fact, General Gouraud could not ready himself in this time, so the attack date was put back further, to November 1.

Liggett, who was less directly exposed than Pershing to pressure from the French, had gained the time he wanted to pull his First Army back into shape. He rotated the divisions, relieving exhausted ones such as the 4th and 32nd and breaking up seven others to provide replacements for those that had been most seriously depleted. He set up "stragglers' posts" on all the roads, sent out patrols to search woods, dugouts, storehouses, and kitchen quarters, and reunited thousands of men with their units. He replaced incompetent commanders, sat down with others to talk through their problems, and introduced new tactical methods. He carried forward the all-important roads and narrow-gauge railways in order to build up stocks of ammunition. Liggett could not work miracles: the AEF as a whole could not supply all his needs, nor could the Allies, particularly where heavy tanks and trucks were concerned. But he was able to ensure that by November 1 the First Army had regained at least the punch it had possessed on September 26.

Liggett's distant objective remained the same: to breach the Sedan-Mézières rail line. His immediate purpose was to move up in conformity

with Gouraud's Fourth Army on the left, enveloping the Bourgogne
Woods. But the Germans were equally determined to hold fast in this particular spot. October had been a disastrous month for them, with the
British bursting through the Hindenburg Line in the north. On October
26, American military intelligence reported, "The retreat of the enemy is
being carried out without confusion. The entire line is pivoting on the territory west of Metz, the greatest retirement being therefore in the north.
The success of this movement depends upon keeping the line intact and
holding the pivot firmly." For the Americans, therefore, success depended
on dislodging that pivot and throwing the retreat into confusion.

The German "pivot" was firmly embedded on commanding terrain: the
Bourgogne Woods on the left, the heights of Barricourt in the center, and
the heights of the Marne on the right, a configuration similar to the terrain
they had defended between the Argonne and the Meuse on September
26. But their positions had little depth, and their manpower situation was
now even more critical.

Three weeks before, Ludendorff had told Gallwitz that in view of the
lack of troops, he must "put into the fighting front every unit which is at all
fit for employment in battle." By November 1, Gallwitz had few men left
and no reserves. To stand any chance of holding Liggett back, his local
commander, Marwitz, had to take a gamble on the Americans' most likely
point of attack—and he favored the west side. For almost two weeks, the
78th Division had battled here to finish what the 77th had begun; Grandpré fell at last on October 27, and the 78th began the push into the Bourgogne Woods. From this Marwitz deduced that the attack must be here,
and he concentrated his best troops on this portion of the line.

Unfortunately for the German commander, Liggett's intelligence
sources, particularly aerial observation, were producing excellent information. The air service went out doggedly in all weather, mostly foul, on reconnaissance missions that provided intelligence of the highest quality on
the entire German front to a depth of three miles, showing the locations of
guns and dumps, troop concentration areas, trenches, roads, light railways, even machine-gun nests. As Marwitz shuffled his troops, Liggett
countered by putting the main weight of his attack into the center, ordering
his divisions on the left merely to press forward.

The center was occupied by V Corps, under Summerall's command. In
the front line Liggett placed John Lejeune's 2nd Division, back from
Blanc Mont, and the 89th Division, with the 1st and 42nd Divisions in

close reserve ready to pass through to the attack. He intended that Summerall should capture the heights of Barricourt by nightfall on the first day. In doing so he would outflank the Germans opposing I Corps on his left and remove any possibility of counterattack from this strong position.

Liggett was combining perfectly the twin American doctrines of rapid maneuver and the application of overwhelming force at a critical point—and his army was well prepared. Roads were repaired, supplies were stockpiled, and all down the line staff work was thorough and well coordinated. Most crucially, Liggett had ensured that for the first time artillery was available to devastate the German positions; using the detailed maps compiled from aerial photographs, his planners could prepare a carefully coordinated barrage to be laid down by army, corps, and divisional artillery. The infantry also benefited; company commanders were issued with maps showing every known machine-gun nest and strong point.

In the days leading up to the attack, airplanes made repeated bombing raids over the German lines while the artillery began a heavy harassing fire. The Navy's huge fourteen-inch guns lobbed their 1,400-pound shells deep into enemy territory. Setting aside their scruples, American commanders made heavy use of gas for almost the first time; the Bourgogne Woods in particular were soaked with all types of gas to neutralize the enemy batteries there. For once the German defenses would be softened up before an American offensive was launched against them.

At 3:30 A.M. on November 1, all the guns opened up in one massive, coordinated blanket of fire. Then, at 5:30 A.M., behind the densest protective barrage that had ever been spread in front of it, the First Army moved forward. At the heart of the attack, led out by the Army's entire remaining stock of tanks—fourteen of them—was the Marine Brigade of the 2nd Division. Their immediate objective was Landres-et-Saint-Georges, where Donovan's 83rd Brigade had been so lavishly expended two weeks before. Now the contrast was almost grotesque. George Hamilton—the hero of the charge up Hill 142 before Belleau Wood, now commanding the 1st Battalion, 5th Marines—reported gratefully that the villages had been "completely reduced by our artillery and gave no resistance."

The First Army's artillery had performed extraordinarily well. Many prisoners taken on this first day claimed that "the reason they were taken was that artillery concentrations were so effective as to confine them to shelters and to isolate them in small groups. Artillery prisoners stated that they were unable to leave their shelters to serve their guns."

But there were some gun emplacements and machine guns that the artillery had not suppressed, and on either side of the 2nd, the attacking divisions were held up, at least at the start. In the center the Marines pressed on, taking advantage of the terrain with great skill, and with the remaining handful of tanks they stormed the Barricourt Heights. "Am digging in," Hamilton reported at 3:20 P.M. "When can we have some chow?"

The day had proved an almost unqualified success. Liggett had begun to show, at last, what a modern American army might be. The First Army had captured 3,602 prisoners, 63 guns, and hundreds of machine guns, and it was finally through the nightmare of the Meuse-Argonne and out into the open on the other side. The 2nd and 89th Divisions advanced about five and a half miles and took all the high ground, as Liggett had instructed, before dark. III Corps on the right similarly took all its objectives. Only in I Corps did tragedy strike. These divisions were facing Marwitz's best troops and had been tasked to do nothing more than "threaten furiously" and protect the left flank of the 2nd Division's thrust. But, as Liggett recalled, "Our men were so eager that part of the Corps got out of hand and the demonstration developed into a real attack. . . . It was magnificent, but it was not war, for it played into the enemy's hands and led to a deplorable waste of life."

Whatever the cost, the pivot of the German line was shattered, and the orderly retreat began to degenerate into a rout. Flying over the lines, Rickenbacker looked down in astonished relief. "Every road was filled with retreating Heinies. They were going while the going was good and their very gestures seemed to indicate that for them it was indeed the finis de la guerre." He was right; it was almost the end of the shooting war. But the battle for the peace had only just begun.

Part Nine

LOSING
the
PEACE

39

Losing to the Allies

The first round of the political battle was fought at home, and it began well for the President. The German decision to address Prince Max von Baden's peace note exclusively to the U.S. government had been a considerable stroke of luck for Wilson. Despite the AEF's relatively minor battlefield role in what now looked like certain victory over Germany, suddenly he seemed to have the opportunity to arrange peace terms that would compel all the belligerents to participate in his program for the postwar world. For almost three weeks, from October 6 to 23, Wilson stood just where he had imagined himself standing, at the helm of world affairs, ignoring the outraged Allies while he alone negotiated with the Germans.

During these heady days, the President exchanged three Notes with the German Chancellor, his own communications growing more imperious and Prince Max's more submissive. The Germans undertook to end submarine warfare, to withdraw "everywhere from invaded territory," and to stop their wanton destruction of French and Belgian towns and villages. They accepted, too, that the terms of the cease-fire—when Wilson had agreed on them with the Allies—would be such as to guarantee "the military supremacy of the armies of the United States and the Allies in the field." Most important of all, Wilson had forced the Germans, at least, to accept his vision of the future: they offered "unqualified acceptance" of the Fourteen Points as the basis for peace negotiations.

At the same time, the President had engineered another significant achievement: the reconstruction of the German Constitution. From the beginning he had been troubled by the notion of negotiating peace with an

autocracy. He had not been fooled by the pseudodemocratic gestures devised by Ludendorff, and in his second message he pointedly reminded
Prince Max of one of the "terms of peace" that he had announced from
Mount Vernon on the Fourth of July, namely "the destruction of every arbitrary power anywhere that can separately, secretly, and of its single
choice disturb the peace of the world." Quite clearly, the militarist regime
operating in the Kaiser's name—"the power which has hitherto controlled
the German nation"—was precisely this kind of arbitrary power, and Wilson suggested that it was now "within the choice of the German nation to
alter it."

Prince Max replied that his administration was supported by "an overwhelming majority of the German people." The proof was the program of
instant reforms that the Reichstag was in the process of pushing through the
system—which included civilian control of the armed forces. But that kind
of synthetic "revolution from above" was not enough for Wilson. In his last
and toughest Note, he warned bleakly that if the United States were forced
to deal with the military masters and the "monarchical autocrats" of Germany, it must demand "not peace negotiations but surrender."

Hindenburg, faithful Prussian servant that he was, was profoundly offended by the implied threat to the throne. Calling his officers together, he
raised his sword above his head and cried, "Long live His Majesty, our
King, Emperor and Master!" Then he signed a proclamation to the Army
denouncing Wilson's Note as a demand for unconditional surrender. "It is
therefore unacceptable to us soldiers."

But as the Western Front buckled inward, soldiers no longer controlled
Germany's destiny. Hoping to save himself, the Kaiser backed civilian
moves to sacrifice the true architect of German militarism, Erich Ludendorff, to America's will. After two years as master of the fate of a nation of
60 million people, Ludendorff found himself without support, deserted
now even by Hindenburg, whom he never forgave.

On October 26, Ludendorff wrote a letter of resignation that the
Kaiser was only too willing to accept. Then he went home to his wife. Two
hours later, one of his staff officers called on him and found the most powerful general in the greatest war yet fought by mankind—a man on whose
instructions hundreds of thousands of German soldiers had gone to their
deaths—sitting quietly in an armchair reading a detective novel.

Prince Max was now in a position to give Wilson the assurances he required: "The peace negotiations are being conducted by a government of

the people, in whose hands rests, both actually and constitutionally, the authority to make decisions. The military powers are also subject to this authority. The German government now awaits the proposals for an armistice."

Woodrow Wilson, by skillfully exploiting both Germany's immediate military predicament and latent, long-suppressed forces for change within her society, had single-handedly forced a full-blown autocracy onto the path to genuine democracy. It was a substantial achievement, but it did not satisfy his fellow Americans; it was not at all what they had had in mind. Once again, the CPI's propaganda backfired. The hatred of Germans and Germany that had festered at home in the spring and summer was fanned by the fighting at Saint-Mihiel and in the Meuse-Argonne and deepened into a hysterical loathing. When the Germans asked for peace on the basis of the Fourteen Points, American public opinion demanded that their request be denied; surrender must be unconditional.

Theodore Roosevelt, his sons dead or maimed, caught the public mood, urging the United States to "dictate peace by the hammering guns and not chat about peace to the accompaniment of clicking typewriters." Turning on Wilson, he declared, "Most of those fourteen points are thoroly mischievous and if made the basis of a peace, such peace would represent not the unconditional surrender of Germany, but the unconditional surrender of the United States." On October 23, Senator Miles Poindexter even tried to make it unlawful for the President to enter into negotiations before the Germans had surrendered. Other voices called for a road of blood leading to Berlin, though the blood, as Wilson pointed out, would not be German alone: for American armies to hack a route into the heart of Germany might cost a million American lives.

To help stem this tide of vengeful bitterness, he looked around for his natural allies, the leading progressives with whose support he had retained the presidency in 1916. But he looked in vain. Liberalism in America had been effectively silenced by the repressive measures that he had himself condoned. Worse, by allowing free speech to be denied by Albert Burleson, the American Protective League, and others, Wilson had helped ensure that his vision of a world governed by a "League of Nations" would not be properly debated in the public arena. Few Americans thoroughly grasped, let alone supported, what Wilson hoped to achieve through his peace maneuvers. The Espionage and Sedition Acts, the military intelligence apparatus, and other war-born instruments of state power had stifled the natural processes of policy making through open debate. So when Theodore Roosevelt boomed that the Fourteen Points were the preserve of "every pro-German and pacifist and socialist and anti-American so-called internationalist," there was no one to dispute the point. Few knew better, and even fewer wished to risk having those labels attached to them.

This gulf between the President's vision and the people's basic instincts could not have opened at a worse moment, with midterm congressional elections approaching. Already, public sentiment was running broadly against the Democrats; terrified of a Republican victory, with all the damage this would do to his prestige and his capacity to fulfill his world vision, Wilson decided to turn directly to the people. They must trust him to deal with Germany and with the Allies and create a new world that only he as yet understood. Aware of the stakes but perhaps not of the odds against him, he made an open appeal for a vote of confidence. BACK UP YOUR PRESIDENT, demanded newspaper advertisements, WHO IS RECOGNIZED EVERYWHERE AS THE TRUE SPOKESMAN OF LIBERALS AND PROGRESSIVES THROUGHOUT THE WORLD. The Allies, warned Wilson, would see a Republican victory in the elections as "a repudiation of my leadership."

With defeat in the elections a real possibility, Wilson sent Colonel House, a coauthor of the Fourteen Points, to Europe to discuss the terms on which Germany might be allowed to end the war. The Allies must now be talked around to a Wilsonian peace. House arrived in Paris in a confident mood. He knew that there was widespread popular enthusiasm in Europe for the President and his manifesto, and he had his President's full backing to use all America's power to secure the appropriate terms for the peace.

In fact, on past performance alone America already had strong claims to a dominant role in the peace process—but the Allies did not care to be reminded of them. No one now spoke of how American divisions had rushed to block the road to Paris during those terrifying days in June. No one mentioned Belleau Wood or the July attack at Soissons and the dreadful price paid in American lives. True, the First Army was not yet punching its full weight in the Meuse-Argonne, but even in failure it had held some thirty German divisions away from other fronts.

Far more significant, and even less willingly mentioned, America's financial contribution to the war had been and would continue to be the foundation of victory. The CPI, raged Walter Lippmann in Paris, seemed determined to present America as "a rich bumpkin come to town with his pockets bulging and no desire except to please." But however much the image offended Lippmann's sensibilities, the bulging pockets had been important to Europe since 1914 and were now crucial. Since early 1918, Britain had been "wholly dependent on the United States for a large proportion of supplies used by both the Services and domestic population."

Of Britain's imported munitions in 1917 and 1918, the United States supplied one sixth of all artillery shells, 100 percent of her smokeless powder, 100 percent of small-arms ammunition, 60 percent of unwrought copper ingots, 100 percent of sulfuric acid—the list was endless and included 80 percent of her wheat. These imports, and similar supplies to the other Allies, were paid for by American loans; only this American support prevented the collapse of the pound sterling on international exchange markets. But all this largesse had not, it seemed, bought America a voice in the victory settlement.

House does not seem to have been prepared for the determination of the Allied politicians not to sacrifice core national interests for the sake of the lofty vision of a president who might not even have the backing of his own people. Everyone was well aware that this first round of negotiations was crucial. Claims staked now would be hard to dislodge at the formal peace conference.

The Allies had a variety of stratagems to keep House at bay. They made sure, for instance, that the armistices with Bulgaria, Turkey, and Austria-Hungary bore no reference to the Fourteen Points, so that even if Wilson did succeed in putting these terms into a peace agreement with Germany, the agreement would not be binding on any of the other Central Powers. American military intelligence noted ruefully that the armistice recently arranged with Austria-Hungary had given the Italians precisely those Austro-Hungarian territories that they had demanded in 1915 as the price of their entry into the war—no "soft peace," this, but an early payoff on one of the "secret treaties."

Then came a full-scale campaign to discount the United States' contribution to the war. The first step was to limit America's physical presence in Europe by undermining Pershing's 80-division program. All the agonizing over the feasibility of the 100-division and then the 80-division plan was now seen to have been a waste of energy. Coolly, Foch made it clear that he no longer required so many American divisions on the Western

Front. Now that the British had triumphed in the Middle East, the danger that they might pull troops out of Europe had receded, and there was no need of the American buffer.

The day before Prince Max sent his first Note, Foch shocked Secretary Baker by telling him that the war would be won with the help of only forty American divisions—and this number was already on the Western Front. No announcement could have been better calculated to derail the American plans for 1919; the timing of the gesture suggests that French intelligence in Germany had got wind of the imminent armistice proposal and, in the knowledge that German capitulation was near, Foch could afford to take a swipe at American pretensions.

The British could, and now obviously would, use their continuing control over transports and merchant shipping to restrict the flow of men and supplies to the AEF. In the face of this démarche, there was very little Wilson, Baker, or House could do to maintain an independent American line. The United States could neither ship men to nor supply a greatly increased AEF on her own. Of their existing shipping, Americans appeared to be devoting to their import trade 2 million tons in excess of their minimum needs—an embarrassing statistic recently turned up by Bernard Baruch's War Industries Board. As for the extravagant quantities of new merchant shipping promised by Hurley and his Shipping Board, the program was disastrously behind schedule. "We're in bad shape on shipping," George Goethals noted gloomily in his diary on October 27. "We based our program of 80 divisions overseas by July next on certain estimates of the Shipping Board, but this body has fallen down most woefully and there seems no chance of gaining enough impetus to make their monthly output, let alone the existing deficiency. I shouldn't be surprised to see the whole shipping situation collapse."

Determined to keep the Americans in a supporting role, the Allies seemed hell bent on denigrating what they had achieved in France. As the American military representative on the Supreme War Council, Tasker Bliss was more exposed than most to Allied criticism, and he observed bitterly that the Allies were working to "minimize the American effort as much as possible." In Washington, Sir Eric Geddes, First Lord of the Admiralty, declared that the American Navy was not doing "anything like her share on the sea in European waters." Pershing came in for vicious criticism for his handling of the Saint-Mihiel and Meuse-Argonne campaigns; throughout October, Paris seethed with rumors that Foch was to remove him.

In fact, nothing could have been less likely. In Pershing, Foch had an American commander whose program perfectly suited French desires for a punitive peace, and he ordered the American Commander in Chief to stay close to his front line, even though command of the First Army had passed to Liggett. So eagerly did Pershing obey, and so tiresome was his constant nagging to attack during the last week of October, that he goaded the even-tempered Liggett into flaring, "Go away and forget it."

But though Foch showed no signs of trying to remove him, Pershing's stance was hardly helpful to House as he struggled to put Wilson's case across to the Allies in Paris. Pershing's unauthorized letter to the Supreme War Council demanding that Germany be forced into an unconditional surrender was a severe embarrassment to a diplomat pleading for a liberal peace. House took steps to muzzle Pershing, but he could not keep him from driving his armies on to the limit of their powers in pursuit of the unconditional surrender, thus sabotaging his own President's plans in the process.

Wilson wanted Germany to come to the peace table with strength enough to negotiate as an autonomous nation. On no other basis could his vision of the postwar world be built; besides, he would then himself assume a uniquely important role as mediator at the peace conference. But to guarantee her autonomy, Germany must not have surrendered unconditionally. She must have an army, must not be reduced to helplessness. Wilson's old foe Henry Cabot Lodge neatly summarized the President's predicament: "If Germany surrenders unconditionally, he will only share in making a peace with the Allies. His hold over the Allies is the German Army in existence, which makes our army and our alliance indispensable." But Pershing was apparently set on blasting that German Army out of existence, and with it Wilson's hopes of stage-managing the negotiations. Each was determined to win America a commanding voice at the peace table, but their means were diametrically opposed. Pershing planned to do it by destroying Germany, Wilson by preserving her.

On October 29, House met the Allied leaders to begin the formal negotiation of the basis for peace. The principal players made an incongruous group. The flowing white hair and shaggy mustache that framed David Lloyd George's features, the glowering eyes and consciously noble brow, the arresting voice, all distracted attention at first from a brain of phenomenal speed and dangerous subtlety, "nimble, unstable and uncertain."

There could be no mistaking Clemenceau's intentions. Beside the restless Welshman, the eighty-year-old French premier was a rock, a squat figure with a massive head permanently covered by a skullcap, a "hard, relentless vulture." And then there was House himself: small, neat, langorous, effete, soft-spoken to the point of incomprehensibility; where he came from, he liked to say, a man could be killed for talking too loud.

The white-and-gold curlicues of the Trianon Palace at Versailles made a perfect setting for what had some of the elements of a French farce. Polite preliminaries out of the way, Lloyd George immediately came to the point: "The question is, do we or do we not accept the whole of President Wilson's Fourteen Points?"

Clemenceau replied drily, "Have you ever been asked by President Wilson whether you accept the Fourteen Points? I never have."

Arthur Balfour, the British Foreign Secretary, attempted to elucidate: "For the moment, unquestionably, we are not bound by President Wilson's terms; but if we assent to an armistice without making our position clear, we shall certainly be bound."

"Then," declared Clemenceau, with mock innocence, "I want to hear the Fourteen Points!"

So House solemnly started to read them out, and immediately the objections began. Lloyd George refused point-blank to countenance the "freedom of the seas" provision. The British, he said, with the security of the Empire to think of, would not "look at" such a notion. If they were to accept this provision, the Royal Navy, defenders of an island nation, would no longer be able to blockade enemy ports in time of war.

As Lloyd George stood immovable, House began to realize just how little power he himself really had. A crude threat to build an American fleet more powerful than the Royal Navy was shrugged off almost contemptuously. Lloyd George, who was perfectly well aware of the political weakness of the administration that House represented, did not bother to beat about the bush: Britain, he stated flatly, "would spend her last guinea to keep a navy superior to that of the United States." When House threatened to make a separate peace with the Germans. Lloyd George called his bluff, with the warning that until Britain had made peace, the Royal Navy would continue to blockade Germany—the implication being that American ships sailing for German ports would once again be intercepted, as they had been during the years of neutrality.

But for all Lloyd George's belligerence, Britain did want peace, and soon. She was bankrupt, and a whole generation of her young men was dead or maimed. What was more, if peace came now, the British would almost certainly do well out of the settlement; the war in the Middle East was won, and Haig's armies could at this point claim the lion's share of credit for the situation on the Western Front. To get a prompt agreement from House, Lloyd George accepted the other thirteen points, including the proposal for a League of Nations (disregarding, for the moment at least, the likely objections from the Dominions, which were hoping to take part in a share-out of Germany's colonies). As a sop to American pride, Lloyd George offered to "discuss" the freedom of the seas issue again at the peace conference. House decided to accept the compromise, though he cannot seriously have believed that the attitude of the Royal Navy was likely to change—and in so doing he made a major concession. America would enter the final peace negotiations having effectively given away one of the main principles for which the nation had ostensibly gone to war.

The British were also adamant that Germany must pay reparations for the damage she had caused in Allied countries. The demand was reinforced by Clemenceau, who wanted the provision inserted in the Armistice agreement itself. "You must not forget that the French people are among those who have suffered most," he argued. "They would not understand our failure to allude to this matter." Again, House gave way—and thus allowed the spirit of retribution to creep into the peace formula—entirely at odds with the ethos of the Fourteen Points.

The French wanted to recoup at least some of what they had lost, but above all they wanted to guarantee their national security. The Prussians had occupied Paris only four decades before; in the last four years, more than a million Frenchmen had died in the effort to prevent their doing so again. The French strategy now centered not simply on forcing a German surrender and, as Wilson had put it, "ensuring Allied and American military supremacy" in the short term but on an Armistice agreement that would crush German military strength for the foreseeable future.

Bliss cabled Washington to warn the President that the French were drawing up cease-fire terms that were "quite as much political as military." But Wilson and House, with their eyes fixed on the formal peace conference, do not seem to have appreciated that the French could achieve these political ends right at the outset, through manipulating the "military" conditions of what should have been a practical cease-fire arrangement.

Bliss advised that the Germans need only be disarmed. Haig wanted only "the evacuation of all invaded territories and of Alsace-Lorraine." But Foch, supported by Pershing, insisted that, in addition to demanding about half of Germany's war matériel, the Allies should occupy the German Rhineland. Astonishingly, House, with his President's consent, accepted this judgment; apparently, Clemenceau had given "his word of honor that France would withdraw after the peace conditions had been fulfilled."

The French had been given the green light: the Allies would occupy the west bank of the Rhine, establish a neutral zone nineteen to twenty-five miles wide on the east bank, and set up three bridgeheads. As American military intelligence pointed out, this arrangement would ensure "complete control of the most important industrial and railroad centers. . . . Essen, Düsseldorf and almost all of the Westphalian industrial section are in the neutral zone. . . . Cologne and the Metz region will be occupied and the Briey iron fields will also fall into Allied hands."

This was no armistice, Bliss concluded, but "a demand for a complete surrender." He was right. The terms in no way served Wilson's purposes; they suited Foch—and Pershing—far better. But it was too late now to draw back. On November 5—the day on which the Republicans gained majorities of two in the Senate and forty-five in the House of Representatives—the President informed the German government that Foch "awaited any representatives they might send to ask for an armistice."

Wilson must have realized that the hopes the German representatives had placed in him were about to be cruelly disappointed. The terms were far more severe than either he or they had hoped for. There was now a real question as to whether Germany would accept an armistice on these conditions; Lloyd George himself had suggested that occupying the east bank of the Rhine was pushing provocation too far. Haig had warned that the German Army was "by no means broken." Had the French asked for too much? Would the Germans agree to the terms? Or would they, as Pershing hoped, require crushing on the field before they would sign what amounted to a death warrant for their national pride?

40

Von Winterfeldt's Tears

James Montgomery Beck, future Attorney General of the United States, was among the first to hear of the German response. He was in London during the second week of November to meet clients and had been hoping to stay at the country home of Lady Paget; but six of the servants had fallen to the influenza epidemic, and she offered him dinner at the Ritz Hotel instead. At the same table sat a French diplomat who had spent the day at his embassy decoding the report of Foch's meeting with the German armistice delegates. Amid the chandeliers, the starched linen, and the glinting silver, mirrors, and glass of the Ritz, Beck sat enthralled as the Frenchman described the scene.

The German delegation crossed the French lines under a flag of truce; on the morning of November 8, they entered Foch's private railroad carriage, halted in a siding in thick woods at Compiègne, several miles southwest of Soissons. The Germans filed into the fusty, spartan interior, formal introductions were made, they sat down, and then:

A profound silence ensued. Finally Foch asked whether they wished to see him. They replied they had come to discuss armistice proposals. He said he had none. They expressed surprise and referred to President Wilson's last letter. Foch asked whether they were asking for an armistice. They evaded the question. Then one of them said if it was a question of terms, they would reply that they were asking for an armistice. Then Foch handed them the Allied terms. They read them with consternation and one of them wiped the tears from his eyes.

The tears were those of Major General von Winterfeldt, chosen to accompany the German delegation because he spoke perfect French. They were tears of bitterness. These terms were not in the spirit of the Fourteen Points, but there were no Americans in the carriage to whom he could appeal. Above all, they were tears of helpless frustration. When Prince Max had first asked for an armistice in October, the German Army had been bruised and battered but still capable of stout resistance. Now complete humiliation was but a few days away—at the hands of the Americans, in whose President the Germans had placed their hopes for a fair peace.

At this moment of truth, Pershing stood in spirit beside Foch as the French commander delivered his uncompromising message. To Haig must go the credit of having seen the opportunity to defeat Germany. The skill and grit of his troops had hurled Germany onto the ropes, but they could not force a final knockout without help. The British Army was exhausted, decimated, pulled back now by the desperate problems of supplying a line extended far into Belgium. With the onset of the winter rains, the roads—ruined by the retreating Germans—had turned into the familiar morasses, impassable by man or machine, and Haig needed time to regroup. Only Pershing could now threaten the Germans with immediate catastrophe; his armies already straddled the Meuse, and the Germans could not break contact. And Pershing, who still sought unconditional surrender, was even then driving his men on.

Liggett's advance in the days following the November 1 breakthrough had been spectacular. On November 2, Gallwitz had praised the courage of the German troops but acknowledged that they "just cannot do anything. . . . It is imperative that the Army be withdrawn behind the Meuse and that this withdrawal be effected immediately."

By dusk on the third day, Liggett had advanced twelve miles along an eighteen-mile front, bringing the German lateral railroad within range of his heavy guns. His men had captured more than a hundred light and medium artillery pieces and stores of all kinds in vast quantities. In this war of rapid movement, Billy Mitchell's aircraft at last began to fulfill some of the soaring hopes of the apostles of airpower. They could now be seen as "winged cavalry" sweeping across enemy lines, not only providing an invaluable reconnaissance and liaison service to the ground troops but sharpening their profile as an offensive weapon, strafing the retreating Germans and bombing roads, rail centers, and supply dumps. Forty-five DH-4s dropped a total of five tons of bombs on Montmédy; thirty aircraft dropped two tons of bombs on Mouzon and Raucourt; American pilots shot down forty-seven enemy aircraft and five balloons in two days, at a cost of fourteen aircraft. At this very last moment, the air forces were putting the "Yankee Punch" into the war and pointing the way to the air combat of the future.

There were now five thousand German prisoners in American cages, thousands more on their way to captivity. Private Oliver Briggs wrote home describing how he had been woken in the early hours by "a great chorus" of prisoners, singing at the prospect of an end to the war. "I sat up and listened. The night was pitch dark and a light rain fell softly on the roof. Had I imagined singing? No! There it was again, beautiful, melodious, voluminous." Going outside into the rain, Briggs was

spell-bound while the tune was continued thru all its variations. . . . Each part was carried to perfection thru all the intricacies. I tried to catch the words but failed because . . . I could not understand German! You cannot conceive the effect of such a chorus. All men. Hundreds in number, trudging along the wet and slimy road in the dead of night, singing. Prisoners of war in the enemy's hand and singing. A few short hours before, they were fighting to defend the Fatherland. Now they were captives marching to the rear guarded by a single American in front and one behind. Can they be called guards, rather guides, I should say.

Gallwitz had no reserves; every single German division was in the line facing the First Army. To shore up his crumbling defenses, he had to shuffle men forward in penny packets. They resorted to desperate, dangerous experiments to halt or even slow the American advance: Hugh Drum cautioned units against "wooden boxes with the inscription 'VORSICHT—INFECTIÖSE MATERIELLE.' . . . These boxes contain tubes in which are enclosed very noxious microzymes. It is dangerous to open them." Booby traps were everywhere; taped to lintels, concealed in radio equipment, waiting under floorboards for the first footfall.

In the rear, the German supply lines were under constant threat from gangs of armed brigands, renegade soldiers among them. Food and other supplies were not reaching the front line; Liggett's men saw dead horses with steaks cut from their flanks. Walter Lippmann recalled that as the surrendering soldiers pressed forward, many were waving the propaganda leaflet devised by American military intelligence, listing the hot coffee, white bread, beef, and other almost forgotten luxuries that could be theirs if they laid down their arms and crossed over to the American side.

The final crushing blow was the American crossing of the Meuse, spearheaded by Hanson Ely's 5th Division. Even as Winterfeldt wept, American troops were almost in possession of the Meuse Heights along their entire length and spilling over onto the Woeuvre Plain. The German hopes of holding on the line of the Meuse were now shattered.

Had the German High Command had any inkling that the armistice terms would bear so little resemblance to a "soft peace," it is conceivable that they might have insisted on a more ferocious last-ditch resistance in the first week of November. Now it was too late. On November 9, the American Second Army under Robert Bullard would launch its first offensive, a hard strike toward Metz, Pershing's cherished objective for so long. Foch put the finishing touches to the German Army's ruin in this sector by asking Pershing to add six divisions to Mangin's Tenth Army and bring both the First and Second Armies as well into a huge coordinated drive for Metz and the Briey iron fields on November 14.

Liggett took great delight in the purely American successes of these last days: "For the first time we were on our own. In the past, French artillery, aviation and other technical troops had made up our deficiencies. . . . [Now] Americans manned the communications, the telegraph lines, water supply, ammunition and supply dumps, and virtually all the services, while other Americans planned the battle and the others fought it."

After the frustrations, disappointments, even humiliations, of the Meuse-Argonne campaign, success was doubly sweet, and Pershing saw a way of crowning this late blaze of glory. Sedan, the scene of France's humiliation in 1870, should be seized by his armies and handed over to the French, so critical and superior these days, with a flourish. Strictly speaking, Sedan was outside the American sector; but the French 4th Division, to which it really should have fallen, had not advanced so fast, and Army Group Commander General Paul Maistre agreed to Pershing's suggestion that the First Army should therefore take the honors.

Pulling rank while Liggett was away from his headquarters, Pershing arranged for Hugh Drum to issue a "memorandum" to the corps commanders on the center and left of the American advance, informing them of the Commander in Chief's "desire" that the "honor of entering Sedan should fall to the First Army." This was not an order; Pershing gave no instructions as such, merely expressed "every confidence that the troops of the I Corps, assisted on their right by the V Corps, will enable him to realize this desire."

Presumably to reassure the corps commanders that the French would not object, Drum added the fatal words "Boundaries will not be considered binding." Unfortunately, Charles Summerall, commanding V Corps in the center, concluded that he had carte blanche to pass one of his divisions through the I Corps area on his left, in order to take Sedan—and this is what he proceeded to do. On November 6, he pulled the 1st Division out of the line and sent it on a night march through the sectors belonging to the 77th and 42nd Divisions, with orders to attack Sedan at dawn. American troops fired wildly at one another in the dark, and the "Big Red One" even managed to get in front of a French unit, which is when Liggett came to hear of the maneuver, from a French officer practically incoherent with astonishment and rage.

"This was the only occasion in the war when I lost my temper completely," Liggett wrote later. "I had been holding this fine division back to be used when we crossed the Meuse, when we might have needed them very badly. . . . Moreover, the movement had thrown the I Corps front and the adjoining French front into such confusion that had the enemy chosen to counterattack in force at that moment, a catastrophe might have resulted." Certainly the 42nd would have been incapacitated, because a unit of the 1st Division, coming across MacArthur poring over a map with some of his officers, had arrested the lot of them as spies.

Mercifully, there was no German counterattack, and the débâcle remained private; Summerall, a favorite commander of Pershing's, was not even reprimanded. The American carryings-on had, as it happened, done nothing to relieve the pressure on the enemy. Late on November 8, the German delegates sent a copy of the proposed Armistice agreement back from Compiègne to Spa, to the waiting German leaders. Technically, they were asking for further instructions; in reality there was only one possible course they could take—they must accept the terms before them.

The military situation along the entire front was critical, if not already lost. Meanwhile, inside Germany the fires of revolution were flaring out of control, leading the armistice delegates to balk at the demand that they surrender 30,000 machine guns; they would need them, they said, to "keep order in Germany." The following day, at the Imperial Headquarters in Spa, Hindenburg asked a specially convened meeting of thirty-nine senior officers whether their troops could be relied upon to suppress the revolution at home. "No," replied a large majority. Suddenly an enemy far more potentially destructive than either America or the Allies was bringing its weight to bear. The delegates in Foch's railway carriage were ordered to sign, while Prince Max wrestled with the more terrifying problem of keeping Germany out of Bolshevik control.

The MID concluded that "the signing of the armistice was compelled by military necessity"—but this was only half the story. In Berlin, almost exactly a year after the Bolsheviks had stormed the Winter Palace in Saint Petersburg, the Spartacists had seized the Imperial Palace, and a large red blanket, acting as a flag, hung from the balcony. Karl Liebknecht, the best-known revolutionary in Germany, proclaimed a soviet, and other cities were quick to follow suit: Leipzig, Hanover, Cologne, Frankfurt, Magdeburg . . . The King of Bavaria had abdicated, and a republic had been declared in Munich. Mutinies, which had been looming for months, had finally broken out in the Army. The principal German naval base at Wilhelmshaven had been in revolt since October 29 and was now under the control of a sailors' soviet; disaffection quickly spread to nearby Hamburg and Bremen as well.

Responsible Germans saw the need to act quickly if the revolution was not to succeed. Prince Max issued a proclamation announcing the Kaiser's abdication; the leader of the Social Democrats proclaimed a socialist republic from the steps of the Reichstag. Socialist deputy Friedrich Ebert became the first President of the German Republic, making a pact with Hindenburg for the Army's support for his administration. And on November 9, Kaiser Wilhelm II abdicated and fled to Holland, where he lived out the rest of his days—even after Adolf Hitler conquered the Dutch and invited him to return home.

While Germany's domestic stability teetered in the balance, while the world outside waited for the eleventh hour of the eleventh day, the soldiers continued to fight. On the afternoon of November 9, not yet convinced that the Germans would sign, Foch sent messages to Pershing, Haig, and Pétain: "Our advance should be kept going and speeded up. I appeal to the energy and initiative of the Commanders in Chief to make the results obtained decisive."

Pershing ordered Liggett to mount a general attack on November 11. At 6:25 A.M., with some troops already over the top, Liggett received the news that the Armistice had been signed that morning and hostilities were to cease at 11 A.M. Urgently he sent word forward, but frontline units were already in action, effectively beyond reach. Hundreds of Americans were wounded in those last hours and minutes, and dozens died, taking Germans with them: the crew of one of the huge naval fourteen-inch guns sent a 1,400-pound shell on its twenty-five-mile trajectory deep into enemy lines, meticulously timed to ensure that the shell's flight ended precisely at 11 A.M.

As the deadline passed, Eddie Rickenbacker walked out into the mud of his airfield. All around him tanks of gasoline were in flames; star shells and Very lights exploded overhead. It was

an aerodrome seemingly thronged with madmen. Everybody was laughing—drunk with the outgushing of their long pent-up emotions. . . . "I've lived through the war!" I heard one whirling Dervish of a pilot shouting to himself as he pirouetted alone in the center of a mud hole. . . . Another pilot, this one an Ace of 27 Squadron, grasped me securely by the arm and shouted almost incredulously, "We won't be shot at any more!"

As for Pershing, he stood staring at the huge map that covered the wall of his bare office, furious and disappointed. "If they had given us another ten days," he complained later, presumably thinking of the planned November 14 attack on Metz, "we would have rounded up the entire German army. . . . What I dread is that Germany doesn't know that she was licked. Had they given us another week, we'd have *taught* them." Even as he reached this conclusion, German officers were originating the theory of the "stab in the back"—the propaganda notion, so successfully exploited by Hitler, that the German Army had never really been beaten, would never have surrendered, had it not been betrayed by enemies within the German state.

On the East Coast of America, it was 6 A.M. The first news flashes had reached New York three hours before, and sleep had been shattered by the hoots of tugs in the harbor, auto horns and air-raid sirens, factory whistles and church bells. The Statue of Liberty prickled with lights in the darkness, and bonfires burned on street corners. As dawn came, Fifth Avenue was already thronged, and by noon the city was one seething celebration: bands competing shrilly, parades emerging from every corner to collide with one another and reconstitute themselves, veterans carried shoulder high for blocks, French and Italian officers mobbed, kissed, pelted with flowers. The Kaiser was hanged, burned, blinded, castrated, dismembered repeatedly throughout the day; ten German internees being taken from the Battery narrowly escaped a similar fate when their guards were rushed and overpowered by hysterical revelers.

The President's statement to his ecstatic people was characteristic; seemingly oblivious to the passions they were feeling—relief, rage, triumph, hatred, grief—it was less a summary of present realities than a projection of lofty hopes for the future: "The Armistice was signed this morning. Everything for which America fought has been accomplished. It will now be our fortunate duty to assist by example, by sober friendly counsel and material aid, in the establishment of just democracy throughout the world."

41

"No Greater Pain"

"Everything for which America fought has been accomplished."
Woodrow Wilson spoke confidently, but his words had a hollow ring. The
war was won, but what laurels had been gathered? Certainly, submarines
were no longer sinking American ships. Germany had accepted peace
based on the Fourteen Points, and so, with reservations, had the Allies.
But Wilson's primary objective—a brave new world of democracies cooperating under the aegis of a League of Nations—had yet to be realized.
The League existed only as a general idea; Wilson had drafted the kind of
constitution he wanted, but the Allies had not been informed, nor had the
Senate. Wilson faced a new struggle—of diplomacy, of politics—and he
decided to take the full burden. He would go to Europe and face the wiles
of Lloyd George and Clemenceau. He would force on the Old World the
vision of the New.

On December 4, 1918, Wilson stood on the deck of the *George Washington* as it slipped down the Hudson past the Statue of Liberty en route
to Europe. There was a widespread sense that something extraordinary
was happening; for the President to leave the country was remarkable in itself, and some even doubted whether the Constitution allowed an incum-
bent to abandon the White House in this way. Flags fluttered all over the
docks, flights of "Flaming Coffins" roared overhead, boat horns sounded
around the harbor. Nine days later, Wilson reached Brest, the AEF's
principal port on France's Atlantic coast. Here, and soon afterward in
Paris, the public response put observers in mind of the Second Coming.

It is almost impossible now to credit the size of the crowds, the scale of the hysteria, the genuine emotion, the sense of deliverance aroused at the end of 1918 by Wilson's appearance in Europe. HONOR TO WILSON THE JUST! proclaimed the banners. VIVE LE PRÉSIDENT WILSON! He had come to redeem his promise to free the oppressed peoples of Europe, to make the Old World new. In London, in Brussels, in Rome and Milan, people literally knelt to kiss the ground he walked on. The world order had been shattered: three empires had burst, spilling their history and peoples into an unknown future. Back in Paris, in a magnificent suite in the Hôtel Crillon on the Place de la Concorde, Wilson received delegation after delegation—Zionists, Armenians, Poles, Slovaks, Swedes, Ukrainians, priests, peasants—all come to beg from the man who had promised universal freedom.

Though the President did not visit Germany, ordinary Germans too saw him as their savior. They wanted the democracy promised in the Fourteen Points, and they wanted protection from the predatory Allies, whose armies had already marched into the Rhineland. The French in particular continued to demonstrate in their occupation of German territory the nakedly vengeful attitude that had shaped the Armistice. Clemenceau was reported to have said, chillingly, "There are twenty million Germans too many." Foch was anxious for an extended, punitive, militarized occupation. "The only possible way for a German to avoid contravening one or other of [the French] by-laws," remarked a British officer, "will be to stay in bed. . . . He will only escape provided he does not snore."

The Americans, on the other hand, in their zone of occupation centered on Coblenz, were easily cast as Germany's natural defenders. According to the *Berliner Tageblatt*, Germans liked "the natural warm-heartedness and kindness of these tall, tanned chaps, who thought but simply and who dealt without duplicity." There was far less bitterness in the hearts of Americans, so many of them of German stock. Billeted in German homes, the soldiers sat around the kitchen stove with the family, "a luxury which can be appreciated only by those who have spent long, cold nights in the field." Mutual suspicion melted all too fast, and within weeks hurried orders went out forbidding fraternization. These were rescinded later, when it was found that, denied easy access to respectable German girls, troops contracted venereal diseases at a vastly higher rate. In the meantime, anti-fraternization orders or no, American soldiers became engaged to local girls in startling numbers. "Why did the Occupation last so long?" asked Will Rogers. "Because two of them weren't married yet."

There were some undercurrents of resentment. American-style sanitary regulations showed a total disregard for European customs: few German farmers were anxious to obey the order that precious manure heaps—their sole surviving source of fertilizer—were to be dispersed in the interests of hygiene. Though Coblenz lay in the heart of Moselle country, American regulations decreed that wine and beer were to be sold only at certain hours, spirits not at all. Passionate huntsmen, the locals chafed against the prohibition on weapons; mail was censored, permission was required to use the long-distance telephone, and carrier pigeons were banned. The penalty for insulting the American flag was sixty days in jail.

The American presence, too, sometimes grated. Locals did not like the rash of souvenir shops, chili con carne stores, and movie theaters spreading through the historic streets of Coblenz. Enlisted men, it was complained, had brought "Wild West manners," spitting in the street and making "insulting" advances to female passersby; meanwhile, their officers' wives patronized the locals and bought up what few items were available in the local stores.

And there were worse things. In the first ten months of occupation, six U.S. soldiers were convicted of murder, five of rape, two of inducing children to commit sodomy, eight of burglary, and eight of robbery—not many, a reporting officer considered, given that many of these young men, coming from states where Prohibition had been in force since 1916, were not used to alcohol.

Abuse and exploitation were not all one-sided. American military courts were forced to punish thousands of crimes by German citizens. The troops were avid consumers, and the majority of German offenses involved the sale of hard liquor to servicemen; a few cases of drug trafficking to troops were also detected. Other common peccadilloes were the theft of American property—soap, boots, blankets, assault on American troops—and "practising prostitution while diseased."

These crimes were often symptoms of desperation. Food had been in short supply for years now; while Americans had been adjusting to "Hooverized" meals, Germans had become specialists in the "Ersatz"— coffee made from roast peas, fat from cockroaches, snails, and worms—and eating pickled walrus or boiled crow. Ill health was widespread—hunger edema, scurvy, tuberculosis, eye ulcers, anemia. (The pegs in many school cloakrooms would be lowered after the war, as the average height of children malnourished in those years markedly declined.) Some surveys also showed a deterioration in mental capacity attributable to dietary deficiencies; later analysts would, with hindsight, identify this with an erosion of moral standards in which Nazism could take root.

The Armistice provided for the Allied blockade to be continued until the Germans met the cease-fire terms. Herbert Hoover, struggling to combat the desperate food crises in the liberated countries of eastern Europe, was appalled: "We do not kick a man in the stomach after we have licked him." A mission sent by him to investigate conditions in Germany early in 1919 reported child mortality up by 30 percent, the population as a whole 20 percent below its normal weight, and eight hundred deaths a day from starvation or disease. General Herbert Plumer, commanding the British occupation force, reported that his men were begging to go home, unable to bear the sight of "hordes of skinny and bloated children pawing over the offal from British cantonments."

Hunger stoked the fires of revolution. As the Left gained control in many towns and cities, the Right struck back. By the new year of 1919, the streets of German cities had become battlegrounds. The sinister paramilitary *Freikorps*, harbingers of Nazism, crushed Spartacist councils and murdered leading revolutionaries Karl Liebknecht and Rosa Luxemburg.

Germans looked to America and Woodrow Wilson for stability in a crazed world, for relief from their suffering, for protection from the greed of the Allies—and they were bitterly disappointed. By the time the terms of the peace agreement were presented to the German representatives in May 1919, the President's posture had changed. He had begun negotiations at Versailles set on a "soft peace": "Our greatest error would be to give [Germany] powerful reasons for wishing one day to take revenge. Excessive demands would most certainly sow the seed of war." But three months later, according to Bernard Baruch, who formed part of Wilson's delegation at Versailles, he was looking on the peace terms that he and the Allies had formulated as "an historic lesson, so that people might know that they could not do anything of the sort the Germans attempted without suffering the severest kind of punishment."

The "historic lesson" was harsh in the extreme, bearing little relation to the moderate sentiments of the Fourteen Points. The guilt for the war was firmly fixed on the Germans. They were to hand over the Kaiser and other leaders for trial. Germany's overseas colonies and concessions were to be carved up among the Allies—including Japan, whose delegates rushed to Versailles demanding German concessions in China and certain islands in the Pacific that they hoped would shield her from an attacker in a future war. Even the German homelands were to be reduced: Poland gained substantial tracts of Prussia and East Silesia, as well as a corridor to Danzig, which was made a free city; part of Upper Silesia went to Czechoslovakia; some of Schleswig went to Denmark; Alsace and Lorraine were returned to France.

The French had succeeded in neutering Germany's military strength, determined that never again should French territory be menaced. The Imperial Navy was restricted to 15,000 men and denied submarines and warships larger than 10,000 tons. The Army was restricted to 100,000 men and forbidden tanks or aircraft; the men were to serve for a minimum of twelve years, to prevent rapid turnover and the training of a large reserve; and the military schools, the infrastructure of Prussian militarism, were abolished, all the way from cadet level to staff college and even the General Staff College itself. The Rhineland was to be permanently demilitarized and occupied by Allied forces until all the other terms of the treaty were fulfilled.

Harshest of all, the Allies demanded enormous, crippling reparations. John Foster Dulles calculated that Germany's potential for repayment had a ceiling of $30 billion. This figure, however, was a small fraction of what the Allies wanted. Ludendorff and his predecessors had fought an exploitative, destructive war. Belgium had been sucked dry of resources and her people enslaved; the coal and iron fields of northern France had fed the German war machine, while the scorched-earth policy of the German Army in retreat had blighted once prosperous farmlands. But the French and British wanted more than direct compensation for damage done; they wanted Germany to pay what it had cost them to defeat her. In the general election held a month after the Armistice, Lloyd George had held on to power by promising to press for huge reparations—in Sir Eric Geddes's phrase, to "squeeze Germany till the pips squeaked." The French, many believed, were calling for repayments they knew the Germans could not make, in order to justify their continued occupation and, eventually, seizure of the Rhineland.

One of the major costs of the war was represented by America's loans to the Allies. The gratitude with which the Allies had accepted these loans was evaporating now. The United States was becoming "Uncle Shylock," shouting for his money from his comfortable bolt-hole across the Atlantic. By McAdoo's reckoning, by November 1920 the Allies had borrowed $9,466,283,000; by 1929, compound interest would bring this to more than $11 billion. On a schedule of repayments stretching into 1987, the total reached $22 billion. In British and French minds, the war debt issue was closely linked to the reparations issue; only if Germany paid her dues could the Allies repay theirs. British economist John Maynard Keynes even promoted a plan that had Germany straightforwardly assuming the inter-Allied war debts.

The Peace of Paris was signed on June 28, 1919. From the very beginning, it was furiously resented by the Germans. "In so far as the French dictated it," declared Walter Simons, the head of the German delegation, the treaty was "a monument of pathological fear and pathological hatred, and in so far as the Anglo-Saxons dictated it, it is the work of a capitalistic policy of the cleverest and most brutal kind."

The tragedy is that Wilson would undoubtedly have engineered a far less punitive settlement had it been within his power; as it was, the conditions were much less vindictive than they would have been had he not gone to Europe. But at Versailles he was too weak—as the Allies had always intended he should be—to dictate terms. Pershing had not dominated the Western Front sufficiently to give his President the moral authority of a victor, but he had done enough to weaken Germany to the point where her powers of negotiation, already undermined by internal revolution, were nonexistent, and now the President had no lever to use against the French. The timing of the war's end, too, had been unfortunate: the Allies were still able to resist America's financial muscle, and at home American voters had undermined Wilson's political credibility. Even the clouds of popular support that had enveloped him on his arrival in Europe soon dispersed, and the mood could not be recaptured. The newly Republican Congress read like a roll call of the enemies of George Creel, and it had axed the CPI's funds on the day after the Armistice. In 1919, Wilson was supported only by a dying wave of old propaganda; there was no longer a megaphone for his views in Europe.

He had to fall back on negotiation—but here he was hopelessly outclassed. "He was not sensitive to his environment at all," wrote Keynes. "What chance could such a man have against Mr Lloyd George's unerring, almost medium-like sensibility to everyone round him? . . . The poor

President would be playing blind man's buff in that party . . . this blind, deaf Don Quixote."

Even if Wilson had possessed the deviousness to outmaneuver Lloyd George and the toughness to outface Clemenceau, he perhaps lacked the will to do so. To get what he most wanted, he was prepared to trade. In a sense, the Germans paid the price for Woodrow Wilson's dream; for he was prepared to sacrifice much of what he had promised them in order to achieve one overriding ambition: securing the Allies' agreement to the League of Nations.

While the French and British had their way with Germany's assets, Wilson pushed forward his scheme for the League. The drafting of a detailed constitution—the "Covenant"—proceeded easily and successfully. By February 14, he had in his hands a Covenant admired by liberals in Europe, one that had been approved in principle by the national delegates to the peace conference.

On this high note, he returned home for ten days. Here he found extravagant praise heaped on what he had done so far. Only a hard core of Republican diehards led by Wilson's implacable enemy Senator Henry Cabot Lodge remained unconvinced. Wilson dined with his opponents and discussed the true meaning of the Covenant in an attempt to win them over—but to no avail. There were several sticking points; as Wilson acknowledged, Article 10 of the Covenant appeared to commit America to protecting the national integrity and political independence of any other member of the League, possibly by force; the means would be for the League's Council to decide. Other well-meant provisions seemed to hold the threat of foreign interference in purely domestic concerns such as tariffs and immigration levels.

This was all too much for Lodge. In a *coup de théâtre* on the eve of the President's return to France, he arranged for thirty senators to sign a document publicizing their opposition to the League. With his credibility further dented, Wilson was forced to go to the Allies and seek certain amendments to the Covenant in an effort to satisfy his Republican opponents. The horse trading at Versailles continued, and the amendments cost Wilson, or rather Germany, favors of various different kinds.

With the treaty signed, Wilson returned to America—but not as a hero, the architect of a new international order. "You Americans are broken reeds," wrote Keynes. To men such as Walter Lippmann and Felix Frankfurter, the peace terms as signed wholly contradicted the spirit of the

Fourteen Points. Abandoning Wilson, even they joined the fight to stop
the Senate ratifying the treaty. At home, Wilson found that the amendments he had made to the Covenant alienated the progressives who had so
admired the draft he had brought home in February—and still failed to
satisfy Lodge and the other Republicans, who had demanded them in the
first place.

Logically, the peace treaty with Germany and the League of Nations
Covenant should have been separate treaties. However, Wilson had decided to tie the Covenant into the peace settlement in order to present
Lodge and his supporters with a package so tightly integrated that they
could not reject the Covenant without rejecting the peace. This had been a
considerable diplomatic feat, achieved against the wishes of many delegates, who wanted the issue of the League postponed until after peace was
achieved; nevertheless, it had within it the seeds of disaster. In this linked
form, it united Left and Right, along with Irish and German Americans,
in opposition to some or all of the terms, be they the vindictive peace settlement or the watered-down Covenant.

But the main focus of the debate was the Covenant itself. Lodge needed
to muster thirty-three votes to defeat Wilson in the Senate and prevent ratification of the treaty (and therefore the Covenant) as it stood. With generous contributions from Henry Clay Frick and Andrew Mellon toward
the cost of intensive anti-League propaganda, he set about accumulating
them by canvassing, jockeying, and striking deals. Wilson, meanwhile, was
showing no such skill in maneuver. He had reached a sticking point: nations, he felt, must now be prepared to sacrifice some of their absolute
freedom of action to achieve a workable system of collective security, and
the Covenant must stand as written.

He was also approaching the limits of his energies. In France in March,
grossly overworking on the Covenant, he had succumbed to a virus that
may have aggravated his existing cerebrovascular disease. He began to
alarm his friends with untypical mood swings and erratic behavior: accus-
ing his French servants of being spies, claiming that someone was stealing
the furniture from his house, changing his opinion without explanation on
matters of crucial importance, such as the possible annexation of the
Rhineland.

Back home, in September 1919, he embarked on a grueling speaking
tour across the country to "reveal" the national consensus for ratification
that he alone believed existed. He was already exhausted and underweight

before he left, with a visible tremor in his hands, and he may well have known that the strain of the tour might cost him his life. After thirty-seven major speeches in twenty-two days—speeches made without the aid of public-address systems—his physical condition had deteriorated to the point where he was suffering from asthma and headaches severe enough to blur his vision. At 2 A.M. on the night of September 25, he was found sitting motionless in the drawing-room compartment of his private railway carriage, ashen and drooling slightly from the left side of his mouth. The next day, in tears, he confessed that he could not go on, and the cavalcade set off back across the country. On October 2, he suffered a massive stroke.

Lodge took full advantage of the President's illness. On November 6, he entered fourteen "reservations" against the peace treaty, each carefully calculated to appeal to one or more of its opponents. On November 19, the Senate rejected the treaty. Whatever capacity for compromise Wilson might once have had was now gone. He would not accept the "reservations"; unless his terms were met, he would not even accept a joint congressional resolution declaring an end to American belligerency. America remained technically at war and left the Europeans to broker their own League of Nations. "America will give lavishly of the blood of her sons to fight for the small nations," observed British pacifist Norman Angell, "[but] she will not be bothered with mandates or treaties in order to make it unnecessary to fight for them."

"There is no pain," wrote Keats, "greater than the pain of failing in a great object," and with his vision of the postwar world in ruins, Wilson clung to the hope that he might seek renomination in 1920. At the first Cabinet meeting he attended after his illness, in April 1920, it was pitifully obvious that he was deluding himself. He could barely stand without help, and more than once he lost the thread of the discussion completely. His doctor begged Democratic Party leaders to spare him further stress and humiliation; his nomination was quietly dropped, and he withdrew into an ill, unhappy retirement.

Epilogue

The
COST

42

Continuing the Search

During the First World War, a torrent of new phenomena overwhelmed the United States: a wash of public money flooding the economy; a hugely inflated federal government; universal conscription; a system for surveillance of the people; a pervasive suspicion and fear of the foreign and unorthodox; and then, with the rise of Bolshevism, a threatening alien ideology that seemed to justify the fears.

The war experience, though short, was explosive because these phenomena made their impact on a society that was already changing rapidly. Their effects were varied and unpredictable; the sheer diversity of people and opinion in America ensured that there would be both damage and gain—but not fixity. All had participated in an experience of such intensity that, whether they knew it or not, their world would never be quite the same again.

The economy had been the most powerful engine of change before the war and proved to be so again during the conflict. Allied spending, the huge federal budget, and the activities of the Alien Property Custodian, the War Trade Board, and the War Industries Board and its committees, all provided learning experiences for businessman and bureaucrat alike.

Abroad, the waging of economic warfare offered extraordinary insights into the workings of the world trading system, which America's new wealth now had the power to dominate. At home, the drive for integration, standardization, and time efficiency revolutionized business methods. Government intervention in the economy during the war fueled calls for greater central involvement in the future. One of George Goethals' key

subordinates—General Hiram "Iron Pants" Johnson—would play a leading role in the New Deal of the 1930s, which would draw heavily on the
wartime experience of federal economic action.

The massive wartime investment, both public and private, in research
and development—in radio technology, aviation, chemicals, mechanical
engineering—affected the way in which postwar Americans lived their
daily lives. Broadcast radio and commercial air travel continued the
process of integrating the country; and fleets of army surplus trucks carried
the concrete to build roads linking the nation's cities. By 1920, there were
9 million automobiles; ten years later, there were almost 30 million. Americans were on the move.

By halting immigration at its source, the war changed the composition
of the working population. The void left by the abrupt removal of 5 million
men from industry and agriculture by the draft could no longer be filled
from outside; suddenly many jobs were opened to women.

Women were operating elevators, directing traffic, running messages for
telegraph companies. They had moved into the realm of finance as tellers
and even department heads, into advertising and communications, into the
"heavy" industries of chemicals, iron, and steel. And as white female
clerks and factory girls moved into men's jobs, black women moved into
the "white" jobs left vacant—out of domestic service and agricultural labor
and into offices and factories previously closed to them. The jobs were
often the least desirable—in tobacco factories and abattoirs, stitching
wings for planes and loading shells—but they represented a shift away
from the traditional occupations of black women that would never be completely reversed.

Women, both white and black, displayed greater confidence and non-
conformity. This was most obviously paraded by women who had already
been notable and independent before the war: novelist Edith Wharton,
who set up refugee hostels in houses she borrowed from aristocratic
Parisian friends; artist Anna Coleman Ladd, who modeled and painted
portrait masks to conceal the hideous face wounds acquired in the
trenches; actress Maxine Elliott, who operated a barge carrying food and
clothing along Belgian canals; writers Gertrude Stein and Alice B. Toklas, who equipped a Model T van they called "Aunt Pauline" to distribute
medicines and bandages to evacuation hospitals in France. But a new
spirit was also obvious in the hundreds of less eminent female volunteers

who worked in France—not just as nurses and entertainers, not just in the ranks of the Salvation Army and the YMCA, but as telephone operators ("Hello Girls" transmitted battlefront messages at Pershing's headquarters during the Meuse-Argonne campaign), anesthetists, translators, statisticians, decoders, laboratory technicians.

When the soldiers began returning home and filling up the labor pool once more, horizons contracted again. In areas where women had begun to gain even before the war, they held on to their gains. White women were now firmly established in white-collar office work as telephone operators, bookkeepers, saleswomen, buyers, designers, copywriters, clerks. But where jobs had opened purely because of the war, women were promptly evicted when the men returned. They found no support from unionists, who feared that employers might use the existence of a huge force of unskilled women as a lever to push down the wages of skilled men; there was also strong resistance to the introduction of day nurseries, which would have permitted a more permanent change in the division of labor.

The most significant reform of all, however, could not be undone. Camped before the gates of the White House, militant women had extracted a price for their support of the war. Enduring abuse, violence, arrest, and force-feeding, they embarrassed the President into telling Congress in 1918 that the vote for women was "vital to the winning of the war." The Nineteenth Amendment, which made suffrage every citizen's right, was passed by the House of Representatives on January 10, 1918, and by the Senate in June 1919.

To some extent, the war had released the younger generation from the grip of the old. Women now regarded cigarette smoking and drinking in public as part of ordinary life. Skirts were shorter and options wider, with more cars on the roads, movies to be seen, mass-circulation magazines to be read, fashions to be followed. Sex could no longer be kept out of conversations or away from public view. Eighteen-year-old boys had been sent three thousand miles from home to kill for their country, to "an essentially lower-order existence," where drinking was cheap and easy, prostitutes plentiful, swearing a mark of masculinity and a shortcut to male bonding. "These kids all cuss whether they want to or not," one YMCA secretary remarked, and he addressed a short lecture on the subject to a unit fresh in from the front line. " 'When you get back,' I said, 'You'll sit down at the family breakfast table. . . . Your mother will want to be filling up your coffee cup again, and your little brother will be crowding up against one side of you and your kid sister against the other, and you'll look across the table and say: 'Goddammit, Ma, where in hell's the butter?' "

In the words of one popular song, "How you gonna keep 'em down on the farm after they've seen Paree?" It was all part of a social upheaval that the war had accelerated dramatically. The prewar guardians of "high culture," who were closely associated with the value system that had brought America into the war, were under siege as never before; the "liquidation of genteel culture" was under way in earnest. One of the most efficient solvents was the war's redistribution of wealth, which had tilted the balance of cultural power away from respectable middle-class, fixed-income America. Those who set the cultural standards now were younger, and the war gave them the opportunity to express their sense of alienation and rejection of conventional values with the extraordinary ferocity that drove the Roaring Twenties.

As new dynamics had been created, other forces for change had been stilled. The enforced assimilation of the war period, the walls now surrounding *Kultur*, the synthetic hatred that had imperceptibly become real, all conspired to limit the role of ethnic Germans in the development of the Republic.

The war had also, as Wilson had found to his cost, stunned the progressive movement, at least temporarily. Before the war, progressives had helped to stir the melting pot, promoting the old American values of individual liberty, equality of opportunity, fairness, and generosity of spirit. Now the prevailing intellectual climate was tinged with the self-interest and intolerance of the last months of the war, sentiments that tended more toward exclusion than inclusion.

Prewar ethnic and religious divisions had been sharpened. Despite the impressive service of Jews in the armed forces, anti-Semitism came closer to the surface; in 1920, the president of Harvard restricted the number of Jews he admitted, in order, he explained, to stop the spread of anti-Semitism among students.

But almost inevitably, it was African Americans who suffered worst of all from the new intolerance. Blacks' cooperation in the war effort was barely recognized, let alone rewarded with reforms. A black adviser to the administration pointed out that "Negro people" had been encouraged by government propaganda—in the Liberty Loan and Food Administration campaigns, in the speeches of the Four-Minute Men, through the work of the Negro Press Division of the CPI—to think of themselves as partners in the service of the nation. They had begun to hope for the vote and the right to serve on juries, for better education and an end to the "Jim Crow" laws, for justice in the courts and access to jobs in the civil service. Instead, they were seeing an escalation in racial violence: thirty-eight lynchings in 1917, fifty-eight in 1918, seventy in 1919 (including the killing of ten veterans in uniform). Ten blacks were burned at the stake in 1919. The Ku Klux Klan was back in action from Texas to New England, with a broad program "for uniting native-born white Christians for concerted action in the preservation of American institutions and the supremacy of the white race." "Americans can see," remarked Norman Angell,

> that the things defended by the British Government in Ireland are indistinguishable from what brought upon Germany the wrath of Allied mankind. But they do not even know . . . that every week there takes place in their country . . . atrocities more ferocious than any which are alleged against even the British or the German. Neither of the latter burn alive, weekly, untried fellow-countrymen with a regularity that makes the thing an institution.

Blacks' protests grew louder when returning veterans reported on their treatment in the American Army during the war, which had been thrown into sharper relief by their warm reception by the French. "The fight against prejudice on the part of those whose hides and homes and families were being protected by the black warriors of the 369th and other Negro units was the hardest fight of all," complained the *Crusader* magazine in April 1919 in an article entitled "Fighting Savage Hun and Treacherous Cracker." White officers "of the white feather variety" who reserved the hottest shell holes and filthiest jobs for blacks; YMCA officials who saved candy and tobacco, unimaginably important to morale, for whites; the "white roses of no-man's-land" who neglected wounded blacks to nurse even wounded Germans in preference; white liaison officers who told French civilians that black troops would rape and butcher their women: "the 'Hell Fighters' might as well have been fighting the AEF for all the support they received from it. It was only after they had been placed with the French that they began to make their fighting qualities tell upon the Hun."

Despite all this, some black soldiers had ambitions to go on serving their country. But these ambitions were dashed when the Chief of Staff of the 92nd Division told them openly that he would disapprove all applications from black officers to be commissioned in the regular army; he filled out the rejection documents while they stood in front of him. At Camp Meade, Captain T. Dent, 368th Infantry, was told by his examining body that he was unqualified to be an officer in the postwar regular army by reason of "the qualities inherent in the Negro race."

The war destroyed any hope of moderate, neighborly black integration in the immediate future, along the lines advocated by Booker T. Washington. The stage was set for confrontation: "Beyond a doubt," the MID noted in August 1919, "there is a new negro to be reckoned with in our political and social life." Black radicals such as W. E. B. Du Bois emphasized the savage irony of fighting for democracy abroad only to return to political and economic oppression at home. The pages of the *Crusader* were filled with calls to action:

> There is a wondrous symbol
> Which has come from 'cross the sea.
> It's worn by every member
> Of the Fifteenth Infantry:
> A snake, curled up, prepared to strike—
> And one can plainly see
> That, by its threatening attitude,
> It says, "DON'T TREAD ON ME!"
>
> O! race! make this your battle cry—
> Engrave it in your heart.
> It's time for us to "do or die,"
> To play a bolder part.
> For by the blood you've spilled in France
> You must—and will—be free.
> So, from now on, let us advance
> With this, "DON'T TREAD ON ME!"

In Washington, D.C., in July, a fight between black and white veterans, over alleged attacks on white women, set off four nights of chaos distinguished from previous riots by the quasi-military tactics and weaponry used at times by both sides, with some soldiers making an "advance movement in circular fashion," others taking to the rooftops with grenades.

A week later, a black boy swimming near a white beach in Chicago was stoned in the water and kept from coming ashore until, exhausted, he drowned. The resulting riots lasted for thirteen days and left fifteen whites and twenty-three blacks dead. These were the first of some twenty-five race riots that would break out before the end of 1919. Leonard Wood, increasingly used as a hard-line troubleshooter in such situations, brought troops to Omaha, Nebraska, in September, when a crowd of almost 20,000 people gathered round a courthouse where a black man accused of "forcibly detaining" a white girl was being held. Wood was not in time to prevent the mob's setting the courthouse afire and dragging out the black suspect and the mayor, who had been trying to keep them out. The mayor was cut down by his detectives from the tree where he was being lynched; the suspect was not so lucky. "A rope was placed around his neck, the body drawn up and riddled with bullets by the mob. The body was afterward cut down and pulled through the streets on the end of a rope to 16th and Doge, where it was burnt."

One striking feature of black radicalism in these years is the enormous volume of intelligence material on the subject in contemporary government files, reflecting a level of monitoring that had simply not been possible before the war. Almost overnight, the very nature of government had changed. America might try now to return to the demilitarized society of prewar days, but the relationship between the American citizen and his government had been permanently altered by the experience of total war.

Manpower was one of the key elements in a nation's war effort, to be "managed" to the same extent as the others, whether financial resources, raw materials, or industrial output. Despite Wilson's insistence that the mobilization should be democratic, the American state had acquired a comprehensive range of tools for manipulating its people—from the grassroots snooping of the American Protective League through the professional propaganda of Creel and Herbert Hoover to the systematized surveillance of the Department of Justice and military intelligence—whose attentions would not be confined to the black population. In its postwar planning, the General Staff produced the remarkable "War Plans—White," whose target "White" was the American people as a whole.

When the war ended, this system of controls might simply have been destroyed with the other war agencies. Creel's propaganda machine was in fact destroyed immediately, but the more negative and un-American function of surveillance could not be allowed to disappear, for it was needed to protect the system from the first genuine international threat to America: the specter of communism.

43

The Abiding Enemy

Amid all the threats to America's peace of mind that were generated by the war, none was more potent or more enduring than that of communism. The fighting around Murmansk, the "revelations" of a Soviet-German conspiracy, shrill press coverage of industrial discontent incited by foreign radicals, all helped ferment a hostility that was increasingly tinged with fear. Across the Atlantic, in the early months of 1919, most of Europe seemed easy prey for revolution. Deeply anxious, Secretary of State Robert Lansing watched "the flames of Bolshevism eat their way into Central Europe and threaten the destruction of the social order. . . . Bolshevism is gaining ground everywhere. Hungary has just succumbed. We are sitting on an open powder magazine and some day a spark may ignite it."

For those who chose to look, it was not hard to detect Bolshevik activity in America. The military attaché in Paris warned that a "deal of money has been sent to United States, France and Great Britain for Bolsheviki propaganda"; some of the propaganda certainly appeared in socialist papers, and handbills were distributed to returning soldiers and sailors. In April 1919, a "Soviet Government Information Bureau" opened in New York, and John Reed became editor of *The New York Communist*. Bolshevik ideas were much discussed in socialist, anarchist, and even liberal intellectual circles; there were marches and mass meetings under the auspices of the Russian Council of Workingmen, calling for the withdrawal of the Allied invaders from Russia.

In January 1919, Lenin decided to hold a meeting of Communist representatives from all over the world—the "Third International"—in

Moscow. The manifesto for the meeting was addressed to named groups, four of which were American, including the left wing of the American Socialist Party and the Industrial Workers of the World. None of these attended, but in the American public's mind, Lenin's summons had conjured up the specter of international revolution even nearer to home.

The year 1919 was a year of mounting unrest, as union leaders watched prices rise and many of their wartime gains evaporate. Now that the administration did not have crucial contracts to fill in a race against time and the labor pool was full again, there was less reason to conciliate the unions. The links formed between the government and business by Bernard Baruch proved stronger than those forged with Samuel Gompers and organized labor. Without such fundamentals as the right to collective bargaining, the unions found they had little on which to build.

Simply to keep what it had won, labor adopted a far more belligerent attitude that played into the hands of Bolshevik agitators eager to raise the temperature—as well as into the hands of employers anxious to discredit organized labor. "The signing of the armistice has removed the checks imposed by the war and labor now feels that it is safe to go as far as it likes," reported the MID. Unfortunately for moderate leaders like Gompers, the first strike—at Seattle—was overtly organized on the Soviet model and colored observers' attitudes toward all the subsequent labor unrest.

At the end of January 1919, seventeen unions of the Seattle Metal Trades Council withdrew their labor in protest over a lowered wage rate in the shipyards. Faced with the virtual certainty that the employers would make no concessions, the Central Labor Council called a general strike for February 6. The mayor of Seattle, Ole Hanson, called in troops and tarred the strikers as Bolsheviks. After four days, the strike collapsed, and Hanson resigned his office to tour the country lecturing on the "Red Peril": "Our terms are Deportation, Incarceration, Annihilation."

By the end of the year, 4 million workers had gone on strike in 3,600 separate actions. The largest, bitterest, and most significant were a police strike in Boston in September that left the city "at the mercy of the mobs"; a steel strike in Gary, Indiana, in October; and coal strikes later the same month. A variety of weapons was used to crush them: in Boston, the National Guard restored order. Leonard Wood sent regular troops into Gary, and the Attorney General issued an injunction against the coal miners. In each case, labor's defeat undid much of the progress of the war years; the strikes were equated with disloyalty, and employers' federations, which were resisting the closed shop, now claimed that unionism "ranked with Bolshevism."

Blacks too were suspected of Bolshevik inclinations. *The New York Times* ran an article in July headed REDS TRY TO STIR NEGROES TO REVOLT. There was some truth in the suggestion that white radical organizations were attempting to mobilize black resentments to serve their own cause. The IWW expressly canvassed blacks, claiming to be the only labor organization to welcome the Negro, and the MID acknowledged that it was "daily winning new converts among negroes."

But the most solid proof that Lenin had indeed arrived in America was the formal foundation of two Communist parties. By 1919, many of the surviving members of the American Socialist Party stood on the extreme left wing. When they captured the National Executive Committee and began to demand that the Socialist Party set up a system of soviets and declare its approval of attempts to overthrow the government by force, the more conservative, old-school leaders expelled them. The outcasts responded by forming two separate Communist parties: the Communist Party of America, whose members were mostly foreign-language speakers under the direct influence of Russia, and the Communist Labor Party, who were mostly native-born Communists under the leadership of John Reed.

Suddenly, Bolshevism in America was more than a shadow; it was concrete enough to provoke a backlash, and its opponents translated their vague fears and suspicions into angry words and actions. An Episcopalian minister caught the mood when he announced that America owed Communists "nothing but sufficient voltage to rid the earth of them." More moderately, *Harper's Bazaar* warned its genteel readers of the "plague abroad in the land," and pressed them to apply the all-purpose cure of Americanization.

The MID took steps to thrust a wedge between blacks and the IWW, both supposed pawns of the Bolsheviks. A carefully faked pamphlet addressed to "Distributors of IWW Literature," supposedly from IWW headquarters, was circulated in Arizona late in 1919, obviously in the hope that it would be seen by blacks and cause them to recoil from men who might otherwise be their natural allies. "Extra activity in realigning the negro is desired," the IWW leaders were represented as saying.

We do not exactly want him in the organization, but we want him to help stir up unrest and general disorder. The negro is rapidly rising to a high position in useful citizenship and standing. We need to break this up. If we can dissociate him from his present tendencies to what they call good citizenship and get capital down on him, we can drop him out of the association later.

Others were less devious and more physical in their methods. Vigilantes, many of them veterans, broke up radical meetings and May Day marches. On May 6, 1919, one ex-sailor in a patriotic crowd noticed that a man—obviously a radical—had not stood up during the singing of "The Star-Spangled Banner"; he shot him three times in the back, to the cheers of onlookers.

The American Legion tended to favor the direct approach. The Legion was the largest of the many veterans' organizations; founded in February 1919 by members of Pershing's staff under the leadership of Colonel Theodore Roosevelt, Jr., it was always intended to be more than merely a social club or lobby group for veterans' rights. First among its stated aims was "to inculcate the duty and obligation of the citizen to the state"—and equally to discourage disloyalty and social indiscipline wherever it was found. To some of its members, Red-baiting was second nature.

In Centralia, Washington, during the 1919 Armistice Day parade, a group of Legionnaires moved fast toward the area's new IWW hall with the intention of running the Wobblies out of town. Without warning, IWW members within the building fired on them and killed four. In the uproar that followed, several Wobblies were lynched. One was said to have been castrated first, and the incident passed into the movement's mythology; it would now seem to have been an elaboration, by Ralph Chaplin, of an occasion that was ugly and brutal enough already.

Later that month, a military intelligence officer in Chicago reported a conversation with the secretary of the Black Hawk post of the Legion in Chicago (a former captain in the 86th Infantry). "He informed me confidentially that the American Legion in the city of Chicago intended to do some night riding or what is known as 'Ku Klux' work against radicalism and the IWW": destroying stores selling radical literature, buildings allowing radical meetings, the IWW's Chicago headquarters, and its printers' premises.

This kind of unofficial action, so common during the war, was not only condoned but often reinforced by the authorities at both state and federal level. By 1921, thirty-five states would have enacted laws against sedition or criminal syndicalism laws, and many would have banned the red flag and other Bolshevik symbols. At the federal level, the leader of the attack on radicalism—now as much a target in peacetime as it had ever been in war—was the new Attorney General, Alexander Mitchell Palmer.

Palmer built an entire career on the American public's fear and hatred. First he had exploited hatred of the Hun, while seizing German assets as Alien Property Custodian; now he played upon the fear of "Reds." He had the good political fortune to become the target of radical ire. In June 1919, a bomb smashed in the front of his Washington home (and scattered fragments of the bomber over the façade of the Franklin Roosevelt residence across the way). The attacker's precise political affiliations were never established, nor were the identities of the men who posted some thirty letter bombs to prominent capitalists, with J. P. Morgan as the first of their targets.

Remarkably, Palmer had been Woodrow Wilson's first choice as Secretary of War, but as a Quaker he had been obliged to decline. Now at last he had a position of real power from which to move against the enemies of the state—and perhaps, in the process, gather enough popular acclaim to win him the Democratic presidential nomination in 1920.

Palmer saw "menace" in the "unrestrained spread of criminal Communism's unspeakable social treason among the masses." His problem was to find a federal law that the Bolsheviks were guilty of breaking. There was no broad-based peacetime sedition law, though he had long been canvassing for one, and the wartime Espionage Act covered only countries with which America was at war—which in 1919 did not include Russia, despite the skirmishing around Murmansk. But Palmer did have available the Deportation Act, which permitted him to remove undesirable aliens from the country—and, as the MID reported, "the core of Bolshevism in the United States [consisted] of certain foreign-born groups . . . principally Russians, Russian Jews, and Finns, with minority representations of Lithuanians, Italians, Magyars, Spaniards and Croatians."

Unfortunately for Palmer, to implement the Deportation Act he needed the cooperation of the Secretary of Labor—and the Scottish-born William B. Wilson, an immigrant himself, was not inclined to aid and abet him. When others had tried their hand at mass deportations to deal with strikers in Seattle, Secretary Wilson had gone in person to Ellis Island to review the deportation orders served on thirty-six foreign-born IWW members implicated in the strike and had reversed twenty-five of them.

He now thwarted Palmer by continuing to insist that simply belonging to the IWW did not in itself constitute grounds for deportation. With some of the biggest fish outside his net, Palmer was forced to focus on the minnows, small radical organizations on the fringes. Hoping to realize the political capital to be made out of Red-baiting, he stifled his sense of the ridiculous and ordered a large-scale dragnet to trawl a puddle. He decided he must have a special assistant to take charge of his sweep, and in July 1919 he turned to a man with a track record: J. Edgar Hoover.

Hoover, too, saw the Bolshevik menace as the path to power. He had made himself the Justice Department's resident expert on aliens. Now he used its Radical Division almost as a personal research establishment, to become the government's "first authority on communism." He selected the targets for Palmer, wrote the briefs justifying their deportation, and argued the government's case at the deportation hearings.

Ideally, Palmer and Hoover would have liked to rid the United States of the agitators with the highest profiles. (Hoover also wanted to get at the "Parlor Bolsheviks" and asked for a "list of 'silk-stockinged' men and women who contribute to the radical cause" compiled by New York's Deputy Attorney General.) Thanks to William Wilson, to be clearly subject to the deportation statute, offenders had either to advocate the overthrow of the government or belong to an organization that advocated it. But most of the radical leaders worked alone and chose their words carefully. The only group that now appeared to fall within the range of the statute was the Union of Russian Workers (URW). It was hardly an imposing target. Even to the most paranoid observer, the URW looked far more like a drinking club for immigrants than a hotbed of subversion. The references in its manifesto to "subverting the government" actually related to the overthrow of the Tsar, and its moving spirits had all gone back to Russia shortly after the Revolution.

Palmer and Hoover were not put off, however. On November 7, 1919—the second anniversary of the Bolshevik coup—they took out warrants against six hundred members of the URW, and in a dozen cities across the country local authorities swooped. The catch was large, including a large surplus for whom there were no warrants, but it was deeply unimpressive; the victims were mostly poor and illiterate, unable to explain in English what they did for a living let alone answer the questions fired at them on the nature of communism and anarchism and whether they had "ever had a venereal disease." Two hundred forty-six were classified as eligible for deportation; many more had to be released. On December 21, the U.S.S. *Buford,* nicknamed the "Soviet Ark," set sail for Russia with 184 of the detainees, plus 51 so-called anarchists, including "Red Emma" Goldman, the pince-nez-wearing feminist, anarchist, and birth control reformer, and her lover, Alexander Berkman, a vision in sombrero and Cossack boots—the last two added to the haul to make the boatload look a little less pathetic.

Two weeks later, Palmer aimed higher, with raids on the two American Communist parties. Hoover had prepared briefs maintaining that the membership documents of both the Communist Party of America (CPA) and the Communist Labor Party (CLP) advocated the overthrow of the government by force. By this reasoning, once membership in either party was proved, the offender, if an alien, could be deported; Hoover now added that if he were a native, he could be prosecuted under the laws concerning criminal syndicalism.

Hoover's methods were even more dubious than this thesis. He got the Labor Department to sign 3,158 warrants—3,068 for the CPA, 90 for the CLP. The warrants all had to be drawn up and served at once, since any advance notice would enable the organizations to destroy their all-important membership documents. But this meant recruiting police and volunteers, including ex–American Protective League members, to help in the raids, and many, as was their habit, exceeded their brief.

On January 2, 1920, Hoover's forces carried out raids in thirty cities in twenty-one states, pouncing on offices, meeting halls, private houses, saloons, and poolrooms and rounding up suspects in their thousands, almost twice as many as the number of warrants. The detainees were not offered bail and were kept in conditions ranging from fair to disgraceful; in Detroit eight hundred were kept cooped up in windowless corridors for days without access to washrooms. Some were handcuffed or chained; intimidation was used on others to get them to admit to membership.

Until this point, the public mood had supported Palmer and Hoover. The wave of antiforeigner hysteria generated during the war had been sustained by the labor troubles and the Bolshevik menace. But in 1920, emotions were beginning to subside. Bolshevism was securely locked inside Russia, a country that presented no military threat to the United States;

Europe, even Germany, had weathered the Bolshevik storm; and labor troubles in America were virtually at an end with the return of prosperity and rising employment figures.

The "Red Scare" now seemed grossly exaggerated, and suddenly the conduct of the hunters was more of a threat to democracy than that of the prey was. Assistant Secretary of Labor Louis B. Post—"Comrade Louie," Hoover called him—was given ultimate responsibility for the deportations in March 1920 and immediately echoed Secretary Wilson's argument that deportation could not be imposed without proof of individual guilt. Thousands of warrants were canceled and deportations were halted while Palmer and Hoover waited for the Supreme Court's ruling as to whether mere membership in a guilty organization was enough, and the momentum of the charge was destroyed. The dragnet raids were abandoned, and the "Red Scare" was over. So, too, was Palmer's career; there was so little interest in his candidacy for the Democratic nomination in 1920 that he was forced to withdraw it. J. Edgar Hoover, however, was firmly entrenched: by 1926, he was able to boast that he had files on 1.5 million Americans.

The collapse of the Palmer-Hoover drive against the "Reds" cleared the air and helped people to see the supposed Bolshevik menace for what it really was. There were probably never more than 70,000 Communist sympathizers in total in America during this period, and while the strength of their convictions was not in doubt, nor their deep indebtedness to Bolshevism, their effective influence was limited. Many were foreign-born radicals, but the majority were recent immigrants and their power was severely restricted by their poverty and illiteracy. There were black sympathizers— but there were no blacks in the Communist parties. As militant leader Marcus Garvey pointed out, "They are all white men to us and all of them join together and lynch and burn negroes."

But though the "Red Scare" itself was over, much of the underlying fear and hatred of aliens lived on. Millions upon millions of potential new immigrants were waiting to leave war-ravaged Europe, but the intolerance generated during the war had given huge impetus to the campaign to stem the incoming tide. New immigration laws were drafted, and inexorably America began to close her gates in the faces of the huddled masses.

44

"When Johnny Comes Marching Home"

Little though the Allies cared to acknowledge the fact, the United States emerged with credit from the Great War. American money, materials, and manpower had saved the Allies from near-certain defeat and built the platform from which the drive to victory could be made. But the cost was immense in money, ecological damage, a fragmented society, and the disillusion of a dream gone sour. And the most painful price was paid, cash on the nail, by the soldiers of the AEF.

The final total of American dead in the First World War was 75,658. Of these, 34,249 would be listed as killed in action—that is to say, they had died before receiving medical attention—while 13,691 had died of their wounds after receiving medical attention. The Marines had the highest percentage of casualties—four out of ten officers dead or wounded, three out of ten men. The 2nd Division had the highest aggregate of casualties (25,232) and the highest number of decorations, including seven Medals of Honor. (For the Army as a whole, the War Department ordered 511 miles of medal ribbon.)

In all, 23,937 men died of disease, the majority from influenza; many caught the disease in the trains taking them to their embarkation points or in the transports crossing to France; many more died without ever leaving the camps. And 3,681 died by suicide, murder, or accident.

Most of the battlefield dead were initially buried where they fell, hastily covered with earth by their comrades; shell holes were used as mass graves, topped by rough crosses or cairns of rubble with indications of the units involved, to attract the attention of the burial parties coming up behind.

Amid the chaos, danger, and misery, the soldiers performed this service as carefully as they could; less than 2 percent of American dead remained unidentified.

Many of the dead were recovered from the battlefield graves after the war and reinterred in eight military cemeteries, one in Belgium, one in England, and six in northern France: 2,200 graves at the cemetery at Belleau, which took most of the dead from the Marne; 6,000 at the Oise-Aisne cemetery; 4,100 at Saint-Mihiel; 1,850 at the Somme cemetery; 1,500 at the Suresnes cemetery; 14,117 at the Meuse-Argonne cemetery at Romagne-sous-Montfaucon.

The mothers and fathers, sisters and brothers of the dead, if they were able to visit the cemeteries, found (and still find) them to be meticulously tended, dignified, peaceful places in the green French countryside. The evidence of the doughboys' suffering, the violence and the horror, was quickly tidied away and grassed over, though the landscape would be scarred for years to come. The human wreckage that came home was often harder to accept.

The wounded came home by the boatload, their numbers increasing all the time. Hoboken, New Jersey, one of the principal ports of disembarkation, received 169 casualties from France in February 1918; the total in July was 539. In September, once the system had processed the wounded from Belleau Wood and the Marne, Soissons, and the Vesle, 1,883 came home; in October, after Saint-Mihiel, it was 2,666; in November, as the wounded poured in from the Meuse-Argonne, the figure was 3,474. During the relative calm of the armistice negotiations, 18,443 came home in December, and this monthly rate would be maintained through the spring of 1919.

Their wounds were specialities of the Western Front. To deal with an unusually high proportion of injuries to the face, typical of trench warfare, American dentists developed a new expertise and American physicians gave medical science the team approach to reconstructive facial surgery.

Gas gangrene was an occupational hazard of fighting over heavily manured agricultural land. Shrapnel carried dirt and scraps of clothing with it and was rarely traveling fast enough to exit; if a fragment lodged in a fleshy part of the body, the flesh closed behind it, shutting off the air and creating the ideal conditions for gangrene, which men rarely survived without amputation. More left arms were lost than right, as the left arm was generally unprotected while the soldier lay in position for shooting in the trench and wounds were aggravated by fragments of the wristwatch.

Injuries to the mind were less conspicuous than the empty sleeve or the artificial leg, but they disabled 69,934 American soldiers temporarily or permanently, and war trauma was still emerging in the late 1920s. In 1918, techniques for the diagnosis of mental illness were not sophisticated. The medical services at home, working under immense pressure, had tried to filter out the mentally unfit from units embarking for France, but often there had been no time to do more than simply ask organizational commanders for lists of "dull, queer or nervous men" in their units. Many cases of "feeblemindedness" slipped through, greatly complicating the task of doctors in France trying to distinguish the shell-shocked and traumatized from the sound but slow. Some were diagnosed as psychoneurotic when they simply had a mental age of less than ten; what life on the battlefield can have been like for them is hard to imagine.

The medical authorities had had no idea of the number of mentally ill casualties they should expect. The debarkation hospital in Newport News, Virginia, was proudly scheduled to open on November 17, 1918, with 30 beds for acute psychoses, 110 for neuroses. Unfortunately, already on October 13 the *Aeolus* had docked with a total of 127 psychoses and 39 neuroses, plus 55 epilepsies, 18 "feebleminded," and 3 diseases of the nervous system. There was no advance notice, and the ship arrived with its crew ravaged by flu. "Two patients hung themselves on the ship, one on the last day of voyage and one while the transfer from boat to train was going on. The ship, of necessity, carried these patients between decks without lights from sunset to sunrise."

To try to understand the nature and effects of the war, Eleanor Roosevelt made herself visit the mental ward of Saint Elizabeth's Hospital in Washington, D.C. To be allowed to talk to the men, she had to be locked into the ward, and she never forgot the time she spent with battle-shocked sailors, "some chained to their beds, others unable to stop shouting of the horrors they had seen."

For the physically disabled, the administration had the best of intentions. Treatment was becoming far more enlightened, with a heavy emphasis on reabsorbing the disabled into the community and helping them to become self-sufficient again. Therapy and vocational training were to be offered to the disabled man "to enable him to enjoy the freedom and hap-

piness afforded by worldwide democracy for which he has given his all."
The Red Cross Institute for Crippled and Disabled Men in New York selected six main trades as suitable for the rehabilitated: the manufacture of
artificial limbs; oxyacetylene welding; mechanical training; monotype casting in printing establishments; motion-picture operation; and jewelry making. Corps of "cheer up men," who had overcome their disabilities with the
right spirit, were to be attached to transports and hospitals; and the Red
Cross Institute organized "cripple parties" to put the wounded in touch
with "successful cripples."

America, courtesy of its Civil War, already led the world, in company
with the Germans and Danes, in the manufacture of artificial limbs. "Italian boys prayed to the Madonna for 'an American leg.' " Experience had
taught that complicated prostheses tended to break, so American manufacturers placed function before appearance. They made artificial feet with
enlarged soles for the disabled agricultural worker needing to walk on
plowed soil, as well as arms to which devices could be attached for grasping the reins of a horse, grips for turning a cream separator, or a hook to
hold a plow handle.

In some trades, of course, such as sales, looks did count. There one
might be given the more attractive, better-groomed *"bras de parade,"* or
"Sunday arm," whose use had otherwise "fallen into disfavor except as a
luxury for dress occasions or for the use . . . of men in occupations where
appearance is an important factor in economic efficiency." Artificial eyes,
remarked the medical officers, "do contribute greatly to availability in the
labor market and to peace of mind," and there was some pressure on the
authorities to provide a type of cosmetic ear that had been developed by
the French. "The wounded man leaves the hospital . . . taking with him
the model of his ear and a jar of paste, tinted to match his complexion, and
he can make himself a new ear when he needs one, which will be usually
about every eight days."

The highly efficient War Risk Insurance plan introduced by the administration had made certain that the great majority of men were insured
against disability. But when the time came to administer the payments
going out, officials found some difficulty in gauging the degree of affliction.
It was safe, they decided, to allot $100 a month for "the loss of both feet
or both hands or both eyes, or . . . becoming helplessly and permanently
bedridden"—though one could never be sure that some of the men with
these disabilities might not be capable of earning a decent living: "A man

who has lost both arms now runs one of the busiest newsstands in New York City. A man who lost two legs, one arm and four fingers of the remaining hand is a flourishing business man in a Western State." One must make an effort, they concluded, to discount "the feeling of compassion that will persist for any visible mutilation of the human body even if it is proved to the intellect that the portion of the body which has been lost is of no economic importance." For all the pious hopes that went into the program, in 1926 veterans of the Civil War were still getting more in pensions than men living on World War disability awards.

As for the survivors, those neither killed nor seriously wounded, at the Armistice 1,980,654 men were in Europe, in transit, or in Russia. Another 1,689,998 were in camp in America. Getting home was the only thought in most men's minds. Captain Harry Truman, the future President, had served his country during 1918 as an artillery officer in the ill-fated 35th Division, so badly mauled in the Exermont ravine. In January 1919, he was still stuck in France, his only hope being that "Woodie" might soon "cease his gallivantin' around and send us home at once and quickly." The AEF, in Truman's opinion, did not "give a whoop (to put it mildly) whether Russia has a Red Government or no Government; and if the King of the Lollipops wants to slaughter his subjects or his Prime Minister, it's all the same to us."

In the cold and mud of winter in northern France, the tension of war relaxed into purposeless military routine and discipline began to be sorely tested. Large numbers of men with previously blameless records went AWOL, ending up in Paris. Others shot the light fixtures out of their billets or picked off chickens in village streets. Fifty-one new companies of military police were created. Trains carrying supplies for the American occupation forces in Germany were looted by gangs of veterans; four soldiers were killed on separate occasions by the same low bridge while riding on the top of a railroad car. A French soldier was killed by an American truck driven, in the words of the court-martial report, "at exaggerated speed, at least 20 kph."

When the veterans finally did reach home, they looked for some recognition of what they had achieved, some understanding of what they had endured; but time after time they were disappointed. After the welcome parades, they returned to their hometowns—to find, very often, that their jobs were gone. The special employment offices simply could not cope with the lines of veterans looking for work; by May 1919, more than eight thousand officers alone had asked for help finding jobs. Former engineers, clergymen, accountants, teachers, clerks, physicians, attorneys, dentists, brokers, all had been squeezed out of their former slots in society. In the ranks, hundreds of thousands of blue- and white-collar workers found their old jobs filled, at least temporarily, by women or blacks.

All around them, men who had stayed at home in war industries commanded what seemed like remarkable wages. The returnees were faced with astonishing price rises—food, clothing, and home furnishings all at nearly double the prices they remembered—and a government that apparently grudged them any help in meeting the bills. The veterans of earlier wars could look to their war bonuses to give them a start in their new life. But this administration was determined to avoid the colossal expenditure of the past, and there was violent argument in Congress over the appropriate reward for veterans' services. Not until 1924 would any allocation of bonuses be finally agreed on, and no actual payments would be made until 1945.

Veterans' bitterness found its way into some of the best and most enduring writing of the period. Some older writers, such as Willa Cather, Edith Wharton, and others who had helped but not fought, still found it possible to revel in the romance of war, and the popular conceptions of heroism and adventure died hard. But for those who had been to Europe with the AEF or the ambulance services, such as John Dos Passos, e e cummings, and Ernest Hemingway, a far more typical reaction was to find creativity in anger, cynicism, and a kind of licensed rebellion. The scarred veteran, it was felt, was entitled to speak his mind. The writing of Laurence Stallings, who had lost a leg after injuries received at Belleau Wood, was powered at this stage, before nostalgia took a hand, exclusively by rancor. In his novel *Plumes*, the protagonist is obsessed by the secret treaties signed by America's allies, all the time "trying to face the fact that he threw himself away [in] . . . a brutal and vicious dance directed by ghastly men. It was the tragedy of our lives that we had to be mutilated at the pleasure of dolts and fools."

In *Company K*, William March attacked one of the standard texts of the old value system in his grotesque burlesque of an official letter of condolence:

Your son Francis, died needlessly at Belleau Wood. You will be interested to hear that at the time of his death he was crawling with vermin

and weak from diarrhea. . . . A piece of shrapnel hit him and he died in
agony, slowly. . . . He lived three full hours screaming and cursing. . . .
He had nothing to hold onto, you see: He had learned long ago that
what he had been taught to believe by you, his mother, who loved him,
under the meaningless names of honor, courage, patriotism, were all lies.

Disillusionment about the war and anguish at its aftermath were not
confined to the ranks. Woodrow Wilson spent a sick, introspective, lonely
retirement until his death on February 3, 1924, at the age of sixty-seven,
living long enough to see his vision of the postwar world in ruins. His son-
in-law William McAdoo, the financial powerhouse of his administration,
had disappointments of his own, failing three times to win the Democratic
nomination. Herbert Hoover, in contrast, would achieve his better-
disguised ambition and win the presidency, only to become one of the most
heavily criticized presidents in American history. Newton Baker turned
his back on the world of the Army and returned to his life as a lawyer, becoming more conservative with age. Josephus Daniels, on the other hand,
emerged more vocally liberal than ever. A newspaperman once more, except for a stretch as the American ambassador to Mexico, he violently attacked the activities of the Ku Klux Klan in North Carolina, championed
the League of Nations and the World Court, and transferred his loyalties
to Franklin D. Roosevelt.

Of the administration's "enemies within," John Reed died of typhus in
Moscow in 1920. He lay in state for seven days guarded by Red Army
soldiers, and thousands of workers came out into the sleet and snow to
watch his interment in the Kremlin wall. "Big Bill" Haywood also took
refuge in Russia, to avoid the twenty-year jail sentence waiting for him at
home. Initially hailed as a revolutionary hero, he was devastated to discover that the Comintern no longer favored the IWW, having higher hopes
of working through the American Federation of Labor. He died in
Moscow in 1929, in his own eyes a traitor to his lifelong cause.

Of the "enemies without," none faced war crimes trials. Ludendorff allied his fortunes with a corporal in the German Army who on Armistice
Day was lying in a hospital, temporarily blinded by mustard gas. In 1923,
Ludendorff appeared on the same platform as Adolf Hitler at a huge rally
in Nuremberg and took part in the failed attempt to seize control of the
government of Bavaria. Acquitted of treason, the Second Reich's former
Supreme Commander stood for the presidency of the new republic in

1925; he came last in a contest that was won by Hindenburg, the man whose name he had made famous.

Ludendorff's end was ultimately less miserable than that of Henri Pétain, who, as the eighty-four-year-old head of the French government in 1940, would seek terms from the Germans; sentenced to death as the principal Vichy traitor and collaborator, Pétain would be spared only because of his age.

Of America's generals, Peyton March was perhaps treated the worst. His acerbic style had made many enemies in Congress, and, humiliatingly, they refused to grant him permanent rank as a full general after the war. Not until 1954, at the age of eighty-eight, would this great soldier receive any official thanks—and then the tribute was carefully worded, referring to his "selfless and patriotic interest in the United States Army *since his retirement.*"

March being what he was, he would not have been hurt half as much by personal pettiness as by the damage inflicted on the army organization that he had helped to revolutionize. Around the globe, other governments and military leaders were digesting the lessons of a first World War—most obviously, the lesson that total war required preparation in time of peace. March handed over piles of documents to staff officers in the Imperial Japanese Army who were anxious to study the American mobilization. His intention was that this evidence of American effectiveness should act as a deterrent: "When those trained Japanese General Staff officers saw precisely what the nation at war meant in men and material, and the rapidity with which we had achieved the results we did . . . there would be no more Japanese problem. . . . It was certain to my mind that Japan would never want to go to war with us." In fact, during the 1920s and 1930s, the Japanese would build elaborate mobilization machinery, listing the nation's resources down to the last chauffeur, which would enable them to go to war with anyone.

In March's own country, on the other hand, Congress deliberately turned its back on the need to prepare in peacetime. Civilian America now balked at funding a large defense establishment. The General Staff had proposed a modified system of universal military service, producing citizen reservists to take the place of the National Army and a greatly increased and professionalized regular army. Congress would have none of either proposal; by mid-1923, the U.S. Army would be down to 131,254 men, little bigger than it had been in April 1917. Only a newly created Industrial College served to remind officers of the intimate connection between the smokestacks and the front line.

Meanwhile, Pershing received the nation's gratitude, a permanent full general commission and the title "General of the Armies of the United States." He became Chief of Staff and won a Pulitzer Prize for his wartime reminiscences (which were sharply critical of March). From time to time he visited Paris and Michette, and late in life he married her. When World War II came, he was an invalid, confined to the Walter Reed veterans' hospital, where the news of war was brought to him by the man his influence had made Chief of Staff: George C. Marshall.

Marshall had defeated another AEF general for the post: Hugh Drum, who had also consistently risen in the postwar army. Douglas MacArthur had already scaled the heights of the Chief of Staff's post. In that role, it had been his task in May 1932, on the orders of President Herbert Hoover, to face the anger of 17,000 AEF veterans who had marched on the Capitol to demand the immediate payment of the bonus, during the depths of the Great Depression. Much as he may have sympathized with their plight, MacArthur had no hesitation in moving on two thousand of the most stubborn with tanks and tear gas, crushing their camps, and scattering the protestors.

The smooth rapidity of MacArthur's rise throws into sharp relief the bumpy passage of Billy Mitchell, another of the most brilliant of the younger men under Pershing's command. For all his drive and inventiveness, Mitchell had been forced to watch the record of America's air service in the war being spoiled by the chaos at home. During the last three months of the fighting, the air forces had been losing planes faster than they were arriving in France. In all, 677 American pilots had died over all, 508 of them in accidents and 263 of those before they ever left America. For every 100 trained pilots who reached the front line, 33 were killed. But just as the war ended, the American air effort was beginning to hit its stride. Satisfactory planes were being built and pilots recruited in large numbers; the service had grown from a mere 1,395 officers and men to almost 200,000.

Mitchell had seen many of his theories vindicated, and he had made the case for equal status for the air service most convincingly. The service was officially recognized as being on a par with the other wings of the Army under the Army Reorganization Act of June 1920. Mitchell's mistake was in the lack of restraint with which he then harried both Army and

Navy commanders to boost their airpower further. In September 1925, he told journalists that the crash of a naval air balloon was the inevitable outcome of the Navy's neglect of aviation; the Army, he added, was no better. He was promptly court-martialed for "conduct prejudicial to good order and military discipline" and seven other offenses. Found guilty, he resigned from the Army the following year.

Saddest of all, perhaps, was the fate of Major Charles Whittlesey. The agony of his "Lost Battalion" stayed with him; he was decorated for his astonishing bravery and endurance, but the burden of suffering he had imposed on his men was too much for him to bear. In 1926, eight years after leading the pathetic remnants of his unit out of their death trap in the Argonne Forest, he put his affairs in order and boarded a boat for Cuba. In midocean he disappeared from the vessel, one more victim of this most terrible of wars.

Acknowledgments

Throughout the research and writing of this book we have received a great deal of help from many people. We should like to thank: Professor Ryuichi Tobe of the National Defense Academy in Tokyo, for drawing to our attention a paper on the Imperial Japanese Army's study of American mobilization; the librarians of the Institute of Historical Research, University of London, in particular Donald Munro for his help in locating microfilmed material; the archivists of the Public Record Office, Kew, London; the staff at the Imperial War Museum, in particular Brad King, Phil Reed, and James Taylor; the staff at the Archives of the Service Historique de l'Armee, Vincennes, Paris; the librarians of the London Library and the British Library; the curators of the Manuscript Division of the Library of Congress, Washington, D.C.; the archivists of the National Archives, Washington, D.C., in particular John Taylor, Rick Peuser, and Mitchell Yockelson. We owe a particular debt to Mitch Yockelson for information that he had collected on the Houston riot and on Native Americans in the AEF, and for his time, effort, and ingenuity in tracking down material to answer our most obscure questions. We owe a similar debt to Dr. Richard Sommers at the Military History Institute, Carlisle Barracks, Pennsylvania. His unique expertise made available a wealth of material we would not otherwise have seen. Through the Western Front Association, we benefited from the chance to discuss themes and topics with scholars and fellow students of American involvement in the Great War, such as Colonel Rod Paschall, Dr. Edward Coffman (who generously gave us a possible lead on the whereabouts of Hunter Liggett's papers), and Professor Charles Burdick (whose paper on Lenin and Woodrow Wilson illuminated our approach to Wilson's world vision). We would like to thank Ian Nish CBE, Professor Emeritus of the London School of Economics, for a contemporary volume of essays from his collection; and Jack Walter, a lifetime student of the First World War, who kindly supplied us with his local historical research on the Calumet region, Indiana. We would also like to thank Charles Burdick for putting us in touch with Agnes Petersen, who greatly helped us in carrying out our research at the Hoover Institution on War, Revolution and Peace at Stanford University.

Any writer depends on his friends to a greater or lesser extent; ours are especially kind and long-suffering, and we should like to thank Joe Stern, Roderick and Kathy Richards, and Evelyn Stefansson Nef, without whom (and Annie) we could not have made our extended stays in Washington, D.C.

We are grateful (as always) to our agent, Peter Ginsberg, for giving life to this book, and encouraging us through the writing. The book was transformed by the sagacity and scrupulousness of our editor, Bob Loomis.

Notes

❧❧❦❧❧

Abbreviations

AAV	Archives of the Service Historique de l'Armée, Vincennes, Paris
AEF	American Expeditionary Forces
AFL	American Federation of Labor
CAB	Cabinet Papers, Public Record Office, Kew, Surrey, England
CIC/WFC	W. Willoughby, *The Capital Issues Committee and War Finance Corporation* (Baltimore: Johns Hopkins U.P., 1934)
CinC	Commander in Chief
CND	Council of National Defense
CO	Commanding Officer
CoS	Chief of Staff
CPI	Committee for Public Information
CWS	Chemical Warfare Service
DoJ	Department of Justice
E	National Archives, Washington, D.C.: Record Group Entry Number
FA	Field Artillery
FAd	Food Administration
FAJ	*Field Artillery Journal*
FDR	Franklin D. Roosevelt

FO	Foreign Office Papers, Public Record Office, Kew, Surrey, England
GHQ	General Headquarters
GS	General Staff
HIoWRP	Hoover Institution on War, Revolution and Peace, Stanford
IWW	International Workers of the World
LoC	Manuscripts Division, Library of Congress, Washington, D.C.
Baker Papers	Papers of Newton Baker
Bliss Papers	Papers of Tasker Bliss
Burleson Papers	Papers of Albert Burleson
Daniels Papers	Papers of Josephus Daniels
Frankfurter Papers	Papers of Felix Frankfurter
Garfield Papers	Papers of Harry Garfield
Goethals Papers	Papers of George Goethals
Gregory Papers	Papers of Thomas Gregory
Harbord Papers	Papers of James Harbord
March Papers	Papers of Peyton March
Mitchell Papers	Papers of William Mitchell
Pershing Papers	Papers of John J. Pershing
Scott Papers	Papers of Hugh Scott
Wilson Papers	Papers of Woodrow Wilson
Wood Papers	Papers of Leonard Wood
M	Microfilm Division, National Archives, Washington, D.C.
MHI	Military History Institute, Carlisle Barracks, Pennsylvania
MID	Military Intelligence Department (later Division)
MIWS	"Military Intelligence Weekly Summary"
MR	Military Representatives
NYT	The New York Times
OUP	Oxford University Press
PRO	Public Record Office, Kew, Surrey, England
PST	Purchase, Storage and Transportation Division

RG	National Archives, Washington, D.C.: Record Group
RIIA	Royal Institute of International Affairs, Chatham House, London
SI	RG 165 Records of War Dept. General and Special Staffs. Office of the Director of Intelligence (G2). General Records. Security Classified *Subject Index* to series 64–65.
SWC	Supreme War Council
USMC	United States Marine Corps
USNIP	*Proceedings of the U.S. Naval Institute*
WD	War Department
WDG&SS	War Department General & Special Staffs
WFA	Western Front Association
WIB	War Industries Board
WIBM	U.S. War Industries Board, *Minutes of the War Industries Board August 1, 1917–December 19, 1918*, 74th Congress, 1st Sess., Senate Committee Print No. 4, Special Committee Investigating the Munitions Industry (Washington, D.C.: U.S. Government Printing Office, 1935)
WTB	War Trade Board
WWI	World War I
WWP	A. Link, ed., *The Papers of Woodrow Wilson*, 69 vols. (Princeton, N.J.: Princeton University Press, 1966–1994)

Prologue: Forgotten Sacrifice

3   "Dark as pitch": Military History Institute, Carlisle Barracks, Pennsylvania, 1st Div. Box, "Tom Carroll's Diary."

4   "All was quiet": Frank Coffman, "And Then The War Began," *American Legion Magazine*, Jan. 13, 1922.

4   "Who are you?": Ibid.

5   "Paul Bordeaux rejoiced": D. Smythe, *Pershing: General of the Armies* (Bloomington: Indiana U.P., 1986), p. 59.

6   "limited capacity . . . for land warfare": J. Terraine, "The Military Structure of the First World War," *Army Quarterly*, 115 (3), July 1985, p. 278.

6   "spent $50.3 billion": J. Franklin Jameson, *Dictionary of United States History* (Philadelphia: Historical Publishing Company. Revised ed., 1931), p. 773. This was the total as of June 30, 1929.

6   "from September 1915": K. Burk, *Britain, America and the Sinews of War* (Boston: George Allen and Unwin, 1985), p. 8.

6   "grotesque $25 billion": Ibid., p. 202 (with exchange rate at $4.76 to the pound).

6   "up to 40 percent": K. Burk, "The Mobilization of Anglo-American Finance During World War I" in N. F. Dreisziger, ed., *Mobilization for Total War: The Canadian, American and British Experience, 1914–1918, 1939–1945* (Waterloo, Ontario, Canada: Wilfrid Laurier U.P., 1981), p. 30. This figure is for September 1916.

6   Pétain's promise: R. F. Weigley, *History of the U.S. Army* (Bloomington: Indiana U.P., 1984), p. 355.

8   "some $38 billion": C. Gilbert, *American Financing of World War I* (Westport, Conn.: Greenwood, 1970), p. 69, gives the cost in 1917–1920 as $38,003.8 billion.

8   "at $192 billion . . . 2 percent": F. Lundberg, *America's Sixty Families* (New York: Vanguard, 1937), p. 499.

1 : The Search for a New America

13   "already as rich": D. A. Shannon, *Progressivism and Post-War Disillusionment 1898–1928* (New York: McGraw-Hill, 1966), p. 20.

13   "traffic cops kept": J. C. Furnas, *Great Times: An Informal Social History of the United States 1914–29* (New York: Putnam, 1974), p. 339.

14   "electricity . . . energy": T. C. Cochran, *The American Business System: A Historical Perspective 1900–55* (Cambridge, Mass.: Harvard U.P., 1957), p. 13.

14   "the gene pool": James R. Doolittle, ed., *The Romance of the Automobile Industry* (1916), quoted in Furnas, *Great Times*, p. 342.

14   "cities were changing": M. H. Yates and B. J. Garner, *The North American City* (New York: Harper and Row, 1971), p. 29.

14   "a dozen cities": G. E. Mowry and B. A. Brownell, *The Urban Nation 1920–1980* (New York: Farrar, Straus and Giroux, 1981), p. 3.

14   "Buildings rose to": Cochran, *American Business System*, p. 20.

14   "Henry James was": W. R. Taylor, *In Pursuit of Gotham: Culture and Commerce in New York* (New York: OUP, 1992), quoted in *Times Higher Educational Supplement* (London), Jan. 8, 1993, p. 21.

14   "single physical entity": A. C. Coolidge, *The United States as a World Power* (New York: Macmillan, 1908), p. 33.

15   "$10,000 a week": Furnas, *Great Times*, p. 128.

15   "Freud . . . first-ever movie": Ibid., p. 44.

15   *"The Negro a Beast":* A. Meier, *Negro Thought in America 1880–1915* (Ann Arbor: U. of Michigan Press, 1963), p. 161.

15   Booker T. Washington: See, e.g., N. A. Wynn, *From Progressivism to Prosperity: World War I and American Society* (New York: Holmes and Meier, 1986), and ibid., pp. 165ff.

15   "Our surest and": Booker T. Washington in *Chapters from My Experience,* quoted in H. Aptheker, ed., *A Documentary History of the Negro People in the United States,* Vol. 2, *1910–1932* (Secaucus, N.J.: Citadel, 1973), p. 5.

15   "wisest among my": I. Katznelson, *Black Men, White Cities* (Oxford, England: OUP/Institute of Race Relations, 1973), p. 49.

16   "Seventy blacks . . . lynched": NAACP Second Annual Report (January 1912) in Aptheker, *Negro People*, p. 38.

16   "peonage": U.S. Attorney General's Report for 1911, in Aptheker, *Negro People*, p. 30.

16   segregation: See D. S. Massey and N. A. Denton, *American Apartheid: Segregation and the Making of the Underclass* (Cambridge, Mass.: Harvard U.P., 1993).

16   "black children . . . per capita": Meier, *Negro Thought*, p. 162.

16   Taft speech and appointments: Katznelson, *Black Men, White Cities*, p. 51.

16   United Colored Democracy manifesto: Aptheker, *Negro People*, p. 21.

16   Du Bois: See, e.g., Meier, "The Paradox of W. E. B. Du Bois" in *Negro Thought*, pp. 190ff.

16   "The function of": *The Crisis*, no. 1, November 1910, in Aptheker, *Negro People*, p. 25.

17   "a dark and . . . It's worth it!": Editorial, *The Crisis*, March 1912, p. 197, in Aptheker, *Negro People*, p. 53.

17   McAdoo fox-trot: W. G. McAdoo, *Crowded Years: The Reminiscences of W. G. McAdoo* (Boston: Houghton Mifflin, 1931), p. 271.

18   "the huge polypus": W. C. Ford, ed., *Letters of Henry Adams 1892–1918* (Boston: Houghton Mifflin, 1938), July 16, 1916.

18   "nesting dingily in": Booth Tarkington, *The Turmoil* (New York: Harper, 1915), p. 183.

18   "ally in Theodore Roosevelt": Furnas, *Great Times*, p. 32.

18   "Edison's son was": E. R. Ellis, *Echoes of Distant Thunder* (New York: Coward, McCann and Geoghegan, 1975), p. 61.

18   "2.4 gallons of": E. Goode, *Drugs in American Society* (New York: McGraw-Hill, 1993).

19   "28,000 patent medicines": Ibid., pp. 286–8.

19   "Gullible Americans will": J. A. Incardi, *The War on Drugs: Heroin, Cocaine, Crime and Public Policy* (Palo Alto, Calif.: Mayfield, 1986), p. 12.

19   "Heroin Square": H. W. Morgan, *Drugs in America: A Social History 1800–1980* (Syracuse, N.Y.: Syracuse U.P., 1981), p. 95.

19   "60 percent of": Ellis, *Distant Thunder*, p. 108.

19   "Dealers laced sweets": Incardi, *War on Drugs*, p. 15.

20   Ludlow massacre: See, e.g., Ellis, *Distant Thunder*, pp. 76ff.

20   " 'lower-level' workers": P. Foner, *A History of the Labor Movement in the United States* (New York: International Publishers, 1965), pp. 122–3.

20   "less for . . . its image": W. Preston, "The Ideology and Techniques of Repression" in H. Goldberg, ed., *American Radicals: Some Problems and Personalities* (New York: Monthly Review, 1957), p. 244.

21   "down in the": William D. Haywood, speech to the First Convention of the IWW, 1905, quoted in A. Fried, ed., *Socialism in America: From the Shakers to the Third International,* 2nd ed. (New York: Columbia U.P., 1990), p. 446.

21   "a son of": Louis Adamic, quoted in Goldberg, *American Radicals,* p. 180.

21   Clarence Darrow: Fried, *Socialism in America,* p. 454.

21   Croly quote: Shannon, *Progressivism and Post-War Disillusionment,* p. 98.

21   "I like a little competition": R. L. Heilbroner and A. Singer, *The Economic Transformation of America: 1600 to the Present* (New York: Harcourt, Brace, 1984), p. 200.

22   "U.S. Steel": B. F. Cooling, ed., *War, Business and American Society: Historical Perspectives on the Military-Industrial Complex* (Port Washington, N.Y.: Kennikat, 1977), p. 50.

22   "Three hundred firms": Heilbroner and Singer, *Economic Transformation,* p. 203.

22   "money monopoly": Cochran, *American Business System,* pp. 81ff.

22   "If monopoly persists": Heilbroner and Singer, *Economic Transformation,* p. 213.

22   "New Freedoms": Woodrow Wilson, *The New Freedom [sic]: A Call for the Emancipation of the Generous Energies of a People* (New York: Doubleday, 1913).

22   "Federal Reserve System": Heilbroner and Singer, *Economic Transformation,* p. 214.

22   antitrust laws and FTC: Cochran, *American Business System,* pp. 56–7.

22   "one third . . . foreign-born": R. H. Ferrell, *Woodrow Wilson and World War I* (New York: Harper and Row, 1985), p. 4.

22   "More than . . . periodicals": S. Vaughn, *Holding Fast the Inner Lines: Democracy, Nationalism and the Committee for Public Information* (Chapel Hill: U. of North Carolina Press, 1980), p. 105.

22   titles from silent films: K. Brownlow, *Behind the Mask of Innocence: Sex, Violence, Prejudice, Crime—Films of Social Conscience in the Silent Era* (London: Jonathan Cape, 1990), pp. 304, 306.

23   "Madison Grant . . . immigration": Furnas, *Great Times*, pp. 53–4.

23   "best of the blood": K. H. Porter and D. B. Johnson, compilers, *National Party Platforms* (Urbana: U. of Illinois Press, 1961).

23   "Their own . . . world": Coolidge, *United States as a World Power*, p. 24.

23   "These men of": J. R. Barrett, "Americanization from the Bottom Up: Immigration and the Remaking of the Working Class in the United States 1880–1930," *Journal of American History*, December 1992, p. 1003.

23   "descend from a": Ibid., p. 996.

24   "In schools and": F. Fitzgerald, *America Revised* (Boston: Atlantic–Little, Brown, 1979), p. 68.

24   Gettysburg Address, etc.: National Archives, Washington, D.C., Record Group RG 12, Office of Education, Entry 6, Box 11, Historical File 1870–1950, File 106, "Americanization War Work."

24   "I take off": "Americanization Committee Issues Primer for Non-English Speaking Adults In Factory Classes," *Chicago Commerce*, in RG 12, Office of Education, Entry 6, Box 11, Hist. File 1870–1950, File 106.

24   "Get the foreign-born": "What a Woman Can Do In Americanization" in ibid.

24   "Trade unions launched": Barrett, "Americanization," p. 1016.

24   "federation of cultures": Randolph Bourne, "Trans National America" in D. Hollinger and C. Capper, eds., *The American Intellectual Tradition*, Vol. 2, *1865—The Present* (New York: OUP, 1989), p. 159. See also L. J. Vaughan, "Cosmopolitanism, Ethnicity and American Identity: Randolph Bourne's Trans National America," *Journal of American Studies* 25 (1991), pp. 443–59.

25   "neither entirely stable": Henry F. May, *The End of American Innocence: A Study of the First Years of Our Own Time* (London: Jonathan Cape, 1960), p. 388.

25   "Nothing is done": Wilson, *New Freedom*, p. 3.

2: On the Edge of the Vortex

26 "Chicago *Record-Herald*": quoted in W. Lord, *The Good Years: From 1900 to the First World War* (London: Longman, 1960), p. 341.

27 "The entrance of": Quoted in Mark Sullivan, *Our Times 1900–1925*, Vol. 5, *Over Here 1914–1918* (New York: Scribner, 1972), p. 21.

27 "the whole world": Ibid., p. 26.

28 export statistics: A. D. Noyes, *The War Period of American Finance 1908–1925* (New York: Putnam, 1926), p. 117.

28 "Bethlehem Steel stock": Ibid., p. 149.

28 "U.S. Steel supplied": Ibid., p. 222.

28 "exports of . . . barbed wire": J. E. Wiltz, "The Nye Munitions Committee 1934" in A. M. Schlesinger, Jr., and R. Bruns, eds., *Congress Investigates: A Documented History 1792–1974*, Vol. 4 (New York: Chelsea House, 1975), pp. 197–8.

29 "old guardians . . . America": Henry F. May, *The End of American Innocence: A Study of the First Years of Our Own Time* (London: Jonathan Cape, 1960), p. 354.

29 "Ten people . . . injured": E. R. Ellis, *Echoes of Distant Thunder* (New York: Coward, McCann and Geoghegan, 1975), p. 270.

29 "district attorney of": Ibid., p. 279.

30 "impartial in thought": C. J. Child, *The German-Americans in Politics 1914–1917* (Madison: U. of Wisconsin Press, 1939), p. 42.

31 "German propagandists . . . 'Mexicans' ": H. D. Lasswell, *Propaganda Technique in the World War* (New York: Knopf, 1927), p. 136.

31 "a secret laboratory": Library of Congress, Manuscripts Division, Woodrow Wilson Papers, Reel 383, memorandum "Improper Activities of German Officials."

31 "Werner Horn": Ibid.

31 "Black Tom Island": see, e.g., Ellis, *Distant Thunder*, pp. 191–2.

32 "apart from . . . Amish": L. J. Rippley, "Ameliorated Americanization: The Effect of World War I on German-Americans in the 1920s" in F. Trommler and J. McVeigh, eds., *America and the Germans: An Assess-*

ment of a 300-Year History, Vol. 2, *The Relationship in the Twentieth Century* (Philadelphia: U. of Pennsylvania Press, 1985), p. 217.

32   "Love of one's": C. Wittke, *The German Language Press in America* (Lexington: U. of Kentucky Press, 1957), p. 222.

32   "The efforts of": Child, *German-Americans,* p. 10.

32   "Ancient Order of": Ibid., p. 6.

32   "backed by the": Rippley, "Ameliorated Americanization," p. 221.

33   "descend to . . . culture": Child, *German-Americans,* p. 169.

34   "I have . . . else.": Quoted in R. H. Ferrell, *Woodrow Wilson and World War I* (New York: Harper and Row, 1985), p. 9.

34   "For two hours": Sullivan, *Our Times,* p. 28.

35   Hoover's physical appearance: G. H. Nash, *The Life of Herbert Hoover,* Vol. 2, *The Humanitarian 1914–1917* (New York: W. W. Norton, 1988), pp. 367–8.

35   "worst public speaker": C. Lloyd, *Aggressive Introvert: A Study of Herbert Hoover and Public Relations Management 1912–1932* (Columbus: Ohio State U.P., 1972), p. 15.

35   "If you . . . about it.": Nash, *Herbert Hoover,* p. 372.

35   "The residents . . . Lafayette Square": Jonathan Daniels, *The End of Innocence* (New York: Da Capo, 1972), p. 146.

35   "Wild West . . . Iroquois": Ellis, *Distant Thunder,* p. 158.

36   "getting the busted": Nash, *Herbert Hoover,* p. 12.

36   "Women all over": H. Hoover, *The Memoirs of Herbert Hoover: Years of Adventure 1874–1920* (London: Hollis & Carter, 1952), p. 177.

36   "Kindly get out": Nash, *Herbert Hoover,* p. 370.

37   "TOURIST SAW SOLDIER": Sullivan, *Our Times,* p. 79.

37   "I was chatting": *NYT,* May 18, 1915, quoted in Elmer Davis, *History of the New York Times 1851–1921* (New York: New York Times, 1921), p. 339.

38   "Many crowded boats": Schwieger's log, quoted in Sullivan, *Our Times,* pp. 114–15.

38   "Find all the": Ellis, *Distant Thunder,* p. 200.

38   "Our propaganda . . . collapsed": Child, *German-Americans,* p. 67. Also see evidence of Dr. Bonn in *Official German Documents relating to the World War: Reports of the 1st and 2nd Subcommittees of the Committee appointed by the National Constituent Assembly to inquire into the Responsibility for the War,* 2d Subcommittee, 15th Sess., April 14, 1920, p. 927. On the weakness of German propaganda in the United States generally, see R. R. Doerries, "The Politics of Irresponsibility: Imperial Germany's Defiance of United States Neutrality During World War I" in H. L. Trefousse, ed., *Germany and America: Essays in Problems of International Relations and Immigration* (New York: Brooklyn College Press, 1980), pp. 6–7.

39   "There are citizens . . . out.": Woodrow Wilson, Third Annual Message to Congress, December 7, 1915, quoted in D. M. Kennedy, *Over Here: The First World War and American Society* (New York: OUP, 1980), p. 24.

3: "To Hell with Peace Talk": Volunteers on the Western Front

41   "To hell with": *Daily Mail* (continental European edition) Feb. 2, 1917.

42   "I have a rendezvous": Alan Seeger, *Poems* (New York: Scribner, 1916).

42   "German-language press commented": See, e.g., "Recruiting Offices in Seattle, Tacoma and Bellingham" in *Seattle German Press,* Mar. 15, 1916; RG 60, Gen. Recs., Class. Sub. Files, Box 78, P1-194.

42   "a blank cheque": Lt. Col. Cuthbert Hoare, Royal Flying Corps, Canada, to L.E.O. Charlton, Director of Air Organisation, Royal Flying Corps, June 1917, quoted in Bradley King, "Americans in the Royal Flying Corps: Recruitment and the British Government," *Imperial War Museum Review* No. 6, p. 89.

42   "the 'American Legion' ": RG 60, Gen. Recs., Class. Sub. Files, Box 78, P1-194.

43   "fed on old": A. G. Empey, *From the Fire Step: The Experiences of an American Soldier in the British Army* (London: Putnam, 1917), p. 28.

43   "The odor . . . party.": Ibid., p. 90.

43   "I felt . . . me.": Quoted in P. L. Hervier, *The American Volunteers With The Allies* (Paris: Éditions La Nouvelle Revue, 1918), p. 183.

44   "terribly distracting": M. A. De Wolfe Howe, ed., *The Harvard Volunteers in Europe* (Cambridge: Harvard U.P., 1916), p. 51.

44   "They whine . . . d'ambulance.": Ibid., p. 119.

44   "I find a positive": Henry James, "The American Volunteer Motor Ambulance Corps in France" (Nov. 25, 1914) in *Within The Rim* (London: Collins, 1918), p. 68.

45   "Anyone who thinks": Howe, *Harvard Volunteers*, p. 196.

45   "the most amazing": Ibid., p. 52.

45   "long lines . . . face.": RG 60, DoJ, Gen. Recs., E 260, Box 1, Woolsey to Judd, Aug. 31, 1917.

46   "office on . . . Fifth Avenue.": King, "Americans," p. 90.

47   "Two valve springs": Quoted in T. C. Leonard, *Above the Battle: War Making in America from Appomattox to Versailles* (New York: OUP, 1978), p. 158.

47   "That our country": Hervier, *American Volunteers*, p. 100.

47   "Raoul Lufbery": B. Robertson, ed., *Air Aces of the 1914–18 War* (Letchworth, England: Harleyford, 1959), pp. 99–100.

48   "villager told them": W. Rawls, *Wake Up, America! World War I and the American Poster* (New York: Abbeville Press, 1988).

4: "I Didn't Raise My Boy to Be a Soldier": The Problem of Preparedness

49   "I didn't raise": Words by Alfred Bryan, music by Al Piantadosi, copyright 1915.

49   "the importance to": P. Karsten, *The Naval Aristocracy: The Golden Age of Annapolis and the Emergence of Modern American Navalism* (New York: Free Press, 1972), p. 369.

49   "a generation behind": B. F. Cooling, ed., *War, Business and American Society: Historical Perspectives on the Military-Industrial Complex* (Port Washington, N.Y.: Kennikat, 1977), p. 38.

50 "Tolstoy . . . Nobel . . . Carnegie": J. C. Furnas, *Great Times: An Informal Social History of the United States 1914–29* (New York: Putnam, 1974), p. 212.

50 "a nice, trim": Entry for Sept. 30, 1918, in *Lord Riddell's War Diary 1914–18* (London: Nicholson & Watson, 1933), p. 364.

50 "a convinced pacifist": D. R. Beaver, *Newton D. Baker and the American War Effort 1917–1919* (Lincoln: U. of Nebraska Press, 1966), p. 1.

51 "a fresh pansy": W. G. McAdoo, *Crowded Years: The Reminiscences of W. G. McAdoo* (Boston: Houghton Mifflin, 1931), p. 342.

51 "exercise world leadership": Woodrow Wilson, *A History of the American People in Five Volumes*, Vol. 5, *Reunion and Nationalization* (New York: Harper's, 1903), p. 299.

51 "collective security . . . new": J. H. Latane, ed., *Development of the League of Nations Idea: Documents and Correspondence of Theodore Marburg* (New York: Macmillan, 1932).

51 "make Don Quixote": *NYT*, Jan. 23, 1917.

51 "the most . . . Independence.": Ibid.

51 "The Pope described": *NYT*, Jan. 26, 1917.

52 "one of the few white men": J. G. Holme, *Life of Leonard Wood* (New York: Doubleday, 1920).

52 "In 1909 . . . maneuvers": Ibid., p. 163.

52 "*The Conquest of America*": J. C. Edwards, "America's Vigilantes and the Great War 1916–1918," *Army Quarterly* 106 (3), July 1976.

54 "Military training is": Furnas, *Great Times*, p. 215.

54 "Take away the": Ibid., p. 219.

54 "Peace Ship": See, e.g., Lella Secor Florence, "The Ford Peace Ship and After" in Julian Bell, ed., *We Did Not Fight: 1914–1918 Experiences of War Resisters* (London: Cobden-Sanderson, 1935).

55 Pulitzer Prize: RG 165, WCD, Gen. Corresp., 1903–1919, Box 172, Aviation Department, 7112-54, Bulletin 139, May 15, 1916.

55 "Edison . . . Daniels": *NYT*, May 30, 1915. See also G. Hartcup, *The War of Invention: Scientific Developments 1914–1918* (London: Brassey's, 1988), pp. 31–2.

55   "Financier Bernard Baruch": R. D. Cuff, *The War Industries Board: Business-Government Relations During World War I* (Baltimore: Johns Hopkins U.P., 1973), p. 32.

56   "engineer Howard Coffin": Ibid., p. 20.

56   "Department of Public Defense": D. R. Beaver, "The Problem of American Military Supply" in Cooling, *War, Business*, p. 77.

56   "prepare adequate programs": Historical Branch, War Plans Division, GS, Monograph 2: *Economic Problems in the United States for the War of 1917* [sic] (Washington, D.C.: War Department Document No. 885, December 1918), p. 7.

57   "In Hawaii": R. S. Kuykendall, *Hawaii in the World War* (Honolulu: Historical Commission, 1928), p. 28.

57   "Beautiful": J. L. Morrison, *Josephus Daniels: The Small-d Democrat* (Chapel Hill: U. of North Carolina Press, 1966), p. 44.

58   "Nuisance and Disturber": *Concise Dictionary of American Biography*, 2d ed. (New York: Scribner, 1977).

58   "Prussianism": Elting E. Morison, *Admiral Sims and the Modern American Navy* (Boston: Houghton Mifflin, 1942), p. 232.

58   "a big, powerful": Bradley Fiske, quoted in A. Rappaport, *The Navy League of the United States* (Detroit: Wayne State U.P., 1962), p. 73.

58   "U.S.S. *Pantalette*": Arthur Grillerman, in *Life*, Sept. 14, 1916, quoted in Morrison, *Josephus Daniels*, p. 74.

58   "campaign against fossilized tradition": Karsten, *Naval Aristocracy*, p. 13.

58   "yeomanettes": E. D. Cronon, ed., *The Cabinet Diaries of Josephus Daniels 1913–1921* (Lincoln: University of Nebraska Press, 1963), entry for Mar. 21, 1917, p. 119. See also F. S. Harrod, *Manning the New Navy: The Development of a Modern Naval Enlisted Force 1899–1940* (Westport, Conn.: Greenwood, 1978), p. 64.

58   " 'gee' and 'haw' ": Jonathan Daniels, *End of Innocence* (New York: Da Capo, 1972), p. 90.

58   "Why should . . . sing?": Mark Sullivan, *Our Times 1900–1925*, Vol. 5, *Over Here 1914–1918* (New York: Scribner, 1972), p. 580.

59 "negotiator on Capitol Hill": Eleanor Roosevelt, introduction to Elliott Roosevelt, ed., *The Roosevelt Letters*, Vol. 2, *1905–1928* (London: Harrap, 1950), p. 17.

59 "global naval dominance": See, e.g., A. Marder, *From the Dreadnought to Scapa Flow: The Royal Navy in the Fisher Era 1904–1919* (Oxford, England: OUP, 1970), pp. 230–3.

59 "too many . . . naval reserve.": D. Trask, "William Shepherd Benson" in R. W. Love, Jr., ed., *The Chiefs of Naval Operations* (Annapolis, Md.: Naval Institute Press, 1980), p. 8. See also M. Simpson, ed., *Anglo-American Naval Relations 1917–1919* (Aldershot, England: Scolar Press/Navy Records Society, 1991), p. 10.

59 "Eight . . . to Mexico": P. Coletta, "The American Naval Leaders' Preparations for War," p. 164.

60 "Under modern . . . struggle.": Baker to Wilson, Apr. 7, 1916, "Memorandum on Preparedness as a Policy" in *WWP*, Vol. 36, p. 431.

60 Baker compromises: Ibid., pp. 431–4.

60 "Council of National Defense": Cooling, *War, Business*, p. 78.

5: "We Can Do No Other": The Decision for War

62 "a battle . . . prepared.": H. Speier, "Ludendorff: the German Concept of Total War" in E. Earle, ed., *Makers of Modern Strategy: Military Thought from Machiavelli to Hitler* (Princeton, N.J.: Princeton U.P., 1941), p. 312.

62 "There was no night": J. Kocka, *Facing Total War: German Society 1914–1918* (Leamington Spa, Warwickshire, England: Berg Publishers, 1984), p. 26.

62 profiteering, black market: Ibid., p. 54.

62 "homosexuality": see, e.g., J. C. G. Rohl and N. Sombart, eds., *Kaiser Wilhelm II* (Cambridge, England: Cambridge U.P., 1982), pp. 287ff., and T. A. Kohut, *Wilhelm II and the Germans: A Study in Leadership* (Oxford, England: OUP, 1991), pp. 104ff.

62 "Jews and mosquitoes": Letter from Wilhelm II to General Mackesen, December 1919, quoted in Daniel Johnson, "Kaiser Bill's Dark Secret of Racial Hate," *The Times*, Oct. 21, 1994.

62 "Freud, who interpreted": *New Introductory Lectures on Psychoanalysis* (1932) quoted in Kohut, *Wilhelm II*, p. 227.

62 "The people wanted": H. W. Gatzke, *Germany and the United States: A "Special Relationship"?* (Cambridge, Mass.: Harvard U.P., 1980), pp. 54–6.

63 "technological and managerial": Kocka, *Total War*, p. 134.

63 "a garrison state": F. Fischer, *From Kaiserreich to Third Reich* (London: Routledge, 1991), p. 68.

63 "live only . . . Fatherland": E. von Ludendorff, *The General Staff and Its Problems: The History of the Relations Between the High Command and the German Imperial Government as Revealed by Official Documents* (London: Hutchinson, 1920), p. 79.

63 "We can only win . . . war.": Ludendorff to Imperial Chancellor, Nov. 2, 1916, "Memorandum on the Extension of Liability to Military Service."

63 "strong resource base": A. Hillgruber, trans. E. Kirby, *Germany and the Two World Wars* (Cambridge, Mass.: Harvard U.P., 1981), p. 43.

63 "strong population program . . . conception.": Ludendorff to Imperial Chancellor, Sept. 9, 1917, in Ludendorff, *General Staff*, pp. 201, 206.

63 "slave labor . . . a week": Hindenburg to von Bissing, Mar. 3, 1917, in ibid., p. 165. See also M. Kitchen, *The Silent Dictatorship: The Politics of the German High Command Under Hindenburg and Ludendorff 1916–1918* (London: Croom Helm, 1976), pp. 95–6.

64 "Objections founded on": War Ministry memorandum, Oct. 7, 1916, in Ludendorff "Memorandum," p. 156.

64 "That the theory": See, e.g., Count Harry Kessler, *Walter Rathenau: His Life and Work* (London: Gerald Howe, 1929), p. 244. See also H. P. von Strandmann, *Walter Rathenau—Industrialist, Banker, Intellectual and Politician: Notes and Diaries 1907–1922* (Oxford, England: Clarendon, 1985), p. 27, entry for July 10, 1917, and C. Paul Vincent, *The Politics of Hunger: The Allied Blockade of Germany 1915–1919* (Athens: Ohio U.P., 1985), p. 47.

64 "boost the morale": Kitchen, *Silent Dictatorship*, p. 121.

65 "This possibility Ludendorff": See, e.g., A. Offer, *The First World War: An Agrarian Interpretation* (Oxford, England: Clarendon, 1989), p. 5, and Doerries, "The Politics of Irresponsibility: Imperial Germany's Defiance

of United States Neutrality During World War I, in H. L. Trefousse, ed., *Germany and America: Essays in Problems of International Relations and Immigration* (New York: Brooklyn College, 1980), pp. 8–9.

65 "amounted to zero": Fischer, *Kaiserreich*, p. 65; Vincent, *Politics of Hunger*, p. 47.

65 "level with Romania's": MIWS, Nov. 17, 1917, "Interrogation of senior member of German General Staff." See also PRO, FO 371 3124 1988838, *Weser Zeitung*, Oct. 14, 1917, criticisms by Major Hoffe of German General Staff.

65 "a fat, rich": James Gerard, quoted in D. Trask, *Captains and Cabinets: Anglo-American Naval Relations, 1917–1918* (Columbia: U. of Missouri Press, 1972), p. 44.

65 "he acted upon": Kessler, *Walter Rathenau*, p. 244.

65 "the Kaiser overruled": G. A. Craig, *Germany 1866–1945* (Oxford, England: OUP, 1978), p. 380.

65 "He did not smile": Memorandum from Lansing to Wilson, Feb. 4, 1917, in *WWP*, Vol. 41, p. 118.

65 striped barber's pole: Mark Sullivan, *Our Times 1900–1925*, Vol. 5, *Over Here 1914–1918* (New York: Scribner, 1972), p. 258.

66 "meticulous, metallic and": B. Tuchman, *The Zimmerman Telegram* (New York: Macmillan, 1966), p. 63.

66 "out every night": Diary of Colonel House, Sept. 9, 1917, in *WWP*, Vol. 44, p. 176.

66 "You stand in": *WWP*, Vol. 40, p. 493.

66 "the liberal element": House to Wilson, Jan. 20, 1917, in *WWP*, Vol. 40.

67 "White civilization": Lansing to Wilson, Feb. 4, 1917, in *WWP*, Vol. 41, p. 120.

67 "sad and depressed": Diary of Colonel House, Feb. 1, 1917, in *WWP*, Vol. 41, p. 87.

67 "man at poker": Memo on neutral countries prepared by British military intelligence, ca. Dec. 30, 1916, in A. Temple Patterson, ed., *The Jellicoe Papers*, Vol. 2, *1916–1935* (Aldershot, England: Navy Records Society, 1968), p. 134.

67　"as fellow pacifists": Jane Addams, *Peace and Bread in Time of War* (New York: 1922), quoted in *WWP*, Vol. 41.

67　"slower than a": F. Lane to G. W. Lane, Feb. 25, 1917, in *WWP*, Vol. 41, p. 282.

67　"pinned merchant vessels": Wilson to joint session of Congress, Feb. 26, 1917, in *WWP*, Vol. 41, p. 283.

68　"public opinion surged": McAdoo to Wilson, Mar. 31, 1917, in *WWP*, Vol. 41, p. 514.

68　"Notwithstanding the difficulties": Robert Russa Moton to Wilson, Mar. 15, 1917, in *WWP*, Vol. 41, p. 412.

69　"I can't keep": J. L. Morrison, *Josephus Daniels: The Small-d Democrat* (Chapel Hill: U. of North Carolina Press, 1966), p. 79.

69　"of calculated outrages": On Mar. 30, 1917, Lansing sent Wilson four memoranda: "Improper Activities of German Officials in the United States," "Violations of American Rights by Germany Since the Suspension of Diplomatic Relations," "Ships Sunk With Loss of American Lives," and "American Ships Damaged or Destroyed by German Submarines"; LoC, Wilson Papers, Reel 383.

69　"wives of American": F. Lane to G. W. Lane, Feb. 25, 1917, in *WWP*, Vol. 41, p. 282.

69　"Three minutes later": Lansing, "Memorandum of the Cabinet Meeting 2:30–5pm Tuesday March 20, 1917" in *WWP*, Vol. 41, pp. 436–44.

70　"disinclined to the": Diary of Josephus Daniels, Mar. 20, 1917, in *WWP*, Vol. 41, p. 445.

70　"had removed . . . objection": Lansing, "Memorandum of the Cabinet Meeting," p. 440.

70　"not desperate for": D. R. Beaver, *Newton D. Baker and the American War Effort 1917–1919* (Lincoln: U. of Nebraska Press, 1966), p. 27.

71　"Apparently he . . . visiting.": Diary of T. W. Brahany, Mar. 21, 1917, in *WWP*, Vol. 41, p. 449.

71　"his own little": Diary of T. W. Brahany, Mar. 31, 1917, in *WWP*, Vol. 41, p. 515.

71　"If the president": Ibid.

71 "Chin shaking, face": E. Sedgwick, *The Happy Profession* (Boston: 1946), pp. 184–5, quoted in R. H. Ferrell, *Woodrow Wilson and World War I* (New York: Harper and Row, 1985), p. 1.

71 "The President spoke": War address, in *WWP*, Vol. 41, pp. 519–27.

72 "Think what it": J. P. Tumulty, *Woodrow Wilson as I Knew Him* (Garden City, N.Y.: Doubleday Page, 1921), in *WWP*, Vol. 41, p. 541.

72 "We are going": *The Congressional Record*, 65th Cong., 1st Sess., Apr. 4, 1917.

73 "Lieutenant Byron McCandless": Diary of T. W. Brahany, in *WWP*, Vol. 41, p. 557.

6: Launching the War Effort

74 "exercise . . . drills . . . profanity!": LoC, Gregory Papers, Box 1, memoranda, July 1917.

75 "plan of sorts": "for conscripting, equipping and training a four-million-man army—a plan Wilson endorsed"—T. Nenninger, "American Military Effectiveness in the First World War" in A. R. Millett and W. Murray, *Military Effectiveness*, Vol. 1 (Boston: Unwin, Hyam, 1988), pp. 116–56.

75 "drawer marked 'J' ": RG 165, Entry 444, Col. John S. Fair, "Fundamentals of Staff Control."

75 "Stephen Ruder": RG 60, DoJ, Gen. Recs. Central Files, Class. Sub. Files, Box 179, Correspondence, P1-194.

75 "without a warrant": Joan M. Jensen, *The Price of Vigilance* (Chicago: Rand McNally, 1968), p. 163.

75 "at the request": See, e.g., RG 60, Entry 114, Boxes 172a–173, File 9-6-12. On Jan. 3, 1918, Merck and Co. of New Jersey put up bonds of $5,000 for 16 employees.

76 "Mr. Otto Mueller": R. G. Powers, *Secrecy and Power: The Life of J. Edgar Hoover* (New York: Free Press, 1987), p. 53.

76 "Ernst Kunwald": RG 60, Gen. Recs., Central Files, Class. Sub. Files, Box 179, Correspondence, P1-194, memorandum from J. E. Hoover to J. Lord O'Brian, Dec. 19, 1917.

76   "One German seaman": RG 60, Gen. Recs., Cent. Files, Class. Sub. Files, Box 180, P1-194, file on George Frank Kuhn.

76   "Preposterously good looking": Arthur Pollen, quoted in M. Simpson, ed., *Anglo-American Naval Relations 1917–1919* (Aldershot, England: Scolar Press/Navy Records Society, 1991), p. 77.

77   "gift for overstatement": Elting E. Morison, *Admiral Sims and the Modern American Navy* (Boston: Houghton Mifflin, 1942), p. 194.

77   "Daniels acknowledged his": Josephus Daniels, *The Wilson Era*, Vol. 2, *1917–1923: Years of War and After* (Chapel Hill: U. of North Carolina Press, 1946), p. 504.

77   "the Warrior's beverage": Morison, *Admiral Sims*, p. 329.

77   "If the time": Ibid., p. 278.

77   "It makes me damn": Ibid., p. 394.

77   "I was fairly": W. S. Sims and B. Hendrick, *The Victory at Sea* (Garden City, N.Y.: 1921), p. 6.

78   "damned un-English weapon": Paul M. Kennedy, *The Rise and Fall of British Naval Mastery* (London: Allen Lane, 1976), p. 245.

78   "on the surface . . . aerial": Karl Doenitz, *Memoirs: 10 Years and 20 Days* (London: Greenhill, 1990, 1st ed. 1958), p. 1.

78   "chattiness . . . British intelligence.": J. Terraine, *White Heat: The New Warfare 1914–1918* (London: Sidgwick & Jackson, 1982), p. 32.

78   "Leading Seaman Stolz": G. Chapman, ed., *Vain Glory: A Miscellany* (London: Cassell, 1968, 1st ed. 1937), p. 625.

78   "captives of our": Terraine, *White Heat*, p. 167.

78   "111 U-boats in": Ibid., p. 17.

78   "hit the periscope": Commander D. Mercer, "Sledge Hammers, Lance Bombs and Q Ships," *USNIP* 87 (4), April 1961, p. 76.

78   Epsom . . . sea lions: A. Marder, *From the Dreadnought to Scapa Flow: The Royal Navy in the Fisher Era 1904–1919* (Oxford, England: OUP, 1970), p. 78.

78   "Gulls were trained": H. G. Herwig, *"Luxury" Fleet: The Imperial German Navy 1888–1918* (London: Allen & Unwin, 1980), pp. 166, 227.

79 "as rude to": Simpson, *Anglo-American Naval Relations*, p. 251.

80 "I shall . . . keep": Sims and Hendrick, *Victory at Sea*, p. 60.

80 "banning American . . . Cork": Sir L. Bayly, *Pull Together! The Memoirs of Admiral Sir Lewis Bayly* (London: Harrap, 1939), p. 233.

80 "Sinn Feiners were": Bayly to Jellicoe, Sept. 1, 1917, in A. Temple Patterson, ed., *The Jellicoe Papers*, Vol. 2, *1916–1935* (Aldershot, England: Navy Records Society, 1968), p. 455. See also E. D. Cronon, ed., *The Cabinet Diaries of Josephus Daniels 1913–1921* (Lincoln: Nebraska Wesleyan U.P., 1963), p. 455.

80 "had severe limitations": Memo by Captain William Wordsworth Fisher, director of Anti-Sub. Division, Sept. 4, 1917.

80 "This subchasing business": An American Officer, "A Destroyer on Active Service" in L. Maxse, ed., *The National Review, 71* (March–August 1918), p. 336.

80 "A saucy . . . Quack": LoC, Daniels Papers, Box 729, "Our Navy in the World War" (1921).

81 "on one vessel": F. Pratt, *The Compact History of the United States Navy* (New York: Hawthorn, 1957), p. 127.

81 "the *Santee*": Lt. Comm. Gosnell, "World War Losses of the U.S. Navy," *USNIP 63* (5), May 1937, p. 632.

82 "Daniels was extremely": LoC, Daniels Papers, Box 729, "Our Navy in the World War"—"Why the Atlantic Fleet Did Not Go As a Unit to European Waters."

82 "submarine cruiser *Deutschland*": Lt. Comm. J. Wise, "U-Boats off Our Coasts," *USNIP 91* (10), October 1965.

82 "I meant to": FDR to Eleanor Roosevelt, July 19, 1917, in Elliott Roosevelt, ed., *The Roosevelt Letters*, Vol. 2, *1905–1928* (London: Harrap, 1950), p. 283.

82 "There are at least": Sims to Page, June 6, 1917, in Morison, *Admiral Sims*, p. 357.

83 "Daniels said we": F. Lane to G. W. Lane, Feb. 25, 1917, in Cronon, *Cabinet Diaries*.

83 "a plain sailor": R. Spector, *Professors of War: the Naval War College and the Development of the Naval Profession* (Newport, R.I.: Navy War College Press, 1977), p. 142.

83 "not . . . 'bright men.' ": Bradley Fiske, *From Midshipman to Rear-Admiral* (London: Werner Laurie, 1919), p. 585.

83 "Not very quick": Marder, *Dreadnought to Scapa Flow*, p. 231.

83 "The real truth": Jellicoe to Vice Admiral Browning, CinC N. America, July 7, 1917 in Temple Patterson, *Jellicoe Papers*, p. 181.

83 "embarrassment and delay": Sims to Pratt, July 3, 1917, in Simpson, *Anglo-American Naval Relations*, p. 238.

84 "mines would eventually": R. M. Grant, *U-Boats Destroyed: The Effect of Anti-Submarine Warfare 1914–1918* (New York: Putnam, 1964), p. 141.

84 "as souvenirs": Herwig, *"Luxury" Fleet*, p. 206.

84 "superior American mine": J. Langdon Leighton, *Simsadus-London: The American Navy in Europe* (New York: Henry Holt, 1920), p. 71.

84 "The closure of": Korvetten-kapitan Hagen, in *Mine- und Seestrategie*, German naval manual M. Dv. 352 (1935), quoted in Marder, *Dreadnought to Scapa Flow*, p. 74.

84 "All we have done": Beatty to Wemyss, Aug. 10, 1918, in Marder, *Dreadnought to Scapa Flow*, p. 68.

84 " 'K-boats' . . . shadow": Lt. H. F. Cope, "U.S. Subs in the War Zone," in *USNIP 56* (8), August 1930, p. 711.

85 *Sterett, Trippe:* Ibid., p. 712.

85 "It is of . . . importance": Simpson, *Anglo-American Naval Relations*, p. 334.

85 "British ships . . . homes.": Ibid., p. 361.

85 " 'a peach' . . . 'Bill H.' ": H. Rodman, *Yarns of a Kentucky Admiral* (Indianapolis, Ind.: Bobbs-Merrill, 1928), p. 276.

85 "incubus": Marder, *Dreadnought to Scapa Flow*, p. 125.

85 "I am sending": Beatty to wife, Feb. 5, 1918, in B. M. Ranft, *The Beatty Papers*, Vol. 1, *1902–1918* (Aldershot, England: Scolar Press/Navy Records Society, 1989), p. 508.

7: The Lists of Honor: Conscription

89   "Hugh L. Scott": See, e.g., Edward M. Coffman, *The War To End All Wars: The American Military Experience in World War I* (New York: OUP, 1968), p. 22.

90   "Walter Lippmann told": Lippmann to Wilson, Feb. 6, 1917, in *WWP*, Vol. 41, p. 134.

91   "Why introduce Prussianism": Joan M. Jensen, *The Price of Vigilance* (Chicago: Rand McNally, 1968), p. 36.

91   "Oh, you call": D. R. Beaver, *Newton D. Baker and the American War Effort 1917–1919* (Lincoln: U. of Nebraska Press, 1966), p. 30.

91   "against having . . . convict.": D. M. Kennedy, *Over Here: The First World War and American Society* (New York: OUP, 1980), p. 18.

91   "What do you know": Beaver, *Newton D. Baker*, p. 33.

91   "A military draft": Coffman, *War To End All Wars*, p. 25.

92   "It would . . . agreeable": May 18, 1917, quoted in R. Stannard Baker and W. Dodd, *The Public Papers of Woodrow Wilson*, Vol. 5 (New York: Harper, 1927), p. 40.

93   "This is . . . arms.": LoC, Scott Papers, Box 28, Scott to McCoy, Apr. 30, 1917; Scott to Dolan, Apr. 26, 1917.

93   draft machinery: For an overview, see J. W. Chambers II, *To Raise an Army: The Draft Comes to Modern America* (New York: Free Press, 1987), pp. 179ff.

93   "Crowder was . . . desk.": Jensen, *Vigilance*, p. 37.

94   "In Hawaii alone": R. S. Kuykendall, *Hawaii in the World War* (Honolulu: Historical Commission, 1928), p. 54.

94   "Ore-passers in Ashtabula": Mark Sullivan, *Our Times 1900–1925*, Vol. 5, *Over Here 1914–1918* (New York: Scribner, 1972), p. 302.

95   687,000, 122,424, etc.: LoC, Baker Papers, Reel 3, p. 507, War Department proclamation, July 12, 1917.

95   "Thousands of doctors": Sullivan, *Our Times*, p. 305.

96   "I was called": E. R. Ellis, *Echoes of Distant Thunder* (New York: Coward, McCann and Geoghegan, 1975), p. 345.

96   gave short shrift: See, e.g., HIoWRP, J. G. Ragsdale Collection, "Conscientious Objection, World War I."

97   "International Bible Students' Association": RG 165, MID Corresp., Box 2770, 10110-510. See also HIoWRP, Ragsdale Collection.

97   "fifteen . . . were killed": Chambers, *To Raise an Army*, p. 212.

97   "saw 164 marriages": Sullivan, *Our Times*, p. 308.

97   "poured carbolic acid": RG 165, WDG&SS, Office of Dir. of Intell. (G2), Gen. Recs., "Service Military, Evasion of," 10101-193, Sept. 10, 1917.

97   "that will make men": Ibid., 10101-160, Jul. 31, 1917.

97   "fitting of eyeglasses": RG 60, DoJ, Centr. Str., Num. Files, 186-233, U.S. vs. Frank T. Hewentine.

98   "to feign malaria": RG 165, WDG&SS (G2), "Service Military, Evasion of," 10101-865, Mar. 12, 1918.

98   "In dealing with": Beaver, *Newton D. Baker*, p. 36.

8: "Bring the Liver Out": Officers of a Democratic Army

99   "Major General Tasker Bliss": Bliss to Baker, May 25, 1917, in *WWP*, Vol. 42, p. 408.

99   "Manifestly a fully-trained": See, e.g., RG 165, CoS Corr., Box 191, "Advance Extract Copy of Program of Training for Training Camps for Candidates for Commission in the Army of the United States, May 15 to August 31, 1918," p. 2, para. 66.

100   "a third . . . corps": *Infantry Journal*, 1919, p. 224.

100   "rich, cultured bourgeoisie": AAV, Le Candidat Inspecteur Auxiliare Mignot to M. le Commissaire Spécial, Chef du Service de Sûreté de la Mission Militaire Français près de l'Armée Américaine, Mar. 18, 1918.

100   "gilded youth and": J. W. Chambers II, *To Raise an Army: The Draft Comes to Modern America* (New York: Free Press, 1987), p. 233.

100   "privileged class": D. R. Beaver, *Newton D. Baker and the American War Effort 1917–1919* (Lincoln: U. of Nebraska Press, 1966), p. 38.

101 "Discipline, precise and": "Advance Extract Copy of Program of Training," op. cit., p. 3, para. 76.

102 "Never hesitate": HIoWRP, Wooldridge Collection.

102 "spirit of . . . again.": Ibid.

103 "27,341": Edward M. Coffman, *The War To End All Wars: The American Military Experience in World War I* (New York: OUP, 1968), p. 57.

103 "Some of the officers": Mignot, op. cit.

103 "I want you": Beaver, *Newton D. Baker*, p. 218.

9: "Are We Still Jim Crow in the Army?"

On this subject generally, see Bernard C. Nalty, *Strength for the Fight: A History of Black Americans in the Military* (New York: Free Press, 1986).

104 "We do not want": LoC, Scott Papers.

104 "The Selective Service": *NYT*, June 10, 1917.

104 "There is no intention": D. R. Beaver, *Newton D. Baker and the American War Effort 1917–1919* (Lincoln: U. of Nebraska Press, 1966), p. 228.

105 "would total 500,000": American Social History Project, *Who Built America? Working People and the Nation's Economy, Politics, Culture and Society* (New York: Pantheon, 1992), p. 240. But see D. S. Massey and N. A. Denton, *American Apartheid: Segregation and the Making of the Underclass* (Cambridge, Mass.: Harvard U.P., 1993), p. 29, which puts the total at 525,000.

105 "a watershed in": A. Meier, *Negro Thought in America 1880–1915* (Ann Arbor: U. of Michigan Press, 1963), p. 170.

105 East Saint Louis riots: P. Foner and R. Lewis, eds., *The Black Worker from 1900 to 1919*, Vol. 5 (Philadelphia: Temple U.P., 1980), pp. 285ff.

105 "scenes of horror": Ibid., p. 287.

106   "In the old": M 1440, War Dept. Papers, Reel 4, M13, "Bulletin for Intelligence Officers" No. 13, Oct. 21, 1918, p. 1.

107   "In talking with": Beaver, *Newton D. Baker*, p. 31.

107   "SOUTH ALARMED BY": PRO, FO, 371 3124/205754, cutting from New York *Tribune*, Oct. 7, 1917.

107   "practically the same": RG 60, Glasser File, Box 9, Mil. Intell. Branch, "Memo re Colored Situation," Nov. 28, 1918.

107   "First Separate Battalion": RG 60, Glasser File, Box 9, memorandum from Provost-Marshal to CoS, Sept. 5, 1917.

107   Houston riot: See, e.g., J. Minton, *The Houston Riot and Courts-Martial of 1917* (Carver Community Cultural Center, n.d.), in file held by Mitchell Yockelson in the Military Reference Branch, National Archives, Washington, D.C. See also Nalty, op.cit., pp. 102–6.

108   "rewarded Baker . . . support": Nalty, *Strength for the Fight*, p. 107.

108   "senior officers had": B. White, "The American Military and the Melting Pot in World War I" in J. Granatstein and R. D. Cuff, eds., *War and Society in North America* (Toronto: Nelson, 1971), p. 46.

108   "widely held stereotype": M. Fletcher, *The Black Soldier and Officer in the U.S. Army 1891–1917* (Columbia: U. of Missouri Press, 1974), p. 155. See also Meier, *Negro Thought*, pp. 161–2.

108   "He had no . . . start with me.": Nancy G. Heinl, "Colonel Charles Young: Pointman" in *Army*, March 1977, p. 31. See also Nalty, *Strength for the Fight*, p. 99.

109   "not only distasteful": See, e.g., Wilson to Baker, June 25, 1917. LoC, Baker Papers, Reel 3, p. 192.

109   "die of nephritis": Heinl, "Colonel Charles Young."

109   "only 45 percent": MHI, "The Colored Soldier in the Army" (Historical Section, Army War College, May 1942), Appendix 27, "Negro Education in the United States."

109   "You who form": Ibid., Appendix 15.

110   "singing plantation songs.": Ulysses Lee, "The Employment of Negro Troops," *The U.S. Army in World War I. Special Studies* 8 (Washington, D.C.: Office of Chief of Military History, U.S. Army, 1966), p. 13.

10: "Over There": Pershing and the Plans for an American Expeditionary Force

112 "The policy we": Lloyd George to Wilson, Sept. 9, 1917, in *WWP,* Vol. 44, p. 126.

112 "Something different should": Wilson to House, Sept. 16, 1917, in Beaver, *Newton D. Baker and the American War Effort 1917–1919* (Lincoln: U. of Nebraska Press, 1966), p. 47.

112 "dismissing the notion": A. R. Millett and W. Murray, *Military Effectiveness,* Vol. 1 (Boston: Unwin, Hyam, 1988), p. 124.

112 "While matters . . . success.": *WWP,* Vol. 44, p. 361.

113 "in uncertain health": D. Smythe, *Pershing: General of the Armies* (Bloomington: Indiana U.P., 1986), p. 3.

113 "an agitator.": May 28, 1917, in *WWP,* Vol. 48, p. 173.

113 Pershing: See generally F. Vandiver, *Black Jack: The Life and Times of John Joseph Pershing* (College Station: Texas A & M U.P., 1977, 2 vols.), and Smythe, *Pershing.*

114 "student of war": Timothy Nenninger, paper presented to 1993 WFA annual conference, Washington, D.C.

114 "Marshall had been": Smythe, *Pershing,* p. 55.

115 "Pershing was appointed": Baker to Pershing, May 26, 1917, in *WWP,* Vol. 42, pp. 404–5.

115 "primitive state of": I. B. Holley, *Ideas and Weapons: Exploitation of the Aerial Weapon by the United States During World War I* (New Haven, Conn.: Yale U.P., 1953), p. 188.

116 "to speak Spanish . . . Philippine Constabulary.": RG 165, WDG&SS, WCD, Gen. Corr., 1903–1919, Box 258, Jan. 19, 1917.

116 " 'earthily profane' . . . 'squeaky' ": Omar Bradley and C. Blair, *A General's Life* (New York: Simon & Schuster, 1983), p. 98.

116 "a most depressed": G. C. Marshall, *Memoirs of My Services in the World War* (Boston: Houghton Mifflin, 1976).

116 "FOR GENERAL PERSHING'S": Edward M. Coffman, *The War To End All Wars: The American Military Experience in World War I* (New York: OUP, 1968), p. 122.

117   "the usual . . . egg . . . lemonade": B. J. Hendrick, *The Life and Letters of Walter H. Page*, Vol. 2 (London: Heinemann, 1923), p. 236.

117   "ambulating refrigerator.": E. L. Spears, *Prelude to Victory* (London: Cape, 1939), p. 33, quoted in D. R. Woodward, ed., *The Military Correspondence of Field Marshal Sir William Robertson CIGS, Dec. 1915–Feb. 1918* (London: Bodley Head/Army Records Society, 1989), p. 7.

117   "separate and distinct": The question of amalgamation is detailed in Army War College Military Records, Historical Section, *The Genesis of the First Army*, at the Military History Institute, Carlisle Barracks, Pennsylvania; and discussed in the cited works of Coffman, Smythe, Woodward, etc.

117   "entirely out of": J. J. Pershing, *My Experiences in the World War* (London: Hodder & Stoughton, 1931), p. 58.

11: "I Hope It Is Not Too Late": The First Division in France

118   "Though I live": J. G. Harbord, *The American Army in France 1917–1919* (Boston: Little, Brown, 1936), p. 80.

119   "I hope . . . not too late.": Edward M. Coffman, *The War To End All Wars: The American Military Experience in World War I* (New York: OUP, 1968), p. 124.

119   "It was . . . touching": J. J. Pershing, *My Experiences in the World War* (London: Hodder & Stoughton, 1931), p. 64.

119   "tactical unit . . . organization.": Historical Branch, War Plans Division, General Staff Monograph No. 6, "A Study in Battle Formation" (Washington, D.C.: U.S. Government Printing Office, February 1920), p. 6.

119   "supplemented by . . . volunteers": C. à Court Repington, *The First World War 1914–1918, Personal Experiences* (London: Constable, 1920), p. 88, gives a ratio of 20 percent regulars.

119   "on puke detail.": MHI, Box, 1st Div., "Tom Carroll's Diary."

119   "One of . . . France.": Mark Sullivan, *Our Times 1900–1925*, Vol. 5, *Over Here 1914–1918* (New York: Scribner, 1972), p. 350.

119   "two miles away": RG 165, WDG&SS, WCD, Gen. Corr., 1903–1919, Box 258, report of Col. Johnson Hagood, Aug. 18–31, 1917.

120 "I have never": G. C. Marshall, *Memoirs of My Services in the World War* (Boston: Houghton Mifflin, 1976).

120 "perhaps . . . most motley": *Field Artillery Journal 13*, in Holbrook, p. 246.

120 "Riding with a": Marshall, *Memoirs*.

120 "Camp surrounded with": MHI, Box, 1st Div., "Tom Carroll's Diary."

121 "This signified": LoC, Mitchell Papers, Box 2, "Before Pershing in Europe," July 1917, p. 8.

121 "They looked": Ibid., p. 9.

121 " 'Père Joffre' . . . 'Père Shing.' ": "Before Pershing in Europe," op. cit., p. 61.

122 "several illegitimate children": D. Smythe, *Pershing: General of the Armies* (Bloomington: Indiana U.P., 1966), p. 122.

122 where to deploy America's forces: See, e.g., D. Smythe, "AEF Strategy in France, 1917–1918," *Army Quarterly, 115* (2), April 1985, p. 192.

122 "The French, too": May 17, 1917. Ibid., p. 11.

123 "a nasty part": Ibid.

123 "one million . . . two years.": LoC, Bliss Papers, Box 318, File "Organization of US Army," memorandum "Report on Organization," July 10, 1918.

124 "with the deep": Harbord, *American Army in France*, pp. 103–4.

124 "most loveable people": This and the other French comments cited in this chapter come from a variety of sources in the French military archives in Vincennes, France, AAV 47/3 17 N 47: "Report on the American troops according to the postal censorship," September–October 1917; "Report of October 1917 from GS of the Army, 2nd Bureau"; "Notes on the U.S. troops in France, Postal Censorship, November 1917"; "Impression made by U.S. troops in the East Postal Censorship, December 1917"; "Police Inspector Louis Bruned's surveillance report on the Gondrecourt area, Jan. 13, 1918"; "Summary Report, Ménil-le-Tar region, Feb. 1–28, 1918"; "Postal Censorship, March 1918"; "Lt. Geais' report on the detachment of gendarmes to the American troops at Saint-Aignan, Mar. 23, 1918"; "Surveillance Summary—various regions, Apr. 1–30, 1918"; "Report of Inspector

S. Hourbette, Special Commissaire in Security Services, May 1, 1918";
"Information Service on the Army, May 27, 1918"; "Postal Censorship,
May 15–June 15, 1918."

125   "Money eventually ruined": LoC, Wood Papers, Container 9, "Report on Trip to England and France December 1917–January 1918," para.
"Pay of Men."

125   "Business is too": Capt. Will Judy, *A Soldier's Diary: A Day-to-Day
Record in the World War* (Chicago: Judy Publishing, 1930), p. 115.

125   "morale among Frenchmen": D. Englander, "The French Soldier
1914–1918" in *French History 1* (1), March 1987, pp. 58–9.

125   "obscene American expressions": Judy, *Soldier's Diary*, p. 127.

126   "These soldiers . . . Gouzeaucourt.": During the last week of August 1917, a Miss Donald, a nurse with the U.S. No. 2 Base Hospital
unit, was wounded by German bombs. RG 60, DoJ, Gen. Recs., E 260,
Box 1, W. C. Woolsey to A. M. Judd, Aug. 31, 1917.

12: The Military Melting Pot: Into the Camps

127   "first Japanese company.": R. S. Kuykendall, *Hawaii in the World
War* (Honolulu: Historical Commission, 1928), p. 40.

127   "The minimum . . . cavalry.": *The Medical Department of the U.S.
Army in World War I*, Vol. 15, Part 1, *Army Anthropology* (Washington,
D.C.: U.S. Government Printing Office, 1921), p. 46.

128   "The Jews and": M. Pearlman, *To Make Democracy Safe for America*
(Urbana: U. of Illinois Press, 1984), p. 150.

128   "the local boards": F. L. Huidekoper, *Illinois in the World War*, Vol. 2,
The History of the 33rd Division (Springfield: Illinois State Historical Library, 1921), p. 8.

128   "if it were known": MIWS, Vol. 28, Sept. 12, 1918.

128   "Private Otto Gottschalk": *NYT*, October 1917. LoC, Stotesbury
Papers, Reel 32.

129   " 'development battalions' ": B. White, "The American Military and
the Melting Pot in World War I" in J. Granatstein, and R. D. Cuff, eds., *War
and Society in North America* (Toronto: Nelson, 1971), pp. 37–51.

129 "Camp Gordon . . . had": MIWS, Vol. 28, Aug. 5, 1918.

129 far higher proportion: N. A. Wynn, *From Progressivism to Prosperity: World War I and American Society* (New York: Holmes and Meier, 1986), p. 41.

129 "The physical condition": See MHI, "The Colored Soldier in the U.S. Army" (Historical Section, Army War College, May 1942), Appendix 22 ("Colored Soldier"), Lytle Brown, June 12, 1918.

129 Camp Hill details: "Special Report on Conditions at Camp Hill, Newport News, Virginia." LoC, Microfilms, "Federal Surveillance of Afro-Americans," Reel 19/0111.

130 "War Department inspector": Charles Williams, "Resume of Conditions Surrounding Negro Troops," Aug. 3, 1918, in ibid., Reel 19/0091.

130 "We have experienced": W. R. Atterbury, AEF CoS, Feb. 15, 1918, in "Colored Soldier," op. cit., Appendix 21.

130 "among the cantonments": Locations listed in RG 120, 92nd Div., Box 1, "Record of Events 92nd Division from Monthly Returns." See also "Colored Soldier," op. cit.

130 "a far-spreading city": Capt. Will Judy, *A Soldier's Diary: A Day-to-Day Record in the World War* (Chicago: Judy Publishing, 1930), p. 75.

131 "Infirmary buildings": The Medical Department of the U.S. Army in the World War, Vol. 4, *Activities Concerning Mobilization Camps and Ports of Embarkation* (Washington, D.C.: U.S. Government Printing Office, 1928), ("*U.S. Army* 4"), pp. 9–10.

131 Camp Logan: Huidekoper, *Illinois in the World War.*

131 "982,500 pounds of": Ibid., p. 14.

132 "semi-solid mass of": Ibid., p. 104.

132 "Mennonites . . . avoid war": H. C. Petersen and G. C. Fite, *Opponents of War 1917–1918* (Madison: U. of Wisconsin Press, 1957), p. 133.

133 "died of pneumonia": Ibid., p. 134.

133 Sheldon W. Smith: Ibid., p. 127.

134 "an estimated 196,000": RG 165, WDG&SS, WCD, Gen. Corr., Box 510, extracts from memorandum of the Surgeon-General.

134   "had foot trouble": *USAMD* 4, op. cit., p. 50.

134   "French Canadians . . . obesity.": Ibid., pp. 46–51.

135   " 'Monkey Chasers.' ": Memo from Capt. James T. Madden to Director, MID, Oct. 28, 1918, "Federal Surveillance of Afro-Americans," op. cit., Reel 20.

136   "men often lied": A. Brandt, *Motor Transport Organization in the AEF* (Washington, D.C.: Historical Section, Army War College, 1942).

136   "Though . . . Western Front.": Census Bureau, 1915, pp. 257–8, quoted in R. L. Barsh, "American Indians in the Great War" in *Ethnohistory*, 38 (3), Summer 1991, p. 291.

136   " 'no colored admixture.' ": RG 75, Indian Office Circulars, 1305-1, May 11, 1918.

136   "In all . . . did so.": Barsh, "American Indians," pp. 277–8.

136   "I felt no": Ibid., p. 282.

137   "Their languages were": Mitchell Yockelson, "Native Americans in World War I" (Washington, D.C.: National Archives, publication).

137   "a scientific basis": Edward M. Coffman, *The War To End All Wars: The American Military Experience in World War I* (New York: OUP, 1968), p. 59.

137   "24.9 percent of men": FO, 371 4247 121389, "General Intelligence Report" to Aug. 16, 1919.

137   "mixture of grades.": D. J. Kertes, "Testing the Army's Intelligence: Psychologists and the Military in World War I" in *Journal of American History* 55 (3), December 1968.

138   "the basis . . . pay.": W. G. McAdoo, *Crowded Years: The Reminiscences of W. G. McAdoo* (Boston: Houghton Mifflin, 1931), p. 426.

138   "My boy . . . three days.": HIoWRP, Papers of Major P. S. Van Cise, Asst. CoS, G2, "Letters on Allotments," Dec. 28, 1918.

138   "London danger zone": FO, 395 85 194048, pamphlet by Lady Lister-Kaye, "Crossing the London Danger Zone," circulated by the National Allied Relief Committee, 300 Madison Avenue, New York, N.Y.

139   "up to thirty-six": RG 165, WD GS, MID, Box 131, 80–73, memorandum, Aug. 15, 1918.

139   "You wouldn't . . . whore?": R. Shaffer, *America in the Great War* (New York: OUP, 1991), p. 101.

139   "Woodrow Wilson . . . price": E. R. Ellis, *Echoes of Distant Thunder* (New York: Coward, McCann and Geoghegan, 1975), p. 363.

140   "MPs were then": Shaffer, *America in the Great War*, p. 105.

140   "by force if necessary.": Harbord, *American Army in France 1917–1919* (Boston: Little, Brown, 1936), p. 146.

140   "Men found lemon": RG 60, DoJ, Centr. Files, Str. Num. Files, Box 2115, Entry 112 185818.

140   "barman 'treated' them": RG 60, DoJ, Centr. Files, Str. Num. Files, Box 2108, Entry 112.

140   " 'Captain Van Blank' ": *FAJ 14*, Wahl, p. 17.

140   "$10 a month": RG 165, WDG&SS, WCD Gen. Corr., Box 510, 10040-8, memorandum to CoS from his office, Nov. 16, 1917.

140   "the Chihuahua . . . morphine.": MIWS, Vol. 28, July 8 and Aug. 13, 1918.

141   drugs in Camp Devens: RG 165, MID Corr., Box 2757, 10110-193.

13: Building the War Machine

145   "boardwalk eighteen inches": Edward M. Coffman, *The War To End All Wars: The American Military Experience in World War I* (New York: OUP, 1968), p. 30.

145   Quartermaster statistics: Noyes, *The War Period of American Finance 1908–1925* (New York: Putnam, 1926), p. 220.

146   "By the fall": LoC, Bliss Papers, Box 319, WCD, memorandum to CoS, Oct. 27, 1918.

146   "for every million . . . hospital care.": "An Address by William C. Gorgas, Late Surgeon General, U.S. Army," Oct. 26, 1917, in M. E. Jenison, *Illinois in the World War*, Vol. 6, *War Documents and Addresses* (Springfield: Illinois State Historical Library, 1923), p. 293.

146   "I think it advisable": LoC, Bliss Papers, Box 319, File "Tanks U.S. Army," July 19, 1917.

146 "Tanks were not": J. Terraine, Western Front Association 1983 presidential address, printed in *Stand To! 10* (24). See also T. Travers, "Could the Tanks of 1918 Have Been War Winners for the BEF?" in *Journal of Contemporary History 27* (3), 1992, pp. 389–406.

146 "more than adequate": PRO, CAB 25/121, SWC, British Section, Versailles, France, Paper 174, "Proposals for the Use of Tanks in the Campaign of 1919."

147 "On September 14": RG 120, CinC Reports, Box 30, Office of Chief of Tank Corps, memorandum, Dec. 27, 1918.

147 "As for chemical": H. R. Slotten, "Humane Chemistry or Scientific Barbarism? America Responds to World War I Poison Gas 1915–1930," *Journal of American History 77* (2), September 1990, p. 476.

147 "would have swamped": L. F. Haber, *The Poisonous Cloud: Chemical Warfare in the First War* (Oxford, England: Clarendon, 1986), p. 13.

147 "Pershing set up": V. Lefebure, *The Riddle of the Rhine: Chemical Strategy in Peace and War* (London: Collins, 1921), pp. 171–2.

147 "rendered soil barren": J. Terraine, *White Heat: The New Warfare 1914–1918* (London: Sidgwick & Jackson, 1982), p. 160.

147 "a large number": FO, 371 3488 16017, "Organization and Development of Gas Service in America," Dec. 20, 1917.

148 "fitted with steam": PRO, CAB 25/121, SWC, Paper 197, "Meeting of Inter-Allied Tanks Committee," May 6, 1918.

148 "several hundred feet": Squiers Report, "Aeronautics in the United States, 1918," p. 64. RG 165, WDG&SS, WCD, Gen. Corr. 1903–1919, Box 172, 7112-102.

148 "Mr Edison came": Cronon, p. 218.

148 "The Board focused": Josephus Daniels, *The Wilson Era*, Vol. 2, *1917–1923: Years of War and After* (Chapel Hill: U. of North Carolina Press, 1946), p. 103.

148 "Lesser brains . . . own hell.": RG 165, WD GS, Special Office of Div. of Organization and Training (G3) Subordinate Offices, Inventions Section, Gen. Corr., 1918–1921, Box 001.

148 "an aerosol system": RG 165, CoS Corr., Box 68, Folder 520, 51-110, "Gas."

149 "In March . . . cheaply?": LoC, Baker Papers, Reel 3, Advisory Commission to Baker, Mar. 31, 1917.

149 "Aviation's champions evoked": See, e.g., M. Paris, "The Rise of the Airmen" in *Journal of Contemporary History* 28 (1), January 1993, and D. Pisano, "Constructing the Memory of Aerial Combat in World War I" in D. Pisano et al., *Legend, Memory and the Great War in the Air* (Washington, D.C.: Smithsonian, 1992), pp. 11–13.

149 "22,625 aeroplanes plus": B. Robertson, *Air Aces of the 1914–18 War* (Letchworth, England: Harleyford, 1959), p. 89.

150 "This represented enormous": See, e.g., Squiers Report, op. cit.

150 "The U-boats . . . bleak.": LoC, Bliss Papers, Box 38, File "Strategy of European War," Lockridge memorandum, Oct. 17, 1917.

150 "eighty-seven enemy vessels": *WWP,* Vol. 43, p. 89, n. 1.

150 Goethals biography: LoC, Goethals Papers.

150 "seventh most useful American": *Independent* magazine poll, 1913, quoted in A. Valentine, *1913: America Between Two Worlds* (1962), p. 109.

150 "hot air artists": LoC, Goethals Papers, Box 4, Apr. 19, 1917.

151 "3,000,000 tons": Goethals to Wilson, June 11, 1917, in *WWP,* Vol. 42, p. 475.

151 "Seamen were similarly": Edward Hurley, *The Bridge to France* (New York: Lippincott, 1927).

151 "At Hog Island": Ibid., p. 77.

152 "$3.5 billion": C. Gilbert, *American Financing of World War I* (Westport, Conn.: Greenwood, 1970), p. 84.

152 "In the thirty-two": Ibid., p. 45.

152 "In the spring": K. Burk, "The Mobilization of Anglo-American Finance During World War I" in N. F. Dreisziger, ed., *Mobilization for Total War: The Canadian, American and British Experience, 1914–1918, 1939–1945* (Waterloo, Ontario, Canada: Wilfrid Laurier U.P., 1991), pp. 25ff.

152 "must have $200 million": Northcliffe to Balfour and Lloyd George, June 30, 1917, in *WWP,* Vol. 43, p. 66.

152   "Sir Richard Crawford": W. G. McAdoo, *Crowded Years: The Reminiscences of W. G. McAdoo* (Boston: Houghton Mifflin, 1931), p. 396.

152   "the ability of": Barclay to Lansing, July 1, 1917, in *WWP,* Vol. 43, p. 67.

153   "The Senate should": McAdoo, *Crowded Years,* p. 376.

14: "Lay Your Double Chin on the Altar of Liberty": Food for the Fighters

154   "Lay Your Double": A. Cornebise, *War As Advertised: The Four-Minute Men and America's Crusade 1917–1918* (Philadelphia: American Philosophical Society, 1984), p. 91.

154   "In February 1917": K. K. Sklar and T. Dublin, eds., *Women and Power in American History,* Vol. 2 (Englewood Cliffs, N.J.: Prentice Hall, 1991).

154   "Whenever a woman": American Social History Project, *Who Built America? Working People and the Nation's Economy, Politics, Culture and Society* (New York: Pantheon, 1992), p. 230.

155   "the man taken": W. C. Mullendore, *History of the U.S. Food Administration 1917–1919* (Palo Alto, Calif.: Stanford U.P., 1941), p. 49.

155   "poor wheat harvest": A. D. Noyes, *The War Period of American Finance 1908–1925* (New York: Putnam, 1926), p. 224.

155   "bidding against each other.": J. H. Shideler, *Farm Crisis 1919–1923* (Berkeley: U. of California Press, 1957), p. 11.

155   "He preferred westerners": G. D. Best, review of G. Nash, *The Life of Herbert Hoover,* in *Journal of American History,* December 1991, p. 1120.

155   "Let the nation": M. MacDonagh, *In London During the Great War* (London: Eyre, 1935), p. 159.

156   "The time is": *Mr Punch's History of the Great War* (London: Cassell, 1920), p. 128.

156   "no sugar bowls . . . Buckingham Palace": Ibid., pp. 170–5.

156   "a King . . . Kaiser": Senator James A. Reed, quoted in M. R. Dickson, *The Food Front in World War I* (Washington, D.C.: American Council on Public Affairs, 1944), p. 16.

156 "dedicated volunteers.": See, e.g., R. D. Cuff, "The Ideology of Voluntarism and War Organization during the Great War," *Journal of American History 64*, September 1977.

156 "I was well aware": H. Hoover, *The Memoirs of Herbert Hoover: Years of Adventure 1874–1920* (London: Hollis & Carter, 1952), p. 244.

157 "price of hogs": T. Saloutos and J. Hicks, *Agricultural Discontent in the Middle West 1900–1939* (Madison: U. of Wisconsin Press, 1951), p. 94.

157 "money abstracted from": Shideler, *Farm Crisis*, p. 14.

157 "particular attention was": See, e.g., F. W. O'Brien, *The Hoover-Wilson Wartime Correspondence 9/24/14–11/11/18* (Ames: Iowa State U.P., 1974), pp. 157, 250–2.

157 "Hoover was perfectly": R. F. Himmelberg, "Hoover's Public Image 1919–1920: The Emergence of a Public Figure and a Sign of the Times" in L. Gelford, ed., *Herbert Hoover: The Great War and Its Aftermath* (Iowa City: U. of Iowa Press, 1979), pp. 207–17.

158 "It isn't 'in' ": E. D. Bullitt, *An Uncensored Diary from the Central Empires* (London: Stanley Paul, 1918), p. 39.

158 "Perhaps it will not": Cornebise, *War as Advertised*, p. 91.

158 "Go back to": FO, 368 5241.

159 "Don't let your": R. H. Ferrell, *Woodrow Wilson and World War I* (New York: Harper and Row, 1985), p. 93.

159 "This will produce": HIoWRP, FAd, Box 5H, Department of Food Conservation, Paper on Division of Cooperating Organizations.

159 "The Loyal . . . members.": HIoWRP, FAd, Box 5H, Home Conservation Division.

159 "Americans were called": Maxcy R. Dickson, "The Food Administration—Educator" in *Agricultural History 16* (1942), p. 94.

159 "The House . . . Hoarder": HIoWRP, FAd, Box 42.

159 "notices requesting readers": Dickson, *Food Front*, p. 70.

159 "Less successful was": Ibid., pp. 88–9.

160 "Black women were": HIoWRP, FAd, 12-H, Box 42.

160   "During the New": HIoWRP, FAd, Box 38.

160   "Do not permit": *Life*, Feb. 21, 1918.

160   "ammonia . . . egg shampoo": HIoWRP, FAd, Box 38.

160   "Making the ten": Elliott Roosevelt, ed., *The Roosevelt Letters*, Vol. 2, *1905–1928* (London: Harrap, 1950), p. 282.

161   "It was . . . mesquite beans.": HIoWRP, FAd, Box 38.

161   "She was urged": Charles Lathrop Pack, "Conserving Our Food Supply," *American Forestry*, July 1918.

161   "In one month": Dickson, *Food Front*, p. 159.

161   "De wise . . . sezee.": Ibid., p. 163.

161   "Catch the carp": Ibid., p. 80.

162   "Hoover's men used": HIoWRP, FAd, 32-33H, Box 64, memorandum, Miles to Lower.

162   "Where the Food Campaign": HIoWRP, FAd, 5-H, Box 3.

162   "How do you suppose": Dickson, *Food Front*, p. 90.

163   "As a being": HIoWRP, FAd, 5-H, Box 3.

15: "One White-hot Mass": Mobilizing Minds

164   "One white-hot mass": George Creel, quoted in S. Vaughn, *Holding Fast the Inner Lines: Democracy, Nationalism and the Committee for Public Information* (Chapel Hill: U. of North Carolina Press, 1980), p. 21.

165   "*Wilson and the Issues*": C. Larson and J. Mock, "The Lost Files of the Creel Committee of 1917–1919," Library of the National Archives, Washington, D.C., p. 9.

165   "His Committee for": Merle Curti, *Peace or War: The American Struggle 1636–1936* (Boston: J. S. Canner, 1959), p. 255.

166   "the trans-Atlantic cable": RG 63, CPI, E1/4, Col. M. Churchill, Chief Military Censor, to CoS, Aug. 5, 1918.

166   "Then, in October": RG 63, CPI, E1/4, "Minutes of Meeting of Censorship Board: Summary," May 22, 1918.

166   "But in letters": RG 63, CPI, E1/4, "Subjects of Interest and Directions for Routing Comments."

166 "guidelines": RG 63 CPI, E1/4, memorandum from Creel, "What the Government Asks of the Press," July 30, 1917.

167 "Why the U-Boats": J. Mock & C. Larson, *Words That Won The War: The Story of the Committee on Public Information* (Princeton: Princeton U. P., 1939), p. 86.

168 "We would rather": M. Ellis, "America's Black Press 1914–1918," *History Today*, September 1991, p. 26.

168 "*The Crisis* says": *The Crisis 16*, September 1918, quoted in Ulysses Lee, "The Employment of Negro Troops," *U.S. Army in World War II. Special Studies 8* (Washington, D.C.: Office of Chief of Military History, U.S. Army, 1966), p. 4.

168 "Victory Boys": HIoWRP, WWI Subject File, Box 21.

169 "The pocket-sized . . . without mercy.": HIoWRP, WWI Subject File, Box 21.

170 "He will come": Reproduced in Vaughn, *Holding Fast*, pp. 178–9.

170 "In gas warfare": RG 63, CPI-1-A12, Box 1, "Censorship of Cables, Division of Advertising—Advertisement No. E-12."

170 "Poison gas, the": Reproduced in Vaughn, *Holding Fast*, pp. 178–9.

171 "It was quite . . . sobbed and cheered.": Mock and Larson, *Words*, p. 129.

171 "Lieutenant Paul Périgord": Vaughn, *Holding Fast*, p. 132.

172 "It became difficult": Mark Sullivan, *Our Times 1900–1925*, Vol. 5, *Over Here 1914–1918* (New York: Scribner, 1972), p. 432.

172 "But in Georgia . . . as well.": A. Cornebise, *War as Advertised: The Four-Minute Men and America's Crusade 1917–1918* (Philadelphia: American Philosophical Society, 1984), pp. 22–6.

172 "You will want": HIoWRP, Oliphant Collection.

172 "My rule for": "A Few Short Talks on the Red Cross" in "The Red Cross War Fund," May 13, 1918, in HIoWRP, Oliphant Collection.

173 "the Master Four-Minute Man": Cornebise, *War as Advertised*, p. 37.

173 "Finish strong and": Ibid., p. 33.

173 "Cut out . . . bunk": Ibid., p. 54.

173   "The Red Cross": *Cartoon* magazine, February 1918.

174   "If you pay": RG 63, CPI, Entry 19, Box 2, Folder 10, Bureau of
Cartoons, "Bulletin for Cartoonists," No. 1, June 7, 1918.

174   "The division worked": RG 63, CPI-1-A12, Box 1, Rufus Steele,
Katherine Hilliker, and Carlyle Ellis, "Progress Report of the Department of
Scenarios and Outside Production," Aug. 10, 1918.

174   "I'd rather you": Cornebise, *War as Advertised*, p. 60.

175   "McAdoo wanted Liberty": W. G. McAdoo, *Crowded Years: The
Reminiscences of W. G. McAdoo* (Boston: Houghton Mifflin, 1938), p. 374.

175   "I have three": M. E. Jenison, *Illinois in the World War*, Vol. 6, *War
Documents and Addresses* (Springfield: Illinois State Historical Library,
1923), p. 188.

176   "It will soon": Cornebise, *War as Advertised*, p. 80.

176   "If the Christ": HIoWRP, Oliphant Collection, Division of Four-
Minute Men, Bulletin 29, Apr. 6, 1918.

176   "Sousa dutifully produced": J. L. Morrison, *Josephus Daniels: The
Small-d Democrat* (Chapel Hill: U. of North Carolina Press, 1966), p. 99.

177   "Enrico Caruso . . . Hall.": A. D. Noyes, *The War Period of American Finance 1908–1925* (New York: Putnam, 1926), p. 184.

177   "not . . . mass market": C. Gilbert, *American Financing of World War
I* (Westport, Conn.: Greenwood, 1970), pp. 119, 123, 126.

177   "The money of": Ibid., pp. 164ff.

177   "In Kona, Hawaii": Kuykendall, *Hawaii in the World War* (Honolulu: Historical Commission, 1928), pp. 320, 324.

16: "I Love My Flag, I Do, I Do":
Discouraging Dissent

179   "mere economic unit": J. Bodnar, *Remaking America: Public Memory, Commemoration and Patriotism in the Twentieth Century* (Princeton,
N.J.: Princeton U.P., 1992), p. 84.

180   "forty cigars a day": F. H. Martin, "Digest of the Proceedings of the
Council of National Defense During the World War" (Senate Doc. No. 193,
73d Congress, 2d Sess.) (Washington, D.C.: U.S. Government Printing
Office, 1934), p. 249.

180 "unions represented directly": *WIBM*, Oct. 25, 1917, p. 100.

180 "discreet word": RG 165, MID, Box 2770, 10110-479, Report on J. T. Brock.

180 "reveals Gompers' collusion": LoC, AFL Letterbooks, 78-51185, Robert Maisel to Gompers, Oct. 10, 1917.

180 "We understand now": S. Gompers, *American Labor and the War* (New York: George Doran, 1919), p. 221.

181 "The president of": LoC, AFL Letterbooks, J. H. Maurer to Gompers, Oct. 12, 1917.

182 "Newspapers cannot say": LoC, Burleson Papers, Vol. 19, Burleson to Editor and Publisher, New York *World*, Oct. 31, 1917.

182 "Burleson 'acted the part' ": W. G. McAdoo, *Crowded Years: The Reminiscences of W. G. McAdoo* (Boston: Houghton Mifflin, 1931), p. 180.

182 "To those who": LoC, Burleson Papers, Vol. 20, "Postmaster General's Statement," May 13, 1918.

183 "You know": LoC, Burleson Papers, Vol. 19, Wilson to Burleson, Sept. 4, 1917.

183 "General Sherman said": M. Dubofsky, *We Shall Be All: A History of the International Workers of the World* (Chicago: Quadrangle, 1969).

183 "I love my flag": Ibid., p. 355.

184 "as many as 95 percent": Ibid., p. 357.

184 "less the destruction": P. Foner, *A History of the Labor Movement in the United States* (New York: International Publishers, 1965), pp. 161–2.

184 "withdrawal of efficiency.": J. R. Conlin, *Bread and Roses Too: Studies of the Wobblies* (Westport, Conn.: Greenwood), p. 105.

184 "Of course you": War Department files, WCD, 10110-362, report by E. N. T. Wright, Sept. 17, 1917.

184 "the saw teeth": RG 165, MID, Box 2770, 10110-480, report by Agent Stansbury.

184 "Blacklegs found cow": RG 165, MID, Box 2770, 10110-480, report by Agent Petrovitsky on IWW at Aberdeen, Wash., Nov. 26, 1917.

184 *"Little Red Songbook":* Foner, *A History of Labor*, pp. 151–7.

185 "And Wobbly leader": RG 60, DoJ, Str. Num. Files, E. 112, Box 2181.

185 "At the same . . . California": LoC, Frankfurter Papers, Reel 94, memorandum "Brief on Labor Situation in California." See also War Department files, A.G.370.61, McCain to Commanding General, Western Department, San Francisco, July 3, 1917.

186 "William B. Wilson": W. Preston, "The Ideology and Techniques of Repression" in H. Goldberg, ed., *American Radicals: Some Problems and Personalities* (New York: Monthly Review, 1957), p. 254.

186 "It is not . . . organization": RG 165, MID, Box 2770, "Report of Special Employee McIntosh for 3-1-1918 re labor situation and the IWW in Western Washington."

187 "They were violating": Preston, "Ideology and Techniques," p. 250.

187 "No violence nor": WD, A.G.370.61, Bisbee, Hornbrook to Adjutant General, June 30, 1917.

187 "The *IWW strike*": WD, A.G.370.61, Bisbee, J. C. Greenway, General Manager, Calumet & Arizona Mining Co. to Baker, June 28, 1917.

188 "Secretary of War": WD, A.G.370.61, Bisbee, McCain to Commanding General, Southern Department, Fort Sam Houston, Tex., Aug. 3, 1917.

188 "a census was held": WD, A.G.370.61, Southern Department, Office of the CoS, "Summary of General Parker's telegram No. 5759 dated August 6, 1917, on the subject of census of men held at Columbus, New Mexico."

188 "wholly without authority": President's Mediation Commission, *Report on the Bisbee Deportations* (Washington, D.C.: U.S. Government Printing Office, 1918).

188 "Samuel Gompers protested": *The Masses*, September 1917, reproduced in W. L. O'Neill, ed., *Echoes of Revolt: The Masses 1911–1917* (Chicago: Elephant/Ivan R. Dee, 1989), p. 296.

189 "Great care should": WD, A.G.014-12, McCain to Commanding General, Southern Department. See also D. R. Beaver, *Newton D. Baker and the American War Effort 1917–1919* (Lincoln: U. of Nebraska Press, 1966), p. 234.

189 "The raiders seized": RG 165, MID, Box 2757, 10110-191, report by Agent William L. Buchanan, Sept. 15, 1917, "In re Kenneth J.

Kennedy: Copy of Letter Dan Buckley, IWW to Fred. A. Raisin, Erie County Jail," Sept. 13, 1917.

189 "Copies of letters": WD, WCD, 10110-362, report by E. N. T. Wright, Sept. 17, 1917.

17: "The Truth About This War": Mobilization Stalled

193 "It will never do": J. M. Grider, *War Birds: Diary of an Unknown Aviator* (New York: George Doran, 1926) quoted in A. Cornebise, *War as Advertised: The Four-Minute Men and America's Crusade 1917–1918* (Philadelphia: American Philosophical Society, 1984), p. 166.

193 "180 days' supply": New York *Tribune*, February 14, 1918, cited in HIoWRP, WWI Subject File, War Department Committee on Education, memorandum to "Mr. O'Higgins."

194 "That winter . . . areas.": J. P. Johnson, "The Wilsonians as War Managers: Coal and the 1917–1918 Winter Crisis," *Prologue: The Journal of the National Archives*, 9 (4), Winter 1977, pp. 203–4.

194 "seventy-one died . . . Funston": LoC, Wood Papers, Container 9, Diaries, Nov. 22, 1917.

194 "Never in the": Ibid., Oct. 12, 1917.

194 "It is pitiless": Ibid., "Report on Trip to England and France, December 1917–January 1918" ("Wood Report").

194 "On December 12": RG 165, E 441, Box 36, "Summary of Hearings of Investigation of War Department by Senate Committee on Military Affairs, December 12, 1917, to March 29, 1918" ("Chamberlain Summary").

194 "National Security League": R. D. Ward, "The Origin and Activities of the National Security League 1914–1919," *Mississippi Valley Historical Review*, 47 (1960–1), p. 51.

195 "We are still": Chamberlain Summary, op. cit., p. 73.

195 "Nine months after": Senator Hitchcock, ibid., p. 60.

195 "Eighty percent of": Ibid., p. 64.

195 "But hospital buildings": Ibid.

195 "hundreds of thousands": Ibid.

195 choice of rifle: D. R. Beaver, *Newton D. Baker and the American War Effort 1917–1919* (Lincoln: U. of Nebraska Press, 1966), p. 56.

195 Lee Enfield rifle: Chamberlain Summary, op. cit., p. 65.

195 "A 'hideous travesty' ": LoC, Wood Papers, Container 9, Wood Report, op. cit.

196 "For its artillery": See, e.g., F. L. Huidekoper, *Illinois in the World War*, Vol. 2, *The History of the 33rd Division* (Springfield: Illinois State Historical Library, 1921), pp. 5–6.

196 "through secret sources.": C. M. Green, H. C. Thomson, and P. C. Roots, *The U.S. Army in World War II—The Technical Services. Ordnance Department: Planning Munitions for War* (Washington, D.C.: Office of the Chief of Military History, Department of the Army, 1955), p. 24.

196 "fearful that a": *WIBM*, Jan. 10, 1918.

196 "Even this was": *Selections from the Correspondence of Theodore Roosevelt and Henry Cabot Lodge 1884–1918* (New York: Scribner, 1925), Dec. 18, 1917, p. 530. See also RG 165, E 441, Box 36, CS, p. 67.

196 "The economy was": C. Gilbert, *American Financing of World War I* (Westport, Conn.: Greenwood, 1970), pp. 204–5.

196 "There was no slack": LoC, Bliss Papers, Box 319, File "Production and Supply of Munitions," CND Report, Dec. 8, 1917, p. 2.

196 naval priority: R. D. Cuff, *The War Industries Board: Business-Government Relations During World War I* (Baltimore: Johns Hopkins U.P., 1973), p. 90. See also Green et al., *Planning Munitions*, p. 25, n. 9.

197 "Often they found": RG 165, E. 445, PST Division, Correspondence, Hugh S. Johnson, memorandum "Some Articles Purchased by More Than One Army Department," Jan. 19, 1918.

197 "Efficiency was threatened": LoC, March Papers, Box 12, memorandum "Description of the Procedure for the Control of the Ordnance Department Supply Program," Dec. 12, 1917.

197 "practically all the": Beaver, *Newton D. Baker*, p. 62.

197 "typewriters piled up": D. Smythe, *Pershing: General of the Armies* (Bloomington: Indiana U.P., 1986), p. 9.

197   "In April 1917": Green et al., *Planning Munitions*, p. 22.

197   "The Quartermaster's Groceries": H. G. Sharpe, *The Quarter Master Corps in the Year 1917 In the World War* (New York: Century, 1921), p. 304.

198   "1,500 separate commodities": RG 165, E. 443, Corr. File, Gerard Swope, Assistant to Director, PST Division, 1918, memorandum, June 25, 1918.

198   "One construction company": RG 61, E. 1-D1, Box 90, Committee on Emergency Construction Report, December 31, 1918.

198   "The president continues": LoC, Goethals Papers, Box 4, July 8, 1917.

198   "In August, Goethals": Ibid., Aug. 5, 1917.

199   "An investigative mission": See, e.g., RG 60, DoJ, Gen. Recs., Box 54, "Hughes Aircraft Investigation" (report by H. Snowden Marshall on air production, May 2, 1918), p. 18.

200   "An airplane engine": Borglum to Wilson, Dec. 25, 1917, in *WWP*, Vol. 45, p. 356.

200   "This would be": RG 63, CPI-1-1A, Box 3, Gen. Corr. of Creel.

200   "often dangerously low.": See, e.g., RG 165, WCD, Gen. Corr. 1903–1919, Box 172, Aviation Department, 7112-96, Col. R. L. Montgomery, GS/CoS, May 20, 1918, on defects in Hall-Scott Motor A-7a. See also "A Mechanic's Story: Dallas L. Darling of the 139th Aero Squadron" in *Over the Front*, 7 (2), Summer 1994; " 'Devil Dog' Sam Richards" in *Over the Front*, 7 (3), Autumn 1994; and Bradley King, "Americans in the Royal Flying Corps: Recruitment and the British Government, *Imperial War Museum Review* No. 6, pp. 92–3.

200   "In the first": LoC, Mitchell Papers, Box 34, "Aviation in America," paper "What Shall We Do With Aviation?" (n.d.).

201   "I don't mind": RG 120, Inspector General's Office, Box 4, report from Col. J. Johnson to Commanding General, First Army, June 8, 1918, "Conditions in 1st Observation Group, Air Service, 1st Army Corps."

201   "criminally constructed fuel": E. V. Rickenbacker, *Fighting the Flying Circus* (New York: Frederick Stokes, 1919), p. 337.

201   "badly delayed the output": RG 120, GHQ, CinC Reports, Box 30, memorandum, Dec. 27, 1918.

201   "Chief of Ordnance . . . Department.": Chamberlain Summary, p. 77.

201   "But the investigating": Ibid., p. 74.

202   "Chamber of Commerce": R. G. Rhett to Wilson, Nov. 15, 1917, in *WWP*, Vol. 46, p. 61.

202   "analogous to the": LoC, Baker Papers, Reel 3, Advisory Commission, op. cit., Mar. 31, 1917.

202   "The world is": LoC, Garfield Papers, Oct. 10, 1917.

202   "Garfield raised prices": Johnson, "The Wilsonians," p. 202.

202   "COAL . . . to—VICTORY.": Ibid., p. 208.

203   "worthy of . . . government": Johnson, "The Wilsonians," p. 206.

203   "There is nothing": House Diary, Jan. 17, 1918, in *WWP*, Vol. 46, p. 23.

18: "The War Is Practically Lost": Crisis on the Western Front

205   "a third . . . supplies": Thomas Page Nelson, Nov. 4, 1917, in *WWP*, Vol. 44, p. 507.

206   "cheer the nation": U.S. Railway Advisory Commission, July 4, 1917, in *WWP*, Vol. 43, p. 440.

206   "Leon Trotsky . . . Library": T. Draper, *The Roots of American Communism* (New York: Viking, 1957), pp. 77, 85.

206   "Judging from what": RG 63, CPI-1-A1, Box 3, Gen. Corr. of G. Creel, Oct. 19–Nov. 1, 1917.

206   "a committee was": MIWS, Vol. 2, p. 23, Nov. 17, 1917.

206   "an informant explained": RG 63, CPI-1-A1, Box 3, Gen. Corr. of G. Creel, December 20, 1917.

206   "Matilda de Cramm": B. D. Rhodes, *The Anglo-American Winter War With Russia 1918–1919: A Diplomatic and Military Tragicomedy* (Westport, Conn.: Greenwood, 1988), p. 7.

207 "besides giving a": F. Lundberg, *America's Sixty Families* (New York: Vanguard, 1937), p. 147.

207 "General W. V. Judson": LoC, March Papers, Box 22, "1919," Judson to March, May 21, 1919 [*sic*].

207 "for the purpose": RG 165, Box 165, File 1240, Lansing to Baker, Feb. 14, 1918.

207 "The Germans are": PRO, CAB 25/121, SWC Document 210, "Manpower from the Conquered Russian Provinces."

207 "the United States": LoC, March Papers, Box 22, "1919," Judson to March, May 21, 1919 [*sic*].

207 "1,150,000 men": LoC, Bliss Papers, Box 38, File "Strategy of European War," Lockridge memorandum, Oct. 17, 1917.

208 War Trade Board: See generally RG 182, E34, Box 232, War Trade Board, Records of the Executive Office, Reports of the Units, Central Bureau of Planning and Statistics, "A Review of the Activities for the Period January 1 to October 1, 1918" ("WTB Report").

208 "worldwide surveillance of": See RG 165, Director of Intelligence, Security Classified Subject Index to Services 64-65, SI WTB and SI War Trade Intelligence, Dept. of Commerce.

208 "In league with": WTB Report, op. cit., pp. 19–24.

208 "Such was . . . borders.": Ibid., Part 4. See also N. Tracey, *Attack on Maritime Trade* (London: Macmillan, 1991), p. 143.

208 "about one half": LoC, Bliss Papers, Box 38, File "Strategy of European War," Lockridge memorandum, Oct. 17, 1917.

208 "On December 15": MIWS, Dec. 15, 1917.

208 "The German internal": MIWS, Jan. 12, 1918.

209 "Pétain confided . . . captured.": *Foreign Relations of the United States*, Lansing Papers, Vol. 2, pp. 199ff, "American Mission to Europe, October 30, 1917–December 16, 1917" ("Bliss Report"), p. 207.

209 "and they have no more": Ibid.

209 "Should she remain": Ibid., p. 203.

209 "It is also . . . died in vain.": LoC, Bliss Papers, Box 319, File "Military Operations Oct. 1917–Feb. 1918," Memorandum to Col. House, Dec. 14, 1917.

209   "he was not": LoC, March Papers, Box 22, March to Pershing, July 5, 1918: "The president handles himself so much of the diplomatic correspondence that heretofore he has been unwilling to definitely assign a civilian representative on the SWC."

210   "We expected to": D. Smythe, *Pershing: General of the Armies* (Bloomington: Indiana U.P., 1986), p. 69.

210   "when an American": D. Smythe, "AEF Strategy in France, 1917–1918," *Army Quarterly, 115* (2), April 1985, p. 193.

210   "At the turn": J. J. Pershing, *My Experiences in the World War* (London: Hodder & Stoughton, 1931), p. 243.

210   "None except the 1st": Edward M. Coffman, *The War To End All Wars: The American Military Experience in World War I* (New York: OUP, 1968), p. 168.

210   "stretch over the": Smythe, *Pershing*, p. 61.

212   "oceangoing tonnage . . . fifty per cent.": LoC, Bliss Papers, Box 319, File "Transport January 1918–November 1918," memorandum, Jan. 7, 1918. See also Baker to Wilson, Jan. 5, 1918, in *WWP*, Vol. 45, pp. 489–91.

212   "Recommend no further": Smythe, *Pershing*, p. 51.

213   "American Army engineers": C. Hendricks, *Combat and Construction: U.S. Army Engineers in World War I* (Fort Belvoir, Va.: Office of History, U.S. Army Corps of Engineers, 1993), p. 5.

213   "The experts of": See, e.g., RG 182, WTB, E177, Box 869, Corr. of George McFadden, WTB representative in Paris.

213   "AEF's logistical system": LoC, Bliss Papers, Box 319, File "Transport Dec. 1917–June 1918," Wilgus memorandum, Dec. 28, 1917.

213   construction projects: Summarized in Hendricks, *Combat and Construction*. See also Wilgus memorandum, ibid.

213   "Americans recently . . . previous day.": RG 200, Pershing Papers, Case Files, etc., Box 8, "Brief History in the case of . . . Sibert."

214   Robert Bullard: For details of his life, see A. R. Millett, *The General: Robert Lee Bullard and Officership in the U.S. Army, 1881–1925* (Westport, Conn.: Greenwood, 1975).

214   "The war is practically": Smythe, *Pershing*, p. 68.

19: American Dreams: Visions of Independence

215 "secondary to the": Dec. 24, 1917, in *WWP,* Vol. 45, p. 439.

215 "Do not think": *WWP,* Vol. 45, p. 439.

216 "Marshal Joffre himself": G. Pedroconcini, ed., *Journal de Marche de Joffre 1916–1919* (Vincennes, France: Service Historique de l'Armée de Terre, 1990), pp. 257–8, diary entry, Jan. 26, 1918.

216 "a fellow Freemason": Alf Peacock, in *Fire Step* (Newsletter of the London Branch of the WFA), Summer 1995, citing "Pick & Knight," *The Pocket History of Freemasonry.*

216 "defend Britain's possessions": D. Woodward, *Trial by Friendship: Anglo-American Relations, 1917–18* (Lexington: U. of Kentucky Press, 1993), p. 131.

216 "My first thought": Dean C. Allard, "Anglo-American Naval Differences During World War I" in *Military Affairs 44* (2), 1980, pp. 75–6.

216 "second to none": M. Simpson, ed., *Anglo-American Naval Relations 1917–1919* (Aldershot, England: Scolar Press/Navy Records Society, 1991), pp. 478–88.

216 "America feared Japan": Dean Allard, "U.S. Naval Strategy in World War I," WFA annual conference, Arlington, Va., October 1993.

217 "Sims . . . Royal Navy": D. C. Allard, "Admiral William S. Sims and United States Naval Policy in World War I," *The American Neptune, 35* (2), April 1975, pp. 99–104.

217 "Don't let the British": D. Trask, "William Shepherd Benson" in R. W. Love, Jr., ed., *The Chiefs of Naval Operations* (Annapolis, Md.: Naval Institute Press, 1980), p. 10.

217 "By early 1917": *NYT,* Jan. 18, 1917.

217 "Chile . . . Nitrates Executive.": RG 165, Entry 248, Recs. of Ordnance Dept. and Chemical Warfare Services 1917–1919, Vol. 19, memorandum from Raw Materials Committee to WIB, Nov. 22, 1917.

217 "closing his eyes": J. G. Harbord, *The American Army in France 1917–1919* (Boston: Little, Brown, 1936), pp. 190–1.

217 "objectives he knew": Senator Nye found circumstantial evidence that Wilson had known of the secret treaties; see J. E. Wiltz, "The Nye Munitions Committee," in A. M. Schlesinger, Jr., and R. Bruns, eds., *Congress Investi-*

gates: A Documented History 1792–1974, Vol. 4 (New York: Chelsea House, 1975), p. 203.

218   "with a big head": J. Reed, *Ten Days that Shook the World* (1919).

218   "secret treaties.": Text received in State Department on Dec. 27, 1917; *Foreign Relations of the United States*, Suppl. 2: *The World War*, Vol. 1, pp. 493ff.

218   Lenin and Wilson: See Charles Burdick, *Aesop, Wilson and Lenin: The End of the World* (San Jose, Calif.: San Jose State U.P., 1975).

219   "to return . . . France": House diary, Dec. 18, 1917, in C. Seymour, ed., *The Intimate Papers of Colonel House* (Boston: Houghton Mifflin, 1926–8), p. 326.

219   "Reports of increasing": MIWS, Vol. 2, p. 21, Dec. 8, 1917.

219   "as Balfour explained": Seymour, *Intimate Papers*, p. 349.

219   text of Lloyd George's speech: WWP, Vol. 45, p. 489.

219   "Privately, even Haig": Woodward, *Trial by Friendship*, p. 129. See also E. B. Parsons, "Why the British Reduced the Flow of American Troops to Europe in August–October 1918," p. 183.

220   "the Russians had": Woodward, *Trial by Friendship*, p. 128.

220   "a voice calling": Jan. 8, 1918, in WWP, Vol. 45, p. 535.

220   "as the 'Inquiry' ": R. Steel, *Walter Lippmann and the American Century* (Boston: Little, Brown, 1980).

220   "powerful liberal offensive . . . idealistic solution.": Seymour, *Intimate Papers*, p. 327. Inquiry report, Jan. 4, 1918, in WWP, Vol. 45, pp. 459ff.

220   "I did not reach": House diary, Jan. 5, 1918, in Seymour, *Intimate Papers*, p. 334.

220   "God only needed": R. Skidelsky, *John Maynard Keynes*, Vol. 1, *Hopes Betrayed 1883–1920* (London: Macmillan, 1992), p. 388.

221   "We demand": Jan. 8, 1918, in WWP, Vol. 45, pp. 536–9.

222   "midday hour . . . bankrupt.": WWP, Vol. 45, p. 465.

222   "one of the great": Quoted in Seymour, *Intimate Papers*, p. 353.

222 "Psychoanalysts . . . as 'psychotic.' ": D. Ross, "Woodrow Wilson and the Case for Psychohistory," *Journal of American History*, 69 (3), December 1982, pp. 661–3.

222 "Edwin Weinstein has": See, e.g., J. George, A. George, and M. Marmor, "Research Note: Issues in Wilson Scholarship: References to Early 'Strokes,' " *Journal of American History* 70 (4), March 1984.

222 "limit of humiliation": House diary, Jan. 9, 1918, in *WWP*, Vol. 45, p. 555.

222 "The President . . . objectives.": House diary, Feb. 24, 1918, in *WWP*, Vol. 46, p. 436.

20: Ludendorff Attacks: Spring 1918

227 "crushing, smashing power": J. Terraine, *To Win a War: 1918, the Year of Victory* (London: Papermac, 1978), p. 59.

227 tactics employed: Historical Branch, War Plans Division, GS, Monograph 1: A Survey of German Tactics (Washington, D.C.: War Department, 1918). See also RG 200, Harbord Papers, Box 1, memorandum "Notes on Recent Fighting," May 16, 1918.

227 "Ludendorff had effectively": For an account of staff work and development of tactics, see H. H. Herwig, "The Dynamics of Necessity: German Military Policy During the First World War" in A. R. Millett and W. Murray, *Military Effectiveness*, Vol. 1 (Boston: Unwin, Hyam, 1988), pp. 95–6, 100–2.

228 "inspired his army": Memorandum, July 29, 1917, "Outline of a Scheme of Patriotic Education for the Troops," in E. von Ludendorff, *The General Staff and Its Problems* (London: Hutchinson, 1920), p. 385.

228 "The whole thing": H. Sulzbach, trans. R. Thonger, *With the German Guns: Four Years on the Western Front 1914–1918* (London: Leo Cooper, 1973), Jan. 18, 1918.

229 "a man of": Quoted in Terraine, *To Win a War*, p. 62.

229 "Pershing's pledge": D. Smythe, *Pershing: General of the Armies* (Bloomington: Indiana U.P., 1986), p. 101.

229 "The principle of": Pershing, *My Experiences in the World War*, (London: Hodder & Stoughton, 1931), p. 332.

230   "There may not be": Smythe, *Pershing*, p. 105.

230   "Instead of cotton": Westman, quoted in R. Parkinson, *Tormented Warrior: Ludendorff and the Supreme Command* (London: Hodder & Stoughton, 1978), p. 159.

232   "by taking boys": LoC, Baker papers, Reel 4, p. 34, Bliss telegram, Mar. 30, 1918.

232   "made available": Ibid.

232   "I have carefully": Ibid., manuscript endorsement.

232   "A better procedure": PRO, CAB 25, Minutes, SWC MR. Mar. 27, 1918.

232   "You are willing": Pershing, *My Experiences*, Vol. 2, May 1–2, 1918, p. 379.

232   "America declared war": Ibid., May 2, 1918, p. 383.

233   "training and service": PRO, CAB 25/121, Paper 18S, "Transportation of American Troops," Apr. 4, 1918.

233   "carry the war": Pershing, *My Experiences*, Vol. 2, p. 383.

234   Peyton March: The definitive biography is E. M. Coffman, *The Hilt of the Sword: The Career of Peyton C. March* (Madison: U. of Wisconsin Press, 1966).

234   "The conception of": LoC, March Papers, Box 2, Army War College lecture, Apr. 20, 1933, pp. 11–12.

235   task of rationalizing procurement: See, e.g., RG 165, WDG&SS, Records of the WD GS PST Div., Gen. Corr., 1918–1920, E 441 Box 36, "History of the PST Division, General Staff."

235   "Empowered by legislation": Overman Act, suggested by Baker to the Chamberlain committee; see RG 165, E 441, Box 36, CS, p. 81.

235   "management-consulting reforms.": See report of first three months in RG 165, PST Div., Gen. Corr., 1918–1920, Box 33, Apr. 15, 1918, "Report of the Purchasing Service and Division of Purchases and Supplies."

235   "the eventual abolition": RG 165, PST Div., Gen. Corr., 1918–1920, Box 33, Aug. 6, 1918, "Report of Activities of Purchase Section" ("Purchase Section Report"). And see also LoC, Goethals Papers, Box 4, Nov. 3, 1918.

235   "The Bureau chiefs are": LoC, Goethals Papers, Box 4, Aug. 5, 1918.

235   "March helped by": LoC, March Papers, Box 22, March to Pershing, Aug. 12, 1918.

235   "timber piling": LoC, Goethals Papers, Box 2, Desk Diary No. 3, Aug. 1, 1918.

235   "only five more": Purchase Section Report, op. cit., p. 5.

235   "My sole desire": LoC, March Papers, Box 22, "Correspondence 1918," Pershing to March, May 5, 1918.

235   "With reference . . . promotions": LoC, March Papers, Box 22, Pershing to March, July 25, 1918.

236   "March therefore suggested": But LoC, March Papers, Box 2, Baker to March, Apr. 4, 1933, claims that the "suggestion originated with Colonel House."

236   "The various Services": RG 182, WTB, E 177, Box 869, McFadden to Auchincloss, Sept. 4, 1918.

236   "There can be": LoC, March Papers, Box 22, Pershing to March, July 19, 1918.

237   "General Order 80": RG 65, E 214, Box 1, "History of the General Staff" (typed ms., 471 pp.).

21: Blood and Propaganda: Setting a Value on the AEF

238   "They had available": F. Fischer, *From Kaiserreich to Third Reich* (London: Routledge, 1991), p. 68.

238   "cartoonists": E. Demm, "Propaganda and Caricature in the First World War," *Journal of Contemporary History*, 28 (1), January 1993, p. 165.

238   "degenerates and . . . transports.": J. Buchan, *A History of the Great War* (London: Nelson, 1922), p. 273.

238   "Our soldiers despise": MIWS, Jan. 12, 1918.

240   "almost three miles": Historical Branch, War Plans Division, GS, Monograph 4: *A Study in Troop Frontage* (Washington, D.C.: U.S. Government Printing Office, 1920), p. 11.

240   "wholly disorganized": J. M. Evarts, *Cantigny—A Corner of the War* (privately printed, 1938), p. 1.

240   "commenced to shake": Ibid., p. 14.

240   "The 1st Division": D. Trask, *The AEF and Coalition Warmaking 1917–1918* (Lawrence: U. of Kansas Press, 1993), p. 65, quoting Alan Millett, "to demonstrate the skill and élan of the AEF."

240   "Pershing nevertheless decided": G. C. Marshall, *Memoirs of My Services in the World War* (Boston: Houghton Mifflin, 1976), p. 97.

241   "one machine-gun company": RG 120, WWI Org. Recs., 1st Div., Box 73, "Cantigny Operation," December 18, 1918 ("McGlachlin Report").

241   "a total . . . 280mm": RG 120, 1st Div., Box 87, "Report of the Capture of Cantigny," June 2, 1918 ("Ely Report").

241   "Ely's force spent": Ibid., p. 4.

241   "A young lieutenant": Marshall, *Memoirs*, p. 92.

242   "At 6:45 A.M. . . . woods.": Ely Report, op. cit., p. 1; McGlachlin Report, op. cit., p. 2.

242   "just as . . . rabbits": Clarence Huebner, quoted in E. Coffman, *The War To End All Wars: The American Military Experience in World War I* (New York: OUP, 1968), p. 157.

242   "An enemy . . . effect.": RG 120, 1st Div., Box 87, "Operations Against Cantigny," CO 3rd Batt., 28th Infantry, June 2, 1918.

243   "shape of a cross": Ely Report, op. cit., p. 2.

243   "The maximum depth": McGlachlin Report, op. cit., p. 4.

243   "Orders for the": Marshall, *Memoirs*, p. 95.

243   "directed by aircraft": Ely Report, op. cit., p. 6.

243   "A 3-inch shell": Marshall, *Memoirs*, p. 96.

243   "the troops had": Ely Report, op. cit., p. 5.

243   "200 yards behind": McGlachlin Report, op. cit., p. 3.

244   "The first wave": McGlachlin Report, op. cit., p. 3.

244   German and American losses: Ely Report, op. cit., pp. 5–6.

244   "The great strain": Ibid., p. 7.

244 "of no strategic": Marshall, *Memoirs*, op. cit.

245 "Pershing ordered Bullard": D. Smythe, *Pershing: General of the Armies* (Bloomington: Indiana U.P., 1986), p. 127.

22: "Know Thine Enemy": The Battle for Belleau Wood, June 1918

Everyone who studies the battle of Belleau Wood is indebted to the detailed work of Robert Asprey in *In Belleau Wood* (New York: Putnam, 1965).

247 "He is attentive": RG 200, Pershing Papers, Case Files, etc., Box 8, Bundy, Report of Col. LeRoy Eltinge, GS, May 7, 1918.

248 "had never commanded": J. Harbord, *The American Army in France 1917–1919* (Boston: Little, Brown, 1936), p. 264.

248 George Barnett: See, e.g., *Marine Corps Gazette* No. 77, Thomas, p. 67.

248 "at least . . . rover": HIoWRP, Allen Neil Papers, "Who Am I?" (recruiting leaflet for U.S. Marine Corps).

248 "Quantico": LoC, Stotesbury Papers, Reel 32, *Philadelphia Inquirer*, ca. October 1917.

248 "60 percent were": R. W. Lamont, "Over There," *Marine Corps Gazette*, June 1993.

248 "With 60 shots": HIoWRP, Allen Neil Papers.

248 "by little, yellow": Harbord, *American Army*, p. 272.

250 "It is absolutely . . . to hold." RG 200, Harbord Papers, Box 1, memorandum from General Degoutte, Cdt. le 21 Corp d'Armée to General Bundy, Cdt. la 2nd Div. U.S., June 1, 1918.

251 "Three times they": M. G. Gulberg, *A War Diary* (Chicago: Drake, 1927), quoted in Asprey, *In Belleau Wood*, p. 133.

251 "Oh, it was": A. W. Catlin, *With the Help of God and a Few Marines* (New York: Doubleday, 1919), quoted in Asprey, *In Belleau Wood*, p. 129.

251 "The hum of": RG 200, Harbord Papers, Box 1, "Diary of 4th Brigade Marine Corps, May 30, 1918–June 30, 1918" ("4BD"), June 5, 1918, p. 5.

251   "Corporal Kirkpatrick was": RG 120, WWI, Org. Rec., 2nd Div. Hist., Box 80, "Diary of a B. C. Battery 'B,' 12th Field Artillery."

251   "Fragments glittered in": Major E. D. Cooke, "We Can Take It," *Infantry Journal*, May–December 1937, quoted in Asprey, *In Belleau Wood*, p. 114.

251   "Retreat? Hell, we": Logan Feland, "Retreat Hell!" in *Marine Corps Gazette*, June 1921, quoted in Asprey, *In Belleau Wood*, p. 127.

252   "I thought trench": Entry for June 11, 1918, in *Lambert Wood: His Job: Letters Written by a 22-Year-Old Lieutenant in the World War to His Parents and Others in Oregon* (Portland: 1930). Wood was killed before Soissons on July 18, 1918.

252   "drawn in 1832": Asprey, *In Belleau Wood*, p. 144.

253   "The division was": MHI, AEF HQ, Arthur L. Conger, WWI.

253   Eddy's intelligence: LoC, Harbord Papers, Container 15, "At Belleau Wood, AEF 1918," patrol report by 2nd Lt. William A. Eddy, Regimental Intelligence Officer, 3:30 A.M., June 5, 1918.

253   "Harbord later claimed": Harbord, *American Army*, p. 289.

254   "properly speaking" . . . "raking fire" . . . "boxing fire," etc.: RG 200, Harbord Papers, Box 1, Orders No. 1 from HQ 2nd FA Brig., signed by Lt. Col. W. C. Potter, FA, for Brig. Gen. Chamberlaine, June 5, 1918.

254   "only two companies": RG 120, 2D/73, interview with Lt. Col. J. H. Turrill, HQ 2nd Div., Dec. 11, 1918.

254   "six hours late.": 4BD, op. cit., June 6, 1918, p. 7.

254   "insure the highest": RG 200, Harbord Papers, Box 1, memorandum No. 52, May 13, 1918.

255   "About 15 prisoners": 4BD, op. cit., June 6, 1918, p. 8.

255   "the enemy . . . driven back": RG 200, Harbord Papers, Box 1, Manus McCloskey, 12th FA, Field Orders No. 3, 7:30 A.M., June 6, 1918.

256   "Among his papers": This point was made by Lieutenant Pete Owen at the 1993 WFA annual conference.

257   "Colonel Albertus Catlin": Asprey, *In Belleau Wood*, p. 165.

257   "The diary for": See, e.g., RG 120, WWI Org. Rec., 2nd Div. Hist., Box 68, "History of 3rd Battalion, 6th Marines," ("3/6 Hist."), p. 6.

257 "What is left": 4BD, op. cit., June 6, 1918, p. 11.

258 "It was one": Catlin, in Asprey, *In Belleau Wood*, p. 177.

258 "so protected in": 4BD, op. cit., June 7, 1918, p. 17.

258 "Lieutenant Clifton Cates": Interview with General Clifton B. Cates, USMC, in Asprey, *In Belleau Wood*, p. 184.

259 "lost 1,087 men": E. Coffman, *The War To End All Wars: The American Military Experience in World War I* (New York: OUP, 1968), p. 217.

259 "The Brigade . . . possible.": 4BD, op. cit., June 7, 1918, p. 17.

23: "Do You Want to Live for Ever?"

260 "Competent observers believe": MIWS, June 15, 1918.

260 "a tool . . . war pay.": Ibid.

261 "We cannot afford": LoC, March Papers, Box 22, June 19, 1918.

261 "The morale, not": MIWS, June 8, 1918.

261 "the Anglo-American claim": D. Smythe, *Pershing: General of the Armies* (Bloomington: Indiana U.P., 1986), p. 139.

262 "at all costs": 4BD, op. cit., June 8, 1918, p. 21.

262 "interrogated with a view": Ibid., June 7, 1918, p. 18.

262 "mowing our men": Ibid., June 8, 1918, p. 19.

262 "We were able": 3/6 Hist., op. cit., p. 8.

262 "many more machine"; 4BD, op. cit., June 8, 1918, p. 20.

263 "Sibley 'became convinced": 3/6 Hist., op. cit., p. 8.

263 "Let your men rest": 4BD, op. cit., June 8, 1918, p. 20.

263 "which by late afternoon": Ibid., p. 22.

263 "Artillery has . . . mince meat.": Ibid., June 10, 1918, p. 27.

263 "Men fall asleep": Ibid., p. 30.

264 "It is a safe": RG 120, WWI Org. Rec., 2nd Div. Hist., Box 67, Wise to CO 5th Regt., June 18, 1918 ("Wise Memo"), p. 2.

264 "The enemy . . . told": 4BD, op. cit., June 8, 1918, p. 23.

264   "One marine later": K. Cowing and C. Cooper, eds., *Dear Folks at Home* (Boston: Houghton Mifflin, 1919), quoted in Asprey, *In Belleau Wood*, p. 245.

264   "Gravitating, according to": Wise Memo, op. cit.

265   "the Germans fought": Company Commander, 5th Marines, Questionnaire, Apr. 6, 1920, No. 45, HS files, quoted in Hist. Section, Army War College, Monograph 13, *The Aisne and Montdidier-Noyon Operations with Special Attention to the Participation of American Divisions* (Washington, D.C.: U.S. Government Printing Office, 1922).

265   "the north half . . . positions.": 4BD, op. cit., June 11, 1918, p. 34.

265   "the biggest thing": Ibid., p. 33.

265   "with a certain": Ibid., June 12, 1918, p. 35.

266   "barrage dropped too far north": Asprey, *In Belleau Wood*, p. 263.

266   "Have now 350": 4BD, op. cit., June 12, 1918, p. 38.

266   "A young . . . lost": Ibid., June 13, 1918, p. 39.

266   "Probably more or": Ibid., June 14, 1918, p. 42.

266   "Wise, expecting 800": Wise Memo, op. cit., note for June 14.

266   "My men physically": 4BD, op. cit., June 14, 1918, p. 42.

266   "8 A.M.": Asprey, *In Belleau Wood*, p. 282.

267   "He could force": 4BD, op. cit., June 15, 1918, p. 46.

267   "The character of": *Records of the 2nd Division (Regular)*, Vol. 6 (Washington, D.C.: Army War College, 1927), quoted in Asprey, *In Belleau Wood*, p. 204.

267   "hospital at Juilly": F. Pottle, *Stretchers: The Story of a Hospital Unit on the Western Front* (New Haven, Conn.: Yale U.P., 1929), p. 108.

267   casualties: Asprey, *In Belleau Wood*, p. 286.

267   "It is understood": 4BD, op. cit., June 18, 1918, p. 47.

268   "Attack ordered on": Ibid., June 20, 1918, p. 47.

268   "Your battalion will": Ibid., p. 48.

268   "I can assure": Ibid., June 21, 1918, p. 51.

268 "Everything is not": Ibid., p. 52.

268 "That when he": Ibid., pp. 52–3.

269 "Imagine the poor": Quoted in Asprey, *In Belleau Wood*, p. 291.

269 "were in groups": 4BD, op. cit., June 21, 1918, p. 54.

269 "The statement made": Ibid., June 22, 1918, p. 56.

269 "temporary nervous breakdown": A suggestion made by Dr. Timothy Nenninger of the National Archives, Washington, D.C., at the WFA annual conference, 1993.

269 "I personally can say": Wise Memo, op. cit., p. 3.

270 "The Boches on": RG 120, 2D.73, interview with Major Shearer, HQ 2nd Div., Dec. 11, 1918.

270 "Every gun that": *Field Artillery Journal, 14*, Wahl, p. 141.

270 "General Harbord had": Shearer interview, op. cit.

270 "*We have taken*": 4BD, op. cit., June 25, 1918, p. 63.

271 "Harbord's estimate was": J. G. Harbord, *The American Army in France* (Boston: Little, Brown, 1936), p. 298.

271 "No-one who has": 4BD, op. cit., June 29, 1918, p. 66.

271 "In stark . . . immaculate.": MHI, AEF HQ, Arthur L. Conger, WWI.

272 "a very good": Lieutenant von Berg, June 17, 1918, quoted in *Infantry Journal*, September 1918.

272 "They are in": MIWS, July 20, 1918, p. 12.

272 "Bois de La Brigade de Marine": 4BD, op. cit., June 30, 1918, p. 68.

24: A Time of Reckoning

275 "There is a . . . danger": June 2, 1918, in *WWP*, Vol. 48, p. 226.

275 "It should be": Pershing to War Department, June 4, 1918, in *WWP*, Vol. 48, p. 246.

275 "General Foch was": *WWP*, Vol. 48, p. 226, June 2, 1918.

275 "We have reached": LoC, March Papers, Box 22, Pershing to March, June 25, 1918.

276   "the Germans . . . shortages": E. von Ludendorff, *The General Staff and Its Problems* (London: Hutchinson, 1920), p. 131.

276   "class of 1920": MIWS, July 20, 1918.

276   "Analysts in Washington": G. Clarkson, *Industrial America in the World War: The Strategy Behind the Line 1917–1918* (Boston: Houghton Mifflin, 1923), p. 228.

276   " 'the Huns . . . a mystery.' ": LoC, Goethals Papers, Box 4, May 31, 1918.

276   Allied machinations: See, e.g., Cabinet meeting of July 1, 1918, discussed in D. Woodward, *Trial by Friendship: Anglo-American Relations, 1917–18* (Lexington: U. of Kentucky Press, 1993), pp. 182–3.

276   "I am thoroughly": LoC, March Papers, Box 22, Aug. 12, 1918.

277   "The immensity of": RG 165, E 443, Box 3, Swope Corr., Rose to Goethals, Dec. 1, 1918.

277   "The reorganization of": LoC, March Papers, Folder 1, "1918," March to Bliss, July 8, 1918.

277   "Sixty percent of": RG 165, E. 248, Ordnance Dept. and CWS (Chemical Warfare Service), Vol. 19, JRS to Pierce, Mar. 20, 1918.

277   "he directly challenged": Ibid., Aug. 19, 1918.

278   "Wilson preferred a": R. Cuff, "American Mobilization for War 1917–45: Political Culture vs. Bureaucratic Administration" in N. Dreisziger, ed., *Mobilization for Total War: The Canadian, American and British Experience 1914–1918, 1939–1945* (Waterloo, Ontario, Canada: Wilfrid Laurier U.P., 1981), p. 5.

278   "gifted (and trustworthy) amateurs": Ibid., p. 76.

278   "He allowed his": W. G. McAdoo, *Crowded Years: The Reminiscences of W. G. McAdoo* (Boston: Houghton Mifflin, 1931), p. 449. See also K. Austen Kerr, "Decision for Federal Control: Wilson, McAdoo and the Railroads 1917," *Journal of American History, 54* (3), December 1967, p. 551.

278   "Clearly, business leaders": R. Cuff, "Business, the State and World War I: The American Experience" in J. Granatstein and R. D. Cuff, eds., *War and Society in North America* (Toronto: Nelson, 1971), pp. 1–19.

278   MacAdoo and Baruch: McAdoo, *Crowded Years*, p. 301.

278 "Your newspaper . . . bully!": Wilson to Baruch, Jan. 19, 1918, in *WWP*, Vol. 46, p. 36.

279 "if I . . . Jew": "Bernard Baruch," entry by M. Coit in *American Dictionary of Biography*, p. 65.

279 Baruch terms of appointment and WIB organization: RG 165, E. 441, Box 36, "Directory of WIB, September 1, 1918" (Washington, D.C.: U.S. Government Printing Office, 1918).

279 "The WIB did": J. R. Gillis, *The Militarization of the Western World* (New Brunswick, N.J.: Rutgers U.P., 1989), reviewed by J. Gooch in *European History Quarterly, 23* (1), January 1993, pp. 92–4.

279 "Military needs were": J. M. Clark, *The Costs of the War to the American People* (New Haven, Conn.: Yale U.P./Carnegie Endowment for International Peace, 1931), p. 159.

279 "allocation of capital": See *CIC/WFC*.

279 "$24.3 billion": C. Gilbert, *American Financing of World War I* (Westport, Conn.: Greenwood, 1970), p. 211.

279 "diverting civilian production": P. A. C. Koistinen, *The Military-Industrial Complex: A Historical Perspective* (New York: Praeger, 1980), p. 8.

279 "Detroit switched almost": RG 61, E1-D1, Box 89, WIB Chairman's Office, Automotive Products Section Report. See also *WIBM*, passim.

279 "Akron Tire . . . pumps." RG 61, E.4-A1, Box 528, Price Fixing Committee, Miscellaneous Correspondence.

280 "required to conserve": RG 61, WIB Chairman's Office, E1-D1, Box 89, Conservation Division Report, Dec. 15, 1918.

280 "steel for stays": J. E. Wiltz, "The Nye Munitions Committee 1934" in A. M. Schlesinger, Jr., and R. Bruns, eds., *Congress Investigates: A Documented History 1792–1974*, Vol. 4 (New York: Chelsea House, 1975), p. 2773.

280 "to reclaim . . . annually.": WIBM, Nov. 16, 1917.

280 "the industrial heartland": Ibid., pp. 261, 284, 308.

280 "Harry Garfield predicted": RG 165, E. 445, PST Div., Corr. of Hugh S. Johnson, Box 3, Baruch to Stettinius, May 13, 1918.

280   railroad tonnage: Interstate Commerce Commission Annual Reports, 1916, 1918, quoted in A. D. Noyes, *The War Period of American Finance 1908–1925* (New York: Putnam, 1926), p. 223.

281   "mergers became as": J. Granatstein and R. D. Cuff, eds., *War and Society in North America* (Toronto: Nelson, 1971), p. 13.

281   "cooperation and control": R. D. Cuff, *The War Industries Board: Business-Government Relations During World War I* (Baltimore: Johns Hopkins U.P., 1973), p. 60.

281   "The limiting factor": *WIBM*, June 27, 1918.

281   "80 divisions of": LoC, March Papers, Box 22, March to Bliss, Sept. 26, 1918.

25: The Will to Fight

282   "They were not laughing": RG 165, WDG&SS, MID, Box 131, File 80-17.

283   "Comprehension of object": RG 165, WDG&SS, MID Corr., 1917–1941, Box 194, 177-28, report by Captain Allen J. Newman, July 23, 1918.

283   "strong and virile": R. Bourne, "Trans National America" in D. Hollinger and C. Capper, eds., *The American Intellectual Tradition*, Vol. 2, *1865–The Present* (New York: OUP, 1989), pp. 153ff.

283   "I go forth": William M. Kelley to Baker, Aug. 1, 1918, in *Federal Surveillance of Afro-Americans 1917–1925: The First World War, the Red Scare and the Garvey Movement* (Frederick, Md.: University Publications of America).

284   "Unrest among . . . present.": MIWS, June 28, 1918, p. 22.

284   "Archie is badly": Roosevelt to Lodge, Aug. 12, 1918, in *The Letters of Theodore Roosevelt*, Vol. 2 (Cambridge, Mass.: Harvard U.P., 1954), p. 534.

284   "Peyton March's son": E. Coffman, in a paper presented to the 1993 WFA annual conference in Washington, D.C.

284   "wise to fix": Willard to Wilson, Dec. 7, 1917, in *WWP*, Vol. 45, p. 233.

285   Brookings: For his account of his methods, see RG 61, Price Fixing Committee, Misc. Corr., E4-A1, Box 528, Brookings to Wilson, Oct. 4, 1918. For WD representative's account, see RG 165, PST Div., Gen. Corr., 1918–1920, Box 33, File 029, report from Young to DPS (Director of Purchasing Section), May 21, 1918, pp. 12ff. See also R. D. Cuff, *The War Industries Board: Business-Government Relations During World War I* (Baltimore: Johns Hopkins U.P., 1973), pp. 225ff.

285   "His committee had": G. Clarkson, *Industrial America in the World War: The Strategy Behind the Line 1917–1918* (Boston: Houghton Mifflin, 1923), p. 175.

285   cost of living: C. Gilbert, *American Financing of World War I* (Westport, Conn.: Greenwood, 1970), p. 213.

285   food prices, etc.: MIWS, Sept. 7, 1918, p. 24.

285   "Mrs Redfield paid": Redfield to Wilson, Dec. 8, 1917, in *WWP*, Vol. 45, p. 216.

285   "The war . . . 2,454 percent": Gilbert, *American Financing*, p. 65.

285   "23.3 percent": Ibid., p. 222. W. G. McAdoo, *Crowded Years: The Reminiscences of W. G. McAdoo* (Boston: Houghton Mifflin, 1931), p. 412, gives the proportion in 1917–1919 as one third.

285   "came from taxes": For the problem of financing the war through taxation, see, e.g., Gilbert, *American Financing*, p. 12.

285   "Secretary McAdoo had": Gilbert, *American Financing*, pp. 177, 179, 194. See also M. Friedman and A. J. Schwartz, *A Monetary History of the United States 1867–1960* (Princeton, N.J.: Princeton U.P., 1963), p. 216.

285   "The volume of": A. D. Noyes, *The War Period of American Finance 1908–1925* (New York: Putnam, 1926), p. 228.

285   "below face value": Josephus Daniels, *The Wilson Era*, Vol. 2, *1917–1923: Years of War and After* (Chapel Hill: U. of North Carolina Press, 1946), p. 280. See also McAdoo, *Crowded Years*, p. 409.

286   "they would receive": WIBM, Feb. 7, 1918.

286   "Similarly, Pierre Du Pont": J. E. Wiltz, "The Nye Munitions Committee 1934" in A. M. Schlesinger, Jr., and R. Bruns, eds., *Congress Investigates: A Documented History 1792–1974*, Vol. 4 (New York: Chelsea

House, 1975), p. 2573. See also RG 165, E248, Recs. of Ordnance Dept. and CWS 1917–1919, Vol. 19, Du Pont to WIB, Dec. 1, 1917.

286   "On the basis": RG 165, E441, Box 36, CS, p. 72.

286   "a small . . . trustees.": J. E. Wiltz, *In Search of Peace: The Senate Munitions Inquiry 1934–1936* (Baton Rouge: Louisiana State U.P., 1963), p. 126.

286   "fulfill their obligations": LoC, Baker Papers, Container 7, Stettinius to Baker, May 4, 1918.

286   "overcontracted its facilities": RG 165, E 44S, PST Div., Hugh Johnson Corr., Box 3, McKay to Pierce, Apr. 6, 1918.

286   "carte blanche as": RG 61, E.1-D1, WIB Chairman's Corr., Box 90, Committee on Emergency Construction Report, Dec. 31, 1918, p. 30.

286   "Wilson told Congress": F. Lundberg, *America's Sixty Families* (New York: Vanguard, 1937), pp. 496ff.

287   "as fine a": McAdoo, *Crowded Years*, p. 494.

287   "Bethlehem Steel . . . large bonuses.": Wiltz, *In Search of Peace*, p. 122.

287   "One executive of": R. Kaufman, *The War Profiteers* (Indianapolis, Ind.: Bobbs-Merrill, 1970), p. 11.

287   "doing everything that": President's statement, July 12, 1917, in *WWP*, Vol. 43, pp. 151–4.

287   "The law of": Hoover to Wilson, Dec. 1, 1917, in *WWP*, Vol. 45, p. 179. Wilson himself used similar words in his State of the Union address, Dec. 4, 1917.

287   "Parents are having": LoC, Baker Papers, Container 6, memorandum, Aug. 10, 1918.

287   "The fact that": J. Mock and C. Larson, *Words That Won The War: The Story of the Committee on Public Information* (Princeton: Princeton U. P., 1939), p. 212.

287   "We cannot hope": Hoover to Wilson, Dec. 1, 1917, in *WWP*, Vol. 45, p. 179.

287   "Just as we": *WWP*, Vol. 45, p. 216.

288 "Why does . . . JOB.": Mock and Larson, *Words That Won*, p. 192.

288 "the principal hotbed": Omar Bradley and C. Blair, *A General's Life* (New York: Simon & Schuster, 1983), p. 145.

288 "written on tissue": RG 60, Glasser File, Box 9, File "1918," report from Dept. Intell. Officer to Director of Mil. Intell., GS, Sept. 21, 1918.

289 "At 4 o'clock": Ibid., Intell. Officer, Spokane, to Dept. Intell. Officer, Oct. 16, 1918.

289 "where Trotzky lived": RG 63, CPI Records, Exec. Div., E 1, Box 2, Feb. 13, 1918.

290 "Lenin's advance guard": See, e.g., RG 65, WD GS, MID, Box 2770, "Report of Special Employee McIntosh for Jan. 3, 1918, re labor situation and the IWW in Western Washington."

290 "throat of America": A. J. Toynbee, "Looking Back Fifty Years" in A. J. Toynbee, *Impact of the Russian Revolution* (London: RIIA/OUP, 1967), pp. 21, 24.

290 "Lenin had written . . . slave.": MIWS, [November 1918], p. 155.

290 "Let us hope": RG 165, WD GS, MID Corr., 1917–1941, 177-56/1; MIWS, Nov. 19, 1918.

290 "There is . . . of Labor.": RG 165, WD GS, MID, Box 2770, "Report of Special Employee McIntosh," op. cit.

291 "Captain Neal Johnson": RG 60, Glasser File, Box 9, File "1918," "Report from Captain N. C. Johnson, 63rd Infantry, to Adjutant General."

291 "highly contentious. . . . the draft.": D. M. Kennedy, *Over Here: The First World War and American Society* (New York: OUP, 1980), p. 269.

291 draft extension: J. W. Chambers, II, *To Raise an Army: The Draft Comes to Modern America* (New York: Free Press, 1987), pp. 188–92.

291 "unpleasant necessity . . . situation.": RG 165, WD GS, MID, report, Sept. 14, 1918.

291 "perceptible slackening": RG 165, WD GS, MID, Box 131, 80-60.

292 "There are many deserters": LoC, Gregory Papers, Box 1, Gregory to Wilson, Sept. 9, 1918.

292 "Ringling Bros. Circus": Joan M. Jensen, *The Price of Vigilance* (Chicago: Rand McNally, 1968), p. 191.

26: "The Spirit of Ruthless Brutality"

293   "Once lead this": Maxwell Anderson, memorandum of conversation
with Frank Irving Cobb in June 1923, printed in New York *World*, Feb. 7,
1924. But see also J. S. Auerbach, "Woodrow Wilson's 'Prediction' to
Frank Cobb: Words Historians Should Doubt Ever Got Spoken," *Journal of
American History*, 54 (3), December 1967, casting doubt on whether Wilson actually said this—and see A. Link's response.

294   "It is difficult": S. Vaughn, *Holding Fast the Inner Lines: Democracy,
Nationalism and the Committee for Public Information* (Chapel Hill: U. of
North Carolina Press, 1980), p. 126.

294   "the largest number": J. Mock & C. Larsen, *Words That Won The
War: The Story of the Committee on Public Information* (Princeton: Princeton
U.P., 1939), p. 152.

294   " 'Withered Willie' . . . gorillas": A. Cornebise, *War as Advertised:
The Four-Minute Men and America's Crusade 1917–1918* (Philadelphia:
American Philosophical Society, 1984), p. 40.

295   "Attorney General Gregory": LoC, Baker Papers, Container 5, Gregory to Baker, Apr. 26, 1918.

295   "Across the country": D. Bennett, *The Party of Fear: From Nativism
Movements to the New Right in American History* (Chapel Hill: U. of North
Carolina Press, 1988). See also J. Higham, *Strangers in the Land: Patterns
of American Nativism* (New York: Atheneum, 1963), p. 208.

295   "King George III": Cornebise, *War as Advertised*, p. 81.

295   "Any book whatever": R. M. Elroy, "German Kultur in American
Schools" in *Win the War for Permanent Peace* (New York: League to Enforce
Peace, 1918), p. 77.

295   "We all know . . . spiked helmet": Ibid., p. 76.

296   "in Willard, Ohio": Cleveland *Plain Dealer*, Mar. 29, 1918.

296   "taking peculiar . . . here.": Cornebise, *War as Advertised*, p. 122.

297   "Night riding and": RG 165, WD GS, MID, Box 2964, 10261-
161.

297   "military and economic cooperation.": D. Stevenson, *The First World
War and International Politics* (Oxford, England: OUP, 1988), p. 207.

297 "Neither he nor": LoC, March Papers, Folder 1, "1918," March to Bliss, July 8, 1918. See also Box 22, March to Baker, June 24, 1918, and Box 2, Apr. 20, 1933, Army War College lecture, p. 32.

298 "But the need": LoC, Baker Papers, Reel 4, cable, July 12, 1918: "military plan mainly is necessarily a compromise."

298 "The reason he": See, e.g., B. Unterberger, *America's Siberian Expedition 1918–1920* (Durham, N.C.: Duke U.P., 1956), p. 231.

298 "Blood from underneath": B. Rhodes, *The Anglo-American Winter War With Russia 1918–1919: A Diplomatic and Military Tragicomedy* (Westport, Conn.: Greenwood, 1988), p. 39.

299 "Living conditions in": E. M. Halliday, *The Ignorant Armies: The Anglo-American Archangel Expedition 1918–19* (London: Weidenfeld & Nicolson, 1961), p. 113.

299 "It's the land": Rhodes, *Anglo-American Winter War*, p. 51. Brig. Gen. W. P. Richardson gives a contrary report; see National Archives Microfilm, M924, "Historical Files of the AEF, North Russia 1918–1919" (Washington, D.C.: National Archives R.A., 1973), 23–11.4, p. 45.

299 "Food was British": Halliday, *Ignorant Armies*, pp. 119–20.

299 "suffer 472 casualties.": Microfilm M924, op. cit., 23-11.1 (68 died of disease, 63 were killed in action, 15 died of wounds).

299 Sisson papers: Text in HIoWRP, CPI Papers; German protest, RG 63, CPI, E1.3, *New Yorker Volkzeitung* to Creel, Oct. 9, 1918.

299 "DOCUMENTS PROVE LENINE": Mock and Larson, *Words That Won*, p. 315.

299 "Their authenticity disputed": See, e.g., Vaughn, *Holding Fast*, p. 77.

27: "Nobody Can Say We Aren't Loyal Now"

300 "We are trying": RG 12, Off. of Education, Hist. File, 1870–1950, Entry 6, Box 11, File 106, "The Great Experiment," Dept. of the Interior, *Americanization Bulletin*, Oct. 15, 1918.

301 "another was to": On the era of 100 percent Americanism, see, e.g., J. F. McClymer, *War and Welfare: Social Engineering in America 1890–1925* (Westport, Conn.: Greenwood, 1980), pp. 75ff. See also J. Higham,

Strangers in the Land: erns *of American Nativism* (New York: Atheneum, 1963), pp. 204–14.

301   "they had no sense": LoC, Daniels Papers, Box 87, Speech by Lane at Americanization conference, Dept. of the Interior, Apr. 3, 1918.

302   "Banque de France's": AAV 6 N 53, Note for the President of the War Council, "War Loans in the United States," June 24, 1918.

302   "spread depressing rumors": *The Spy Glass, 1* (1), June 4, 1918.

302   "gave the dignity": John Lord O'Brian, "Civil Liberty in War Time," address to the 42nd Annual Meeting of the New York State Bar Association, New York, Jan. 17–18, 1919 (Washington, D.C.: U.S. Government Printing Office, 1919), p. 18.

303   "American Protective League": The fullest study is Joan M. Jensen, *The Price of Vigilance* (Chicago: Rand McNally, 1968).

303   "spy hysteria had": O'Brian, "Civil Liberty," pp. 5–6.

303   "I'd rather . . . blamed place": Daniels diary, Mar. 30, 1917, in *WWP,* Vol. 41, p. 506.

303   "I wonder if": Jensen, *Price of Vigilance,* p. 45.

304   "agents had to": HIoWRP, Hanford Collection.

304   "organizations . . . or crime.": Supplement to *The Spy Glass, 1* (8), Sept. 21, 1918.

304   "I am not shure": Jensen, *Price of Vigilance,* p. 48.

304   "Let us call": Emerson Hough, quoted in ibid., p. 149.

304   "Contrary to my": LoC, Gregory Papers, Box 1, Gregory to Wilson, Sept. 9, 1918.

305   "more than 100,000": Jensen, *Price of Vigilance,* p. 146.

305   "The beloved leader": T. Draper, *The Roots of American Communism* (New York: Viking, 1957), p. 75.

305   "The speedy outcome": *The Spy Glass, 1* (8), Sept. 21, 1918.

305   "They carried out": Jensen, *Price of Vigilance,* p. 180.

305   "traveling salesmen": RG 165, WD GS, MID, Box 3052, 10325-8, T. J. Phelps of the United Commercial Travelers of America to William F. Garcelon, Oct. 27, 1917.

306 "suspect cards . . . buffet luncheons.": RG 165, MID, Box 3053, 10320-5, H. T. Hunt to R. T. Bullen re Travelers' Protective Association.

306 "Volunteers were used": RG 60, AG 370.6, MID, Adjutant General to Baker, May 16, 1917.

306 "An agent from": J. M. Jensen, *Army Surveillance in America* (New Haven, Conn.: Yale U.P., 1991), pp. 145–159.

306 "councils of defense": See, e.g., S. J. Keillor, review of C. H. Chrislock, *Watchdog of Loyalty: The Minnesota Commission of Public Safety During World War I* (St. Paul: Minnesota Historical Society Press, 1991), in *Journal of American History*, Sept. 1992, pp. 702–3.

306 "enjoying the liberty . . . Liberty Loans.": R. Schaffer, *America in the Great War* (New York: OUP, 1991), p. 19.

306 "Economic Vigilance Committees": CIC/WFC, p. 37.

307 "In New York": MIWS, Aug. 3, 1918.

307 "Elsewhere there flourished": H. C. Peterson and G. C. Fite, *Opponents of War 1917–1918* (Madison: U. of Wisconsin Press, 1957), p. 18.

307 "through accusations of": McClymer, *War and Welfare*, p. 76.

307 "In the summer": LoC, Gregory Papers, Box 1, Gregory to Dr. R. E. Vinson, University of Texas, May 13, 1918.

307 "The young . . . Eugene O'Neill": E. R. Ellis, *Echoes of Distant Thunder* (New York: Coward, McCann and Geoghegan, 1975).

308 "The university president": H. L. Mencken, "On Patriots" in *Prejudices: Third Series* (New York: Knopf, 1922), pp. 211–13.

28: Attack and Counterattack: July 1918

312 "McAlexander had taken": RG 120, 3rd Div., Box 42, C. H. Lanza, "The 38th Infantry in the Second Battle of the Marne" ("Lanza Report"), p. 2.

312 McAlexander's defensive plan: RG 120, 3rd Div., Hist., 38th Regt., Box 44, "Plan of Defense—East Subsector."

312 "facing the French sector": RG 120, WWI, Org. Recs., Hist., 3rd Div., 38th Regt., Box 46, U. G. McAlexander, Report of Battle of 15–16 July, 1918: "I had also made provision . . . in the event of the withdrawal of

the French." But see also Lanza Report, op. cit., p. 2: "Their original intention was to face to the west."

312 "intended to do": *Field Artillery Journal*, 23, Anderson, p. 380.

312 "in exactly 120": HIoWRP, Wooldridge Papers, Wooldridge letter, July 28, 1918.

312 "behind which at forty: Ibid.

313 "The regiment which . . . on my sector.": RG 120, Hist., 3rd Div., 38th Regt., Box 45, "Report of Operations of Company G, 38th Infantry, July 15–21, 1918" ("Co. G Report").

313 "kitchen personnel, company": Ibid.

313 "lost 19.8 percent": Lanza Report, op. cit., p. 4.

314 "division's own artillery": Co. G Report, op. cit.

314 "The Americans kill": *Journal of the Royal Artillery*, 49, 1922–23, p. 339.

314 "compressing . . . three miles.": Lanza Report, op. cit., p. 4.

314 "He had been": E. Coffman, *The War To End All Wars: The American Military Experience in World War I* (New York: OUP, 1968), p. 234. See also H. Liggett, *Commanding an American Army: Recollections of the World War* (Boston: Houghton Mifflin, 1925), p. 33, and RG 200, Harbord Papers, Box 1, "The Operations Southwest of Soissons, July 18–25, 1918."

315 "Harbord had replaced . . . Bundy": RG 200, Pershing Papers, Case Files, etc., Box 8, Bundy.

315 "The divisional surgeons": RG 120, First Army, Box 30, Files 27.2–31.2, "Notes on Recent Operations No. 2 (Sanitary Service)."

315 "hub to hub": RG 120, 2nd Div., Box 80, G. D. Wahl report (n.d.).

316 "it was thronged": J. M. Evarts, *Cantigny—A Corner of the War* (privately printed, 1938), p. 85.

316 "Weary drivers were": J. G. Harbord, *The American Army in France 1917–1919* (Boston: Little, Brown, 1936), p. 324.

317 "last hot meal": RG 120, 2nd Div., Box 73, F. J. Grayling report (n.d.).

317 "The 5th Marines": Harbord, *American Army*, p. 331. See also RG 120, 2nd Div., Box 73, E. D. Cooke report, July 2, 1919 [*sic*].

317 "no telephone links": RG 200, Harbord Papers, Box 1, Daily Report, July 18, 1918.

317 "Lieutenant, where are": R. W. Kean, *Dear Marraine 1917–1918* (privately printed, 1969), p. 158.

317 "the wheat was": RG 120, 2nd Div., Box 73, L. H. Vandoren report, Jan. 28, 1919.

317 "it was difficult": RG 120, 2nd Div., Box 73, F. J. Grayling report.

317 "could evacuate only": Harbord, *American Army*, p. 332.

318 "walking slowly down": Kean, *Dear Marraine*, p. 158.

318 "It is not practicable": RG 200, Harbord Papers, Box 1, Daily Report, July 18, 1918, 11:45 P.M.

318 "The large number": RG 120, 2nd Div., Box 73, R. L. Keyser report, July 22, 1918.

318 "practically continuously": RG 200, Harbord Papers, Box 1, Daily Report, July 18, 1918.

319 "a mixed blessing.": RG 120, 2nd Div., Box 73, F. J. Grayling report.

319 "We are advancing": RG 120, 2nd Div., Box 68, Field Message, July 19, 1918, 9:50 A.M.

319 "the commander of": RG 120, 2nd Div., Box 73, F. W. Clarke report, July 20, 1918.

319 "70 percent losses": RG 120, 2nd Div., Box 68, "A Brief History of the 2nd Battalion, 6th Marines During the Period July 13–25, 1918" by L. H. Vandoren (n.d.).

320 "losses at 5,000": Harbord, *American Army*, p. 336.

320 "Let no man": *Field Artillery Journal*, 13, Holbrook, p. 249.

29: Hope and Glory

322 "victory through attrition.": D. Trask, *The AEF and Coalition Warmaking 1917–1918* (Lawrence: U. of Kansas Press, 1993), p. 93.

322 "In his preliminary": RG 120, AEF GHQ, G3 Reports, Box 3152, File 1033, "Preliminary Study of Offensive Operation Against the St. Mihiel Salient," Aug. 6, 1918.

323   "I have had . . . grade": LoC, March Papers, Box 22, Pershing to March, July 27, 1918.

323   "In return for": RG 165, E. 445, Hugh Johnson, Box 1. The June 1918 replacements included 30,719 metric tons of steel, 6,782 tons of copper, and 3,285 tons of smokeless powder.

323   "We did not": J. Hagood, *The Services of Supply: A Memoir of the Great War* (Boston: Houghton Mifflin, 1927), p. 313.

324   "These were deficiencies": A. Brandt, *Motor Transport Organization in the AEF* (Washington, D.C.: Historical Section, Army War College, 1942).

324   "We cannot hold": LoC, March Papers, Box 22, Pershing to March, June 25, 1918.

324   "Officers cannot learn": Ibid.

324   "Recalling his training": W. J. Schierholt, *Diary of William J. Schierholt in World War I* (Manhattan, Kans.: Military Affairs/Aerospace Historian Publishing, 1978).

325   "There were also": See, e.g., D. Woodward, "The Military Role of the United States in World War I" in J. Carroll and C. Baxter, eds., *The American Military Tradition from Colonial Times to the Present*.

325   "Pershing, however, believed": Leonard Wood supported both open warfare and Pershing's faith in the rifle; see Wood Report, op. cit., para. "Training."

325   "It seems . . . misunderstood": RG 165, CoS Corr., Box 191, 1450.

326   "The company of": Historical Sub-Section, GS, AEF, Monograph 1: *A Survey of German Tactics* (Washington, D.C.: War Department, Document 883, December 1918), p. 23.

326   "On August 29": RG 120, WWI, Org. Recs., First Army, Box 30, "Combat Instruction for Troops of First Army."

326   "Among Harbord's papers": RG 200, Harbord Papers, Box 1, Col. J. H. Parker, 102nd U.S. Infantry, "Organization of Infantry for Victory."

327   "strong right arm": LoC, Mitchell Papers, Box 34, memorandum from Chief, Air Service, 1st Army Corps [Mitchell] to Commanding General, 1st Army Corps, n.d. (March–April 1918?), pushing for the creation of a separate AEF Air Service.

327 "If we create": LoC, Mitchell Papers, Box 2, "Before Pershing in Europe," May 17, 1917, p. 12.

328 "more or less": Ibid., Sept. 18, 1917, p. 277.

3o: The Dream Shattered

329 "in view of": MIWS, Aug. 10, 1918.

330 "imperil the supply": RG 165, Dir. Intell., Gen. Recs., Summary of Information Reports, June 1918–January 1919, Box 2, Summary, Nov. 16, 1918, quoting German document, Aug. 5, 1918.

330 "70% of the": MIWS, Aug. 10, 1918.

330 "But nothing was": M. Kitchen, *The Silent Dictatorship: The Politics of the German High Command Under Hindenburg and Ludendorff 1916–1918* (London: Croom Helm, 1976), p. 235.

331 "Haig was the": H. Liggett, *AEF: Ten Years Ago in France* (New York: Dodd, Mead, 1927), p. 161: "The war could not have been won in 1918, in all likelihood, had not [Haig] been willing to take on his own individual shoulders a responsibility which his government refused to accept."

331 "We ought to": Quoted in J. Terraine, "The Final Offensive," 1993 Presidential Address to the WFA, printed in *Stand To!*, *40* (Spring 1994), pp. 10–11.

331 "to get a decision": D. Woodward, *Trial by Friendship: Anglo-American Relations, 1917–18* (Lexington: U. of Kentucky Press, 1993), p. 195.

331 "Foch's message was": J. J. Pershing, *My Experiences in the World War* (London: Hodder & Stoughton, 1931), pp. 568–79. See also E. Coffman, *The War To End All Wars: The American Military Experience in World War I* (New York: OUP, 1968), pp. 270–3, and D. Smythe, "AEF Strategy in France, 1917–1918," *Army Quarterly*, *115* (2), April 1985, pp. 198–9.

331 "It would be": Liggett, *AEF*, p. 172.

332 "means of maintaining pressure": Smythe, "AEF Strategy," p. 177.

333 "even an . . . three months?": Liggett, *AEF*, p. 203.

334 "It was now": J. Hagood, *The Services of Supply: A Memoir of the Great War* (Boston: Houghton Mifflin, 1927), p. 315.

335   "Throughout August, according": RG 120, AEF GHQ, G3 Reports, Box 3152, File 1033/1088, "Report of the Tank Corps at St. Mihiel, Oct. 22, 1918" ("Rockenback Report").

335   "150 of them": Ibid.

335   "could not . . . going on.": RG 120, AEF GHQ, G3 Reports, Box 3152, 1033/1078, Aug. 22, 1918.

31: The First Battle: Saint-Mihiel

339   "In early September . . . Alsace-Lorrainers": RG 165, Dir. Intell., Gen. Recs., June 1918–January 1919, Box 1, "German Official Reports of the Battle of St. Mihiel" ("German Reports"), p. 1.

340   Belfort ruse: RG 120, AEF GHQ, G3 Reports, Box 3152, 31/535. See also R. Paschall, *The Defeat of Imperial Germany 1917–1918* (Chapel Hill, N.C.: Algonquin, 1989), p. 173, and "St. Mihiel: Deception or Getting Over, Over There," 1993 WFA annual conference.

340   "prepare detailed plans": RG 120, AEF GHQ, G3 Reports, Box 3152, "Operations in Upper Alsace," Aug. 28, 1918.

340   "definitely select bridgeheads": Ibid., Sept. 4, 1918.

340   "Both the French": Pershing, *My Experiences*, p. 573.

341   "Every taxi driver": E. V. Rickenbacker, *Fighting the Flying Circus* (New York: Frederick Stokes, 1919), p. 230.

341   "without waiting for": German Reports, op. cit., pp. 1–2.

341   "documents captured in June": RG 120, AEF GHQ, G3 Reports, Box 3152, File 1033/1085, "Notes on the Operation by Fox Conner" ("Fox Conner Report").

341   "would fall back": D. Trask, *The AEF and Coalition Warmaking 1917–1918* (Lawrence: U. of Kansas Press, 1993), p. 104.

342   "Mitchell then pleaded": LoC, Mitchell Papers, Box 2, draft manuscript "Before Pershing in France," pp. 283–4.

342   "posts rotted and": Rockenback Report, op. cit.

343   "the 2,971 guns": Fox Conner Report, op. cit.

343   "The enemy's attack": German Reports, op. cit., pp. 2, 4.

343 "Their intelligence had": Army Service Schools, *Report on St. Mihiel Offensive, 89th Division* (Fort Leavenworth, Kans.: Army Service Schools, 1919), p. 17.

343 "cut . . . by artillery fire": Fox Conner Report, op. cit.

343 "according to Patton.": RG 120, AEF GHQ, G3 Reports, Box 3152, File 1033/1088, George Patton, "Report of Operations of the Tank Corps," Oct. 22, 1918 ("Patton Report").

343 "Closely pressing came": Rickenbacker, *Flying Circus*, p. 236.

344 "They laughed and": F. P. Duffy, *Father Duffy's Story: a tale of humor and heroism, of life and death with the Fighting 69th* (n.d.), p. 238.

344 "Can I go back": Ibid., p. 239.

344 "Dipping down at": Rickenbacker, *Flying Circus*, p. 232.

344 "huge quantities of": Ibid., p. 234.

345 "at all costs": German Reports, op. cit., p. 3.

345 "only 1,100 men": Ibid.

345 "13,251 prisoners . . . 11,000.": Fox Conner Report, op. cit.

345 "favorable conditions . . . withdrawn.": AAV, 16 N, 1927, "Report of the Mission Attached to the U.S. 1st Army, Sept. 21, 1918."

346 "failed to press their advantage.": German Reports, op. cit., p. 3.

346 "with impunity.": Fox Conner Report, op. cit.: "A further advance could undoubtedly have been made on the Metz and the Briey region."

346 "a vague reservation": P. F. Braim, *The Test of Battle: The American Expeditionary Forces in the Meuse-Argonne Campaign* (Newark: U. of Delaware Press, 1987), p. 82.

346 "a well-oiled, fully": Ibid., p. 85. See also H. Liggett, *AEF: Ten Years Ago in France* (New York: Dodd, Mead, 1927), p. 159.

346 "perhaps the most": Fox Conner Report, op. cit.

347 "back to Jonville": Patton Report, op. cit.

347 "From a point": Rockenback Report, op. cit.

347 "vim, dash and courage": Ibid.

347 "The greatest result": Fox Conner Report, op. cit.

347   "Command, Staff—Lacking": AAV, 16 N, 1927, "Analysis of the French Mission's Note on the Operations of the 1st U.S. Army, Sept. 26, 1918."

348   "This fact materially": Patton Report, op. cit.

348   "The machinery for": RG 120, First Army, Box 3240, "Special Report . . . St. Mihiel."

32: "The Most Ideal Defensive Terrain": Between the Meuse River and the Argonne Forest

349   "The most ideal": See E. Coffman, *The War To End All Wars: The American Military Experience in World War I* (New York: OUP, 1968), p. 300. See also A. Kaspi, *Les Temps des Américains 1917–1918. Le Concours américain à la France en 1917–1918* (Paris: Sorbonne, Série Internationale 6, 1976), p. 332.

350   "through fixed defenses": MIWS, Dec. 8, 1917.

350   "We must, above": MHI, V Corps Box, Truesdell Papers, memorandum, Jan. 27, 1919, "A Development of Highly Organized Warfare" ("Truesdell Memo"), p. 15. See also RG 120, GHQ, CinC Reports, Box 30, Russell, lecture "Intelligence Section 5th Army Corps, Meuse-Argonne Operations," Jan. 19, 1919 ("Russell Lecture"), p. 10.

350   "an extensive infrastructure": Russell Lecture, op. cit.

350   "six hundred . . . heights.": RG 120, GHQ, CinC Reports, Box 30, lecture by Maj. Gen. W. S. McNair, Chief of Army Artillery, Fourth Army, "Explanation and Execution of Plans for Artillery for St. Mihiel Operation and Argonne-Meuse Operations to November 11, 1918," Dec. 23, 1918 ("McNair Lecture"), p. 12.

350   "to target enemy infantry": LoC, Mitchell Papers, Box 2, draft manuscript, "Before Pershing in France," p. 309.

350   "problems would really begin.": The German defensive system is discussed in detail in Truesdell Memo, op. cit.

350   "another outpost zone": Ibid., p. 13.

351   "one spadeful deep.": Ibid., p. 4.

351   "The Kriemhilde Position": Ibid., p. 14.

351 "eight to one": H. Essame, *The Battle for Europe, 1918* (London: Batsford, 1972), p. 167.

351 "Absolute secrecy": *Les Armées Françaises Dans Le Grand Guerre (LAFDLGG)*, Tome VII, Ier Vol.; Annexes, 2de Vol.; Annexe No. 1163, "Instruction personelle et secret," Sept. 16. 1918.

351 "River Codes": MHI, First Army, Folder Col. Parker Hitt, memorandum, Sept. 10, 1931, "Comments on Certain Statements in H. O. Yardley's book *The Black Chamber.*"

352 "Pétain's headquarters spread": *LAFDLGG*, Tome 7, Ier Vol., Quatrième Partie, p. 347. See also Kaspi, p. 314.

352 "some camouflage radio": MHI, First Army, Folder Col. Parker Hitt, memorandum, Sept. 18, 1918, Hitt to Capt. Loghry, Radio Detachment.

352 "The civilians in Metz": Kaspi, *Les Temps*, p. 315.

352 "The circulation in": Russell Lecture, op. cit., p. 6., See also Truesdell Memo, op. cit., p. 11.

353 "Brown uniforms having": Ibid., p. 10.

353 "5th Guard Division": RG 120, AEF GHQ, G3, Box 3241, "Field Orders and Instructions, 1st Army Corps: 'The Battle of the Argonne.' "

353 "appears to be . . . echeloning": Ibid. See also McNair Lecture, op. cit., p. 13.

353 "Pershing intended that": RG 120, GHQ, CinC Reports, Box 30, R. T. Ward, lecture, Dec. 18, 1918, "Explanation and Execution of Plans and Operations, 1st American Army, for Meuse-Argonne Operation to Nov. 11, 1918," p. 11, para. 17(d).

354 "going over the top": V. R. Nicholls, *Infantry Journal*, September 1919, pp. 183ff.

354 "moppers up": Ibid.

354 "3,980": McNair Lecture, p. 15.

355 "two 75mm guns.": RG 120, AEF GHQ, G3, Box 3241, I Corps, Field Orders No. 57, Sept. 22, 1918.

355 "GIVE THEIR ESPECIAL": Ibid.

33: Over the Top:
The First Day on the Meuse-Argonne

356 " 'Fix bayonets!' . . . acrid powder fumes": V. R. Nicholls, *Infantry Journal*, September 1919.

356 "Now here I was": MHI, 35th Division, Box Milton B. Sweningsen.

357 "Sergeant William Triplett": MHI, 35th Div. Box.

357 "barely forty feet": RG 120, 35th Div., Box 15, "Report . . . 138th Infantry, September 25–26, 1918–October 1, 1918." ("Howland Report").

357 "luminous compass . . . etc.": RG 120, 35th Div., H. W. Thompson, "Report of Operations, September 26–October 2," Oct. 4, 1918.

357 "given twenty-five minutes": RG 120, 79th Div., Box 18, "Report of Operations for 314th Infantry and 158th Infantry Brigade" ("314th Report").

357 "they bunched up": Nicholls, op. cit., p. 188.

357 "At 8:55 A.M.": RG 120, IGO Inspections (5), V Corps, 91st Div., W. H. Johnston, statement, Sept. 29, 1918.

357 "Many dead are": MHI, 79th Div., L. Y. Haile, 304th Engineers.

357 "Some of them . . . wounded": MHI, 79th Div., E. A. Davies, 315th Regiment.

357 "We came across": MHI, 79th Div., C. W. Swartz, 314th Regiment.

358 "The shelling was": Howland Report, op. cit.

358 "My left hand": RG 120, WWI, ORH, 35th Div., Regimental Box 15, telegram, Sept. 29, 1918.

358 "Now, as ordered": Historical Division, U.S. Department of the Army, *The United States Army in the World War (USAWW)*, Vol. 9, *General Missions*, (Washington, D.C.: U.S. Government Printing Office, 1948), p. 130.

359 "Liggett had . . . objectives": H. Liggett, *AEF: Ten Years Ago in France* (New York: Dodd, Mead, 1927), p. 175.

359 "a bad mistake": H. Liggett, *Commanding an American Army: Recollections of the World War* (Boston: Houghton Mifflin, 1925), p. 80.

359 "No substantial resistance": *USAWW*, Vol. 9, pp. 163–4.

359 "The two outer . . . assist V Corps": Ibid., p. 130.

359 "More than half": RG 120, 79th Div., Box 16, G. E. Thorne report.

360 "Toward 4 o'clock": 314th Report, op. cit.

360 "The tanks I": RG 120, 79th Div., Box 16, "Report of Operations of 313th Infantry," Nov. 18, 1918.

360 Robert Noble story: RG 200, Pershing Papers, Case Files, Box 8, "Brief History in the Case of the Relief and Reduction of Brigadier-General Robert H. Noble."

361 "one great belching": MHI, 79th Div., J. W. Kress, 314th Regiment.

361 "Montfaucon captured 11 H 45.": RG 120, 79th Div., Box 16, "Pigeon Service," Sept. 27, 1918.

361 "The 313th dead": MHI, 79th Div., E. A. Davies, 315th Regiment.

34: "Retrograde Movements": The Second, Third, and Fourth Days

362 "infantry and artillery": V. R. Nicholls, *Infantry Journal*, September 1919.

363 "As far as": E. V. Rickenbacker, *Fighting the Flying Circus* (New York: Frederick Stokes, 1919), p. 303.

363 "give the men . . . support.": O. L. Spaulding, "A Study in Ammunition Supply," *Field Artillery Journal*, 13 (4), July–August 1923, p. 327. See also RG 120, 35th Div., Box 15, J. E. Reiger, "Tactical Lessons," Oct. 8, 1918: "There were no accompanying guns." See also RG 120, 35th Div., Box 15, P. A. Carmady, "Tactical Lessons," Oct. 10, 1918: "After the first day we had little or no artillery support."

363 "2nd Cavalry . . . tanks": RG 120, 35th Div., Box 15, "Report of Operations . . . of 35th Infantry, September 29, 1918," Oct. 4, 1918 ("Kalloch Report").

364 "Picking up all": Ibid.

364 "None materialized.": Ibid. See also MHI, WWI, AEF HQ, Arthur Conger, "Attack of 35th Division."

364   "It was now": RG 120, 35th Div., Box 15, "Operations of 137th Infantry, September 26–October 2, 1918," Oct. 4, 1918.

365   "We executed": RG 120, 35th Div., Box 15, "Chronological Report, 1st Platoon, M/G Co., 138th Infantry."

365   "looked terrible": Triplett, MHI, 35th Div. Box.

365   "Major General C. S. Farnsworth": RG 120, IGO (2), 37th Division, "Statement of Major-General C. S. Farnsworth."

366   "from shell holes.": RG 120, 79th Div., Box 19, "Chapter 1," n.d.

366   "again drifted to": RG 120, 79th Div., Box 18, Untitled report, Nov. 16, 1918.

366   "come nearer than": 314th Report, op. cit.

366   "the French staff": AAV, 47/3, 6 N 53, "Opérations de l'Armée U.S. entre Meuse et Champagne Sept. 26–30, 1918" gives a damning critique of the First Army's efficiency.

366   "heavy army artillery": McNair Lecture, op. cit., p. 18.

367   "Essentially, the First": J. Jaffin, M.D., "Medical Support in the Meuse-Argonne," 1993 WFA annual conference.

367   "a sanitary train": MHI, WWI, AEF HQ, Arthur L. Conger, memorandum, W. R. Eastman, "Evacuation of Sick and Wounded During the Meuse-Argonne."

367   "suspended the offensive.": RG 120, First Army, Box 3240, Field Order No. 32.

367   "I believe that": RG 120, First Army, Box 30, W. Howell, "Memo for Chief of Staff," 8:30 P.M., Sept. 29, 1918.

368   "Failure of artillery": RG 120, IGO (2), J. C. Johnson, "Memo for Corps Inspectors," Oct. 2, 1918.

369   Frank Luke: See, e.g., B. Robertson, *Air Aces of the 1914–18 War* (Letchworth, England: Harleyford, 1959), pp. 96–8.

369   "a deliberate sacrifice": Rickenbacker, *Flying Circus*, p. 253.

369   "Watch three Hun": But Rickenbacker, *Flying Circus*, p. 281, says "two balloons."

35: In the Argonne Forest

370   "own private war.": See generally RG 120, 77th Div., Box 3, monograph by Capt. N. M. Holderman, "Operation of the Force Known as the Lost Battalion," 1925.

370   "almost totally unexpected.": *LAFDLGG*, Tome 7, Ier Vol., Quatrième Partie, p. 355: "en vue de faire tomber par encerclement."

370   "it may be": R. T. Ward, "Study of First Army Situation," in *The United States Army in the World War*, Vol. 9, *General Missions* (Washington, D.C.: U.S. Government Printing Office, 1948), 1:30 P.M., Sept. 29, 1918. See also A. Kaspi, *Les Temps des Américains 1917–1918. Le Concours américain à la France en 1917–1918* (Paris: Sorbonne, Série Internationale 6, 1976), pp. 313–4.

370   "Its support weapons": RG 120, 77th Div., Box 15, "Report of Operations, September 26–November 8," Nov. 19, 1918, p. 2.

370   "Huge trees": MHI, 77th Div., 1st Lt. A. McKeogh.

371   "who held up": RG 120, 77th Div., Box 15, "Conversation with Dakota," Sept. 27, 1918.

371   "orders not to surrender": RG 120, Holderman, op. cit., p. 13.

372   "Badly wounded in": MHI, McKeogh, op. cit.

372   "before they had begun.": AAV, 47/3, MMF, 17 N 138, Metz Noblat report, Oct. 5, 1918 ("Noblat Report"). See also 17 N 138, Lestre to Chef MMF, Oct. 16, 1910 ("Lestre Report").

372   "Liaison was quickly": Lestre Report, ibid.

372   "Every time the": MHI, *The Colored Soldier in the U.S. Army* (Historical Section, Army War College, May 1942), Appendix 33, J. N. Merrill Report, Oct. 3, 1918.

372   "93rd Division's . . . had done well": AAV, 47/3, MMF, 6 N 53, M. Tardieu to French Commissioner, New York, May 28, 1918.

372   "a cold, authoritarian man": AAV, MMF, GS-3, MN 138, "Confidential Statement—Notice on the Command of the 92nd Division" ("Confidential Statement").

372   "They observed that": Ibid.

373   "The relatively restricted": Lestre Report, op. cit.

373   "still to be ignorant": Ibid.

373   "very mediocre": AAV, 47/3, MMF, 17 N 138, Metz Noblat, "Special Report," July 25, 1918.

373   "crushing responsibility": AAV, 47/3, MMF, 17 N 138, Lestre to Chef MMF, Sept. 15, 1918.

373   "You are of": Lestre Report, op. cit.

373   "Unless this decision": Ulysses Lee, "The Employment of Negro Troops," *The U.S. Army in World War II. Special Studies* 8, (Washington, D.C.: Office of Chief of Military History, U.S. Army, 1966), p. 9.

374   "actually did more": M 1440, Reel 4, memorandum from W. H. Loving to Director of Military Intelligence (DMI), "Treatment of Negro Officers and Soldiers in France as published in the May issue of *The Crisis*," May 6, 1919.

374   "Aware that their": Noblat Report, op. cit.

375   "sent a message": The pigeon messages from Whittlesey are in RG 120, 77th Div., Box 9, with copies in Box 27. The field messages from relieving units are in RG 120, 77th Div., Box 22.

375   "sealed his unit off.": See generally RG 120, Holderman, op. cit.

375   "in a pocket": RG 120, 77th Div., Box 27, C. W. Whittlesey, "Report of 1st and 2nd Battalions, 308th Infantry from October 2–October 8, 1918" ("Whittlesey Report"), Oct. 9, 1918.

375   "a motley force": Listed in RG 120, 77th Div., Box 9, B. O. Buchanan memorandum, Apr. 10, 1919.

375   "Our mission is": RG 120, Holderman, op. cit., p. 18.

376   Stacey story: RG 200, Pershing Papers, Case Files Relating to the Reclassification of Officers, Box 9, "Brief History in the Case of Col. Cromwell Stacey, 30th Infantry."

377   "2,100 raw recruits": RG 120, 77th Div., Box 21, Operations Report, 305th Infantry; this regiment alone received 900 replacements on Sept. 24. See also RG 120, IGO (5), "Report by A. T. Rich—77th Division, cutting off of seven companies," Oct. 8, 1918.

377   "many of them": RG 120, IGO (5), 77th Div., "Sworn Statement of Lt. Weston Jenkins," Oct. 6, 1918.

377   "down to 375 men.": Whittlesey Report, op. cit., p. 4.

378   "All the time": RG 120, IGO (5), 77th Div., E. M. Johnson, "Report—Further Use of 154th Infantry Brigade in Action," Oct. 7, 1918, p. 2.

378   "took the dressings": RG 120, Holderman, op. cit., p. 28.

378   "six years ... in Seattle.": MHI, 77th Div., L. C. McCallum, *History and Rhymes of the Lost Battalion* (Bucklee Publishing, 1939), pp. 63ff.

378   "The suffering of": RG 120, Holderman, op. cit., p. 28.

379   "Whittlesey said nothing": Whittlesey Report, op. cit., p. 15.

36: "They Are Learning Now": The First Two Weeks of October

380   "south of Montfaucon": R. T. Ward, "Study of First Army Situation," in *The United States Army in the World War (USAWW)* Vol. 9, *General Missions* (Washington, D.C.: U.S. Government Printing Office, 1948).

380   "the problems which": Quoted in A. Kaspi, *Les Temps des Américains 1917–1918. Le Concours américain à la France en 1917–1918* (Paris: Sorbonne, Série Internationale 6, 1976), p. 319.

380   "a firm proposal": J. J. Pershing, *My Experiences in the World War* (London: Hodder & Stoughton, 1931), p. 622.

380   "Clemenceau had declared": AAV, 47/3, 6 N 53.

381   "your attacks start": D. Smythe, *Pershing: General of the Armies* (Bloomington: Indiana U.P., 1986), p. 204. See also Kaspi, *Les Temps*, p. 319.

381   "There is no": *USAWW*, Vol. 9, p. 549, Gallwitz to Fifth Army, Oct. 13, 1918.

381   "It is on": MIWS, Oct. 26, 1918, Marwitz to Fifth Army, Oct. 1, 1918.

382   "causing five hundred": MHI, WWI, AEF HQ, Arthur L. Conger, memorandum "The Attack of the 1st Division on the Argonne Forest" ("Conger Memo").

382   "the frontline units": RG 120, 1st Div., Box 83, "Report on Operations of 26th Infantry, Oct. 18, 1918" ("26th Infantry Report"), p. 3. MHI, Box "1st Division HQ," Summerall memorandum, Oct. 17, 1918, says, "communications from regiments to front line battalions were working 85% of

the time." But other divisions complained that the wire was cotton-covered and useless in wet conditions—cf. RG 120, Inspector-General's Reports, AEF, First Army Reports on 79th Div., J. Johnson to CoS First Army, Sept. 30, 1918.

382 "voice control . . . disappeared": J. Terraine, *White Heat: The New Warfare 1914–1918* (London: Sidgwick & Jackson, 1982), p. 148.

382 "the pitiful sight": MHI, Box "1st Division No. 1," Donald Kyler.

382 "Casualties were heavy.": 26th Infantry Report, op. cit.

383 "One of the shells": MHI, Donald Kyler, op. cit.

384 "across the Aire.": Liggett, not Malin Craig, thought of the idea. MHI, Box "1st Army Corps—HQ," Liggett to Craig, n.d.

385 Alvin York story: 74th Congress, 1st Sess., Senate Report No. 64, Feb. 6, 1935.

385 "the 307th Infantry": Whittlesey Report, op. cit.

386 "177 officers and 8,370 men": Conger Memo, op. cit., p. 2. See also MHI, Box "1st Div. HQ," Summerall memorandum, Oct. 19, 1918, p. 3.

386 "Lt Hyde reports": RG 120, 1st Div., Box 79, Field Message, Oct. 9, 1918.

386 "Legge totaled up": RG 120, 1st Div., Box 79, Oct. 10, 1918, 8:20 A.M.

386 "My phone will not": RG 120, 1st Div., Box 79, L. S. Frazier, Field Message, Oct. 11, 1918, 8:15 A.M.

386 "No sound of": RG 120, 1st Div., Box 79, Field Message, Oct. 10, 1918, 12:15 P.M.

37: Crisis Before Kriemhilde

388 "he realized his mistake.": D. Trask, *The AEF and Coalition War-making 1917–1918* (Lawrence: U. of Kansas Press, 1993), p. 130.

390 "create a Second Army": A. R. Millett, *The General: Robert Lee Bullard and Officership in the U.S. Army, 1881–1925* (Westport, Conn.: Greenwood Press, 1975).

390 "on October 10": H. Liggett, *AEF: Ten Years Ago in France* (New York: Dodd, Mead, 1927), p. 198.

390 "a big man": Josephus Daniels, *The Wilson Era*, Vol. 2, *1917–1923: Years of War and After* (Chapel Hill: U. of North Carolina Press, 1946), p. 391.

390 "refusing to assume command": Ibid., p. 205.

391 "Doctors blamed some": RG 120, IGO, files of Inspector General, AEF, 1917–1923, OIG, First Army, Inspections (6).

391 "the overwhelming epidemic": LoC, March Papers, Box 22, Oct. 18, 1918.

391 "there were 286": RG 61, E. 1-D1, Box 89, WIB, Chairman's Office.

391 "Of the 100,000": Liggett, *AEF*, p. 206.

391 "only 4,316 men": R. C. Hamber, "Absences and Desertions During World War I" (Historical Section, Army War College, November 1942).

391 "one enterprising trio": RG 120, GHQ, CinC Reports, Box 30, Lt. Col. Troup Miller, lecture "Plan of Communication, Supply and Evacuation, 1st Corps, for St. Mihiel and Meuse-Argonne Offensive," Jan. 20, 1919 ("Troup Miller Lecture"), p. 10, para. "Stragglers."

391 "limited disciplinary training": RG 120, IGO, Box 7, memorandum "Information for Report on AEF," Mar. 22, 1919. See also RG 120, E. 765, Box 1, Files 1.4–10.6, Folder 8, 191-10.2: "The causes for the excessive straggling in the 1st Army are . . . ," Nov. 11, 1918, and RG 120, IGO (2), Appendix 30, "Report on Stragglers," Oct. 24, 1918.

392 "the YMCA came in": Troup Miller Lecture, op. cit., p. 10.

392 "We immediately went": Omar Bradley and C. Blair, *A General's Life* (New York: Simon & Schuster, 1983), p. 46.

392 "50,000 fewer horses": J. Hagood, *The Services of Supply: A Memoir of the Great War* (Boston: Houghton Mifflin, 1927), p. 314.

393 "ordered to economize": Memorandum, Oct. 15, 1918, in F. L. Huidekoper, *Illinois in the World War*, Vol. 1 (Springfield: Illinois State Historical Library, 1921), p. 145.

393 "We ran up": F. P. Duffy, *Father Duffy's Story: a tale of humor and heroism, of life and death with the fighting 69th* (n.d.), p. 296.

393 "Foch's refusal to": Trask, *AEF*, p. 153. Foch decided on occupation and reparations from Oct. 8 onward.

394   "On October 29 . . . unconditional surrender": B. Lowry discusses his motivation in "Pershing and the Armistice," *Journal of American History*, 55 (2), September 1968.

38: "The Big Man":
Liggett Pulls the Army into Shape

396   "he was taking 45 seconds": Timothy Nenninger, "J. J. Pershing and Relief for Cause—The Failure of Combat Commanders in the AEF," 1993 WFA annual conference.

396   "immediately relieved him": Ibid.

397   "Groups of our": F. P. Duffy, *Father Duffy's Story*, p. 272.

397   "results, no matter": Ibid., p. 276.

397   Châtillon story: For a full account of the Châtillon operation, see D. C. James, *The Years of MacArthur*, Vol. 1 (Boston: Houghton Mifflin, 1970).

399   "on October 16.": H. Liggett, *AEF: Ten Years Ago in France* (New York: Dodd, Mead, 1927), p. 206.

399   "piecemeal operations": Ibid., p. 214.

399   "a vary advantageous": H. Liggett, *Commanding an American Army: Recollections of the World War* (Boston: Houghton Mifflin, 1925), p. 107.

400   "put into . . . fighting front": *USAWW*, Vol. 9, p. 549, Ludendorff to Gallwitz, Oct. 10, 1918.

400   "The air service": Russell Lecture, op. cit., p. 13.

401   "by nightfall on": Liggett, *AEF* p. 219.

401   "outflank the Germans": Liggett, *Commanding*, p. 110.

401   "twin American doctrines": R. W. Lamont, "Over There," *Marine Corps Gazette*, June 1993, p. 77.

401   "staff work was": See, e.g., RG 120, AEF GHQ, G3 Reports, Box 3241, "Annex No. 5 to Field Orders No. 85, 1st A.C.—Battle Instructions."

401   "the detailed maps": McNair Lecture, op. cit., p. 20.

401   "completely reduced by": RG 120, 2nd Div., Box 73, memorandum from G. W. Hamilton, "Report of Operations covering period October 17–November 16, 1918," Nov. 16, 1918.

401   "Many prisoners taken": For other interrogation reports along the same lines, see *Field Artillery Journal, 13*, McGlachlin, p. 15.

401   "the reason they": Russell Lecture, op. cit., p. 14.

402   "Am digging in": RG 120, 2nd Div., Box 63, Field Message, Nov. 1, 1918.

402   "The First Army": RG 165, D.I., Summary of Information Reports June 1918—January 1919, Box 1, "Summary of Information, November 1, 1918."

402   "Our men were so eager": Liggett, *AEF,* p. 222.

402   "Every road was": E. V. Rickenbacker, *Fighting the Flying Circus* (New York: Frederick Stokes, 1919), p. 352.

39: Losing to the Allies

405   "The German decision": See, e.g., K. Schwabe, "U.S. Secret War Diplomacy, Intelligence and the Coming of the German Revolution in 1918: The Role of Vice Consul James McNally," *Diplomatic History, 16* (2), Spring 1992, p. 190.

405   text of exchange of notes: See *Foreign Relations of the United States 1918*, Suppl. 1, Vol. 1.

406   "Long live His Majesty": M. Kitchen, *The Silent Dictatorship: The Politics of the German High Command under Hindenburg and Ludendorff 1916–1918* (London: Croom Helm, 1976), p. 263.

406   "a detective novel.": R. Parkinson, *Tormented Warrior: Ludendorff and the Supreme Command* (London: Hodder & Stoughton, 1978), p. 183.

407   "a substantial achievement": Schwabe, "Secret War Diplomacy," p. 193.

407   "dictate peace by": Roosevelt to Lodge, Oct. 24, 1918, in *WWP,* Vol. 51, p. 456.

407   "On October 23": T. J. Knock, *To End All Wars: Woodrow Wilson and the Quest for a New World Order* (Oxford, England: OUP, 1992), p. 176.

407   "million American lives.": H. C. F. Bell, *Woodrow Wilson and the People* (New York: Doubleday, 1945), p. 248.

407 "Liberalism in America": Knock, *To End All Wars*, p. 185, quoting George Creel.

408 "a repudiation of": Ibid., p. 178.

409 "a rich bumpkin": R. Steel, *Walter Lippmann and the American Century* (London: Bodley Head, 1980), p. 147.

409 "wholly dependent on": K. Burk, "The Mobilization of Anglo-American Finance in World War I" in N. F. Dreisziger, ed., *Mobilization for Total War: The Canadian, American and British Experience, 1914–1918, 1939–1945* (Waterloo, Ontario, Canada: Wilfrid Laurier U.P., 1991), p. 40.

409 "Of Britain's imported": Customs and Excise Department, Statistical Office, *Annual Statement of the Trade of the United Kingdom* (London: H.M. Stationery Office, 1920).

410 "danger . . . had receded": D. Woodward, *Trial by Friendship: Anglo-American Relations, 1917–18* (Lexington: University of Kentucky Press, 1993), p. 203.

410 "The British . . . shipping": See, e.g., Geddes to Lloyd George, Aug. 26, 1918, in M. Simpson, ed., *Anglo-American Naval Relations 1917–1919* (Aldershot, England: Scolar Press/Navy Records Society, 1991), p. 507. See also J. Safford, "Anglo-American Maritime Relations During the Two World Wars: A Comparative Analysis," *The American Neptune, 41* (1), October 1981.

410 "minimize the American": E. B. Parsons, "Why the British Reduced the Flow of American Troops to Europe in August–October 1918," p. 186.

410 "anything like her share": House diary, Oct. 9, 1918, in *WWP*, Vol. 51, p. 279.

411 "In Pershing, Foch": Pershing telegram, Oct. 26, 1918, urging "no tendency toward leniency," in *WWP*, Vol. 51, p. 454.

411 "Go away and": D. Smythe, *Pershing: General of the Armies* (Bloomington: Indiana U.P., 1986), p. 218.

411 "If Germany surrenders": Woodward, *Trial by Friendship*, p. 209.

412 "rock . . . 'hard relentless vulture.' ": C. Seymour, ed., *The Intimate Papers of Colonel House*, Vol. 4 (Boston: Houghton Mifflin, 1926–8), p. 197.

412 Lloyd George–Clemenceau exchange: Ibid., p. 167.

412 "would not 'look at' ": Ibid., p. 190.

412 "would spend her": Ibid. See also Simpson, *Anglo-American Naval Relations*, p. 489.

413 "to 'discuss' the freedom": Woodward, *Trial by Friendship*, p. 218.

413 "given away . . . war.": Simpson, *Anglo-American Naval Relations*, p. 487.

413 "You must not": Seymour, *Intimate Papers*, p. 127.

413 "quite as much political": LoC, Bliss Papers, Box 245, "October 1918–October 1919," cable, Oct. 23, 1918.

414 "Bliss advised that": Ibid.

414 "Astonishingly": Knock, *To End All Wars*, p. 183, suggests that this was Clemenceau's price for accepting the Fourteen Points.

414 "his word of": Seymour, *Intimate Papers*, p. 121.

414 "awaited any representatives": Ibid., p. 139.

414 "by no means broken": Ibid., p. 123.

40: Von Winterfeldt's Tears

415 Beck account of armistice: J. M. Beck, *A Diary of Armistice Days* (privately printed, 1923), p. 33.

416 "just cannot do": D. R. Beaver, *Newton D. Baker and the American War Effort 1917–1919* (Lincoln: U. of Nebraska Press, 1966), p. 209.

417 "a great chorus . . . say.": HIoWRP, O. Briggs Papers, letter, Nov. 3, 1918.

417 "wooden boxes with": RG 120, E 765, Box 1, Files 1.4–10.6, Folder 11, memorandum from H. Drum, Nov. 11, 1918.

417 "dead horses . . . flanks.": Imperial War Museum, Sound Archives, Leon Diament, 4076/C/C.

418 "For the first time": H. Liggett, *AEF: Ten Years Ago in France* (New York: Dodd, Mead, 1927), p. 224.

418 "memorandum": *USAWW*, Vol. 9, p. 385, "Drum, Chief of Staff, by Command of Lt. Gen. Liggett: 'Memorandum for Commanding Generals I Corps, V Corps.' "

419 "This was . . . lost my temper": Liggett, *AEF*, p. 228.

419 "fires of revolution": T. J. Knock, *To End All Wars: Woodrow Wilson and the Quest for a New World Order* (Oxford, England: OUP, 1992), p. 183.

420 "the signing of": MIWS, period ending Nov. 11, 1918.

420 "not . . . would sign": J. G. Harbord, *The American Army in France 1917–1919* (Boston: Little, Brown, 1936), p. 460.

420 "Our advance should": Liggett, *AEF*, p. 234.

421 "an aerodrome seemingly": E. V. Rickenbacker, *Fighting the Flying Circus* (New York: Frederick Stokes, 1919), p. 359.

421 "If they had given us": Smythe, p. 232.

422 "The Armistice was": A. Walworth, *Woodrow Wilson* (New York: Longman, 1958), p. 197.

41: "No Greater Pain"

424 "Zionists . . . peasants": See Bliss summary, "The Proposed Jewish State in Palestine," Dec. 21, 1918, in LoC, Bliss Papers, Box 358, File "Jewish Question and Zionism."

424 "There are twenty million": C. Paul Vincent, *The Politics of Hunger: The Allied Blockade of Germany 1915–1919* (Athens: Ohio U.P., 1985), p. 85.

424 "The only possible way": K. Nelson, *Victors Divided: America and the Allies in Germany 1918–1923* (Berkeley: U. of California Press, 1975), p. 35.

424 "the natural warm-heartedness": *Berliner Tageblatt*, ca. Jan. 16, 1923, quoted in Henry T. Allen, *The Rhineland Occupation* (Indianapolis, Ind.: Bobbs-Merrill, 1927), p. 525.

424 "a luxury which": U.S. Armed Forces in Germany, Assistant Chief of Staff, G2, *American Representation in Occupied Germany 1920–1921, 1922–1923*, Vol. 2, ("*USAFG*"), p. 203.

424   "contracted venereal diseases": Ibid., p. 204.

425   "Why did the": Nelson, *Victors Divided*, p. 257.

425   "manure heaps . . . hygiene.": *USAFG*, op. cit., p. 211.

425   "Passionate huntsmen, the": Historical Division, U.S. Department of the Army, *The United States Army in the World War* (*USAWW*), Vol. 11, *The American Occupation of Germany* (Washington, D.C.: U.S. Government Printing Office, 1948), p. 152.

425   "chili con carne": Allen, *Rhineland Occupation*, p. 420.

425   "Wild West manners": Nelson, *Victors Divided*, p. 60.

425   "six U.S. . . . robbery": *USAFG*, p. 208.

425   "Germans had become": James Taylor, "The Drama of the Larder: Germany's Food Crisis 1914–1918," *Imperial War Museum Magazine*, 1995, pp. 104–5.

425   "hunger edema, scurvy": Vincent, *Politics of Hunger*, p. 137.

426   "The pegs in": R. O. Cummings, *The American and His Food: A History of Food Habits in the United States* (Chicago: U. of Chicago Press, 1940), p. 6.

426   "erosion of moral standards": Vincent, *Politics of Hunger*, pp. 148–51, 161–4.

426   "We do not kick": H. Hoover, *The Memoirs of Herbert Hoover: Years of Adventure 1874–1920* (London: Hollis & Carter, 1952), p. 347.

426   "hordes of skinny": Vincent, *Politics of Hunger*, p. 110.

426   "an historic lesson": Quoted in R. Skidelsky, *John Maynard Keynes*, Vol. 1, *Hopes Betrayed 1883–1920* (London: Macmillan, 1992), p. 374.

427   "John Foster Dulles": Ibid., p. 363.

427   "squeeze Germany till": Sir Eric Geddes, speech in Cambridge, England, Dec. 9, 1918, quoted in ibid., p. 356.

427   "to justify . . . Rhineland.": Ibid., p. 357.

427   "The gratitude . . . now.": P. A. Grant, "France and the American War Debt Controversy 1919–1929" in *Proceedings of the Ninth Annual Meeting of the Western Society for French History* (Lawrence, Kans.: U. of Kansas Press, 1982), p. 372.

428 "Uncle Shylock": B. D. Rhodes, "Reassessing Uncle Shylock—The United States and the French War Debt 1917–1929," *Journal of American History*, 55 (4), March 1969, p. 787.

428 "On a schedule": J. M. Clark, *The Costs of the War to the American People* (New Haven, Conn.: Yale U.P./Carnegie Endowment for International Peace, 1931), p. 180.

428 "John Maynard Keynes": Skidelsky, *Keynes*, pp. 368–70.

428 "In so far": Simons to wife, May 5, 1919.

428 "He was not sensitive": *The Collected Writings of John Maynard Keynes*, Vol. 2 (1971), pp. 25–6. See also Keynes, quoted in G. Chapman, ed., *Vain Glory: A Miscellany* (London: Cassell, 1937), p. 720.

429 "You Americans . . . broken reeds": Keynes to Norman Davis, June 5, 1919, in Skidelsky, *Keynes*, p. 374.

429 "Lippmann . . . joined the fight": T. J. Knock, *To End All Wars: Woodrow Wilson and the Quest for a New World Order* (Oxford, England: OUP, 1992), p. 257.

430 "Irish and German Americans": L. E. Ambrosius, "Ethnic Politics and German-American Relations after World War I: The Fight over the Versailles Treaty in the United States" in H. C. Trefousse, ed., *Germany and America: Essays in Internal Problems of International Relations and Immigration* (New York: Brooklyn College Press, 1980), p. 33.

430 "With generous contributions": D. M. Kennedy, *Over Here: The First World War and American Society* (New York: OUP, 1980), p. 360.

431 "America will give": Norman Angell, *The Fruits of Victory* (London: Collins, 1921), p. 150.

42: Continuing the Search

436 "opened to women.": See, e.g., M. W. Greenwald, *Women, War and Work: The Impact of World War I on Women Workers in the United States* (Westport, Conn.; Greenwood, 1980); M. R. Higonnet, J. Jensen, S. Michel, and M. C. Weltz, eds., *Behind the Lines: Gender and the Two World Wars* (New Haven, Conn.: Yale U.P., 1987); and A. Kessler-Harris, *Out to Work: A History of Wage-earning Women in the United States* (New York: OUP, 1982), pp. 219–20.

436   "black women moved": Summary Report of George E. Haynes, Director of Negro Economics, "The Negro At Work During the World War and During Reconstruction: Negro Women in Industry" in P. Foner and R. Lewis, eds., *The Black Worker from 1900 to 1919*, Vol. 5 (Philadelphia: Temple U.P., 1980), pp. 401–5.

436   "notable and independent": Dorothy and Carl Schneider, *Into the Breach: American Women Overseas in World War I* (New York: Viking Penguin, 1991), pp. 40–2, 52, 102, 103.

437   "of day nurseries": Higonnet et al., *Behind the Lines*, p. 36.

437   "vital to the winning": D. M. Kennedy, *Over Here: The First World War and American Society* (New York: OUP, 1980), p. 284.

437   "an essentially lower-order . . . the butter?' ": J. C. Burnham, *Bad Habits* (New York: New York U.P., 1993), p. 217.

438   "liquidation of genteel culture": Edmund Wilson, quoted in Bevis Hillier, *The Style of the Century 1900–1980* (London: Herbert Press, 1983), p. 68. See also ibid., pp. 24–7, 94–7.

438   "anti-Semitism came closer": G. Sorin, *A Time for Building: The Third Migration 1880–1920*, Vol. 3, *The Jewish People in America* (Baltimore: Johns Hopkins U.P., 1992), p. 237.

439   "They had begun": Emmett J. Scott, *Scott's Official History of the American Negro in the World War* (Chicago: Homewood Press, 1919), p. 459.

439   "ten veterans in uniform": Bernard C. Nalty, *Strength for the Fight: A History of Black Americans in the Military* (New York: Free Press, 1986), p. 126.

439   "Americans can see": Norman Angell, *The Fruits of Victory* (London: Collins, 1921), p. 157.

439   "Fighting Savage Hun": FO, 371 4244 12335, *Crusader Magazine*, *1* (8), April 1919.

440   "the rejection documents": M 1440, Reel 5, 10281-331, memorandum from Major W. H. Loving to Dir. Mil. Intell., Mar. 3, 1919, "Conditions Among Officers (Colored) at Camp Meade."

440   "the qualities inherent": M 1440, Reel 4, 10218-279, memorandum from Capt. J. E. Cutler to General Churchill, May 9, 1919.

440   "Beyond a doubt": RG 60, Glasser File, Box 9, File "1919," memorandum from Maj. J. E. Cutler to Dir. Mil. Intell., Aug. 15, 1919, "The
Negro Situation," p. 1.

440   "There is a": FO, 371 4244 12335, *Crusader Magazine*, *1* (8), April
1919.

441   Chicago: See, e.g., Nalty, *Strength*, p. 125.

441   "troops to Omaha": LoC, Wood Papers, Container 12, diary, Sept.
29, 1919ff.

441   "War Plans—White": See, e.g., J. M. Jensen, *Army Surveillance in
America* (New Haven, Conn.: Yale U.P., 1991), pp. 189ff. See also RG
60, Glasser File, Box 9, Files "War Plans White Nos. 1 and 2."

43: The Abiding Enemy

443   "the flames of": J. M. Thompson, *Russia, Bolshevism and the Versailles Peace* (Princeton, N.J.: Princeton U.P., 1966), p. 389.

443   "deal of money": RG 165, WDG&SS, MID, Security Classified
Subject Index to Services 64-5, Box 19, 10058-293, Military Attaché,
Paris, Nov. 12, 1918.

443   "Soviet Government Information Bureau": T. Draper, *The Roots of
American Communism* (New York: Viking, 1957), p. 162.

443   "John Reed became": Ibid., p. 146.

444   "four of which": Ibid., p. 150.

444   "The links . . . labor.": See, e.g., D. M. Kennedy, *Over Here: The
First World War and American Society* (New York: OUP, 1980), pp. 141–2.

444   "The signing of": RG 60, Glasser File, Box 9, File "1918," Nov. 22,
1918.

444   "Our terms are": M. J. Heale, *American Anti-Communism: Combating
the Enemy Within 1830–1970* (Baltimore: Johns Hopkins U.P., 1990), p. 63.

444   "a police strike": RG 60, Glasser File, Box 9, File "1919," MID Report, Nov. 25, 1919.

444   "in Gary, Indiana": LoC, Wood Papers, Container 12, diary entry,
Oct. 5, 1919.

445   "ranked with Bolshevism.": Heale, *American Anti-Communism*, p. 67.

445 "white radical organizations": See, e.g., Mark Ellis, "J. Edgar Hoover and the Red Summer of 1919," *Journal of American Studies*, 28 (1), April 1994, p. 41, and RG 60, DoJ, E 112, 2181, "Memo for Mr. Rathom in re attempt to turn the Negro from his allegiance to the United States," July 28, 1919.

445 "The IWW expressly": P. Foner, *A History of the Labor Movement in the United States* (New York: International Publishers, 1965), pp. 124–7.

445 "the MID acknowledged": See, e.g., RG 60, Glasser File, Box 9, reports on race riot at Elaine, Ark., October 1919. See also M 1440, Reel 5, 10218-348 "Memo in re Riot at Bisbee between Soldiers of 10th Cavalry and Civil Officers, July 4."

445 "two separate Communist parties": Draper, *Roots*, pp. 176ff.

445 "A carefully faked": LoC, Microfilms, "Federal Surveillance of Afro-Americans," Reel 22, 10110-B-2, 1919, Dec. 15, 1919.

446 "he shot him": S. Coben, "A Study in Nativism: The American Red Scare of 1919–1920," *Political Science Quarterly*, 79 (1), p. 52.

446 "In Centralia, Washington": RG 60, DoJ, Str. Num. Files, Box 768, 186701, B. H. Lampman, "Centralia Tragedy and Trial—The American Legion's account of the Armistice Day Massacre."

446 "One was said": T. Copeland, *The Centralia Tragedy of 1919: Elmer Smith and the Wobblies* (Seattle: U. of Washington Press, 1993), p. 89.

447 "By 1921, thirty-five": Heale, *American Anti-Communism*, p. 73.

447 "attack on radicalism": See generally R. Murray, *Red Scare: A Study in National Hysteria* (Minneapolis: U. of Minnesota Press, 1955), and W. Preston, *Aliens and Dissenters: Federal Suppression of Radicals 1903–1933* (Cambridge, Mass.: Harvard U.P., 1963).

447 "Wilson's first choice": W. G. McAdoo, *Crowded Years: The Reminiscences of W. G. McAdoo* (Boston: Houghton Mifflin, 1931), p. 183.

447 "Democratic presidential nomination": Coben, "Study in Nativism," p. 73.

447 "menace . . . the masses.": RG 60, DoJ, Central Files, Str. Num. Index, 1904–1937, E 112, Box 3214, Palmer to Lyman Abbott, Jan. 27, 1920.

447 "the core of": RG 165, WDG&SS, MID Corr., 1917–1941, 177-56/2, "M.I.4. Weekly Situation Report," Nov. 26, 1918.

448 "continuing to insist": RG 60, DoJ, Central Files, Str. Num. Index, 1904–1937, E 112, Box 3214, Palmer to Senator C. C. McNary, Mar. 24, 1920.

448 "Hoover . . . Radical Division": R. A. Kaplan, *An Historical Inquiry into the Organization and Activities of the United States Intelligence Establishment and its Relationship to Foreign Policy* (M.A. thesis, San Francisco State University, December 1977), pp. 25–30.

448 "personal research establishment": R. G. Powers, *Secrecy and Power: The Life of J. Edgar Hoover* (New York: Free Press, 1987), p. 96.

448 "first authority on communism.": Hoover personally prepared briefs on the CPA and CLP for distribution; see, e.g., Hoover to Senator W. H. King, Jan. 7, 1920, and Hoover to U.S. Attorney F. G. Caffey, Jan. 9, 1920, RG 60, DoJ, Central Files, Str. Num. Index, 1904–1937, E 112, Box 3214.

448 "He selected . . . hearings.": Powers, *Secrecy and Power*, p. 67.

448 "Parlor Bolsheviks": RG 60, DoJ, Central Files, Str. Num. Index, 1904–1937, E 112, Box 3214, Hoover to Lamb, Jan. 6, 1919.

448 URW details: Powers, *Secrecy and Power*, p. 76.

449 "a venereal disease.": RG 60, DoJ, Central Files, Str. Num. Index, 1910–1937, E 112, Box 3200, "Transcript of interrogation of Pete Mironovich," Nov. 18, 1919.

449 "sombrero": Powers, *Secrecy and Power*, p. 88.

449 "ex–American Protective League": The APL was dissolved on Feb. 1, 1919; RG 65, FBI-APL, E. 12/1, Jan. 30, 1919.

449 "windowless corridors": Powers, *Secrecy and Power*, p. 104.

449 "emotions were beginning": Coben, "Study in Nativism," p. 74.

450 "on 1.5 million Americans.": Kaplan, *Historical Inquiry*, p. 29. (It is not clear if this figure included the older 750,000-name index compiled since 1900.)

450 "70,000 Communist sympathizers": Heale, *American Anti-Communism*, p. 65. Draper, *Roots*, p. 190, puts the figure at 40,000 enrolled members.

450 "They are all white": RG 60, Glasser File, Box 9, memorandum "Negro Agitation" from Executive Div., Mil. Intell. Branch, July 1, 1919, p. 2.

44: "When Johnny Comes Marching Home"

451   "75,658 ... 34,249 ... 13,691 ... 23,937 ... 3,681": R. Gabriel and K. Metz, *A History of Military Medicine*, Vol. 2, *From the Renaissance Through Modern Times* (Westport, Conn.: Greenwood, 1992), p. 249.

451   "The Marines had": FO, 371 4247 121389, general intelligence report for period ending Aug. 16, 1919.

451   "511 miles": *Infantry Journal*, November 1919, p. 422.

451   "Most of the battlefield": RG 120, IGO (6).

452   "2,200 ... 6,000 ... 4,100 ... 1,850," etc.: Col. H. Howland, *America in Battle* (Paris: Herbert Clarke, 1920), pp. 584–9.

452   "Hoboken, New Jersey": The Medical Department of the United States Army in the World War (USAMD), vol. IV (Washington, D.C.: U.S. Government Printing Office, 1924), p. 291.

452   "More left arms": E. T. Devine, *Disabled Soldiers and Sailors: Pensions and Training* (New York: OUP/Carnegie Endowment, 1919), p. 9.

453   "they disabled 69,934": William Hanigan, "Wind of a Ball—Shell Shock During the Great War," address to the 1993 WFA annual conference, Washington D.C.

453   "dull, queer or": *USAMD*, p. 435.

453   "diagnosed as psychoneurotic": Ibid., p. 441.

453   "in Newport News": Ibid., p. 436.

453   "Eleanor Roosevelt made": G. C. Ward, review of B. Cook, *Eleanor Roosevelt*, Vol. 1, *1884–1933*, in *New York Review of Books*, Sept. 24, 1992.

453   "to enable him": Devine, *Disabled Soldiers*, p. 320.

454   "cripple parties": Ibid., p. 380.

454   "Italian boys prayed": Ibid., p. 394.

454   *"bras de parade ... days."*: Ibid., pp. 396–8.

454   "the loss of both feet": Ibid., pp. 415–7.

454   "A man who": HIoWRP, WWI, Subject Collection, Box 27, Lewis B. Moore, "How the Colored Race Can Help In the Problems Issuing From the War" (Patriotism Through Organized Education Series: National Security League, ca. 1919).

455   "the feeling of compassion": Devine, *Disabled Soldiers*, p. 417.

455   "1,980,654 . . . 1,689,998": FO, 371 4247 79331, Maj. Gen. J. D. McLachlan, Mil. Att., "Report on Demobilization," May 1, 1919.

455   "cease his gallivantin' ": Truman to Ethel Nolan, Jan. 20, 1919, quoted in R. H. Ferrell, *Woodrow Wilson and World War I* (New York: Harper and Row, 1985), p. 179.

455   "Trains carrying supplies . . . 20 kph.": RG 120, IGO (4) and (8).

455   "jobs were gone.": See, e.g., F. L. Paxson, "The Great Demobilization," *American Historical Review*, *44* (18), January 1939, pp. 244–5.

455   "more than eight thousand": FO, 371 4247, "Report on Return to Civil Life of Officers of U.S. Army," May 19, 1919.

456   "trying to face": Quoted in J. S. Auerbach, "Woodrow Wilson's 'Prediction' to Frank Cobb: Words Historians Should Doubt Ever Got Spoken," *Journal of American History*, *54* (3), December 1967, p. 614.

456   "Your son Francis": Quoted in D. M. Kennedy, *Over Here: The First World War and American Society* (New York: OUP, 1980), p. 226.

458   "selfless and patriotic": E. M. Coffman, *The Hilt of the Sword: The Career of Peyton C. March* (Madison: U. of Wisconsin Press, 1966), p. 245.

458   "March handed over": LoC, March Papers, Box 2, Army War College lecture, Apr. 20, 1933.

459   "his influence . . . Marshall.": R. F. Weigley, *History of the U.S. Army* (Bloomington: Indiana U.P., 1984), p. 422.

459   "17,000 AEF veterans": See, e.g., R. Daniels, *The Bonus March: An Episode of the Great Depression* (Westport, Conn.: Greenwood, 1971).

459   "677 . . . 508 . . . 263": *The Great War in the Air*, p. 340.

459   air strength at end of war: Ibid., p. 338.

459   "Army Reorganization Act": I. B. Holley, *Ideas and Weapons: Exploitation of the Aerial Weapon by the United States During World War I* (New Haven, Conn.: Yale U.P., 1953), p. 149.

460   "In midocean he disappeared": John Toland, *No Man's Land: The Story of 1918* (London: Methuen, 1978), p. 474, says Whittlesey "jumped overboard."

Index

Adams, Henry, 17–18
Addams, Jane, 16, 54, 67, 171
Aire River, 349, 356, 358, 363, 369,
    382–84, 395–96
air power, 46–48, 55, 149–50, 169,
    198, 327–28, 346–47,
    416–17, 459–60
Aisne River, 231, 240, 242–43, 246,
    314
Alexander, Gen. Robert, 370, 374–76,
    378, 395–96
Alien Property Custodian, 148, 208,
    435, 447
Allies, behavior to United States, 5, 8,
    30, 42, 46, 216, 229, 276,
    297, 409–14, 428–29, 451
Allies, relations with, 43, 79–80, 113,
    124–25, 162, 199, 206,
    209–10, 217–21, 229–33,
    240, 245, 272, 297–98,
    316, 323, 325, 331–35,
    345, 393, 409–14, 423
amalgamation, Allied pressure for, 117,
    215–16, 231–33, 245,
    249

American Expeditionary Force (AEF),
    70–71, 113, 122–23, 140,
    146, 150, 166, 195, 210,
    213, 230, 232, 234–38,
    240, 243, 245, 248, 261,
    265, 275–76, 281, 288,
    297, 302, 322, 324–25,
    327, 331, 351–52, 354,
    381, 388, 391–92, 399,
    405, 410, 439, 451,
    455–56, 459
American Federation of Labor,
    179–81, 188, 290, 451
Americanization, 24, 104, 136,
    178–79, 301, 445
American Legion, 446
American Protective League (APL),
    303–5, 407, 441, 449
Anaconda Copper Co., 186, 188, 286,
    288
Angell, Norman, 431, 439
Argonne Forest, 332, 349, 353, 356,
    358–59, 363–64
Armistice, 413, 418–22, 424, 426,
    455

Army
British, 6, 122, 209, 215, 227–28,
231–32, 246, 394, 416
French, 6, 118, 122, 123, 205, 209,
211, 215, 228, 243,
246–47, 249–52, 254–55,
261, 267, 269, 311–20,
325, 328, 332, 342, 353,
372, 375, 380–81, 386,
393–94, 399–400, 418–19,
439
German, 4, 27, 31, 49, 60, 63, 92,
123, 209, 227–28, 230,
243, 247, 249, 256–57,
261–62, 264–65, 269–70,
276, 311–12, 314, 316–20,
329–31, 339–46, 349–53,
358, 362, 368, 371,
377–79, 381, 383, 385–86,
389, 400, 402, 411, 414,
416–18, 420–21, 427
Italian, 205, 311, 314
Japanese, 234, 458
American, 49, 56–57, 65, 89, 119,
234, 261, 354, 458–59
size, 123, 145, 186–89, 194,
196–98, 210, 234, 275–77,
281, 290, 292, 323–34,
340, 392, 409–10
divisions
1st, 119–21, 124–26, 210–12,
214, 238–45, 249, 315,
318–21, 324, 342, 345,
382–84, 386–87, 389, 398,
402, 419
2nd, 210–11, 245, 247–59,
260–72, 315–20, 324, 340,
342, 386, 400–2, 451
3rd, 127, 247, 249, 261,
267–69, 311–14, 324, 381

4th, 342, 353, 359, 361, 399
5th, 340, 342, 395–96, 398,
418
26th, 210, 239, 342, 345
28th, 311, 353, 358, 384
29th, 340
32nd, 395, 398–99
33rd, 128, 131, 353
35th, 353, 356–58, 363–65,
383, 387, 455
37th, 353, 365
42nd ("Rainbow"), 210–11,
213, 314, 324, 340, 342,
344, 387–88, 393, 395–98,
400, 419
77th, 128, 353, 370–72,
374–79, 384–85, 395–96,
400, 419
78th, 396, 400
79th, 325, 353, 357–61, 366,
389, 392
80th, 132, 353
82nd, 342, 347, 384–85
85th, 298–99
89th, 342, 400, 402
90th, 342
91st, 354, 358, 362, 365
92nd, 135, 284, 372–74, 440
93rd, 372
regiments (infantry)
5th (Marine), 120, 124, 248,
252, 254–59, 260–72,
316–20
6th (Marine), 248, 251, 253,
256–59, 260–72, 316,
319–20
7th, 267–69
9th, 271–72, 316
16th, 3–5, 382–83
18th, 241, 382

23rd, 256, 271–72
26th, 382–83, 386
28th, 241–45, 316, 382–83
30th, 312–13
38th, 103, 312–14, 339
126th, 399
137th, 363–65
138th, 353, 365
140th, 365
164th, 396–98, 401
165th, 396–98, 401
306th, 371, 375–79
307th, 375–79, 385
308th, 371–72, 375–79
313th, 360–61
314th, 357–60
315th, 359–60, 366
328th, 384–85
339th, 298–99
368th, 372, 374, 440
369th, 439
Army War College, 100, 116, 120

Baden, Prince Max von, 389, 405,
    406, 410, 416, 420
Baker, Newton D., 50–51, 57, 60, 70,
    91, 93–95, 98, 103–4,
    106–8, 111, 113–14, 116,
    132–33, 138, 140, 188–89,
    196–97, 204, 210, 215,
    232, 236–37, 275, 281,
    283, 286, 291, 325, 334,
    410, 457
Baldwin, Roger, 96
Balfour, Arthur, 6, 83, 217, 219, 412
Ballou, Gen. Charles C., 109, 372–74
Barnett, Gen. George, 50, 76, 91,
    248
Barricourt Heights, 349, 351, 395,
    400–2

Baruch, Bernard M., 55, 60, 278–80,
    410, 426, 444
Bayly, Admiral Lewis, 79–80
Beatty, Admiral David, 83–85, 89
Belfort ruse, 340
Bell, Gen. George, 128
Belleau Wood, 7, 245, 250, 252–53,
    255–59, 261–72, 275, 282,
    311, 314, 317, 319, 401,
    408, 452, 456
Benson, Admiral William S., 59, 83,
    85, 216–17, 222
Berkman, Alexander, 449
Bernstorff, Count Johann von, 65–66
Berry, Maj. Ben, 254–58, 262, 264,
    270
Bethlehem Steel, 28, 31, 82, 286–88
Bielaski, A. Bruce, 303
Bisbee deportations, 187–88
black forces
    officers, 108–10, 372–74
    men, 106–8, 129–30, 135, 139,
        284, 372–74, 439
blacks, treatment of, 15–16, 31, 58,
    104–10, 160, 164, 168–69,
    283–84, 292, 296–97, 436,
    438–41, 445
"Black Tom," 31, 49
Blanc Mont, 386, 393
Bliss, Gen. Tasker, 99, 107, 111–12,
    114–15, 119, 209, 212,
    228, 232, 235, 277, 281,
    297, 410, 413–14
blockade, Allied, 30, 61, 207–8, 426
Boehn, Gen. von, 311–12, 314, 319
Bohm, Gen., 261
Bolsheviks, Bolshevism, 206–8,
    219–20, 289–90, 297–99,
    301, 330, 420, 435,
    443–50

Bouresches, 250, 252, 255–59, 262–63, 266–67, 272
Bourgogne Woods, 395, 400–1
Bourne, Randolph, 24, 283
Bradley, Lt. Omar, 116, 288, 392
Brest-Litovsk, Treaty of, 289
Briey-Longwy, 123, 414, 418
Brookings, Robert, 285
Broun, Heywood, 193
Brown, Col. Preston, 247, 249
Bryan, William Jennings, 57
Bryce, Sir James, 37
Buford, U.S.S., 449
Bullard, Gen. Robert, 214, 239, 241–42, 245, 315, 353, 359, 381, 390, 418
Bundy, Gen. Omar, 211, 247, 249, 251–54, 259, 265, 269, 272, 315, 340
Burleson, Albert, 167–68, 182–83, 407
Butte, Montana, 186, 188, 288

Cameron, Gen. George, 342, 344–45, 353, 358, 367, 381, 386, 390
camps and cantonments, 129–32, 134, 163, 169, 194–95, 305, 324, 392
Cantigny, 7, 240–45, 261, 382, 396
Caporetto, 205, 209
Capps, Washington L., 198
casualties, American, 5, 210, 212, 240, 244, 271, 313–14, 320–21, 345, 367, 383, 391, 398, 451–55
Cates, Lt. Clifton, 258, 269
Cather, Willa, 456
Catlin, Col. Albertus, 257–58, 262
Cavell, Edith, 170

censorship, 8, 166–68, 182–83
Centralia, 446
Chamberlain, Senator George, 194–95, 201, 203, 278
Chaplin, Charlie, 15
Chaplin, Ralph, 185, 189, 446
Château-Thierry, 247, 249, 261, 271–72, 314–15, 320
Châtel-Chéhéry, 384
Châtillon, Côte de, 351, 387, 396–98
Chaumont, 124, 212, 390
Churchill, Winston, 331
Clabaugh, Hinton, 189
Clark, Champ, 91
Clemenceau, Premier Georges, 140, 220, 229, 275, 380–81, 394, 412–14, 423–24, 429
Cobb, Frank, 293
Coblenz, 424–25
Coffin, Howard, 55, 199
Cole, Maj. Edward, 258
Commission for Relief in Belgium, 155
Committee for Public Information (CPI), 165–77, 179, 181, 193, 200, 202, 206, 282, 288, 290, 293–94, 299, 307, 383, 407, 409, 428, 439
communism, 8, 301, 442–45, 447–50. *See also* Bolsheviks
Compiègne, 415, 419
Conger, Col. Arthur, 253, 271, 340
Conner, Col. Fox, 116, 341, 343, 345–47
conscientious objectors, 96–97, 132–33
conscription, 89–98, 174, 183, 435
Conta, Gen. von, 246, 249–50
convoys, 82–84
costs of war, 6, 8, 151–52, 210, 285

Council of National Defense (CND),
        60, 75, 149, 180, 194, 199,
        202, 278
Craig, Col. Malin, 390
Cramm, Matilda de, 206
Crawford, Sir Richard, 152
Creel, George, 165–69, 171–72, 174,
        193, 200, 206, 221,
        282–83, 287–88, 294, 299,
        308, 428, 441–42
Croly, Herbert, 21
Crosby, Oscar T., 74
Crowder, Gen. Enoch, 91, 93–95,
        97–98, 291–92
cummings, e e, 456

Daly, Dan, 257
Dame-Marie, Côte de, 395–99
Daniels, Josephus, 55, 57–60, 66, 69–
        70, 73, 76–77, 81–83, 91,
        138, 148, 165, 390, 457
Darrow, Clarence, 21
Dawes, Col. Charles, 213
Debs, Eugene, 53, 182, 305
Degoutte, Gen. Jean, 249–50, 252,
        314
Denman, William, 198
Dewey, John, 16
Dickman, Gen. Joseph, 311–13, 342,
        345–46, 390
dissent, repression of, 8, 167, 177,
        182–83, 186–89, 277,
        302–8, 435, 441–42,
        446–47
Donovan, Col. William "Wild Bill,"
        396–97, 401
Dos Passos, John, 456
Doyen, Gen. Charles, 211
draft, 8, 90, 93–98, 134, 179, 184,
        290–92

draft dodgers, 97–98, 292
drugs, 19, 140–41
Drum, Gen. Hugh, 116, 326, 349,
        417–19, 459
Du Bois, W. E. B., 16–17, 104, 168,
        306, 440
Du Pont, Pierre, 28, 31, 286–87
Dulles, John Foster, 427

East Saint Louis riot, 105–6, 297
Eastman, Crystal, 54
Ebert, Friedrich, 420
Eddy, Lt. William, 253, 256
Edison, Thomas, 18, 54–55, 148
Edwards, Gen. Clarence "Daddy,"
        210, 239–40
Ely, Gen. Hanson, 241–46, 312, 396,
        418
Emergency Fleet Corporation, 151,
        198, 235
Empey, Arthur Guy, 42–43, 171
Enright, Thomas, 4–6
Espionage Act, 167–68, 182, 189,
        302, 307, 407, 447. See
        also Sedition Act
espionage, German, 31, 49, 167
Exermont, 363–65, 381–83, 387,
        455
Etzel Position, 350–51

Fairbanks, Douglas, 159, 176
Farnsworth, Gen. C. S., 365–66
Federal Reserve System, 14, 22, 285
Feland, Col. Logan, 255, 266–67
First Army, 322–23, 332–34, 342–49,
        351–55, 358–60, 362–63,
        366–68, 380–81, 386,
        390–93, 396, 399, 401–2,
        418
Fiske, Admiral Bradley, 49

Foch, Marshal Ferdinand, 229–30,
        232, 247, 275–76, 314–15,
        322, 329, 331–33, 341,
        359, 380–81, 388, 393–94,
        409–11, 414–16, 418, 420,
        424
Folz, Gen. F. S., 357
Food Administration, 155–63, 193,
        198, 202, 385, 438
Ford, Henry, 13, 23, 54–55
Fosdick, Raymond, 138–40
Four-Minute Men, 171–73, 175–76,
        294, 439
Fourteen Points, 220–22, 389, 394,
        405, 407–9, 412–13, 416,
        423–24, 426, 430
Frankfurter, Felix, 188, 429
Freud, Sigmund, 15, 62, 222
Frick, Henry Clay, 430
Fuchs, Gen., 341, 344–46
Fuel Administration, 202, 285

Gallwitz, Gen. Max von, 352–53, 381,
        395, 400, 416–17
Garfield, Harry, 202–3, 278, 280
Garvey, Marcus, 450
gas warfare, 147–48, 266, 401
Geddes, Sir Eric, 410, 427
General Staff, U.S. Army, 56–57,
        90–91, 99, 100, 106, 112,
        119, 135, 197, 208,
        234–37, 279, 286, 291,
        325, 441, 458
German Americans, 30, 32–33,
        38–39, 49, 93, 128, 283,
        293–96, 438
Germany, conditions in, 30, 61–64,
        208, 330, 419–20, 425–26
Gibson, Charles Dana, 173
Giselher Position, 350–51, 381

Goethals, Gen. George, 150–51, 198,
        235–37, 276–77, 279, 410,
        435
Goldman, "Red Emma," 449
Gompers, Samuel, 60, 179–81, 188,
        288, 444
Gondrecourt, 124, 211
Gorgas, Surgeon General William,
        146, 195, 235
Göring, Hermann, 319
Gouraud, Gen. Henri, 314, 399
Grandpré, 395–96, 400
Grant, Madison, 23
Greer, Col. Allen, 374
Gregory, Attorney General Thomas,
        188–89, 202, 291, 295,
        303–4, 307
Gresham, James "Boo Boo," 4–6
Griffith, D. W., 14, 174

Haan, Gen. William, 398–99
Hagood, Johnson, 323, 334
Haig, Field Marshal Douglas, 116,
        122, 209, 216, 219,
        228–33, 246, 315, 322,
        331–32, 335, 381, 389,
        413–14, 416, 420
Hamilton, Maj. George, 244–45,
        401–2
Hanson, Ole, 444
Harbord, Gen. James, 115–16, 118,
        124, 245, 248, 250–53,
        255–56, 259–71, 315–20,
        326
Hawley, William, 127
Hay, Merle, 4–6
Haywood, William "Big Bill," 21, 184,
        186, 189, 289, 457
Hearst, William Randolph, 167, 295,
        299

Hemingway, Ernest, 44, 456
Hexamer, Charles, 33–34, 293
Hill 223, 384–85
Hill 142, 250, 252–56, 263, 267, 272, 401
Hill, Joe, 184
Hillquit, Morris, 182
Hindenburg, Gen. Paul von Benecken-dorff und von, 52, 62–63, 66, 118, 208, 406, 419–20, 458
Hindenburg Line, 64, 69, 123, 205, 330–32, 346, 389, 400
Hines, Gen. John L., 396
Hitler, Adolf, 63, 420–21, 457
Hog Island, 151
Holcomb, Maj. Thomas, 256, 258, 266–67
Hoover, Herbert, 35–36, 155–62, 164, 198, 278, 287, 425–26, 441, 457, 459
Hoover, J. Edgar, 76, 448–50
House, "Colonel" Edward, 26–27, 66–67, 112, 182, 203, 218–220, 222, 408–9, 410–14
Houston riot, 107, 284
Howell, Col. Willey, 367–68
Hughes, Maj. John, 263–64
Hurley, Edward, 278, 410

immigrants, 18–19, 22, 24, 128, 178–79, 186, 283, 300–1, 450
Industrial Workers of the World (IWW), 20–21, 29, 183–89, 193, 288–90, 301, 304, 444–46, 448, 457
inflation, 28–29, 285, 456
influenza, 298, 391–92, 451–52

Inquiry, The, 220
instructors, British and French, 134–35, 211, 325
intelligence tests, 137
internment, 75–76

James, Henry, 14, 44
Japan, America and, 68, 169, 216, 297–98
Jaulgonne, 247
Jellicoe, Admiral John, 76–78, 83
Joffre, Marshal Joseph, 119, 121, 216, 394
Johnson, Gen. Evan, 371, 375–78
Johnson, Gen. Hiram "Iron Pants," 436
Judson, Gen. W. V., 207
Justice, Department of, 75–76, 189, 292, 302–4, 441, 448

Kerensky, Aleksandr, 206
Keynes, John Maynard, 428–29
Kriemhilde Position, 351, 353, 359, 361–62, 380–81, 386–87, 390–96, 399
Kuhn, Gen. Joseph E., 359–61, 366
Ku Klux Klan, 297, 439, 446, 457

labor, 8, 19–20, 29–30, 98, 178–81, 287–88, 292, 301, 304, 306, 444–45, 450
Lafayette Escadrille, 46–48, 327–28
La Follette, Robert, 68, 72
Landres-et-Saint-Georges, 396, 398, 401
Lane, Franklin (Secretary of the Inte-rior), 24, 67, 83, 169, 171, 178–79, 222, 300
Lansing, Robert (Secretary of State), 65–68, 70, 161, 443

League of Nations, 51, 66, 221, 407,
       413, 423, 429–31, 457
Lee, Lt. Col. Harry, 262, 319
Lejeune, Gen. John, 400
Lenin, Vladimir Ilich, 206–7, 218–20,
       289–90, 297, 299, 305,
       389, 443–45
Liberty Bonds, 174–77, 285, 302,
       306, 438
Liberty engine, 199–201
Liebknecht, Karl, 420, 426
Liggett, Gen. Hunter, 342, 344, 346,
       353, 358–59, 362–63,
       380–82, 384, 390–91, 393,
       399–402, 411, 416–21
Lippmann, Walter, 41, 52, 90, 220,
       409, 417, 429
Little, Frank, 188
Lloyd George, David, 83, 112, 117,
       156, 209, 215–16,
       219–220, 232, 275, 331,
       411–14, 423, 427–29
loans, American, 6, 69, 152–53,
       408–9, 427–28
Lodge, Henry Cabot, 165, 194, 196,
       411, 429–31
"Lost Battalion," 375–79, 384, 460
Lucy-le-Bocage, 250, 253
Ludendorff, Gen. Erich, 7, 62–66, 75,
       111, 205–9, 216, 227–28,
       230–31, 233, 238, 240,
       242–47, 249, 260–61,
       275–76, 295, 301, 308,
       311, 315, 322, 326,
       329–30, 332, 334, 354,
       389, 400, 406, 427,
       457–58
Lufbery, Raoul, 47–48
Luke, Frank, 369
Lusitania, 37–39, 49, 59, 79, 171, 294

Luxemburg, Rosa, 426
Lys River, 231, 275

MacArthur, Gen. Douglas, 114, 210,
       346, 387, 397–98, 419,
       459
Maistre, Gen. Paul, 418
Mangin, Gen. Charles, 314–16,
       319–20, 418
March, Gen. Peyton, 234–38, 261,
       276–77, 281, 284, 297–98,
       324, 391, 458
March, William, 456
Marine Brigade, 120, 211, 247–48,
       250–72, 401–2, 451
Marine Corps, 50, 76, 282
Marne River, 5, 7, 124, 246–47, 249,
       261, 275, 311–14, 319,
       400
Marne salient, 249, 311, 314, 320,
       329, 398, 452
Marshall, Gen. George C., 114, 116,
       119–20, 242–44, 322, 326,
       333, 343, 346, 356, 459
Marwitz, Gen. Georg von der, 381,
       400, 402
materials, 6, 28, 164, 185, 277
McAdoo, William G. (Secretary of the
       Treasury), 6, 17, 28, 51, 70,
       138, 151–53, 174–75, 177,
       182, 217–18, 278, 285–87,
       303, 428, 457
McAlexander, Gen. Ulysses Grant,
       312–13, 339
McCloskey, Maj. Manus, 255
McCormick, Vance, 208
McFadden, George, 236
McMahon, Gen. John, 396, 398
MacRae, Gen. James, 396
medical services, 43–46, 146, 267, 367

Mellon, Andrew, 430
Mencken, H. L., 308
Menoher, Gen. Charles T., 387, 396
Merrill, Maj. J. N., 372–73
Metz, 331, 342, 346, 352, 400, 414,
       418, 421
Meuse-Argonne front, 332–35, 345,
       347–55, 356–402, 407–8,
       418, 437, 452
Meuse River, 332, 339, 345, 349–50,
       352–54, 356, 359, 369,
       380–81, 389–91, 400, 416,
       418–19
Michel Position, 339, 341, 343–47
Military Intelligence Division (MID),
       303, 305–7, 330, 420, 440,
       444–45, 447
mines, 78–79, 84, 146
Mitchell, Gen. William "Billy,"
       121–23, 200, 327–28,
       314–42, 346–47, 355, 369,
       416, 459–60
mobilization, 75, 145–46, 177, 458
   economic and industrial, 55, 60,
       150–51, 154–64, 178,
       277–81
   failures in, 193–205
Moffett, Cleveland Langston, 52–53, 103
Montdidier, 249, 275
Montfaucon, 334, 349–51, 353,
       357–62, 366–67, 370, 380,
       386, 389, 392
Montrebeau Wood, 363, 365, 382
Mont Sec, 212, 239, 339
Mooney, Thomas, 29–30
Mordacq, Gen. Jean-Henri, 388
Morgan, J. Pierpont, 21, 28, 281, 447
Moselle River, 339–40, 352
Moton, Robert Russa, 68, 108
Murmansk, 298, 443, 447

NAACP, 16
National German-American Alliance,
       32–33, 36
National Guard, 50, 56–57, 92, 95,
       100, 107–9, 123, 128, 131,
       134, 145, 210, 239, 444
Native Americans, 136–37, 174
nativism, 8, 300–8
Navy
   Imperial German, 64–65, 67, 78,
       84, 427
   Royal, 30, 77–79, 84–85, 150,
       155, 217, 412–13
   U.S., 49, 57–59, 76–85, 146, 166,
       196, 216–17, 410
neutrality, American, 5–6, 26, 34
Neville, Col. Wendell, 235
Nicholls, Private Vernon, 354, 362
Nivelle, Gen. Robert, 6, 118, 205,
       209, 261
Noblat, Capt. Metz, 374
Noble, Gen. Robert, 360–61
Norris, George, 72
Northcliffe, Lord, 41, 152
North Sea barrage, 84, 146
Norton, Richard, 44–45
Noyon, 276

Occupation, American, of Germany,
       424–25, 455
officers, 89–90, 100–1, 111, 120, 123,
       134–35, 324, 368
O'Neill, Eugene, 307
Ordnance Department, 195–97
Oury, Col., 360–61

pacifism, 50, 67, 97
Page, Walter Hines, 68–70, 82, 152
Palmer, Attorney General A. Mitchell,
       447–50

Papen, Fritz von, 31
Paris, 3, 6–7, 41–42, 44, 118–19,
    121–24, 210, 231, 242,
    245–47, 249, 251–52, 260,
    272, 314, 322, 327, 341,
    394, 408–10, 413, 423–24,
    428, 438, 446, 455
Passchendaele, 205
Patton, Lt. Col. George S., 116,
    342–43, 347–48, 355
Périgord, Paul, 171
Pershing, Gen. John J., 108, 115–17,
    135–37, 145–47, 149, 197,
    210, 212–13, 228, 239–41,
    245, 247, 261, 275, 314,
    320, 322–28, 418–20, 437
  biography, 113–14
  personality, 114–15
  responsibilities, 115
  arrival in France, 118–19, 121–24
  and American independence, 117,
    215–16, 222, 230, 232–33,
    240, 245, 328–29, 332–34,
    394
  supply problems, 212–13, 236, 278,
    323
  and morale, 213–14
  and Peyton March, 235–37
  Belleau Wood, 247, 251, 261, 265
  and 100 divisions, 275–76, 281,
    409–10
  Soissons, 318
  Saint-Mihiel, 322, 326, 328,
    331–35, 340–46, 410
  and First Army, 322–23, 326, 332
  training and methods of warfare,
    324–26, 388
  Meuse-Argonne, 349–55, 359, 361,
    367, 370, 380–82, 384,
    386, 388–99, 410

and unconditional surrender of
    Germany, 411, 414, 416,
    421, 428
  death, 459
Pétain, Gen. Henri, 6, 118–19, 209,
    228–30, 347, 340, 350–52,
    420, 458
Pickford, Mary, 5, 159, 176
Plattsburg, 53, 55, 57, 99
Plumer, Gen. Herbert, 426
Poindexter, Senator Miles, 407
Post, Louis B., 450
Prager, Robert, 296, 302
preparedness, 7, 49–60, 196
Price-Fixing Committee, 285
Prince, Norman, 46–47
procurement, military, 196–201,
    277–78
profiteering, 285–87
Prohibition, 280, 425
propaganda, 30–31, 36–38, 49, 90,
    94, 128, 149, 164–65,
    167–78, 189, 238, 240,
    260, 293, 417, 428, 441–43
Pulitzer, Ralph, 55
Putnam, Irving, 295

Quantico (Virginia), 248, 266
Q-ships, 81

Rainbow Division. See Army, Divisions
Rankin, Jeanette, 72
Rathenau, Walther, 64
Red Cross, 169–70, 172–74, 207,
    295, 302, 454
Redfield, William (Secretary of Com-
    merce), 285, 287
"Red Scare," 447–450
Reed, John, 41, 188, 218, 443, 445,
    457

Reims, 242, 246, 249, 311, 314, 329, 332

reparations, 427–28

Resco, Micheline "Michette," 121–22, 394, 459

Retz, Forest of, 311, 314, 316

Rhineland, 394, 414, 424, 427, 430

Rickenbacker, Eddie, 201, 341, 343–45, 363, 369, 392, 402, 421

Robertson, Gen. William "Wully," 117, 209

Rockenbach, Samuel, 335, 347

Rodman, Admiral Hugh, 85

Rogers, Will, 425

Romagne, Côte de, 351, 381, 387, 395–96

Roosevelt, Eleanor, 82, 160, 279, 453

Roosevelt, Franklin D., 74, 80, 82, 84, 161, 447, 457

Roosevelt, Quentin, 284

Roosevelt, Theodore "Teddy," 13, 17, 39, 53, 56, 92, 113–15, 121, 182, 194, 196, 284, 407–8

Roosevelt, Theodore, Jr., 115, 284, 446

Root, Elihu, 89–90, 111, 206

Russia, 9, 204–5, 218–21, 289, 301, 447, 457

Russia, American intervention in, 111, 297–99, 443, 447, 455

Russian Revolution, 70, 283, 290, 299, 448

Saint-Mihiel, 123, 211–12, 238, 322, 327–28, 331–35, 339–48, 351, 353, 369, 396, 407, 452

Schiff, Jacob, 16

Schwieger, Leutnant-Kapitan, 38

Scott, Emmett, 108

Scott, Gen. Hugh, 89–92, 99–100, 104, 111, 136

Seattle, 289, 444, 448

Second Army, 390, 418

Secret Service Division, Treasury, 162, 302–3

"secret treaties," 217–19, 389, 409

Sedan, 332, 334, 394–95, 399, 418–19

Sedition Act, 302, 307, 407

Seeger, Alan, 41

Seicheprey, 239–40, 322, 339

Shearer, Maj. Maurice, 270

"shell shock," 453

shipping, 33, 64, 117, 150, 212, 287, 392, 410

Shipping Board, 150–51, 198, 410

Siberia, 217, 298

Sibert, Gen. William, 214, 245

Sibley, Maj. Berton, 251, 256–59, 262–63, 267

Simons, Walter, 428

Sims, Admiral William S., 76–83, 116, 122, 150, 216–17

Sisson, Edgar, 299, 301, 308

"slacker raids," 292

Smith, Lt. Col. Fred, 371–72

Socialists, 53–54, 133, 155, 181–83, 193, 305, 444–45

Soissons, 7, 242, 246, 249, 315–20, 322, 326, 383, 386, 389, 408, 415, 452

Spartacists, 420, 426

Sparks, Cpl. Lee, 107

Stacey, Col. Cromwell, 376–78

Stallings, Laurence, 456

State, Department of, 64, 207

Stein, Gertrude, 436

Stevens, John F., 206
Stokes, Rose Pastor, 182
stragglers, 365–66, 368, 386, 391–92, 399
submarines, American, 84–85
Sullivan, Mark, 172
Summerall, Gen. Charles, 243–44, 315, 318, 320, 382, 386, 390, 397–98, 400–1, 419
supplies, American sale of, 28, 33, 65, 152–54, 161, 409
supply system, 212–23, 277, 323–24, 348, 354, 362–63, 366–67, 380, 392
Supreme War Council, 209–10, 232, 334, 394, 410–11
Surmelin valley, 312–14
Sweezey, Col. Claude, 360–61

Taft, William H., 16, 76
tanks, 146–47, 335, 342, 347, 355, 360, 401
Taussig, Joseph K., 79
Thomas, Captain Shipley, 383
Thompson, Col. William B., 207
Thurber, James, 95–96
Toklas, Alice B., 436
training
  officers, 90, 99–103, 109–10, 391
  men, 99, 134–37, 317, 323–24, 354, 373, 377
Trans-Siberian Railway, 298
Traub, Gen. Peter, 356, 358, 363, 365
Trenchard, Gen. Hugh, 327
Trotsky, Leon, 206–7, 289, 297, 299
Truman, Capt. Harry, 455
Tumulty, Joseph, 72, 169
Turrill, Maj. Julius, 252, 254–56, 267

U-boats 31, 39–40, 61, 64–66, 69, 77–84, 119, 150, 238, 298

Vanderbilt, Alfred G., 37–38
Vaux, 271–72
venereal disease, 129, 131, 134, 139–40, 424, 449
Verdun, 5–6, 30, 46, 60, 119, 252, 335, 339, 350, 352, 357, 381
Versailles, 5, 8, 394, 412, 426–29
veterans, 452–56, 459
Vigneulles, 342, 344–45
Vladivostok, 298
volunteers, 41–48, 90, 92, 121

War Department, 93, 99–101, 103, 105, 107, 108–9, 113, 115, 117, 119, 132, 134, 137, 139, 147, 155, 169, 194–96, 198, 201, 203, 207–8, 234, 236–37, 277, 288, 291, 305, 325, 373, 451
War Industries Board, 278–80, 284, 391, 410, 435
"War Plans—White," 441
War Trade Board, 208, 213, 236, 435
Washington, Booker T., 15, 104, 108, 440
Western Front, 27, 30, 43, 45–47, 60–61, 69, 112, 115, 122–23, 166, 193, 208–9, 211, 228, 236, 238, 248, 276, 297, 328, 333–35, 350, 366, 381, 395, 397, 406, 413, 452
Wharton, Edith, 436, 456
Whittlesey, Maj. Charles, 371–72, 375–80, 384–85, 460
Wilhelm II, 30, 34, 62–64, 85, 175, 177, 288, 294–95, 406, 420, 422, 426
Wilson, William B. (Secretary for Labor), 186, 447–50

Wilson, Woodrow, 26–27, 30, 33–34,
        74, 76, 83, 90, 92–94, 98,
        103, 111–14, 119, 122, 133,
        138–40, 151–52, 155, 161,
        165, 178, 180–82, 193–94,
        198, 201, 204, 208–9,
        222–23, 232, 260–61,
        275–76, 279, 283, 286–87,
        289, 293, 297–99, 307, 331,
        389, 408, 437, 447
    political philosophy, 21–22, 25, 39,
        50–51, 60, 91, 179, 202–3,
        278, 281, 283–84
    decision for war, 39–40, 53, 56, 59,
        60–73, 91
    war aims, 51, 59, 70, 111, 117, 156,
        217–22, 283, 323, 333–34,
        389, 393–94, 405, 408,
        411
    and American independence, 70, 117,
        217–19, 223, 232, 410–11
    and repression of dissent, 76, 183,
        189, 291, 293, 302–3,
        307–8, 407, 441
    negotiations for peace, 405–8,
        410–16, 422
    and League of Nations, 51, 66, 221,
        407, 423, 429–31
    and Peace Conference, 5, 411,
        423–24, 426–31, 455
    collapse and death, 431, 457
Winterfeldt, Maj. Gen. von, 416, 418
Wise, Maj. Frederic, 263–67, 269–70
Wobblies. See IWW
Woeuvre Plain, 331–32, 352, 418
women's organizations, 17, 54
women, status of, 17, 163, 436–37
Wood, Gen. Leonard, 52–53, 56–57,
        90, 99, 113–14, 121–22,
        132, 194–95, 441, 444
Wooldridge, Capt. Jesse, 312–14

Yerkes, Robert M., 137
YMCA, 139, 366, 392, 437, 439
York, Sgt. Alvin, 97, 385
Young, Col. Charles, 108–9

Zimmermann telegram, 68, 83, 169

ABOUT THE AUTHORS

MEIRION HARRIES studied law at Cambridge University and worked as an attorney in Hong Kong and Japan before taking up an appointment as deputy director general of the Society of Authors. He is also a member of the Institute for Strategic Studies and chairman of the PEN Archives Committee, and he ran the 1996 Authors' Foundation appeal.

SUSIE HARRIES studied classics at Cambridge and Oxford universities and worked for several years for the Independent Commission Against Corruption in Hong Kong. She reviews for the *Times Literary Supplement* and is a member of the PEN Books to Prisoners Committee.

They started their writing partnership in 1979 and have since co-authored seven books, two of which have been short-listed for national prizes in England. *The Last Days of Innocence* is their fourth book on military history.

ABOUT THE TYPE

This book was set in Cheltenham, a typeface created by a distinguished American architect, Bertram Grosvenor Goodhue, in 1896 and produced by Ingalls Kimball of the Cheltenham Press in New York in 1902, who suggested that the face be called Cheltenham. It was designed with long ascenders and short descenders as a result of legibility studies indicating that the eye identifies letters by scanning their tops. The Mergenthaler Linotype Company put the typeface on machine in 1906, and Cheltenham has maintained its popularity for almost a century.